DYNAMICS OF
INTERNATIONAL RELATIONS

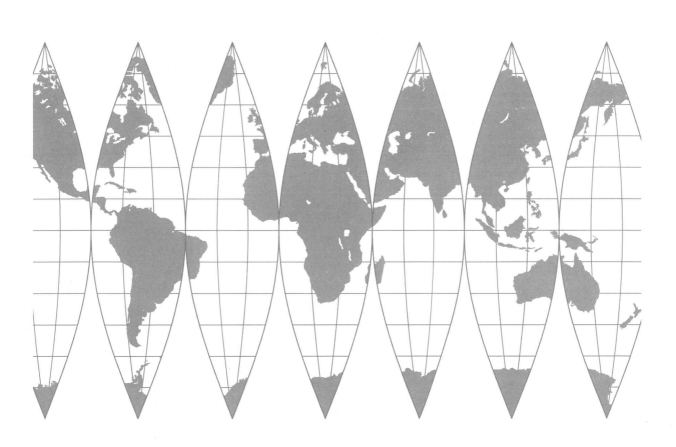

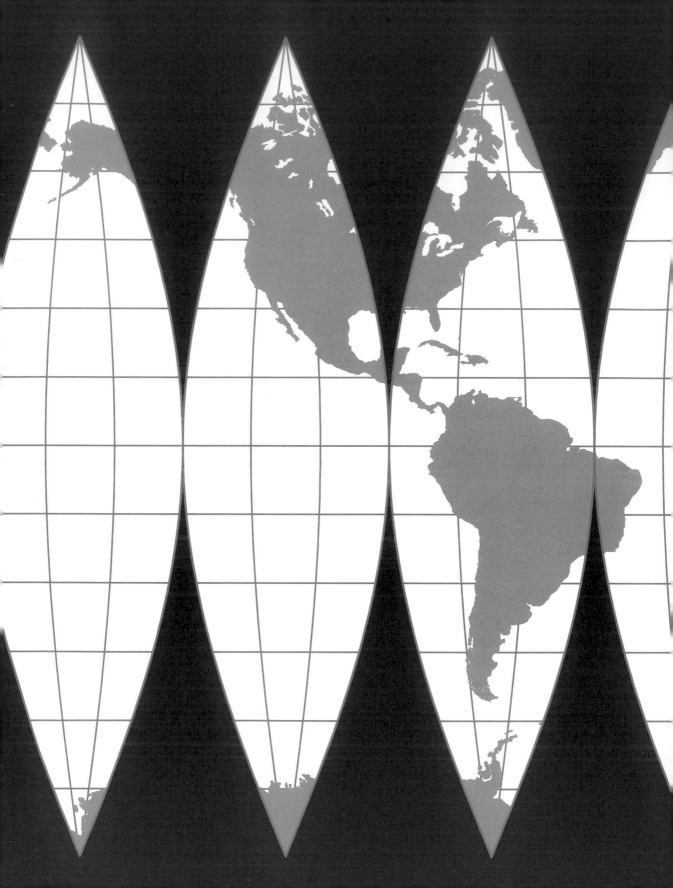

DYNAMICS OF INTERNATIONAL RELATIONS

CONFLICT AND MUTUAL GAIN IN AN AGE OF GLOBAL INTERDEPENDENCE

Walter C. Clemens, Jr.

ROWMAN & LITTLEFIELD PUBLISHERS, INC.
Lanham • Boulder • New York • Oxford

ROWMAN & LITTLEFIELD PUBLISHERS, INC.

Published in the United States of America
by Rowman & Littlefield Publishers, Inc.
4720 Boston Way, Lanham, Maryland 20706

12 Hid's Copse Road
Cumnor Hill, Oxford OX2 9JJ, England

*Book design, typesetting, and maps by Kachergis Book Design, Pittsboro,
North Carolina*

British Library Cataloguing in Publication Information Available

LIBRARY OF CONGRESS CATALOGING-IN-PUBLICATION DATA
Clemens, Walter C.
    Dynamics of international relations : conflict and mutual gain in an era
of global interdependence / by Walter C. Clemens, Jr.
        p.   cm.
    Includes bibliographical references and index.
    ISBN 0-8476-8851-8 (pbk. : alk. paper)
    1. International relations.   I. Title.
JZ1242.C57   1998
327.1'01—dc21   98–13242
                                                                     CIP

ISBN 0-8476-8851-8 (pbk. : alk. paper)

Printed in the United States of America

∞ The paper used in this publication meets the minimum requirements of
American National Standard for Information Sciences—Permanence of
Paper for Printed Library Materials, ANSI Z39.48-1984.

謹致愛妻

何丽蓮

If I am not for myself, who will be for me? Yet if I am for myself only, what am I?
—Hillel

Let us get out of our grooves and study the rest of the globe.
—Voltaire, *On Toleration*

More and more, the interdependence and complexity of international and political and economic relations render it incumbent on all civilized and orderly powers to insist upon the proper policing of the world.
—Theodore Roosevelt

That people inevitably think in terms of their self-interest is something very little can be done about. But is it not equally tenable that a great deal can be done about influencing people to think and act in terms of their *true* self-interest? In this dangerous international age, notions of exalted and exaggerated nationalism, national egocentrism and isolationism, of chauvinism, of group superiority and master race, of group exclusiveness, of national self-righteousness, of special privilege, are in the interest of neither the world nor of any particular group in it. They are false views of self-interest and carry us all toward the disaster of war.
—Ralph Bunche, "The International Significance of Human Relations," Lincoln's Day Address, Springfield, Illinois, February 12, 1951

The building of peace is like the building of a beautiful cathedral. It is a work that may not be done in my lifetime nor shall it be done in yours. But you ought to add a stone to it. There ought to be at least one spiral that is yours or one edifice that belongs to you. You ought to be able to point to it and say that I helped place that building block in the cathedral of peace.
—Vice President Hubert H. Humphrey on International Cooperation Year, Washington, D.C., June 2, 1965

If the world has survived to this day, it is because at tragic moments in its history, the forces of evil were always opposed by the forces of good, arbitrary power by the rule of law, treachery and meanness by honor and decency, violence by the strength of the spirit and belief in justice.
—Soviet Foreign Minister Eduard Shevardnadze to the United Nations, September 25, 1990

BRIEF CONTENTS

DETAILED CONTENTS

LIST OF TABLES, FIGURES, AND MAPS

FIGURES

LIST OF SIDEBARS AND TIMELINES

PREFACE

What are the dynamics of international relations (IR)—the driving forces of conflict and cooperation across frontiers? Today's news as well as history books assure us that conflict abounds within and among the key players in IR. Is there also a role for mutual gain? This book examines conflict—ethnic and economic, geopolitical and strategic. But the text also shows how governments and other international actors have often cooperated to mutual advantage, and why they might do so even more in the future.

At the cusp of the 21st century more people enjoy peace, prosperity, and freedom than ever before. But more than one-fourth of humanity suffers abject poverty, often combined with brutal repression. Food harvests stay a notch ahead of world population growth, but environmental disasters can strike at any time. Arms controls multiply but weapons become cheaper and more accessible. Fighting may have slowed, but land mines make farming a lethal occupation from Angola to Cambodia.

Dynamics of International Relations introduces the reader to IR as a fact of life and as a field of study. Both the practice and the study of IR are problem oriented, focused on issues of survival, development, justice, and the environment. These issues challenge both our minds and our character, pressing us to fuse knowledge from many fields to grasp complex realities and suggest constructive policies.

THE APPROACH OF THIS BOOK

How can an introductory text make sense of these multiple challenges and opportunities? This book tries to integrate theory with practice, in-depth case studies with broad surveys, foreign policy perspective from many capitals with an overview of global interactions. Each chapter outlines how classic and "neo" schools of realism and idealism explain, prescribe, and predict. The text suggests, however, that a more balanced perspective may be found in a paradigm of global interdependence.

Global interdependence has been a fact of life for centuries, but ours is a time of escalating interdependence. Not just states but transnational corporations and nongovernmental organizations (NGOs) join in webs of mutual vulnerability. Interdependence is a fact, but humans have choices: They can pursue policies that yield gain or pain for one, some, or many players.

Applying theory to bargaining behavior, the book weighs the utility of zero-sum, win-win, and conditional cooperation approaches to negotiation. It finds that a value-creating strategy oriented toward mutual gain tends to serve each actor's long-term interests better than efforts to claim values and exploit others. Zero-sum exploitation generates conflict, while mutual gain policies are conducive to a positive peace. Cooperation contributes to domestic and international system fitness—the ability to cope with complex challenges.

Mutual gain, of course, depends upon reciprocity. In the real world most actors both compete and cooperate. Why don't they cooperate more? The book uses prisoner's dilemma and other social science models to explain distrust and free-riding. Borrowing from game theory and psychology, we see that tit-for-tat policies can put actors on a treadmill of mutual punishment. To break deadlocks, graduated initiatives to reduce tension have proved useful. The book shows how—sometimes—actors learn and institutions develop to shape an emergent structure to mutual advantage. Reality is richer than our models of rational choice allow.

The starkest mutual vulnerability is that of the two nuclear weapons giants, the United States and Russia, each hostage to the other's restraint. But most of the countries of Europe and North America, as well as Japan, gravitate toward a multilayered, complex interdependence in which war is virtually unthinkable.

Interdependence and complex interdependence do not nullify governments. But many forces of globalization transcend political borders—the bits and bytes of the Information Revolution pulsing through the air waves and cyberspace; electronic money transfers; consumer aspirations; drug trafficking; migrations; epidemics; fads and fashions; religions and other transnational ideologies. Good or bad, all are facts of international life.

To understand synergy across frontiers, this book analyzes five action levels—the individual (Level 1), the state (Level 2), the international system (Level 3), transnational actors (Level 4), and the biosphere (Level 5). No level is taken for granted.

Level 1: Our cases show how personal characteristics affected the policy successes and defeats of John F. Kennedy and Nikita Khrushchev; Henry Kissinger and Zhou Enlai; Jimmy Carter, Anwar Sadat, and Menachem Begin; and Richard Holbrooke and other mediators. Many world figures are ranked by their mastery of fifteen skills useful for the negotiator.

Level 2: States remain the weightiest players in IR, but we assess the internal cleavages and bureaucracies that often thwart a unified foreign policy.

Levels 3 and 4: We assess the strengths and weaknesses of the evolving state system, the United Nations, specialized agencies such as the World Health Organization, and NGOs such as the International Committee of the Red Cross. We see that the International Campaign to Ban Land Mines united more than a thousand NGOs with the Canadian and other governments to generate a treaty signed by most countries in 1997 (though not by the largest powers). The 21st century will probably witness more global governance—collaboration between governments and nonstate actors.

Level 5: The biosphere is an action level that shapes and is shaped by IR. We review the debate between Malthusians and Cornucopians, study the "Aswan syndrome" from the Nile to the Yangtze, and analyze how environmental diplomacy deals with climate change.

THE STRUCTURE OF THIS BOOK

The book is organized into four parts. Part 1 analyzes theories of realism, idealism, and interdependence in relation to war, peace, and power. Fitness, within societies and international systems, is defined as the capacity to cope with complexity. Security, we see, has domestic as well as external dimensions. Part 2 analyzes how order can arise from anarchy, for example, by regimes to limit nuclear arms, by direct and mediated negotiation of differences, and by power-sharing among ethnic groups. Much attention is given to the uses of hard and soft power and how they influence other actors. Part 3 addresses the international political economy—the impact of domestic regimes on international peace and prosperity; the contest between Adam Smith's "invisible hand" and neomercantilism; and the competitive partnerships of Japan, the U.S., and Europe. The chapters in Part 3 look at how some "poor" countries achieve high scores in health, education, and welfare. We review evidence that raising female literacy is a powerful tool for economic development as well as for social justice. We examine the transitions facing the developing and former Communist countries in quest of higher living standards. Can they—should they—try to buck the system or join the world of commerce now dominated by the West and Japan?

Part 4 asks, How can we build a better world? How can we override the shortsighted, parasitic logic that often confounds policies meant to enhance public goods such as clean air and security? We examine environmental diplomacy and review case studies of how nonstate actors contribute to collective security and peacekeeping, how individuals combat the scourges of smallpox and HIV, and how relief agencies contend with complex humanitarian emergencies. Human rights—sham or revolution?—is the bottom line in our treatment of international law. In the final chapter we consider the lessons of nearly eighty case studies and summarize the conditions under which it has paid policymakers to pursue a hard line, a win-win approach, or conditional cooperation. After sketching six alternative futures, we end by proposing modes of global governance that tap the complementary assets of governments, interstate players, and transnational actors.

PEDAGOGICAL FEATURES

Theory informs case studies, while cases inform both theory and policy. How cases were chosen is explained in To The Reader. Each chapter presents several cases in depth to help the reader track decisions and outcomes. These cases are assessed against broader surveys such as Correlates of War, Minorities at Risk, and the Human Development Index.

Each chapter engages the student in problem-solving and negotiation. Each starts with a tough question: "Does it pay to fight?" "How can foes become partners?" "What is the role of women in development?" Some chapters task the reader to don an official hat and look at IR from the standpoint of the U.S. secretary of state, the Brazilian foreign minister, the European Commissioner for Competition, the president of India, or the leader of Kazakstan. Other chapters ask the reader to advise the UN Secretary-General on how to reduce ethnic conflict, the European Parliament and U.S. Congress on how to balance business with human rights concerns in China and an NGO on how to establish a University of the Middle East.

How can we present sufficient history to understand the past and future of IR? Rather than attempting to summarize the relevant facts in an introductory survey, each chapter integrates past events into IR analysis. Chapter 2, for example, analyzes the new world orders that victors sought to establish in 1648, 1815, 1918, 1945, and 1991. It contrasts the value-creating orientation of the Marshall Plan with the value-claiming policies pursued by the victors at Versailles and by the USSR toward Eastern Europe after 1945.

Declassified Russian and U.S. documents are applied to various action levels in Chapter 3 to explain how individuals and bureaucracies pushed Moscow and Washington to the brink of nuclear war in October 1962 and then pulled away.

Having presented a problem to be solved, each chapter follows a three-part structure: (1) Contending Concepts and Explanations—a tool box of definitions, frameworks, and theories on the chapter's central questions; (2) Comparing Theory and Reality—case studies of major events in 20th-century IR that illustrate how the contending theories do or do not explain reality; and (3) What Propositions Hold? What Questions Remain?— evaluation of possible insights from these cases. These insights are woven into a closing role play incorporating the material covered and applying it to the questions asked in the opening scenario. The replies, of course, are tentative, and students are encouraged to develop alternative recommendations.

Key Names and Terms, Questions to Discuss, and Recommended Resources (including books, journals, and web sites) round out each chapter. A glossary of key names and terms appears at the end of the book along with a study and resource guide (Learning About International Relations) that outlines how to write a research paper and how to locate the requisite materials (bibliographies, documentary collections, journals, web sites) with which to do it.

The text is fleshed out with sidebars, figures, and tables that contrast rival arguments, juxtapose historical events, and summarize economic and military trends. For example, tables show the investment rates and the weight of foreign trade in several developed and less-developed economies. Female literacy is plotted against infant mortality and other social-economic indicators. Several tables depict what the U.S. spends on international affairs, including foreign aid, and R&D. At each juncture we see how domestic and external entwine.

Maps, photos, and the biting cartoons of Jeff Danziger help to illustrate the main themes.

ACKNOWLEDGMENTS

Many individuals and institutions helped stimulate, support, and improve this book—more than can be named here. Thanks to them all! Professor B. Welling Hall, Earlham College, read several drafts and made many helpful suggestions; she prepared the instructor's manual and provided many web site references. William E. Griffith, Massachusetts Institute of Technology, and John J. Schultz, Boston University, also critiqued much of the manuscript.

Other reviewers included William H. Baugh, University of Oregon; Robert Breckinridge, St. Francis College; Glen Chafetz, University of Memphis; Nader Entessar, Spring Hill College; Richard Frese, Bentley College; Roger Hamburg, Indiana University at South Bend; Jonathan Harris, University of Pittsburgh; Derick L. Hulme, Alma College; Clair W. Matz, Marshall University; Karen Mingst, University of Kentucky; Marie D. Natoli, Emmanuel College; Kenneth A. Rodman, Colby College; Kendall Stiles, Loyola University, Chicago; Charles S. Taber, State University of New York, Stony Brook; Primo Vannicelli, University of Massachusetts, Boston; Thomas J. Volgy, University of Arizona.

Other scholars who have read or discussed parts of the book include Andrew Bell-Fialkoff, Michael Corgan, Karl W. Deutsch, Michael Doyle, Hermann Fr. Eilts, Roger Fisher, David Fromkin, Deborah J. Gerner, Paul Goble, Clark Johnson, Roger Kanet, Stuart Kauffman, Robert Keohane, William Keylor, Jacek Kugler, Igor Lukes, José Garcia-Pico, David Mayers, Alexander Motyl, Daniel Partan, Sofia Perez, Howard Raiffa, Maria Rodrigues, John Rothgeb, James Sebenius, J. David Singer, S. Frederick Starr, Stephen Van Evera, and Frank Zagare.

Mentors, colleagues, and friends whose insights find their way into the book include Hayward Alker, Graham Allison, James Billington, Lincoln P. Bloomfield, Walter Connor, Mark Greuter, Philip C. Jessup, George F. Kennan, Joseph S. Nye, Andrei D. Sakharov, Jeremy J. Stone, J. Ann Tickner, Elie Wiesel, and Jerome B. Wiesner.

A Rockefeller Foundation Humanities Fellowship helped initiate this book. The book benefited greatly from colleagues and facilities at Boston University and Harvard University's Center for Science and International Affairs and Davis Center for Russian Studies. Related research was supported by the Ford Foundation, the U.S. State Department, and the Woodrow Wilson International Center for Scholars.

Darin Foster, Julie George, Justin Schardin, David Young, and Jun Zhan conducted research and helped the project in many ways. Viktoria Tripolskaya-Mitlyng provided encouragement and crucial connections. Rowman & Littlefield editors Jennifer Knerr and Brenda Hadenfeldt brought intelligence, grace, cheer, and efficiency to the project. Tracy Villano and Kachergis Book Design carefully prepared the manuscript, tables, and figures. Internet Presence Inc. provided many web sites. My wife Ali Ho Clemens helped think through many questions, prepared graphics, and sustained the work. The dedication in Chinese is to her.

TO THE READER

WHY STUDY INTERNATIONAL RELATIONS?

Why study international relations (IR)? Because, like a mountain, it is there—challenging, interesting to explore, sometimes beautiful, potentially useful (with rich ore), and often dangerous. Why attempt the climb? To understand where humanity has come from and where it can go. To survive. To make the world a better place. Also, to get ahead—to find a job. To live and prosper in a world where, as naturalist John Muir noted: "When you touch anything, you find it is hitched to everything else in the universe."

The dynamics of international relations—the driving forces behind conflict and cooperation across borders—are important not only to diplomats, soldiers, and peacekeepers. They shape the safety and prosperity of everyone. They awaken the imagination of every alert human being, every seeker for patterns in the great chain of being. They are a "must know" for the banker, the commodity trader, the public health worker, the ecologist, and for those working at many other professions.

A better understanding of IR can enhance rather than destroy life. We owe it to ourselves and to future generations to seek knowledge that could alter our dance of the dinosaurs—the shortsighted routines that invite extinction.

WHO GETS WHAT, HOW, AND WHY?

The basic IR question is how to enhance the interests of one's own group—whether it be a tribe, nation, party, state, business corporation, social movement, or church—in a global setting where each group's interests may conflict as well as harmonize with others'. Whether we see our group in narrow terms (for example, Bosnian Serbs) or in broad terms (all humanity), we must deal with others whose objectives may parallel but also differ from ours.

The underlying patterns in IR have for thousands of years been viewed through the lenses of competing theories: realism and idealism. Realists describe what they see as hard fact—world politics as a struggle for power. Idealists prescribe what could be—IR as a quest for law and morality. There are many varieties of realism and idealism, including late-20th-century updates. Despite many strong points and refinements, however, neither theory explains or anticipates large swaths of what happens; neither offers a dependable guide to action.

A third perspective focused on interdependence took shape in the late 20th century. This theory posits an international stage where actors are linked so closely that they can both hurt and help one another. The key players are governments of countries (states), but other actors are gaining influence, from the World Trade Organization to General Motors, Amnesty International, MTV, and drug cartels.

Our world is one of escalating interdependencies. How should we cope with our shared vulnerabilities? Governments and other IR actors may seek one-sided or joint gains. They may claim values (wealth, power, influence) for themselves or create and share such goods with others. Which road should IR actors take?

This book examines two policy guidelines. The first suggests that IR actors are more likely to achieve their own objectives in the long run if they cooperate for mutual gain than if they exploit others for one-sided gain. It warns, however, that cooperation among competitors depends upon reciprocation and may require safeguards to promote compliance. In contrast to mutual gain policies, efforts to exploit others may yield short-run benefits but tend over time to boomerang against the exploiter.

A second guideline concerns communication among actors able to help or harm one another. It predicts that the more all parties communicate, the more likely these parties will find solutions useful to all sides.

FOR DEPTH AND BREADTH: HOW THIS BOOK IS ORGANIZED

The book tries to provide a full picture, both deep and wide. Depth comes from detailed analysis of important cases structured to permit meaningful comparisons. For example, two chapters compare efforts to build a new international order after the two world wars and after the Cold War. The three settings were similar in many ways, but also quite distinct: Germany in the 1920s and again in the 1950s resembled but also differed from Russia in the 1990s. History is not a perfect laboratory. The global scene refuses to hold still for repeated experiments.[1] The policy implications of earlier cases must be sifted carefully if applied to a different time and place.

Trying to fill in the entire canvas, the book supplements its case studies with summaries of wide-reaching survey studies. The chapter on war, for example, examines several pairs of comparable wars (for example, Vietnam and Afghanistan) but also reports on the severity and frequency of all major wars since the late 18th century. The chapter on nationalism focuses on ethnic strife in Sri Lanka and the Balkans, but relates these cases to surveys of minorities worldwide.

How were the cases selected? They were chosen for four reasons. First, each exemplifies an important IR problem that recurs in different settings, for example, how to defuse explosive confrontations. Thus, Europe's leaders in 1914 stumbled into a major war that few wanted. In 1962, however, Soviet and U.S. leaders managed to step back from their confrontation over Cuba. What lessons, if any, do such cases suggest for policymakers?

---

1. To supplement history we can mimic the "real world" with games and simulation exercises using humans, computers, or both. Role-playing games and simulations can provide insights but they are not what happened or will happen. Usually they omit important variables, most significantly, the personalities of decision makers.

Second, the cases help to assess the three IR theories and our twin policy guidelines in a variety of contexts—from arms control to environmental protection. A sampling of case studies cannot fully test a hypothesis or theory. But if a theory fails in important cases, we must doubt its validity. If it seems to explain some key cases, we must study it further.

Third, the cases help us evaluate which types of foreign policies have met or failed to achieve their objectives—an important exercise for the scholar and politician alike. Many cases examine what experts see as the major achievements and failures of U.S. and Russian foreign policy since 1917.[2] For example, the reconstruction of Europe and Japan after World War II ranks at the top of U.S. successes abroad. On the other hand, both Washington and Moscow failed ignominiously when they tried to keep clients in power in Vietnam and Afghanistan.

Fourth, doors have opened since the collapse of the USSR in 1991, permitting many of our case histories (for example, the Korean War and Cuban crisis) to embody recent disclosures made in memoirs, interviews, and declassified archives. As still more facts emerge, of course, interpretations of recent history undergo continuous revision.

The combination of depth and breadth should help us grapple with the deepest paradox of IR: how cooperation and "order" can exist in a global system that lacks an overarching government.

DO WE NEED THEORY? WHERE DOES IT COME FROM?

Every field of knowledge has a dominant image, or paradigm, guiding its explorations. If the image is wrong (the sun circles the earth), we misinterpret what we see. If correct (the earth circles the sun), the phenomena we perceive can fall into their proper places. Many thousands of years passed before humans dropped their image of the earth as the center of the universe.

A correct paradigm is essential to a good IR theory—the principles, rules, and as-

2. The author surveyed experts associated with the Woodrow Wilson International Center for Scholars and the Kennan Institute for Advanced Russian Studies in 1976–1977 and again in 1987. The latter study was supplemented by surveys of foreign policy experts at Boston University and the Harvard Center for Science and International Affairs. Most respondents were Americans, but some were from Canada, Europe, Israel, Korea, and Japan. Most were political scientists and historians, but a few were diplomats, including four former ambassadors. The open-ended survey instrument asked them to list five to fifteen major successes and failures of U.S. or Soviet foreign policy since 1917, given what they presumed were the objectives of U.S. or Soviet leaders, and to list several of the underlying reasons for those successes and failures. Follow-up discussions were held with George F. Kennan, Henry S. Commager, J. William Fulbright, Fred W. Neal, Peter H. Vigor, and Hermann Fr. Eilts.

The survey results were reported in Walter C. Clemens, Jr., "Soviet Foreign Policy Since 1917: Achievements and Failures," *Survey: A Journal of East & West Studies* 30, no. 4 (June 1989): 87–112; Clemens, *Can Russia Change? The USSR Confronts Global Interdependence* (New York: Routledge, 1990), chap. 1; and op-ed essays published in the *Christian Science Monitor,* including "Let Us Not Fear to Negotiate," May 27, 1980; "The Fulbright Program: It's a Bargain," November 18, 1981; "Of Generations, Experience, and Peace," August 7, 1986; "America's Greatest Achievement in Foreign Affairs," June 4, 1987; "70 Years of Soviet Power," November 5, 1987; and "Communism's Milestones of Failure," October 27, 1989.

sumptions by which we analyze IR problems and accumulate knowledge. The two long-dominant IR theories, realism and idealism, this book argues, start from simplistic, often misleading paradigms. We need a paradigm shift to construct a more accurate theory.

Can theory also be relevant to practice? The answer is yes, for wise policymaking depends upon an insightful theory. Every diplomat and politician consults some kind of theory—if only the maxims learned at a parent's knee.[3] Better an accurate theory than a warped one. Scholars, of course, need theory to spur and organize their search for discovery.

Grand, comprehensive theories of IR view the world as through a telescope. There are also partial and medium-range theories that peer at details as through a microscope. A comprehensive theory can give birth to a partial theory: For example, realism implies that wars are inevitable and should be treated as just another tool in the quest for power. Partial theories also help build grand theories. Interdependence draws upon medium-range theories of collective action and negotiation.

Theory-building begins with questions about what causes what or how to solve a problem. Starting from a basic image (paradigm) of the system, we can cultivate hunches and turn them into tentative explanations (hypotheses) and test them against experience. IR theory should make sense of the scrambled signals we take in daily from a world pulsing with both conflict and harmony.

Our trove is history—the data bank of all experience. To analyze this experience we adapt insights and tools from all of the social sciences as well as from statistics, law, and philosophy. To understand the diverse civilizations on the world stage, we study sacred texts such as the *Koran,* epic tales such as *Ramayana,* and novels such as *Bridge on the Drina* by Ivo Andric and *Guerrillas* by V. S. Naipaul. We consult other relevant disciplines, from biology (symbiosis) to physics (missiles) to plant genetics (hybrid wheat).

Recommended books, journals, and web sites are listed at the end of each chapter. Additional sources and suggestions on how to conduct research are supplied at the end of the book in Learning About International Relations: A Study and Resource Guide.

We cannot sit forever before books and computer screens. While we can communicate far and wide from our PC, we should also visit distant places and learn how others see and feel about the world—preferably in their own language.

No theory endures unchallenged—not even in the physical sciences. At a minimum, theories are refined. Sometimes the underlying paradigm is replaced, giving rise to a new process of search and discovery.

3. The longest-serving Soviet foreign minister often recalled how his father and a friend traced U.S. wealth to "cunning and wise" presidents such as Theodore Roosevelt. Did he see the U.S. presidents he met—from Franklin Roosevelt to George Bush—through his father's lens? See Andrei Gromyko, *Memoirs* (New York: Doubleday, 1989), 4.

Changes come quickly in IR. Some two dozen new countries appeared in the 1990s. Name changes caused journalists and map makers to pull their hair. The study of IR seeks to understand why and how such transformations take place.

FACING COMPLEXITY

The streams and rivers of international studies flow into an ever-expanding effort to comprehend life—its chaos, its complexity, its order. Analysis of IR gains from and contributes to many branches of knowledge—history, philosophy, and science—as they study all spheres of life.

Students of IR, like all scientists, ponder whether the real world is too intricate to fathom. Perhaps the answers to some questions will remain beyond our reach. The human psyche and other variables shaping IR are even more complicated than the "quarks and jaguars" studied by other disciplines. And even if our understanding of IR is on target, our policy recommendations will be subjective: Where we stand depends heavily on where we sit. Indeed, we form part of what we are trying to comprehend.

The study of IR is in flux. After much searching, our questions will probably outnumber our answers. We must build on and improve one another's findings, making knowledge cumulative. With better data and more insightful models, perhaps we can improve IR theory and in so doing possibly raise the quality of life worldwide.

Our efforts to understand IR may resemble the waxed wings of Icarus, bound to melt as he rose toward the sun. But we hope rather that they will rise more like the first flight of the Wright Brothers—primitive, yet open to improvement.

PART 1

Hard Realities, High Ideals, and Global Interdependence

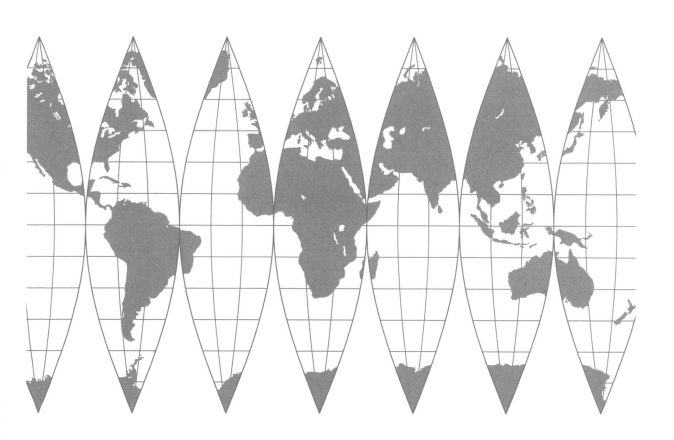

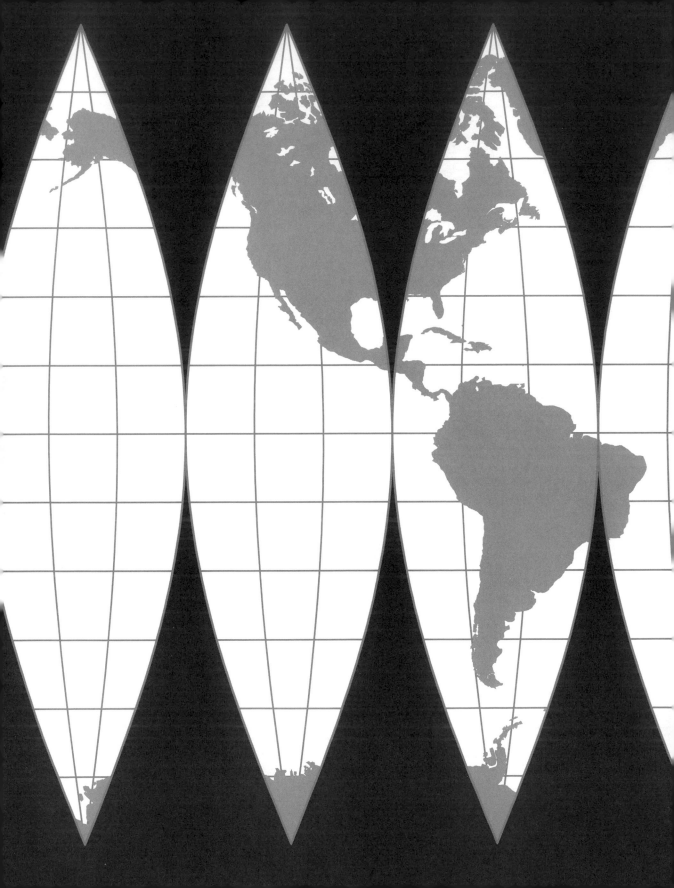

CHAPTER ONE

IS IR "WINNER-TAKE-ALL"? CAN IT BE MUTUAL GAIN?

THE BIG QUESTIONS IN CHAPTER 1

- How does international relations (IR) differ from foreign policy?

- Who or what are the key players in IR? What and where are the main playing fields?

- Through what lens should you view IR—the realist focus on the struggle for power, the idealist vision of a world order based on law and morality, or the interdependence image of shared danger with opportunity?

- What is negotiation? What are the main types of negotiators?

- Should you go it alone or cooperate with other IR players?

- What happens when players seek a free ride?

- Games that IR actors play: Defection or coordination?

- Can agreements serve the interests of both sides if they have divergent interests?

- Is it wiser to do your business behind closed doors or in the open?

- Are there any principles that guide foreign policy?

When You Become Secretary of State.... Imagine that, not too far into the 21st century, the newly elected president asks you to be her Secretary of State. She asks you to recommend a strategy for building a world in which U.S. interests can flourish. Everywhere she sees both danger and opportunity. Partners, such as Germany and Japan, are also rivals. More than one-fourth of humanity lives in dire poverty—a source of chaos and a challenge to conscience. Globalization of knowledge, industry, and commerce is a boon and a bane. The Internet and electronic banking skim across political frontiers, but so, too, do cocaine, AIDS, and global warming.

The president endorses international cooperation. She would like to "grow the pie" with other actors for mutual gain. But she notes that China, Singapore, and Indonesia assert that Western values are not their values. She also knows that a Hitler or a Stalin could return to the world stage. Russia is down but not out. When Russia recovers, will it be with us or against us? When, if ever, can we trust other governments whose view of the world is very different from ours?

Given all this, the president asks, "how can we negotiate agreements that serve the interests of all parties? When we negotiate, should we try to coerce, persuade, or accommodate the other side? Should we hold fast to our basic positions or go more than halfway to reach a deal? Should we put our cards openly on the table or hold them close to the chest?

"What is the bottom line? Must we depend more on muscle or on persuasion? How likely is it that we will need to use military force during my coming term? How should we apply our resources? How much to defend and deter, to protect allies and back the United Nations? How much to safeguard our commerce and our space stations? Can we—should we—cut back on military outlays and concentrate instead on economics and education?

"How can we handle world affairs in a way that improves our life at home? Last, but not least, how can foreign policy help me be reelected?"

This is a big order. The president wants both theoretical and practical advice. You agree to report first on how to view the world stage, and second on how to act on it—how to negotiate with others over divergent and shared interests. Other briefings will follow.

IR AS A FACT AND AS A FIELD OF STUDY

As Secretary of State your task is to direct foreign policy, as viewed from Washington. You have a full plate. "Foreign affairs" includes any problem a foreign minister must worry about as part of the job. The "high politics" of security merges with the "low politics" of trade and other cross-border concerns. Global problems require global solutions. Your portfolio expands from wars and weapons to trade deficits, climate change, and AIDS. You must also deal with issues such as child labor and women's rights, issues once considered matters of domestic jurisdiction where outsiders should not meddle. Since the 1970s, however, Congress has required the Department of State to report each year on human rights in every country receiving U.S. assistance and, indeed, in every UN member-state. Thus domestic and foreign affairs overlap.

International relations (IR) is even broader than foreign policy—broader than the policies of all governments combined. IR is both a fact of life and a field of study. As an existential fact, IR is what happens when diverse players interact across borders; as a field of study, IR searches for patterns in these interactions. IR takes in *any* development—governmental or private, material or spiritual—that shapes political relations across borders.

IR is our object of study, but we are its subjects. When we examine IR, we also examine ourselves and the values we hold. While governments try to advance their own interests, scholars must strive to be open-minded as they look for truth. But because IR shapes life and death, scholars, too, may feel the need to take a stand before all the facts have been analyzed. It is important to distinguish between what we may want to believe from what we actually know.

IR studies what has been and what is in order to know what can be and what should be. The discipline faces three tasks: (1) to explain what happened and why, (2) to forecast the probability of alternative futures (if x and y, then z), and (3) to guide and set norms for policy.

Scholars and statesmen must search wide and deep to grasp the dynamics of IR—the driving forces of conflict and cooperation across frontiers.[1] Conflict arises because interests clash and/or **actors** lack vision. We shall study how some conflicts can be managed or transcended through cooperation for mutual gain. There is a growing demand for "honest brokers"—intermediaries who can help parties resolve conflict without war.

Individuals can change history. Everything is complicated. Women play leading roles on the world scene. These themes of this book come to life in Madeleine Albright, named first female U.S. Secretary of State in 1996.

1. "Dynamics" comes from Greek *dinamis*—"power"—probably derived from the Indo-European *deu*—"to do" or "perform." The same roots give us "dynamo," "dynasty," and "dynamite"—a word coined by its inventor, Alfred Nobel, who used some of his earnings to establish a famous peace prize. See *American Heritage Dictionary of the English Language*, 3d ed. (Boston: Houghton Mifflin, 1992), 574, 2100.

When we study IR, we also investigate ourselves and our values.

We scan history for trends and lessons. We want to know not only *what* happened, but also *why* and *how*. Why did one policy succeed and another fail? Did *x* cause *y* or merely coincide with it? Why did one event occur rather than another? Might such an event recur? What conditions might abet or thwart it? To build such knowledge is not easy. Inspiration and hard work are necessary for insight.

WHERE THE ACTION IS: KEY ACTORS AND LEVELS OF IR ANALYSIS

To begin to understand IR, you must know who the key players are and where to find them. There are many kinds of international actors, and they perform on many levels, as outlined in Figure 1.1. These actors and levels are distinct but interlocked.

Level 1: Individuals and Human Nature

Humans are the designers, implementers, beneficiaries, and often the victims of world politics. Individuals can shape IR from outside as well as inside government. The Nobel Peace Prize has been awarded not only to UN officials such as Ralph Bunche and government ministers such as Henry Kissinger, but also to private individuals such as Jane Addams, Martin Luther King, Jr., Lech Walesa, Mother Teresa, and Elie Wiesel.

Level 2: Domestic Factors—State and Society

The 1648 **Treaty of Westphalia** established that the state should be seen as the basic unit of the international (or, more accurately, the inter-*state*) system. A **state** must have four features: a defined territory; a permanent population; a stable government; and independence—that is, the sovereign right to deal with other states. This view of the state developed in the 16th century when the French kings asserted their **sovereignty** (supreme power) over feudal lords and Protestant princes in northern Europe established their independence from the Catholic Church.[2]

We often speak of the state as a unified actor ("France"), but no country is monolithic. Every state contains regional, ethnic, social, and other groups with unique views and interests. These groups, as well as provincial and even town governments, can be weighty players in IR. We may also speak of the state in IR as the "nation-state" or "nation," but this, too, is a misnomer. Most states contain more than one nation. In Canada, for example, many French speakers and Native Americans see themselves as members of distinct nations.

The international law doctrine that every state is an independent, sovereign actor has always been a legal fiction, one that grows increasingly implausible in the face of globalization—the easy movement across borders of ideas, capital, knowledge, production, sales, and weapons.[3]

Level 3: The International System of States

A unified Christendom broke apart during the 16th and 17th centuries, but states created international law to regulate trade and limit war. Even though states are sovereign, they pledge to obey the laws they have established. The International Court of Justice, an organ of the United Nations, and other courts hear cases between states, but, as the 21st century begins, there is no world government—no supranational authority—over individual states.

An **intergovernmental organization (IGO)** is an organization created and funded by states. The United Nations is an example of an IGO. Its founders wanted it to enhance international peace and security, but they also assigned it wide economic and social goals. Other IGOs strive to promote narrower, "functional" tasks—from delivering mail across borders to fostering peaceful uses of atomic energy (see Chapter 15). IGOs belong to the state system and yet can be seen as nonstate actors because they are not states. The **European Union (EU)**, on the other hand, began as an IGO but increasingly acts like a state. The EU is a hybrid organization—

Fig. 1.1 Five Levels of IR Action and Analysis

The Biosphere

Transnational Organizations and Movements

The International System of States

Domestic Factors—State and Society

Individuals

2. The Treaty of Westphalia affirmed the independence of the United Dutch Provinces and the Swiss cantons from Spanish Hapsburg rule. The treaty ended the Thirty Years wars of religion and upheld the principle: "Whoever rules, his religion will prevail."

3. Robert K. Schaeffer, *Understanding Globalization: The Social Consequences of Political, Economic, and Environmental Change* (Lanham, Md.: Rowman & Littlefield, 1997).

part international, part supranational, part regional. We detail its evolution in Chapter 15.

Like any system, the system of states may be seen as a patterned relationship between the whole and its parts. Though it lacks a supranational authority, the interstate system is structured, with a pecking order, rules, and a hierarchy of power and influence. There are regional subsystems within the larger international system. Some regions have their own organizations, such as the Organization for African Unity and the Organization of American States.

Levels 1, 2, and 3 have been the focus of most IR analysis, but two other levels are gaining in salience.

Level 4: Transnational Organizations and Movements

Levels 2 and 3 are bounded by governments. But "international" refers not just to interstate relations, but also to **transnational** relations—the realm of nongovernmental actors whose membership and actions transcend official state borders. Some transnational actors are backed by governments, but many operate independently; some even work against governments. Trade, commerce, and missionary activity have for millennia operated across borders and continents. British trading companies, for example, dominated India before diplomats and troops made it part of the British Empire.

Transnational organizations and movements come in many shapes and sizes.[4] The biggest **transnational corporations (TNCs),** such as General Motors and Ford, have revenues larger than many states. But a small business can offer its services worldwide on the Internet. Religions unite millions of believers across borders. **Nongovernmental organizations (NGOs)** such as Greenpeace and Doctors Without Borders often challenge governments. Mafias, terrorists, and drug traffickers can be powerful transnational players. Music, tastes, and fashions shape life across borders, as do economic practices such as **Fordism** (mass production techniques plus mass consumption). Even brand names such as "Coke" can move people. In post-Communist Albania, for example, many people viewed their first Coca-Cola plant as a sign of a good life to come.

The importance of states declines as TNCs leap political frontiers. Level 4 of IR action sometimes outweighs Levels 2 and 3. General Motors is based in Detroit, but it has offices and plants around the globe. TNC managers look worldwide for settings that promise lower costs and higher profits. If their global outlook calls for a move to greener pastures, local workers and governments can be left high and dry.

4. Richard J. Barnet and John Cavanagh, *Global Dreams: Imperial Corporations and the New World Order* (New York: Simon & Schuster, 1994); Kenichi Ohmae, *The Borderless World: Power and Strategy in the Interlinked Economy* (New York: HarperBusiness, 1990).

Transnational influences can be seen in many ways. Electronic money transfers go on twenty-four hours a day from Hong Kong to London to New York, eluding government controls. Drug dealers and others escape taxes by laundering profits via offshore banks—for example, on several Caribbean islands. Governments that still seek to control the minds and tastes of their citizens (as in China) are fighting an uphill battle as exotic sights and sounds bounce from satellites to local TV screens.

Few individuals can be more transnational than George Soros. Both his business and his philanthropy transcend all borders. One of the world's richest men, the Hungarian-born Soros lives in the U.S. but has mutual funds headquartered offshore. His funds seek bargains around the globe—from overvalued currencies to real estate to oil reserves. Critics see his funds as pirate ships that raid state treasuries, such as the Bank of England, through currency speculations. But Soros also underwrites and steers the Soros Foundation, a sponsor of progressive educational-economic reforms worldwide. In the late 1990s the Soros Foundation gave more aid to Russia than the U.S. government. For more on Soros and his philanthropy, see the sidebar in this chapter entitled "Who Is an Idealist in the 1990s?"

Apart from "interstate" and "transnational," we may also classify IR actors as belonging to North and South, East and West, or the First, Second, Third, or Fourth Worlds (see Table 1.1). The idea of a **Third World** developed during the Cold War to distinguish those countries that were neither part of the First (or Free) World nor part of the Second (or Communist) World. In fact, most nonaligned countries were in the South. Unlike the **First World,** led by Washington, or the **Second World,** led by Moscow, most Third World countries were nonwhite, non-Christian, and not developed industrially. However, each division contained enormous diversity. For example, the First World contained both Greece and New Zealand. The Second World embraced not just the USSR and Poland, but also China and Cuba. The Third World included India, Yugoslavia, and Guyana. Some analysts even spoke of a **Fourth World,** made from the very poorest ranks of the Third. Thus, reality is far more variegated than our categories, which are humble starting points for analysis.

Level 5: The Biosphere

Population pressures and resource shortages remind us that IR, like all human activity, depends upon the earth's thin envelope of stone, water, soil, fauna, flora, and atmosphere. Humans are part of this biosphere, and

Globalization reduces each government's ability to control its own borders. Global drug trafficking challenges the health, finances, and political stability of many states. With UN support, however, this Thai farmer has replaced opium poppies with other crops.

Table 1.1 North and South

The North, or First World

The North consists of Western Europe, the U.S. and Canada, Japan, Australia, and New Zealand. These countries are highly "developed," economically industrialized, capitalist, high-income, democratic, located largely in the northern hemisphere, largely Caucasian and Christian. This "club of rich nations" makes up the **Organization for Economic Cooperation and Development (OECD),** founded in 1960 to discuss and coordinate economic policies. Most of the North is allied militarily with the U.S. in bilateral pacts or through the **North Atlantic Treaty Organization (NATO),** founded in 1949 to protect the West from Soviet attack.

↑ ? The Second World ? ↑	↑ Newly Industrializing Countries (NICs) ↑
Most of the former Communist states of Eastern Europe and the Soviet Union have been striving since the late 1980s to join the First World. Cuba and North Korea are still Communist. China and Vietnam have a foot in each "world."	Many countries in the South were acquiring a "northern" status in the 1990s. They include the four Asian "Little Tigers" of Singapore, Hong Kong, Taiwan, and South Korea. Other NICs include Chile, Malaysia, Thailand, Argentina, Brazil, and Indonesia.

The South, or Third World

The Third World includes the "developing" or "less developed countries" (LDCs) of Asia, Africa, the Middle East, and much of Latin America. Many of these countries have adhered to the Nonaligned Movement that emerged in the mid-1950s and the Group of 77 (numbering more than 125 member states), a caucus on economic affairs within the UN since the mid-1960s. The Third World also includes the Central Asian states (such as Tajikistan) that emerged from the former USSR.

The Fourth World

The Fourth World is drawn from the poorest of the poor: African states such as Guinea, Mozambique, and Somalia; Asian states such as Bangladesh and Maldives; and in the Americas, Haiti and some Native American communities.

international activity, from reforestation to war, can enlarge or weaken the globe's carrying capacity for life. Level 5 is the broadest arena for IR action and analysis.

On every level we find nonstate actors—important IR players that are not states. At Level 1 these players are key individuals; at Level 2 they are substate actors such as ethnic groups and economic interests. At Level 3 IGOs such as the United Nations often act independently of governments. Level 4 players consist of NGOs; TNCs; religions; foundations; the

The biosphere is the broadest arena for IR action. Environmental protection became a major UN concern in the 1970s. "Think globally, act locally" is an important principle of global environmentalism, illustrated here by recycling and the use of wind power.

Internet and World Wide Web; the Cable News Network (CNN), the BBC, and MTV; and terrorist organizations and global crime syndicates. On Level 5 is the biosphere—another nonstate actor.

With so many players and stages to explore, students of IR face the **level-of-analysis problem:** Which level(s) must they study to understand a given issue? Which level(s), if any, can be neglected? There is no easy answer. Knowledge from many disciplines must be integrated to comprehend how each level interacts.

THROUGH WHAT LENS SHOULD YOU VIEW IR?

To understand the myriad events and forces shaping IR, we need a good lens—a theoretical perspective that helps us to explain the past, describe the present, anticipate alternative futures, and provide sound guidelines for policymaking. Two opposing perspectives have long dominated the practice and study of IR—realism and idealism. A third view, focused on interdependence, emerged in the last decades of the 20th century. Let us look through each lens in turn.

Image 1: Realism—IR as a Struggle for Power

The Growth of Realism. Most realists agree that international relations is a struggle for power, which can be defined as the military, economic, and other means for obtaining material wealth, influence, and prestige. Four centuries before Christ, the realist's bottom line was clearly stated by an Athenian commander: "The strong do what they have the power to do and the weak accept what they have to accept." The Athenian officer demanded that the people of Melos, an island in the Cretan Sea, fight with Athens against Sparta. But the Melians wanted to remain neutral and appealed to an ideal: "It is to the general good of all men" to uphold the principles of "fair play and just dealing." Impatient with idealistic talk, the Athenians seized Melos, slaughtering or enslaving its people.[5]

We learn much about **realism** and **idealism** in ancient Greece from Thucydides, an Athenian general turned historian. He explained the Peloponnesian war on all levels: the **hubris** (arrogant pride) and caution of individual leaders, the spirit of Athenian democracy and Spartan dictatorship, the growth of Athenian power relative to Spartan power, the cultural ties that linked Athens and other city-states, and the environmental pressures that pushed certain people to settle Athens and make it into a great seafaring power.

The tactics of realism were elaborated by Niccolò Machiavelli in 16th-century Italy. Machiavelli focused on Level 1, the ambition and courage of great leaders. He advised the statesman to be both the lion and the fox—powerful and clever. "Let a prince win and maintain the state—the means will always be judged honorable and praised by everyone."[6]

Living during England's 17th-century Civil War, Thomas Hobbes targeted Levels 2 and 3. He focused on what realists see as the structural cause of the struggle for power: **anarchy**—the absence of government. In a "state of nature" without government, Hobbes argued, every person would do whatever seemed necessary to survive, unleashing a "war of all against all" where life is "nasty, brutish, and short." To escape this turmoil, Hobbes wrote, people contract to obey a supreme political authority. This government provides security within the state.[7]

For Hobbes, a student of Thucydides' work, IR is a state of nature.[8] Among diverse societies and states, however, there is anarchy—no overarching government to define and impose rules. Hence, each society must depend on its own strengths and cunning—what today's realists call **self-help**—to survive. The only way to check others' tyranny is to amass power, either alone or with allies.

But the realist politician utilizes persuasion as well as coercion. Thus, German Chancellor Otto von Bismarck blended force with other forms of diplomacy to unify Germany and defeat France in 1870–1871 and prevent for two decades an aggrieved France from aligning with Russia against Germany. Bismarck's *realpolitik* (realist policy) brought a German word into common English usage.

There are various kinds of realists. The ultrarealist—a follower of

5. Thucydides, *The Peloponnesian War* (New York: Penguin Books, 1956), Book 5, chap. 7.

6. Niccolò Machiavelli, *The Prince* (Prospect Heights, Ill.: Waveland Press, 1980), 109. For his ties with Leonardo da Vinci, see Roger D. Masters, *Machiavelli, Leonardo, and the Science of Power* (Notre Dame, Ill.: University of Notre Dame Press, 1996). For applications, see Harvey C. Mansfield, Jr., *Taming the Prince: The Ambivalence of Modern Executive Power* (New York: Free Press, 1989).

7. Thomas Hobbes, *Leviathan* [1651] (New York: Penguin, 1981), 185–188; chaps. 14–17.

8. Hobbes' first published work was his 1628 translation of Thucydides' *Peloponnesian War*.

Machiavelli or Hobbes—is a hard-liner who assumes that conflict is inevitable. The ultra goes all out to defeat rivals, treating war as just another tool of policy. The founder of the Soviet state in 1917, Vladimir Lenin, endorsed a kind of ultrarealism for Communists. He taught that politics is "*kto kovo*" (who [conquers] whom). Lenin endorsed any and all means likely to promote a worldwide dictatorship of the working class.

Moderate realists, however, often hope to avoid war. They seek compromise accords and strong webs of international law to promote long-term stability. U.S. policy since World War II has been guided basically by moderate realism, though laced at times with the ultra's belief that "anything goes." World War II taught Americans that aggressive dictators must be contained, if necessary by force. In 1946–1947 U.S. diplomat George F. Kennan articulated a strategy for containing Soviet expansion by building up the economic, political, and military strengths of the U.S. and its partners.

Americans also learned moderate realism from theologian Reinhold Niebuhr, geographer Nicholas Spykman, and IR scholars such as professor **Hans Morgenthau**.[9] Taken together, their writings suggested six axioms of realism:

1. Human nature: Humans are self-centered, greedy, and often aggressive.

2. State centrism: The state is now the primary actor in world politics. The United Nations is an instrument of states.

3. Power as interest: The basic interest of each state is to increase its power. Politics is a struggle for power. At home, states build military and economic strength; externally, they form alliances against others. Power is an end in itself, but it is also a tool. It is a means, fungible like gold or money, toward many ends.

4. Rationality: Governments calculate rationally how to maximize state power. Knowing this, we can read between the lines of flowery messages that one foreign minister sends to another.

5. Amorality: There is no common moral code among states. Individual morality stops at the border. As Morgenthau put it, "realism refuses to identify the moral aspirations of a particular nation with the moral laws that govern the universe." Ultras go further: Among states, they say, might makes right.

6. History over science: A wise reading of history is the best guide to understanding IR. Scientific models and statistical analyses cannot measure the vitality of politics.

 Can Realists Favor International Institutions?

Moderate realists are often institutionalists—proponents of international law and organization. They see a constructive role for international institutions, though they are reluctant to surrender power to them. They welcome institutions that reduce anarchy, believing that law can benefit the strong as well as the weak, because rules make cheating on treaties and sneak attacks less likely. Institutions can make IR more predictable and reduce the cost of transactions across borders.

In 1919 the Republican-controlled U.S. Senate did not approve President Woodrow Wilson's plan for a League of Nations. Wilson wanted to end power politics; Republican leaders expected it to continue. But most Republican senators were not isolationist; most were conservative internationalists in the moderate realist traditions of former presidents Theodore Roosevelt and William Howard Taft. Taft himself served as president of the League to Enforce the Peace (founded in 1915), which endorsed collective security though it said nothing about economic reform or national self-determination. Moderate Republicans engineered the 1922 Washington Naval Treaty to limit battleships and heavy cruisers, and backed other internationalist policies such as the 1932 Stimson Doctrine (see Chapter 16).

In the 1990s ultrarealists, including some U.S. senators and congressional leaders, wanted to dissolve the United Nations. Moderate realists saw a constructive role for international institutions.

9. Hans J. Morgenthau, *Politics Among Nations: The Struggle for Power and Peace* (New York: Knopf, 1948), updated and revised by Kenneth W. Thomp-

U.S. containment policy, based on these axioms, proved relatively effective from the late 1940s to the mid-1960s. In the late 1960s and 1970s, however, the American superpower foundered in Vietnam and then reeled in the face of sharp increases in the price of oil demanded by the Organization of Petroleum Exporting Countries (OPEC). What had gone wrong? Critics assailed each axiom of realism:

1. Human nature: Human behavior is not uniform. Some leaders and followers are more aggressive than others. Individuals can change; so can societies. Life across borders can be improved.

2. State centrism: States are not the only important players on the world stage. The evening TV news, antiwar folk singer Joan Baez, and OPEC all challenged U.S. "super power" in different ways.

3. Power as interest: Military-political power is no longer fungible. The heavily armed U.S. was being eclipsed by "trading states" such as Japan and West Germany.[10] To understand IR, critics advised, study **international political economy (IPE)**—how politics and economics, both domestic and across borders, combine to shape world affairs.[11]

4. Rationality: Governments do not always act rationally. They often foul up due to fatigue, misperception, partisan politics, and bureaucratic rigidity.

5. Morality: There is a growing worldwide consensus on morality—for example, on human rights—making morality a weighty factor in IR.

6. Science: Analysts of IR go astray when they trust their instincts and generalize from a few incidents. A scientific approach is necessary to understand IR. Otherwise, bias takes over.

Dissatisfaction with realism strengthened the quest to develop better approaches to international studies. Two new approaches sought to improve the scientific rigor of IR and to pay more attention to economics.

Neorealism/Structuralism. A school of **neorealism,** or structuralism, developed in the last decades of the 20th century, led by professor **Kenneth N. Waltz.** Adapting Thomas Hobbes, Waltz explained IR by one key variable: the underlying structure of the international system—its anarchy and the distribution of power. According to this view, wars happen because there is nothing to prevent them—no government over states. For neorealists IR is less a struggle for power than for security. When push comes to shove, states respond to the power structure in which they operate, regardless of leaders' personalities or form of government.[12]

Critics say that structuralism is too mechanistic and claims far more than it proves. For example, Waltz asserts that the bipolar structure of the

son (New York: McGraw-Hill, 1993). For realist views in the 1990s, see John Mersheimer, "The False Premises of International Institutions," *International Security* 19, no. 3 (winter 1994–1995): 5–49, and others' essays in the same volume called "GET REAL." See also "Realism Reconsidered," *National Interest* (special issue), no. 30 (winter 1992–1993).

10. Richard Rosecrance, *The Rise of the Trading State* (New York: Basic Books, 1986).

11. See Robert Gilpin, *The Political Economy of International Relations* (Princeton, N.J.: Princeton University Press, 1987). For a literature review, see Dennis J. Gayle, Robert A. Denemark, and Kendall W. Stiles, "International Political Economy: Evolution and Prospects," *International Studies Notes* 16, no. 3, and 17, no. 1 (fall–winter 1991–1992): 64–68.

12. Kenneth N. Waltz, *Theory of International Politics* (New York: McGraw-Hill, 1979). See also Waltz, *Man, the State, and War: A Theoretical Analysis* (New York: Columbia University Press, 1959). For a structuralist IR textbook, see Robert J. Lieber, *No Common Power: Understanding International Relations*, 3d ed. (New York: HarperCollins, 1995).

system under the two superpowers explained both their Cold War rivalry and their restraint. This assertion is plausible but not established. Thus, the bipolar structure could as well have triggered World War III or given rise to a cooperative Soviet-U.S. partition of the globe. Bipolarity does not assure peace. Other bipolar systems—Athens/Sparta and Rome/Carthage—ended in major wars. Why did the long cold peace prevail? To answer, we must study not only the pyramid of interstate power but individuals such as Stalin and Harry Truman, the societies that spawned them, and the interactions of particular states.[13]

The World-System (Dependency) School. Updating Karl Marx and Lenin, **world-system theory** (or dependency theory) posits that for centuries there has been a world system divided into a core of rich capitalist states, a dependent periphery of poor states, and a semi-periphery between the core and outer circle. What Waltz calls anarchy, world-system theorists say is really the structural dependency of the periphery on the core. They charge that Waltz and other non-Marxists ignore dynamic forces such as the class struggle pushing toward a revolutionary transformation of the world system.[14]

Critics say the world-system model is too simplistic. It downplays the role of individuals, ignores the emergence of some poor countries into the ranks of the rich, and glosses over the mutual dependence of North and South.

On balance, both neorealists and dependency theorists are too deterministic. Over and over we shall see that policy choices are conditioned— not decided—by the structures of power. Let us turn now to idealism, the major alternative to realism for more than two thousand years.

Image 2: Idealism—IR as a Quest for Harmony, Law, and Morality

The Growth of Idealism and Liberalism. Many idealists and liberals expect all peoples to live in harmony thanks to nature, law, or morality. Realists anticipate conflict and war; idealists, cooperation and peace. Realists focus on what is good for the state; many idealists think more about the good of humanity.

Idealism is also ancient. The Melians, as we saw, called on the Athenians to practice "fair play and just dealing." But realists like the Athenian commander treat rules as nothing more than dictates of the strong. Idealists, in contrast, view legal and moral norms as sacred—built into IR by God or Nature or human contract.

Idealists trust in Reason to reform the world and bring peace; realists doubt that social science can subdue greed. Idealists hope for the best; re-

13. See also Randall L. Schweller and David Priess, "A Tale of Two Realisms: Expanding the Institutions Debate," *Mershon International Studies Review* 41, Supplement 1 (May 1997): 1–32, which reviews some two hundred sources.

14. See, for example, Immanuel Wallerstein, *The Rise and Future Demise of the World Capitalist System* (New York: Cambridge University Press, 1979); Wallerstein, *Geopolitics and Geoculture: Essay on the Changing World-System* (New York: Cambridge University Press, 1991); Robert W. Cox, "Social Forces, States and World Orders: Beyond International Relations Theory," *Millennium: A Journal of International Studies* 10 (summer 1981): 126–155; and "The South in the New World (Dis) Order," *Third World Quarterly* 15, no. 1 (March 1994).

Table 1.2 Three Images of IR: Diverse Assumptions

	Realism	Idealism	Interdependence
Focus	the means (power); the possible	the moral objective; the desirable	the means and ends
Nature of IR	anarchy; often win-lose; self-help	harmony (win-win)	potential for mutual gain or pain
Human Nature	egotistical, aggressive, greedy	good	malleable, variable
Values at Stake in IR	survival and influence	peace, justice, welfare, the biosphere	survival, influence, and quality of life
Source of Most IR Conflicts	struggle for power	misperception	struggle for power and misperception
How to Plan	learn from the past	visualize the future	learn from the past and visualize the future
What to Study	history	social sciences, law	all relevant knowledge
Outlook	pessimism, caution	optimism, hope	cautious hope
Key IR Actors	states and systems of states	international and transnational actors	both state and nonstate actors
International Law	undependable—a weak reed to rely on	an independent force for cooperation	weak but growing—an "emergent property"
Human Rights and Morality	irrelevant to IR	central to IR	increasingly relevant
Criterion for Action	national interest	humane ideals	enlightened self-interest and humanism
How to Negotiate	claim values and seek gains relative to your rivals'	seek absolute gains for all parties	greatest possible gains for self and others

alists fear the worst. These and other differences are summarized in Table 1.2.

Like realists, idealists fall into many camps. Philosophical idealists, like Plato, believe that ideal forms underlie the imperfect, material bodies we see. They agree with St. John: "In the beginning was the Word. . . ." Utopians, like Sir Thomas More, sketch models of ideal worlds to stimulate thought and action. Grotians (named for Hugo Grotius, a founder of international law) seek to codify the norms imbedded in nature or wise practice. Liberals are a new breed, dating only from the 17th century. Lockean liberals (followers of John Locke) stress liberty and the sovereignty of the individual. Utilitarians (followers of Jeremy Bentham) believe that public policy should seek the greatest utility for the most people. Their 20th-century offshoots favor welfare programs for the dispossessed. Commercial pacifist liberals (followers of Adam Smith and Joseph Schumpeter) hold that free trade contributes not only to wealth but to peace. Liberal pacifists (followers of Immanuel Kant) believe that representative democracy leads to peace and international codes of behavior.

Global idealists proclaim the equality of all men and women. But there are also narrow idealists who struggle on behalf of the "one true faith" or the "master race." They have often spawned so-called holy wars and campaigns to wipe out other peoples. Arguing against such narrow idealisms, Soviet President Mikhail Gorbachev called in the 1980s for the "humanization" of international relations—the placing of universal human needs above those of race, religion, or class. As awareness of our common fate grows, he told the United Nations, "every nation would be genuinely interested in confining itself within the limits of international law."[15]

Idealism in U.S. Policy. American policy has long carried the stamp of strong ideals—its founders' confidence that they were destined to build a New World better than the Old, the claim that "all men are created equal," and trust in scientific progress.

President Woodrow Wilson became the world's most famous idealist in 1917–1919 when he summoned Americans to a crusade to make the world safe for democracy and demanded that a League of Nations supplant old-style power politics.

Later, President Franklin Roosevelt championed his "four freedoms" (freedom of speech, freedom of worship, freedom from want, and freedom from fear) and the establishment of the United Nations. From 1945 until 1976 Democratic and Republican presidents alike spoke up for freedom while also emphasizing pragmatic containment of communism.

More than any other U.S. president, Jimmy Carter, elected in 1976, made human rights the central objective of U.S. policy. But when Iranian ayatollahs and Soviet militarists made Carter look "soft," U.S. voters swung the other way: starting in 1980 they voted for what became twelve years of Ronald Reagan–George Bush *realpolitik.*

In 1992 the wheel turned again as U.S. voters rejected Bush in favor of Bill Clinton, who, as a candidate, promised to achieve welfare ideals at home and promote human rights abroad—for example, in China. President Clinton's foreign policy turned out to be more pragmatic than idealistic, but he often dispatched diplomats to mediate as "honest brokers" and soldiers to act as the policemen of the world.

The New Idealists. Just as neorealists have sought to improve on Morgenthau's axioms, neoidealists and neoliberals seek to remedy blind spots in the Wilsonian tradition. Neoidealists, like neorealists, try to apply scientific methods of analysis to IR. Neoidealists are more attuned to the IPE than traditional idealists, but reject the neorealists' material determinism.

International relations is not a males-only arena, but many people see IR through gender-tinted lenses. In Chapter 5 we shall see how the UN Development Programme grades societies by the opportunities they leave open to women.

15. For the evolution of Gorbachev's foreign policy, see Walter C. Clemens, Jr., *Can Russia Change? The USSR Confronts Global Interdependence* (New York: Routledge, 1990), chaps. 7–8.

Who Is an Idealist in the 1990s?

Various forms of neoidealism abound as another millennium begins.

Endism. Since the conflict of ideas drives history, the victory of Western liberalism over Communist ideology has meant the "end of history."[1]

Civilizationism. "History" continues in the clash of civilizations (defined as the "broadest level of cultural identity"). The end of the Cold War pits "the West against the Rest"—Confucian, Muslim, Hindu, and other civilizations.[2]

Postmodernism. Sophistry still thrives, magnified by the power of sound bites. Disgusted by inflated rhetoric, postmodernists read between the lines to deconstruct political language and show its hollow or self-serving character. So-called facts are often propaganda to buttress existing power structures.[3] Postmodernists are correct in seeing ethnic and other identities as more manufactured than organic. All texts have multiple meanings. But deconstruction can also go too far. It is good to punch holes in empty claims, but not necessary to throw away all faith in language.

Feminism. Feminist scholars try to deconstruct the language of IR to reveal its gender bias; then they hope to reconstruct IR by putting women back in.[4] Feminists contend that men and patriarchal political systems have dominated the practice and the study of IR. Man the hunter and fighter has shut out woman the nurturer and cooperator. The prevailing stereotype in many countries is that women are "soft"—not tough enough for the brutal game of politics. Hence, they should be IR spectators or should be relegated to "low politics."

There are many varieties of feminism in IR studies—liberal, essentialist, postmodern, Third World, and others. But most focus on a central question: If women were more influential in the study and process of IR, would the world be different? Would policy-makers behave differently? Would there be more or less peace?

As we will see in Chapter 5, the UN Development Programme has devised measures of gender bias to ascertain the extent to which women are deprived economically and shut out politically in countries around the world. In Chapter 12 we will learn that "keeping women down" helps to keep entire countries backward and poor; Chapter 16 details women's rights abuses.

Feminists caution that we cannot infer much from the exceptional cases of Margaret Thatcher and other women who have led countries such as Israel, Britain, Pakistan, Israel, Turkey, Bangladesh, India, Ireland, Iceland, and Norway. A man or a woman who gets to the top in politics is probably tougher than most. Secretary of State Madeleine Albright advocates more forceful policies than most other U.S. policy-makers.

In sum, feminism provides a valuable lens when kept in focus.

"Worlding" IR. Not just women but many men have been omitted from traditional IR. Ethnic minorities and peoples without states, such as the Kurds, need to be better represented in both the practice and the study of IR. A more comprehensive view would combine gender with ethnicity and other variables. White women in Scarsdale, New York, for example, differ greatly from most black women in a Congolese village, but both play roles in IR.

A Note on George Soros

While other idealists theorized, financier George Soros acted. He doubted that liberalism would take hold in the former Second World unless it was nourished. In the 1990s his Soros Foundation invested in free-market economics, democracy, and public health in two dozen former dictatorships ranging from Hungary to Haiti and South Africa. A believer in ideas, Soros financed hookups to the Internet and the writing of new history texts. But his politics antagonized authoritarian regimes from Belarus to Burma, and his financial speculations aroused critics from Moscow to Kuala Lumpur.

1. Francis Fukuyama, *The End of History and the Last Man* (New York: Avon, 1992).

2. Samuel P. Huntington, *The Clash of Civilizations and the Remaking of World Order* (New York: Simon & Schuster, 1996).

3. See, for example, Francis A. Beer and Robert Hariman, eds., *Post-Realism: The Rhetorical Turn in International Relations* (East Lansing: Michigan State University Press, 1996); and Pauline Marie Rosenau, *Post-Modernism and the Social Sciences: Insights, Inroads, and Intrusions* (Princeton, N.J.: Princeton University Press, 1992).

4. For example, Jan Jindy Pettman, *Worlding Women: A Feminist International Politics* (London: Routledge, 1996); J. Ann Tickner, *Gender in International Relations: Feminist Perspectives on Achieving Global Security* (New York: Columbia University Press, 1992); and the many works by Cynthia Enloe on ethnic minorities and on women.

Traditional, Wilsonian idealists still hope that governments (Level 2) and organizations such as the United Nations (Level 3) can generate progressive reforms. Many new idealists focus on Level 4 and hope that transnational networks can transcend IR's state borders and centers of power. They count on NGOs and communities of experts and cultural leaders to outflank governments.[16]

Some neoidealists believe that realists ignore social constructs—the deep beliefs of each society about other societies and other ways of life. Thus, if the nuclear arsenals of Britain and China were identical, Americans would fear the British less than the Chinese because they trust British intentions. Uncertain about Chinese intentions, Americans worry about their military capabilities.

In focusing on the biosphere (Level 5), many neoidealists are biophiliac. Furthermore, they see threats to whales, wolves, coral, insects, and trees as threats to all life. They call for "green accounting" (calculating environmental costs along with other production costs) and oppose those who resist any restraints on their quests for power and wealth.

Feminism, postmodernism, and other forms of neoidealism are outlined in the sidebar on page 18.

Appraising Realism and Idealism. Each school of realism and idealism contributes to our understanding of IR. But neither greed nor reason governs the world; few humans are basically evil or basically good. Our sight will be impaired if we assume, as realists do, that no better system can emerge. We will be disappointed if we believe, as idealists do, that the future is entirely open-ended.

The very terms are misleading. One person's realism may be another's folly; one person's idealism may be another's self-righteous naïveté or dogma. The term "liberalism" is also problematic, because its meaning has shifted from the 18th to the 20th century. We need a more complete paradigm, less given to either/or categories. If realism is thesis and idealism its antithesis, where is a constructive synthesis?

Image 3: Interdependence—Mutual Vulnerability

A world view anchored in global **interdependence** offers a broader lens with fewer distortions than either realism or idealism. The concept of interdependence fits our complex world where high-low politics converge and domestic-external realms intertwine. This world view affirms both the difficulties and the possibilities of greater cooperation in IR. It acknowledges the continuing importance of states but also the rising tide of cross-border transactions by nongovernmental actors.

Two nongovernmental organizations cooperated across borders to press for an end to nuclear testing. In 1989–1990, the Nevada-Semipalatinsk Movement (NSM) linked those who wanted to end testing in Nevada and at Semipalatinsk in Soviet Kazakstan. The NSM worked with International Physicians for the Prevention of Nuclear War (IPPNW), winner of the 1985 Nobel Peace Prize. Here the president of the Kazak branch of the IPPNW signs a petition calling for a halt to nuclear testing.

16. Thus, the World Order Models Project seeks transnational support for four goals—peace, economic well-being, justice, and environmental protection—and a timetable to achieve them. It has sponsored books by scholars from the U.S., African, Indian, Scandinavian, and other political cultures. See Richard A. Falk, *A Study of Future Worlds* (New York: Free Press, 1975); and Falk, *Explorations at the Edge of Time: The Prospects for World Order* (Philadelphia: Temple University Press, 1992). See also works by Ali A. Mazrui, Rajni Kothari, and Johan Galtung.

What is interdependence? It signifies mutual dependence—a point on the spectrum between absolute dependence and independence. Interdependence means mutual vulnerability. It is a relationship in which the well-being of two or more actors is vulnerable, or at least sensitive, to changes in the condition or policies of the other.[17]

To assess mutual vulnerability we must first ask: Is it balanced? If dependence is basically one-sided, it is not interdependence. Second, is there vulnerability or mere sensitivity? Two countries share strategic vulnerability if they cannot defend against one another. A country is sensitive if it can be hurt by effects from outside before it takes countermeasures. When the U.S. set limits on wheat exports to the USSR in the 1980s, Soviet importers turned out to be merely sensitive to the limits; they could still buy wheat from Argentina and Australia. Third, does the interdependence apply to one issue or many? Some states share vulnerability in just one or two arenas. Canada and the United States, on the other hand, interdepend on a wide range of issues. Fourth, how is interdependence perceived? Parties may interdepend but not perceive it; alternatively, actors may exaggerate their vulnerability. Fifth, does interdependence occur by choice? Interdependence can result from accidents, choice, or coercion. Hoping to tame Soviet expansionism, Washington in the 1970s sought to enmesh the USSR in a web of security, commercial, and scientific cooperation. Some Soviet leaders resisted this web.

Sources and Limits of Interdependence. Mutual vulnerability arises from many sources, each of which has a capacity to enhance or diminish life. Sources of vulnerability include weaponry—vulnerability to mass destruction can spur cooperation or inspire a surprise attack; commerce—trade ties can bolster peace or generate frictions; communications—shared information can lead to mutual appreciation or disdain; science and culture—shared knowledge enriches our lives but can also endanger individuality; and coevolution—having evolved together, humans have become interdependent with one another and with their shared habitat.

Is interdependence good or bad? Does it engender peace or conflict? Interdependence by itself is neither good nor bad. How humans deal with this condition can generate gain or pain. The impact of interdependence on peace is difficult to assess because multiple factors are at work. Some studies suggest that extensive trade ties inhibit violence.[18] But such ties do not exclude violent conflict. Many peoples have fought one another despite their interlocked economies—for example, Americans during their Civil War and Europeans in 1914.

17. The argument here follows Robert O. Keohane and Joseph S. Nye, *Power and Interdependence*, 2d ed. (New York: HarperCollins, 1989), chap. 1. But Waltz argues that to accept interdependence as sensitivity guts the term of any political meaning.

18. Susan M. McMillan, "Interdependence and Conflict," *Mershon International Studies Review* 41, Supplement 1 (May 1997): 33–58.

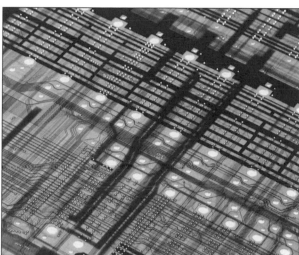

(Left) Trade links countries and may contribute to peace. Beginning in 1963, most Soviet moves toward arms control agreements with the U.S. took place in years when the USSR needed to import grain. Here, a Soviet grain ship docks in New Orleans in 1989—the same year that the Berlin Wall fell.

(Right) International communication, international finance, international technology transfer—all are both cause and effect of growing global interdependence and globalization.

The relationship between the U.S. and Japan shows how interdependence can cut in opposite directions. The two countries bicker over trade and U.S. bases but have been partners in security and commerce since the late 1940s. Japanese and Americans can enrich or diminish one another. If Americans and Japanese did not interact, as was the case during the 18th century, they would not quarrel. Neither would Americans drive Hondas or Japanese play baseball. Without its U.S. ally, Japan would probably arm more and invest less.

Is interdependence growing? Experts disagree on the extent of interdependence and what it means for IR. But the overall picture at the onset of another millennium is one of escalating interdependence—on many issues and among many partners—worldwide. As Soviet President Gorbachev put it in the late 1980s, the world is "contradictory but also integral and interdependent." Humans face many "global problems too complex to be resolved by any single country."[19] To deal with these problems requires cooperation by all "worlds"—including both genders, all races, all cultures, all classes, all regions, and all religions.

In the late 20th century global interdependence coexisted with globalization. The two phenomena are related but distinct. Interdependence—mutual vulnerability—implies the continued existence of states. **Globalization**—global processes that ignore borders—suggests the weakening or even disappearance of state sovereignty as it was known after 1648.[20] The implications and prospects of globalization are discussed in the last chapters of this book.

19. In the 1960s and 1970s Soviet spokesmen asserted that American talk of interdependence masked U.S. ambitions to dominate the world. See Walter C. Clemens, Jr., *The USSR and Global Interdependence: Alternative Futures* (Washington, D.C.: American Enterprise Institute, 1978), chaps. 3–4; and Clemens, *Can Russia Change?*, chaps. 5–6.

20. Wolfgang H. Reinicke, "Global Public Policy," *Foreign Affairs* 76, no. 6 (November–December 1997): 127–139.

Fig. 1.2 Visions of the World

Hierarchy of realism and structural
neorealism

World-system dependency

One-world idealism

Interdependence

Complex Interdependence. Some countries are more than trading partners or allies. They are linked in **complex interdependence,** a relationship with three characteristics: (1) There is a complex agenda with no hierarchy. These countries share many concerns, but no single issue stands out so that, if unresolved, it jeopardizes the entire relationship. (2) Interaction occurs at many levels of government and society. Multiple channels connect these societies—not just the meetings of ministers and presidents. (3) Parties bargain hard and long on various issues, but regard military threats as virtually unthinkable.

Complex interdependence and peaceful cooperation can strengthen one another. Canada and the U.S. have moved toward complex interdependence since the late 19th century, even though their governments and many basic values have remained distinct. All West European countries have gravitated toward complex interdependence since the 1950s. This movement may continue and form a closer union, or it may stall or switch directions. It may expand to include East Europeans and other, more distant actors.

How interdependence theorists view the world compared to other theorists is suggested in Figure 1.2. Traditional and structural realists emphasize the hierarchy of power. World-system theorists divide the world into concentric circles of power. Idealists visualize one world—united despite differences. The interdependence perspective accepts that units have both divergent and shared interests, and that the units can harm or help one another.

THE ART OF THE DEAL: DIVERGENT AND SHARED INTERESTS

Interdependence is a fact. How to respond to this reality is a question for policy-makers. Let us review the basics of negotiation, the tools of the diplomat's trade.

HOW TO NEGOTIATE: CLAIM OR CREATE VALUES?

"Negotiate" is from Latin for "do business." One way to negotiate is to "bargain," derived from the Old French for "haggle."

Most of us negotiate every day, on everything from house chores to terms for a new car. When you haggle about who washes the dishes, the stakes are minor. Between states they are often major.

Negotiation is a process by which parties communicate about ways to deal with issues on which they have different viewpoints. Negotiation is a major tool in **diplomacy**—the conduct of foreign policy. "The essence of diplomacy," said U.S. diplomat Lawrence Eagleburger in 1986, "is how you manage the day-to-day business, the confidence you build, the atmosphere you create, so that when the tough times come, you can do business."[21] But diplomats do not always negotiate to reach an agreement. Often they seek side benefits such as scoring propaganda points or keeping open a channel of communication.

21. Quoted in *Dictionary of Twentieth-Century World Politics*, compiled by Jay M. Shafritz et al. (New York: Holt, 1993), 216.

What Is Diplomacy?

The word "diplomacy" comes from the Latin diploma—a passport or other official document conferring a privilege. By the 18th century "diplomatic" referred to the conduct of foreign policy, especially by ambassadors or other official representatives, as well as to IR documents such as treaties.

Diplomacy has become nearly a synonym for foreign policy. Accordingly, diplomacy comes in many forms. There is open and closed diplomacy, conducted openly or in secret. The diplomacy of force (including gunboat diplomacy and atomic diplomacy) depends on military threat or coercion. Yen or dollar diplomacy uses commercial penetration and economic influence. Media diplomacy directs some messages through press and television. Public diplomacy (such as Voice of America radio broadcasts) addresses the public on the other side.

Cultural diplomacy uses the arts, including film, music, and literature. Sports or ping-pong diplomacy uses athletics to win friends or influence people. All this gives rise to two-track diplomacy—a public track conducted by governments and a private track of citizen and nongovernmental diplomacy. The public and private tracks may harmonize, compete, or conflict.

There is also parliamentary diplomacy (exchanges between parliaments), summit diplomacy (between top leaders), sauna diplomacy (a Russian favorite), shuttle diplomacy (used by U.S. envoys traveling between Israel and Arab capitals), and tin cup diplomacy (asking others to pay for one's own adventures).[1]

There is also diplomacy of deception, disinformation, and half-truths. One story holds: "When a diplomat says 'yes,' he means 'maybe.' When he says 'maybe,' he means 'no.' If he says 'no,' he is not a diplomat." Another saying is that "an ambassador is someone sent abroad to lie for her country."

In this book we argue the case for a diplomacy of truth—at least in peacetime. While secret diplomacy appeals to many governments, it often backfires. Accords reached by open diplomacy are more likely to endure, because they must address the interests of all concerned parties.

1. On Bismarck's cigar diplomacy, see *Dictionary of Twentieth-Century World Politics*, 217.

As Secretary of State you negotiate at home as well as abroad. In Washington you negotiate with the White House and Congress about appointments, budgets, and policy priorities. With the Department of Defense and other agencies you negotiate to dovetail your actions. You must also negotiate with a host of private actors such as the news media, corporations, and churches. From Belgium to Bangladesh you negotiate with governmental and nongovernmental organizations on everything from military alliances to currency reforms to disaster relief.

Pursuing your goals, you may utilize hard or soft power—coercion or persuasion. Negotiators often try to back their words with carrots and sticks. You may reward or penalize, smile or frown, appoint conciliatory "doves" or antagonistic "hawks" to key posts, spend less or more on defense, keep ships at home or "show the flag" abroad. You may welcome, reject, or ignore overtures by others. (Silence, too, can be eloquent.) Your gov-

ernment may also negotiate with force, using war as an instrument of policy. If neither hard nor soft power works, you may give in or withdraw.

Many values or utilities can hinge on negotiations—tangible goods such as land and wealth and intangibles such as honor and credibility. You seek to advance a range of values—those of your country, your government, your department, your own. If the cost is not exorbitant, you may also wish to help other peoples and make the world a better place. You often face hard trade-offs: more of value x at the expense of value y.

IR actors may try to claim *values for themselves or* create *values jointly with others; in short, they can pursue exploitation or mutual gain. Which approach will you adopt? You may choose between three basic types of negotiator.*[22]

Approach 1: The Win-Lose Hard-Liner. *You claim and seek values for your side alone. You want to cut the pie so your side gets the largest possible share from a finite asset. You assume that what one side gains, the other must lose. You reject even a win-win solution unless you gain relatively more than your rivals.*

Your only rule is to win. A lion and a fox, you blend force and deception. You mask your assets, weaknesses, and goals, and expect others to do the same. You value immediate profits more than a reputation for integrity.

If you can't win alone, you partner with others for joint gains at the expense of third parties, as Hitler and Stalin did in 1939 when they split Poland between them. If weak, you can still follow win-lose logic: you "bandwagon" and join the king of the jungle or play the "jackal," following the lion to pick up what remains.[23]

Approach 2: The Win-Win Cooperator. *You want accords—almost for their own sake—trusting that win-win outcomes are always available. You value candor and put all your cards on the table. You focus on absolute gains, not relative benefits. So long as you gain, who cares if others profit more?*

Approach 3: The Conditional Cooperator. *You try to advance your interests by creating values with other actors for mutual gain. You strive to create values that profit each side and help the deal to endure. If you can expand ("grow") the pie, it will be easier to divide and achieve joint benefit. You seek to replace expectations of win-lose with a shared quest for win-win.*

You condition your cooperation on reciprocal action by others. But you take precautions lest the other side feign cooperation while seeking a one-sided victory. To break a spiral of conflict, however, you sometimes initiate exploratory steps to reduce tensions.

You are neither malevolent nor altruistic. You employ leverage gracefully—not with a sledgehammer. Though slightly distrustful, you foster openness. You share information about preferences, beliefs, and even minimum requirements. You cultivate habits of joint problem-solving. You nourish conditions where neither party needs to worry if the other side gains marginally more. You honor commitments and demand that others do the same.

You understand that joint gains are possible but not inevitable. You reject the settlement unless it looks better than the alternatives to no deal at all.

---

22. See also the works by Raiffa, Fisher and Ury, and Lax and Sebenius cited at the end of this chapter in Recommended Resources.

23. See Randall J. Schweller, "Bandwagoning for Profit: Bringing the Revisionist State Back In," *International Security* 19, no. 1 (summer 1994): 72–107.

WHY COOPERATION IS DIFFICULT

If interdependence is a fact, why do IR actors often act like hard-liners and pursue win-lose outcomes? The realist statesman and hard-line negotiator see many reasons to go it alone. They know that each level of international action generates obstacles to mutual gain solutions, beginning with individual greed. These obstacles are multiplied by parasitism and distrust.

Free-Riding: The Logic of Collective Action

Some actors seek to **free ride.** Free riders follow the egotistical **logic of collective action.** This logic appeals to narrow self-interest. It advises the actor to exploit the goods that others provide and contribute as little as possible. Far from augmenting mutual gain, free riders undermine it because they act like parasites. Parasitism is often feasible because some actors are willing and able to produce public goods such as clean air and security even if others contribute less than their fair share.[24] Free riders often make just enough of a token payment to keep major contributors in the game.

If parasitism prevails, public goods will be underfinanced.[25] An interested party may pay the lion's share but still fail to do all that is needed. Parasitism can harm even the parasites. It weakens alliances and pollution controls leaving even the free riders endangered and impoverished. As we shall see in Chapter 4, efforts by Britain and France to "pass the buck" encouraged Hitler to commence World War II. Later, free-riding weakened the anti-Soviet alliance.[26] It continues to threaten the biosphere, as we shall see in Chapter 14.

The Security Dilemma

The **security dilemma** is that action by one state to increase its security may actually weaken it. John and Ivan, for example, say they wish to live in peace. John, however, decides to heighten the walls around his city. John says the walls are purely for defense, but Ivan fears John may be preparing a surprise attack backed by defenses against a counterattack.

Ivan also faces a dilemma: failing to react to John's improved defenses could increase Ivan's vulnerability. But if Ivan takes countermeasures, they may intensify John's insecurity. Action and reaction may produce an arms race—even a war—that neither wanted. This pattern has recurred throughout history. Many players have followed the slogan, "Best safety lies in fear"—often with tragic consequences.

24. Mancur Olson, *The Logic of Collective Action* (Cambridge, Mass.: Harvard University Press, 1965); see also Olson, *The Rise and Decline of Nations* (New Haven, Conn.: Yale University Press, 1982).

25. The Greek *parasitos* means someone who dines at another's table; Latin *parasitus* is one who lives by amusing the rich. Parasitoid insects eventually kill their hosts.

26. Europe and Japan could assume that Washington, for its own reasons, did not want them to fall under Soviet domination. U.S. allies contributed just enough to keep Americans from turning inward. For most of the Cold War Americans devoted more than 6 percent of their economic production to defense; Europeans, about 3; Japanese, 1 or 2. The result was that Western forces could never match Soviet forces man-for-man, tank-for-tank. Had the Soviets attacked, Washington might have felt compelled to respond with nuclear weapons.

Prisoner's Dilemma (PD)

IR negotiations often resemble a game—sometimes played for high stakes. Game theory outlines four kinds of contests.[27] First, a game is called **zero-sum,** or win-lose, when the winnings of one side equal the other's losses, as in poker. Whatever John wins Ivan loses. Hard-line realists often perceive their contest with rivals as zero-sum. Second, a game is **negative-sum,** or lose-lose, if both sides lose more than they gain—the likely result of a nuclear exchange. Third, if both contestants win (as in a friendly race), a game is **positive-sum,** or win-win.

But neither pure conflict nor 100 percent harmony occurs often in world affairs. The fourth and most common IR game is **variable-sum:** each side may win, each side may lose, or one side may win and the other lose.

Variable-sum situations compel each side to decide whether to cooperate or defect from what could be a common cause. Such choices can be difficult, as we see in the **Prisoner's Dilemma (PD):**

The police charge John and Ivan with a crime and put them in separate cells so they cannot talk with each other. The prosecutor wants one or both to confess because she cannot prove their guilt.[28] She tells Ivan: "If you confess that you both did it, and John remains silent, I will set you free and reward you with $500. If you clam up and John squeals, you will stay in jail for 40 years. If both of you admit your guilt, however, each will receive a 10-year jail term. But if you both stay silent, I must free you both."

The prosecutor offers John the same choices. Each player would like to go free and get the reward. But neither knows if the other will confess or hold his tongue. (As we see in the sidebar on page 27, alleged terrorist conspirators cannot always trust one another.) Both players' choices are plotted in a decision matrix (see Table 1.3). The matrix assigns a numerical value to each of the four possible outcomes. Thus, the upper right cell posits a 20-point gain for Ivan and a 40-point loss for John. These numerical values are quite subjective and could vary depending on how much each player values his freedom.

Looking at these choices, Ivan decides to defect ("squeal"). Why? He wants to minimize his risk (at worst, -10) while maximizing his gain (+20). John follows the same rationale and also defects. To their shock, each must spend a decade in jail.

Here is the paradox: In pursuing their self-interest, both Ivan and John suffer a poor outcome. Had they cooperated with each other, neither would have scored the maximum possible gain but each would have at-

27. Game theory is a branch of mathematics that analyzes decisions in terms of the stakes and likely outcomes. See Frank C. Zagare, *Game Theory: Concepts and Explanations* (Beverly Hills, Calif.: Sage, 1984), and articles on IR "games" in the *Journal of Conflict Resolution.*

28. The exercise focuses on the self-interest of John and Ivan—not on their possible guilt or the merits of honesty.

Table 1.3 The Prisoner's Dilemma (PD)

		IVAN'S CHOICES	
		Be silent (cooperate with John)	Confess (defect from cooperation with John)
JOHN'S CHOICES	Be silent (cooperate with Ivan)	(+10) good for Ivan (+10) good for John	(+20) great for Ivan (- 40) catastrophic for John
	Confess (defect from cooperation with Ivan)	(- 40) catastrophic for Ivan (+20) great for John	(-10) poor for Ivan (-10) poor for John

tained a substantial good: liberation from jail and freedom to pursue other opportunities (+10).

How Relevant Is PD to IR?

PD oversimplifies, but it makes us think. It is a heuristic device—a tool to stimulate insights. PD is just one of many games that approximate particular IR situations. In other chapters we shall consider games such as "Chicken," "Stag hunt," and "Deadlock."

The ultrarealist will always defect, because she/he sees all relationships as zero-sum. A win-win idealist will always cooperate, ignoring the danger that her/his goodwill may be abused. But sophisticated realists and idealists see that consistent gains come from cooperation—provided neither side defects. Where realists and idealists disagree is on the stability of conditional cooperation. The realist worries that, after repeated plays, the other side may defect and inflict heavy punishment on the rival. The idealist, counting on human goodness and progress, trusts that cooperation will persist and expand.

The student of interdependence rejects both perspectives. Mutual cooperation is neither impossible nor assured. World politics is nothing if not complex. Some players are generous and open; others are aggressive and deceptive. Players can and do "learn," but rivals may infer different lessons. Sometimes players unlearn. Or they reverse gears as circumstances change, causing amity to sour.

WHY COOPERATION IS POSSIBLE

Neither suckers nor cynics do well in PD situations. Suckers are abused and cynics condemn themselves to persistent losses. Is the same true for countries? How do they cooperate without being exploited?

PD in New York

PD came to life in February 1995 when one of the persons accused of a terrorist conspiracy broke ranks with his co-defendants in a New York court. Siddiq Ali pleaded guilty and said that he and eleven other defendants had worked to assassinate and bomb. The other defendants were shocked, unaware that their associate had been talking with prosecutors for weeks.

To get a feel for the dilemma, present it as a real choice to a small group. Isolate each "prisoner" and ask her/him to write on a slip of paper "confess" or "silent." Then bring the "prisoners" together and announce the outcome. If you repeat the exercise several times, the roles of trust and trickery will become more evident. Afterwards, discuss with the players why they chose to cooperate or defect.

As we shall see in later chapters, skilled negotiators have often overcome the problems inherent in the security dilemma and PD. They are free to do so because real world IR is not a one-shot affair. It is a process that continues year after year, with more than two players and no all-powerful authority. Most important, real IR negotiators can communicate and learn from experience. They can build trust and install safeguards against cheating.

Coordination Games

Coordination games come readily to lovers, friends, business partners, and allies. The point of a **coordination game** is to increase the gains for each party. Such games can also be played by antagonists who have some common interests. They may transform a conflict (as between Armenia and Azerbaijan) into a coordination game in which the issue is how to increase gains for each party (oil, revenue, trade, and—above all—peace).

Negotiators can generate rewards for cooperation and penalties for defection. They can help one another to view their relationship not as a private prisoner's dilemma—"What's in it for me?"—but as a shared *prisoners'* dilemma—"What outcomes will benefit us both and harm neither?"

Breaking the Spiral of Conflict

Many governments believe that their diplomacy should match the tough moves of their rivals. When people play repeated rounds of computerized sequential Prisoner's Dilemma, the winning strategy turns out to be **tit-for-tat (TFT).** The formula is simple: "Cooperate on your first move and after every cooperative move by the other side. If the other side defects, however, do the same until the other side cooperates."[29]

Once any party defects, however, a strategy of TFT locks both sides onto a treadmill of mutual defection. To escape the treadmill, one side must take the first step and initiate a pattern of cooperation. To make coordination games possible, unilateral initiatives may be needed, as we shall see in Chapters 6 and 7.

The Best Alternative to No-Agreement (BATNA)

Should you accept a negotiated settlement even if it fails to meet all your needs? Is half a loaf better than none at all? You weigh the settlement available by negotiation against the **best alternative to no-agreement (BATNA)** and deliberate: "If I reject this accord, will my side be better off with some other alternative?"[30]

29. Robert Axelrod, *The Evolution of Cooperation* (New York: Basic Books, 1984). Tests show that if just two computer messages are permitted, sequential PD players learn more quickly how to act on their common interests. Hayward R. Alker, Jr., Roger Hurwitz, and Karen Rothkin, "Fairy Tales Can Come True: Narrative Constructions of Prisoner's Dilemma Game Plays," unpublished paper, Massachusetts Institute of Technology, 1993.

30. On BATNA, see Fisher and Ury in Recommended Resources at the end of this chapter.

Mutual gain may be found in a deal that meets diverse needs. Assume that Ivan has surplus oil while John has excess wheat. Joint gains for both sides are shown in Figure 1.3. No agreement is shown as zero while an oil-wheat trade is marked A on the axis pointing up and to the right. But security concerns rank even higher for Ivan and John than a commodity exchange. If they could agree to reduce Ivan's tanks and John's bombers, this deal would improve security *and* save money. Therefore we place an accord on tanks and bombers at B, even higher on the axis.

Joint gains need not mean equal gains. If John is desperate for oil, he may barter a great deal of wheat for a small supply of oil. If Ivan fears John's air force, he may give up many tanks for some reduction of John's bombers. Agreements with unequal values are shown in Figure 1.4. An agreement at A would be an improvement for both sides compared to no agreement at zero, but an accord at either B or C would be even better for both parties than A. Ivan, however, would prefer the B settlement while John likes C better.

The Frontier of Possibilities

Hard-line realists reject deals that benefit the other side more than themselves. By contrast, a value-creating orientation seeks a compromise accord as high as possible up the axis. How far can the parties move up the axis? If John gives up new planes for Ivan's old tanks, John's interests may suffer. Figure 1.5 shows the **frontier of possibilities.**

From any point along the frontier neither side can gain more except at the other's expense. Ivan cannot get a better deal unless John becomes worse off. Within the frontier, one or both sides can gain. But Ivan profits more from vertical moves above the axis while John gains more from horizontal moves to the right. The higher along the axis the two sides move, the more the mutual gain. Joint but asymmetrical gains are possible in many realms. If absolute gains are substantial, Ivan and John may not worry about which side profits more.

The concepts of BATNA and the frontier of possibilities help negotiators to know when mutual gain is possible. Ultimately, however, accords depend on diplomats who can surmount difficult circumstances. Our case studies will show that effective negotiators possess an array of personal strengths, as summarized in the sidebar on page 30. Some diplomats have more of one quality than another, and express these qualities in different ways. A "winning personality," for example, could be gruff or suave.

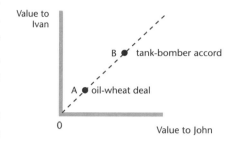

Fig. 1.3 Joint Gains from Trade and Arms Control

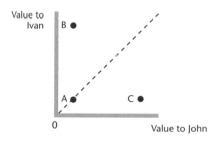

Fig. 1.4 Joint and Asymmetrical Trades

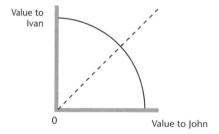

Fig. 1.5 The Frontier of Possibilities

Qualities of the Effective Negotiator or Mediator

1. Knowledge of the players and the issues

2. Management skills to coordinate his/her own team

3. Timing—when to wait, pull back, initiate, persist, and follow through

4. Empathy with all whose interests are at stake

5. Communication skills in speech, writing, and gestures

6. Constructive imagination to identify or create mutual-gain solutions

7. Leverage—carrots or sticks—to motivate an accord

8. Toughness to stand pat, threaten, bluff, fight

9. Flexibility to accommodate when appropriate

10. Stamina and patience to endure long hours, frustration, and travel

11. Integrity to inspire trust

12. A winning personality interesting to work with

13. Draftsmanship to produce treaty language that copes with differences either by precision or by creative ambiguity

14. Domestic support from your government and society

15. Internal drive to achieve

HOW TO APPROACH NEGOTIATION: TWO GUIDELINES

The hard-line approach to negotiation may produce immediate gain if the other side is bullied or deceived. But this gain can be short-lived since it depends on coercion or deceit. The win-win approach may succeed with friends but risks catastrophic abuse by hard-line antagonists. The lion may overpower you; the fox deceive you. Not every deal is advantageous. The conditional cooperation approach limits exposure to exploitation while offering a good platform for mutual gains.

Combining the concepts of interdependence and conditional cooperation, we suggest two guidelines for policy. First, actors are more likely to enhance their objectives if they can frame and implement value-creating strategies aimed at mutual gain than if they pursue value-claiming policies aimed at one-sided gain. Exploitation may yield short-run benefits for one side but tends to boomerang in the long run, so that costs outweigh benefits. The long run may have earlier been measured in decades or centuries, but in our world of escalating interdependencies, it becomes ever shorter. Profitable exploitation is difficult to sustain for more than a decade.

Few IR conflicts are mere misunderstandings, but creating values requires informed discussion by all concerned parties at home and abroad. The second guideline suggests that the more all parties communicate, the greater the prospect of finding solutions useful to all sides. The more intelligence estimates are publicly available, the fuller will be the public discussion preceding and accompanying each foreign policy thrust, and the higher the probability it will achieve its objectives.

Mutual gain policies and openness, if reciprocated, can lead IR actors toward a multifaceted, complex interdependence with a strong capacity to diminish discord and sustain peaceful cooperation. As we shall see in Chapter 5, the life sciences as well as social science suggest that a society's well-being—its overall fitness—may depend on a capacity to cooperate both within and outside the group. To sustain our common life-support system, humans need to cooperate—not free ride or exploit one another.

Complex interdependence can make its participants stronger than the sum of their parts. Their interlocking relationship is like that of diverse life forms coevolved into an ecosystem. A coral reef, for example, protects its members from the ravages of storms and alien species. The resultant structure of mutual aid may be seen as an "emergent property" or "order for free."[31]

31. An emergent property is a kind of "self-organization." See Roger Lewin, *Complexity: Life at the Edge of Chaos* (New York: Macmillan, 1992); and Stuart A. Kauffman, *The Origins of Order: Self-Organization and Selection in Evolution* (New York: Oxford University Press, 1993). Compare with James N. Rosenau, *Turbulence in World Politics: A Theory of Change and Continuity* (Princeton, N.J.: Princeton University Press, 1990).

The arguments for mutual gain and openness are hypotheses that must be validated or refined by experience. Consider them as you ponder today's news and the case histories in the chapters that follow. Are the arguments valid? Must they be refined? Under what conditions?

What Do You Tell the President? … *What do these nuts and bolts add up to?*

What approach do you recommend to the President? You draft your initial brief to the White House:

Our world contains danger and opportunity. We are linked with others—countries, peoples, movements—in networks of global interdependence. We can help or hurt one another.

We should approach other actors in the spirit of conditional cooperation. The optimal way to enhance each actor's interests is by cooperating to create values with other actors—not by playing winner-take-all.

Openness at home and abroad is another key to success. Effective policies are likely to flow from strategies oriented toward mutual gain, incubated and nourished by relatively open dialogue at home and across borders. Policy failures, on the other hand, are most likely to arise from zero-sum, exploitative strategies conceived behind closed doors and implemented without meaningful dialogue at home or with the target country.

KEY NAMES AND TERMS

actors (in IR)	interdependence	Prisoner's Dilemma (PD)
anarchy	intergovernmental organization	realism
best alternative to no-agreement	(IGO)	Second World
(BATNA)	international political economy (IPE)	security dilemma
complex interdependence	international relations (IR)	self-help
coordination game	level-of-analysis problem	sovereignty
diplomacy	logic of collective action	state
European Union (EU)	Hans Morgenthau	Third World
feminism (in IR)	negative-sum	tit-for-tat (TFT)
First World	neorealism	transnational
Fordism	nongovernmental oranization (NGO)	transnational corporations (TNCs)
Fourth World	North Atlantic Treaty Organization	Treaty of Westphalia
free ride	(NATO)	variable-sum
frontier of possibilities	Organization for Economic Coopera-	Kenneth N. Waltz
globalization	tion and Development (OECD)	world-system theory
hubris	positive-sum	zero-sum
idealism	postmodernism	

QUESTIONS TO DISCUSS

1. With what lens have *you* viewed world affairs? Did your viewpoint come from your home, your schooling, your outside reading, your travels, other experiences? How do your assumptions about IR match those outlined in Table 1.2?

2. What kinds of people have won the Nobel Peace Prize? Compare Ralph Bunche and Martin Luther King, Jr.; Jane Addams and Mother Teresa; Lech Walesa and Elie Wiesel.

3. If you were locked in a cell separate from another prisoner charged with the same offense, would you plead guilty to win your freedom? What if your admission meant a jail term for the other accused? Can you be sure that she won't plead guilty and implicate you? What are the prerequisites of trust?

4. Does international cooperation depend on trust or on interest, or both? Give examples of each.

5. From your knowledge of recent events, point to a foreign policy action that can be explained by the structure of the international system. Point to another event better explained by the personality of the decision maker or the society where she/he operates.

6. Do idealists ever win?

7. How does interdependence theory differ from idealism?

8. How does complex interdependence differ from other forms of interdependence?

RECOMMENDED RESOURCES

BOOKS

Baldwin, David A., ed. *Neorealism and Neoliberalism: The Contemporary Debate.* New York: Columbia University Press, 1993.

Dougherty, James E., and Robert L. Pfaltzgraff, Jr. *Contending Theories of International Relations: A Comprehensive Survey.* 3d ed. New York: HarperCollins, 1990.

Doyle, Michael W. *Ways of War and Peace: Realism, Liberalism, Socialism.* New York: Norton, 1997.

Fisher, Roger, and William Ury. *Getting to Yes: Negotiating Agreement without Giving In.* New York: Penguin, 1985.

Fisher, Roger, et al. *Beyond Machiavelli: Tools for Coping with Conflict.* Cambridge, Mass.: Harvard University Press, 1994.

Kegley, Charles W., Jr., ed. *Controversies in International Relations Theory: Realism and the Neoliberal Challenge.* New York: St. Martin's, 1995.

Keohane, Robert O., ed. *Neorealism and Its Critics.* New York: Columbia University Press, 1986.

Knutsen, Torbjörn L. *A History of International Relations Theory.* Manchester and New York: Manchester University Press, 1992.

Lax, David A., and James K. Sebenius. *The Manager as Negotiator: Bargaining for Cooperation and Competitive Gain.* New York: Free Press, 1986.

Luard, Evan, ed. *Basic Texts in International Relations: The Evolution of Ideas about International Society.* New York: St. Martin's, 1992.

Raiffa, Howard. *The Art and Science of Negotiation.* Cambridge, Mass.: Harvard University Press, 1982.

Stein, Janice Gross, and Louis W. Pauly, eds. *Choosing to Cooperate: How States Avoid Loss.* Baltimore: Johns Hopkins University Press, 1992.

JOURNALS

General journals such as *Foreign Affairs* and *International Studies Quarterly* are listed at the end of the book in Learning About International Relations: A Study and Resource Guide. Journals relevant to specific chapters, however, are listed with Recommended Resources for those chapters.

WEB SITES

Online Interactive Prisoner's Dilemma Game
    http://serendip.brynmawr.edu/playground/pd.html
Council on Foreign Relations
    http://www.foreignrelations.org
Foreign Affairs
    http://www.foreignaffairs.org
International Studies Association
    http://csf.colorado.edu/isa
Foreign Policy Association
    http://www.fpa.org
U.S. Department of State
    http://www.state.gov/

C H A P T E R   T W O

HOW TO WIN AT PEACE: CREATING NEW WORLD ORDERS

After Victory, What? ... *The White House asks your advice: "The West won the Cold War when the Soviet empire collapsed in 1991. How can we now win at peace? We are considering three strategies. Which is most likely to succeed? Shall we try to repress our longtime rivals in Moscow? Or forgive and forget? Or seek a partnership for mutual gain?"*

How do you give a well-considered reply to the White House? You recall the words of a former Secretary of State: "The rise and fall of previous world orders . . . is the only experience on which one can draw in trying to understand the challenges facing contemporary statesmen." The study of history, however, "offers no manual of instructions that can be applied automatically." History teaches by analogy between comparable situations.[1] *How* comparable *is a tough issue, though, because sharp differences usually mark even the most similar diplomatic constellations.*

You decide to review other attempts at forging a new world order after major wars of the 19th and 20th centuries. You find that the challenge has been to blend tough with conciliatory measures to build a stable peace based on mutual gain.

---

1. Henry Kissinger, *Diplomacy* (New York: Simon & Schuster, 1994), 26. For a symposium on diplomatic history, IR theory, and statecraft, see *International Security* 22, no. 1 (summer 1997).

CONTENDING CONCEPTS
AND EXPLANATIONS

WHAT IS A WORLD ORDER? WHAT IS PEACE?

Nothing is constant. International life contains both stability and turmoil. Where stability prevails, there is some kind of order. Each **world order** embodies a hierarchy of power (a kind of pecking order), with rules dictated by the most influential actors. Often a new order emerges after a previous one has been destroyed by war, after which the victors establish rules that favor them. As their power ebbs, the erstwhile victors try to delay their decline by manipulating the structures they created while strong.

Order implies peace—within society and across borders. **Negative peace** is the absence of war. **Positive peace** is more—it is a harmony based on satisfaction with things as they are.[2]

A cold, negative peace can be built upon any of five different principles: (1) the **hegemony** ("leadership" in Greek) of one major power; (2) the **condominium** (shared domination) of two or more powers; (3) an **alliance** uniting several states against others; (4) **collective security**, a system of "one for all and all for one" requiring each partner to reply to an attack on another member as an attack on itself; or (5) **deterrence**, restraint achieved by fear of retribution. A negative peace may coexist with structural violence—structures that repress and exploit, and that breed rebellion. The absence of war is not a stable or positive peace, especially if it depends upon mutual fear. If the power to intimidate erodes, negative peace can become war.

A positive and stable peace can emerge not from deterrence but from a value-creating order that generates mutual gain. Peace would be rooted in widely shared perceptions of prosperity, social justice, and environmental well-being. It would be buttressed but not guaranteed by complex interdependence (see Chapter 1). Parties to a positive peace do not see war as a legitimate or likely recourse; instead, they foster extensive forms of dispute avoidance and conflict resolution.

Does external peace among governments require internal peace and harmony *within* individuals and societies? Can a tormented individual lead the way to peace?[3] Can a repressive dictatorship cooperate peacefully with other countries? Tormented leaders and conflicted societies may take part in a negative peace, but positive peace is far more likely between

2. Kenneth E. Boulding, *Stable Peace* (Austin: University of Texas Press, 1978). Each civilization has a distinctive vision of peace. See Johan Galtung, "Peace," in *The Oxford Companion to Politics of the World*, ed. Joel Krieger (New York: Oxford University Press, 1993), 688–689.

3. Some teachers hold that peace must begin *within* a person and radiate outward to other people, groups, and all living things. A Sioux medicine man labored to integrate his personal hoop as a condition for helping his tribe rebuild its hoop. Ultimately he wanted the hoops of all nations to interact in harmony. See Black Elk, as told to John G. Neihardt, *Black Elk Speaks* (Lincoln: University of Nebraska Press, 1961).

internally peaceful actors than when one or more parties is deeply conflicted. As we shall see in Chapter 10, authoritarian regimes—most of them led by egomaniacal dictators—started most major wars of the 20th century.

Hopes arose in the early 1990s for a new world order more positive than the mutual deterrence practiced during the Cold War. But these hopes proved short-lived. As one century ended and another began, there was a new world disorder with few rules. Dealing with this condition raised many burning questions, which we will take up in later chapters. Let us first examine the failures and successes of previous efforts to establish a new world order.

THREE WAYS TO MAKE PEACE AND BUILD A NEW ORDER

Each negotiating type outlined in Chapter 1 takes a distinct approach to building a new order. Each approach can be illustrated by important cases.

Approach 1: Carthage

The win-lose hard-liner favors repression to prevent the vanquished from upsetting the victors' new order. If successful, repression can produce a negative peace. The hard line worked fairly well when ancient Rome subdued its longtime rival Carthage (located in today's Tunisia) in 146 B.C. The term **Carthaginian peace** symbolizes not just defeat but all-out destruction of the vanquished. Rome razed Carthage, killed or enslaved its people, and salted its fields. Victory over Carthage permitted Rome to establish a *pax Romana* ("peace of Rome") from North Africa to the British Isles. Still, Rome needed Carthage, and later rebuilt it to become a granary of the Roman Empire and capital of its province "Africa."

Total victory requires total defeat. Total victory like Rome's over Carthage is rare. Usually the victor inflicts halfway measures that permit the other side to survive, determined some day to strike back. Absolute subjugation is seldom practical. A punitive peace requires the victors, drained by their wartime exertions, to hold down a defeated country determined to overthrow the settlement. The countries that feel exploited by the new order may combine forces against the victors.[4]

Repression can hurt both victor and vanquished. It stifles production and creativity. If mines and fields are to be exploited, subject peoples must have the will and strength to work. If the vanquished die or flee, workers must be imported.

4. Kissinger, *Diplomacy*, 81.

DANZIGER
The Christian Science Monitor

Hope for a new world order rose when the Berlin Wall fell in 1989 and Moscow agreed to the unification of East with West Germany. Soon, however, there was a new world disorder, symbolized here by a Bosnian graveyard, chosen because it was beyond the range of most Serbian artillary.

How France and Prussia Enraged Each Other

Napoleon defeated Prussia in 1807 and forced its king to sign the **Treaty of Tilsit.** The treaty compelled Prussia to cede territory to France and pay indemnities so vast that they consumed nearly all Prussian government revenues for several years. The treaty limited Prussia to only 42,000 troops, but Prussia evaded this limit and, when Napoleon weakened, denounced the treaty and declared war on France in 1813.

All this was reversed after Prussia and other German states defeated France in 1870; then it became Berlin's turn to dictate terms. The 1871 Treaty of Frankfurt compelled France to pay Germany heavy indemnities and accept German occupation until these debts were paid (which was accomplished in two years). France ceded two border regions, **Alsace and Lorraine,** to Germany. Adding insult to injury, the King of Prussia had himself crowned Kaiser (Emperor) of the Second German Reich (Empire) at the Versailles Palace outside Paris. The French swore *revanche* (revenge). They took it, as we shall see, in 1919—in the same Versailles Palace.

In many wars the winner takes booty, for "to the victor go the spoils." Sometimes the victor claims financial indemnities or other **reparations** (from "repair") as compensation for damages caused by the other side. Indemnities may be paid from gold and currency reserves or from future earnings; reparations may be paid in cash or in kind—labor, coal, ships, shoes.

Such compensation can be difficult to extract. The defeated country may have no more gold; its money may be worthless. Goods taken as reparations, such as factory parts, may not be usable elsewhere. For a country to pay reparations, it must recover economically. The victor cannot repress the defeated and simultaneously get substantial reparations from current production.

Approach 2: Appomattox

The win-win negotiator does not punish the vanquished but trusts in conciliation ("bringing together") to restore harmony. An idealist is more likely to seek a "time to heal and to build" than an ultrarealist. Still, a moderate realist might agree that "no lasting settlement can be made in a spirit of revenge."[5]

A magnanimous settlement—the opposite of a Carthaginian peace—was initiated at Virginia's Appomattox Court House in 1865, ending the Civil War between the U.S. North and South. **Appomattox** stands for a generous, forgiving approach to the defeated. When Union General Ulysses S. Grant accepted the surrender of Confederate General Robert E. Lee at Appomattox, Grant was not vindictive. He required Lee's troops to disarm but allowed them to take their horses and mules home to work their farms. Lee said this concession "will do much toward conciliating our people."

President Abraham Lincoln and his successor, Andrew Johnson, wanted to heal wounds and rebuild the Union. But few Southern elites felt gratitude or obligation—in fact, they felt quite the opposite. Many exploited Johnson's forbearance and moved to reestablish the prewar planter aristocracy. A French newspaper reporter, Georges Clemenceau, who later became the French premier, opined that the North was letting itself "be tricked out of what it had spent so much trouble and perseverance to win."

After the Civil War, neither the North nor the South found the right mix of firmness and generosity. The approach begun at Appomattox failed because most Southern planters would not change their ways with-

5. This was what the Spartans told the Athenians when the latter had the upper hand. Thucydides, *The Peloponnesian War* (New York: Penguin Books, 1956), Book 4, chap. 1.

out pressure. Northern liberality gave way to severity. In 1867 Congress put most of the defeated South under a military administration that lasted for nearly a decade. When troops were withdrawn, resentful whites in the "solid South" defied Washington and repressed blacks again. North-South animosities lingered for generations.

Thus, a peace based on indulgence can also fail. Generosity risks abuse (as in Prisoner's Dilemma, Chapter 1). If the victor offers a friendly hand, the vanquished may feign cooperation for a time but then defect when the erstwhile victor eases its grip.

Approach 3: Congress of Vienna

The conditional cooperator assumes that most cross-border relationships are variable-sum. This negotiator blends tough and conciliatory measures to establish three conditions: first, a power structure that prevents another war; second, a system of shared values that removes any wish for violent change; and third, a web of interdependence that rewards cooperation and punishes defection. The more these conditions are met, the easier it should be to replace hostility with partnership.

The victors over Napoleon combined firmness with healing when they dealt with France at the **Congress of Vienna** in 1815. The victors—led by Britain, Austria, Russia, and Prussia—could not ignore the fact that France had ravaged Europe for twenty-five years, but they opted to reintegrate France quickly into the new order. The victors sent Napoleon into exile; stripped France of territories it had seized since 1790; and exacted heavy reparations (more than 700 million francs), occupying France until they were paid. But they also restored the French monarchy; admitted France to the Congress; and, in 1818, enlarged the four-power alliance of Europe's major powers to make a seat for France.

The Congress of Vienna set the stage for a century of relative peace. Why the long peace? The three conditions for enduring peace were met. No state had the means to challenge the new order, nor, for many decades, the desire. The Congress fostered a power equilibrium that would prevent any one state from dominating the others. To uphold this equilibrium, the Congress inaugurated what became known as the **Concert of Europe**, a precursor to the United Nations Security Council. The concert was a loose agreement by the major European powers to act together on European questions of common interest. Austria, Prussia, England, Russia, and France aimed to uphold the peace by concerted diplomatic action and by periodic meetings to deal with threats to stability.

Divergent Memories of Another War

In Paris in 1919 the idealist Woodrow Wilson had to negotiate with an archrealist—French Premier Georges Clemenceau, the same reporter who had questioned the North's indulgence toward the South in 1865. Clemenceau returned to France and climbed to the summit in French politics. Known as "the Tiger," he pressed for a tough line toward Germany. But Wilson had far different memories of the U.S. Civil War than did Clemenceau. At age seven, Wilson watched wounded Confederate soldiers die inside his father's church in Augusta, Georgia. Later he saw Confederate President Jefferson Davis paraded under Union guard. Wilson recalled that he once looked up into the face of General Robert E. Lee. Perhaps these childhood memories helped President Wilson—fifty-four years later—to oppose a vindictive peace. As Wilson once observed, "A boy never gets over his boyhood, and never can change those subtle influences which have become a part of him."

6. This term has many meanings, however, as we shall see in Chapter 4.

7. Other settlements were imposed on Austria-Hungary, Bulgaria, and Turkey.

8. Thomas J. Knock, *To End All Wars: Woodrow Wilson and the Quest for a New World Order* (New York: Oxford University Press, 1992).

Shared values underlay these arrangements. All of Europe's leaders accepted the new order and the need to preserve the "balance of power."[6] The 1815 order began to falter in the 1850s, but Europe was spared another system-wide war until 1914.

COMPARING THEORY AND REALITY: REBUILDING AFTER EACH WORLD WAR

A century of relative peace ended in the most devastating war yet known. World War I began in 1914, sucked in the U.S. in 1917, ended in 1918, and served as a prelude to World War II. The reasons for both world wars are discussed in Chapter 4. Here we focus on the victors' attempts after each war to build a new world order. Did these experiences produce lessons for those who sought to erect a new world order in the 1990s after the Cold War?

THE NEW ORDER AFTER WORLD WAR I: THE VERSAILLES SYSTEM

The post–World War I order was planned by the victors and imposed on Germany at the Versailles Palace outside Paris in 1919.[7] The so-called **Versailles system** was stamped by the divergent views and personalities of U.S. President Woodrow Wilson and French Premier **Georges Clemenceau**. Had the victor states been led by other individuals, the new order might have been quite different.

The U.S. and French Role

Somewhat like President Lincoln in 1865, Wilson in 1918 proposed a lenient peace—a peace without indemnities or territorial annexations. Wilson wanted to replace *realpolitik* with collective security. He called for an international organization to guarantee the independence and territorial integrity of all countries large and small. This dream, inspired by many sources, became the League of Nations.[8]

Exhausted but not yet defeated in late 1918, Germany sought soft peace terms like those Wilson had proposed. The parties agreed to an armistice on November 7, 1918. The twenty-seven victor governments then met at Versailles to decide the precise content of the peace treaty while the vanquished waited offstage.

The peacemakers confronted unprecedented loss of life and property. Some 40 million soldiers and civilians had been killed by fighting, hunger, or disease; another 20 to 30 million people had been maimed.

The Big Four peacemakers at Versailles in 1919: David Lloyd George of England, Baron Sidney Sonnino of Italy, Georges Clemenceau of France, and Woodrow Wilson of the United States. In this case, realists and idealists combined to produce not conditional cooperation but rather a patchwork peace marred by vindictiveness.

Some French leaders hoped that the U.S. would finance reconstruction, but Americans had already contributed one-fourth of their economic product to the war effort in 1917 and 1918 and were in no mood to keep lending or giving. Indeed, Wilson insisted in 1919 that London and Paris repay the huge sums that the U.S. had loaned them during the war. Many Europeans thought that the U.S., having profited from the war, should write off its loans. But Americans leaned toward the view later expressed by President Calvin Coolidge: "They hired the money, didn't they?"

Rebuffed by Washington, French leaders looked to Germany. France had paid indemnities in 1815 and again in 1871. Now Paris wanted Germany to pay for the damage it had caused. This goal, however, contradicted another French objective: to keep Germany down. With only half Germany's population, France feared German economic and military growth. But how could Germany pay reparations unless it revived economically?

British Prime Minister David Lloyd George also claimed reparations —not for physical damage but to pay pensions for Britain's widows, orphans, and the disabled. He explained: "I could not face my people and say that human life was of less value than a chimney."

Wilson regarded Clemenceau and Lloyd George as shortsighted and

The Communist Vision of a New Order

Like Wilson, Russian Communist leader Vladimir Lenin also denounced power politics, secret treaties, and imperialism. But Lenin had a Communist agenda—global revolution to destroy the capitalist class and capitalist states responsible for imperialism and war. In their place he proposed a Communist-led "dictatorship of the working class." Disdaining law and religion, Lenin championed class warfare; Wilson believed in sacred covenants and a natural harmony among all humans.

Despite their opposing visions of a new world order, Lenin in 1919 expressed an interest in coming to terms with the victors at Versailles. But Britain and France, joined by the U.S. and Japan, chose to intervene militarily in the Russian Civil War against the Communists. By 1921 it was clear that the West could not soon unseat the Communists and that the Soviets could not soon ignite a revolution in the West. But each side gave the other grounds for long-lasting distrust.

greedy. But the idealist compromised with the realists: He approved their demands for reparations since they agreed to his priority, a League of Nations.[9]

Wilson also abandoned his earlier opposition to secret diplomacy. In January 1918 Wilson had insisted on "open covenants openly arrived at." At Versailles, however, most of the treaty terms were decided behind closed doors by Wilson, Clemenceau, and Lloyd George. Other victors—even Italy and Japan—had little say. The major players treated China as a passive object and did not even invite Soviet Russia. The German delegation was also excluded from the deliberations, kept under house arrest. Finally, the Germans were shown the treaty and told to sign it—or else. Thus, in 1919 "open diplomacy" meant only that the final text of agreements would be published.

The treaty imposed on Germany was signed on June 28, 1919, in the same Versailles Palace where in 1871 the Second German Empire had been proclaimed.[10] Was the 1919 treaty harsh, lax, or a blend? It contained 361 articles—some severe, others not. The 1919 treaty was not significantly tougher than the Treaty of Tilsit that Napoleon forced on Prussia in 1807, the treaty that Germany imposed on France in 1871, or the Brest-Litovsk Treaty that Imperial Germany inflicted on Soviet Russia in March 1918. But the 1919 treaty was far more vindictive than the 1815 Congress of Vienna settlement. The terms of all four treaties are compared in Table 2.1.

The 1919 compromise between idealism and realism was a patchwork that satisfied nobody. The Versailles system was too harsh to conciliate Germany and too weak to keep Germans down. Versailles was not so extreme as Carthage or Appomattox; but neither was it wisely balanced like the 1815 Vienna settlement.

The 1919 settlement compelled Germany to return Alsace-Lorraine to France and give up other lands in Europe and abroad. Parts of Germany would be occupied for fifteen years. Territorial changes are shown in Map 2.1 on page 44. As in 1807, Germany was restricted to a low level of armaments. Germany had to pay extensive reparations—52 percent for France. In an unprecedented move, the treaty demanded that the German Kaiser be tried for war crimes.

Why Did the Versailles System Fail?

The Versailles system—peace treaties, financial settlements, League of Nations—collapsed like a deck of cards in the 1930s as Tokyo, Rome, Berlin, and Moscow embarked on wars of conquest. Many factors combined to undermine the Versailles peace.

9. President Franklin D. Roosevelt made a similar tradeoff in February 1945: He approved many British and Soviet demands for the postwar world so long as they approved his concept of a United Nations.

10. The signing took place precisely five years after the event that triggered World War I, the assassination of Austria's Archduke Franz Ferdinand as he visited Bosnia.

Table 2.1 How Victors Treated Losers in 1807, 1815, 1871, and 1919

Peace Settlement	1807 (Tilsit)	1815 (Vienna)	1871 (Frankfurt)	1919 (Versailles)
Loser	Prussia	France	France	Germany
Defeated in battle?	Yes	Yes	Yes	No
Occupied?	Yes	Yes	Yes	Yes
Formally accused of responsibility for war?	No	Yes	No	Yes
Deprived of territory?	Yes	Yes	Yes	Yes
Indemnities (payments to victors) required?	Yes	Yes	Yes	Yes
Leaders condemned?	No	Yes	Yes	Yes
Compelled to disarm?	Yes	No	No	Yes
Assisted economically?	No	No	No	No
How long before reintegrated into the international community?	Not excluded	1 to 3 years	Not excluded	3 to 7 years
Mechanism for assuring peace	French army	Concert of Europe	Concert, then alliances	League of Nations

German Revisionism. Victor states seek to uphold the status quo; **revisionist** states seek to alter or even overthrow the existing order. France and other victors tried to uphold the new status quo based on the Versailles Treaty; Germany worked to revise it. Many German leaders regarded the 1919 treaty as unjust.[11] They resented the territorial losses and reparations imposed on Germany, the "war guilt" clause (see sidebar on page 45), one-sided disarmament, and Germany's exclusion from the League of Nations.

Instead of complying with Versailles, key German leaders schemed to cast off Germany's obligations. To evade the arms limitations established at Versailles, the German military in the 1920s secretly developed modern weapons on Soviet territory. The treaty stipulated severe limits on German arms so that *all* states could reduce arms. Hitler, who became Germany's chancellor in 1933, charged that the Versailles victors still denied Germany equality by keeping Germany disarmed while refusing to bind themselves by any disarmament treaty. In 1935 Germany began openly to rearm, in 1936 remilitarized the left bank of the Rhine and denounced what Hitler called the "war-guilt lie," annexed Austria in 1938, and dismembered Czechoslovakia and invaded Poland in 1938 and 1939.

Nations Without States. Four multinational realms disappeared during the war—the German, Austro-Hungarian, Russian, and Ottoman empires. What would rise from their ashes? Wilson and others had raised expectations of national self-determination—that each nation (defined

11. Speech by the president of the German delegation, May 29, 1919, in *The Treaty of Versailles and After: Annotations on the Text of the Treaty* (Washington, D.C.: Government Printing Office, 1947), 39–44.

Alsace and Lorraine were restored to France. Plebiscites—direct elections by the local populations—resulted in the transfer of certain border lands to Belgium and Denmark. The rich Saar territory came under French administration for fifteen years. France was allowed to occupy the Rhineland until 1935, while the right bank of the Rhine was to be permanently demilitarized.

Poland was reconstructed from the German, Austro-Hungarian, and Russian empires. Parts of Germany—West Prussia, Posen, and the southern part of East Prussia—went to Poland, separating East Prussia (Kaliningrad after 1945) from the rest of Germany. Danzig (Gdansk in Polish) became a "free city" administered by the League of Nations. Upper Silesia was split between Germany, Poland, and Czechoslovakia. Poland expanded eastward and took lands inhabited by Lithuanians, Belarussians, and Ukrainians.

The Austro-Hungarian empire dissolved, and "rump" Austria ceded southern Tyrol to Italy and other borderlands to Yugoslavia.

Many new countries were born or reborn after World War I: Finland, Estonia, Latvia, Lithuania, Czechoslovakia, Poland, and Hungary. Serbia and Montenegro expanded into Yugoslavia. Four other countries expanded: Italy, Romania, Albania, and Greece, while Germany, Bulgaria, Russia, and Turkey lost territory.

The Russian Empire also dissolved, giving birth to an independent Finland, Estonia, Latvia, Lithuania, and Poland. Ukraine and other border regions of Russia were briefly independent.

Map 2.1 How the Versailles System Changed Europe

Central Europe, 1914

Germany, 1914

Central Europe, 1924

—— Boundary of Germany

Plebiscite areas under Versailles Treaty

Demilitarized zone under Versailles Treaty

mainly by language) would have its own state. But this was not feasible, for many populations were mixed. Failure to meet expectations for self-determination weakened support for the entire settlement. In the late 1930s some disgruntled minorities, as in Slovakia, looked to Nazi Germany for support.[12]

A Power Vacuum in Eastern Europe. The structure of power no longer contained but rather encouraged German expansionism. When the Kaiser looked east or south in 1913, Germany was hemmed in by the Russian and Austro-Hungarian empires. By 1919 these barriers were gone, their places taken by weak states that had emerged from the former empires. Once Germany recovered, Berlin wanted to regain its former eastern domains. Feuds among the newly independent states of Eastern Europe (for example, between Poland and Lithuania) would help Berlin and Moscow to divide and conquer.

Economic Nationalism. Between the two world wars most countries ignored their economic interdependence. Instead of enlarging the pie, they practiced beggar-thy-neighbor, hoarding gold and discouraging imports.[13] Continuing a wartime addiction, the German government in the early 1920s printed huge quantities of paper money. The ensuing inflation wiped out the savings of Germany's middle class, many of whom blamed the Versailles victors and Germany's Jews for damage done by Berlin's printing presses. U.S. bankers kept the international financial system afloat by loaning money to Germany so Berlin could pay France and England so that Paris and London could repay their loans to the U.S. In theory the money would recycle:

U.S. ➤ Germany ➤ France and England ➤ U.S.

But German leaders managed to delay, reduce, and eventually halt payments both on reparations and on loans from U.S. banks. Borrowers made lenders their prisoners.[14]

Germany attained financial stability in the late 1920s, but tight money policies and high tariffs in key countries hurt investment, trade, and jobs worldwide. A deep and prolonged depression began in 1929. World trade fell after President Herbert Hoover signed the punitive Smoot-Hawley tariffs in 1931. That same year the major actors agreed to a one-year moratorium on all intergovernmental debts. Germany stopped all reparations payments. Generations later, U.S. creditors were still holding the bag.[15]

National egotism yielded economic chaos and mutual impoverishment, which helped spawn militarism in Japan and Germany.

No Collective Security. Wilson wanted the League of Nations to ensure peace by means of collective security. Such a system would require

The "War Guilt" Clause: Misperception or Propaganda?

German officials passionately denounced what they called the "war guilt" clause—Article 231 of the Versailles Treaty. The German delegation saw guilt where it was not mentioned. From the victors' standpoint, Article 231 merely explained why Germany should pay reparations. It required Germany to accept responsibility for damages to the "Allies and their Associated Governments and their nationals" caused by Germany's aggression. Article 232, moreover, sharply limited Germany's obligations. It required Germany to pay only for damage done to the Allies' civilian populations and property—not to their military establishments. Nonetheless, Article 231 was a burr in the German consciousness. Hitler later used it to whip up resentment against the Versailles system.

12. For more on "minorities at risk," see Chapters 8 and 9.

13. When Germany paid reparations in gold, France and Britain used little of this wealth to buy German goods. The 1920s differed from the 1870s when Germany recycled French indemnities, contributing to prosperity in both Germany and France.

14. Germany devoted about one-fourth of its exports to reparations in the 1920s, but only 5 to 7 percent of its national income—less than the 5 to 11 percent of French income that Paris paid to Berlin in 1871–1873. Stephen A. Schuker, *American "Reparations" to Germany, 1919–1933: Implications for the Third-World Debt Crisis* (Princeton, N.J.: Princeton Studies in International Finance No. 61, July 1988), 56; see also Steven B. Webb, *Hyperinflation and Stabilization in Weimar Germany* (New York: Oxford University Press, 1989).

15. In the 1970s West Germany paid back the principal on Germany's 1920s debts to foreign bond holders. In 1995 a reunified Germany issued new bonds to pay off the interest due (at 3 percent) by 2010. Caveat junk bonds investor!

that, if a League member were attacked, all other members come to its aid. But the U.S. Senate did not approve U.S. membership in the League. It also spurned a treaty commitment with Britain to assist France if attacked by Germany.

The League of Nations Covenant required each member to carry out economic sanctions against an aggressor, but permitted members to choose whether to join in military sanctions. Such loopholes worried France and buoyed aggressors.[16]

U.S. isolationism made it even more imperative for the other victors to reintegrate Germany into a new world order (as the Congress of Vienna did France in 1815). Instead, they treated Germany as an outcast for most of the 1920s. When there was still hope to accommodate Germany, Paris and London were too tough. After 1933, when they confronted a Hitler hell bent on conquest, French and British leaders were too soft. They tried to appease the Nazi beast by letting it feed on other countries. Their concessions gave appeasement a bad name.

Is collective security an impossible dream? It did not get a fair test in the 1920s and 1930s, because the U.S. never joined the League of Nations and other key players—Germany, the USSR, Japan, and Italy—were absent for years. We shall see later (in Chapters 4 and 15) that collective security fared better under the United Nations with strong U.S. leadership.

Zero-Sum Perspectives. All of these challenges to the post–World War I order stemmed from a value-claiming approach: The key actors behaved like egotists in Prisoner's Dilemma. Failing to cooperate, all suffered. Washington had the ideas and power to forge a more viable world

16. Inis L. Claude, Jr., *Swords into Plowshares: The Problems and Progress of International Organization*, 4th ed. (New York: Random House, 1984), chap. 12.

Table 2.2 The Results of Value-Claiming Policies, 1919–1939

Going It Alone	Results
1919–1931: U.S. insists on repayment of its wartime loans to Europe	Deepens financial pressures on France and Britain
1919–1932: France and Britain require Germany to pay reparations	Antagonizes Germans and strains international banking
1920s: U.S. leads in high tariffs and other forms of economic nationalism	Limits trade, growth, and jobs
1920s–1930s: U.S. spurns League of Nations	Aborts collective security
1930s: Japan, Italy, and Germany embark on militarist expansion	Leads to World War II and their complete defeat
1930s: Britain, France, and U.S. pass the buck, doing little to contain the aggressors	Opens the way to war and makes defeat of the aggressors more costly

Could the blunders of the 1920s and 1930s be avoided following the defeat of Germany and Japan in 1945? If President Harry S. Truman had asked you for advice on rebuilding a war-torn world, what strategy would you have recommended? Had Soviet leader Josef Stalin asked your advice, would you have answered any differently?

order, but Americans turned inward, denying that their well-being depended on that of others. France and Britain were consistently myopic, while the heirs of J. S. Bach, Kant, and Goethe, like lemmings to the sea, followed Hitler and his racist manias. The rewards for such myopia are summarized in Table 2.2.

AFTER WORLD WAR II: CONFLICT AND MUTUAL GAIN

The Big Four victors—Britain, France, the U.S., and the USSR— agreed in 1945 to each occupy a zone of Germany and a sector of Berlin. They also agreed to carry out a policy of the four D's: they would democratize, de-nazify, demilitarize, and deindustrialize Germany. De-nazification began at once. A special court set up at Nuremberg tried twenty-two Nazi leaders for war crimes and crimes against humanity.[17] The court condemned twelve of the accused to death, jailed seven, and acquitted three. The Allies purged and excluded from public office more than 400,000 people charged with contributing to German militarism. Critics said the trials and purges went too far; others, not far enough. Defenders maintained that they were both just and necessary.

Demilitarization also proceeded quickly. Unlike 1918, German forces in 1945 were defeated on German soil. All of Germany was occupied and Hitler's forces disbanded. (The Soviet occupiers of East Germany, however, formed a heavily armed "People's Police" that later became the "People's Army [*Volksarmee*]," another tool of Soviet policy.)

U.S. policy emphasized the first D, democratization, and soon replaced deindustrialization with what amounted to a fifth and quite different D—economic development. The Americans wanted Germans to feed and support themselves. Washington believed that Germany and the rest of Europe had to be rebuilt together.

The Cold War got colder. In 1946 Josef Stalin said that the USSR must prepare for another war. Winston Churchill declared that an **Iron Curtain** had descended to divide Europe. In March 1947 the Truman Doctrine proclaimed U.S. readiness to help Greece and Turkey defend

17. The importance of these developments for human rights law is analyzed in Chapter 16.

their independence against Communism. Still, neither Washington nor Moscow closed the door to accommodation. Each alternated tough with conciliatory moves. For example, U.S. Secretary of State George C. Marshall went to Moscow in March 1947 to reaffirm a U.S. proposal for a four-power alliance—the U.S., USSR, UK, and France—to keep Germany demilitarized. But Marshall left Moscow feeling that he had hit a stone wall.

The Marshall Plan/European Recovery Program (ERP)

The winter of 1946–1947 was harsh in Europe, giving urgency to three forces—power politics, idealism, and interdependence—that pushed the Truman administration to develop a strategy to boost European recovery.

Power Politics. Most Americans regarded Soviet Communism not just as immoral but also as dangerous. Washington decided in 1946–1947 to contain and, if possible, undermine the Soviet empire. Washington also sought to halt domestic unrest in France and Italy that could help Communist parties there to seize power, assisted perhaps by Soviet tanks.

Idealism. Washington wanted to relieve human suffering. The U.S. delivered some $10 billion in food and other relief supplies to Western Europe in the years 1945 to 1947. Emergency aid reduced misery but did not put Europeans on their feet. Marshall saw first-hand in March 1947 the shortages of food and coal that left France hungry and cold nearly two years after the war.

Interdependence. Washington sought to build powerful economies able to buy U.S. goods. When pent-up demand from the war years waned, the U.S. economy would need foreign markets. Washington also wanted Europe to drop protectionism and embrace free trade.

These interlocked motives gave birth to the **European Recovery Program (ERP),** or **Marshall Plan,** named for Secretary of State George C. Marshall. Outlining what became the ERP on June 4, 1947, Marshall presented no master plan; rather, he urged European governments to spell out their needs so that U.S. aid could be integrated into a long-term cure for Europe's economic ills. The job could not be done by the U.S. alone. "The program should be a joint one, agreed to by a number of, if not all, European nations."[18]

Marshall invited participation by the USSR and the states of Eastern Europe as well as Western Europe. Washington feared that Stalin would try to sabotage the ERP, but gambled that Moscow would rebuff the plan. In late June 1947 Soviet Foreign Minister **Viacheslav M. Molotov** traveled to a meeting in Paris to look this gift horse in the mouth, but he soon pro-

18. The occasion was a commencement speech at Harvard University, where honorary degrees were given to Marshall, poet T. S. Eliot, and J. Robert Oppenheimer ("father" of the atomic bomb). For the speech, analysis, and many references, see "The Marshall Plan and Its Legacy," *Foreign Affairs* 76, no. 3 (May–June 1997): 157–221.

Unlike the Versailles system at the end of World War I, the Marshall Plan provided for the rebuilding of victors and losers after World War II. Here, West Berlin's biggest concert hall and cultural center is repaired with the help of ERP funds.

nounced it unfit and returned to Moscow. When Molotov said *nyet*, Western officials breathed a sigh of relief.

Why did the war-ravaged USSR reject economic aid? The Kremlin rejected any notion of mutual dependence with the capitalist world. Molotov asserted that the U.S. plan would enslave European states and destroy their independence. The whole scheme, he said, was designed to save the *American* economy.[19] Probably the Kremlin wanted to hide Soviet weaknesses and guard against any intrusion that could diminish Soviet domination of Eastern Europe. Pressured by Moscow, Czechoslovakia and Poland also kept away from the ERP.[20] The Kremlin imposed a harsh, "all-roads-lead-to-Moscow" imperial rule wherever the Red Army had driven back German or Japanese forces.[21]

Sixteen West European states promptly met to coordinate a response to the U.S. offer.[22] They estimated each country's likely budget deficit and proposed a four-year recovery program. Then came the billion-dollar question: Would the Republican-controlled U.S. Congress foot the bill for foreign aid endorsed by a Democratic administration? Would the Republicans scuttle Truman's ERP as they had Wilson's League of Nations?

But the Democrats had learned from Wilson's mistakes. Unlike 1919, in the 1940s they did not exclude Republicans from foreign policymaking. Instead, they cultivated a bipartisan policy in which Republican-Democrat rivalries stopped at the water's edge. For example, the four-power alliance that Marshall proposed to the Soviets in March 1947 was the brainchild of Republican Senator Arthur Vandenberg.

19. V. M. Molotov, *Problems of Foreign Policy* (Moscow: Foreign Language Publishing House, 1949), 466; see also Scott D. Parrish and Mikhail M. Narinsky, "New Evidence on the Soviet Rejection of the Marshall Plan, 1947: Two Reports," *Working Paper No. 9,* Cold War International History Project (Washington, D.C.: Woodrow Wilson International Center for Scholars, March 1994).

20. What Czech sources told the U.S. ambassador in Prague is reported in Laurence Steinhardt to George C. Marshall, July 10, 1947, in *Foreign Relations of the United States: 1947,* Vol. 3 (Washington, D.C.: Government Printing Office, 1972), 319–320. For Molotov's recollections on this point, see *Sto corok besed c Molotovym: Iz dnevnika F. Chueva* (Moscow: Terra, 1991), 88–89.

21. "Kremlin" means "citadel" or "walled city." The Moscow Kremlin, dating from the 14th century, has housed the government of tsarist, Soviet, and post-Communist Russia.

22. All West European countries (even neutral Switzerland) and Turkey took part, with the exceptions of Portugal and Spain, both of which were under the sway of a dictator.

Powerful Economies Can Bolster Free Trade

British Foreign Minister Ernest Bevin compared the U.S. economic position after World War II with Britain's after the Napoleonic wars. In 1815 Great Britain had 30 percent of the world's wealth; in the late 1940s the U.S. had 50 percent. After the Napoleonic wars the British practically gave away their exports for eighteen years, said Bevin, but this had contributed to stability and peace for a century.

This course also held hazards. Some economists believed that Great Britain in the 19th century undermined its economic strength by practicing free trade while its competitors hid behind protectionist barriers. These economists argued that the U.S. after World War II risked following Britain's route to self-destruction; others claimed the two situations defied comparison.

23. See Michael J. Hogan, *The Marshall Plan: America, Britain, and the Reconstruction of Western Europe, 1947–1952* (New York: Cambridge University Press, 1987), 432; and Immanuel Wexler, *The Marshall Plan Revisited: The European Recovery Program in Economic Perspective* (Westport, Conn.: Greenwood, 1983), 251; see also Charles S. Maier, "The Two Postwar Eras and the Conditions for Stability in Twentieth-Century Western Europe," with comments by Stephen A. Schuker and Charles P. Kindleberger, in *American Historical Review* 86 (April 1981): 327–367. For a political science perspective, see Hadley Arkes, *Bureaucracy, the Marshall Plan, and the National Interest* (Princeton, N.J.: Princeton University Press, 1972); and Charles P. Kindleberger, *Marshall Plan Days* (Boston: Unwin Hyman, 1987), 246.

24. Confirmed by the author's surveys noted in the introduction and by numerous publications on the fortieth and fiftieth anniversaries of Marshall's 1947 proposal.

Whereas U.S. policy in 1919 bore Wilson's personal seal, the ERP was very much a team effort, conceived by leading economists and some of America's most experienced diplomats, including George F. Kennan and Dean Acheson. Its first administrator was a Republican industrialist, Paul G. Hoffman. Truman had the plan named for Marshall, a luminary widely viewed as above party politics.

The Marshall Plan operated from 1948 through 1951. It was both a burden and a boon for the U.S. economy. How large was the burden? Under the ERP the U.S. dispensed $13.2 billion in grants and loans (mostly grants)—nearly $90 billion if measured in 1990s dollars. ERP transfers initially amounted to 2.3 percent of U.S. gross national product (GNP), but over four years averaged 1.2 percent. (In the 1990s, in contrast, U.S. developmental aid was less than one-fifth of 1 percent of U.S. GNP, spread over the globe instead of concentrated in one region.) But the U.S. economy also gained. Many ERP dollars quickly came home because Europe bought two-thirds of its imports from the United States. Thus, European and U.S. well-being became entwined.

The ERP became a model of mutuality in planning, inputs, and perceived gains. The U.S. proposed and subsidized the ERP, but Europeans helped plan and implement it. Americans catalyzed Europeans' energies and pressured them to cooperate with the U.S. and with one another—France with Germany, Belgium and the Netherlands with France. U.S. aid was probably a necessary though not a sufficient condition for Europe's recovery.[23] With financial reserves provided by Washington, Europeans did not need to pursue self-sufficiency (their fantasy between the world wars). Instead they could trade with each other and make purchases abroad. Total U.S. grants and loans amounted only to 10–20 percent of total investments in Europe in 1948–1949, but they sparked a multiplier effect. They facilitated essential imports, eased bottlenecks, encouraged capital formation by Europeans, and curtailed inflation. The ERP could wind down in 1951 because it was no longer needed.

Historians and statesmen from many countries viewed the Marshall Plan as the outstanding success of U.S. foreign policy in the 20th century—perhaps ever.[24] The ERP helped build a trans-Atlantic community of like-minded democracies for economic development and security. None of these countries fought each other again after 1945. The ERP inaugurated an era of peace and prosperity more durable than any other in modern European history. At the end of the 20th century there was still no "United States of Europe," but the ERP had laid the foundations for a dynamic European Union (EU).

General MacArthur and Postwar Japan

U.S. policy to Japan also converted a vanquished foe into a partner. Unlike U.S. policy in Europe, however, Washington dealt with Japan and with other Asian countries one-on-one instead of multilaterally. And Washington saw no reason to coordinate its Asian policy with the USSR, even though Soviet troops attacked Japanese in the last days of the war.[25]

Another difference was that U.S. policy in Japan depended heavily upon one person—General **Douglas A. MacArthur**, commander of the occupation forces. MacArthur believed that U.S. occupation of Japan should express America's influence "in terms of essential liberalism"— not "in an imperialistic manner or for the sole purpose of commercial advantage." Though known for his huge ego and self-confidence, MacArthur preferred to negotiate with Japanese authorities rather than dictate. MacArthur developed a good working relationship with the emperor and Prime Minister Yoshida Sigeru. Instead of issuing proclamations, MacArthur gave orders, which the Japanese government carried out. This approach provided a low-cost way to meet U.S. goals while helping to maintain Japan's bureaucratic system and pride.[26]

Having received initial directives from Washington, MacArthur, on August 30, 1945, summarized his tasks in Japan:

First, destroy the military power. Punish war criminals. Build the structure of representative government. Modernize the constitution. Hold free elections. Enfranchise the women. Release the political prisoners. Liberate the farmers. Establish a free labor movement. Encourage a free economy. Abolish police oppression. Develop a free and responsible press. Liberalize education. Decentralize political power. Separate church from state.

By the time MacArthur left in 1951, most of these tasks had been accomplished.

As in Germany, suspected Japanese war criminals were tried. Twenty-five were condemned to die (more than in Germany). Another 200,000 Japanese were excluded from public office (far less than in Germany). The Americans did not indict the emperor, despite his probable complicity in initiating and prolonging the war. Kid-glove treatment of Hirohito facilitated U.S. occupation, but also helped Japanese to avoid confronting the past. Many Japanese felt that the war had been a disaster and that their government had misled them, but few were penitent.[27] Many claimed there had been no surrender—only an end to the war. The U.S. position was that Japan had surrendered unconditionally, but MacArthur seldom pressed the issue.

In 1946 the U.S. closed down all production of military goods,

 Is Aid Good or Bad? The Cases of Germany and Japan

Is aid useful? The two countries that received relatively little U.S. aid after World War II, Japan and Germany, grew faster than those that collected more. Germany got only $8.50 per capita in 1949; the UK, $24.03; and France, $23.96. The Japanese got even less than the Germans (as did Italy, at $7 per capita).[1] Does this mean that "the less aid, the better growth"? Probably not. Even Japan and Germany needed a boost. As we will see in Chapters 11 and 12, many factors shape economic growth.

1. See analysis and data in A. F. K. Organski and Jacek Kugler, *The War Ledger* (Chicago: University of Chicago Press, 1980), esp. chap. 3 and app. 2.

25. U.S. and British authorities excluded Soviets from the occupation of Italy and the Soviets excluded Westerners from the countries they had conquered or liberated, such as Bulgaria. The rule seemed to be: Only the state that pays in blood may occupy another.

26. The following draws largely from Richard B. Finn, *Winners in Peace: MacArthur, Yoshida, and Postwar Japan* (Berkeley: University of California Press, 1992); see also Daikichi Irokawa, *The Age of Hirohito: In Search of Modern Japan* (New York: Free Press, 1995).

27. Japan's Ministry of Education made sure that Japanese textbooks excused the attack on Pearl Harbor and Japanese atrocities in China, Korea, the Philippines, Indonesia, and elsewhere. Not until 1995 did the Japanese prime minister offer even personal regret for Japan's wartime treatment of British prisoners.

stripped Japanese factories of equipment to provide reparations for China and the Philippines, and tried to break up Japan's industrial conglomerates. But such policies made U.S. occupation of Japan expensive. By 1947 the victor was subsidizing the vanquished to the tune of $400 million a year. In 1949 Washington reversed course and ordered that all Japanese industrial facilities be used for economic recovery. As in Germany, deindustrialization gave way to development.

MacArthur's staff drafted a new constitution for Japan, which was adopted by the Japanese legislature in 1946. Article 9 disavowed war as an instrument of policy and pledged Japan not to maintain armed forces for offensive purposes.

U.S. occupation formally ended in 1951 with the signing of a Japanese-U.S. peace treaty. Unlike Tilsit or Versailles, the 1951 peace treaty was not punitive. It placed no restrictions on Japan's peacetime activity and made no provision for reparations. The treaty recognized Japan's right to self-defense. Japan and the U.S. also signed an alliance in 1951 (renewed with modifications into the 1990s)—a mutual security treaty that permitted U.S. troops to be stationed in Japan. Over time Japan's self-defense forces steadily improved, but Washington often urged Japan to do more. The Americans feared not Japan but Communist China, North Korea, and the USSR.

How did U.S. occupation policies affect Japan? The country's economic attainments built upon efficient work habits. But the U.S. gave Japan "an indispensable push" toward prosperity as well as toward democracy. Both Japan and the U.S. won. Japan's longtime prime minister reflected: "The Americans came into our country as our enemies, but after an occupation lasting a little less than seven years, an understanding grew up between the two peoples which is remarkable in the history of the modern world."[28]

By the 1960s Japan was joining North America and Western Europe in a trilateral community—the world's fulcrum of economic development and democracy.

Unlike the Americans, the Soviets hung tough with Japan: Moscow spurned Tokyo's demand for return of Japan's northern islands annexed by Stalin in 1945. In the 1990s there was still no peace treaty between Japan and Russia, even though both countries could gain from closer ties.

The Soviet Empire: Exploitation and Dependency

Sharing the tasks of reconstruction could have united Communist and non-Communist Europe. Instead, the ERP sharpened East-West

28. Finn, *Winners,* 316. In April 1951 President Truman sacked MacArthur because he had exceeded orders in Korea. But Japanese-U.S. relations were not harmed. Indeed, Japan got a lesson in how a civilian government should handle an insubordinate general. At age 86, Yoshida traveled to Virginia in 1964 to attend MacArthur's funeral.

Table 2.3 How Victors Treated Losers After 1919 and 1945

Peace Settlement	1919 Versailles	1945 Settlements U.S.-UK-French occupation	U.S. occupation	Soviet occupation
Loser	Germany	West Germany	Japan	East Germany
Defeated in battle?	No	Yes	Yes	Yes
Occupied?	Yes	Yes	Yes	Yes
Formally accused of responsibility for war?	Yes	Yes	Yes	Yes
Deprived of territory?	Yes	Yes	Yes	Yes
Reparations?	Heavy	Light	Light	Heavy
Leaders condemned?	Yes	Yes	Yes, but emperor spared	Yes
Compelled to disarm?	Yes	Yes	Yes	Yes
Assisted economically?	No	Yes	Yes	No
How long before reintegrated into the international community?	3 to 7 years	3 years	6 years	4 to 28 years
Mechanism for assuring peace	League of Nations	Occupation armies; NATO after 1949	U.S. Army; after 1951, the U.S.-Japan Mutual Security Treaty	Soviet Army; Communist parties; bilateral alliances and 1955 Warsaw Pact

differences. Stalin claimed and extracted values *from* Moscow's subjects instead of creating values *with* them and with the West. From 1945 to 1956 the Kremlin's policy toward Eastern Europe was far more harsh than the 1919 Versailles system had been to Germany.

In the years 1945–1956 the USSR extracted from Eastern Europe goods valued at $14 to 20 billion—more than the $13.2 billion the U.S. transferred to Western Europe under the ERP. Like Clemenceau in 1919, Stalin in 1945 felt that the aggressor should pay. The Soviets carted off machinery and factories from the former enemy countries—East Germany, Hungary, and Romania. But even in "liberated" countries such as Czechoslovakia, the Kremlin set up joint stock companies to divert East European output to the USSR. Moscow paid less than world market prices for Eastern Europe's commercial exports. A Polish joke conveyed the bitter truth: "Moscow sells Poland coal-mining machinery at higher than world prices so Poles can dig coal and sell it to Russia for less than world prices." Table 2.3 compares the post-1945 settlements in Europe and Japan with the Versailles system after World War I.

The Iron Curtain dividing Eastern from Western Europe had many elements—not just barbed wire and mine fields. Countering Marshall's initiative, Soviet ideologists declared in 1947–1948 that "two camps" faced each other on the world stage. In 1949 Moscow sponsored what some called the "Molotov Plan"—the 1948 Council on Mutual Economic Assis-

As Churchill put it in 1946, an Iron Curtain divided Europe from the Baltic to the Black Sea. Each government in Eastern Europe was subservient to Moscow. Czechoslovakia, however, did not have a Communist government until 1948—the same year that Yugoslavia bolted from the "Soviet camp."

Map 2.2 An Iron Curtain Sunders Europe, 1945–1948

Occupation zones of Germany (4)

Occupation zones of Austria (4)

States that became Communist, 1945–1948

"Iron Curtain," 1948

Annexed by the USSR between 1939 and 1945

✳ Cities divided into four occupation sectors

tance (**COMECON**) to promote economic integration of Eastern Europe and the USSR. In practice, however, COMECON cultivated bilateral ties that kept each East European country dependent on the USSR. All roads, it seemed, led to Moscow. Cut off from Western ideas and competition, Eastern Europe stagnated.

The Cold War intensified. In 1949 the Western powers merged their occupation zones into a new state, the Federal Republic of Germany (West Germany), and established the **North Atlantic Treaty Organiza-**

Table 2.4 Mutual Gain vs. Zero-Sum Politics, 1945–1956

Cooperate	Results	Claim Values	Results
United Nations formed in 1945	Limited but unprecedented achievements	Many Soviet vetoes at UN	Debilitates UN Security Council
World Bank and International Monetary Fund begin operations in 1946	Helps economic reconstruction and growth	USSR subjugates and pillages Eastern Europe	Impoverishes the Second World
U.S. relief aid to Europe and Japan after the war	Allays suffering	USSR fosters bilateral trade with Communist states	Isolates the Second World
General Agreement on Tariffs and Trade (GATT) begins in 1948	Helps liberalize trade		
Marshall Plan, 1948–1951	A community for peace and security linking North America, Europe, and Japan—a compromise between old-style alliances and universal collective security	USSR spurns Marshall Plan and organizes COMECON in 1949	Isolates the Second World
NATO forms in 1949			
"Police Action" taken by UN in Korea in 1950		USSR demands bases and joint stock companies in China in 1950	USSR alienates Communist China
U.S.-Japanese security treaty signed in 1951	Enduring alliance		
European Coal and Steel Community formed in 1952	A start toward European Union	Soviet tanks crush East German revolt in 1953 and Hungarian uprising in 1956	Deepens animosities between Soviet hegemon and Eastern Europe
West Germany joins NATO in 1955	Enduring alliance		

tion (**NATO**). Later that year the USSR countered by setting up the German Democratic Republic in East Germany.[29]

The boomerang returned, however, as Soviet exploitation generated uprisings in East Germany in 1953 and in Hungary in 1956. After suppressing these revolts with Soviet tanks, Moscow reversed gears. After 1956 the Kremlin sought to stabilize its empire by subsidies—selling Soviet oil to Communist regimes in Eastern Europe at far less than world prices. For reasons discussed in Chapters 5 and 13, however, Moscow's grip loosened, and in 1989 its empire dissolved.

A balance sheet of cooperation versus zero-sum politics in the decade after World War II is outlined in Table 2.4. Some events in the table are discussed in later chapters, but we note them here to sketch the big picture. Most of the cooperative practices (first column) continued to operate into the 1990s, because they generated ongoing mutual advantage. Most value-claiming practices (third column) were short-lived, because they benefited only one side.

29. The Kremlin did not form its own Warsaw Pact alliance until 1955, a riposte to West Germany's entry into NATO that year. East Germany and its borders were not recognized by the West until the early 1970s. East and West Germany joined the UN as seperate states in 1973.

Map 2.3 European Union Expansion in the 1990s

1. SLOVENIA
2. CROATIA
3. BOSNIA
4. ALBANIA
5. MACEDONIA
6. SERBIA and MONTENEGRO

■ Existing members   ▨ Potential future members

The "twelve" became "fifteen" when Sweden, Finland, and Austria joined the EU in 1995. Norway and Switzerland were also invited to join the EU in 1995, but a majority of their voters preferred to stay aloof. Cyprus, Turkey, and most states formerly in the Soviet sphere wished to join the EU but, as of 1997, were not admitted for political or economic reasons. The EU is analyzed in more detail in Chapter 15.

Half a century after Moscow prevented them from joining the ERP, Czechs and other East Europeans struggled in the 1990s to rejoin the world economy. Most East European countries obtained associate status in the European Union, shown in Map 2.3, and hoped for full membership one day. Like the Marshall Plan, the EU could bind together a long-divided continent—or perpetuate its divisions. The same question loomed in the 1990s as in 1947: Would Russia and the West cooperate or struggle against each other?

WHAT PROPOSITIONS HOLD? WHAT QUESTIONS REMAIN?

REPRESSION, LENIENCY, INTEGRATION

What lessons flow from the past? Efforts to create a new global order in the 19th and 20th centuries suggest that integrative, mutual-gain policies work better than either brutal repression or hope-for-the-best indulgence.

Relations between the strong and the weak can help or harm each side. As a wise Athenian put it: The basis for the security of an empire lies in "good administration"—not harsh repression. The right way to deal with dependent people is not to punish but to "take tremendous care of them."[30] Updating this insight, we can say that alliances and empires resemble businesses where "competitive advantage grows fundamentally out of the value a firm is able to create for its buyers."[31]

Repression generates a boomerang effect. The ultrarealist victor who exacts a harsh peace risks rebellion. Zero-sum policies backfired after 1919, as they had after 1807 and 1871. France wanted to keep Germany pinned to the mat after World War I, but Germany rose up for another onslaught.

Similarly, Moscow's heavy hand alienated East Europeans after World War II. The Kremlin repressed its vassals, and in so doing undermined its own power, violated Marxist ideals, and obstructed the interdependence that Karl Marx had celebrated in his *Communist Manifesto* (1848) a century before. The East Europeans might have become genuine partners of the USSR. Instead, they labored as disgruntled serfs until they could break free.

Forbearance also failed. It was abused by Southern planters after the U.S. Civil War and by German officials pleading for revision of the Versailles Treaty in the 1920s and 1930s.

A wiser course was set by the moderate realists who dominated the 1815 Congress of Vienna. They dealt firmly with France but then welcomed their former foe into the Concert of Europe.

Power, idealism, and interdependence converged in the U.S. quest for a new order after World War II. Americans defanged militarists in Germany and Japan but then made partners of their former foes. These policies were realistic—firm but conciliatory and idealistic—based on vision and empathy and imbued by a search for mutual gain.

30. Diodotus, quoted in Thucydides, *Peloponnesian War*, Book 3.

31. See Michael E. Porter, *Competitive Advantage: Creating and Sustaining Superior Performance* (New York: Free Press, 1985), xvi.

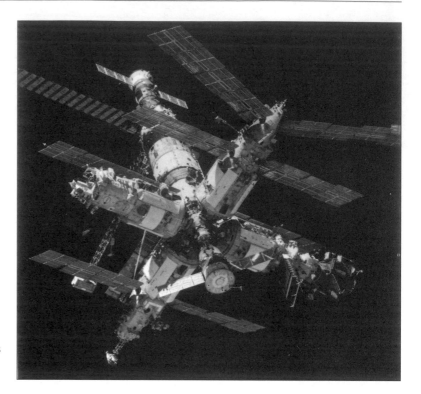

International cooperation in space benefits from shared expertise, equipment, and financing. It also reduces prospects of an arms race in outer space. U.S. astronauts and other foreign crew members joined Russian cosmonauts aboard the Russian space station Mir in 1996–1997.

THE USES OF OPEN DIPLOMACY

Closed diplomacy undermined peace efforts after World War I. The Versailles Treaty was drafted behind closed doors and presented as an accomplished fact. Germans were expected to comply with the treaty and Republican senators in Washington were supposed to approve the pact even though they had played no role in its writing. Had the views of all concerned parties been heard, the new order might have been more viable.

By contrast, the Marshall Plan represented a triumph of openness. U.S. planners conceived the program in their Washington offices, but it was proposed, negotiated, and implemented in a relatively open setting. The ERP was widely debated by each concerned society—except in Eastern Europe and the USSR, where Moscow dictated a party line for all Communists.

U.S. officials, however, doubted the ability of the American public to respond to arguments based on the economic interdependence of Europe and the United States. As a result, officials gave a heavy anti-Communist spin to the Marshall Plan, emphasizing its role in stopping Communism. Thus, Americans supported the ERP, but not for all the right reasons.

What Do You Tell the White House? ... *You draft your brief for the White House: The reconstruction of Western Europe and Japan after 1945 showed that mutual-gain policies can be both useful and feasible. Washington blended firmness with value-creating to overcome differences and spur recovery. The U.S. extended incentives to cooperate while establishing safeguards against defection. U.S. policies spawned a trading and security community in North America, Western Europe, and Japan that lived in peace and prosperity. Governments sometimes learn the right lessons.*

These lessons can guide us as we try to help damaged societies recover from dictatorship, harsh imperial rule, or civil war—from Angola and Haiti to Cambodia and Ukraine.[32] But these damaged societies and their leaders must also learn. They should note that Germany and Japan relied mainly on their own efforts to rebuild.

Can we—should we—mobilize a Marshall Plan for subjects of the former Soviet empire? We should pursue a mutual-gain orientation toward these countries, but cannot expect quick successes. Russia, Ukraine, and Kazakstan in the 1990s are not Germany or Japan in the 1940s or 1950s. The foundations for democracy and a market economy in the former Soviet Union are much weaker. Furthermore, the West has limited leverage because it did not defeat Russia in war and occupy it. Last but not least, Westerners see little reason to invest huge sums to rebuild the ex-Communist economies. To obtain popular support for enlightened diplomacy, foreign affairs specialists and the public must educate one another—communicate openly about the facts and values at stake. Honest dialogue and wise planning require us to elevate foreign affairs beyond party politics.

To sum up, the success of U.S. policy to Europe and Japan flowed from a strategy oriented toward mutual gain, rooted in a relatively open dialogue both at home and internationally. The failures of Soviet policy toward Eastern Europe derived from an exploitative approach imposed with no meaningful discussion at home or with target countries.

The utility of mutual gain and openness in other arenas will be examined in the chapters that follow. We must learn more about many issues before we attempt to evaluate transitions and whether the Second World can join the First (see Chapter 13).

Unlike the problems of rebuilding after a long conflict, our next case study (Chapter 3) focuses on a sharp crisis—how it arose and how it was defused. Each policy problem has its specific characteristics. Principles, we shall see, are difficult to apply; but without guidelines, we stagger in the dark.

32. See Anthony Lake et al., *After the Wars: Reconstruction in Afghanistan, Indochina, Central America, Southern Africa, and the Horn of Africa* (Washington, D.C.: Overseas Development Council, 1990).

KEY NAMES AND TERMS

alliance
Alsace and Lorraine
Appomattox
Carthaginian peace
Georges Clemenceau
collective security
Council on Mutual
   Economic Assistance
   (COMECON)
Concert of Europe
condominium
Congress of Vienna
deterrence
hegemony

Iron Curtain
Douglas A. MacArthur
Marshall Plan/European
   Recovery Program (ERP)
Viacheslav M. Molotov
negative peace
North Atlantic Treaty
   Organization (NATO)
positive peace
reparations
revisionist state
Treaty of Tilsit
Versailles system
world order

QUESTIONS TO DISCUSS

1. Why would a Western leader in the 1990s care about the outcomes of earlier wars? To what extent does history repeat itself? Why?

2. How open was the diplomacy that produced the Versailles system? The Marshall Plan? Soviet policy to Eastern Europe?

3. Why did General MacArthur work with Japanese officials instead of dictating policy?

4. Compare U.S. policies toward Germany and Japan after 1945.

5. Why did Republicans spurn President Wilson's plans for the postwar world but accept Truman's?

6. Compare the pros and cons, financial and political, of the ERP and the Soviet treatment of Eastern Europe after 1945.

7. Had Stalin asked you to recommend an overall strategy toward Eastern Europe in 1945, what guidelines would you have endorsed?

8. What kinds of peace settlement would be sought by a realist, an idealist, and a student of interdependence?

9. What factors make it difficult to adopt a mutual-gain approach with defeated foes?

10. What are the pros and cons of open diplomacy? When is it feasible? Desirable?

RECOMMENDED RESOURCES

BOOKS

Acheson, Dean. *Present at the Creation: My Years in the State Department.* New York: Norton, 1987.

Albrecht-Carrié, René. *A Diplomatic History of Europe Since the Congress of Vienna.* Rev. ed. New York: Harper & Row, 1973.

Craig, Gordon A., and Felix Gilbert, eds. *The Diplomats, 1919–1939.* Princeton, N.J.: Princeton University Press, 1953.

Fromkin, David. *In the Time of the Americans: FDR, Truman, Eisenhower, Marshall, MacArthur—The Generation That Changed America's Role in the World.* New York: Knopf, 1995.

Gaddis, John Lewis. We *Now Know: Rethinking Cold War History.* New York: Oxford University Press, 1997.

Hoffmann, Stanley. *World Disorders.* Lanham, Md.: Rowman & Littlefield, 1998.

Kennedy, Paul. *The Rise and Fall of the Great Powers: Economic Change and Military Conflict from 1500 to 2000.* New York: Random House, 1987.

Kissinger, Henry A. *Diplomacy.* New York: Simon & Schuster, 1994.

Leffler, Melvyn P. *A Preponderance of Power: National Security, the Truman Administration, and the Cold War.* Stanford, Calif.: Stanford University Press, 1992.

Mastny, Vojtech. *The Cold War and Soviet Insecurity.* New York: Oxford University Press, 1996.

Ulam, Adam B. *Expansion and Coexistence: Soviet Foreign Policy, 1917–73.* 2d ed. New York: Praeger, 1974.

Zubok, Vladislav, and Constantine Pleshakov. *Inside the Kremlin's Cold War: From Stalin to Khrushchev.* Cambridge, Mass.: Harvard University Press, 1996.

WEB SITES

General MacArthur and Postwar Japan
   http://www.earlham.edu/JIC/menu.html
General Military History
   http://www.cfcsc.dnd.ca/links/milhist/index.html
Marshall Plan
   http://www.usis.usemb.se/topical/pol/marshall.html
   This is a U.S. Embassy site. Follow the gopher link to pam-toc.
U.S. Civil War
   http://www.cfcsc.dnd.ca:80/links/milhist/usciv.html
Versailles Treaty
   http://www.lib.byu.edu/~rdh/
   Follow the links to World War I, treaties, and Versailles.
World War I
   http://www.cfcsc.dnd.ca:80/links/milhist/wwi.html
World War II
   http://www.cfcsc.dnd.ca:80/links/milhist/wwii.html

C H A P T E R   T H R E E

FOREIGN POLICY DECISION MAKING: DO INDIVIDUALS COUNT?

T H E   B I G   Q U E S T I O N S   I N   C H A P T E R   3

- How could Washington and Moscow in 1962 go to the brink of a war that neither wanted?

- How could the two major nuclear powers so badly misread each other?

- Was their trip to the brink due to the helmsmen or to the seas on which they sailed? Which action levels were responsible? Who—or what—was in charge?

- In crises, do domestic and international factors overshadow individuals— or the reverse?

- How can the Marshall Plan and Washington's handling of the missile crisis *both* be regarded as major achievements of U.S. foreign policy? Despite their apparent differences, did these policies have any significant similarities?

- Can *governments* learn?

"We Don't Make Mistakes." . . . *The White House asks you, "How did it come about—humanity's closest brush with a thermonuclear exchange? Could the Cuban missile crisis of 1962 have been avoided? How can we avoid getting onto such collision courses in the future? If we find ourselves heading for a collision, how can we avert disaster? How can we improve decision making?"*

You review what happened: Both Soviet and U.S. leaders played IR as zero-sum poker. Stakes were high. Bluffs and bullying overshadowed sweet-talk. Secrecy aggravated suspicion.

President John F. Kennedy met Soviet leader Nikita S. Khrushchev for two days in Vienna, June 3 and 4, 1961. JFK warned Khrushchev that the consequences would be horrific if "our two countries should miscalculate."

Khrushchev retorted: "We don't make mistakes. We will not make war by mistake." He exploded: "All I ever hear from your people . . . is that damned word miscalculation." Moscow would defend its vital interests whether the U.S. called it miscalculation or not. "You ought to take that word and bury it in cold storage and never use it again," said Khrushchev.

Kennedy reminded Khrushchev that Europeans had earlier misjudged Hitler. During the Korean War the U.S. in 1950 had "failed to foresee what the Chinese would do." JFK admitted that he too had made "certain misjudgments." Kennedy wanted to introduce "precision in judgments of the two sides and to obtain a clearer understanding of where we are going."[1]

Despite Kennedy's warnings, both Washington and Moscow misread each other in 1962. That year the Soviets attempted to deploy nuclear-tipped missiles secretly in Cuba just ninety miles from Florida. Discovering the operation as it neared completion, Washington offered the Kremlin either war or mutual concessions. Moscow chose the latter. Like teenage drivers playing "Chicken," JFK and Khrushchev found themselves on a collision course. Fortunately for the planet, they veered to avoid a crash. Sobered by their brush with disaster, both sides found that they were locked in mutual vulnerability—their very survival hostage to each other's restraint. In 1963 they took steps to improve communications and promote mutual gain. Having risked disaster by value-claiming, both sides turned to value-creating.

What lessons can you derive for the President? You begin by reviewing what psychologists and social scientists say about perception and decision making.

---

1. Interpreter's notes, cited in Michael R. Beschloss, *The Crisis Years: Kennedy and Khrushchev, 1960–1963* (New York: HarperCollins, 1991), 196–197.

CONTENDING CONCEPTS AND EXPLANATIONS: IS ANYBODY IN CHARGE? HOW ACTION LEVELS INTERACT

Who or what produced the key decisions in the Cuban missile crisis? Let us look for answers on the first three levels of IR action. We will examine the fourth and fifth levels (transnational and environmental factors) in later chapters.

LEVEL 1: INDIVIDUALS AND HUMAN NATURE

Do individuals count? Proponents of **determinism** say that individuals are the puppets of great forces such as divine will, fate, economics, and eros. The neorealists (discussed in Chapter 1) are also determinists: They hold that the structure of power leaves little role for individuals or social systems. If impersonal forces control our lives, it makes little difference who occupies the White House. Against determinists, voluntarists argue that IR is the product of individuals exercising their free will.

This book contends that individuals are conditioned—not determined—by nature and nurture. Genes and life experiences make individuals unique. Each person responds differently to the demands of time and place. Whenever we look closely at world-shaking events, one sees the imprint of individuals.[2] Compare, for example, Woodrow Wilson and Vladimir Lenin—one a rigid liberal, the other a pragmatic Communist.

How Personal Characteristics Can Shape Political Outcomes

Here is a mystery: Wilson was the most influential person in the world in 1919, but he failed to achieve U.S. membership in the League of Nations. By contrast, Lenin was then a political unknown attempting to retain power in war-ravaged Russia. Despite attacks from all sides, Lenin succeeded in establishing Soviet rule in most of the old Russian empire.

Wilson's personal characteristics were evident as he sought Senate approval of the Versailles Treaty and League of Nations Covenant. Senate Republicans demanded modification in the treaty language. Wilson refused to bargain. He insisted that the Senate vote on the treaty "as is." He lost, and the U.S. never joined the League.

All his life Wilson had insisted on unquestioning support. On several key issues he had split from close friends who urged him to moderate his stands. Why? Some scholars say that Wilson's domineering father, an ar-

2. Many political scientists say that individual personalities should be left to historians and psychohistorians. An exception is John G. Stoessinger. See his *Crusaders and Pragmatists: Movers of Modern American Foreign Policy* (New York: Norton, 1979). On the pros and cons of psychohistory, see Saul Friedlaender, *History and Psychoanalysis: An Inquiry into the Possibilities and Limits of Psychohistory* (New York: Holmes & Meier, 1978); and David E. Stannard, *Shrinking History: On Freud and the Failure of Psychohistory* (New York: Oxford University Press, 1980). On the physical burdens of leadership, see Robert E. Gilbert, *The Mortal Presidency: Illness and Anguish in the White House* (New York: Basic Books, 1992).

ticulate, good-looking Presbyterian minister, left him profoundly inse-cure. But body as well as mind played a role. Wilson's health often failed under pressure. His hypertension exploded in a major stroke as he whis-tle-stopped the U.S. in 1919 seeking public backing for the League.[3]

Like Wilson, Lenin came from a cultivated, middle class family—his father was a reformist school administrator under the tsar. But the future Communist leader had no self-doubt. Growing up in a happy family, Vladimir was a brilliant student and strong sportsman.[4] After his expul-sion from university for political agitation, however, Lenin became a ruthless, professional revolutionary who saw all politics as "who, whom?" Still, Lenin's operational code advised flexibility. Against strong opposi-tion Lenin suggested "one step backward to go two steps forward."

Lenin's ability to compromise—or to seem to—helped him save his Communist regime. When Soviet Russia's ragged troops faced an advanc-ing German juggernaut, some Russian Communists favored revolution-ary idealism. Lenin, however, called for a Communist *realpolitik*. The ide-alists believed Soviet Russia should not negotiate with Imperial Germany but should instead foment a workers' revolution there. Lenin urged self-help. Put aside dreams of revolution, he said. Buy "breathing space" by giving Germany a swath of Russia's territory in exchange for peace. Lenin did not split with his opponents (as Wilson did when colleagues dis-agreed with him). Instead he persuaded his comrades to endorse the deal—the Treaty of Brest-Litovsk in March 1918. Expediency paid off. Six months later the Kaiser fled Germany and the Soviets tore up the pact.

The world and the U.S. needed a strong League of Nations, but good ideas do not always prevail. Wilson's behavior undermined his ability to influence the U.S. Senate. Lenin's personality, in contrast, helped his party to prevail. Many leaders fail despite trumps while others make the most of a weak hand.

The Right Person at the Right Time

To be effective a leader's personality must fit the situation.[5] Very differ-ent personality types can win political power in different times and places.[6] Another U.S. president, Franklin D. Roosevelt (FDR), avoided Wilson's mistakes while absorbing positive lessons from his cousin Theodore Roosevelt, president from 1901 to 1909. FDR's pragmatism and charm, combined with his wife's idealism, helped him transform the country. While Eleanor Roosevelt thought about what *should* be done, Franklin focused on what *could* be done. Crippled by polio at age 39, FDR was frailer than Wilson, but he remained upbeat to his last day.[7]

3. On Wilson's psyche, see Juliette L. George and Alexander George, *Woodrow Wilson and Colonel House: A Personality Study* (New York: Dover, 1964); on Wilson's physical frailties, see Edwin A. Wein-stein, *Woodrow Wilson: A Medical and Psychological Biography* (Princeton, N.J.: Princeton University Press, 1981); for George and George's comments on Weinstein, see *Political Science Quarterly* 96, no. 4 (winter 1981–1982): 642–665. Several Wilson biogra-phies published in the late 1980s downplayed George and George's thesis.

4. This portrait is gathered from reminiscences by family members and others who knew Lenin.

5. William Howard Taft, for example, made a fine chief justice but a clumsy president—at least in the circumstances he faced. Alexander L. George, *Presidential Decisionmaking in Foreign Policy: The Effective Use of Information and Advice* (Boulder, Colo.: Westview, 1980), 7.

6. For contrasting views, see James David Bar-ber, *The Presidential Character: Predicting Perfor-mance in the White House*, 3d ed. (Englewood Cliffs, N.J.: Prentice-Hall, 1985), and Theodore Lowi, *The Personal President: Power Invested, Promise Unful-filled* (Ithaca, N.Y.: Cornell University Press, 1985).

7. David Fromkin, *In the Time of the Americans* (New York: Knopf, 1995); Doris Kearns Goodwin, *No Ordinary Time: Franklin and Eleanor Roosevelt: The Home Front in World War II* (New York: Simon & Schuster, 1994).

Politics may help insecure persons such as Wilson overcome self-doubt; for expansive, confident persons like Lenin, it offers a way to impose their will on others. But both Wilson and Lenin sought to implement their (rival) visions. Some leaders, however, seek power for its own sake, to acquire personal wealth, or to win acclaim. Idealists as well as realists may seethe with anger over personal grievances that they elevate to matters of principle.

Why Do Decision Makers Sometimes Misjudge?

Rationality in politics is to make decisions by calculating probable gains and losses from alternative courses of action and choosing the course most likely to maximize values. Such thinking is not morality or even wisdom, for evil and unwise goals may be pursued rationally.

But single-minded, rational pursuit of one goal is rare. Most of us—even presidents—"satisfice" rather than maximize: We settle for enough of one value (for example, wealth) to meet our needs while pursuing another value (such as leisure). When a president juggles conflicting goals, such as "guns and butter," the resulting policy mix may appear far from rational.

Foreign policy is also affected by **bounded rationality**—limits on time, intellect, and information that can keep decision makers from fully weighing their values and options. The sheer number and complexity of problems may outstrip their capacity to cope. Pressure to act under a deadline can bring on stress and fatigue that fog the brain. Signals are often ambiguous. Is the other side offering to shake hands to improve relations or to break your wrist?

How can a decision maker keep an open mind and remain alert to change without being drowned in streams of conflicting alarms? She may take shortcuts. But each entails risk. Instead of looking for all relevant data, she may halt the search when she seems to possess sufficient information. But if she stops the quest too early, she may lack the ingredients for a wise decision. Other dangers are outlined in the sidebar on page 66.

Still, not everyone performs worse under stress. Many students find that exams clear away the cobwebs. Richard Nixon claimed to function *better* under pressure. He described crises as "mountaintop experiences" in which his performance peaked. But even Nixon met a threshhold: He broke after Watergate. Andrei Gromyko, Soviet foreign minister for three decades, seemed to put dogma aside and focus on practical solutions during crises.

Warning: What You See May Not Be What You Get

Memo to Foreign Ministers: Beware these pitfalls as you make decisions under pressure and uncertainty.[1]

1. *Reduced capacity:* Your ability to cope with and learn during a crisis is hindered by fatigue and by the same factors that led the challenger to misjudge your resolve in the first place.

2. *Selective attention:* You pay more attention to news that seems to affect you immediately.

3. *Stereotyping and simplification:* You pay less attention to facts that contradict your previous views; you are reluctant to throw out the old and build anew.

4. *Self-righteousness:* You fail to empathize with the other side and are blind to change.

5. *Source bias:* You pay more attention to news from familiar, trusted sources.

6. *False postulates:* You leap to sweeping conclusions from a few statistics or anecdotes. You forget, ignore, or confuse facts. As a professor, Woodrow Wilson understood that the president must work with Congress; as president, however, Wilson disdained the Senate in 1919.

7. *Overgeneralization:* You overrate your past successes and trust "tried-and-true" policies. You may depend upon what you think is a sound operational code—beliefs and decision rules on how to respond to challenges.[2] But rules that work in one context may fail in others. Neither Lenin's pre-diction of class warfare nor Wilson's trust in global harmony was a sound guide to all settings.

8. *False analogies:* Past experiences may not fit today's problems. Americans learned from the 1938 Munich deal not to appease aggressors. This lesson worked well enough in Korea in the 1950s but went awry in Vietnam.[3]

9. *Attention space:* You pay more attention to facts that you will have to act upon and neglect others.

10. *Saliency:* As events become more important, they crowd out others and reduce the number of events on which you can focus.

11. *Momentum:* You pay more attention to facts bearing on actions in which you are already involved.

12. *Utility:* You pay attention to news if it may prove useful. You are less likely to react to warnings unless you also perceive remedies.

1. See Ithiel de Sola Pool and Allen Kessler, "The Kaiser, the Tsar, and the Computer: Information Processing in a Crisis," in *International Politics and Foreign Policy: A Reader in Research and Theory,* rev. ed., ed. James N. Rosenau (New York: Free Press, 1969), 664–678; Robert Jervis, "Hypotheses on Misperception," in ibid., 239–254; and Richard Ned Lebow, *Between Peace and War: The Nature of International Crisis* (Baltimore: Johns Hopkins University Press, 1981), 272.
2. Alexander L. George, "The 'Operational Code': A Neglected Approach to the Study of Political Leaders and Decision-making," *International Studies Quarterly* 13 (1969): 190–222.
3. Richard E. Neustadt and Ernest R. May, *Thinking in Time: The Uses of History for Decision Makers* (New York: Free Press, 1986).

LEVEL 2: DOMESTIC FACTORS—STATE AND SOCIETY

A Unified Rational Actor?

Splits within governments and society also undermine the rational consistency of government policies. We often talk of entire countries as though they were monolithic actors. For example, we say *France* demanded that *Germany* pay reparations. This phrasing implies a **rational actor model**. It presumes that states are united and rational in pursuit of their "national interests." But this image is too simple. "France" is an abstraction. Not all French leaders and citizens agreed with Premier Clemenceau on how to deal with Germany. Every French politician and interest group had a particular view of the "national" or "state" interest.

Sex, SOPs, and Different Drummers

States are rarely single-minded, unified players. Most are divided by gender, age, ethnic ties, economic interests, education, region, and religion. Each group may push for a different policy at home and abroad.

In addition, most governments are split by partisan and by bureaucratic politics. Rival parties chase their own visions. Each bureaucracy has its own interests and routines.[8] Each department's **standard operating procedures (SOPs)** aim at efficiency but often yield rigidity and contradiction as each unit follows its own drummer. Thus, the Pentagon tested nuclear weapons in 1990 just as the White House sought to arrange a cordial setting for Gorbachev's visit to Washington. Did the Americans conspire to intimidate the Soviet president? Or were the weapons laboratories just "doing their own thing"?

LEVEL 3: THE INTERNATIONAL STATE SYSTEM

The international system, as we saw in Chapter 1, consists of states and the organizations they establish, such as the United Nations. The existing system is anarchic, for it lacks an overarching supranational government, but is not chaotic. The system is defined by its key actors; their interaction; the hierarchies of power and influence among them; and how the system permits, encourages, or limits certain behaviors.

How did each level impact the 1962 missile crisis?

COMPARING THEORY AND REALITY: THE CUBAN MISSILE CRISIS

The 1962 confrontation had deep roots. Arriving in the Caribbean in 1492, Spaniards exterminated most Native Americans and replaced them with slaves from Africa and settlers from Spain. Chafing under Old World rule, most of Latin America obtained independence by 1826. But Cuba and Puerto Rico remained under Spain. Cubans launched wars for independence in 1868 and again in 1895.

In 1823 U.S. President James Monroe warned that Washington would view as "unfriendly" any effort by Europe to regain colonies in the New World. Monroe worried about Spain, France, and Russia, still expanding down America's northwest coast. The **Monroe Doctrine**, as it was later called, combined isolationism with latent interventionism. It pledged the U.S. not to meddle in the Old World or in Europe's existing colonies. But the doctrine also set the stage for the U.S. not just to guard but to dominate the Caribbean and Latin America.

8. See Graham T. Allison, *Essence of Decision: Explaining the Cuban Missile Crisis* (Boston: Little, Brown, 1971). A Marxist would offer still another explanation: Each government represents the economic interests of the ruling class. There is also a cybernetic model—government as a steering mechanism that responds quickly or slowly to signals, for example, from public opinion or the stock market.

U.S. forces in 1898 helped Cuba gain independence from Spain. But Cuba then came under heavy U.S. influence. Washington's paternalism and U.S. exploitation set the stage for an anti-Yankee revolt. In 1959 rebels led by Fidel Castro overthrew the local dictator long supported by U.S. commercial interests, and took power.

Could revolutionary Cuba and the U.S. achieve a working relationship? Castro visited the U.S. and Latin American countries in spring 1959. He enjoyed rousing welcomes at Harvard University (where his application for admission had been rejected a decade before) and at Princeton, but got a cooler reception at Yale. In Washington he was not received by President Dwight Eisenhower, who was playing golf in Georgia. Castro did meet Vice President Richard Nixon, however, and Nixon concluded that the U.S. should oust the new Cuban leader (as it had the leftist leader of Guatemala five years before).

Castro in 1959 valued his independence and disdained Communist discipline. In Soviet terms he was then more a "bourgeois nationalist" than a Communist. But two close colleagues, brother Raúl Castro and Ernesto ("Che") Guevara, were Communists. They pushed for leftist reforms and close contacts with the USSR even as Castro, Cuba's prime minister, sought U.S. economic aid. The prime minister himself was mercurial. In May 1959 Cuba nationalized much agricultural land owned by U.S. interests. Washington responded by reducing the amount of sugar Cuba could sell to the U.S. In September 1959 Khrushchev approved a

A Guide to Soviet Weapons in Cuba

Medium-range ballistic missiles (MRBMs) have a range of 600 to 1,500 nautical miles (n.m.); **intermediate-range ballistic missiles (IRBMs),** a range of 1,500 to 3,000 n.m. MRBMs fired from Cuba could hit Washington and population centers such as New York; IRBMs were counterforce weapons, because they could reach U.S. ICBM (intercontinental ballistic missile) bases in the Midwest. Soviet MRBM sites were discovered by U-2 cameras on October 14; IRBM sites the next day.

By October 22 the Soviets had completed deployment of 24 MRBM launchers equipped with 36 missiles—12 of them "refires" for a second barrage. The Soviets had not yet completed deployment of 16 IRBM launchers—the missiles for which were still in transit. Nearly 100 nuclear warheads were already in Cuba—for the MRBMs, IRBMs, short-range rockets,

and Il-28 bombers (1950 vintage, four jet engines, 4,000 pound bomb load capacity, 740 mile radius of action). Warheads, however, were kept at some distance from missiles.

Soviet troops had six short-range tactical rocket launchers (30–40 km. range) with nine tactical nuclear warheads (2–25 kiloton range). In case of a U.S. invasion, the local Soviet commander was authorized to fire these, even though this could start a thermonuclear war.[1]

1. Soviet spokesmen later revealed that 42,000 Soviet ground, naval, and air defense personnel were in Cuba in 1962—twice as many as Washington estimated then. These forces included motorized rifle regiments, coastal defense cruise missiles, patrol boats, 24 SAM sites with 144 launchers, 42 MiG-21 fighters, 42 Il-28 jet light bombers, and—undetected by the U.S.—20 launchers with 80 conventionally armed cruise missiles for tactical ground support. Raymond L. Garthoff, "The Havana Conference on the Cuban Missile Crisis," *Cold War International History Project Bulletin* (Woodrow Wilson International Center for Scholars), 1 (spring 1992): 2–5.

secret sale of Polish arms to Cuba. Soon there was a major Soviet presence in the Western hemisphere, undercutting the Monroe Doctrine.[9] What started as an irritant to Washington became a threat to world peace. Let us review the key events.

THE UNFOLDING OF THE CUBAN MISSILE CRISIS

The events of 1960–1962 leading up to the Cuban missile crisis are described in the timeline on page 70.

After a U.S. U-2 spy plane on October 14, 1962, brought back evidence of the missile deployment, the White House did not immediately broadcast this information. It used the time before the missiles could be made operational to plan an effective response. How could Kennedy get the best advice? How avoid both raucus discord and **groupthink** conformity? Some presidents had asked advisers to play "devil's advocate" for unpopular views. President Eisenhower often requested a list of formal options with pros and cons.[10] Kennedy favored a less formal approach. He set up a working group, later called the **ExComm** (Executive Committee), comprised of some fourteen to twenty officials from various branches of government, each thinking like a generalist. Sometimes the president stayed away so ExComm members could debate more freely.

A psychologist's study concluded that the ExComm approach minimized groupthink.[11] But in fact the group paid little attention to noncoercive options. The ExComm rejected any course that allowed the Soviets to stall while they made the missiles operational. Adlai Stevenson, U.S. ambassador to the United Nations, and others who favored a nonmilitary solution were branded **doves** while proponents of tough, unilateral measures became **hawks**. (These caricatures persisted in U.S. politics, making it difficult for political figures to propose anything less than a fully macho approach to Vietnam and other conflicts.)

The ExComm focused on six options: (1) do nothing and accept Soviet missiles in Cuba; (2) mend fences with Castro; (3) use diplomacy to squeeze or buy them out; (4) invade Cuba with conventional forces, eliminating the missiles and Castro; (5) take out the missiles with a surgical air strike; or (6) stop further military shipments by imposing a naval blockade of Cuba. Map 3.1 on page 71 shows the tactical situation.

JFK's desire to look firm excluded options 1 and 2. Even option 3 was initially rejected, because any "deal" to remove the Soviet weapons could be seen as a reward for Moscow's duplicity. For a time the ExComm and Kennedy leaned toward an air strike against Soviet missiles in Cuba. But when military chiefs could not guarantee destruction of all the missiles,

9. Gaddis Smith, *The Last Years of the Monroe Doctrine, 1945–1993* (New York: Hill and Wang, 1994), 95–103.

10. Another approach would be "multiple advocacy." See George, *Presidential Decisionmaking,* chaps. 11 and 12.

11. I. L. Janis, *Victims of Groupthink* (Boston: Houghton Mifflin, 1972).

TIMELINE

1960

2/4–13
Soviet First Deputy Prime Minister **Anastas Mikoyan** visits Cuba and signs trade and aid agreements

3/10
President Eisenhower authorizes CIA to explore ways to overthrow Castro

6/29
U.S. oil companies Texaco and Esso refuse to refine Soviet oil in Cuba; Cuban government nationalizes its refineries

7/9
Khrushchev offers to protect Cuba with rockets and buy its sugar

10/6
Cuba nationalizes all U.S. holdings without compensation

12/19
Cuba claims solidarity with the Sino-Soviet bloc

1961

1/3
U.S. terminates diplomatic and consular relations with Cuba

3/31
U.S. cuts Cuban sugar quota to zero

4/17–19
Anti-Castro exiles backed by CIA are defeated at Cuba's **Bay of Pigs**

6/3–4
Khrushchev meets JFK in Vienna and announces a six-month deadline to resolve the problems of divided Germany and Berlin

6/12–13
Berlin Wall erected by East Germans with Soviet backing

10/21
Pentagon reveals that "missile gap" favors the U.S.

1962

1/22–31
Organization of American States (OAS) ousts Cuba from its ranks and agrees to collective defense measures against it

2/3
U.S. embargoes all trade with Cuba except critical medicines

April–May
U.S. troops, planes, and ships take part in large-scale maneuvers off North Carolina and Puerto Rico; activity denounced by Havana as preparations to invade Cuba

5/14–20
Khrushchev conceives plan to install nuclear missiles in Cuba[12]

5/29
Soviets propose missile deployment and Castro agrees

7/3–8
Cuban and Soviet leaders initial secret treaty governing Soviet forces in Cuba

7/27
Castro announces that Cuba, with Soviet aid, is taking measures to make any U.S. attack on Cuba the equivalent of a world war

8/10
CIA Director John McCone reports to JFK his belief that Soviet MRBMs will be deployed in Cuba

8/27–9/2
Khrushchev rejects Cuban proposal to publicize the missile deployment

9/4
Soviet Ambassador **Anatoly Dobrynin** conveys to Attorney General Robert F. Kennedy assurances from Khrushchev that no ground-to-ground or offensive weapons will be deployed in Cuba

9/15
The first Soviet MRBMs arrive in Cuba

9/19
U.S. Intelligence Board concludes that Soviet policy does not support establishment of nuclear missiles on foreign soil

9/21
Soviet Foreign Minister Andrei Gromyko warns UN that a U.S. attack on Cuba would mean war with USSR

late September
Soviet **surface-to-air missiles (SAMs)** are deployed in Cuba and are operational, but are under orders not to fire at U.S. reconnaissance planes

12. See Nikita S. Khrushchev, *Khrushchev Remembers*, 3 vols. (Boston: Little, Brown, 1970–1990), 1: 492–494. How Khrushchev's memoirs were composed and published is explained by his son, Sergei Khrushchev, in *Khrushchev on Khrushchev: An Inside Account of the Man and His Era* (Boston: Little, Brown, 1990).

Map 3.1   U.S. Targets Within Range of Soviet Missiles

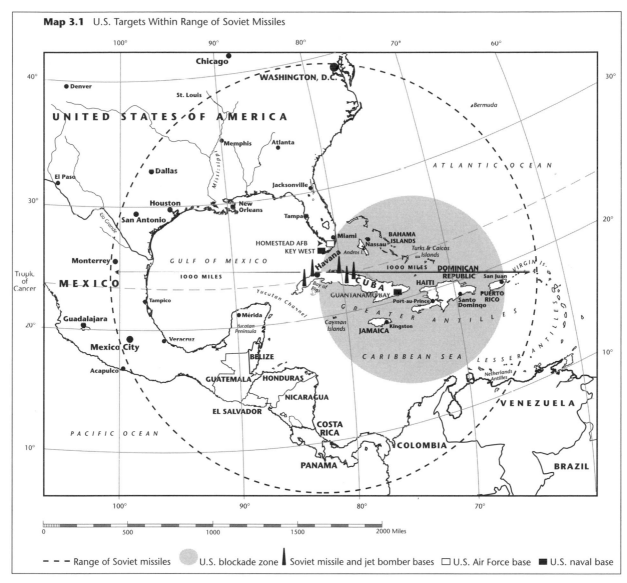

- - -   Range of Soviet missiles   ● U.S. blockade zone   ▮ Soviet missile and jet bomber bases   ☐ U.S. Air Force base   ■ U.S. naval base

the president ordered a blockade instead—dubbed a "quarantine" since a blockade is an act of war.

On October 22 JFK told the world that the Soviets had mounted a "secret, swift, and extraordinary buildup" to change the "status quo" in an area with a special relationship to the U.S. Washington's "initial" course of action would be to impose a "quarantine on all offensive military equipment under shipment to Cuba." Ships with such equipment would be turned back. Kennedy called upon the USSR to withdraw all offensive

MRBMs fired from Cuba could hit Washington and population centers such as New York; IRBMs were counterforce weapons, because they could reach U.S. ICBM bases in the Midwest. Even Il-28 bombers could easily hit the southern U.S. and return to Cuba.

SOURCE: Adapted from *Hammond Atlas of the 20th Century* (Maplewood, N.J.: Hammond, Inc., 1996), 110.

A new form of open diplomacy served the U.S. as U.S. Ambassador Adlai Stevenson, on October 25, 1962, showed the UN Security Council photos of Soviet missile sites in Cuba.

weapons from Cuba. The same message was conveyed in a private letter to Khrushchev that began "Dear Sir" instead of "Dear Mr. Chairman," the usual and more courteous address. The alert status of U.S. forces worldwide was raised from Defcon ("Defense Condition") 5 to Defcon 3.

The clock ticked.

During these tense days Kennedy and his team tried to micromanage U.S. policy. They violated military SOPs by skirting the chain of command and denying autonomy to local commanders. The ExComm knew all Soviet ships by name and followed their movements on a large map. The president personally directed many operations of the quarantine to make sure that needless incidents or reckless subordinates did not escalate the crisis.[13]

Four days after the quarantine began, Khrushchev tried to defuse the crisis. On Friday, October 26, he sent a long, rambling letter to Kennedy offering to declare that Soviet ships carried no weapons to Cuba in exchange for a U.S. pledge not to invade Cuba, which would mean that the need for Soviet "military specialists in Cuba would disappear." On Saturday, however, Khrushchev sent a second letter—this one demanding a parallel withdrawal of U.S. missiles from Turkey. Why the Soviet leader wrote two letters is a mystery. Nor do we know whether he grasped that the second letter would be interpreted as more assertive than the first.

It was not until October 27 that Khrushchev proposed to trade Soviet missiles in Cuba for U.S. missiles in Turkey. He did so by means of a radio broadcast made even before his second letter reached Washington. Not only did the Americans regard his second proposal as more aggressive,

13. Defense Secretary Robert S. McNamara asked Admiral George Anderson, Chief of Naval Operations, what U.S. ship would make the first interception of a Soviet ship headed for Cuba. Were Russian-speaking officers on board? What would the Navy do if a Soviet captain refused to disclose his cargo? The chief pointed to the *Manual of Naval Operations* and shouted: "It's all in there." McNamara shot back: "I don't give a damn what John Paul Jones would have done. I want to know what you are going to do, now." Elie Abel, *The Missile Crisis* (Philadelphia: Lippincott, 1966), 155–156.

but, because it was so different from the first offer, they doubted that Khrushchev was bargaining in good faith. Alternatively, some wondered if he had lost control in the Kremlin.

From the onset of the crisis the White House had considered a trade of U.S. missiles in Europe for a pullback of Soviet missiles from Cuba. Such a deal would be low-cost in that U.S. missiles in Europe had become redundant—in some respects, a liability. Not based in silos, they were vulnerable to a Soviet first-strike. Nor were they needed for "extended deterrence"—preventing an attack on U.S. allies—because this task could now be accomplished by more secure weapons based in the U.S. and on U.S. submarines. British Prime Minister Harold Macmillan several times offered to trade off the sixty or so U.S. missiles based in Britain against the Soviet missiles in Cuba. Kennedy considered the offer but did not utilize it.

Moscow focused on the missiles closest to the USSR—those in Turkey, not those in the UK, in Italy, or elsewhere. Washington was reluctant to ask Turkey to give up its U.S. missiles, however, because Ankara—unlike London—attached great weight to the U.S. missiles on its soil. The warheads were still owned and controlled by the U.S., but the missiles were technically owned by Turkey. The White House believed that Ankara had not fully considered how the U.S. missiles might attract a Soviet attack on Turkey and debated whether their withdrawal might be compensated by stationing a missile-firing Polaris submarine near Turkey. The ExComm preferred to avoid any act implying that a clandestine Soviet deployment in Cuba deserved a U.S. concession elsewhere. U.S. leaders believed they had the right to surround the USSR with missiles; Moscow had no comparable right to station its missiles close to U.S. shores. And if U.S. missiles were removed from Turkey, Soviet forces aimed at Turkey should also be disarmed.

Kennedy opted to publicly welcome Khrushchev's first letter and respond to the second only in private. At 8:05 P.M. on October 27 JFK declared that if the USSR withdrew its offensive weapons and undertook, "with suitable safeguards," not to introduce them again, and with "adequate arrangements through the United Nations" to verify these commitments, the U.S. would lift its quarantine and "give assurances against an invasion of Cuba."

Khrushchev's second letter got a positive reply later that night when Attorney General Robert F. Kennedy (the president's brother) met with Soviet Ambassador Anatoly Dobrynin. When Dobrynin asked about Turkey, Robert Kennedy replied that the White House was willing to pull

TIMELINE

1962

10/23
Cuba calls for UN Security Council meeting; Moscow accuses U.S. of violating international law with provocations that could lead to war; the OAS votes 20–0 to endorse U.S. actions; Khrushchev agrees to a proposal by UN Acting Secretary General U Thant to halt Soviet arms shipments if U.S. lifts quarantine, an idea rejected by Washington

10/24
Most Soviet ships en route to Cuba slow or reverse course but one tanker continues; U.S. quarantine goes into effect; Strategic Air Command alert climbs to Defcon 2—one step away from war

10/25
A dozen Soviet ships turn back but one tanker is intercepted and allowed to proceed without boarding

its missiles from Turkey in four to five months, but insisted that this side deal be kept secret. Kennedy coupled this concession with an ultimatum that he termed a "request": Washington needed a Soviet commitment "by tomorrow" that the Soviet missiles would be removed.

Poor communications and the time lag (8:05 P.M. in Washington was 3:05 A.M. in Moscow) added to fatigue and frayed nerves. At least eight hours were needed to get a message from the Soviet embassy in Washington to Khrushchev. Dobrynin sent coded messages to Khrushchev in telegrams taken to Western Union by a bicycle messenger. In Moscow they were decoded and typed out at the Soviet Foreign Ministry and delivered to Khrushchev. The fastest way for either side to communicate was to read a speech over the radio. (Anxious to improve the flow, Washington and Moscow in 1963 set up a direct communication link, the "hotline.")

October 27 was filled with tension. Castro urged Khrushchev to launch a preemptive nuclear strike on the U.S. if the Americans invaded Cuba.[14] The Soviet SAM network in Cuba shot down an American U-2. Soviet fighters scrambled to intercept still another U-2, this one based in Alaska, as it overflew Soviet territory, but did not fire on it.

Fearing a U.S. attack on Cuba or the USSR or both, Khrushchev on October 28 advised the Presidium of the Soviet Communist Party to accept the U.S. offer not to attack Cuba if Soviet weapons were withdrawn from Cuba. Robert Kennedy's offer to Dobrynin to pull back the U.S. missiles from Turkey seems to have arrived some time *after* Khrushchev's decision to retreat. In the days that followed, however, Khrushchev tried to nail down the U.S. commitment on Turkey. Robert Kennedy reiterated the U.S. pledge orally but absolutely refused to confirm it in writing.[15]

On October 28 Khrushchev informed President Kennedy that he had given an order to "dismantle the arms which you described as offensive."[16] The crisis had peaked. On October 29 there were still signs that Soviet crews were continuing to prepare missile sites. Soon, however, they started to disassemble the missile sites and crated the equipment for shipment back to the USSR.

Had Khrushchev not backed off within a day of the Attorney General's "request," what would have been Washington's next step? The White House hinted that it might soon launch an air strike against the missiles and an invasion force. Bluff or reality? Kennedy told a visiting congressional delegation that invading Cuba during the crisis would be "one hell of a gamble." Decades later the former Defense Secretary, **Robert S. McNamara,** said that Kennedy would probably have tightened the quaran-

14. For the text, see James G. Blight et al., *Cuba on the Brink: Castro, the Missile Crisis, and the Soviet Collapse* (New York: Pantheon, 1993), 481–491.

15. Because the Secretary of State, Dean Rusk, was reluctant to broach these issues with the Turkish government, the deal was made without consulting Ankara. Kennedy chastised Rusk for negligence on this matter on October 29.

16. Khrushchev denied that these arms were anything but "defensive" and avoided using the word "missile." Washington seized on this vagueness to specify the weapons it wanted withdrawn: The Americans included not just the Soviet MRBMs but also aging short-range Il-28 bombers. Since Moscow had promised some of these planes to Castro, their removal struck another blow to Soviet-Cuban relations.

Fig. 3.1 "Chicken"

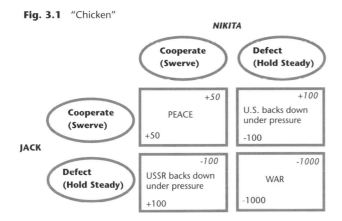

NIKITA

	Cooperate (Swerve)	**Defect (Hold Steady)**
Cooperate (Swerve)	*+50* PEACE +50	*+100* U.S. backs down under pressure -100
Defect (Hold Steady)	*-100* USSR backs down under pressure +100	*-1000* WAR -1000

JACK

tine, while the former Secretary of State, Dean Rusk, recalled that the president, to overcome a continued crisis, considered orchestrating a public UN proposal for a Turkey-Cuba deal. If the Soviets did not budge, the U.S. could still have used force. U.S. military forces stayed on high alert through November 1962.[17] There was no sign, however, that Washington ever contemplated a first-strike on the Soviet homeland.

"We were eyeball to eyeball," Rusk observed, and "the other side just blinked." But the reality was more complex. Each side gave the other time and space to avoid a collision. Neither backed the other into a corner from which it could exit only by fighting. To be sure, the U.S. gained the most—it had compelled Moscow to back down. But Khrushchev could claim that he had won major U.S. concessions. And while Castro felt betrayed by the Soviet retreat, he gained a qualified U.S. pledge not to invade Cuba. All three countries survived intact.

Kennedy did not rub salt in Soviet wounds or crow over the Soviet retreat. Rather, as we will see in Chapters 6 and 7, both U.S. and Soviet leaders in 1963 and in later years looked for ways to prevent confrontations and improve relations.

But the 1962 U.S.-Soviet understandings were left hanging. Fuming that he had not even been consulted, Castro refused UN inspection of Cuban territory. Moscow and Washington then devised an alternative: Soviet missiles were lashed to the decks of Soviet ships where they could be observed and photographed by U.S. planes. But there was no on-site inspection to verify withdrawal of nuclear warheads. And no "suitable safeguards" were established against future weapons deliveries. Lacking these assurances, the U.S. gave no formal promise that it would not attack Cuba. Indeed, the White House continued to sponsor sabotage in Cuba and assassination plots against Castro. Only in 1970, when Moscow asked

The Game of "Chicken"

The Cuban confrontation resembled what game theorists call Chicken: Two rivals drive straight at each other. The first to swerve is deemed "chicken"— she or he loses "face" but not life (see Figure 3.1). The unflinching rival wins applause. If both swerve at the same time, neither wins but both survive. If both hold a steady course, neither survives. In game theory terms, to swerve is to cooperate while to hold a steady course is to defect.

Chicken differs from Prisoner's Dilemma (see Chapter 1) in that both sides share a deep interest in avoiding mutual defection—catastrophe. In Chicken, being exploited is not as bad as a head-on crash. Still, each driver will try to look firm so the other swerves. Players like Kennedy or Khrushchev may demonstrate commitment by fixing the wheel, feigning insanity, or appearing not to understand the dangers. If one plays Chicken with a committed player, it pays to back down. A sensible actor would avoid such games altogether! A minor player (like Castro), if rational, would avoid getting caught between two juggernauts.

17. Defense Minister Rodion Malinovskii reported to the Central Committee, Soviet Communist Party, on November 17, 1962, on the status of U.S. forces worldwide. He said that 75 B-52 flights took place each day and that 178 B-47s were based in Europe and 36 in Asia along with two B-52s. Five U.S. missile-firing submarines were on patrol off Norway while two were at their base in Scotland and one in Charleston. Soviet reconnaissance was not so bad either! See *Diplomaticheskii vestnik* 19–20 (October 15–31, 1992): 62–63.

Washington for a confirmation, did the White House confirm privately that the 1962 understanding was "still in full force."[18]

How the outcome of the crisis benefited each side is suggested in Table 3.1.

Table 3.1 How the Deal Served Both Sides, Though Unequally

What Khrushchev Could Say	What Kennedy Could Say
We avoided war.	We avoided war.
The imbalance of forces is no worse and I can confide to my critics in Moscow that Kennedy agreed to pull back U.S. missiles from Turkey.	The balance of power is unchanged. We got a Soviet retreat in exchange for our redundant missiles in Turkey—a swap that Moscow has agreed not to publicize.
Castro is angry, but we got a U.S. pledge not to invade Cuba. We worsened U.S. ties with Turkey.	We pledged not to invade Cuba contingent on an inspection that Castro has prevented, which leaves us with a free hand.
My leadership looks weaker, but we avoided disaster and I can claim victory.	Our domestic and international position is much stronger. We can try to improve relations now with the USSR.

WHY DID THE CRISIS TAKE PLACE?

We are now in a better position to understand how and why the confrontation began. The likely perceptions of each side are outlined in Table 3.2 on page 77 and elucidated in the text that follows.

Why Did Khrushchev Gamble?

The Balance of Strategic Power. Khrushchev sought to obtain a quick-fix—a cheap and ready way to restore Soviet bargaining power. From 1957 until 1961 Khrushchev had enjoyed what the broad public saw as a "missile gap." He claimed that the USSR was turning out missiles "like sausages." Washington did little to rebut Khrushchev in public, but U.S.

18. Henry Kissinger, *The White House Years* (Boston: Little, Brown, 1979), chap. 16.

UN Secretary-General U Thant (center left) met with Cuban leader Fidel Castro (third in on right) in Havana on October 30, 1962, to discuss UN verification of the dismantling of Soviet missiles in Cuba. Castro rejected outside inspection as an infringement of Cuban sovereignty. Unlike Saddam Hussein in the 1990s, Castro was not compelled to accept UN inspections.

Table 3.2 How Each Side Saw the Other Before October 1962

How Moscow Saw Washington	How Washington Saw Moscow
We can equalize the balance of power by putting MRBMs in Cuba. We can slip the missiles in and Washington will have to accept a new situation.	The Soviets would not dare confront us in our own backyard. They have never conducted large operations far from their own territory.
Our MRBMs will balance U.S. missiles in Turkey.	Our missiles in Turkey are for defense of the West.
We can protect an outpost of revolution from U.S. aggression.	We don't intend to invade Cuba so the Soviets have no need to protect Castro.
Kennedy is weak and Americans degenerate. They were irresolute at the Bay of Pigs, the Vienna Summit, on Berlin, and on other issues.	Khrushchev is impetuous. Perhaps we looked weak to him before, but we've made clear we will not abide offensive missiles in Cuba.
We can and should teach Washington to fall back before our power.	We must stop Soviet expansion. The Kremlin has no right to intrude in the Caribbean.

spy planes (1956–May 1960) and satellites (after August 1960) revealed that the USSR produced and deployed very few ICBMs.[19] Khrushchev delayed mass production until an improved model was perfected.

Taking office in 1961, the Kennedy team did not know precisely how many missiles the USSR possessed, but Pentagon officials began to tell the public that the missile gap favored the U.S. Khrushchev's bluff was exposed. Moreover, the Kennedy administration stepped up U.S. missile production, aiming to deploy more than 1,000 ICBMs. Looking back, we know that in 1962 the U.S. already had 200 nuclear-tipped ICBMs plus thousands of additional nuclear weapons on bombers, aircraft carriers, and submarines able to strike the USSR. The Soviet Union then had only about 20 ICBMs—all liquid-fueled, difficult to launch; no nuclear-tipped missiles in submarines; no intercontinental bombers; and no aircraft carriers.

What Moscow had in spades was medium- and intermediate-range missiles that could reach many U.S. targets if deployed in Cuba. Khrushchev planned to deploy these missiles secretly in October 1962 and reveal their existence after the U.S. midterm elections in November. Kennedy would then have to accept them as accomplished facts and give way to Moscow on such issues as West Berlin.[20]

Thus, Khrushchev's primary motive was probably to redress the strategic balance of power.

19. See sample photos and documents in Kevin C. Ruffner, ed., *CORONA: America's First Satellite Program* (Washington, D.C.: Center for the Study of Intelligence, Central Intelligence Agency, 1995); on "learning to live with transparency," see John Lewis Gaddis, *The Long Peace: Inquiries into the History of the Cold War* (New York: Oxford University Press, 1987), chap. 7.

20. Anastas Mikoyan, discussion with Castro on November 3, 1962. *Diplomaticheskii vestnik* 19–20 (October 15–31, 1992): 58–62 at 62. Once the crisis began, however, Berlin remained calm, and afterwards Moscow never again threatened West Berlin directly.

21. U.S. intelligence agencies concluded in 1958 that Moscow would not use force in response to U.S. deployment of IRBMs on the Soviet periphery, because the USSR could depend on its own ICBM capability. "Probable Sino-Soviet Reactions to US Deployment of IRBMs on the Soviet Bloc Periphery," National Intelligence Estimate No. 100-4-58, April 15, 1958, in *Selected Estimates on the Soviet Union, 1958–1959,* ed. Scott A. Koch (Washington, D.C.: Center for the Study of Intelligence, Central Intelligence Agency, 1993), 271–279.

22. How Castro felt in 1962 we do not know, but decades later he stated that the idea for the nuclear missile deployment came from Moscow. Castro said he approved the scheme because he wanted Cuba to do its part in "defending socialism." To protect Cuba against a U.S. invasion, he added, could have been achieved merely by better conventional forces. For an interpretation that probably overstates Khrushchev's commitment to Cuba, see John Lewis Gaddis, *We Now Know: Rethinking Cold War History* (New York: Oxford University Press, 1997), 260–280.

23. Similar uncertainties confronted President George Bush and Iraqi leader Saddam Hussein as they faced one another over Kuwait. For how to do "psychology at a distance," see Stanley A. Renshon, ed., *The Political Psychology of the Gulf War: Leaders, Publics, and the Process of Conflict* (Pittsburgh: University of Pittsburgh Press, 1993), published in Persian in Teheran in 1997.

24. Also in 1894 Nicholas II became tsar, Lenin published his first political tract, and Stalin entered a seminary.

25. But Beijing commentators afterwards hit Khrushchev going and coming: To send missiles to Cuba, they said, was "adventurism"; to pull them out, "capitulationism." Concurrent with the missile crisis, Khrushchev had sided with New Delhi as India and China skirmished in the Himalayas.

26. First Deputy Minister Mikoyan predicted Castro would refuse the missiles; Foreign Minister Gromyko warned that the Americans would discover them early and respond vigorously. But Khrushchev got Castro's OK and ignored Gromyko. Khrushchev discussed the missile venture with a handful of high officials, including Defense Minister Malinovskii and rocket specialist S. S. Biriuzov, in late May or early June. Then he briefed the entire Communist Party Presidium. Mikoyan, Gromyko, and Presidium member Otto Kuusinen expressed deep reservations, but others kept their doubts to themselves.

Second, Khrushchev wanted equal treatment. If the USSR had to live with U.S. missiles in Turkey, Americans should also agonize over missiles close to their homeland.[21]

Third, Khrushchev probably hoped to deter a U.S. invasion of Cuba.[22] Some analysts believe this was Khrushchev's main reason for deploying missiles to Cuba. They say that the aging Soviet leader seemed to gain new life from Castro and his revolution, and wanted to protect Cuba. But when push came to shove, Khrushchev put Soviet security above all else.

Individuals: The High Stakes Risk-Taker. How could Khrushchev bolster Soviet power and preserve his own rule while avoiding nuclear war?[23] Khrushchev's personal make-up generated a bold, idiosyncratic solution. Khrushchev was sure he could deceive and then bully the pampered millionaire, twenty-three years his junior.

Khrushchev was born in 1894 to a coal miner's family.[24] He once boasted to Western diplomats: "You all went to great schools. I went about barefoot and in rags. When you were in the nursery, I was herding cows. And yet here we are, and I can run rings around you all."

CIA psychiatrists called Khrushchev "a gambler . . . expert in calculated bluffing." Khrushchev often moved with bold strokes, burning bridges without considering how to retreat. A different Soviet leader might have reasoned: "Why gamble? The Soviet nuclear arsenal is already sufficient to frighten the Americans. Let Castro save his own skin."

Few if any other Soviet leaders would have risked the Cuban venture. Lenin, in 1918, took "one step backward" when he faced overwhelming German force. Previous Soviet leaders had been cautious about projecting military forces, but Khrushchev departed from the norm—and got the Soviet bureaucracy to go along.

Soviet Politics. Khrushchev hoped that a dazzling success in the Caribbean would silence his critics—Soviet officers displeased with his 1960 plan to cut the armed forces by one-third; party officials opposed to his radical reorganizations, others who blamed Khrushchev for the flagging Soviet economy, and anti-Western hard-liners (backed by Chinese leaders) who argued that Khrushchev was soft on Western imperialism.[25]

Though many Soviet experts doubted the wisdom of Khrushchev's gambit, none tried to halt it. Khrushchev's bold style fed on the compliant Soviet political system—too obedient to thwart its risk-prone leader. Khrushchev surrounded himself with yes-men he had known since the 1940s. He went through the motions of consulting, but ignored any dissident voices.[26] To make matters worse, the KGB fed Khrushchev unreliable

Table 3.3 A Unified Soviet Policy vs. What Actually Happened

A Fully Unified Policy	What Actually Happened
1. Prepare surface-to-air missiles (SAMs) and make them operational before MRBM deployment begins.	1. The SAMs were deployed but not authorized to fire on U.S. reconnaissance planes until *after* MRBM deployment began.
2. To avoid detection, deploy MRBMs at night and camouflage the work by day.	2. No camouflage was used at the missile sites until *after* detection by the U.S.
3. Avoid deployment patterns (such as those used in the USSR) that could alert U.S. observers.	3. The SAM, MRBM and IRBM sites were laid out in the same patterns used in the USSR—familiar to U.S. intelligence.

reports—for example, that Soviet tests of giant hydrogen bombs in 1961 had deterred an American nuclear first-strike on the USSR. (Had Washington considered attacking, the tests would have provided good cause to get on with it.) To understand Kennedy's plans during the missile crisis, the KGB depended heavily on a hot tip from an émigré bartender in Washington who overheard the best guesses of two U.S. journalists.

Khrushchev's gambit was irrational in the sense that it contained a high risk of disaster for goals not crucial to Soviet life. Still, the Soviet system was organized to behave like a rational monolith in pursuit of Kremlin objectives. The system's output, however, did not look like the work of a rational monolith. If there were a master plan, some parts did not dovetail, as we see in Table 3.3.[27] Soviet habits of secrecy kept one hand from knowing what the other was doing.

Why Did Washington Doze?

Why, given a host of cues and clues, was the Soviet deployment not discovered earlier? Why were Americans again dozing, as they had been when Japan advanced toward Pearl Harbor?[28] We begin with the hubris of Kennedy and his top men.

The Pragmatic Liberal vs. the Communist Gambler. The Soviet leader was inquisitive but had been trained mainly in the school of hard knocks; Kennedy, at prep school and Harvard. Khrushchev's father was a coal miner; Kennedy's, a multimillionaire and U.S. ambassador to England. Khrushchev spoke in peasant proverbs; Kennedy's senior thesis became a book, *Why England Slept,* its foreword written by the publisher of Time-Life. Khrushchev had been a propaganda commissar in the Red Army; Kennedy was an authentic war hero whose wounds never fully healed. (He asked his doctor for a painkiller just before meeting Khrushchev in 1961.) Kennedy, his aide Ted Sorensen wrote, had "limitless curiosity about nearly everything"; read constantly and rapidly; and grew

27. Soviet military personnel were disguised in civilian slacks and sport shirts when they stepped onto Cuban shores, but they then lined up by fours and moved out in truck convoys. Missiles protruded from some trucks carried along Cuban roads. The commanding officer, an Army general, lacked experience with missiles.

28. See Roberta Wohlstetter, *Pearl Harbor: Warning and Decision* (Stanford, Calif.: Stanford University Press, 1962); and Gordon W. Prange, *At Dawn We Slept: The Untold Story of Pearl Harbor* (New York: Penguin Books, 1981).

The U.S. was equipped to intercept enemy air-craft but had no defenses against missiles. Here, President John F. Kennedy looks over a Hawk anti-aircraft missile battery at the Naval Air Station at Key West, Florida.

and profited from experience. He combined tough politics and reckless womanizing.[29]

Kennedy called himself a pragmatic liberal. Where Khrushchev was ideological, Kennedy was uneasy with the idealism of some of his fellow Democrats. On Cuba, however, Kennedy (like many other U.S. leaders) could be emotional. Castro symbolized Khrushchev's claim that Communism was on the march and reminded Kennedy of his 1961 failure at the Bay of Pigs.[30]

The self-assured Kennedy sought out the best and brightest—men he had never met—as top aides to head the Departments of Defense, State, and Treasury. But these luminaries had little empathy for others. Blinded by self-righteousness, they believed it proper for the West to encircle the USSR with rockets but wrong for the Soviets to have a base in Cuba.

The Americans noted every Soviet move that might threaten West Berlin, but they ignored how U.S. training exercises known as "Quick Kick" and "Whip Lash" in April–May 1962 might look to Havana and Moscow. Kennedy's team knew that Washington had not decided to invade Cuba; it presumed that the other side would interpret U.S. maneuvers as mere contingency planning.

Bureaucratic Logjam. U.S. intelligence failed Kennedy repeatedly on Cuba. In 1961 the CIA assured him Cuban exiles could overthrow Castro, but they were stopped on the beach at the Bay of Pigs. On September 19, 1962, the U.S. Intelligence Board concluded that the USSR would not in-

29. His affairs included a possible Nazi agent in 1942, a Mafia courtesan in 1960–1962, and a possible East German–Soviet agent in 1963. Beschloss, *Crisis Years,* 141, 613–617.

30. Dean Rusk was surprised that "this man with ice water in his veins" was so "emotional" about Castro. However, McNamara recalled that they were all "hysterical" about Castro. Beschloss, *Crisis Years,* 375.

troduce offensive missiles into Cuba.[31] Surely the Soviets would not challenge the Americans in their own backyard.

U.S. officials gathered relevant information from many sources—shipping reports, agents in Cuba, refugees, sporadic aerial reconnaissance. One report had Castro's private pilot boasting that Cubans had "everything, including atomic weapons." There was evidence of SAM sites, missile patrol boats, and Il-28 bombers, but *not* of offensive missiles.

Much of this data was as yet undigested when the U.S. Intelligence Board made its report on September 19. SOPs required methodical collecting and sifting of information, much of which was inconclusive. Neither planes nor satellites surveyed every inch of Soviet territory, and U.S. satellites did not target Cuba.

Adding to uncertainty, the West's ace spy in Moscow was silent. For two years, beginning in August 1960, **Oleg V. Penkovsky**, a colonel in Soviet military intelligence, transmitted to British and U.S. agents more than 10,000 pages of military information on 111 rolls of film—from Soviet war plans to diagrams of missiles. This information explained the pattern ("footprint") of deployed missiles discovered on October 14 and told how many days' grace before the MRBMs would be operational. But no word came from Penkovsky after August 1962; he was arrested by Soviet agents in Moscow on October 24, just as the missile crisis neared its climax.[32]

The president's Foreign Intelligence Advisory Board concluded later that before October 14 the intelligence community lacked the "focused sense of urgency or alarm which might well have stimulated a greater effort."[33] Flights by U-2 spy planes over Cuba were risky and provocative. They took place at fixed intervals and could not cover all of Cuba with one sweep.[34] Increasingly alarmed about reports of missile activity, the CIA on October 4 got high-level approval for a U-2 flight over Cuba, but the flight was delayed ten days by a dispute within the bureaucracy: Would the U-2 be operated by the CIA or by an Air Force pilot in uniform?

When the October 14 flight brought evidence of MRBM deployment, the fragments of gathered information fell into place. The White House had been deceived by Moscow and misled by the CIA.

Republicans and Democrats. Before October 14 the evidence of a Soviet missile deployment was ambiguous. Partisan bias conduced to divergent interpretations. Some Republicans charged that Kennedy was ignoring danger in Cuba. Indeed, the president could not afford to look soft before November's midterm elections. If the Soviets *dared* send missiles

31. By August 1962 CIA Director John McCone, a conservative Republican businessman, believed a Soviet missile deployment likely. But his was a lonely voice and he departed for Europe on his honeymoon.

32. In 1963 Penkovsky was tried for treason, found guilty, and shot. See Jerrold L. Schecter and Peter S. Deriabin, *The Spy Who Saved the World: How a Soviet Colonel Changed the Course of the Cold War* (New York: Scribner's, 1992).

33. Top secret memorandum for the president, February 4, 1963, in Mary S. McAuliffe, ed., *CIA Documents on the Cuban Missile Crisis 1962* (Washington, D.C.: Central Intelligence Agency, 1992), 362–371.

34. CIA Director McCone said later that his order in late August for daily overflights of Cuba had been cancelled by McNamara and Rusk who feared "a hell of a mess" if a plane were shot down. Schecter and Deriabin, *The Spy,* 332.

to Cuba, this implied that the president appeared weak to Moscow and was less discerning than Republicans. Once proof of the Soviet missiles existed, partisan politics pushed Kennedy to make a strong response. Why did he risk Armageddon over a few dozen missiles? Kennedy claimed later that, had he done nothing, he would have been impeached.

WHAT PROPOSITIONS HOLD? WHAT QUESTIONS REMAIN?

INTERTWINING THE LEVELS OF ANALYSIS

Are individual humans mere puppets pulled by the structure of power, as neorealists say? The key roles played by Khrushchev and Kennedy—and by other leaders such as Lenin and Wilson—belie any view that humans are marionettes of great forces. The shifting distribution of nuclear missiles was the stage; the U.S. and Soviet political systems established key parameters; but the origins of the missile crisis and how it played out depended on the personal qualities of Khrushchev and Kennedy.

Political leaders are often like captains on the high seas. In the maelstrom of world politics the helmsman can make or break the voyage. He is often more important than the crew, the ship, the sea, or the weather. If the helmsman ignores the portents, falls asleep at the wheel, or provokes a mutiny, the ship may never reach harbor. A skillful captain, on the other hand, will steer the ship safely whatever the conditions. If the wind is slack, he will use the time to rest and make repairs. If a head wind lashes the vessel, the captain tightens the sail or tacks. Braced by a strong wind from aft, the helmsman unfurls the sails and advances. At all times the skilled helmsman attends both crew and ship, preparing them for the perils ahead.

Neither Soviet nor U.S. policy was determined inexorably by the strategic balance. So-called American policy was imprinted by Kennedy's beliefs and style. He and his top advisers helped provoke the crisis by their bluster toward Castro and their rapid missile buildup. Former President Eisenhower, for one, thought that a more gradual buildup of U.S. strategic forces would suffice against the slowly emerging Soviet threat.

Once the Soviet missiles were discovered, Kennedy again put his personal stamp on U.S. policy. Had Adlai Stevenson been president and not UN ambassador at the time, he probably would have placed less emphasis on force. Had Lyndon Johnson been president and not vice president, he might have acted without deliberating for a week. Had Eisenhower still been president, he probably would have left more authority with local commanders—a riskier approach than Kennedy's micromanagement.

To be sure, no person is a completely free agent. Personal inclinations are tempered by the logic of situations. As dangers become more visible, reality can dispel wishful thinking. Kennedy under pressure became more pragmatic.[35] He objected to rewarding Soviet duplicity, but—reluctant to play at Chicken—privately agreed to pull back U.S. missiles from Turkey.

What role did domestic factors (Level 2) play in 1962? Both Khrushchev and Kennedy were energized and constrained by state and society. "Russian" and "American" political values helped to shape Soviet and U.S. actions in 1962, but "political culture" and "civilization" do not predict how individuals will behave—particularly under stress. If political culture determined behavior, all Soviet and U.S. leaders would have responded identically to the problems they faced in 1962.

The impact of individuals is greatest at times of crisis. At critical moments decision makers must choose which fork to take and at what speed. The inertia and routines of bureaucracies carry most weight in normal times, but Khrushchev and Kennedy bent their bureaucracies to become their servants in October 1962.

Individuals at all levels can act like wild cards to disrupt all calculations. In 1962, for example, Western intelligence benefited from the unprecedented revelations of Colonel Penkovsky. Other individuals could have easily brought on disaster, for example, the Soviet commanding officer in Cuba able to fire tactical nuclear weapons if Americans invaded with or without authorization from Moscow. As it happened, this same man gave the order to the Soviet SAM unit that shot down the U-2 on October 27, an act that Khrushchev feared might unhinge his deal with Washington.[36]

We face a knowledge gap. Few leaders are ready to bare their souls or share their medical records with foreign analysts. Even when leaders have been intensively scrutinized, as was Wilson, experts disagree about what made them tick. CIA psychiatrists knew much about Khrushchev but could not predict his behavior in specific situations. Individuals count, but are often unpredictable.

WHAT THE CRISIS IMPLIES FOR MUTUAL GAIN AND OPEN DIPLOMACY

How can the Marshall Plan and Washington's handling of the missile crisis *both* be regarded as major achievements of U.S. foreign policy?

35. Lenin became more realistic and persuaded most of his comrades to modify their dreams as the Kaiser's armies drew closer. Wilson, on the other hand, refused to compromise, despite warnings that the Senate would otherwise turn down the League.

36. See Khrushchev-Castro letters in Blight et al., *Cuba on the Brink*, 482–484, and many references indexed as *U-2 shootdown*.

Some differences were stark. The Marshall Plan was characterized by open planning for mutual gain with Europe. By contrast, the Kennedy team saw the missile crisis as part of a zero-sum struggle. The Marshall Plan was launched with "carrots"; the Cuban blockade, with "sticks"—prepared in secret. Kennedy masked the U-2 discovery while preparing a firm response.

Yet there were also similarities. Both the ERP and Cuban crisis emerged from a bipolar structure of power with intense competition. U.S. diplomacy in each case was bolstered by support from Western Europe. Both in 1947 and in 1962 U.S. policy was well planned by experts with diverse skills.

The ERP was a coordination game—a problem of coordinating convergent interests. The missile crisis looked more like Chicken. Still, both Washington and Moscow converted their confrontation into a coordination game. Each avoided backing the other into a corner. Having made a deal, they found ways to implement it. Thus, when Castro refused to permit UN verification that the missiles were gone, Moscow and Washington cooperated on shipboard inspection from the air. Sobered by their trip to the brink, Kennedy and Khrushchev embarked on a strategy to reduce tensions (analyzed in Chapters 6 and 7).

The near catastrophe of October 1962 confirms the warning that zero-sum politics and deception are inferior to joint strategies of mutual gain and open diplomacy. Khrushchev worked for a one-sided triumph. His deceit—of the Soviet people, of world public opinion, of the White House, and even of Fidel Castro—was integral to the missile crisis.

Secrecy and deception bore bad fruit. Had the Kremlin *publicly* announced a missile deployment in Cuba (as Castro suggested), Washington would have had few grounds to protest. No law barred a Soviet presence. The Monroe Doctrine was never international law.

Moscow manipulated Cuba and embarrassed Castro. Trying to assuage Castro's hurt feelings after the crisis, Soviet First Deputy Prime Minister Mikoyan told him: "It's all right to deceive enemies." With friends, however, "sincerity and openness" are necessary to "resolve differences and reach a consensus. With enemies things are different." But then Mikoyan lied to Castro as well, implying that Moscow's only goal had been to protect Cuba.[37]

Castro later said that if he had known that the Soviets were thinking how to improve the balance of power, and how few missiles they had in 1962, he would have "advised them to be more prudent."[38]

37. "*S vragami, drugoe delo, ikh mozhno i obmanut'*" (Meeting on November 3, 1962), *Diplomaticheskii vestnik* 19–20 (October 15–31, 1992): 58–62 at 61.

38. Quoted in Blight et al., *Cuba on the Brink,* 203.

U.S. policy before the crisis would have been on far sounder footing had the public been better informed. Few Americans understood how U.S. policy since 1898 had bred anti-U.S. feelings in Cuba. Americans knew very little about U.S. missile superiority or U.S. schemes against Castro. Ignorance kept Americans from anticipating Soviet or Cuban anxieties. For decades after the crisis, Americans did not know that Kennedy had promised Moscow to pull back U.S. missiles from Turkey (a pledge fulfilled in 1963).

How to Improve Decision Making.... *You draft the following memo to the President: How can we avoid another collision course? How should we deal with such crises if they arise? Here are ten guidelines:*

*1. **Pursue mutual gain and openness.** Even with strong rivals, explore conditional cooperation buttressed with safeguards against defection. Better to compromise and create joint values than retreat or march toward war.*

*2. **Blend firmness and flexibility, potential punishment and reward.** Be sure your strength is evident and credible, but do not bluster needlessly. Consider what the changing balance of power means for potential foes as well as for ourselves.*

Be aware of how hard it is to communicate. A Khrushchev may read conciliatory gestures as weakness and ignore stern warnings. Only when Kennedy blockaded Cuba did Khrushchev get the message.

If deterrence fails and you find yourself on a collision course, try to compel the other side to retreat. But if the other side can inflict major damage, consider adjusting to a changed situation. Had the Soviets not veered in 1962 but instead detonated just one hydrogen bomb over U.S. cities, few Americans would have applauded Kennedy's firmness. Americans soon learned to live with a far larger Soviet missile threat than the force Khrushchev tried to deploy in 1962.

*3. **Strive to see ourselves as others see us.** Had the Kennedy team seen itself through Khrushchev's eyes—as materially strong but irresolute—Washington might have predicted Khrushchev's gamble.*

*4. **Expect surprise.** Beat down preconceptions and wishful thinking. Investigate how worst-case and least likely scenarios might unfold. Ask whether rationality and value for the other side may differ from your definition.*

5. *Expect duplicity—certainly from foes who endorse any means to their ends—but try to prevent it.* Lying was part of the Soviet operational code. Do not trust assurances, especially those with ambiguous terms such as "offensive" weapons.

6. *Do not stereotype others. Allow that they may change.* Khrushchev became a sober statesman as the crisis evolved. Had Kennedy typed Khrushchev once and forever as a cheat, give-and-take negotiations would have been unthinkable.

7. *Things often go wrong. Do not assume that crises can be readily managed.* Luck as well as skill avoided a catastrophe in 1962. Do not count on good fortune.

8. *Distance major foreign policy issues from partisan politics.* Republicans and Democrats joined forces to organize the United Nations, the Marshall Plan, and NATO; their rivalry helped kill the League of Nations in 1919 and set the stage for the 1962 crisis.

9. *Learn. Do not make the same mistakes twice. But do not learn the wrong lessons.* Review assumptions and SOPs to cope with change. Decide beforehand what evidence would count for or against your expectations. Weigh competing hypotheses. Integrate new data methodically with your existing beliefs. If an event comes as a surprise, reevaluate your expectations. Discuss misjudgments internally and perhaps with the other side.

10. *Do not merely adapt to circumstances but seek deep learning and new solutions.* It is easier to adjust tactics than to make substantive changes. After the Cuban crisis both sides adapted because they wanted to avoid more collisions. But Soviet leaders also pledged: "Never again"—never again would they have to back down before overwhelming U.S. power. The Kremlin "learned" to intensify its arms buildup—a major reason for the eventual collapse of the Soviet empire.

You need confidence but not hubris; willingness to use force but only when needed; tolerance for ambiguity but ability to act under uncertainty; ability to get advice without producing paralyzing splits within your team. You need both memory and openness: Without memory, you are driftwood in the streams of life; without openness, a bullet fired on an unchangeable path.

We have learned much from 1962, but these lessons are only rough guidelines. Tomorrow's challenges will probably come from countries further from Western values and more desperate than the USSR in 1962.

KEY NAMES AND TERMS

attention space
Bay of Pigs
bounded rationality
Chicken
determinism
Anatoly Dobrynin
ExComm
groupthink
hawks and doves
intermediate-range ballistic missiles (IRBMs)

Robert S. McNamara
medium-range ballistic missiles (MRBMs)
Anastas Mikoyan
Monroe Doctrine
Oleg V. Penkovsky
rational actor model
standard operating procedures (SOPs)
stereotyping
surface-to-air missiles (SAMs)

QUESTIONS TO DISCUSS

1. Why do governments find it hard to plan and execute coherent policies?
2. When, if at all, should politicians compromise? What are the alternatives?
3. How can a government make other "drivers" back down? Is it wise to try? Was it right for Kennedy to take a tough stand even if he risked nuclear war?
4. Compare action levels in the Cuban crisis with those shaping a foreign policy problem today.
5. If structures of power dictate policy, as neorealists say, did Khrushchev have any options except the Cuban gambit?
6. If "civilizations" shape decisions, how were their influences manifest in the October 1962 confrontation?
7. What good are spies? Spy planes? Satellites? What are the dangers of each?
8. Is it ever possible to overcome narrow bureaucratic and partisan interests to produce a rational and unified foreign policy?
9. What were the negative and positive aspects of secrecy during the October 1962 crisis?
10. Can governments learn? What are the obstacles? Are any lessons from 1962 applicable to foreign policy problems in the 1990s, for example, between Washington and Baghdad?

RECOMMENDED RESOURCES

BOOKS

Allison, Graham T. *Essence of Decision: Explaining the Cuban Missile Crisis.* Boston: Little, Brown, 1971.

Beschloss, Michael R. *The Crisis Years: Kennedy and Khrushchev, 1960–1963.* New York: HarperCollins, 1991.

Blight, James G., et al. *Cuba on the Brink: Castro, the Missile Crisis, and the Soviet Collapse.* New York: Pantheon, 1993.

Blight, James G., and David A. Welch. *On the Brink: Americans and Soviets Reexamine the Cuban Missile Crisis.* New York: Hill and Wang, 1989.

Breslauer, George W., and Philip E. Tetlock, eds. *Learning in U.S. and Soviet Foreign Policy.* Boulder, Colo.: Westview, 1991.

Chang, Laurence, and Peter Kornbluh, eds. *The Cuban Missile Crisis, 1962: A National Security Archive Documents Reader.* New York: New Press, 1992.

Dobrynin, Anatoly. *In Confidence: Moscow's Ambassador to America's Six Cold War Presidents (1962–1986).* New York: Times Books, 1995.

Farnham, Barbara, ed. *Avoiding Losses/Taking Risks: Prospect Theory and International Conflict.* Ann Arbor: University of Michigan Press, 1994.

Fursenko, Aleksandr A., and Timothy Natalfi. *"One Hell of a Gamble": Khrushchev, Castro, and Kennedy, 1958–1964.* New York: Norton, 1997.

Gaddis, John Lewis. *We Now Know: Rethinking Cold War History.* New York: Oxford University Press, 1997.

Garthoff, Raymond L. *Reflections on the Cuban Missile Crisis.* Washington, D.C.: Brookings Institution, 1987.

Hopple, Gerard W. *Political Psychology and Biopolitics: Assessing and Predicting Elite Behavior in Foreign Policy Crises.* Boulder, Colo.: Westview, 1990.

Lebow, Richard Ned, and Janice Gross Stein. *We All Lost the Cold War.* Princeton, N.J.: Princeton University Press, 1994.

May, Ernest D., and Philip D. Zelikow, eds. *The Kennedy Tapes: Inside the White House During the Cuban Missile Crisis.* Cambridge, Mass.: Harvard University Press, 1997.

McAuliffe, Mary S., ed. *CIA Documents on the Cuban Missile Crisis 1962.* Washington, D.C.: Central Intelligence Agency, 1992.

Nathan, James A., ed. *The Cuban Missile Crisis Revisited.* New York: St. Martin's, 1992.

Singer, Eric, and Valerie Hudson, eds. *Political Pyschology and Foreign Policy.* Boulder, Colo.: Westview, 1992.

Snyder, Glenn H., and Paul Diesing. *Conflicts Among Nations: Bargaining, Decision Making, and System Structure in International Crises.* Princeton, N.J.: Princeton University Press, 1977.

Tetlock, Philip E., et al., eds. *Behavior, Society, and Nuclear War.* 3 vols. New York: Oxford University Press, 1989–1993.

Utz, Curtis A. *Cordon of Steel: The U.S. Navy and the Cuban Missile Crisis.* Washington, D.C.: Naval Historical Center, U.S. Department of the Navy, 1993.

JOURNAL

Political Psychology

WEB SITES

"Fourteen Days in October: The Cuban Missile Crisis"
http://library.advanced.org/11046

Library of Congress archive site (also leads back to Russian archive)
http://lcweb.loc.gov/exhibits/archives/colc.html

National Security Archive on the Cuban crisis
http://www.seas.gwu.edu/nsarchive/nsa/cuba_mis_cri/cuba_mis_cri.html

U.S. State Department, *Foreign Relations of the United States, 1961–1963,* Vol. XI: Cuban Missile Crisis and After
http://www.state.gov/www/about_state/history/frusxi

C H A P T E R   F O U R

WHY WAGE WAR? DOES IT PAY TO FIGHT?

- Was/is war inevitable? If so, why? Is war merely another tool to conduct policy and negotiate? Or does it represent a malfunction—something wrong within individuals, societies, the state or transnational systems, or even the biosphere?

- Can war be a rational means to an end? Can war be "just"? Can it be rational or just in the nuclear era?

- Are wars increasing in frequency? In the damage they wreak? Are there any patterns over time?

- What caused the major wars of the 20th century? Are there any similarities in the factors that brought on World Wars I and II? The interventions in Korea and the Persian Gulf? The U.S. campaign in Vietnam and the Soviet campaign in Afghanistan?

- Who gained and who lost from these conflicts?

- If you want peace, should you prepare for war? Or do war preparations lead to war?

One Week After Her Election the *President-to-be asks you to serve as Secretary of Defense. She asks you to provide a grand design for U.S. force planning. For starters, she wants your views on some deep and vexing questions: "The Kennedy team," she recalls, "avoided war with Moscow over Cuba, but U.S. forces have taken part in two world wars and many smaller ones. Why have Americans fought in distant places when few of us have any desire to conquer foreign lands?*

"Haven't weapons become so destructive that war is now outmoded—like dueling and slavery? Why do we and other states keep large nuclear arsenals if nuclear war is unwinnable?"

You need time to reply. You tell the President-elect that you will assess the major viewpoints on the uses and causes of war. Next, you will review for her how this century's major wars began and why the U.S. became involved. Later, you will examine options for sizing and structuring U.S. forces. However, you can anticipate the conclusion: Perhaps war is obsolete but in some forms is still thinkable—even likely.

CONTENDING CONCEPTS AND EXPLANATIONS

WAR—CREATOR, DESTROYER, REFORMER

War is overt, organized violence of one community against another. It is a means to hold or seize territory, wealth, resources, prestige, and influence—the ultimate tool for value-claiming and resolving conflict. War can be an adventure—a stage for heroism and glory. For most participants and bystanders, however, it is hell.

War destroys and creates. It can make, break, or reform a state.[1] Wars have made states more powerful. Europe's princes used war to expand their realms and form a "body politic" from disparate peoples. War audits the efficiency of the state and can spur reforms meant to improve fighting capacity. Wars encourage governments to expand and streamline their bureaucracies; raise taxes; put more people into government service; reduce social barriers based on sex, race, class, or region; and promote literacy and training. But war can also dissolve a state and devour its human and material resources.

THE PATTERNS OF WAR

The Scale and Frequency of War

World Wars I and II were the most destructive in history. As we see from Figure 4.1, however, there has been no clear trend in the frequency, size, or destructiveness of war.

Nor is there evidence that a series of smaller wars means that a larger war is about to erupt—like tremors before a major earthquake. To be sure, several lesser wars took place in the decade before each world war, but the many small- and medium-sized wars since 1945—from roughly twenty to forty each year—have not (as yet) been followed by World War III.

War can be more or less destructive thanks to changes in technology and in politics. From the end of the Thirty Years War in 1648 until the French Revolution in 1789, Europe's wars usually spared civilians and workshops. Europe's princes fought with relatively small armies, often mercenaries. The French Revolution, however, gave birth to the "nation in arms" and much larger armies. Soon, the Industrial Revolution turned people and factories into prime targets. The U.S. Civil War (1861–1865)

 War as Glory, War as Hell

Pinned down by the Russian winter and the Red Army in 1943, a German officer sent home a letter on the last flight to Berlin from Stalingrad: "You must tell my parents [to] remember me with happy hearts." The officer wrote that he planned to face God not as an angel, but as a "soldier, with the free, proud soul of a cavalryman, as a *Herr* [noble gentleman]!"

Most Germans entrapped at Stalingrad had lost any romantic feelings about war. One wrote home: "You were supposed to die heroically," but what was death at Stalingrad? "Here [our soldiers] croak, starve . . . freeze to death. . . . They drop like flies; nobody cares and nobody buries them. Without arms or legs and without eyes, with bellies torn open, they lie around everywhere. . . . It is a death fit for beasts."

These and thousands of other letters from Stalingrad were never delivered. Nazi analysts screened them to learn about morale. Only 2 percent had a positive attitude toward Germany's leadership; 61 percent were negative or actively opposed.[1]

1. See *Last Letters from Stalingrad* (Westport, Conn.: Greenwood, 1974). For rather different perspectives, see Frank Gibney, ed., *Senso: The Japanese Remember the Pacific War* (Armonk, N.Y.: M. E. Sharpe, 1995).

1. Bruce D. Porter, *War and the Rise of the State: The Military Foundations of Modern Politics* (New York: Free Press, 1994).

Fig. 4.1 Dimensions of Major Wars, 1775–1998

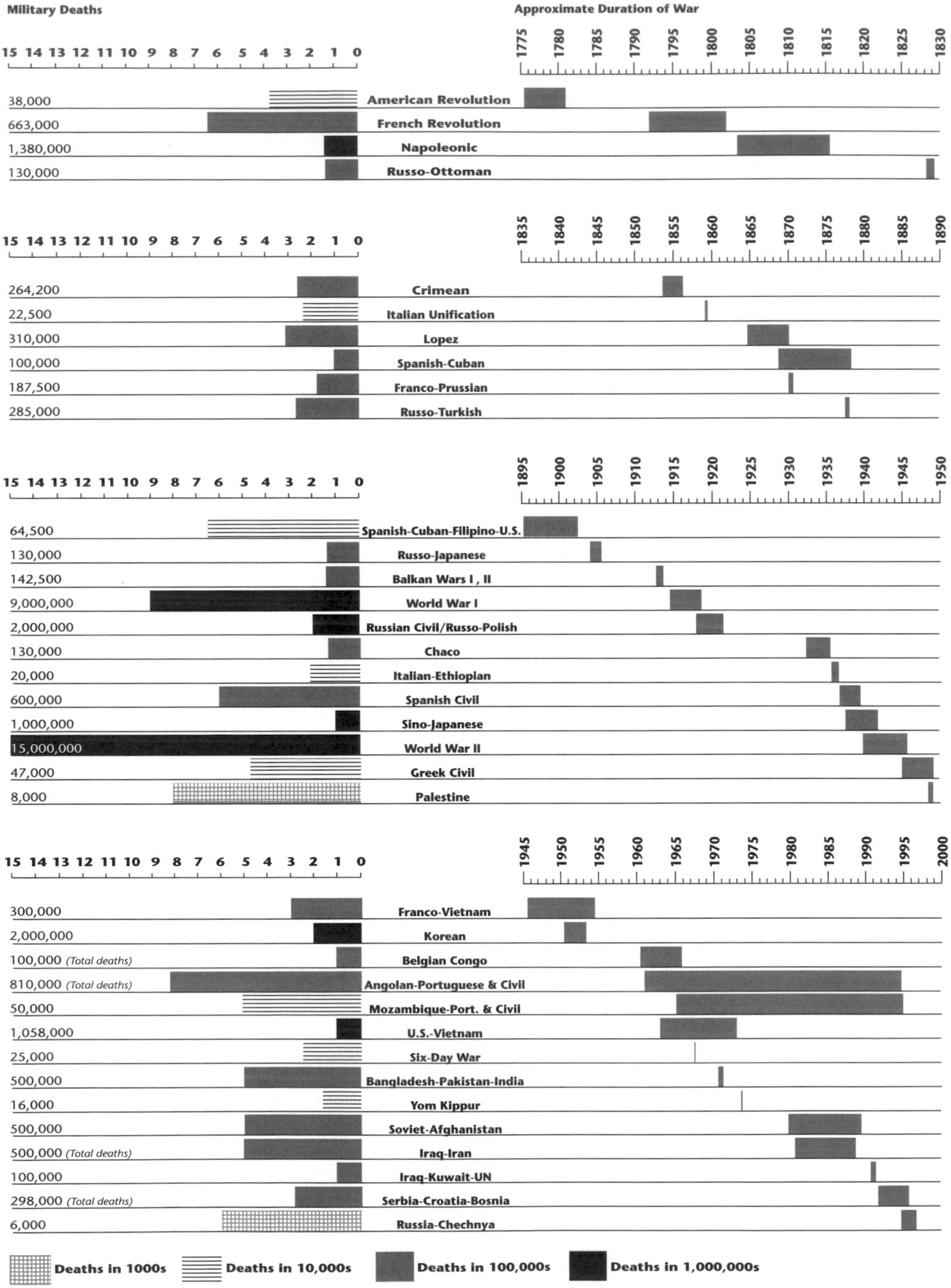

Military Deaths

Approximate Duration of War

Deaths	War	Duration (1775–1830)
38,000	American Revolution	
663,000	French Revolution	
1,380,000	Napoleonic	
130,000	Russo-Ottoman	

15 14 13 12 11 10 9 8 7 6 5 4 3 2 1 0

1775 1780 1785 1790 1795 1800 1805 1810 1815 1820 1825 1830

Deaths	War	Duration (1835–1890)
264,200	Crimean	
22,500	Italian Unification	
310,000	Lopez	
100,000	Spanish-Cuban	
187,500	Franco-Prussian	
285,000	Russo-Turkish	

15 14 13 12 11 10 9 8 7 6 5 4 3 2 1 0

1835 1840 1845 1850 1855 1860 1865 1870 1875 1880 1885 1890

Deaths	War	Duration (1895–1950)
64,500	Spanish-Cuban-Filipino-U.S.	
130,000	Russo-Japanese	
142,500	Balkan Wars I, II	
9,000,000	World War I	
2,000,000	Russian Civil/Russo-Polish	
130,000	Chaco	
20,000	Italian-Ethiopian	
600,000	Spanish Civil	
1,000,000	Sino-Japanese	
15,000,000	World War II	
47,000	Greek Civil	
8,000	Palestine	

15 14 13 12 11 10 9 8 7 6 5 4 3 2 1 0

1895 1900 1905 1910 1915 1920 1925 1930 1935 1940 1945 1950

Deaths	War	Duration (1945–2000)
300,000	Franco-Vietnam	
2,000,000	Korean	
100,000 (Total deaths)	Belgian Congo	
810,000 (Total deaths)	Angolan-Portuguese & Civil	
50,000	Mozambique-Port. & Civil	
1,058,000	U.S.-Vietnam	
25,000	Six-Day War	
500,000	Bangladesh-Pakistan-India	
16,000	Yom Kippur	
500,000	Soviet-Afghanistan	
500,000 (Total deaths)	Iraq-Iran	
100,000	Iraq-Kuwait-UN	
298,000 (Total deaths)	Serbia-Croatia-Bosnia	
6,000	Russia-Chechnya	

15 14 13 12 11 10 9 8 7 6 5 4 3 2 1 0

1945 1950 1955 1960 1965 1970 1975 1980 1985 1990 1995 2000

▦ **Deaths in 1000s**   ≡ **Deaths in 10,000s**   ▨ **Deaths in 100,000s**   ■ **Deaths in 1,000,000s**

Fig. 4.1 *(continued)*

Name of War	Duration	Number of Primary Participants	Battle Deaths	Total Deaths (Military and Civilian)
American Revolution	1775–1781	3	38,000 *(Levy)*	n.a.
French Revolution	1792–1802	6	663,000 *(Levy)*	n.a.
Napoleonic	1803–1815	6	1,380,000 *(Sivard)*	2,380,000 *(Sivard)*
Russo-Ottoman	1828–1829	2	130,000	191,000 *(Sivard)*
Crimean	1853–1856	5	264,200	n.a.
Italian Unification	1859	4	22,500	40,000 *(Sivard)*
Lopez (War of the Triple Alliance)	1864–1870	4	310,000 *(Sivard)*	600,000 *(Sivard)*
Spanish-Cuban	1868–1878	2	100,000	200,000 *(Sivard)*
Franco-Prussian	1870–1871	5	187,500	250,000 *(Sivard)*
Russo-Turkish	1877–1878	3	285,000	n.a.
Spanish-Cuban, Spanish-Cuban-Filipino-U.S., Filipino-U.S.	1895–1898, 1898, 1899–1902	2, 4, and 2	50,000, 10,000, and 4,500	300,000, 200,000, and 12,000 *(Sivard)*
Russo-Japanese	1904–1905	2	130,000	n.a.
Balkan War I and Balkan War II	1912–1913	5	142,500	n.a.
World War I	1914–1918	15	9,000,000	n.a.
Russian Civil/Russo-Polish	1917–1921	12 or more	2,000,000 *(Somin)*	9,000,000 *(Somin)*
Chaco (Bolivia-Paraguay)	1932–1935	2	130,000	200,000 *(Sivard)*
Italian-Ethiopian	1935–1936	2	20,000	n.a.

(Continues)

Fig. 4.1 *(continued)*

Name of War	Duration	Number of Primary Participants	Battle Deaths	Total Deaths (Military and Civilian)
Spanish Civil	1936–1939	5 or more	600,000 *(Sivard)*	1,200,000 *(Sivard)*
Sino-Japanese	1937–1941	2	1,000,000	2,150,000 *(Singer and Small, Sivard)*
World War II	1939–1945	29	15,000,000[a]	n.a.
Greek Civil	1945–1949	5 or more	47,000	160,000 *(Sivard)*
Franco-Vietnam	1945–1954	2	300,000 *(Sivard)*	600,000 *(Sivard)*
Palestine	1948–1949	6	8,000	n.a.
Korean	1950–1953	16	2,000,000	2,889,000 *(Sivard)*
Belgian Congo	1960–1965	5 or more	n.a.	100,000 *(Sivard)*
Angolan-Portuguese and Civil	1961–1975; 1975–1995	7	n.a.	810,000 *(Sivard)*
Mozambique-Portuguese and Civil	1965–1975; 1975–1995	6	50,000	1,080,000 *(Sivard)*
U.S.-Vietnam	1963–1973	5 or more	1,058,000 *(Sivard)*	2,058,000 *(Sivard)*
Six-Day War (Arab-Israeli)	1967	4	25,000	75,000 *(Sivard)*
Bangladesh-Pakistan-India	1971	3	500,000 *(Sivard)*	1,000,000 *(Sivard)*
Yom Kippur (Arab-Israeli)	1973	5	16,000	n.a.
Soviet-Afghanistan	1979–1989	6	500,000 *(Sivard)*	1,500,000 *(Sivard)*
Iraq-Iran	1980–1988	2	n.a.	500,000
Iraq-Kuwait-UN	1990–1991 (Desert Storm lasted 6 weeks)	21	100,000	200,000 *(Sivard)*
Serbia-Croatia-Bosnia	1991–1995	3	n.a.	298,000 *(Sivard)*
Russia–Chechnya	1994–1996	2	6,000	35,000 *(Sivard)*

SOURCES: Data drawn from J. David Singer and Melvin Small, *The Wages of War, 1816–1965: A Statistical Handbook* (New York: Wiley, 1972), unless otherwise specified. Additional sources include Ruth Leger Sivard, *World Military and Social Expenditures* (Washington, D.C.: World Priorities, 1988 and 1997); Jack S. Levy, *War in the Modern Great Power System, 1495–1975* (Lexington: University Press of Kentucky, 1983); and Ilya Somin, *Stillborn Crusade: The Tragic Failure of Western Intervention in the Russian Civil War* (New Brunswick, N.J.: Transaction, 1996).

  a. Figure represents low estimate.

was the first great war of industrial civilization. Union General William T. Sherman became one of the first modern strategists because he struck at the sources of the opponent's armed power—its economic and social foundations. Sherman sought to break civilian morale.

Technology has expanded the might and reach of weapons, while changes in political organization have turned entire populations into key participants in war. Many countries have lost over 10 percent of their population in a single war. War turns millions into refugees. To put this in perspective, however, Communist and other dictators of the 20th century killed more of their compatriots than all of those killed in this century's wars combined (see Chapter 10).

Modern technology can kill more people, but it can also pinpoint destruction. Many countries participated in the 1990–1991 Persian Gulf War, but its duration was brief and relatively few military personnel or civilians were killed while the fighting raged. In the years that followed, however, Iraqi civilians suffered greatly from damage to the country's infrastructure and from economic sanctions.

Cold statistics, of course, mask the pain suffered by those killed or wounded, their families and friends. And while we can estimate the effects of a war by the number of babies not conceived, we can never know what those killed or wounded would otherwise have contributed to culture or to economic well-being.

U.S. losses in war, compared to many other countries, have been small in scale. Table 4.1 on page 96 shows total U.S. battle deaths since 1775. Some estimates have been much higher, placing total battle deaths at about 1.3 million, with nearly half of those occurring during the Civil War. By comparison, the Soviet Union suffered between 25 and 40 million deaths—military and civilian—during World War II.

The indirect consequences of war—disease and epidemics—have often been more lethal than the fighting. Figure 4.1 and Table 4.1 show only the number of military casualties—military personnel killed in combat or who died from wounds, accidents, or disease. Civilian deaths have often been at least twice those suffered by military forces in most wars since 1789. Spared by geography, few U.S. civilians have been killed as a result of war, except in the Civil War and in the global influenza epidemic (more than 20 million deaths worldwide) following World War I.[2]

The civilian share of war deaths increased in the 1970s and 1980s to 75 percent or more in Angola, Mozambique, and elsewhere where land mines killed without discrimination, and where even children became soldiers.[3] Indeed, some 2 million children died from wars in 1985–1995 while another 10 to 15 million were maimed physically or psychologically.

A Note on War Statistics

The raw numbers in Figure 4.1 require interpretation. First, some data are missing. Second, these data do not show severity—deaths per capita. A million deaths in 1945 represented a much smaller share of the population than in 1815 or 1915, when populations were smaller. Third, total deaths rose in the 20th century as more countries fought in a single war. Finally, death rates in industrialized countries were restrained by better health care for the wounded; technologies that put fewer troops on the front lines; and by a shift of the fighting from Europe to Asia, the Middle East, and Africa. Table 4.1 shows how U.S. military deaths decreased per 1,000 soldiers from the 1860s through the 1990s.

2. William H. McNeill, *Plagues and People* (New York: Anchor, 1977), 255.

3. Civilian casualties are estimated in Ruth Leger Sivard, *World Military and Social Expenditures* (Leesburg, Va.: World Priorities, 1988 and 1997).

Table 4.1 U.S. Military Casualties, 1775–1991

	American Revolution (1775–1781)	War of 1812 (1812–1815)	Mexican War (1846–1848)	Civil War (1861–1865)[a]	Spanish-American War (1898)	WWI (1917–1918)	WWII (1941–1945)	Korea (1950–1953)	Vietnam (1963–1973)	Gulf War (1990–1991)
Total military personnel during the war	ca. 217,000	286,730	78,718	2,213,363	306,760	4,734,991	16,112,566	5,720,000	8,744,000 worldwide; 3,385,000 in Southeast Asia	2,029,600; 467,539 in Gulf region
Battle deaths	4,435	2,280	1,733	140,414	385	53,402	291,557	33,746	47,369	148
Other deaths	n.a.	n.a.	11,550	224,097	2,061	63,114	113,842	20,617	10,799	145
Wounded but survived	6,188	4,505	4,152	281,881	1,662	204,002	670,846	103,284	303,648	467
Annual death rate per 1,000	n.a.	n.a.	n.a.	104.4	36.6	35.5	11.6	5.5	n.a.	n.a.

SOURCES: U.S. Department of Commerce, *Historical Statistics of the United States: Colonial Times to 1970*. 2 parts (Washington, D.C.: Government Printing Office, 1975), Pt. 2, 1140; Congressional Reference Service, *U.S. Military Personnel and Casualties in Principal U.S. Wars* (Washington, D.C.: Government Printing Office, 1973). Updated by the author using Department of Defense sources.
  NOTE: n.a.= not available.
  a. Figures are for Union Forces only. Confederate troops suffered at least 133,821 deaths, of which 74,524 were in battle.

Internal War

In the 20th century many international wars acquired a strong internal component and many "civil" wars (within one state or society) involved outside intervention. For example, the Spanish Civil War (1936–1939) drew in "volunteers" from many countries (as depicted in Ernest Hemingway's *For Whom the Bell Tolls*).

Civil and combined civil-international wars have outnumbered international wars since 1945.[4] The Arab-Israeli, Korean, Vietnamese, Afghan, and 1990s Balkan wars all began as internal wars that soon attracted foreign intervention. Each became an internal-international war kept within local borders. For Saddam Hussein, even the Persian Gulf War began as a civil war, for he viewed Kuwait as part of Iraq.

From the 17th until the late 20th century, most wars were waged by governments. In the 1990s, however, a "new world disorder" erupted in which war often became a private enterprise. In the former Yugoslavia and elsewhere, much of the fighting was conducted by bands of irregulars who served out of personal loyalty, hope for booty, or lust for revenge.[5] They were often joined by volunteers and mercenaries from near and far.

The U.S. armed forces in the 1990s, however, began to do less fighting and more peacekeeping—for example, in Bosnia. The Pentagon even adopted a new acronym: **MOOTW**—Military Operations Other Than War. It covered everything from peacekeeping to disaster relief to intimidation.

4. See surveys reported by Roy Licklider, ed., *Stopping the Killing: How Civil Wars End* (New York: New York University Press, 1993), 6.
5. In the twenty recognized states and eleven unrecognized mini-states that replaced Yugoslavia and the USSR, there were at least 12 party or movement militias, 8 armed criminal groups, and 6 warlord units operating within official armies. Charles H. Fairbanks, Jr., "The Postcommunist Wars," *Journal of Democracy* 6, no. 4 (October 1995): 23.

THE SPECTRUM OF VIOLENCE

The gradient of hostility begins with tension, scowls, and curses and continues toward annihilation. What follows are some stages in the spectrum of violence.

Cold War

Cold war is a multifaceted struggle to defeat the other side without overt ("hot") war between the major adversaries. It may include **economic warfare** (trade restrictions, economic blockades), **psychological warfare** (propaganda to subvert the enemy and rally supporters), espionage and sabotage, and even **proxy wars**—hot war by clients.

Cold war may entail military threats to compel or deter certain behavior by others. From 1945 into the 1990s both Moscow and Washington used "force without war" hundreds of times. Soviet/Russian forces often practiced tank maneuvers to intimidate their neighbors. The U.S. Navy often "showed the flag" to remind others of American power.[6] When China practiced firing missiles into the sea near Taiwan in 1996, two U.S. aircraft carrier groups arrived. These actions conveyed two messages: Beijing warned Taipei not to declare its independence while Washington warned it would stand by Taiwan.

Unconventional War

Unconventional war encompasses assassination of notables, terrorism (taking hostages, blowing up airplanes and buildings, spewing gas into subways, poisoning reservoirs), and guerrilla warfare (hit-and-run strikes by irregular forces). Such methods are often favored by stateless peoples such as the Kurds and by rogue states (seen as berzerk or unprincipled by others).[7] Some actors have accused the U.S. of state terror—intimidation by overwhelming might. But the availability of high-tech weapons helps to even the playing field. In the 1980s and 1990s, for example, many irregular armies acquired anti-aircraft missiles and cannon. Tomorrow's terrorists may carry "suitcase" nuclear bombs.

Conventional War

Conventional war employs regular forces such as tanks, planes, and missiles but avoids nuclear weapons, poison gas, and germ warfare. It may be local (restricted to a specific locale) or global. It may be limited or all-out in terms of weapons and targets.

6. Barry M. Blechman and Stephen S. Kaplan, *Force Without War: U.S. Armed Forces as a Political Instrument* (Washington, D.C.: Brookings Institution, 1978); and Stephen S. Kaplan, *Diplomacy of Power: Soviet Armed Forces as a Political Instrument* (Washington, D.C.: Brookings Institution, 1981).

7. A rogue elephant is a vicious, solitary animal, separated from the herd. "Berzerk" probably comes from the Old Norse for a warrior who wore bear [*bera*] hides for a shirt [*serkr*], became frenzied in battle, howled, and foamed at the mouth. *American Heritage Dictionary of the English Language*, 3d ed. (Boston: Houghton Mifflin, 1992), 177.

Détente— A "Loaded" Term

Détente in most European languages and Russian now signifies a relaxation of tensions. In French it also means "trigger," from the medieval name for the latch that, when released, fired a crossbow. The traditional Russian term for détente, *razriadka,* refers to the discharge of electrical energy.

Nuclear War

Nuclear weapons have been detonated in war only in August 1945. Since 1945 they have been used mainly for deterrence—dissuasion by terror. The threat that nuclear weapons would be used to retaliate is supposed to deter any country from launching a first-strike. Nuclear weapons may have helped prevent World War III, so far, but they have not averted scores of other wars.

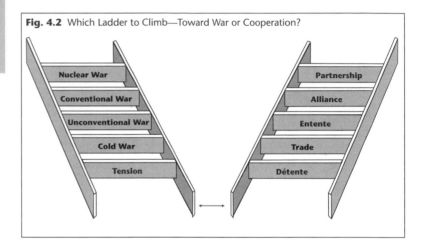

Fig. 4.2 Which Ladder to Climb—Toward War or Cooperation?

Inexorable Rise or Escalation Ladder?

Conflict need not move inexorably from cold to hot war. Tensions can escalate or diminish. Actors can move up or down on two ladders, as suggested in Figure 4.2. To de-escalate from conflict, actors must climb down the **escalation ladder** on the left and move up the ladder toward détente and cooperation on the right. In theory each rung on each ladder marks an interval—a pause on the path toward violence or cooperation; in practice, however, actors may race up each ladder, skipping rungs. Reversing metaphors, actors sometimes appear to slide on a slippery slope toward war.

CAN WAR BE RATIONAL?

Realists say that war is just another arrow in the quiver of a rational foreign policy. The realists' bible, *On War,* was written by the Prussian officer **Carl von Clausewitz** in the early 19th century. Clausewitz defined war as the "continuation of policy by other (violent) means." War should be a "light, handy rapier"—not a campaign for all-out destruction, unless policy seeks to eliminate entirely the other side.[8] Battle tactics must be

8. Carl von Clausewitz, *On War,* rev. ed. (Princeton, N.J.: Princeton University Press, 1984), 604–610; see also Peter Paret, "Clausewitz," in *Makers of Modern Strategy: From Machiavelli to the Nuclear Age,* ed. Paret (Princeton, N.J.: Princeton University Press, 1986), 186–213.

subordinated to strategy. There can be no "purely military" decision except in details such as when and where to patrol.

Clausewitz prescribed model behavior. But today's "rational choice" analysts claim to describe actual behavior. Some contend that governments decide on war as if they seek rationally to maximize gains and minimize losses. Expected utility is key. The theory says that most governments act in a rational manner: They calculate the war potential of each side, including that of the home front.[9]

The classic realists, however, did not believe that war outcomes could be dependably predicted. "The longer a war lasts," Thucydides warned, "the more things tend to depend on accidents." For his part, Machiavelli stressed the role of *fortuna* (luck). Even Clausewitz warned of "friction"—all that can go wrong in war. For example, reinforcements expected in three hours arrive in ten, because rain turned roads to mud.

Many analysts deny that war is inevitable or rational. They see war as a malfunction, a mistake, or a madness that can and should be cured. Humans, they say, can rise above violence.

CAN WAR BE JUST?

If might makes right, the morality of war is a non-issue. But some idealists distinguish just and unjust wars. A war's justice hinges on three factors: (1) Motive—is the cause just? Most people accept self-defense as a justifiable motive, but some political and spiritual leaders initiate what they call just wars or holy wars (crusades, jihads) to promote their ostensibly spiritual goals. (2) Consequences—are the evils the war seeks to remedy greater than the evils the fighting is likely to produce? (3) Legality—is the war lawful within the framework of international law and the belligerent country's constitution?

Nuclear weapons raise new questions: Can any cause justify mass destruction and probable suicide?[10] Nuclear weapons may be good to deter war, but bad if used to wage war.

THE ALTERNATIVE OF NONVIOLENCE

Pacifists reject war as a policy option. They say war is irrational or unjust or both. Some contend that no cause can justify violent means. Others are pragmatists: They hold that nonviolent methods, properly funded and organized, can be as effective as armed struggle while causing less suffering. If they are right, millions of lives could be saved, along with billions of dollars, yen, and rupees.

What Is Strategic?

Strategic doctrine, a theory on how and when to wage war, can make states more or less likely to fight. "Strategic" comes from *strategos*, Greek for "general," the commander of a *stratos* (army). **Strategy** is a military plan or any long-range design to achieve a major goal, while **tactics** are means to that end, often quite flexible. Tactics may include one or more stratagems—tricks to deceive the other side, such as presenting a Trojan Horse. Indeed, some authors use "strategic" as a euphemism for deceitful.

Strategic Arms Reduction Talks in the 1980s treated as **strategic weapons** those arms able to strike deeply into the other side's homeland—in contrast to "battlefield" or "tactical" weapons. Strategic bombing aims at key industries or population centers in an effort to force surrender; strategic goods are those needed for war—for example, oil.

Strategic logic is full of paradox: A good road may be bad, because it is well guarded; a bad road may be good, because it is not.

---

9. Bruce Bueno de Mesquita, *The War Trap* (New Haven, Conn.: Yale University Press, 1981). If country A experiences widespread domestic resistance to war, its leaders may launch a war anyway lest country B try to take advantage of A's weak home front. Bruce Bueno de Mesquita and David Lalman, *War and Reason: Domestic and International Imperatives* (New Haven, Conn.: Yale University Press, 1992).

10. Joseph S. Nye, Jr., *Nuclear Ethics* (New York: Free Press, 1986); see also *Ethics and International Affairs*, published annually by the Carnegie Council on Ethics and International Affairs.

Could Nonviolence Win If Preplanned?

Could a civilian-based system of **nonviolent sanctions** and defense replace armed force? Against a ruthless occupier, nonviolent action risks violent reprisals. But nonviolent resistance helped India (1947) and Poland (1980s) to regain independence. A blend of nonviolent with violent action helped U.S. and South African blacks resist racial discrimination.

Nonviolent methods include protest—mass demonstrations, symbolic funerals, renouncing honors, walkouts; noncooperation—civil disobedience, strikes, tax withholding, providing sanctuary, resignations; and intervention—sit-ins, creating parallel institutions, guerrilla theater, exposure of who did what.[1] These methods aim to make a subject people virtually ungovernable. But they require mass training and discipline of civilians—quite unlike the quick-fix promised by professional soldiers with high-tech weapons.

1. Peter Ackerman and Christopher Krueger, *Strategic Nonviolent Conflict: The Dynamics of People Power in the Twentieth Century* (Westport, Conn.: Praeger, 1994).

11. See Jack S. Levy, "The Causes of War: A Review of Theories and Evidence," in *Behavior, Society, and Nuclear War*, 3 vols., ed. Philip E. Tetlock et al. (New York: Oxford University Press, 1989), 1: 247-251.

12. Lenin thought that war between capitalist countries was inevitable as they struggled to gain secure investment opportunities in less-developed countries. See V. I. Lenin, *Imperialism—The Highest Stage of Capitalism* (1916) (New York: International Publishers, 1933). But Western economists such as Joseph Schumpeter and Kenneth Boulding argued that the profit motive favors peace and civilian industry. Only small sectors of capitalist economies benefit from war, arms competition, or imperialist expansion.

WHY WAR? INPUTS AT EACH LEVEL OF IR ACTION

There are numerous factors operating at each level of IR action that promote war. Some factors act as long-term, underlying conditions; others, as proximate factors emerging in the five or so years before warfare erupts; still others as catalysts—sparks that ignite the combustible material. Causation presents many puzzles: Does a factor really "cause" war or merely precede it? Mere correlation is not causation. Is it a "necessary" or a "sufficient" cause? Are any factors both necessary and sufficient to produce a war?[11] Following is a list of factors at each level that often encourage war:

Level 1: *Individuals and Human Nature*

1. Aggressive personality
2. Beliefs in personal superiority
3. Misperceptions, miscalculations, hubris, wishful thinking

Level 2: *War-Prone States and Societies*

4. A culture of violence and assertive value-claiming
5. "Us vs. them" mentality
6. Dictatorship
7. A unifying cause, a distraction
8. *Realpolitik* that sees war as a useful tool of policy
9. Estimate that victory is likely
10. War-prone military doctrine and technology
11. "Just war" doctrines
12. Economic pressures (surplus people, capital, or goods)[12]
13. A military-industrial complex of makers and merchants of arms and a warrior caste
14. Imperialism vs. national liberation

Level 3: *The Interstate System—Anarchy and Self-Help*

15. Absence of a supranational government to keep the peace
16. Territorial or other claims in dispute
17. Altered threat perception (provoking alarm or complacency)
18. The "security dilemma" (one state's "defensive measures" may prod rivals into countermeasures)
19. A shifting balance of power (or new weapon) generates incentives for war

Level 4: *Transnational Competition*

20. Profit drive of transnational corporations
21. Militant political and religious movements

Level 5: *Environmental Pressures*

22. Resource scarcities

DOES THE "BALANCE OF POWER" SPELL WAR OR PEACE?

Everyone agrees that the **balance of power** is important, but analysts use the term in many ways. It can be a description, a prescription, or a prediction. As a description, it can refer to *any* distribution of power assets—equality of assets (for example, 500 tanks on each side) or superiority of one side (for example, 1,000 tanks vs. 500), as shown in Figure 4.3. As a prescription it suggests: "Maintain a balance of power so that no rival gains an advantage." As a prediction it anticipates that states will attempt to balance their power in certain ways. Some analysts limit "power" to hard assets such as oil wells and tanks; others, including the author of this book, understand "power" to include also intangible assets such as morale. A careful writer will specify what sense is intended.

Woodrow Wilson blamed World War I on "balance of power" politics. By contrast, realists and neorealists contend that war may be prevented— or at least postponed—by maintaining the "balance of power." Unfortunately, these analysts do not agree *which* power balance—which kind of **polarity**—is most stable. Following are five favorites:

1. Unipolarity—power concentrated in one center that maintains order, such as Imperial Rome

2. Bipolarity—two poles of power balance each other, as in the Cold War

3. Tripolarity—a third center, perhaps China, balances two main rivals

4. Multipolarity—five or more major actors align so that no country can dominate others, as in 19th-century Europe

5. Unit-veto—each government is so strong it can block actions by others

Sooner or later, the strong get weaker. **Power transition theory** holds that a shifting balance of power induces **hegemonic war**—a war either to uphold or overthrow the existing hegemon ("leader"). If the hegemon is slipping, it may try to beat down challengers.[13] Alternatively, rising powers may seek to topple the faltering hegemon. Hegemonic wars often suck in all actors in the system.[14] A new hegemon generates a new international order with new rules and distributions of wealth.

Are any of these theories true? For better or worse, we shall see that no mechanical distribution of power has assured either war or peace in the

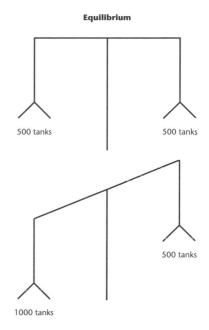

Fig. 4.3 Two Balances

Equilibrium

500 tanks   500 tanks

500 tanks

1000 tanks

Superiority-Inferiority

13. The underlying reason for the Peloponnesian War, Thucydides wrote, "was the growth of Athenian power and the fear that this caused in Sparta." *The Peloponnesian War* (New York: Penguin Books, 1956), Book 1, 25. For a rebuttal, see Donald Kagan, *The Outbreak of the Peloponnesian War* (Ithaca, N.Y.: Cornell University Press, 1969), 345–346.

14. But the Seven Weeks' War, fought only by Austria and some German states in 1866, transformed the entire system by vastly increasing Germany's power. Bueno de Mesquita and Lalman, *War and Reason*, chap. 7.

How Power Transitions May Spur Preventive and Pre-emptive Wars

A **preventive war** is one launched by the weakening party before the challenger can consolidate power in the months or years ahead. Thus, some U.S. leaders suggested preventive war against the USSR in the late 1940s before the Kremlin acquired nuclear weapons. A **pre-emptive strike**, in contrast, seeks to disarm the enemy's forces just minutes, hours, or days before they are launched. Fearing an imminent Egyptian attack in 1967, Israel struck first and destroyed Egypt's air force on the ground. Most governments, however, "wait and see" rather than risk bold actions.

20th century. Even a negative peace requires more than a certain balance of power; a positive peace, far more. Power transition theory, our cases show, explains few of the century's major wars.

COMPARING THEORY AND REALITY: GLOBAL AND LOCALIZED WARS

Let us now turn from theory to cases. We examine two global wars that transformed the IR system; two localized conflicts that merely restored the territorial status quo; and two superpower interventions, one of which helped bring down the Soviet empire and destroy the Second World.

TWO GLOBAL WARS

The Riddle of World War I

The Concert of Europe after 1815 gave way in the late 19th/early 20th century to a confrontation between two rival coalitions: the **Triple Alliance** of Germany, Austria-Hungary, and Italy against the **Triple Entente** of France, Russia, and Great Britain. Now comes a riddle: Realists say that World War I resulted from the challenge of a rising Germany to the declining hegemon, Great Britain. But the immediate catalyst was a political murder in Bosnia—an incident affecting not the principals but their allies. Would the German-British competition have led to a major war absent the Bosnian spark? We cannot know.

Germany was dangerous because it was strong; Austria-Hungary, because it was weak. Unable to cope with the ethnic minorities it already ruled, the Austrian court tried to take over still more land and diverse peoples. Thus, Austria-Hungary annexed Bosnia-Herzegovina in 1908. Adjacent Serbia asked Russia to prevent the annexation, but St. Petersburg felt too weak to intervene. The Russian court then swore "never again" to back down before Austrian expansion.

How and why World War I began is summarized in the timeline and in Table 4.2 on page 103. Why did Europe leap into darkness while Kennedy and Khrushchev stepped back from the abyss?

Level 1: Incompetence at the Top. Unlike Kennedy and Khrushchev in 1962, Europe's leaders in 1914 lacked the skill and determination to veer from disaster. German Kaiser Wilhelm II, for example, focused on himself and his Second German Empire. He once declared: "There is no balance of power in Europe but me—me and my twenty-five army corps," and tagged God as the "ancient Ally of my house." He looked down on

Table 4.2 World War I: Action Levels and Likely Causes

Individuals	Incompetent leaders at the top; aggressive ministers and generals in Vienna, Berlin, and St. Petersburg
State and Society	Febrile nationalism throughout Europe and Japan; authoritarian regimes in Germany, Austria-Hungary, and Russia; cult of the offensive (see page 104)
International System	Loose bipolar confrontation of two alliances; U.S. initially neutral
Underlying Factors	Germany challenges Britain; Ottoman Empire is dying; Concert of Europe declines and anarchy gains
Proximate Causes	Russia swears "never again" to abide Austro-Hungarian expansion after Vienna annexes Bosnia-Herzegovina
Catalysts	Assassination in Sarajevo → German "blank check" to Austria → mobilizations → chain-ganging (see page 104)

Slavs and other non-Germans.[15] By 1914 he imagined a Russian-English-French conspiracy to encircle and destroy Germany. Wilhelm rejected information disputing his hope that Russia would just watch while Austria-Hungary triumphed over Serbia.

Poor judgment became worse under stress. Like Wilhelm, most of Europe's leaders ignored or denied facts that contradicted their existing convictions. Most were self-righteous and treated their own actions as justified. Each was fatalistic. Resignation to war's inevitability made it more likely.

Level 2: Expansionist Forces in State and Society. A coalition of generals, shipbuilders, munitions makers, and others in quest of glory or profit energized Germany's expansion. These lobbies shaped policy much more than the Soviet or U.S. military-industrial complexes of the Cold War era.

Top leaders in Berlin, Vienna, and St. Petersburg were manipulated by aggressive war ministers, generals, and foreign ministers. After authorizing troop trains to move toward Belgium in 1914, Wilhelm panicked and tried to halt them. Germany's chief of staff told the Kaiser that it would be impossible to mobilize German troops only for the Russian front. This advice—a lie—made sure that Germany would fight France as well as Russia.

U.S. capitalists and Soviet Communists in 1962 believed their own system superior, but few Americans or Soviets were fanatic nationalists. Neither country had major territorial claims against the other; neither nursed old wounds caused by the other. Many Europeans in 1914, how-

---

HOW WORLD WAR I UNFOLDED

1914

6/28
Serbian nationalists assassinate Austrian Archduke Franz Ferdinand in Sarajevo, capital of Bosnia-Herzegovina

7/15
German Kaiser Wilhelm II offers Austria-Hungary a virtual blank check to punish Serbia, but then goes on vacation

7/23
Vienna issues a ten-point ultimatum: Within 48 hours Serbia must agree to wipe out agitation against the Austro-Hungarian Empire

7/25
Hoping to avoid war, Serbia accepts all Austrian demands except one: It will not permit Austro-Hungarian officials to take part in a "judicial inquiry against those implicated" in the assassination

7/28
Austria-Hungary declares war on Serbia but takes no major action

7/29–30
Russian Tsar Nicholas II orders a partial, then a general, mobilization of Russian forces—an order that he cancels and then reinstates

7/31
Germany sends a twelve-hour ultimatum to Russia demanding that it demobilize, to which Russia does not reply

8/1–23
Declarations of war: Germany on Russia and France; Britain on Germany; Austria-Hungary on Russia; Britain and France on Austria; Japan on Germany

The Ottoman Empire and Bulgaria eventually join Germany and Austria-Hungary; Italy and Romania, however, switch and join the other side

---

15. Barbara W. Tuchman, *The Proud Tower: A Portrait of the World Before the War, 1890–1914* (New York: Bantam, 1972), 280.

ever, were ardent nationalists. When war was declared, many people cheered; parliaments voted credits to finance the war; most Socialists voted for war, even though it meant killing working class comrades; even bankers went along, despite the risk to their foreign holdings.

Level 3: The System—Loose vs. Tight Bipolarity. The tight bipolar balance of power in 1962 helped keep the missile crisis in check. By contrast, the two opposing alliances in 1914 constituted a loose bipolarity. The 1914 system was precarious because it had neither the discipline of tight bipolarity nor the flexibility of multipolar balancing.

Furthermore, there were no superpowers in 1914. Germany dominated the Triple Alliance but had fewer ships than Britain and fewer soldiers than Russia. The Triple Entente had no clear leader. Britain was strong at sea; Russia, on land.

For a coalition to deter attack, it must inspire fear. But no one could be sure if the Triple Alliance and Triple Entente would hold in time of war. Many of their terms were kept secret.

An **entente** is a mere understanding. Britain refused to enter a formal alliance with Russia or France. France and Russia had a "military convention" that specified how many troops each would field in the common defense, but Britain made no such promises. British officers discussed with French officers where British troops would land if they joined a war on the Continent, but it was never clear *if* Britain's government would send them. Indeed, British leaders held back from declaring war in 1914 until Germany attacked Belgium, whose neutrality London had sworn to uphold.

Europeans in 1914 did not fear war as Americans and Soviets did in 1962. Europe's strategists in 1914 saw war as another tool of a rational policy. They embraced a **cult of the offensive**, a belief that wars could be fought and won in short order, with victory going to the army that struck first, troops charging with fixed bayonets.

Good logistics would be crucial: Germany had the best train system and could mobilize its entire army within two weeks; Russia had more troops, but needed forty days to fully mobilize. German generals were so confident that they planned to hit France first and then shift troops eastward to meet the late-arriving Russians.

Strategic doctrine and different mobilization capacities pressured each set of partners to move quickly and together—**chain-ganging**, as it were—their fates inseparable. If war seemed imminent, each side wanted to start mobilizing, even though this would compel the rival alliance to do the same. Here was the security dilemma in action. If any country started to mobilize, even for its own defense, its rival saw this as a threat to be countered. The 1914 situation was far more incendiary than that of 1962, because neither Kennedy nor Khrushchev had much incentive to strike first.

All parties in 1914 counted on a quick victory. They did not reckon with Clausewitzian "friction"—all that can go wrong. The generals' faith in the offensive proved to be misplaced. Germany's advance into France stalled in mid-September 1914. Machine guns minced advancing infantry and forced their replacements into trenches. Soon Germany faced a stalemate on two fronts. A long war of attrition began, wearing down Germany's initial advantages.

Germany had not counted on having to fight the U.S. Berlin hoped that the U.S. would not join the Entente or, if it did, could not mobilize in time to make a difference. For its part, the U.S. tried to remain neutral. But when German submarines resumed unrestricted attacks on U.S. ships delivering supplies to Britain and France on credit, Congress in April 1917 declared war.

Europe stumbled into a war that none had sought. Europe's leaders did not appreciate the dangers they faced in 1914. "Reason" told each party that "not fight" was a worse option than "fight." Looking back, we see that almost any choice would have served the protagonists better than war.

While many factors made the conflict likely, none made it inevitable. Nothing compelled Austria to attack Serbia, or Germany to issue Austria a blank check, or Germany to mobilize as soon as Russia began its slow mobilization. World War I ended the West's faith in Progress and set the stage for an even more bloody collision.

World War II: Similar but Different

The Versailles system lasted less than twenty years. In retrospect the two world wars look like one long effort by Germany to dominate the world stage. But there were differences as well as similarities between 1914 and 1939. Compare Table 4.3 with Table 4.2.

Let us look more closely at each factor.

Level 1: Aggressive Egomaniacs vs. Appeasers. Weak leaders in England and France faced aggressive egomaniacs in Rome, Berlin, and Moscow. Politics for Benito Mussolini, Adolf Hitler, and Josef Stalin gave meaning to lives that in childhood and young manhood were filled with hurt feelings and disappointment. Mussolini and Hitler dreamed of recreating mythic empires run by a master race. Stalin imagined himself

Authoritarian leaders started and lost most major wars of the 20th century. Italian Premier Benito Mussolini conquered Ethiopia in 1936, the same year that German Chancellor Adolf Hitler remilitarized Germany's Rhineland, setting the stage for World War II. Here, the two dictators review a parade honoring Mussolini's visit to Munich in 1937.

Table 4.3 World War II: Action Levels and Likely Causes

Individuals	Egomaniacs in Rome, Berlin, and Moscow; militarists in Tokyo
State and Society	Totalitarian dictatorships in Japan, Italy, Germany, and USSR; irresolute democracies in France, UK, and U.S.; cult of the defensive faces Blitzkrieg
International System	Multipolarity, with uncertainty about Soviet and U.S. power and intentions
Underlying Factors	Japan, Italy, and Germany challenge the Versailles order; collective security fails as U.S. stays aloof and Britain and France pass the buck; economic nationalism and the Great Depression
Proximate Causes	Japan invades China; Italy conquers Ethiopia; Britain and France appease Hitler as Germany rearms, annexes Austria, and takes Czechoslovakia
Catalysts	Germany and USSR invade Poland after their August 1939 pact to divide Eastern Europe

another tsar and wished to restore Russia's borders to their pre-1905 configuration. Similar in some ways, Stalin bonded with Hitler in 1939–1941.[16] Japan's leaders were driven more by a shared nationalism than by personal pathologies.

Level 2: Totalitarian Dictatorships vs. Irresolute Democracies. Contrary to Woodrow Wilson's hopes, democracy did not flourish after 1919. Dictatorship took hold in the USSR, Italy, Japan, and Germany. Each dictatorship mobilized nationalist feelings to acquire more resources and land (*Lebensraum*—living space). Traumatized by World War I and internally divided, France and Britain favored peace at any price and tried to appease Hitler.

Level 3: Multipolarity + Cult of Defensive + Egotism = Buck-Passing. The interwar balance of power was even more ambiguous than that preceding World War I. The cohesion of Britain, France, and Russia (USSR) was weaker in the 1930s than it had been in 1914. The old Triple Alliance, however, was stronger: Hitler annexed Austria in 1938 and found a willing partner in Mussolini. Japan allied with Germany and Italy in 1940. The U.S., once again, stood aside.

The aggressors met little opposition as they dismantled the Versailles system. The League of Nations was too weak to provide collective security. There was no Concert of Europe, no loose or tight bipolarity as in 1914 and 1962, and no unit-veto or deterrence based on terror.

Searching for security, many countries entered alliances in the 1920s and 1930s. But these pacts were weaker than those existing before 1914.

16. Alan Bullock, *Hitler and Stalin: Parallel Lives* (New York: Knopf, 1992).

HOW WORLD WAR II UNFOLDED

1931

9/18
Japan begins to detach Manchuria
from China

1936

5/9
Italy annexes Ethiopia

1937

7/28
Japanese troops take Beijing

1938

3/13
Germany annexes Austria (the *Anschluss*)

9/29
Britain, France, and Italy agree at Munich
that Germany may take the largely German-
speaking Sudetenland from Czechoslovakia

1939

3/31
Britain and France guarantee Poland's
independence

8/23
Germany and USSR sign Nonaggression
Pact and plan to partition the Baltic and
Eastern Europe

9/1
Germany invades Poland, leading France
and Britain to declare war on Germany

9/17–27
Poland divided between Germany and USSR

1940

6/5–22
Germany invades France and accepts
its capitulation

7/10
Germany starts to bomb Great Britain

9/22
Japan invades Indochina

1941

3/11
Roosevelt signs Lend-Lease Act to transfer
war matériel abroad

4/13
USSR and Japan sign a five-year Nonaggression Pact

6/22
Germany attacks USSR

July–November
Britain, U.S., and Holland freeze Japanese
assets and cancel oil sales; Washington conditions lifting of trade restrictions on Japanese withdrawal from China and Indochina

12/7–8
Japan attacks Pearl Harbor, Philippines,
Hong Kong, and Malaya

12/11
Germany and Italy declare war on U.S.

The USSR, for example, entered a mutual security treaty with France in 1935, but Moscow and Paris never discussed how to implement it. The Kremlin promised to aid Czechoslovakia if it were attacked, but only if France upheld its own pledge to do so. Soviet troops, however, could not even reach Czechoslovakia without transiting Poland or Romania, each hostile to Moscow. Neither Paris nor Moscow would discuss military plans with Prague. When France betrayed Czechoslovakia in 1938, Moscow did nothing to help its Czech ally. Instead, Moscow instructed Czech Communists to try and grab power in Prague.

Alarmed by Japan and Germany, the USSR labored from 1934 until 1938 to strengthen the League of Nations. Shunned by London and Paris, Moscow switched directions in 1939. As we see in the above timeline, the Soviet and Nazi dictators divided the spoils of Eastern Europe for two years, until Hitler double-crossed Stalin in 1941.

The defenders of the status quo did not chain-gang; instead, they passed the buck. **Buck-passing** is to let another actor take responsibility.[17] Why did this happen? In the 1930s French and British strategists became devoted to a **cult of the defensive**—a belief that the defense had an inherent advantage over the offense. This attitude lowered incentives to unite against aggressors. French and British planners hoped someone else would stop or sate Hitler. If not, the French would depend on their

17. "Buck" is for the "buckhorn" knife formerly used to designate the next dealer in poker. To pass the buck was to transfer responsibility to the next player.

Maginot Line of giant forts; the British, upon the English Channel and Royal Air Force interceptors.

The Germans, however, believed in the offensive—what they called **Blitzkrieg** ("lightning war") by bombers, tanks, and motorized infantry. In June 1940 German gliders and paratroopers landed on Belgian forts and compelled their immediate surrender. Since France had never bothered to complete its defense line, German forces swept around the Maginot forts and marched into Paris.

The 1930s cult of defense, like the earlier cult of offense, made war more likely.[18] In 1914 chain-ganging fostered a wide war by chain reaction. In the 1930s buck-passing made it easier for Germany to expand. Having betrayed Czechoslovakia, Paris and London declared war on Germany when Hitler invaded Poland. France then had to resist Germany without Czechoslovakia (dismembered by Hitler in 1938–1939); then Britain had to fight without France (which quickly surrendered in 1940)—attacked by German bombers that could not have reached Britain without the forward bases Hitler acquired in 1940. Britain's salvation came when Hitler opted to attack the USSR in June 1941 and declare war on the U.S. in December.

Perhaps the aggressors' initial conquests could be seen as rational continuations of realist diplomacy. But Tokyo gambled wildly in taking on the U.S. Hitler's fantasy was the most far-fetched: How could Germany simultaneously conquer Europe, Russia, and the U.S.? By 1945 Italy, Japan, and Germany were defeated and their empires destroyed.

The only country to have made significant gains relative to its losses (less than half a million dead) was the U.S. The USSR—one part aggressor, one part liberator—made huge territorial gains in Europe and the Far East, but paid with 25 to 40 million dead. Great Britain and China also suffered greatly and profited little, except to regain the pre-war status quo. France paid little and gained nothing, except to be counted a victor.

FOUR LOCALIZED WARS, TWO PARTIAL VICTORIES FOR COLLECTIVE SECURITY

Korea, 1950–

18. Thomas J. Christensen and Jack Snyder, "Chain Gangs and Passed Bucks: Predicting Alliance Patterns in Multipolarity," *International Organization* 44, no. 2 (spring 1990): 137–168; see also Randall L. Schweller, "Tripolarity and the Second World War," *International Studies Quarterly* 37, no. 1 (March 1993): 73–104.

Japan annexed Korea in 1910 and used it as a platform to invade China in the 1930s. U.S. and Soviet troops liberated Korea from Japan in 1945, but their subsequent occupation divided a homogenous and long-interdependent nation. By 1948 there were two states: South of the 38th parallel there were 21 million people in the Republic of Korea (ROK) under the

Table 4.4 The Korean War: Action Levels and Likely Causes

Individuals	Egomaniacs in Pyongyang, Beijing, and Moscow vs. strong-willed U.S. president and ROK dictator
State and Society	Korean nationalism; Communist dictatorships in DPRK, PRC, and USSR; anti-Communist dictatorship in ROK; presidential democracy in U.S.
International System	Bipolar world and Cold War, with Communist actors feeling stronger
Underlying Factors	Kim Il-sung believes DPRK can and should unify Korea
Proximate Causes	U.S. and USSR depart from Korea; Washington declares Korea beyond its defense perimeter
Catalysts	DPRK invades ROK after Mao and Stalin approve

anti-Communist dictatorship of President Syngman Rhee; to the north were 9 million in the Democratic People's Republic of Korea (DPRK) headed by Communist dictator **Kim Il-sung**.

Kim Il-sung thought his regime could unify the nation by force without U.S. interference. Why? The factors that led to war in 1950 are outlined in Table 4.4. Most Soviet and U.S. forces departed the two Koreas in 1948–1949, but Soviet aid made North Korea far stronger militarily than the South. The world was bipolar in 1950, similar to 1962. But even tight bipolarity did not assure stability. The Communist world seemed to be gaining on the West. In 1949–1950 the USSR tested its first atomic bomb and gained Communist China—formally the People's Republic of China (PRC)—as an ally. In January 1950 U.S. Secretary of State Dean Acheson said that the U.S. military defense "perimeter" stopped with Japan.

Kim Il-sung assured Stalin that an invasion by DPRK troops would trigger a popular uprising in the South.[19] Deliveries of Soviet equipment increased. DPRK troops invaded the South on June 25, 1950. But the White House saw Kim Il-sung as a Soviet puppet. U.S. President Harry Truman acted on the lesson of the 1930s: no appeasement of aggressors. Truman did not pass the buck.[20] The U.S. acted unilaterally but also mobilized international support. Responding to a U.S. request, the UN Security Council, by a vote of 9 to 0, with one abstention (Yugoslavia) and one absent (the USSR), declared that an "armed attack" had taken place in Korea and called for an immediate end to hostilities and withdrawal of North Korean forces from the South.[21] Two days later the Security Council (7 to 1) adopted a U.S. resolution calling on all members to furnish such assistance as necessary to repel the armed attack.

19. Kim sent forty-six telegrams to Moscow pressing his case. He went to Moscow in late 1949 and again in March–April 1950 to seek Stalin's go-ahead; Kim got Mao Zedong's backing during an April visit to Beijing. Kathryn Weatherby, "New Findings on the Korean War," *Cold War International History Project Bulletin* (Woodrow Wilson International Center for Scholars, Washington, D.C.), 3 (fall 1993): 1, 14–18.

20. Many State Department officials wanted to recognize the PRC, but President Truman worried this might bolster Republican opposition to the Marshall Plan and to containment of the USSR. See Thomas J. Christensen, *Useful Adversaries: Grand Strategy, Domestic Mobilization, and Sino-American Conflict, 1947–1958* (Princeton, N.J.: Princeton University Press, 1996).

21. The USSR did not veto this decision because the Soviet delegate stayed away, protesting that "China's" seat was occupied by Nationalist China (Taiwan) rather than the People's Republic of China—which did not get China's seat until 1971.

The Commander-in-Chief and Congress

Can the U.S. president make war without Congress? The Constitution makes him "commander-in-chief" but leaves it to Congress to declare war. Many presidents have sent U.S. troops on military missions without congressional approval. But 1950 marked the first time that a president ordered U.S. forces to take part in what became a prolonged, large-scale combat without a declaration of war by Congress. Truman initiated a half century in which the U.S. often acted like a world policeman, with or without congressional approval—and never with a formal declaration of war. Instead, war became the "continuation of policy by other means." It was waged for limited political purposes—not the total defeat of the other side. The U.S. Congress sometimes tried to limit the president's powers as commander-in-chief. In 1964 Congress endorsed the "Tonkin Gulf" resolution giving President Johnson a virtual free hand in Vietnam. When Indochina became a quagmire, however, Congress wanted to rein in the executive. In 1973 it passed the **War Powers Resolution**—a requirement that the president withdraw U.S. troops from combat missions within sixty days unless Congress extended the period. Every president from Nixon to Clinton complained that the 1973 act infringed executive prerogatives. Each president requested congressional approval for certain combat missions, but did what he pleased anyway.[1]

1. Francis D. Wormuth and Edwin B. Firmage, *To Chain the Dog of War: The War Power of Congress in History and Law*, 2d ed. (Urbana: University of Illinois Press, 1989); and John Hart Ely, *War and Responsibility: Constitutional Lessons of Vietnam and Its Aftermath* (Princeton, N.J.: Princeton University Press, 1995).

Map 4.1 Korea and Its Neighbors: A Dagger in Every Direction

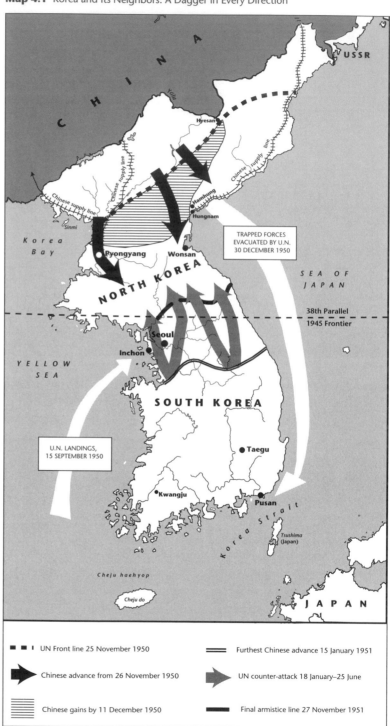

General Douglas MacArthur, still based in Japan, commanded "United Nations" forces. But most UN members sent only token units, leaving U.S. and ROK troops to bear the brunt. North Koreans advanced south and nearly drove the U.S. and ROK troops into the sea. But MacArthur's forces landed at Inchon and cut the DPRK lines. Soon UN troops liberated Seoul, capital of South Korea (see Map 4.1).

Authorized by the UN General Assembly to "insure a stable situation in the whole of Korea," MacArthur ordered his troops to move north from Seoul across the 38th parallel. Neither PRC leader **Mao Zedong** nor MacArthur deterred one another. MacArthur ignored Beijing's warnings that it might intervene, and Mao Zedong downplayed U.S. superiority in weaponry. Fearing that the UN advance threatened China, Beijing in October 1950 sent PRC "volunteers" to join the war.[22] For a time Chinese volunteers reversed the tide, but soon UN forces drove them back to approximately the 38th parallel.[23]

The three Communist powers followed the parasitic logic of collective action. None chain-ganged. Beijing helped North Korea only when China felt endangered. **Pyongyang** (capital of North Korea) later criticized China for not joining the war earlier. PRC and Soviet officials, in turn, blamed Kim Il-sung for many bad decisions. China had to expend many lives and much material wealth to save Kim Il-sung. The USSR provided equipment plus some 26,000 advisers and pilots who served in Korea in 1951–1953. But the USSR maintained a low profile to avoid provoking a U.S. attack on the Soviet Union. Moscow demanded that Beijing pay for military aid—an enormous debt not discharged until 1965.

The UN Command and North Korea agreed to a cease-fire in July 1951, but both sides practiced "talk-and-fight" until they signed a truce on July 23, 1953. Why did the North finally agree to a truce? Its backers in Moscow sought a wide-ranging détente after Stalin died in March 1953. There is no evidence that any of the Communist powers were swayed by U.S. hints that Washington might use nuclear arms to end the fighting.[24]

The truce established a demilitarized zone that ran just below and above the 38th parallel. The UN coalition won a qualified victory for collective security by driving back North Korea. Some two million soldiers died in a war that barely altered the boundary. China lost 900,000; the DPRK, 520,000; the ROK, 415,000; and the U.S., 54,000. Civilian deaths were uncounted.

While the UN-approved **police action** contained Kim Il-sung, he continued to tighten his dictatorship and defy the international community.

22. Thomas J. Christensen, "Threats, Assurances, and the Last Chance for Peace: The Lessons of Mao's Korean War Telegrams," *International Security* 17, no. 1 (summer 1992): 122–154; also Gennady Vasilyev, "A Russian War in Korea," *Moscow News* 30 (1992): 12.

23. Soviet archives say that in 1951 there were 2 million Chinese troops plus 337,000 North Koreans facing 700,000 troops in the South—380,000 South Koreans, 280,000 Americans, and 40,000 other UN forces. Mao Zedong sought a 4:1 numerical advantage for Communist forces to outweigh their foe's superior equipment.

24. See Richard K. Betts, *Nuclear Blackmail and Nuclear Balance* (Washington, D.C.: Brookings Institution, 1987): 32–47.

Following Kim's death in 1994, the two Korean governments were still at odds—the ROK backed by nearly 40,000 U.S. troops in the South.

Vietnam: The U.S.'s Biggest Foreign Policy Blunder

Governments sometimes learn the wrong lessons. President Truman learned from Munich 1938 that appeasement invites larger wars. Having applied this lesson to Korea in the early 1950s, the U.S. inferred that staunch resistance could stem Communist expansion. The administration of President John F. Kennedy thought that it saw another Korea in Vietnam. The Communist North, backed by China and the Soviet Union, wanted to conquer the South. Washington embraced the **falling dominoes theory**—a belief that if a critical country falls to the other side, its neighbors will fall as well. Washington feared that if Vietnam became Communist, this event would knock Laos, Cambodia, Thailand, Indonesia—like falling dominoes—into the Sino-Soviet camp (see Map 4.2). Washington chose Vietnam as the place to stem the Communist tide. "If we don't stop them in Vietnam," said one soldier, "we'll have to fight them in Hawaii or California."[25] Table 4.5 outlines the broader context of the U.S. intervention in Vietman.

After 1954 the U.S. replaced France as patron of South Vietnam's anti-Communists and backed the refusal of President Ngo Din Diem to take part in all-Vietnamese elections. By 1960 Saigon was receiving $300 mil-

Table 4.5 The U.S. and the Vietnam War: Action Levels and Likely Causes

Individuals	Determined leadership of Ho Chi Minh vs. overconfident Kennedy and insecure (in foreign affairs) Johnson (see page 114)
State and Society	Communist discipline in North Vietnam; corruption in South Vietnam; party politics in the U.S.—Democrats fear Republican challenge
International System	Bipolar confrontation is qualified by China's split from the Soviet camp, virtually ignored by U.S. presidential advisers
Underlying Factors	Legacy of French imperialism; Vietnamese nationalism; Cold War rivalry
Proximate Causes	Apparent Communist successes in many parts of the world confront U.S. hubris and ignorance of Indochina
Catalysts	Johnson gets a virtual free hand from Congress in the form of the 1964 Tonkin Gulf Resolution and starts to bomb North Vietnam in 1965 (see page 114)

25. Marvin E. Gettleman et al., eds., *Vietnam and America: A Documented History,* 2d rev. ed. (New York: Grove, 1995). This book includes a long bibliographic essay including references to the several versions of the "Pentagon Papers," a once classified history of U.S. involvement by Defense Department analysts.

Map 4.2 Vietnam and Prospective Dominoes

lion worth of U.S. military aid annually. Hanoi, for its part, received aid from both Moscow and Beijing. But North Vietnam's greatest assets were strong political cohesion rooted in tight organization and Hanoi's determination to achieve national unity.

The Kennedy administration increased the number of U.S. advisers in Vietnam from 900 in 1961 to 16,500 by late 1963. With Americans coaching South Vietnamese patrols and co-piloting aircraft, Washington believed that U.S. proxies were fighting those of Russia and China, and said: "Our little tigers can beat their little tigers."

The Kennedy team urged President Diem, a U.S.-educated Catholic, to "win the hearts and minds" of his people—to carry out land reform and stop harassing Buddhists. Frustrated by his corrupt dictatorship, Washington winked when South Vietnamese officers, most of them Buddhists, murdered Diem on November 1, 1963. Three weeks later, Kennedy himself fell to an assassin.

The new president, Lyndon B. Johnson, insecure but ambitious, wanted to look as internationalist as Kennedy. But in May 1964 Johnson complained to colleagues that U.S. engagement in Vietnam was "the biggest damn mess I ever saw." He lamented: "I don't think it's worth fighting for, and I don't think we can get out." He worried about sacrificing U.S. soldiers in a pointless cause. While Johnson believed that public opinion already opposed the war, he feared Congress would impeach him if he tried to pull back. Johnson did not want to sacrifice young Americans to a pointless cause. Just to imagine sending a sergeant who worked for him, the father of six, to Vietnam, he said, "makes the chills run up my back."[26]

Still, Johnson persuaded Congress in August 1964 to give him a blank check. Both houses endorsed the **Gulf of Tonkin Resolution**, authorizing "the President, as Commander-in-Chief, to take all necessary measures" to combat North Vietnamese aggression.[27] Responding to a Communist attack on a U.S. air base in the South, U.S. planes in February 1965 began large-scale bombings of the North. In March the first U.S. combat troops arrived. By the end of 1965 U.S. forces in Vietnam numbered over 184,000; in February 1969 they peaked at 542,000.

Vast U.S. military and economic assets did not derail Hanoi. High-tech weapons did not staunch the streams of Communist guerrillas heading south on jungle trails. U.S. ignorance of the local language, culture, and values made it difficult to "win hearts and minds" for Saigon.

President Johnson never escalated sufficiently to win the war, because that would have required even more troops or crueler weapons. He wanted to avoid provoking another large-scale Chinese intervention, which, he feared, could trigger a nuclear war. Instead, he increased U.S. forces only enough to forestall a Communist victory. Johnson feared a rerun of the havoc wreaked on the Truman administration by Republican charges that Truman "lost" China to Communism in 1949. But the U.S. home front crumbled in 1968 as the numbers of casualties mounted—many of the maimed and dead conscripted, middle-class whites. Johnson withdrew from politics, setting the stage for a Republican to become president.

Richard M. Nixon was sworn in as president in 1969. He and National Security Assistant Henry Kissinger sought a face-saving retreat. They wanted to "Vietnamize" the war—make South Vietnam capable of fighting its own military and political battles against the North. The U.S. intensified its bombing of the North to "buy the time needed to make our ally self-sufficient." Seeking to destroy a North Vietnamese sanctuary,

26. Tapes of Johnson's telephone conversations on May 27, 1964, with National Security adviser McGeorge Bundy and with Senator Richard Russell, released by the presidential library at University of Texas, Austin, on February 14, 1997. See Michael R. Beschloss, ed., *Taking Charge: The Johnson White House Tapes, 1963–1964* (New York: Simon & Schuster, 1997).

27. The previously drafted resolution was sent to Congress immediately after skirmishes—whether real or imagined—between U.S. destroyers and North Vietnamese torpedo boats in the Gulf of Tonkin at a time when South Vietnamese commandos were raiding the North.

"War is hell." Here a U.S. Marine rounds up villagers in South Vietnam in September 1965 after discovery that most males had fled the area, perhaps recruited by Communist forces (the "Vietcong"). The Marines feared that some villagers could be armed for sniper attacks. Such events precipitated the My Lai massacre three years later when U.S. Army troops murdered hundreds of men, women, and children.

U.S. forces entered Cambodia in 1970, triggering a civil war in which nearly a third of the population perished.

In January 1973 Kissinger and Hanoi negotiator Le Duc Tho signed a truce establishing a cease-fire throughout Vietnam. It provided that all U.S. fighting forces would depart, but North Vietnamese troops could remain where they were in the south.

After U.S. forces left, Hanoi broke the truce and took all the south in April 1975. Within months Vietnamese Communists overthrew a pro-U.S. regime in Cambodia and a non-Communist one in Laos. But Thailand, Burma, and Indonesia did not become Communist, one after another, as the falling dominoes theory predicted. In the mid-1990s Vietnam opened its doors to foreign investors; the first U.S. ambassador to Hanoi was an ex-pilot long held captive in the "Hanoi Hilton"; and former Defense Secretary Robert McNamara discussed with Vietnamese leaders how each side could have curtailed the war (drawing a blank from them).

The Vietnam War was probably the greatest U.S. foreign policy failure

One of the "best and brightest," Robert S. Mc-Namara served as U.S. Secretary of Defense when the U.S. entered the Vietnam War. Three decades later, in his book *In Retrospect: The Tragedy and Lessons of Vietnam* (Random House, 1995), McNamara stated: "[We] acted according to what we thought were the principles and traditions of this nation. . . . Yet we were wrong, terribly wrong. We owe it to future generations to explain why."

28. This was the opinion of most experts polled in surveys conducted by the author at the Woodrow Wilson International Center for Scholars in 1976 and 1987 and at the Harvard Center for Science and International Affairs in 1987. There was little disagreement among the U.S. and foreign observers, or the academics and diplomats polled.

29. Estimates of dead and wounded vary depending on source. Compare, for example, figures in Table 4.1. Many of the 2.7 million veterans alive in the 1990s were haunted by nightmares of blood and jungles. The U.S.'s direct expenditures and aid to Saigon made up a large share of the federal budget, from 1965 to 1973, but they were dwarfed by the billions that would later go to veterans' benefits.

30. See *New York Times*, March 24 and April 17 and 30, 1985; David Fromkin and James Chace, "What Are the Lessons of Vietnam?" *Foreign Affairs* (spring 1985); George McT. Kahin, *Intervention: How America Became Involved in Vietnam* (New York: Knopf, 1986); George K. Osborn et al., eds., *Democracy, Strategy, and Vietnam: Implications for American Policymaking* (Lexington, Mass.: Lexington Books, 1987).

in the 20th century—perhaps ever.[28] A 1985 Gallup poll indicated that 63 percent of the American people believed that U.S. involvement there had been a mistake. U.S. costs included 58,721 American dead and 519,000 disabled veterans.[29] War-induced inflation derailed U.S. economic growth and movement toward income equality. Washington's ability and will to lead the First World declined. Political cohesion plunged within the U.S. while racial, ideological, and generational conflicts soared.

Some supporters of the war blamed the U.S. defeat on self-imposed restraint—"fighting with one hand tied behind us"; they also blamed the press and TV for ruining American morale and South Vietnam for wasting U.S. aid. Critics said that Washington misjudged: Vietnam was the wrong war in the wrong place waged for the wrong reasons. Washington should have backed Vietnamese nationalists, even if they were Communists, against French imperialists, and kept Hanoi from dependency on Moscow or Beijing.[30]

In the 1970s the U.S. lost its drive to resist Communist advances around the globe. When Soviet troops invaded Afghanistan in 1979, however, Americans awoke.

Moscow's "Vietnam"—Afghanistan

Afghanistan is a land-locked country with some 15.5 million people divided by religion (85 percent **Sunni** and 14 percent **Shiite Islam**), by language, and by way of life (urban vs. rural). Of educated Afghans, some have looked to the West, others to Moscow, and still others to Pakistan, Iran, or Egypt for cultural and political cues.

Unlike the U.S. in Vietnam, Russia had long been concerned with Afghanistan. Both superpowers gave economic aid to Afghanistan in the 1950s, but Washington cut back its involvement in the 1960s. The USSR aided Afghanistan but took out natural gas and minerals at cut-rate prices. "Aid" became a tool for Soviet exploitation.

Afghanistan's feudal monarchy ended in 1973 when the king's cousin, Daud Khan, staged a coup d'état and proclaimed himself president. In April 1978 Daud was killed by military officers who handed power to the Communists—the People's Democratic Party of Afghanistan (PDPA).

The 1978 coup caught Moscow by surprise. But Soviet leaders now asked themselves: With our aid, what kind of regime is possible in Afghanistan? What changes could take place without provoking U.S. intervention?[31]

But Afghanistan's Communists feuded among themselves. The PDPA was split between two factions: The "Banner" faction drew from the lower ranks of the Persian-speaking elite in the capital, Kabul; the "Masses" wing appealed to some newly educated persons from rural backgrounds. Masses leader Nur Mohammed Taraki took power in April 1978 and embarked on a revolution by decree and terror. His land reforms and anti-religious policies drove traditional Afghans into armed rebellion, supported by Pakistan and Iran. Taraki solicited Soviet aid but Moscow was cool. The USSR supplied some military advisers and weapons, but Soviet generals feared another "Vietnam" if the USSR intervened heavily in Afghanistan.

By the late 1970s Soviet President Leonid Brezhnev was ill and senile. Key decisions were made by three or four other top Communist Party leaders. They would meet visiting Afghans and then draft speeches for Brezhnev to read to them.

In September 1979 Taraki was killed by his rival within the Masses leadership, Hafizullah Amin. From Moscow's perspective, Amin was even worse than Taraki. Top Soviet leaders concluded that Amin was "insincere and two-faced": He planned to purge rivals and continue policies that would strengthen the counter-revolution; but he also flirted with conservative Muslim leaders and even with the West. The Kremlin heard that Amin spread anti-Soviet rumors and stories that Moscow plotted to end his life. On the other hand, Amin begged Moscow to send special troops to protect him.

31. The following account is based on "top secret" Soviet documents from the period January–December 1979 published in *Journal of South Asian and Middle Eastern Studies* 17, no. 2 (winter 1994). The documents appear to be authentic but incomplete. See also Henry S. Bradsher, *Afghanistan and the Soviet Union*, rev. ed. (Durham, N.C.: Duke University Press, 1985).

Table 4.6   The Soviet War in Afghanistan: Action Levels and Likely Causes

Individuals	Blood feuds in Kabul: Tarakai kills Daud and Amin kills Taraki; Soviet President Brezhnev becomes senile; President Carter appears irresolute
State and Society	Afghan society split between traditionalists and modernizers as well as between many ethnic groups; Communist policies of Taraki and Amin spur armed resistance
International System	Bipolar IR, but the USSR and Iran seem to be gaining at the expense of the U.S.
Underlying Factors	Longstanding Russian interest in dominating Afghanistan and Iran; Soviet advances throughout the Third World in late 1970s unchallenged by U.S.
Proximate Causes	Soviet worries that Communist regime in Kabul will fall to anti-Communists backed by Iran, Pakistan, and the West
Catalysts	Afghan Communists seek Soviet aid; Soviets intervene militarily in December 1979

These and other factors set the stage for Soviet intervention—as outlined in Table 4.6.

Moscow, like Washington, worried about falling dominoes. In 1979 the Kremlin came to fear that unless Soviet forces intervened Moscow would lose a client state—the first time that an established Communist regime had been overthrown. If Afghanistan fell, what might follow? In early December the Politburo decided to act. It airlifted special forces to Kabul on December 25, 1979. Instead of shielding Amin, however, the Soviets killed and replaced him with Babrak Karmal—a Banner faction leader who Moscow hoped would obey its directives. The Kremlin declared that it had sent a "limited contingent of Soviet forces to Afghanistan at the request of its government." Moscow claimed also that its actions were consonant with the Soviet-Afghan friendship treaty of December 1978 and with Article 51 of the UN Charter, which authorizes "self-defense." The Soviet Politburo received rubber-stamp approval for the Afghan intervention from the Soviet Communist Party Central Committee five months later (unlike President Johnson, who got his Tonkin Gulf resolution from Congress before escalating the U.S.'s combat role in Vietnam).

The Soviet "limited contingent" quickly grew to 120,000 men (more than twice the size of the Afghan government's forces) and remained for nine years. Signs multiplied that Moscow wanted also to use Afghanistan as a springboard to move south, east, and west. A Sovietized Afghanistan could bully Iran, Pakistan, and the Arab oil-producers.

Stirred from its post-Vietnam slumbers, the U.S. acted to oppose the Soviet intervention. Washington backed the UN majority that yearly called for a withdrawal of "foreign" forces from Afghanistan; the U.S. boycotted the 1980 Moscow Olympics; the White House strove to block grain and high technology sales to the USSR; the Pentagon built a U.S. Rapid Deployment Force to help vulnerable countries such as Saudi Arabia; and the CIA helped arm the Afghan resistance with the cooperation of Pakistan, Saudi Arabia, Egypt, and China.

A stalemate developed in which Soviet and local Communist forces controlled Afghanistan's major cities while the anti-Communist *mujahideen* ("holy warriors")[32] dominated the countryside.

Those who defend their own territory have deep reasons to fight despite great suffering. Like Vietnamese Communists, the mujahideen struggled against aliens, most of whom felt no deep reason to fight. Unlike the disciplined Vietnamese Communists, the mujahideen had little cohesion. Still, their combined efforts produced steadfast resistance. Soviet hopes in Afghanistan were already flagging when the U.S. began to supply "Stinger" missiles to the mujahideen in late 1986. This shoulder-braced weapon permitted the Afghan tribesmen to shoot down an average of one Soviet plane or helicopter a day. Stinger hard power combined with mujahideen will power snapped Soviet overall power.

Soviet casualties mounted. By the mid-1980s Moscow could no longer hide the horrors of the Afghan war from Soviet citizens. Draft-age men began to injure themselves or pay bribes to avoid military service in Afghanistan. While most Soviet citizens initially supported the Afghan expedition, by 1987 many actively opposed it.[33]

In 1988 the Kremlin announced it would withdraw all Soviet troops from Afghanistan within one year. At the same time Pakistan agreed to end interference in Afghan internal affairs and the U.S. promised to terminate support to the mujahideen in tandem with the halting of Soviet aid to the Communists in Kabul.

As in Vietnam, there were many losers and no clear winners in Afghanistan. The war killed more than a million Afghans—mostly civilians—and produced the world's largest refugee problem: Two million Afghans were uprooted while another five million sought refuge in Pakistan or Iran.

At least 13,000 Soviet troops—perhaps 50,000—died in Afghanistan. Drug addiction multiplied and morale fell within the Soviet armed forces. Overreaching, Moscow undermined its entire empire.

32. More precisely, a *mujahid* (plural, *mujahideen*) is a fighter in a holy war for the faith, a *jihad*. In other contexts, Western governments opposed Muslim jihads. Ralph H. Magnus and Eden Naby, *Afghanistan: Mullah, Marx, and Mujahid* (Boulder, Colo.: Westview, 1997).

33. Based on interviews with Soviet citizens traveling in Europe. "The Soviet Public and the War in Afghanistan: Discontent Reaches Critical Levels," Radio Free Europe/Radio Liberty, May 1988.

Each superpower allowed itself to be sucked into a conflict where it had few deep interests and where victory would be hard to achieve.[34] The reality was that factional strife in Saigon and Kabul prevented either superpower from forming a cohesive regime there. Neither client obeyed its paymaster; each persisted in policies that alienated much of the local population.[35]

The U.S. gained something from its rival's burdens, but the Afghan War, like that in Vietnam, imposed opportunity costs on both superpowers. Global rivalry inflated their military spending and curtailed mutually useful cooperation in science and other fields.

In the 1990s active mines littered the Afghan landscape (as they did too in Indochina), making farming extremely hazardous. Having expelled the Soviets and ousted the Communists, the mujahideen factions turned their knives on one another. Washington pulled away; Pakistan backed the most radical Muslim fundamentalists; and Moscow labored to keep religious and factional struggle from penetrating what had been Soviet Central Asia, especially Tajikistan and Uzbekistan.

The Persian Gulf, 1990–

Iraqi President Saddam Hussein faced many foes in 1990—both at home and abroad. He wanted to restore to Iraq the glory and power of ancient Babylon. As in North Korea, personal and family lust for power and wealth also underlay a cruel dictatorship.

Unlike Koreans, Iraqis are not one people. Sunni Muslims rule Iraq but make up just 20 percent of the population. Some 60 percent of Iraqis are Shiite Muslims (as are most Iranians). Some 20 percent (perhaps 25 percent) of Iraq's population are Kurds—Muslims with their own customs and language.

How action levels and likely causes interlaced to spur the Gulf War is suggested in Table 4.7.

Repeating its 1950 Korean error, Washington failed to warn Iraq that the U.S. would resist a takeover of the country's southern neighbor. U.S. diplomats curried favor in Baghdad, trying to use Iraq against Iran, which Washington saw as the greater evil. (On one occasion U.S. officials even apologized to Iraq for a Voice of America broadcast on the evils of police states!) On July 25, 1990—eight days before Iraq invaded Kuwait—President Hussein summoned U.S. Ambassador April C. Glaspie. He told her that his problem with Kuwait was an inter-Arab dispute. Iraq would negotiate with Kuwait, "but if we are unable to find a solution, then it will be natural that Iraq will not accept death." He warned Americans: "We

34. Neither U.S. nor Soviet officials admitted their mistakes until too late. In 1989, however, the Soviet Foreign Minister told his parliament that Soviet intervention in Afghanistan had been "immoral." No top U.S. leaders issued a mea culpa until Robert S. McNamara's book *In Retrospect: The Tragedy and Lessons of Vietnam* (New York: Times Books) appeared in 1995.

35. The Americans urged the anti-Communist regime in Saigon to carry out land reform to win favor among poor peasants, while the Soviets pressed the Kabul Communists to go easy on their land reforms that alienated rich landlords.

Table 4.7 The Gulf War: Action Levels and Likely Causes

Individuals	Egomaniac in Baghdad (Saddam Hussein) faces effective team leader in Washington (George Bush)
State and Society	Dictatorship in Iraq faces feudal dynasty in Kuwait and presidential democracy in U.S.
International System	World becomes unipolar with decline of USSR → UN no longer polarized → collective security becomes feasible
Underlying Factors	Bristling with Soviet arms, Iraq challenges Kuwait's independence and covets its borders, oil, and wealth
Proximate Causes	Kuwait pumps oil beyond OPEC quotas and demands that Iraq repay loans; U.S. appeases Iraq
Catalysts	Iraq invades and annexes Kuwait and refuses to withdraw despite UN resolutions and U.S.-led military buildup

 Saddam Hussein: A Psychological Portrait

A megalomaniac like Hitler and Kim Il-sung, **Saddam Hussein** also became a dictator who brought his country into costly struggles that led nowhere. Hussein's father, a landless peasant, died before he was born. Hussein was brought up by his mother's uncle, an army officer who taught the youth to hate British colonialism. In power he surrounded himself with docile ministers—many of them his own relatives, often from his own community. Hussein compared himself with Nebuchadnezzar II, who destroyed Jerusalem in the 6th century B.C., and with Saladin, the Muslim warrior who drove back Christian crusaders in the 12th century. Still, Saddam Hussein—like Hitler and Stalin—could also talk like a reasonable man who had legitimate grievances.[1]

1. See Stanley A. Renshon, ed., *The Political Psychology of the Gulf War: Leaders, Publics, and the Process of Conflict* (Pittsburgh: University of Pittsburgh Press, 1993); see also Judith Miller and Laurie Mylroie, *Suddam Hussein and the Crisis in the Gulf* (New York: Times Books/Random House, 1990); also Efraim Karsh, "In Baghdad, Politics Is a Lethal Game," *The New York Times Magazine*, September 30, 1990, 39 ff.

too can harm you. We cannot come all the way to the United States, but individual Arabs may reach you." Following what she thought were her orders, Glaspie indicated to Hussein that the U.S. would take no side in this border dispute between neighbors, though it could never "excuse" any settlement by force.[36] If Iraq did invade Kuwait, many U.S. specialists expected Hussein to take only disputed borderlands and islands.

Hussein had five complaints. First, he maintained that, since Ottoman times, Kuwait was part of Iraq.[37] Second, Kuwait pumped oil from wells in Iraqi territory. Third, Kuwait refused to give Iraq two islands blocking its access to the Persian Gulf. Fourth, Kuwait exceeded the oil production quotas set by OPEC (Organization of Petroleum Exporting Countries) and thus lowered the world price of oil. Fifth, Kuwait refused to cancel its loans to Iraq during the 1980s war that Hussein had waged against the common Arab foe—Iran.

Iraq's forces quickly took Kuwait in August 1990. Some of U.S. President George Bush's advisers urged acceptance of this as an accomplished fact. Like Truman in 1950, however, Bush wanted to prevent one state from extinguishing another. He saw Hussein as "another Hitler" and did not want Iraq to control half or even a quarter of the world's oil. If Hussein conquered Kuwait and Saudi Arabia, Iraq would control nearly half of the world's known oil deposits (Iraq, 12.5 percent; Kuwait, 12.2 percent; Saudi Arabia, 21 percent).

In 1990 Iraq's armed forces were the largest and best equipped in the Middle East. But Iraq was far from having nuclear weapons and would face practical difficulties in using its germ and poison gas weapons. Had

36. Lawrence Freedman and Efraim Karsh, *The Gulf Conflict, 1990–1991: Diplomacy and War in the New World Order* (Princeton, N.J.: Princeton University Press, 1993), 52–55.

37. What is now Iraq had been three provinces of the Ottoman Empire until 1920 and then a British Mandate under the League of Nations until Iraq became independent in 1932. Kuwait formally belonged to the Ottoman Empire too, but—at the request of the ruling family—became a British protectorate from 1897 until 1961. Iraq then tried to annex newly independent Kuwait but was prevented by British troops.

HOW THE GULF WAR UNFOLDED

1980–1988

Iraq fights Iran

1981

Israeli bombs destroy Iraqi nuclear plant

1990

July

Iraq accuses Kuwait and United Arab Emirates of conspiring with "imperialists" and "Zionists" to keep oil prices low

7/23–25

Iraq masses troops on Kuwait border

7/25

U.S. Ambassador April Glaspie conciliates Hussein

8/2–3

Iraq occupies Kuwait and oil prices double

8/6

UN Security Council imposes sanctions on Iraq

11/29

UN Security Council authorizes UN coalition forces in the Persian Gulf to use "all necessary means" to expel Iraq from Kuwait

1991

1/12

U.S. Congress authorizes "all means necessary" to expel Iraq

1/17

Coalition air attacks begin on Baghdad and on Iraqi troops

2/24

Coalition forces advance on the ground

2/27

Washington orders a cease-fire, to start the following day

38. The number of Iraqi soldiers killed was probably about 1,500 and no more than 10,000; Iraqi civilians, about 1,000. John G. Heidenrich, "The Gulf War: How Many Iraqis Died?" *Foreign Policy* 90 (spring 1993): 108–125.

39. The Chairman of the Joint Chiefs of Staff, General Colin Powell, had never favored the war and jumped at an excuse to suspend operations. See Michael R. Gordon and Bernard E. Trainor, *The Generals' War* (Boston: Little, Brown, 1995). For essays on "After the Gulf War," see *International Journal* 49, no. 2 (spring 1994).

Baghdad possessed a credible weapon of mass destruction, the United Nations might have been less ready to drive Iraq from Kuwait.

As in 1950, the UN Security Council endorsed actions favored by the U.S. In 1990–1991, however, the USSR was never absent and voted with the majority on every issue. Only Albania and Cuba opposed the majority; China sometimes abstained.

As detailed in Chapter 15, the UN Security Council immediately denounced Baghdad's action and imposed sanctions against Iraq to cut off its oil revenues. Iraq did not budge. After the Security Council and U.S. Congress authorized "all necessary measures" to expel Iraq, a U.S.-led coalition attacked Iraqi forces in January–February 1991. Allied planes waged an air war for five weeks before launching a ground attack.[38] Advised that Iraq had been driven from Kuwait, President Bush ordered an end to the ground war after just one hundred hours. Retreating Iraqis set six hundred Kuwaiti oil wells ablaze, wasting a valuable asset and devastating the fragile Persian Gulf environment.[39] The military operations are outlined in Map 4.3.

Expecting Hussein to fall soon, Secretary of State James Baker wanted

The biosphere sustains and suffers from war. Some 950 Kuwaiti oil wells were damaged or set ablaze by Iraqi forces as they retreated in early 1991, poisoning the air and waters of the Persian Gulf region and impeding Kuwait's economic recovery—estimated to cost more than $100 billion.

Map 4.3 The Gulf War

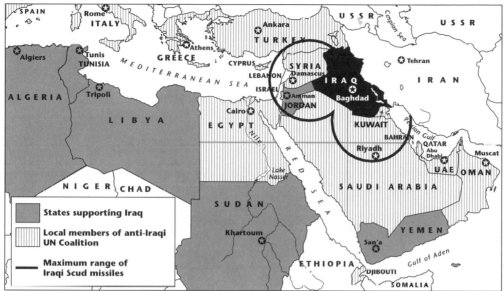

to include a post-Hussein Iraq in efforts to construct a more stable region. Baker told Congress in February 1991: "The time for reconstruction and recovery should not be the occasion for vengeful actions against a nation forced to war as a result of a dictator's ambition." Baker's vision for the Middle East resembled the U.S. policies that integrated Western Europe after World War II. But the Arab states backed away from a peacekeeping force and President Bush opposed any scheme to finance Iraq's reconstruction.[40]

The 1991 Gulf campaign represented another qualified victory for collective security. As in Korea, however, the egomaniacal dictator remained. His troops massed again near Kuwait in 1994, pulled back only after the U.S. again sent a large force to the region. Hussein complied with many UN demands, but not all. The UN Security Council blocked Iraq from selling oil so long as it concealed facilities for making mass destruction weapons. Without oil revenues, Iraq could not import food and medicines. This meant malnutrition and disease for the masses while Hussein's entourage got richer by manipulating the black market. The UN eventually permitted Iraq to sell some oil to generate money for food and medicine, but Saddam Hussein wanted all sanctions lifted. Here was grist for another "just war" debate: Was it right—was it *just*—to keep pressure on a brutal dictator if the principal victims were his hapless subjects?

40. James A. Baker, III, *The Politics of Diplomacy: Revolution, War & Peace, 1989–1992* (New York: G. P. Putnam's, 1995), 411–415.

WHAT PROPOSITIONS HOLD?
WHAT QUESTIONS REMAIN?

IS WAR A RATIONAL TOOL OF FOREIGN POLICY?

Has war been a rational tool of foreign policy in the 20th century? The answer is seldom, if ever.[41] No war that we have examined was launched after a systematic study of the alternatives, along with their likely gains and losses. To be sure, the top leaders and their advisers talked as though they had analyzed everything, but their analysis was usually slanted to favor a decision already made—often for reasons extraneous to the war.[42]

Judging by the results, all the aggressors erred. All were defeated, after large losses.

Contrary to what neorealists expect, neither the decision to fight nor the outcome of war can be dependably predicted. The structure of power does not foretell who will fight or who will win. It does not forecast skill or morale or the role of accidents, luck, and friction.

Has it been wise to resist aggression? In some cases, yes; in others, the reply is not so clear. To answer we must weigh the cost of submitting to a conqueror versus the cost of resisting. Those who resisted Germany in World Wars I and II "won," but for many the price was dreadfully high. Submission to Hitler would have been much more horrific than to Wilhelm's Reich. But was it worthwhile for Soviet citizens to drive back Hitler at the price of 25 to 40 million Soviet lives—and then continue to be ruled by Stalin? Poles fought Nazi invaders; Czechs did not. Poles lost far more lives, but gained more self-respect. Which course was better? Both Poles and Czechs soon fell into Stalin's empire.

Only the U.S. escaped from the world wars with relatively few casualties and a stronger power position. The U.S. also gained stature from its role in driving back North Korea and Iraq. But U.S. social cohesion and prestige suffered greatly from the attempt to stop Communism in Indochina.

The bottom line is that it has generally been more rational, as well as just, to resist than to attack. But expected victory is neither a necessary nor a sufficient condition to fight.

Has it been rational to fight for national liberation? The U.S. war of independence from Great Britain cost fewer than 5,000 American combat deaths. Almost two centuries later, however, some three million Vietnamese died fighting to drive out foreign forces and unify Vietnam. Hanoi's leaders thought the price worthwhile. But not every struggle for

41. One possible exception was the 1967 Israeli attack meant to pre-empt an Egyptian attack on Israel.

42. See, for example, Mao Zedong's telegrams quoted in the appendices to Christensen, *Useful Adversaries*.

Was it "burden sharing" or "tin cup diplomacy"? Interested governments—Germany, Japan, Saudi Arabia, Kuwait—reimbursed the U.S. about $54 billion for the Gulf War effort whose direct costs to the U.S. ran to $40–45 billion. But indirect and long-term costs for medical and other veterans' benefits far exceeded the differential.

liberation succeeds. Afghans drove out a superpower but then fell to fighting among themselves.

CONFLICT AND MUTUAL GAIN

The bad news is that history, as Edward Gibbon noted, is the record of the follies, crimes, and inhumanities of man to man. The good news is that none of the wars studied in this chapter was inevitable. Each war resulted from pursuit of one-sided gain.

The wars begun in 1914, 1939, 1950, and 1990 flowed from the aggressor's myopic greed for more resources, glory, or influence. None explored or rationally pursued its deepest interests. Almost any negotiated revision of existing arrangements—or just maintaining the status quo—would have benefited the challengers more than war.

HOW DO WARS BEGIN? HOW LEVELS INTERTWINE

Individual Leaders: "Bundles of Mysteries"

As we saw in the 1962 missile crisis, it matters who is at the helm. Most leaders who authorized or ordered the first shots in the wars we have studied had an ego so large that it blocked the light. Each gave in to wishful thinking, pride, and a lust for power. Each suffered a failure of imagination.[43] Most expected a quick victory and substantial gains at a reason-

43. Adapted from Kagan's verdict in *The Outbreak of the Peloponnesian War*, 356.

able price. Few considered the consequences of miscalculation or the ruin that war could engender. Hitler persuaded his generals to attack the USSR without outfitting the troops for winter weather.

Aggressive tendencies are stronger in some persons than others. Some kings and presidents fight when others keep talking or walk away. Why these differences? How individuals respond to challenges depends heavily upon personal make-up. Both Hitler and Hussein, for example, seemed to love violence and war. Stalin was sadistic, but cautious about risk-taking abroad.

Do the more aggressive personalities seek to compensate for physical or emotional slights? Wilhelm II had a withered arm; Hitler, just one testicle; Stalin, a pock-marked face; Johnson, anxieties about his ability to fill Kennedy's shoes. But real or imagined shortcomings need not produce aggressive behavior. Three U.S. presidents in our cases—Wilson, Roosevelt, and Kennedy—suffered from severe physical disabilities, but each sought to avoid a major war. Individuals are crucial, but the psyche remains a bundle of mysteries.

The State: Aggressive Dictatorships

The most powerful explanation of war-proneness is domestic constitution. Dictatorships started and lost all the 20th century's major wars. They also committed **demicide**—mass murder of their own people (*demos*). By contrast, as we shall see in Chapter 10, established democracies have seldom, if ever, fought other democracies or exterminated their own citizens. They have, however, often resisted dictatorships and attacked national liberation movements.

Did any of the aggressors we have studied behave like a rational monolith bent on maximizing power? The answer is no. If these regimes calculated, they miscalculated.

Except for 1914, bureaucracies usually influenced how rather than whether a war was fought. Industrialists never called the shots in the century's wars even if some pressed for arms buildups.

Partisan politics played little role in initiating the wars we have studied. No aggressors started a war to divert the public from domestic problems.[44] Wars helped produce modern states but were not needed to sustain them.

None of our wars resulted from imperialist pressures like those expected by disciples of Karl Marx and Vladimir Lenin. Capitalist states did not fight one another for markets or resources. Strategic or ideological

44. See Jack S. Levy, "Domestic Politics and War," *Journal of Interdisciplinary History* 18, no. 4 (spring 1988): 653–673.

concerns far outweighed economic in the U.S. and Soviet forays into Indochina and Afghanistan.

Clashes between civilizations helped evoke hostility, but caused no major wars. Often one culture fought its supposed soul mates or allied with a rival culture. "Western" France and England allied with "Eastern" Serbia and Russia against "Western" Germany in two world wars. Shinto-Buddhist Japan attacked the West in the 1940s but soon after allied with the leading Western power. In short, power political interests predicted alignments better than civilizational unity.

The International Balance of Power

No Formula for Stability. Major wars took place in spite of—or perhaps due to—various power balances often touted as keys to peace. Blends of loose bipolarity and multipolarity did not prevent World War I or II. Tight Soviet-U.S. bipolarity yielded no world wars but allowed and perhaps encouraged localized wars such as in Korea and Vietnam. Unipolarity did not prevent the Gulf War or the Balkan wars of the 1990s (discussed in Chapter 8 and 9).

Neither equality nor superiority ensures stability, for each order, each balance, will be challenged by expansionist regimes; by new weapons and military tactics; by new, crusading ideologies; by intervention of actors outside the system; and by the disappearance of smaller states crucial to the balance. The only structure without war has been the unit-veto: None of the countries with nuclear arms has yet attacked another.

Whatever the balance, war becomes more likely if the status quo states show no capacity or will to curb aggression. In World Wars I and II, Korea, and the Gulf War, the combined defenders were stronger than the challengers. Washington's weight was always decisive, but the U.S. failed to warn Wilhelm, Hitler, Kim, or Hussein that it would fight aggression. (Mere words, of course, may not suffice: Khrushchev sloughed off U.S. warnings not to deploy offensive weapons in Cuba.)

No foreign policy method can assure peace, but the most promising approach has been conditional cooperation to promote peaceful change. Win-lose hard-liners started four of the century's major wars. Many of those who hoped to avoid the flames—win-win cooperators, stand-patters, and isolationists—were pulled into the fire.

Power Shifts Need Not Produce War. The evidence for power transition theory is weak. World War I started over Austrian greed and Russian honor in the Balkans—not over Germany's drive to overthrow Britain's

Table 4.8 Alternative Responses to Power Transitions

Underlying Condition		Policy Response
Strength	**Weakness**	**Policy Response**
U.S. in 1898; USSR in 1970s	Austria-Hungary and Russia in 1914	Militant expansionism
U.S. in 1919	U.S. in 1970s	Isolationisim
U.S. in 1945 and 1990	USSR in 1930s and late 1980s	Support for collective security

hegemony. In the late 1930s, however, Hitler hoped to overthrow the existing order before his foes geared up to fight. Similarly, Tokyo in 1941 decided to strike the U.S. fleet before Japanese supplies diminished and the U.S. got stronger.[45] Washington intervened in Indochina and Moscow in Afghanistan to prevent expansion by their global rivals.

Power transition theory does not explain the Korean, Gulf, or Balkan wars. Neither Kim Il-sung in 1950 nor Saddam Hussein in 1990 nor Serbian President Slobodan Milosevič in the mid-1990s aspired to displace a hegemon. They hoped rather to defeat weak targets.

The evidence shows that an improving or worsening power base can lead to a variety of policies—militant expansionism, restraint, or pursuit of collective security, as outlined in Table 4.8.

Where power transition theory could have been truly relevant—the rapid demise of the Soviet empire—it utterly failed: The Second World went down in 1989–1991 not with a bang but a few whimpers. Thus, there is nothing predetermined about the ways that nations respond to shifts in the balance of power. Leaders have choices.

45. In 1941 Japanese strategists reached a consensus: "Now! The time for war will not come later." Michael A. Barnhart, *Japan Prepares for Total War: The Search for Economic Security, 1919–1941* (Ithaca, N.Y.: Cornell University Press, 1987), 258.

What to Tell the President.... Is war obsolete? Now that you are ready to share your conclusions with the the commander-in-chief, you draft the following memo: For thousands of years, war held the potential for profit. It could bring more land for farmers, more glory or wealth for kings. But the Industrial and Information Revolutions changed the calculus. Raw materials can be obtained by trade or replaced more cheaply than by war. A growing moral consensus sees occupation of conquered territory as illegitimate. Weapons are unprecedentedly dangerous.[46]

46. Carl Kaysen, "Is War Obsolete? A Review Essay," *International Security* 14, no. 4 (spring 1990): 42–64. The article reviews John Mueller, *Retreat from Doomsday: The Obsolescence of Major War* (New York: Basic Books, 1989), and other works.

Still, such conditions do not guarantee peace: Neither deep vulnerability nor shared values sufficed to prevent the American Civil War or World War I. Instead, admixtures of emotion laced with calculation or miscalculation seem to trigger one war after another.

Perhaps war should be obsolete, but it is not. Governments may still hope to fight short, decisive wars that win solid gains. Or a crazed leader, expecting defeat, may decide to pull down the roof and evoke universal disaster. War will be harder to eliminate than dueling or slavery. Incentives for war arise from individual personalities, societal pressures, uncertain power balances, and shrinking resources. If just one government opts for conquest, the others must resist or submit. For war to disappear, all governments—for all time and with no exceptions—would have to accept that it cannot be profitable

Individuals and societies will forgo violence only if the prospects of resistance are strong or if their interests can be better advanced under conditions of peace. Thus, the ancient Romans captured part of the truth when they said: "If you want peace, prepare for war."

Conclusion: We continue to need a substantial military establishment. The foundation of our security, however, is not just military strength but overall fitness—a topic addressed in my next memo.

KEY NAMES AND TERMS

balance of power	economic warfare	nonviolent sanctions	strategic weapons
Blitzkrieg	entente	polarity (uni-, bi-, multi-)	strategy
buck-passing	escalation ladder	police action (UN)	Sunni Islam
chain-ganging	falling dominoes theory	power transition theory	tactics
Carl von Clausewitz	Gulf of Tonkin Resolution	pre-emptive strike	Triple Alliance
cold war	hegemonic war	preventive war	Triple Entente
conventional war	Saddam Hussein	proxy wars	unconventional war
cult of the defensive	Kim Il-sung	psychological warfare	war
cult of the offensive	Maginot Line	Pyongyang	War Powers Resolution
demicide	Mao Zedong	Shiite Islam	
détente	MOOTW	strategic doctrine	

QUESTIONS TO DISCUSS

1. Is war rational if it brings destruction to one's own people?
2. If we knew precisely who had what forces, could wars be fought out on computer screens and actual combat be avoided?
3. Which action level was most important in bringing on World War I and World War II? The wars in Korea, Vietnam, Afghanistan, and the Persian Gulf?
4. Do personal frailties incline leaders toward or away from war?
5. Which balance of power, if any, is most conducive to peace?
6. Can weapons of mass destruction make war obsolete?
7. How did U.S. participation in the Vietnam War resemble Soviet intervention in Afghanistan? How did it differ?
8. As the heir to Saddam Hussein's presidency, you still want to annex Kuwait. How should you go about it? What are the optimal conditions for you to act?
9. Using the framework of Tables 4.2–4.7, outline the possible causes of another war. Which level proved decisive?
10. Was it right to keep sanctions on Iraq if they hurt ordinary people rather than the rulers?

RECOMMENDED RESOURCES

BOOKS

Clausewitz, Carl von. *On War*. Princeton, N.J.: Princeton University Press, 1984.

Freedman, Lawrence, ed. *War*. New York: Oxford University Press, 1994.

Gilpin, Robert. *War and Change in World Politics*. Cambridge: Cambridge University Press, 1981.

Holmes, Robert L., ed. *Nonviolence in Theory and Practice*. Belmont, Calif.: Wadsworth, 1990.

Howard, Michael. *The Causes of War*. 2d ed. Cambridge, Mass.: Harvard University Press, 1989.

Institute for National Strategic Studies. *Strategic Assessment*. Washington, D.C.: Government Printing Office, 1995–.

International Institute for Strategic Studies (IISS). *The Military Balance*. London, annual.

Levy, Jack S. *War in the Modern Great Power System, 1495–1975*. Lexington: University Press of Kentucky, 1983.

Khalilzad, Zalmay M., and David A. Ochmanek, eds. *Strategic Appraisal 1997: Strategy and Defense Planning for the 21st Century*. Santa Monica, Calif.: RAND, 1997.

Sawyer, Ralph D., trans. *Seven Military Classics of Ancient China*. Boulder, Colo.: Westview, 1993.

Schelling, Thomas C. *Arms and Influence*. New Haven, Conn.: Yale University Press, 1966.

Sivard, Ruth Leger. *World Military and Social Expenditures*. Washington, D.C.: World Priorities, annual.

Small, Melvin, and J. David Singer. *Resort to Arms: International and Civil Wars, 1816–1980*. Beverly Hills, Calif.: Sage, 1982.

Snyder, Jack. *Myths of Empire: Domestic Politics and International Ambition*. Ithaca, N.Y.: Cornell University Press, 1991.

Stockholm International Peace Research Institute. *World Armaments and Disarmament*. Stockholm: SIPRI, annual.

Stoessinger, John G. *Why Nations Go to War*. 7th ed. New York: St. Martin's, 1997.

Tilly, Charles. *Coercion, Capital, and European States, AD 900–1990*. Cambridge, Mass.: Basil Blackwell, 1990.

U.S. Department of Defense. *Annual Report to Congress* [title varies].

Vasquez, John A., and Marie T. Henehan. *The Scientific Study of Peace and War: A Text Reader*. New York: Lexington Books, 1992.

Waltz, Kenneth N. *Man, the State, and War: A Theoretical Analysis*. New York: Columbia University Press, 1960.

Walzer, Michael. *Just and Unjust Wars*. 2d ed. New York: Basic Books, 1992.

JOURNALS

Adelphi Papers

International Security

Journal of Conflict Resolution

Journal of Peace Research

Journal of Strategic Studies

Strategic Survey

Survival

WEB SITES

Afghanistan
    http://enterprise.aacc.cc.md.us/~haq/
General Military History
    http://www.cfcsc.dnd.ca/links/milhist/index.html
Gulf War
    http://www.cfcsc.dnd.ca:80/links/milhist/gw.html
Korea
    http://www.cfcsc.dnd.ca:80/links/milhist/korea.html
Vietnam
    http://www.cfcsc.dnd.ca:80/links/milhist/viet.html
    http://jefferson.village.virginia.edu/sixties/HTML_
        docs/Bibliographies/VN_on_TV/VN_on_TV_01.html
    http://acs.oakton.edu/~wittman/
World War I
    http://www.cfcsc.dnd.ca:80/links/milhist/wwi.html
World War II
    http://www.cfcsc.dnd.ca:80/links/milhist/wwii.html

C H A P T E R   F I V E

POWER AND INFLUENCE: WHAT WINS?

"How Should We Use Our Assets?" ... *You are one of the wise men and women whom presidents seek out for their view of the big picture. Seeing the rapid changes confronting the nation on every front, the President asks you to advise her: "How should we allocate our resources to help the country become more fit, more secure, more influential?"*

The President details her concerns: "Great Britain had the world's largest empire. Britain survived but never recovered from World War I. The USSR was a superpower, but its empire fell apart after the Afghan campaign. While the superpowers engaged in cold and hot war, Japan surpassed the USSR and became the world's second largest economy. The U.S. bounced back after defeat in Vietnam, but now faces severe challenges at home and abroad. China is rising. Europe is uniting.

"U.S. material power is unmatched, but more of our babies die than in most other industrialized countries. Our scientists win a majority of Nobel prizes, but our kids do worse in school than those in Hong Kong or Germany.

"Why do we and other states spend so much money on the tools of death and destruction when we lack funds for better roads and schools? To be influential in world affairs, shouldn't we rely less on military power and more on commerce, science, and diplomacy?

"Why doesn't our influence better reflect our military and economic power? Our closest partners go their own ways. Even countries we aid spurn our recommendations. We opened our markets to China, but Beijing did little to reciprocate.

"To raise America's fitness, must others' well-being decline? Or can all peoples climb together?"

As usual, the President probes deeply. You promise her to survey the debate on what it means to be fit, to analyze how power translates into fitness and influence, and to outline the nature and distribution of power at the onset of another millennium.

CONTENDING CONCEPTS
AND EXPLANATIONS

HOW TO BE FIT—RUGGED INDIVIDUALISM
OR MUTUAL AID?

You begin by reviewing the concept of **fitness**.[1] The theory of evolution teaches that the fittest organisms and species pass on their genes. By analogy, a fit society is one able to enhance and pass on its way of life. For organisms and for societies, fitness may be thought of as an ability to cope with complexity—to survive challenges and make the most of opportunity.

In the late 19th century Social Darwinists taught that the fittest survive thanks to rugged individualism. Imperialists agreed that strong races should rule the weak: "Might makes right." Other analysts of evolution opposed this view, arguing that fitness depends heavily upon mutual aid and adaptation: The species that cooperate among themselves and harmonize with their habitat have the best prospects to flourish.[2] Egotistical self-seeking (like the logic of collective action discussed in Chapter 1) can backfire. Many societies decline when members fail to pool their strengths for the common good.

A society that does not utilize the potential of all its members weakens its fitness. Discrimination against women, ethnic minorities, regions, or other groupings undermines total capabilities. A society that fails to support its frailest members cannot tap the genius, for example, of a Stephen Hawking, the physically disabled but brilliant holder of Newton's chair at Cambridge University.

A society at peace with itself, whose members believe their society just, is more likely to be fit than one roiled by internal strife or one where repression achieves only a negative peace. Positive peace (discussed in Chapter 2) helps fitness.

Table 5.1 Who Is Fittest?

View of Human Evolution and IR	Survival Depends On
Social Darwinism and *realpolitik*	Individual strength in a mutual struggle for survival
Mutual help and interdependence	Ability of group to cooperate and adapt for mutual gain

1. For background, see *International Studies Quarterly* [special issue: Evolutionary Paradigms in the Social Sciences] 40, no. 3 (September 1996); for applications and an extensive bibliography, see Joshua M. Epstein and Robert Axtell, *Growing Artificial Societies: Social Science from the Bottom Up* (Cambridge, Mass.: MIT Press, 1996).

2. See Thomas Huxley, "The Struggle for Existence" (1888), and the reply by Petr Kropotkin, *Mutual Aid* (1902), both published in Kropotkin, *Mutual Aid: A Factor of Evolution* (Boston: Extending Horizons Books, 1955); see also Kropotkin, *Ethics, Origin and Development* (New York: Dial Press, 1924).

Table 5.2 Infant Mortality Among Rich and Poor, Selected Years

	1960	1991	1994
Industrial countries	35	14	14
Developing countries	149	71	64
Least developed countries	170	114	103

SOURCE: United Nations Development Programme, *Human Development Report* [*HDR*] *1993* (New York: Oxford University Press, 1993), 143; and *HDR 1997* (1997), 175.

NOTE: Figures are deaths per 1,000 live births in first year.

Internal Fitness

One measure of fitness is **infant mortality**. The fewer babies that die in their first year, the fitter the society. Infant mortality reflects other fitness factors such as education and access to social services. Infant mortality declined worldwide in the late 20th century, but remained far higher in most poor countries than in rich, as shown in Table 5.2.

A broader indicator of fitness is the **human development index (HDI)** designed by the United Nations Development Programme to measure health, education, and income. Since HDI rankings are often skewed by gender, the UN Development Programme developed indexes to measure differences between the sexes in HDI and in political participation.[3]

Some Measures of Internal Fitness

GDP—gross domestic product is the value of all goods and services produced in the country, usually stated in U.S. dollars

GDP per capita—average income (omits discrepancies among classes)

PPP—purchasing power parity is the number of units in a local currency (say, Swiss Francs) needed to purchase the same basket of goods and services that a U.S. dollar would purchase in the U.S. Switzerland, with a strong currency relative to the dollar, has a lower PPP than its GDP measured by official currency exchange rates; India, with a weak currency, has a higher PPP than GDP.

Real GDP per capita—PPP per capita, measured in the purchasing power of the local currency; also expressed in **BMT** (Big Mac Time), the number of minutes the average worker has to work to buy a Big Mac. In 1997 the numbers were as follows: Houston and Tokyo, 9; Hong Kong, 11; Toronto and New York, 12; Montreal and Zurich, 14; Copenhagen and Taipei, 20; Prague, 56; Mexico City, 71; Bombay, 85; Budapest, 91; Jakarta, 103; Moscow, 104; Caracas, 117; Nairobi, 193 (calculations by the Union Bank of Switzerland).

HDI—the human development index is based on three measures: life expectancy, educational attainment (adult literacy and combined primary, secondary, and tertiary enrollment), and PPP per capita

HPI—the human poverty index measures poverty within a country based on percentages of people expected to die before age 40, illiterate adults, people without access to health service and safe water, and underweight children under age 5

GDI—the gender-related development index is the HDI adjusted for gender

GEM—the gender empowerment measure shows economic and political participation by gender

There are many other possible measures of fitness—for example, low crime and inflation rates. Even very fit societies have shortfalls. Most Canadians live well, but many French-speakers and "First Nations" (Native Americans) assert that they are deprived. Japan and Sweden have low homicide but high suicide rates. Thanks to high life expectancy and education, countries such as Costa Rica, Belize, Cuba, and Sri Lanka rank high on the HDI even though their per capita incomes are modest. From limited economic resources they invest heavily in health and education.

Internal fitness also requires a strong life support system. Harvesting

3. See its *Human Development Report* [*HDR*] (New York: Oxford University Press, annual).

Demilitarized and democratic, Costa Rica has achieved a high level of fitness relative to other Central American countries. In the 1990s Costa Rica's former president, Oscar Arias Sanchez (above), lobbied other governments in the region to disband their armies and concentrate on internal development.

trees on hillsides may produce good income this year but cause serious losses in the future. Environmental accounting, based on satellite surveys, suggests that in many countries the value of wealth lost in the 1990s (for example, topsoil) exceeds that of wealth produced. Quality as well as quantity is at stake: Japanese and Americans replant trees on many hillsides, but the new growth often lacks biodiversity.

To evaluate a country's internal fitness is not easy. To do so it is necessary to review many variables and how they interact.

External Fitness

Fitness in foreign relations requires an ability to defend a society against external threats while preserving its way of life. External fitness depends upon internal fitness and vice versa. But there is no set formula for overall fitness. Both Costa Rica and Sweden, for example, demonstrate high domestic fitness. Each country has invested heavily in social welfare and has long avoided foreign wars. Costa Rica, however, spends almost nothing on defense, while Sweden spends heavily for military preparedness. Low defense expenditures do not assure domestic fitness, but neither do high defense outlays preclude it.

International System Fitness

The fitness of an international system can also be evaluated by its capacity to sustain life and help its members fulfill their potential. The first

Fig. 5.1 Exploitation, Mutual Gain, and Fitness: Likely Linkages

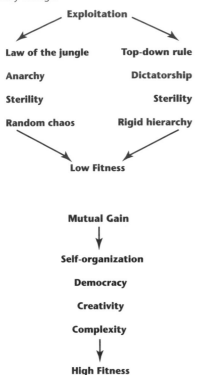

half of the 20th century witnessed unprecedented destruction. In the second half, however, there were no world wars, the number of humans increased, and their HDI ranking improved. Political participation became broader, for females as well as males. Every state—nearly two hundred by the late 1990s—had an equal vote in the UN General Assembly. While some trends were positive, others were not. Many analysts worried that humans would exhaust their life support system, the biosphere.

Coevolution: The Rise and Fall of Fitness Landscapes

What we call evolution is really **coevolution**. Every species and society coevolves with other species and their shared environment. Fitness can be assessed only in relative terms—relative to that of other actors and to a changing life support system. Survival depends upon internal mutation in tandem with a changing environment.

A fit society thrives on complexity, just as marine life teems on the cusp of the steep slope that leads from shallow, warm waters toward the cold currents of the depths.[4] A very fit society can adapt to challenges—from drought and disease to hostile neighbors; a less fit society will cope poorly with domestic and external problems. Fit societies can process information efficiently and create values. These societies take hold and flourish in a life zone between unstable, random movement and ultrastable, rigid hierarchy.

A fit society finds resilience in a combination of many strengths coevolved to deal with a changing environment. Like a coral reef, its diverse members benefit from their interdependence. They exist in a symbiosis that nourishes individuals and shields the community from surging currents, extremes of cold and heat, and predators. In this kind of emergent structure everything is both a means and an end.[5] The society becomes self-organizing—in political terms, it has self-rule (democracy). Mutual gain produces and benefits from such complexity, as outlined in Figure 5.1.

Like the species coexisting within an ecosystem, human communities—locally or globally—may cultivate a fitness that gives stability to their way of life. Mutual gain may result from each member doing what it does best, as though guided by an "invisible hand."[6] But it can also flow from wise, far-sighted policies. Either way, fitness benefits from cooperation. By this logic, we should not be surprised that the U.S. and Swiss constitutions are among the world's oldest. Less fit systems have come and gone. In political life as in business, long-term fitness and "profit" come from creating value—not from exploitation.

4. On coevolution and complexity, see Stuart A. Kauffman, *The Origins of Order: Self-Organization and Selection in Evolution* (New York: Oxford University Press, 1993); Charles J. Lumsden and Edward O. Wilson, *Genes, Mind, and Culture: The Coevolutionary Process* (Cambridge, Mass.: Harvard University Press, 1981); Martin A. Nowak et al., "The Arithmetics of Mutual Help," *Scientific American,* June 1995, 76–81; and Roger Lewin, *Complexity: Life at the Edge of Chaos* (New York: Macmillan, 1992). For a skeptical view of Kauffman and Lumsden and Wilson, see John Horgan, *The End of Science: Facing the Limits of Knowledge in the Twilight of the Scientific Age* (Reading, Mass.: Addison-Wesley, 1996), chaps. 5–9. For a more balanced appraisal, see "Edge of Chaos" and other relevant entries in Ian Marshall and Danah Zohar, *Who's Afraid of Schrödinger's Cat: All the Science Ideas You Need to Keep Up with the New Thinking* (New York: Morrow, 1997).

5. Society is more than a mechanical device in which the parts exist only for one another, but is less than an organism in which the parts exist for one another and by means of one another.

6. Adam Smith's term, in *The Wealth of Nations* (1776), discussed in Chapter 11.

We can picture fitness as a peak rising from a plain.[7] If A is a truly fit society, its peak will tower like the Matterhorn; if B is an unfit society, its "peak" will be a low mound. If B becomes more fit, its mound will rise. Each actor's peak, however, reflects external security as well as internal health. If A's peak rises in ways threatening to B, the latter's fitness may suffer and its peak decline. But if actors cooperate for mutual gain, each of their peaks may rise. Free trade among Mexico, Canada, and the U.S. seeks to push all three North American peaks upward.[8]

HOW DOES POWER RELATE TO FITNESS AND TO INFLUENCE?

Fitness and power can build upon one another. **Power** includes basic resources, economic strength, political cohesion, military strength, brain power, culture, and alignment with international institutions. If well used, these assets contribute to fitness at home and abroad.

Power is the *potential* to actualize—to get things done, to claim or create values, to be fit and to influence others.[9] Unless power is used effectively, it will not enhance fitness or influence.

Power assets differ in their **fungibility**—the extent to which they can be interchanged with other assets. For Christopher Columbus, spices and gold were highly fungible; in today's markets, dollars and yen are more useful. One of the most fungible assets is information.

To actualize power—make real its potential—it must pass from the latent stage, through the mobilized or developed stage, and into the kinetic stage. **Kinetic power** is power in motion. Table 5.3 illustrates how different kinds of power transit these three stages.

Power is not the same as **influence**. Power is potential. Power can be a

Table 5.3 Three Stages of Power Realization

Domain	Stage 1: Latent	Stage 2: Developed and Mobilized	Stage 3: Kinetic
Agriculture	fertile soil	cultivated fields	harvested grain being eaten
Minerals	oil deposits	oil being pumped and refined	fuel being converted to energy
Communications	power lines	PC modems connected to a network	Internet operating online
Military	available recruits	soldiers trained and ready to move	soldiers attacking

7. On the structure of rugged fitness landscapes, see Kauffman, *Origins of Order*, chaps. 2–3.

8. If a landscape is too smooth or too rugged, its occupants may fail to achieve their full potential. This concept of fitness echoes the theory of Arnold Toynbee that civilizations rise and fall in response to an optimum or an excessive challenge. See Toynbee, *A Study of History*, 12 vols. (New York: Oxford University Press, 1934–1961).

9. From Latin *potentia* we get "potential," "potent," and "power"—similar to French *pouvoir*. "Might" in English corresponds to *macht* in German and *moshchnost'* (capability) in Russian. "Dynamics"—that which makes something move—probably derives from the Indo-European *deu*, which also gives us "do."

Who or What Influenced Whom?

In 1993 Venezuela staked out activist positions in support of Bosnia. Working with Pakistan and several other non-aligned delegations on the UN Security Council, Venezuela pushed through resolutions 819 and 824 establishing "safe areas" in Bosnia. Venezuela also campaigned, unsuccessfully, for lifting the arms embargo against Bosnia. The U.S. in the next two years became much more active in support of Bosnia. Who or what influenced whom? Did Venezuela influence the U.S. or did Washington listen to its own drummer?

These questions imply that countries or governments influence one another. We should also look at individuals. Venezuela's permanent representative to the United Nations, Diego Arria, had strong views and a persuasive manner. If another person had represented Venezuela, its UN delegation might have been less supportive of Bosnia.

10. See, for example, Russell J. Leng, "Influence Techniques Among Nations," in *Behavior, Society, and International Conflict*, 3 vols., ed. Philip E. Tetlock et al. (New York: Oxford University Press, 1991–1993), 3: 71–125.

11. Adapted from Joseph S. Nye, Jr., *Bound to Lead: The Changing Nature of American Power* (New York: Basic Books, 1990).

12. See Nurit Kliot and Stanley Waterman, eds., *The Political Geography of Conflict and Peace* (London: Belhaven Press, 1991); Martin Ira Glassner, *Political Geography* (New York: Wiley, 1993); and Saul B. Cohen, *Geography and Politics in a World Divided*, 2d ed. (New York: Oxford University Press, 1973).

cause. Influence is an effect. To influence others is to sway their minds and affect their behavior. Influence is difficult to measure. A behavioral measure of influence would show the extent to which the U.S., for example, can alter the behavior of Mexico and Venezuela. We might review how often these countries voted with the U.S. at the United Nations. But more study would be needed to learn whether Mexico City and Caracas voted as they did for their own reasons or in response to pressure from Washington—or vice versa.

States and other IR actors try to influence one another using a wide range of instruments and techniques.[10] They negotiate using "hard" and "soft" power. **Hard power** is the ability to coerce others (by force) and command (by threat). Hard power uses mainly tangible assets, such as military, economic, and geographic resources, but can also employ intangibles, such as scarce information. **Soft power** is the ability to inspire consensus (agreement) and to coopt (persuade others to share the same goals). **Conversion power** is the ability to translate hard and soft power into fitness and influence.[11]

A hard-liner seeks influence by coercion and command, often supplemented by deception. Gains from this approach are unstable, however, because exploitation provokes resistance; deception, when discovered, yields a boomerang effect. Both the win-win and the conditional cooperator seek consensus and cooption. If they succeed, cooperation may become a stable, emergent property—a "security community" like that evolved from the Marshall Plan. The conditional cooperator, however, may also use hard power if cooperation fails.

The simplest method to measure power is the **bean count**—summing and comparing assets such as people, rifles, and PCs. The bean count, even if accurate, leaves open many vital questions: What is the quality of the asset being counted? Its availability? Location? Can it be replaced?

Let us analyze some key ingredients of power and examine the debates about how to assess each factor.

Basic Resources. A country's physical setting—its location, climate, size, shape, and resources—provides a foundation for its economic and political life. How physical spaces relate to politics is the focus of political geography.[12]

Is there an ideal physical space? Humans can prosper in many settings. Great states have been anchored to rivers (Babylon, Egypt), islands (Crete, Java), deserts (Arabia, the Silk Road), jungles (Yucatán, Cambodia), as well as to temperate climes (Europe, North America). Size is not critical. Small city-states (ancient Athens, medieval Venice, today's Singapore) have achieved power and influence, but so have medium-sized states (Germany) and large empires (Mongolia). Raw materials are not essential if they can be imported or substituted by technology. Holland, England, and Japan became prosperous without a rich resource base. The same resource can be both a plus and a liability. Thus, China's large population assures a large supply of workers for every task, but they must be fed and housed on limited land.

The IR student and diplomat must not only know political geography, but must also be able to distinguish fact from myth. Today's geopolitical certainty often becomes tomorrow's absurdity. Analysts may lapse into "environmental determinism": They exaggerate the role of a physical restraint or the weight of a single factor such as oil or weather. Geopolitical thinking can also be twisted by self-centered ambition. For example, ancient Chinese saw their "Middle Kingdom" as the hub of the universe. Similarly, most U.S. maps show the Americas at the center of the world. Like statistics, maps are selective. They can illuminate or mislead.[13]

How geography conditions IR is sometimes called **geopolitics**. Soviet and U.S. leaders often justified their Cold War policies by reference to political geography—for example, to the importance of controlling the "heartland" or marine "choke points."[14] Both sides viewed the planet as a chessboard where the loss of even the smallest piece could decide the game.

13. On postmodern and poststructuralist geography, see John Paul Jones III et al., eds., *Postmodern Contentions: Epochs, Politics, Space* (New York: Guilford, 1993), and other Guilford books on mappings.

14. See Colin S. Gray, *The Geopolitics of the Nuclear Era: Heartland, Rimland, and the Technological Revolution* (New York: Crane, Russak & Co., 1977); Zbigniew Brzezinski, *Game Plan: A Geostrategic Framework for the Conduct of the U.S.-Soviet Contest* (Boston and New York: Atlantic Monthly Press, 1986); and Brzezinski, *The Grand Chessboard: American Primacy and Its Geostrategic Imperatives* (New York: Basic Books, 1997).

Geopolitics: Science, Policy, or Propaganda?

Whether true or false, geopolitical beliefs can shape or rationalize policy. Geopolitics took root in 19th-century universities and helped inspire imperialist expansion. From London to Tokyo, aspiring imperialists drew on theories of geopolitics and Social Darwinism to justify expansionist policies. German professors asserted Germany's need to unify German-speakers and give them *Lebensraum* ("living space"). Japanese geopoliticians assayed the raw materials of neighboring countries. British and U.S. advocates of big navies stressed the role of sea power in history.

As the Versailles Treaty was debated in 1919, British geographer Sir Halford Mackinder warned his countrymen not to depend upon sea power alone. Whoever controls Eastern Europe, he argued, could dominate the entire Eurasian land mass (or **World Island**):

Who rules East Europe commands the Heartland:
Who rules the Heartland commands the World Island:
Who rules the World Island commands the World.

Similar views were voiced by German geopoliticans in the 1930s as Hitler planned his eastward march and by Kremlin spokesmen in 1968 when Soviet forces invaded Czechoslovakia.

American geographer Nicholas J. Spykman in 1942 provided a rationale for U.S. containment policy: "Who controls the Rimland rules Eurasia; who rules Eurasia controls the destinies of the world." Technology shortened distances, but Washington sought to keep Moscow from dominating the World Island—its heartland or its rimland.

But geopolitics can serve peace as well as war. Its assumptions can rationalize a tough *realpolitik,* but critical geography in tune with ecology underscores mutual vulnerability and the need for cooperation.

Economic Strength. Economic power undergirds military, cultural, and other forms of power. **Economic statecraft** uses rewards and penalties to shape other states' behavior. Positive rewards include lowered tariffs, subsidized trade, aid, and investment guarantees. Negative sanctions may entail boycotts, tariff increases, trade quotas, dumping of surpluses, preclusive buying, freezing of assets, and aid cutoffs.[15]

Geonomics (or "geo-economics")[16] contends that economic factors have replaced geopolitics (understood as geography plus military power) as the material basis for IR. One view is that **trading states**, whose wealth and influence are based on international commerce and not on territorial extent or military might, have supplanted militarized states as influential actors in world affairs.[17] Geoeconomic power, some analysts say, requires the government to foster key industries at home and internationally.[18]

Political Leadership and Cohesion. All other components of power come to naught unless a society has good leadership and the body politic holds together—even under stress. Conversion power also depends on leadership and cohesion.

Leadership is key to the design and implementation of effective policies. Good leadership can work wonders with meager resources; bad management wastes rich resources.

Political cohesion boosts a government's extraction capability—its ability to tax and mobilize assets for public purposes. Extraction capability is part of conversion power. If two societies are equal in GDP and GDP per capita, that with the higher extraction rate can field more resources. But a high extraction capability may merely postpone defeat (as happened to Germany and Japan in World War II) if the other side commands far more resources.[19]

Political cohesion also contributes to **cost-tolerance**—a society's ability to endure hardship. The ultimate victor in any competition must be able to persist despite pain and sacrifice. A study of forty wars showed that almost half were won by the party that suffered more than its antagonist.[20]

Do leadership, cohesion, extraction capability, and cost-tolerance develop more readily under authoritarian or democratic rule? There is no formula. Good leadership and strong cohesion—and their opposites—are possible whether a society is ruled from the top down or bottom up.

Military Strength. To prevail in war it is useful to have every asset—

15. See David A. Baldwin, *Economic Statecraft* (Princeton, N.J.: Princeton University Press, 1985), 41–42.

16. In Greek *geo* means earth, *ekos* means house or habitat, and *nemein* means management.

17. Richard Rosecrance, *The Rise of the Trading State: Commerce and Conquest in the Modern World* (New York: Basic Books, 1986).

18. See Edward N. Luttwak, *The Endangered American Dream: How to Stop the United States from Becoming a Third-World Country and How to Win the Geo-Economic Struggle for Industrial Supremacy* (New York: Simon & Schuster, 1993); and Wayne Sandholtz et al., *The Highest Stakes: The Economic Foundations of the Next Security System* (New York: Oxford University Press, 1992). For a different perspective, see Jagdish Bhagwati, *The World Trading System at Risk* (Princeton, N.J.: Princeton University Press, 1991). See also Chapters 11 and 12.

19. Jacek Kugler and William Domke, "Comparing the Strength of Nations," *Comparative Political Studies* 19, no. 1 (April 1986): 39–69 at 51.

20. Steven Rosen, "War and Power and the Willingness to Suffer," in *Peace, War, and Numbers,* ed. Bruce Russett (Beverly Hills, Calif.: Sage, 1972), 166–183 at 175.

hard, soft, and conversion power. But the optimal blend of military strengths depends upon circumstances—on time and place, the mission, the adversary, the available technology, and other factors as well.

If resources are tight, is it wiser to invest in men or machines? There are few guidelines valid for all time. We know that Hitler's "lightning war" skirted French forts but stalled in Russia's frozen vastness. Trying to buttress Soviet cohesion, Stalin assured his subjects that Hitler's surprise attack gave Germany only a transitory advantage. War, said Stalin, pits entire societies against each other, testing all their strengths and weaknesses. Though he implied that people could best machines, Stalin also ordered a crash program to develop atomic bombs.

Lessons from a previous war can mislead. The U.S.'s first computer-guided "smart bombs" failed in Vietnamese jungles, but later versions proved more effective against targets in Iraqi deserts.[21] Insights from the 1991 Gulf War, in turn, gave no guidance to peacemakers trying to restore order to divided societies such as Somalia and Bosnia.

Brain Power. Brain power is key to unleashing all other power. It includes education (mass and elite), science, technology, information, and communication. Brain power helps societies to avoid both stagnation and chaos while adapting to complexity. The ability to acquire and use information can help actors to adjust and innovate more efficiently than their rivals. An Information Revolution seems to be supplanting the Agricultural and Industrial Revolutions. Information technology depends upon human capital, universities, and a stable supply of electricity.[22]

Education, like a strong economic base, provides the foundation from which other assets may derive. The educated citizen can invent, utilize, repair, and improve the means of production and destruction. As we see in Table 5.4, on page 142, the highest-ranked country by HDI, Canada, has invested heavily in education but not in defense. Second-ranked France, however, has invested heavily in both; so have the U.S., Singapore, Israel, and South Korea.

Users of modern libraries and the Internet are deluged with information. But bits and bytes must be analyzed to become knowledge. And knowledge must be refined—perhaps nurtured by compassion and empathy—to become wisdom.

To develop and apply brain power, a society needs many assets in combination: the leisure and wealth to pursue knowledge + a critical mass of knowledge-seeking organizations + the means to collect and analyze data + the freedom to reflect on and debate their implications + wis-

Paradoxes: The Bear and the Porcupine

Despite its great mass, the Russian "bear" astride its broad plain has often been attacked. Switzerland, on the other hand, is a prickly porcupine in a mountain fortress; though small and centrally located, Switzerland has not been invaded since Napoleon. Russians are resource-rich but poor; the Swiss have modest resources but are rich. Russians have long been anxious about their place in the world; the Swiss, confident. Russians have often intervened militarily abroad; the Swiss have not threatened others for hundreds of years. The Swiss have converted their power assets far more efficiently than the Russians. How they profited from World War II and the Holocaust, however, is another matter.

21. In the Gulf War the kill rate was not "one bomb, one target," as some Pentagon reports claimed. The ratio was more like "four bombs, one target"—still a very high rate.

22. *The Global Competitiveness Report 1997* (Cologny, Switzerland: World Economic Forum, 1997), 59–65.

Table 5.4 How HDI Correlates with Education and Defense Expenditures

HDI Ranking and Country	Education as Percentage of GDP	Defense as Percentage of GDP
1. Canada	7.4	1.6
2. France	6.0	3.1
3. Norway	7.6	2.6
4. U.S.	7.0	3.8
7. Japan	5.5	1.1
15. UK	5.3	3.1
22. Singapore	3.3	5.9
23. Israel	6.0	9.2
32. South Korea	4.5	3.4
108. China	2.6	5.7
138. India	3.8	2.5
Public expenditures in all industrial countries	5.4	2.7
Public expenditures in all developing countries	3.6	3.1

SOURCE: *HDR 1997*, Tables 15, 19, 31, 38.
NOTE: Data are from 1993–1995.

23. *Global Competitiveness Report 1997*, 60.
24. *The Economist*, February 15, 1997, 98.
25. International Research Institutes, *Business and Consumer Attitudes to the Internet: A 22 Country Study*, 3d ed. (Brussels: IRIS, 1997), Executive Summary.
26. U.S. diplomats gained when cryptographers broke Japan's diplomatic code in 1922. Washington and London intercepted and decoded many German and Japanese messages during World War II.
27. In 1990s Washington spookspeak HUMINT stood for "human intelligence"; SIGINT for "signal intelligence"; MASINT for "measurement and signature intelligence," as from acoustic and seismic sensors; RUNINT for rumors; and FUSS for "Fleet Undersea Surveillance System."
28. Dulles, *The Craft of Intelligence* (1963), analyzed in Thomas Powers, *The Man Who Kept the Secrets: Richard Helms and the CIA* (New York: Knopf, 1979), 342, n. 51; see also Gregory F. Treverton, *Covert Action: The Limits of Intervention in the Postwar World* (New York: Basic Books, 1987), 11.

dom, freedom, and opportunity to apply what has been learned + mechanisms for corrective feedback. This blend is not easy to attain. Soviet scientists, for example, achieved many scientific and engineering breakthroughs but lacked intellectual freedom and free markets in which to introduce innovations. Indeed, the Soviet government blocked direct-dial telephones and limited fax machines to prevent easy access to the outside world. Such lags are not readily overcome. Ranked by availability of information technology in 1997, Russia and Ukraine placed just above India, Poland, and China.[23]

Computerization is a by-product and probably a source of knowledge and wealth. But modem access does not correlate perfectly with GDP. In 1996 some 60 percent of the world's Internet hosts were in the U.S., though Finland and Norway had more per capita. But other economic giants—Germany, Singapore, and Japan—had far fewer hosts per capita. Italy, with one of the world's largest GDPs, had fewer Internet hosts than Spain or Hungary.[24] In most of Western Europe about 10 to 15 percent of the population had access to the Internet in 1996 compared with about one-fourth of Canadians and Australians and one-third of U.S. citizens. Among people with access to the Internet, men were more likely to use it than women; Internet awareness was lower among women than men in Latin America and southern Europe.[25] The number of Chinese owning PCs shot up at a fast rate in 1996 from a low base. Some educators believe that the Internet can complement, reinforce, and enhance traditional approaches to learning. Others speculate that it lowers critical abilities and reading skills.

One aspect of brain power is **intelligence**—information about other IR actors. Good intelligence collection and interpretation can make a weak power strong; faulty intelligence can undercut strength.[26] Useful information may come from spies, from open sources such as publications, and from machines that watch and listen.[27] "Gentlemen do not open each other's mail," said U.S. Secretary of State Henry Stimson in 1929. But Allen Dulles, for many years director of the Central Intelligence Agency (CIA), later replied: "When the fate of a nation and the lives of its soldiers are at stake, gentlemen do read each other's mail—when they can get their hands on it."[28]

The track record of U.S. intelligence has been mixed. As we saw in Chapter 3, U.S. planners benefited greatly from information provided by reconnaissance flights and from sources within the USSR such as Colonel Penkovsky. On the other hand, the CIA often misled the White

House about Cuba and the USSR. Ostensible CIA successes in overthrowing governments, as in Iran in 1953 and Guatemala in 1954, netted long-term difficulties for all parties.[29] In the 1980s the CIA had so many problems—traitors, "moles," toadies, and whitewashers—that some experts said the U.S. would have been better off with no intelligence service at all.

The most expensive kind of intelligence comes from satellites and electronic snooping. After the USSR's demise, Americans debated whether they should continue to spend some $28 billion per year to support intelligence gathering and analysis, and clandestine operations against other states. Should government limit itself to research and halt operations such as coups and other "dirty tricks"? Should all intelligence work, long scattered across the State, Defense, and Commerce Departments and the CIA, be merged? Should the CIA focus on geonomic challenges rather than security issues? If the CIA collects proprietary information, should it be shared with private firms? If so, which firms—and how? Should the U.S. spy on Japanese or French competitors—risking alliances for commerce? Or should Americans learn what they need from newspapers and trade journals? Virtually all useful information, George F. Kennan estimated, could be gleaned from open sources. Spying is bad for its authors as well as their victims, he wrote, because it produces unlimited cynicism.[30] Given the growth of international crime and terrorism, however, one observer concluded that, unless human nature changes, the U.S. could not afford to bring its spies in from the cold.[31]

Universal Culture. If a country's way of life and values seem legitimate to others, this adds to soft power to persuade and coopt. The U.S. gained influence in the Cold War competition because its path, charted by Adam Smith and John Locke, had more worldwide appeal than the Communist ways endorsed by Karl Marx and Vladimir Lenin. The U.S. gained also because Coke, Levis, and Hollywood had greater allure than Stolichnaya vodka, fur hats, or the Bolshoi Ballet. But the appeal of Western culture is often superficial. Devotion to Magna Macs does not assure respect for the Magna Carta. A taste for jeans and Marlboros is no endorsement for U.S. views on human rights.

International Institutions. The structure and policies of international institutions are shaped by the dominant actors. The U.S. gained in the Cold War because the world's major economic institutions—the World Bank, the International Monetary Fund (IMF), and the General Agreement on Trade and Tariffs—harmonized with U.S. preferences for free markets and free trade. (See Chapters 11 and 12 for discussion of these in-

Navajo Code

Not all codes require expensive machinery. During World War II Navajos serving with U.S. forces in the Pacific sent messages to one another in their own language—an undecipherable code to the Japanese.

29. The CIA planned to assassinate dozens of individuals in Guatemala in 1954, but this proved unnecessary. For a review of a memoir and documents relating to such operations, see Theodore Draper, "Is the CIA Necessary?" *The New York Review of Books,* August 14, 1997, 18–22.

30. George F. Kennan, "Spy & Counterspy," *New York Times,* May 18, 1997, op-ed.

31. David Fromkin, "Daring Amateurism: The CIA's Social History," *Foreign Affairs* 75, no. 1 (January–February 1996): 165–172.

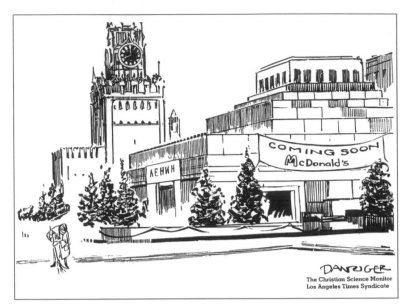

The ability of the Soviet system to compete with other ways of life collapsed in the 1980s. Lenin remained in the mausoleum on Red Square, but the world's largest McDonald's opened in Moscow, not far from the Kremlin (soon eclipsed by an even larger McDonald's in Beijing).

stitutions.) States whose values conflict with prevailing institutions must struggle harder just to survive. The USSR stood apart—isolated and self-isolated—from the World Bank and IMF for most of the Cold War. In the UN Security Council the USSR cast its veto more often than the other four permanent members because Moscow often was the odd man out.

COMPARING THEORY AND REALITY: POWER AND INFLUENCE AT A.D. 2000

FROM EMPIRES TO GLOBAL COMPETITORS

Five great empires collapsed in the first two decades of the 20th century—the Chinese, Russian, Ottoman, Austro-Hungarian, and German. The Italian, Nazi, and Japanese empires perished in World War II. Most of the Dutch, French, British, and Portuguese empires had disappeared by the mid-1970s. The Soviet empire perished in 1989–1991. The U.S. controlled several islands but otherwise had no formal empire. Its global influence was indirect, based largely on economic and soft power.

The main economic trends at the end of the 20th century are sketched in Table 5.5. The rich industrial countries grew at about 2.5 percent per year. The developing countries, led by East Asia, grew at two or three times that rate; Africa, however, grew little faster than its population increase. The former Second World had a negative growth rate after the fall of communism, but entered onto positive ground in 1996.

Table 5.5 Growth Rates in Real Gross Domestic Product, Selected Years (1978–1996)

Area	1978–1987	1991	1994	1995	1996
Industrial countries	2.7%	0.8%	2.8%	2.1%	2.3%
U.S.	2.8	-1.0	3.5	2.0	2.4
Canada	3.2	-1.8	4.1	2.3	1.4
Japan	3.7	4.0	0.5	0.9	3.5
Germany	1.8[a]	5.0	2.9	1.9	1.3
EU[b]	2.1	1.6	2.8	2.5	1.6
Developing countries	4.5	5.1	6.6	5.9	6.3
Africa	2.1	1.8	2.9	3.0	5.0
Asia	6.8	6.9	9.1	8.6	8.0
Middle East and Europe	2.5	3.5	0.5	3.6	3.9
Western Hemisphere	3.1	3.3	4.7	0.9	3.0
Countries in transition	3.0	-11.5	-8.8	-1.3	0.4
Central and Eastern Europe	—	-10.8	-2.9	1.2	1.6
Russia, Transcaucasus, and Central Asia	—	-12.0	-14.8	-4.1	-0.9

SOURCE: *Economic Report of the President* (Washington, D.C.: Government Printing Office, 1997),
Table B-110.
   a. Figure for West Germany only.
   b. Includes Germany.

Fig. 5.2 The Pyramid of Power ca. A.D. 2000

The world's richest states at century's end did not have large imperial holdings. They competed with one another but were also partners. On the whole, their fitness peaks rose in tandem. The most competitive had institutions that cultivated long-term growth in the global economy. Of large industrialized countries, the most competitive in 1996 were the U.S., Canada, the UK, Japan, France, and Germany; of small states, Singapore, Hong Kong, New Zealand, Switzerland, and Taiwan; of rising developing countries, Malaysia, Chile, Indonesia, Thailand, South Korea, Egypt, and China. The least competitive were countries where socialism had imposed rigidity: Greece, Vietnam, Poland, Zimbabwe, Ukraine, and Russia.[32] In late 1997, however, many East and Southeast Asian economies overheated and were compelled to seek huge loans from the IMF and other potential donors such as Japan and the U.S. to stabilize their currencies. In 1997 South Korea negotiated the largest external "bailout" ever in world history—some $55 billion.

WHO HAS WHAT: THE PYRAMID OF POWER

The pattern of power at the cusp of the millennium resembled a pyramid, as in Figure 5.2. Each unit in the pyramid can be ranked by military, economic, and cultural power. The U.S. is preeminent in all three, and therefore stands at the apex. The great powers in the second rung are strong in two kinds of power but preeminent in none.[33]

32. *Global Competitiveness Report 1997.*
33. See Brian Nichiporuk, "Pivotal Power: America in the 1990s," MIT Defense and Arms Control Studies Working Paper, Cambridge, Mass., May 1991; for another approach, see Lars-Erik Cederman, "Emergent Polarity: Analyzing State-Formation and Power Politics," *International Studies Quarterly* 38, no. 4 (December 1994): 501–533.

The U.S.

No other country or coalition could rival the U.S.'s combined hard and soft power at the end of the 20th century. American popular culture influenced tastes the world over while U.S. space vehicles sent back images from Mars. English was the world's lingua franca for commerce, transportation, and science; it also ruled the Internet.

The Internet, like television, spread an American way of looking at the world. In 1997 the Iraqi newspaper *Al-Jumhuriya* denounced the Internet as "the end of civilizations, cultures, interests, and ethics"—as "another American means to enter every house in the world." The paper charged that Americans "want to become the only source for controlling human beings in the new electronic village." Not surprisingly, the Internet was not readily accessible in Iraq.

Economic Strength. At the end of the 20th century, as at its onset, the U.S. still produced almost one-fourth of the world's goods and services. After World War II the U.S. produced nearly half of the world's GDP. As Europe and Japan recovered, the U.S. share of global GDP declined. Still, in the 1990s one-twentieth of the world's population produced and consumed one-fourth of its wealth. The U.S. real GDP was about twice the size of Japan's and four times that of Germany, though it might be exceeded by China's in the 21st century.

In the mid-1990s the U.S. had the lowest inflation and lowest unemployment of any large industrialized state. Ratings of economic competitiveness in 1996–1997 placed the U.S. at the top, just behind two special cases, Singapore and Hong Kong.[34] One ingredient of competitiveness is good governance. One survey placed the U.S. as the sixteenth least-corrupt country, less corrupt than seven European Union members and Japan.[35]

Military: Systems of Systems. The U.S. and Russia were the only states with thousands of nuclear warheads; the British, Chinese, French, and Israeli arsenals numbered in the hundreds. The U.S. deterrent stood on three strong legs—ICBMs, submarines, and bombers. Russia, however, depended mainly on ICBMs. Russia's nuclear weaponry was deteriorating from age and poor care, while U.S. forces were well maintained and modernized.

No other country had large conventional forces, able to fight anywhere on short notice. To deploy a sizeable force in the Persian Gulf in 1979 would have required three months; in 1991, three weeks; in 1995, three days—thanks in part to pre-positioned equipment and some twenty ships stationed in or near the Persian Gulf. No other country had even

34. *Global Competitiveness Report 1997.*
35. Of the fifty-two countries surveyed, the least corrupt were Denmark, Finland, Sweden, New Zealand, and Canada; China ranked forty-first; at the bottom were Russia, Colombia, Bolivia, and, most corrupt, Nigeria. "1997 TI Corruption Index," issued by Transparency International (TI), Berlin, 1997.

Table 5.6 The Difference That Leadership (Conversion Power) Makes

The Problem	U.S. Hard and Soft Power Available	U.S. Leadership Commitment	Influence
Iraq in Kuwait, 1990–1991	High	High	High
Hunger and chaos in Somalia, 1992–1993	High	Low	Low
Chaos in Haiti, 1994–1998	High	Low-Medium	Medium
Chaos in the Balkans, 1991–1995	High	Low	Low
Chaos in the Balkans, 1995–1998	High	Medium-High	Medium

one U.S.-style aircraft carrier group, but the U.S. maintained eleven, plus one in reserve.

On the other hand, the U.S. was vulnerable to attack by ballistic and cruise missiles, poison gas sprays, and bacteriological agents. Truck bombs caused major damage in New York and Oklahoma City.

Hard power was empty without conversion power. President George Bush organized a strong coalition against Iraq in 1991, but the White House did little in the early 1990s to thwart the warlords of Somalia and the Balkans. In 1994–1995, however, President Bill Clinton intervened with force in Haiti and the Balkans. U.S. influence improved, even though serious problems remained in both regions. Energetic leadership and commitment made a big difference, as suggested in Table 5.6.

In the 1990s U.S. defense expenditures surpassed the total military outlays of the other eight leading industrial powers combined. It may

U.S. influence in the world depended upon hard, coercive power as well as soft, persuasive power. In the 1990s, the U.S. military budget declined as a percentage of GDP but nearly equaled that of the rest of the world combined. The Pentagon argued that it needed forces capable of fighting and winning two regional wars simultaneously while conducting peacekeeping or humanitarian operations.

Table 5.7 U.S. Federal Outlays for Discretionary Programs, 1978 and 1998 *(billions of constant 1992 dollars)*

Category	1978	1998 (estimate)
National defense	217.7	225.3
International affairs	17.0	16.0
General science, space, technology	9.8	13.6
Energy	10.5	4.2
Natural resources and environment	24.1	17.7
Agriculture	2.7	3.5
Commerce and housing credit	6.7	2.8
Transportation	29.8	31.5
Community and regional development	21.7	9.9
Education, training, employment, and social services	45.1	36.7
Health	14.8	20.8
Medicare	1.9	2.3
Income security	13.4	35.7
Social security	2.8	2.8
Veterans benefits and services	12.2	16.0
Administration of justice	7.6	19.8
General government	9.4	10.0
Total domestic	212.5	227.2
Total discretionary budget authority	447.2	468.6

SOURCE: *Historical Tables, Budget of the United States Government, Fiscal Year 1998* (Washington, D.C.: Government Printing Office, 1997), Table 8.8.

36. The federal budget has functional categories that classify government activities by their primary purpose. Most Department of Defense activities are Function 50 but some are in 150 as well. See Stanley E. Collender, *The Guide to the Federal Budget: Fiscal 1998* (Lanham, Md.: Rowman & Littlefield, 1997), app. D.

37. For example, see Robert D. Reischauer, ed., *Setting National Priorities: Budget Choices for the Next Century* (Washington, D.C.: Brookings Institution, 1997).

38. Joseph S. Nye, Jr., and William A. Owens, "America's Information Edge," *Foreign Affairs* 75, no. 2 (March–April 1996): 20–36; see also Eliot A. Cohen, "A Revolution in Warfare," in the same issue, 37–54.

have equalled that of all other countries. Was the money well spent? Should it have been allocated differently for defense? Should more have gone to nonmilitary pursuits?

In the mid-1990s the federal government budget totaled some $1.5 trillion—about 21 percent of GDP. Nearly $1 trillion of this was uncontrollable—mandated by law. This part of the budget included entitlements such as social security (22 percent of the total) and medicaid/medicare (16 percent), and interest payments on government debt (15 percent). That left about half a trillion for discretionary spending, which included defense (about 18–20 percent of the total federal budget). Defense and other categories of discretionary spending are listed in Table 5.7. The subset devoted to international affairs is outlined in Table 5.8.

By comparison with the Defense Department ("Function 50"), the rest of the budget for international affairs ("Function 150")—for the State Department and other agencies involved in export promotion, food aid, foreign affairs, foreign military sales, security assistance, U.S. contributions to the World Bank and IMF—is modest.[36] Even including nearly $6 billion in military and economic aid for Israel and Egypt, Function 150 is less than two-thirds the estimated budget for intelligence. Assessed contributions to the United Nations and its agencies are just over $1 billion per year.

Do these allocations seem reasonable? Most of these outlays could contribute to internal or external fitness. How should they be balanced? Experts disagree.[37] Before we formulate an answer, let us consider other ingredients of power and their financial implications.

The Information Revolution. The U.S.'s greatest comparative advantage was its leadership in the Information Revolution. Communications and information technology is a force multiplier of both hard and soft power.[38] It buttressed military prowess, enhanced the soft power attraction of democracy and free markets, and earned export dollars. Information technology, aerospace products, and electronics ranked high among U.S. exports.

By sharing selected information, the U.S. could add to its power to persuade. Information gathered by U.S. reconnaissance was shared not only with allies (as in the Falklands conflict) but with the United Nations and the International Atomic Energy Agency (leading the IAEA to intensify its inspections of North Korea and Iraq).

U.S. military power gained from continuing advances in ISR and C4I. (ISR stands for intelligence collection, surveillance, and reconnaissance; C4I refers to command, control, communications, and computer pro-

Table 5.8 U.S. International Affairs Budget Request, Fiscal Year 1998 *(millions of dollars)*

Promoting trade and investment		**525**
Includes Export-Import Bank		
Building democracy in former Second World		**1,629**
Sustainable development		**3,848**
Includes:		
World Bank, IMF, debt reduction	1,557	
Protection of global environment	342	
Peace Corps	258	
Promoting peace		**6,438**
Includes:		
Aid to Israel and Egypt	5,686	
Peacekeeping	376	
Nonproliferation and disarmament	127	
Counter-narcotics and crime	230	
Anti-terrorism	19	
Humanitarian assistance (refugees, disasters, food)		**1,727**
Advancing diplomacy		**5,390**
Includes:		
State Department operations	2,754	
United Nations and affiliates	1,023	
Total Function 150 (Discretionary Programs)		**$19,451[a]**

SOURCE: U.S. Department of State, *International Affairs Function 150: Budget Request and Objectives, Fiscal Year 1998* (Washington, D.C.: Government Printing Office, 1997), iv.

a. Total differs from $16 billion estimate in Table 5.7 because the lower figure is expressed in 1992—not current—dollars and because the FY 1998 request was unlikely to be fully honored; it exceeded the FY 1997 appropriation by $1.2 billion.

cessing.) These technologies can provide an ability to gather, sort, process, and display information in real time about complex events occurring in all kinds of weather over wide areas. Both technologies contributed to the "system of systems" that facilitated the use of precision force during the Gulf War.

U.S. military R&D provided spinoffs for nonmilitary applications, for example, improvements in civil aeronautics and the creation of the Internet. But a large amount of industrial high technology rested on "public science"—research funded by the government and by foundations. One study showed that 73 percent of the scientific papers cited by U.S. industrial patents were based on research financed by government or nonprofit agencies. Only 27 percent of the papers were funded by private industry.[39] Public science seemed to be more rewarding than private.

U.S. federal R&D in the 1990s amounted to just 1 percent of GDP—.06 for military and .04 for nonmilitary research (see Table 5.9). Federal R&D expenditures plateaued at about $70 billion per year in the mid-1990s, while private industry invested nearly twice this amount. Outlays for the National Science Foundation in 1998 were just over $2 billion, a pittance in the federal budget. Nonetheless, Republicans and Democrats alike aimed in 1996–1997 to trim federal R&D by up to one-fifth.

39. William J. Broad, "Study Finds Public Science Is Pillar of Industry," *New York Times*, May 13, 1997, C1, C10.

In the late 20th century an Information Revolution began to supplant the Industrial Revolution. Communication and information technology was crucial to U.S. hard and soft power.

Control and communications for power, industry, and military purposes depend heavily on computer networks, at risk from programming errors, sabotage by hackers, overload, and power outages.

Table 5.9 U.S. Federal Outlays for Research and Development, 1978 and 1998
(millions of current dollars)

Category	1978	1998 (estimate)
National defense	**12,077**	**37,416**
Department of Defense	10,726	35,067
Atomic energy	1,351	2,349
Nondefense general science	**4,429**	**10,707**
NASA	3,454	7,767
National Science Foundation	701	2,201
Atomic energy	274	739
Energy	**2,542**	**2,796**
Transportation	**705**	**2,135**
Department of Transportation	326	941
NASA	379	1,194
Health	**2,764**	**12,896**
National Institutes of Health	2,439	12,060
Other	325	836
Agriculture	**499**	**1,185**
Natural resources	**675**	**1,673**
Other	**841**	**1,398**
Total nondefense	**12,455**	**32,790**
Total R&D	**24,532**	**70,206**

SOURCE: *Historical Tables, Budget of the United States Government, Fiscal Year 1998,* Table 9.8.

40. *Statistical Abstract of the United States 1996: The National Data Book* (Washington, D.C.: Government Printing Office, 1996), Table 962.

Total R&D outlays in the U.S. (private and public, defense and civilian) amounted to 2.7 percent of GDP in the early 1990s—less than Japan's share (2.8 percent) but more than Germany, France, or the UK (2.5 or less). For nondefense R&D, however, both Japan (2.8 percent) and Germany (2.4 percent) invested a larger share of their GDP than the U.S. (2.05 percent).[40] As U.S. investment slackened, others caught up. In the 1980s and 1990s the number of foreign contributions in *Physical Review Letters,* a leading science journal, grew from 30 percent to just over 50 percent.

Americans in the 1990s continued to win more than half of the Nobel prizes awarded in science and economics (and more than their share in literature and peace). But the science awards tended to reflect work done at least fifteen years before. U.S. preeminence in science owed much to the creative talent of refugees from Nazi Europe and their U.S.-born protégés.

U.S. brain power was uneven in the 1990s. Its universities were among the world's best, and more than one-third of Americans aged 25 to 65 graduated from college. Still, many others were functionally illiterate. Money was no cure-all. The U.S. spent 7 percent of GDP on education—more than most countries. (Canada invested 7.4 percent; Singapore, only 3.3 percent; and South Korea, 4 percent.) But the results were disappointing. Compared against forty other countries, U.S. students performed below average in mathematics and straddled the average in science .[41] The country's most prevalent educator—television—glorified consumerism, violence, sexism, and promiscuity. Education mirrored social health.

Social Health. Internal fitness can deteriorate even though wealth accumulates. Despite a gradual rise in GDP per capita, U.S. social health declined from the early 1970s into the mid-1990s. The gulfs separating a growing underclass, a shrinking middle class, and an expanding, ever richer upper class grew wider.[42] America's rich-poor gaps exceeded those in any other First World country.

Infant mortality decreased in the 1990s, but more babies in the U.S. died in their first year than in most of Europe, Singapore, or Hong Kong. A larger share of children in the U.S. lived below the poverty line than in most industrial democracies.[43]

At century's end public goods got less funding than in earlier decades. School buildings, bridges, and public transportation cried out for renewed investment.[44] Funding for the arts was cut back even more than for science. New Deal welfare programs were jettisoned in the hope that young mothers with children would find jobs.

Why a Public Goods Deficit? Why did the world's richest country not provide more resources for public goods and social welfare? Many voices cried out against "big government" and the "dole." The logic of collective action suggested that somebody else should care for the public good (provided, of course, that one's own entitlements and tax deductions remained untouched).

U.S. budget and trade deficits fed the image of a declining hegemon spending beyond its means. But the numbers looked different when placed against a GDP approaching $8 trillion in 1997–1998. To be sure, the federal budget deficit grew in the 1980s, with government outlays exceeding tax collections. But U.S. economic growth picked up in the late 1980s and by 1997 the budget deficit shrank to less than 1 percent of GDP (small also compared to deficits of more than 3 percent in most European Union countries). The U.S. **trade imbalance**—more imports than exports for goods and services—remained between $100 and $200 billion per year in 1996–1997. A drop in demand from East Asia could raise this gap (part of the "current accounts balance") to $250 billion in 1998. But even this would represent only a tiny fraction of U.S. economic activity. A more important factor was that currency turmoil in East Asia could cut demand for U.S. exports so that U.S. economic growth declined from 3 to 2 percent in 1998.

41. Some 500,000 seventh- and eighth-graders were examined in forty-one countries. The top scorers in mathematics were Singapore, South Korea, Japan, Hong Kong, and Belgium; the U.S. was 28th. In science top marks went to Singapore, the Czech Republic, Japan, South Korea, and Bulgaria; the U.S. placed 17th. See *New York Times,* November 21, 1996, B14.

42. In 1994, however, six measures of U.S. social health improved: infant mortality, percentage of children in poverty, unemployment, average weekly earnings, poverty among those over 65, and homicide. Six other indicators worsened: child abuse, teen suicide, drug abuse, high school dropouts, food stamp coverage, and rich-poor gap. Another four indicators remained stable: health insurance coverage, alcohol-related traffic fatalities, out-of-pocket health costs for those over 65, and access to affordable housing. Fordham Institute for Innovation in Social Policy, *1996 Index of Social Health* (Tarrytown N.Y.: Fordham Graduate Center, 1996). For official explanations of income inequality, see *Economic Report of the President* (Washington, D.C.: Government Printing Office, 1997), chap. 5.

43. Lee Rainwater and Timothy M. Smeeding, "Doing Poorly: The Real Income of American Children in a Comparative Perspective," Luxembourg Income Study Working Paper No. 127, Centre d'Etudes de Population, de Pauvreté et de Politique Socio-Economiques, Walferdange, Luxembourg, August 1995.

44. And what about the trade-offs between education and jail? To jail someone for a year cost $25,000 to $30,000 in 1997—more than the average college education. Would not economic power and brain power gain from greater investments in whatever kinds of education help to keep people out of jail?

A much greater burden was payments on debts accumulated since 1969—the last year of a budget surplus. Presidents Lyndon Johnson and Ronald Reagan increased military outlays without raising taxes; indeed, Reagan cut taxes in the early 1980s at the same time a deep recession reduced revenues. U.S. and foreign investors loaned Washington funds to make up the gap. The U.S. public debt quintupled between 1980 and 1995, rising from $709 million to $3.6 billion. Interest payments on this debt devoured 15 percent of federal outlays in 1995 (up from 7 percent in the 1970s).[45]

In sum the U.S. had the resources to fund public goods more fully if it chose to do so. In 1997, however, Congress and the White House agreed to cut taxes and eliminate the budget deficit within five years. Critics called for a more prudent balance between reducing the U.S. debt—a burden on later generations—and investing in health, education, and infrastructure—a benefit for future generations. The defense budget, if cut by half—or even by one-tenth—could fund many alternative investments.

The Other Major Players

None of the other great powers approached the lone superpower in overall assets, but each had regional and global strengths.

Japan. Recovering from World War II, Japan became a model trading state, exporting far more than it imported. Japan's economy, education, and social cohesion were strong. Japanese lived longer than most other peoples even though Japan's consumers received fewer protections than their Western counterparts.[46] Shielded by the U.S. nuclear umbrella, Japan conquered markets rather than foreign territories.[47] Japan invested about 1 percent of GDP on its "Self-Defense Forces" and nearly another 1 percent to support U.S. forces stationed in Japan. Just this sliver of Japan's wealth yielded the world's third- or fourth-largest military budget. In the 1990s, however, Japan's economy stalled and the ruling party lost its grip. Japanese dynamism could wilt if the country's youth refused to work like and for the growing numbers of their elders.

Despite economic clout, Japan's external influence was curtailed by its inward-looking culture, dependency on the U.S., a post-1945 allergy to militarism, and neighbors' fears of revived Japanese imperialism.

China. In the 1990s China was medium-strong in hard power but weak in soft. Its troop strength was the world's largest (nearly double that of Russia, India, or the U.S.). China also boasted a growing nuclear arsenal, including regional and intercontinental ballistic missiles and some missile-firing submarines. China's per capita income in the late 1990s did

45. Still, U.S. total public debt in 1995 was "only" 64 percent of GDP—less than Belgium (133), Italy (123), Greece (111), Canada (99), Denmark (80), and Japan (83). U.S. debt was slightly more than the UK (58), France (58), and Germany (62). But it was much more than Switzerland, with 45 percent, and Taiwan, which had no public debt.

46. Japan Tobacco Inc., owned and operated by the Ministry of Finance, was the largest corporate taxpayer in Japan in 1993. Lung cancer killed 3 out of 100,000 in 1955; 31 of 100,000 in 1991.

47. The sharing of burdens was uneven. The U.S. spent a much greater share of its GNP on defense than did Japan or Germany. Still, the U.S. also gained: Japan and Germany aligned with Washington on nearly every security issue of the Cold War. Absent ties with Washington, Japan and Germany would surely have felt compelled to build a nuclear deterrent. Had this happened, neighboring states—recalling World War II—would probably have been far cooler to their ex-foes.

not exceed $600, but its total GDP promised soon to overtake Japan's. Still, China had multiple vulnerabilities: too many people cultivating too little land, environmental degradation, no visible alternative to one-party dictatorship, rampant corruption, resistance to global norms on human rights and free trade, and discontent among Tibetans and other subject peoples.

China's influence fluctuated considerably. China looked like a paper tiger when it "test"-fired missiles into the Taiwan Strait in 1996 in a vain attempt to influence Taiwanese elections. In 1997, however, China regained Hong Kong and President Jiang Zemin received red carpet treatment when visiting the U.S.

Russia. Though the USSR appeared in the 1970s to be fit, its foundation proved weak and the Soviet peak collapsed in the 1980s. Russia emerged as a separate state, along with more than fourteen other states along Russia's borders. The core of the former Soviet Union was still the world's largest country, with vast resources and a huge nuclear arsenal. But Russia's internal fitness plunged in the 1990s. Infant mortality continued to rise while male life expectancy fell to 58 years. Russia's fledgling democracy foundered while corruption and criminality mounted. Russia's leaders in the 1990s tried to raise a new peak, but they wandered in a swampy labyrinth, quarreling over how to get out. Their prospects are analyzed in Chapter 13.

Germany. In the 1990s Germany was strong in most respects except in military power. Its population and GDP were Europe's largest, but less than one-third those of the U.S. Domestic cohesion was strained by the burdens of integrating East and West Germany; discontent over "guest workers" and political refugees; high unemployment, which reached over 20 percent in the provinces of former East Germany; and general belt-tightening to reduce debt and qualify for membership in the European Monetary Union.

Like Japan, Germany had to cope with memories of its previous aggression. But Germany in the 1990s became the dominant force in the European Union.

The European Union. In the 1990s the European Union (EU) had great economic power and internal fitness but modest influence. It had a larger population and GDP than the U.S. but no common military or foreign policy. The EU pioneered the "common marketization" of IR—downgrading security/sovereignty issues while cooperating in a single trading bloc. Most EU countries had very high HDI scores, but were much less competitive and more corrupt than the U.S.

The EU resembled a troika—the strongest horse, Germany, ran straight ahead; the French horse pulled to the left (toward big government); and the British horse to the right (toward less government). Both London and Paris possessed nuclear forces, but neither was willing to share them. Europeans talked much but did little to stop the bloodshed at their Balkan doorstep. The union split on how far to expand its membership. Few Europeans except business elites and a smattering of politicians were keen on closer integration and a single currency. Still, the economic muscle of the common market grew steadily, as we shall see in Chapter 11.

Wild Cards. Apart from these established players, the deck is loaded with wild cards. Some countries will make the most of their potential while others waste their assets. The personal qualities of individual leaders—their vision or blindness, heroism or cupidity, energy or sloth—will boost some countries and harm others. Bad luck—an earthquake or drought—will knock some actors to their knees.

Given these trends, what does the future hold? Best- and worst-case scenarios are sketched in Chapter 17.

DID GEONOMICS SUPERSEDE GEOPOLITICS AND MILITARY FORCE?

Did the end of the Cold War mean that hard power—military and geopolitical assets—had become irrelevant? That a strong economy rooted in global trade was the key to fitness and influence? Military power could be a useful backdrop but faced severe limits. Without a Soviet threat, Americans and Europeans saw few reasons to put their troops in harm's way. The world spent much less on defense in the late 1990s than in the late 1980s.

But geonomics and economic statecraft also faced limits. Japan and Germany could focus on trade only because their basic security was still assured by the U.S. Both Japan and Germany depended on Middle Eastern oil, but neither country could keep sea lanes open. Others could ride piggyback and help pay the bill, but U.S. military power was their last resort.

Reluctant to fight, actors tried economic statecraft. But it produced no miracle cures. Economic carrots and sticks had little impact on states pursuing "vital interests." Thus, Tokyo's financial offers did not spur impoverished Russia to hand back to Japan the northern islands taken by the Red Army in 1945. German financial carrots did help persuade Soviet President Mikhail Gorbachev to pull Soviet troops from East Germany, but

Iraq's fitness withered under UN sanctions intended to compel Saddam Hussein to permit the dismantling of Iraqi facilities for weapons of mass destruction. In 1995, the UN Security Council relaxed sanctions to permit limited sales of Iraqi oil to purchase food and medical supplies.

German marks merely sweetened a bitter pill: The USSR had no supply line to East Germany after Poland and Hungary threw off Soviet controls.

Washington employed a wide range of economic levers for political ends, often in ways that impaired U.S. business interests. Washington debated each year whether to condition most-favored-nations tariffs for China on its human rights and arms policies. A study for the National Association of Manufacturers identified sixty cases in 1993–1997 in which the U.S. imposed sanctions against thirty-five countries. Washington targeted not just Cuba and Iran but corporations doing business with them. Other targets included Iran and Libya for terrorism, Colombia and Myanmar for drug trafficking, Pakistan for pursuing a nuclear weapons program, Brazil and Taiwan for environmental violations, Saudi Arabia and Mauritania for abusing workers' rights, African countries for not banning female circumcision, and Balkan states for not handing over their indicted leaders to the UN war crimes tribunal.

Few such pressures had much effect. Fidel Castro, Saddam Hussein, and Libya's Colonel Moammar Qaddafi remained in power. China's policies on human rights and arms exports barely budged. Despite their need for food imports, North Korea and Iraq specialized in defiance—not compliance. The Balkan countries delivered few alleged criminals to the UN tribunal.

Economic sanctions work best when backed by many countries.[48]

48. See Gary Clyde Hufbauer et al., *Economic Sanctions Reconsidered: History and Current Policy,* 2d ed. (Washington, D.C.: Institute for International Economics, 1990); and Lisa L. Martin, *Coercive Cooperation: Explaining Multilateral Economic Sanctions* (Princeton, N.J.: Princeton University Press, 1992).

Thus, UN sanctions added to the reasons why South Africa gave up racist policies in 1994 and why Serbia recognized Bosnia in 1995. Economic statecraft also gains from linkage to other carrots and sticks.

No asset guarantees clout. Oil and grain offer leverage, but no single supplier controls prices. Oil was a kind of black gold in the 1970s but lost purchasing power in the 1980s and 1990s. Cartels such as the Organization of Petroleum Exporting Countries cannot readily enforce production quotas on their members. Kuwait's bulging purse did not deter aggressors. Neither oil nor money nor air-conditioned classrooms could assure longer life spans, good science, or social cohesion.

WHAT PROPOSITIONS HOLD? WHAT QUESTIONS REMAIN?

POWER DOES NOT ASSURE INFLUENCE OR FITNESS

We see that every power asset faces limits. No single asset guarantees influence or fitness. Fitness requires the capacity to cope with multiple challenges at home and abroad, converting them into opportunities. This capacity is multifaceted and requires many kinds of strength.

Memo to the President: The U.S. enjoys super power and high influence abroad but only low to medium fitness at home. We face great challenges with vast resources. We must balance means and ends. Humans do not live by bread alone. Without power, however, even noble ideals will be hard to achieve.

Long-term fitness is more likely to arise from cooperation (as in the Marshall Plan) than from zero-sum politics (as in the Cold War and Vietnam War). The optimal way to convert power resources to fitness is through value-creating on a broad scale.

The world is unipolar but interdependent. How actors react to interdependence is an open issue. Americans have the means to take bold measures to nudge the world toward mutual gain. Here are six policy guidelines:

1. Strive to increase the country's overall fitness. Internal and external fitness depend on one another.

2. Cultivate a consensus at home and abroad for our policies. Persuade and co-opt.

3. To stop rogue aggressors, maintain sufficient strength to command and coerce.

4. With no military rival, we can spend less on defense. Given our internal needs, we should invest more in health, education, and other features of domestic well-being. Not just money but wise choices and leadership are required on all fronts.

5. Promote informed dialogue at home and abroad. Value-creation thrives on openness; value-claiming and misjudgment on secrecy. Greater openness and better communication are needed to make our country and the whole world more fit.

6. Look for solutions that grow our fitness with that of others. We can climb higher with others than we can alone.

KEY NAMES AND TERMS

bean count	geonomics	kinetic power
coevolution	geopolitics	power
conversion power	hard power	soft power
cost-tolerance	human development index (HDI)	trade imbalance
economic statecraft	infant mortality	trading states
fitness	influence	World Island
fungibility	intelligence	

QUESTIONS TO DISCUSS

1. What country is most fit—by what measure?
2. Select two countries whose influence you believe exceeds their hard power. Point to two other countries whose influence is less than their power might warrant. What is the evidence for your assessment?
3. Can/should the U.S. adopt the Japanese approach to security and economic development?
4. You must advise the U.S. president about discretionary spending. What outlays will you keep, increase, or reduce?
5. As defense minister of Lithuania, should you build a modern army, train the entire population in civilian resistance, or both? If both, how will you allocate resources?
6. Do you agree with the Pyramid of Power in Figure 5.2? If not, why?
7. Will states such as Brazil, Ukraine, and Kazakstan play the same, a smaller, or a larger role in IR in 2020? What factors and trends must you consider to answer this question?
8. Consider two of the potential great powers. What would it take for them to actualize their potential?
9. Point to a situation where State A wishes to change the behavior of State B. How could State A utilize economic levers to accomplish its objective?
10. How does oil affect peace, security, and economic well-being in the countries bordering the Caspian Sea? The South China Sea? The Caribbean?

RECOMMENDED RESOURCES

BOOKS

Demko, George J., and William B. Wood, eds. *Reordering the World: Geopolitical Perspectives on the Twenty-first Century.* Boulder, Colo.: Westview, 1994.

Epstein, Joshua M., and Robert Axtell. *Growing Artificial Societies: Social Science from the Bottom Up.* Cambridge, Mass.: MIT Press, 1996.

Kennedy, Paul. *Preparing for the Twenty-first Century.* New York: Random House, 1993.

——. *The Rise and Fall of the Great Powers: Economic and Military Conflict from 1500 to 2000.* New York: Random House, 1987.

Nye, Joseph S., Jr. *Bound to Lead: The Changing Nature of American Power.* New York: Basic Books, 1990.

Rosecrance, Richard. *The Rise of the Trading State: Commerce and Conquest in the Modern World.* New York: Basic Books, 1986.

Thurow, Lester. *Head to Head: The Coming Economic Battle Among Japan, Europe, and America.* New York: Morrow, 1992.

World Bank. *World Development Report.* New York: Oxford University Press, annual.

United Nations Development Programme. *Human Development Report.* New York: Oxford University Press, annual.

JOURNALS

Daedalus

The Economist

European Journal of the History of Economic Thought

Far Eastern Economic Review

International Studies Quarterly [special issue: Evolutionary Paradigms in the Social Sciences] 40, no. 3 (September 1996)

Journal of East Asian Affairs

WEB SITES

Electronic Industries Association
    http://www.eia.org/

Internet Society
    http://www.isoc.org

Japan's Ministry of Posts and Telecommunications
    http://www.mpt.go.jp/

Middle East Internet Directory
    http://www.arab.net/meid/

Organization for Economic Cooperation and Development Information and Communications Policy
    http://www.oecd.org/dsti/sti/it/index.htm

PART 2

From Anarchy, Order?

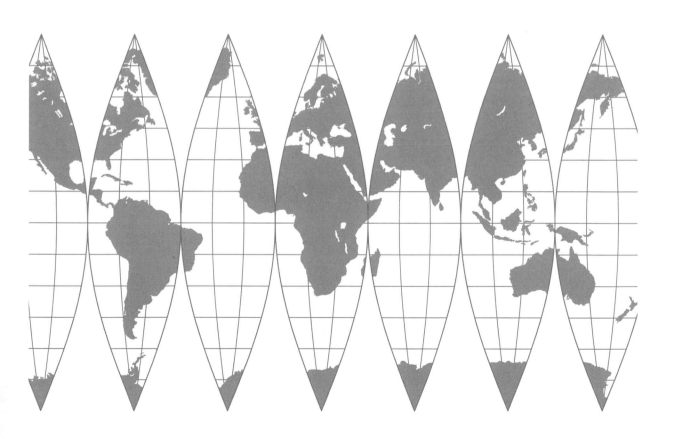

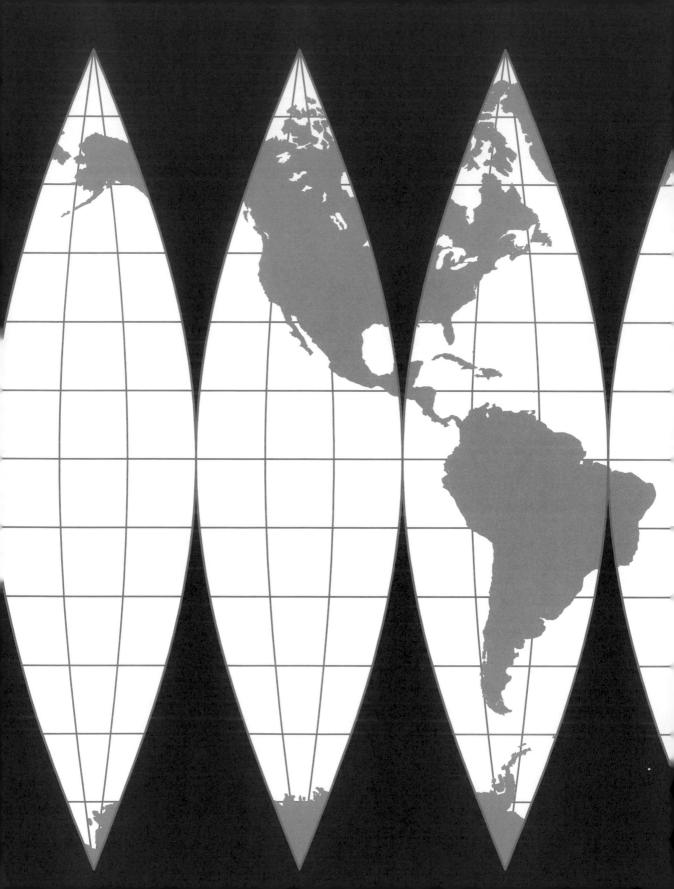

C H A P T E R   S I X

WHY ARM? CAN SWORDS BECOME PLOWSHARES?

The President Asks You to chair a policy review. Participants include analysts from the Defense and State Departments, the U.S. Arms Control and Disarmament Agency, and the Central Intelligence Agency. Your task is to answer two basic questions: First, given the foreseeable threats to world security, what should be the mission and size of U.S. armed forces? Should they continue to be prepared to fight and win "two plus" medium-intensity regional wars? Can we scrap all nuclear weapons? Can we retire to a "Fortress America"?

Second, how should we think about disarmament? Are negotiations merely a public relations gimmick to make each side look like a champion of peace? Are arms limits good or bad for our security? for the economy? for our overall fitness?

The President recalls that the Bible has words for and against arms control. The ancients knew that many assets are "dual-use": What builds or defends can also attack. The blade of a plow can cut a furrow or kill. Favoring arms reductions, the prophet Isaiah (2:4) told his people to "beat their swords into plowshares, and their spears into pruning hooks." But Joel (3:10–21) voiced the opposite message. He told the Israelites that God ordered them to "beat their plowshares into swords and pruning hooks into spears" to fight their oppressors.

The Israelites learned the dangers of disarmament. The Philistines imposed on them an arms control regime to make sure the Hebrews did not turn plowshares into swords. The Philistines forbade the Hebrews to forge iron tools and required them to sharpen their plowshares only on Philistine soil. When war came, only two Hebrews had a sword or spear (1 Samuel 13:19–22).

The President suggests that nuclear power is like plowshares. Both are dual-use. She asks: "How can we channel nuclear and other modern technologies to build rather than destroy?"

You share this goal but know that the obstacles are enormous. The eagle on the U.S. official seal clutches sharp arrows in one set of talons; in the other, an olive branch. The symbols are clear: Fitness requires a blend of strength and conciliation. But what is the right mix of arms and arms control? You promise the President to review how self-help and mutual aid can be linked to enhance security.

CONTENDING CONCEPTS
AND EXPLANATIONS

WHAT IS SECURITY?

Security is freedom from danger. A wise security policy seeks to uphold a country's fitness—its physical survival and way of life. But absolute security is impossible. Governments must balance their resources between problems at home and problems abroad. Fitness can erode from failure to meet internal or external challenges.

Human security depends upon a favorable environmental support system. Arms buildups and war do extreme damage to the biosphere. The nuclear powers, trying to achieve external security, poisoned their own wells and peoples, leaving archipelagos of radioactive hot spots across the former USSR, China, and the U.S. The Pentagon was spending $6 billion a year to clean up some 20,000 hazardous sites in the mid-1990s.

For security we depend first of all on our own efforts. But when each actor is vulnerable, security may depend on mutual aid as well as on self-help. Governments say that they arm to be secure, but forces for and against arming spring from every level of IR.

HOW LEVELS OF IR GENERATE AND RESTRAIN ARMS COMPETITION

Key Individuals. The man who supervised development of the first atomic bombs, U.S. Secretary of War Henry Stimson, became the first U.S. leader to advocate internationalization of atomic energy. Albert Einstein and many other physicists who had urged creation of nuclear weapons, lest Germany acquire them first, later sought their abolition. Some founded the journal *Bulletin of the Atomic Scientists*, with its famous clock showing a few minutes before midnight.

Josef Stalin ordered crash programs to build nuclear and thermonuclear weapons for the USSR. In the 1940s the "father of the Soviet H-bomb," Andrei Sakharov, thought of himself as a soldier in a "new scientific war" to break the U.S. monopoly in advanced weapons. In the 1950s, however, he worried about the health consequences of nuclear testing.[1] Convinced that the two superpowers had achieved a balance of terror in the 1960s, Sakharov devoted his life to arms control and human rights.

Not every weapons scientist becomes an advocate of arms control.

1. Sakharov urged the Kremlin (often in vain) to move local populations far from the test sites. Sakharov calculated that a one-megaton test would cause 10,000 deaths worldwide from radiation-induced cancers and genetic illnesses. By 1957 the total power of nuclear bombs tested around the world added up to nearly fifty megatons—500,000 casualties by his estimates. Despite Sakharov's pleas, the USSR in 1961 tested an H-bomb that he helped to design. This single explosion had the force of more than 50 megatons—perhaps 100 megatons! When he failed to stop duplicate tests, Sakharov was overcome by "unbearable bitterness" and wept. Andrei D. Sakharov, *Memoirs* (New York: Knopf, 1990), 201–229.

Never forgetting the Communist takeover of his native Hungary, the "father of America's H-bomb," Edward Teller, labored for more than fifty years to advance U.S. superiority in weapons.

State and Society. Strong forces within society press for and against arms. President Dwight D. Eisenhower in 1961 cautioned Americans against the influence of the "military-industrial complex"—an "immense military establishment and a large arms industry." In democratic countries antimilitarists can become informed but they find it hard to mobilize against "requirements for national security." Still, U.S. public opinion swings up and down on "how much is enough." In dictatorships, however, few people have any knowledge let alone voice on such matters. Soviet defense spending during the Cold War may have consumed a quarter of the country's GDP, but official figures were far lower.

International Dynamics: The Security Dilemma and Multiple Symmetry. Anarchy leaves each state insecure. As we saw in Chapter 1, the security dilemma is that the very steps that State A takes to make itself more secure may goad State B into countermeasures that threaten A.

A model of **multiple symmetry** holds that each rival must match or surpass every asset of its adversary or lose the competition. Multiple symmetry must be maintained—in troops, weapons, alliances, and spies.[2] Compelled to anticipate expected growth of State A's forces, its rival B tends to overshoot.

Some scholars believe that arms races always end in war.[3] Others disagree. The race may peter out if one or both sides focus on other problems, become friends, or reach exhaustion. Qualitative competition in laboratories is probably safer than quantitative rivalry in the field.

The model of multiple symmetry oversimplifies how states interact. Still, it helps us grasp the anxieties that could drive two parties to a deadlock. In game theory terms "deadlock" is continual mutual defection where D,D > C,D (see Table 6.1). Once either side defects, deadlock continues because neither side has a sufficiently strong incentive to break off the competition.[4]

Another way to understand arms racing is through the parable of the Stag Hunt.[5] Imagine five hunters waiting for a stag. If they kill a stag, they can feed their families for a week. But hours pass and no stag appears. Instead, a hare emerges from the bush. One hunter shoots the rabbit even though the noise scares any stag from the area. The single hunter defects from the common cause to get meat sufficient for his stew tonight, ruining prospects for a larger bounty for all. Tomorrow he, like the others, may be hungry.

2. For a summary of this theorem, see Jan F. Triska and David D. Finley, *Soviet Foreign Policy* (New York: Macmillan, 1968), 284–309.

3. Samuel P. Huntington pointed to at least eight arms races that did not end in war, including France vs. England (1840–1866), Argentina vs. Chile (1890–1902), Japan vs. the U.S. (1916–1922), and—as he wrote—the U.S. vs. USSR since 1946. See Huntington, "Arms Races: Prerequisites and Results," *Public Policy* 8 (1958): 41–86.

4. See George W. Downs, David M. Rocke, and Randolph M. Siverson, "Arms Races and Cooperation," *World Politics* 38, no. 1 (October 1985): 118–146, and other articles in this special issue on cooperation under anarchy.

5. This story is adapted from Jean Jacques Rousseau, *A Discourse on the Origin of Inequality* (1754), analyzed also in Kenneth N. Waltz, *Man, the State, and War: A Theoretical Analysis* (New York: Columbia University Press, 1959), 167–168.

Each hunter, like a rival state, has a preference order:

1. Cooperate and trap the stag—limit the costs of defense and share the benefits of prosperity

2. Get the rabbit by yourself—build up arms while others are passive (if this produced a major advantage, it might be the first choice for some states)

3. You and others chase the rabbit—arms race, risk war

4. Stay in place while others chase the rabbit—remain unarmed while others arm.

The Soviet-U.S. confrontation for decades resembled a mix of Chicken and Stag Hunt. Moscow and Washington were locked in a costly and dangerous security dilemma. The costs included the price of arming, unrealized gains from cooperation (CC), and augmented danger of war (DD). But states, like hunters, may decide that their joint interests require safeguards to prevent defection.

CAN SWORDS BECOME PLOWSHARES?

Security Regimes: Arms Control and Disarmament

A state may seek security by matching or bettering the armed might of its foes. Alternatively, a state may seek security without making adversaries feel threatened. To deal with their security dilemma Washington and Moscow developed **security regimes**—rules, informal norms, decision-making procedures, and other incentives to cooperate rather than defect.[6] Security regimes are valuable because self-help is costly and dangerous. But they are also difficult to achieve, because foes fear their rivals may cheat.

Arms limitations offer one kind of security regime. There are two main types of arms limitation: **Disarmament** means the reduction or elimination of armaments. **Arms control** is broader. It includes any regulation of arms. Arms control could entail disarmament—fewer arms— but it could also mandate more arms or a freeze at existing levels.

Why Limit Arms—or Talk About It?

Throughout the 20th century, Russia and the U.S. took the lead in promoting arms control. Why should two of the strongest powers call for arms limitation? Arms control diplomacy can serve many goals:

• *Make war less likely and enhance crisis stability:* Reduce incentives to shoot first. Take steps to prevent accidental war and uncontrolled escalation.

Table 6.1 Arms Choices and Arms Race Deadlock

Country A		Country B	
		Cooperate	Defect
	Cooperate	C,C	C,D
	Defect	D,C	D,D (deadlock)

6. On regimes, see Stephen D. Krasner, ed., *International Regimes* (Ithaca, N.Y.: Cornell University Press, 1983), and many essays appearing in the journal *International Organization.*

The Parable of Eagle, Lion, Dragon, and Bear: How Each Wanted the Other to Disarm

Eagle offered a simple solution to arms control: "Let us do away with claws and sharp teeth." Lion called for abolishing fiery breath. Dragon demanded the abolition of talons and speed. Smiling, Bear countered: "Comrades, let us replace all weapons with the great universal embrace."

• *Limit damage if war occurs:* Reduce unnecessary destruction. Develop "clean" bombs that destroy military objects and minimize civilian losses. Use **smart bombs** featuring computerized guidance systems that avoid enemy defenses and zero in on military targets.

• *Shape economic growth:* Convert military resources to civilian uses. Alternatively, intensify arms competition for domestic purposes and to bankrupt the other side.

• *Control the climate of world politics:* Promote détente to raise mutual understanding or mask hostile operations.

• *Shape politics in the rival camp:* Divide foes and support partners.[7]

• *Win political support:* Appear both strong and reasonable.

• *Improve the military balance:* If you are Eagle (see the sidebar), try to de-claw Lion. If you have no nuclear weapons, call for their abolition. If you have plenty, stop others from acquiring them. So long as each player depends on self-help, each seeks to retain its own strengths and abolish the weapons it lacks.

How to Control Arms

Diplomats, generals, scientists, business entrepreneurs, and peace activists have devised a multitude of ways by which to limit the engines of destruction. Governments have used five main methods:

• *Practice unilateral restraint:* Produce and deploy fewer forces. Make them less threatening. For example, build fewer tanks and more tank traps.

• *Disarm defeated foes:*[8] Examples include Germany in 1919 and again in 1945; Iraq after 1991.

• *Take parallel action:* Sometimes states limit their arms in tandem, with or without an understanding. Soviet leader Nikita Khrushchev in 1963–1964 endorsed "disarmament by mutual example."

• *Buy them out:* The First World in the 1990s virtually paid the Second World to disarm—from Russia and Kazakstan to North Korea.

• *Negotiate:* Negotiations to limit arms are difficult if the parties have unequal or different assets. As we shall see, however, skilled diplomats have often parlayed asymmetries into deals that serve both sides.

Scientists have invented ingenious ways to monitor nuclear testing, dismantle arms, and verify arms reductions. Engineers and business entrepreneurs have found ways to neutralize chemical weapons and land mines. Peace activists have generated strong pressure on governments to limit arms.

7. Thus, Lenin advised Soviet diplomats in 1922 to do everything possible to strengthen the "pacifist wing" of the bourgeoisie so as to divide Moscow's foes. Ultimately Lenin wanted to arm the proletariat in capitalist countries and "disarm [*obezoruzhit*'] the bourgeoisie." See Walter C. Clemens, Jr., *Can Russia Change? The USSR Confronts Global Interdependence* (New York: Routledge, 1990), chaps. 3 and 4.

8. The German and Russian languages have two different words for "disarm": *entrüsten* and *obezoruzhit*' mean to disarm by force; *abrüsten* and *razoruzhit*', to disarm voluntarily.

COMPARING THEORY AND REALITY: CONTROLLING VERTICAL AND HORIZONTAL PROLIFERATION

Could policymakers cap the twin volcanoes of the arms buildup? One volcano expanded upward after 1945 as the major powers piled one new weapon on top of the other; the other volcano expanded sideways as additional countries attempted to acquire nuclear and other arms. The two volcanoes have been linked. As one reached higher, the other broadened. If the first subsides, will the second shrink?

HOW THE VERTICAL VOLCANO GROWS AND SUBSIDES

The Genie Escapes the Baruch Plan

The U.S. tested the world's first nuclear bomb in New Mexico on July 16, 1945. In August U.S. planes dropped two atomic bombs—"Little Boy" and "Fat Man"—on Hiroshima and Nagasaki.

With Nazi Germany and Japan defeated, what should the U.S. do with this new power? Secretary of State James Byrnes advised President Harry Truman to use the U.S. nuclear monopoly as a lever in negotiations with Stalin. But Secretary of War Henry Stimson argued that the bomb was no diplomatic "master card."[9] Stimson advised Truman to internationalize nuclear power in order to avoid a dangerous arms race. It mattered less

Nuclear and Thermonuclear

Nuclear, atomic, fission—each term signifies an "A-bomb" that splits uranium or plutonium atoms. Thermonuclear, hydrogen, fusion—all signify an "H-bomb" that uses a nuclear trigger to detonate hydrogen atoms. But "nuclear" has become shorthand for both A- and H-bombs.

9. See Daniel Yergin, *Shattered Peace: The Origins of the Cold War and the National Security State* (Boston: Houghton Mifflin, 1977), 123; and James Chace, "Sharing the Atom Bomb," *Foreign Affairs* 75, no. 1 (January–February 1996): 129–144.

Hiroshima, the first of two Japanese cities struck by atomic bombs in August 1945, became a symbol of the destructiveness of atomic weapons—a major impetus behind the quest for nuclear arms control. The initial blast and firestorm alone killed more than 70,000 of Hiroshima's 200,000 residents and destroyed some 80 percent of its structures.

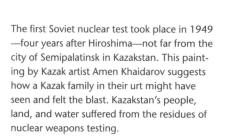
The first Soviet nuclear test took place in 1949 —four years after Hiroshima—not far from the city of Semipalatinsk in Kazakstan. This painting by Kazak artist Amen Khaidarov suggests how a Kazak family in their urt might have seen and felt the blast. Kazakstan's people, land, and water suffered from the residues of nuclear weapons testing.

whether the Soviets mastered the atom in four years or in twenty than that they be peace-loving partners when they did.

Implementing Stimson's suggestion the Truman administration in 1946 proposed to the United Nations the creation of an International Atomic Development Authority to control all nuclear plants and materials throughout the world. The proposal became known as the **Baruch Plan**, named for Bernard Baruch, a financier chosen by Truman to present the idea. But Baruch loaded the plan with one-sided **jokers**—provisions that virtually assured its rejection by the USSR. For example, the plan's first stage required the Soviets to open their secrets to inspection but permitted the U.S. to keep its nuclear monopoly so long as it chose.

The Soviets rejected the Baruch Plan, demanding nuclear disarmament first, inspection later. The U.S. sought inspection first, disarmament later. Though Soviet diplomats talked tough at the United Nations, Khrushchev later recalled that Stalin "trembled with fear" because the USSR lacked nuclear arms, and surrounded Moscow with 100-mm anti-aircraft guns.

The USSR soon mastered the nuclear genie. The first Soviet atomic explosion took place on August 29, 1949—little more than four years after the first U.S. test.

Having lost its nuclear monopoly, the Truman administration decided to develop a "super" or thermonuclear bomb. The first U.S. hydrogen bomb was tested in February 1954 and yielded 15 megatons. The Soviets were not far behind. Their first H-bomb explosion occurred in November 1955 and yielded 1.6 megatons.[10]

What could have been seen as a shared "Stag Hunt" problem turned into an ongoing arms competition expensive to each side. Could it have been avoided? What if professional U.S. diplomats (not a cranky Wall Street speculator) had talked directly to Stalin instead of conducting a public sparring match at the United Nations? What if, after the Soviets tested their first atomic bomb in 1949, Truman had pledged not to develop a U.S. H-bomb and called on Stalin to exercise similar restraint?

Soviet scientist Sakharov later opined that U.S. moderation would have achieved nothing: Stalin would have pursued a thermonuclear bomb anyway. Had Washington suspended work on the H-bomb, Stalin would have seen this as "a cunning, deceitful maneuver or as evidence of stupidity or weakness." Stalin would have sought "to avoid a possible trap, and to exploit the adversary's folly at the earliest opportunity."[11] We cannot know if Sakharov was correct, but his opinion helped explain why Moscow and Washington deadlocked at D,D.

Similar problems recurred throughout the Cold War. Usually ahead in technology, the White House had to decide: "Shall we try to abort this new weapon with Soviet cooperation or try to stay ahead?" Usually Washington chose the second track, and Moscow played catch-up.

Many realists have claimed that the clash over atomic energy confirmed their view that disarmament diplomacy is cold war by other means.[12] It masks an underlying struggle for hegemony. Distrust causes arms—not vice versa. Significant arms limitations cannot be negotiated between a have and a have-not. Lacking parity (rough equality), the only arms accords possible will be cosmetic—for show. Once a weapon has been developed, it will be deployed. The Soviets will never accept on-site inspection. Conclusion: Exploit rather than be exploited. Arm.

Much water would flow over the dam before each side learned that arms controls, if well crafted, can enhance mutual security. It took decades for Moscow and Washington to master conditional cooperation.

How Much Terror for Deterrence?

From the late 1940s into the 1990s the West staked its security upon deterrence—a strategy to paralyze the other side with terror.[13] If the adversary is intimidated, deterrence succeeds. If the foe attacks, deterrence fails.[14]

U.S. strategists said that stability depended on a capacity for "mutual

10. For other crucial dates, see David Holloway, *The Soviet Union and the Arms Race* (New Haven, Conn.: Yale University Press, 1983), 26.

11. Sakharov, *Memoirs*, 99.

12. The propositions here derive from John W. Spanier and Joseph L. Nogee, *The Politics of Disarmament: Soviet-American Gamesmanship* (New York: Praeger, 1962); Colin S. Gray, "The Purpose and Value of Arms Control Negotiations," in U.S. Senate Committee on Foreign Relations, *Perceptions: Relations between the United States and the Soviet Union* (Washington, D.C.: Government Printing Office, 1978); and Joseph J. Kruzel, "From Rush-Bagot to START: The Lessons of Arms Control," *Orbis* 30, no. 1 (spring 1986): 193–216.

13. "Deterrence" derives from the Latin for "terror." The same root exists in German and Russian: *Abschreckung* and *ustrashenie*. Sometimes Soviet writers used instead *sderzhivanie*, which approximates "containment" (from *derzhat'*—"to restrain"—and *derzhava*—"power"). For Washington, deterrence was *part* of containment.

14. For more on deterrence, methodology, and simulation, see *International Studies Notes* 22, no. 1 (winter 1997).

and assured destruction"—MAD. To strike the first blow—with conventional or nuclear arms—would be suicidal if the other side could retaliate with nuclear weapons.

The White House reckoned that the U.S. had to be able to absorb a first-strike and still inflict "unacceptable punishment" on the USSR. Some analysts said that a **minimum deterrent**, small but adequate, might be achieved with a few dozen or perhaps a few hundred nuclear weapons. But the Kennedy team decided to build more than a thousand land-based ICBMs (intercontinental ballistic missiles) and more than thirty submarines armed with many SLBMs (submarine-launched ballistic missiles). Washington said that U.S. forces must be able to destroy at least one-fifth of the people and one-half of the industry of the USSR to dissuade the Kremlin from striking first. To overcome "all that can go wrong" (what Carl von Clausewitz called "friction") many warheads would be required.[15]

To obtain a dependable **second-strike** force the Pentagon built a **triad** of long-range bombers, land-based missiles, and SLBMs. Any leg of the triad would have to be able to retaliate if the other two were destroyed. Some U.S. bombers were always aloft to assure they would survive a Soviet attack.[16]

The Soviet deterrent rested far more on land-based missiles than the U.S. deterrent. This was an important asymmetry. Soviet planes and submarines were less dependable than those of the U.S. On the other hand, Moscow held all of Europe hostage to its combined nuclear and conventional forces.

Critics said each side engaged in overkill. But military planners replied that large and diverse forces were needed to demonstrate that a first-strike could never disarm the victim to the extent that it could not strike back. Such calculations faced a new twist in the 1960s: What if one or both sides could blunt a retaliatory blow with anti-missile defenses?

Can Defense Be Bad? How Do Attack and Defensive Weapons Interact?

Governments would like a defense against missiles because deterrence may fail. Deterrence depends on shared ways of thinking and no mistakes; it offers no protection against a nuclear missile launched by a madman or by accident.

Before reading further, please answer this question: "If Moscow launched 1,000 ICBMs against the U.S. in the next few years, approximately how many would U.S. defenses likely shoot down? About 900? 750? 500? 250? Zero?" Why did you make this estimate?

15. Some planes, missiles, and warheads would malfunction; some would miss their targets; some would be intercepted; others would be countered by "hardening" of Soviet sites; some would destroy each other ("fratricide").

16. A spoof of the resulting dilemmas was the film *Dr. Strangelove, or How I Stopped Worrying and Learned to Love the Bomb.*

Most Americans reply in the 250 to 750 range. Better-educated persons expect fewer intercepts, because they respect Murphy's Law. Very few Americans—even those concerned with the defense industry—know that the correct answer is "zero."[17] Even fewer know why: one of the most important arms control agreements ever concluded—the 1972 treaty limiting **antiballistic missile (ABM)** defenses.[18]

ABM, SALT, and MIRVs. In the 1960s the USSR deployed a first-generation ABM defense system around Moscow. By 1972 the Moscow system contained sixty-four ABM launchers with interceptor missiles, directed by radars to track incoming missiles.

Here was the classic security dilemma—one side's defense looked threatening to the other. Washington tried to persuade Moscow that ABM systems were a bad idea. First, an ABM deployment would provoke the other side to build more attack missiles. Second, no ABM system could shoot down more than a fraction of a large attack force.

Moscow was deaf to such arguments until President Lyndon Johnson in 1967 called for a "limited" ABM defense. Eureka! Suddenly the Kremlin understood how one side's defense could affect the other's security. **Strategic Arms Limitation Talks (SALT)** began in 1969. Three years later, President Richard Nixon and Soviet leader Leonid Brezhnev signed the SALT 1 accords. Faced with mutual vulnerability, Washington and Moscow renounced defense and made their security hostage to mutual restraint.

SALT 1's cornerstone was the ABM treaty obliging Moscow and Washington not to build an ABM system for the "defense of the territory of its country." Moscow and Washington agreed to deploy no more than 100 launchers and interceptors, plus necessary radars, at each of two sites: one to defend the "national command authority" and one to protect an ICBM field. A follow-up accord in 1974 permitted each country only one site with 100 launchers. This allowed the Soviets to keep their puny Moscow defense but Washington chose to have no ABM at all. What good are 100 launchers against thousands of incoming warheads?

SALT 1 also included a five-year freeze on offensive strategic missiles—ICBMs and SLBMs. It permitted the U.S. to keep the missiles it had and authorized the Soviets to continue deploying weapons already in production. But SALT 1 did nothing to curb other weapons such as bombers, cruise missiles, and multiple warheads on one missile. Multiple warheads, or **multiple individually targetable reentry vehicles (MIRVs)**, were designed to overwhelm any Soviet ABM defenses. Reluctant to give up such a "sweet" technology even after ABMs were limited, the U.S. proceeded to

17. Try putting this question to a journalist covering national news, a stock broker concerned with high-tech stocks, a weapons engineer, or a political scientist not specializing in arms control.

18. This was the conclusion of repeated surveys by Boston University students conducted among diverse audiences across the country from the early 1970s into the 1990s. Their basic question was: "If Moscow launched 1,000 ICBMs against the United States, what percentage would we shoot down?" See Walter C. Clemens, Jr., "A Quiz for a Peaceful Sunday," *Los Angeles Times*, March 22, 1981, op-ed, summarized in *Fortune*, October 19, 1981, 142, and Clemens, "Americans in the Dark on Defense," *Christian Science Monitor*, August 31, 1993, 20. Republican pollsters got similar results in 1994 as did pollsters in a 1992 survey conducted at the University of Copenhagen among students of Russian affairs, who believed U.S. defenses superior to Russian.

President Ronald Reagan in 1983 committed the U.S. to a Strategic Defense Initiative (nicknamed "Star Wars"). The SDI aimed to provide an astrodome-like shield over the U.S. Critics labeled Star Wars a fantasy that would either waste tax dollars or provoke the USSR into building more attack missiles, or both.

"MIRV" (deploy multiple warheads). In the 1970s the U.S. mounted three warheads on many ICBMs; on SLBMs, many more. Soon the Soviets also began to MIRV. The results were dramatic. The number of missile launchers remained stable, as required by SALT 1, but stocks of strategic warheads more than tripled in the 1970s.

Brezhnev and U.S. President Jimmy Carter signed a SALT 2 treaty in 1979 far more ambitious than SALT 1. It set ceilings on long-range bombers as well as on ICBMs and SLBMs. But the treaty was unpopular in Washington, partly because it did not constrain mobile ICBMs, possessed only by the USSR. The Soviet invasion of Afghanistan in December 1979 killed any chance of U.S. ratification. Still, Moscow and Washington generally kept their arsenals within the limits of the unratified treaty. As new weapons were deployed, old ones were retired. Far from a minimum deterrent of a few hundred weapons, the U.S. by 1984 had about 11,000 strategic nuclear warheads; the USSR, nearly 10,000—larger but less accurate than U.S. warheads.

The Strategic Defense Initiative, or "Star Wars." President Ronald Reagan in 1983 announced plans for the **Strategic Defense Initiative (SDI)**, also dubbed "Star Wars." He promised a virtual "astrodome" to protect the U.S. from missile attack. For the rest of the decade Congress authorized some $3 billion a year for SDI—about 1 percent of Pentagon outlays.

SDI funded research on new forms of anti-missile technologies not available when the ABM treaty was signed in 1972. U.S. scientists researched satellites with lasers intended to zap Soviet missiles on takeoff, interceptors to stop Soviet missiles in flight, and huge catapulted "nails" to bash surviving missiles as they descended toward U.S. territory.

Was SDI legal? Critics of SDI argued that the ABM treaty banned development and testing of *new* forms of anti-missile defense. State Department lawyers retorted that SDI tests of "subcomponents" (such as lasers and satellites) were permitted so long as actual weapons systems were not deployed. Furthermore, the White House charged that the Soviets were developing their own SDI.[19]

Moscow worried that SDI would produce defenses that undermined the Soviet deterrent. Like a boxer, the USSR feared that if its opponent combined a powerful defense with a long reach, it might seek a knockout; such fears, some U.S. experts worried, could tempt Moscow to strike soon, before U.S. defenses were ready.

The Kremlin did not accept Reagan's assurances that he would share SDI discoveries with the USSR. Moscow beefed up its offensive forces to

19. While the USSR seems not to have matched the U.S. research effort, Soviet engineers erected a large radar at Krasnoyarsk that, if switched on and tied to ABM launchers, could have shielded a large swath of Soviet territory. After the U.S. government and some NGOs charged that the Krasnoyarsk installation violated the ABM treaty, the Soviet government dismantled the radar in the late 1980s.

ensure penetration. For several years the Kremlin demanded a halt to SDI as a precondition for any arms control. In 1987, however, Moscow relented. Seeing that SDI would not yield any sudden breakthroughs, Soviet President Mikhail Gorbachev signed arms controls with Washington despite continued SDI activity.

Theater Ballistic Missile Defense. U.S. support for Star Wars waned in the 1990s. A decade of SDI research costing more than $30 billion yielded no signs that an effective country-wide defense would ever be feasible against a large-scale ICBM attack. Russia continued to possess thousands of nuclear weapons able to wipe out the U.S. in half an hour, but their new masters seemed less hostile since the demise of the USSR.

In the 1990s the Pentagon put less emphasis on developing a **national missile defense (NMD)** of the entire country. Instead it focused on **theater ballistic missile defense (TBMD)** to protect U.S. forces abroad and allies from short- and intermediate-range missiles, improved versions of the scud missiles used by Iraq and other countries in the 1980s and early 1990s. No potential rogue state (such as Iraq or North Korea) was likely to get ICBMs for many years, but U.S. partners such as Japan and Israel were already vulnerable to the short- and intermediate-range missiles of hostile neighbors.[20]

The Pentagon investigated both low- and high-altitude TBMD technologies. Low-altitude systems (such as upgraded "Patriot" missiles) would target short-range (1,000 km or less) ballistic missiles within the earth's atmosphere, while theater high altitude area defense (THAAD) systems aimed at intermediate-range (ca. 1,000–3,000 km) missiles above the atmosphere.

Arms controllers worried that upper-level defenses could degrade Russia's deterrent and subvert the stability achieved by the ABM treaty. In 1996 the Pentagon bowed to this logic and decided to emphasize low altitude TBMD, slowing but not stopping work on high-altitude systems.

Rejecting this logic, the Republican-dominated Congress in 1995 called for deployment of a multi-site ABM force to protect the entire U.S. by 2003. President Bill Clinton vetoed the bill, however, saying it would put the U.S. on a collision course with Russia and the ABM treaty. Instead, the Pentagon pledged to improve components of a single-site ABM defense compatible with the ABM treaty that could be deployed within three years after an actual long-range threat was identified (other than from Russia). A single ABM site, of course, might protect the capital or a nest of ICBMs but would leave most of the country defenseless.

Russia's arsenal was getting smaller but also older, and perhaps more

Airborne Lasers and TBMD

The U.S. Air Force in the late 1990s wanted to test multimegawatt lasers carried by B747-400 planes on a mission to destroy ballistic missiles during their boost phase. The life cycle of the program, including deployment and twenty years of operations, was expected to cost $11 billion. The defense system would have to detect an enemy missile on takeoff, track it, and hold a heat beam on it—at a distance of up to 500 kilometers—until the missile's pressurized casing exploded. The beam would have to do its job in the 30 to 140 seconds after the missile cleared cloud tops and before the rocket booster burned out. Critics doubted whether the laser could reach its target in turbulent air conditions difficult even to predict. See U.S. General Accounting Office, *Theater Missile Defense: Significant Technical Challenges Face the Airborne Laser Program*, GAO/NSIAS-98-37 (Washington, D.C.: Government Printing Office, October 1997).

20. Michael Klare, *Rogue States and Nuclear Outlaws* (New York: Hill & Wang, 1995).

accident-prone. The Pentagon wanted a hedge against "limited strikes, whatever their source"—which could include Chinese as well as Russian ICBMs. Therefore the U.S. continued to investigate technologies useful for NMD or TBMD. At the same time, Washington tried to treat Russia more as a partner than an adversary. The U.S. invested more than one billion dollars in the mid-1990s to help Russia implement arms control treaties and develop **cooperative security** programs to promote shared security interests. One of these brought Russian specialists to Falcon Air Force Base, Colorado, in 1996 to conduct a joint TBMD command post exercise to simulate joint operations against a common foe armed with tactical missiles.

China had a small but growing stock of nuclear weapons in the 1990s (about 17 ICBMs, 46 IRBMs, and 12 SLBMs on one submarine in 1996). Washington assumed that Beijing, like Moscow, was a sober actor not likely to start a nuclear war. Still, some PRC leaders threatened in 1996 to nuke Los Angeles if the U.S. interfered in PRC efforts to incorporate Taiwan. Few PRC leaders shared the cooperative security mentality of their U.S. and Russian counterparts. In late 1997, however, China agreed (more explicitly than before) not to send nuclear equipment to other countries.

As a new millennium approached, all countries were vulnerable to nuclear and other forms of terror. The task of hitting a fly in the sky (or a swarm of hornets) remained technologically daunting. Even if antiballistic missile defenses were improved, they would not stop low-flying cruise missiles. Nor would they help against weapons smuggled into a country. A nuclear sword of Damocles could fall at any moment. What if just one or two missiles penetrated and struck any city with **nuclear, biological, or chemical (NBC) weapons**? Every country with nuclear power stations was vulnerable to terrorists. A conventional bomb could rip open a reactor and spew deadly radioactivity far and wide. Most Americans lived oblivious to these dangers. As noted above, most U.S. citizens assumed that their government had already deployed a defense that could destroy a large percentage of attacking missiles.

Real Disarmament: INF, START 1 and 2, and CFE

INF. As the Cold War melted, many fresh streams bubbled through the ice. Presidents Reagan and Gorbachev in 1987 signed the first major disarmament agreement between Washington and Moscow—the **Intermediate-Range Nuclear Forces (INF) Treaty**. Reagan demanded and got from Gorbachev a commitment to zero-INF. The INF Treaty obliged Washington and Moscow to destroy all their ground-based missiles, both ballistic and cruise, with a range of 500 to 5,500 km. To reach zero, the Kremlin had to remove over three times as many warheads and destroy more than twice as many missiles as Washington, a process both sides completed in 1991. Skeptics noted, however, that both sides retained other missiles able to do the same work as those destroyed, and that INF warheads and guidance systems could be recycled.

START. In 1991 Gorbachev and U.S. President George Bush signed the first **Strategic Arms Reduction Treaty (START)**, known as START 1. It obliged Washington and Moscow within seven years to cut their forces by more than one-third to 1,600 strategic delivery vehicles (ICBMs, SLBMs, heavy bombers) and 6,000 warheads. When the USSR dissolved later that year, Russia (or, more precisely, the Russian Federation) took the Soviet Union's place in START and other arms control regimes. Three other successor states inherited nuclear weapons—Ukraine, Belarus, and Kazakstan—but they agreed to send all nuclear warheads in their territories to Russia. START 1 became legally binding in 1994 and each party began steps to meet the ceilings set for seven years hence—2001.

President Bush and Russian President Boris Yeltsin in 1993 signed another treaty, START 2, requiring each side to cut its arsenal by 2003 to no more than 3,500 strategic nuclear warheads. To reduce any capacity for a disarming first-strike, the parties agreed that ICBMs could have only one warhead each and that no more than half the allowed warheads could be deployed on submarines.

START 2 was approved by the U.S. Senate in 1996, but the Russian parliament was apprehensive. Confronted by the likely expansion of NATO and by deteriorating Russian conventional forces, many Russian leaders wanted to keep or improve their nuclear arsenal. The Kremlin's military doctrine changed in the mid-1990s to allow Moscow "first use of nuclear arms" even against a conventional attack. Since many Russian missiles were deteriorating from old age, however, some strategists proposed a much cheaper solution—a START 3 requiring Russia and the U.S. to reduce its arsenals to a thousand or so nuclear weapons.

CFE. The 1990 **Conventional Forces in Europe (CFE) Treaty** set equal ceilings for ground and air forces of two groups of states—in effect, NATO and the Warsaw Pact—"from the Atlantic to the Urals." On average, one-third of existing tanks and artillery were destroyed or removed from the designated region. Again, Russia made the largest cuts.

By 1995 all CFE Treaty signatories had met their obligatory reductions except Armenia, Azerbaijan, Belarus, and Russia. Russia exceeded its quota on its southern flank where it had moved large conventional forces to fight in Chechnya and to shape events in Azerbaijan and Georgia. Russia asked for and got adjustments on its "flank" limitations, because its alliance system had dissolved and it stood nearly alone.

Given NATO's planned expansion, Russia and other CFE states began negotiations in 1997 to revise the CFE Treaty by late 1998 in order to abolish bloc-to-bloc limitations; reduce most quotas for individual states; keep flank limits that constrain Russian deployments in the Baltic, the Caucasus, and along Norway's border; allow existing NATO countries to deploy forces for a time in new NATO countries (such as Poland) within regional limits; and increase transparency.

A Revolution in Arms Control and Disarmament: How Did It Happen?

INF, START, and CFE differed from earlier treaties: First, Moscow and Washington disarmed. They did not merely limit arms—they junked weapons, new and old. Generals winced to see modern missiles and bombers literally sawed in half! Second, cuts were asymmetrical. In each case the Kremlin agreed to make larger cuts than Washington to reach zero or similar force levels. Third, verification of earlier treaties depended on "national means" (mainly satellite reconnaissance). But INF, CFE, and START mandated highly intrusive on-site inspections that would continue for years even after arms reductions had been completed.

Why these breakthroughs? Each side believed that it could gain more from mutual cooperation than from armed rivalry. The real world inhabited by Presidents Reagan and Gorbachev, Bush and Yeltsin, differed sharply from the artificial confines of Prisoner's Dilemma.

• *Direct communications:* Unlike PD's isolated players, Washington and Moscow communicated directly about common problems—even their mutual distrust.

• *Repetition and learning:* Unlike a single round of PD, relations between states go on and on. Americans and Soviets gathered from decades of experience that mutual defection is costly.

• *Limited payoffs:* Unlike the PD structure that posits "catastrophe" for the sucker, Washington and Moscow retained a nuclear deterrent so that, even if one side cheated, it could not dictate terms.

• *Safeguards:* Most Soviet-U.S. agreements were backed by elaborate "verification" systems.

• *Multiple players:* More than two actors played key roles. If Washington or Moscow defected, it would face repercussions in Berlin, Beijing, Tokyo, and New Delhi.

• *Multiple options:* Each player had many options beyond "cooperate" or "defect." Package deals could be worked out with sweeteners.

All of these factors—more nuanced than the basic PD exercise—helped the U.S. and Russia become contingent cooperators.

HORIZONTAL PROLIFERATION: HOW MANY PLAYERS SHOULD HAVE THE BOMB?

While the vertical volcano rose and then slumped, a second volcano grew and broadened. Britain tested its first atomic bomb in 1952; France, in 1960; China, in 1964. Each went on to conduct hydrogen bomb tests and wed warheads to missiles.

The Chain Reaction: Who, Whom?

A dozen or so other countries pursued the nuclear weapons option. Israel started assembling bombs in the 1960s and had 100 to 200 bombs by the mid-1990s; Israel insisted on keeping its "Samson option" until a stable peace took hold in the Middle East.[21]

India tested a "peaceful" nuclear device in 1974; India had components for 30 to 100 bombs in the 1990s. This "can deploy but have not yet" mode of deterrence was emulated by Pakistan. Islamabad started nuclear R&D in the 1970s and had components for at least fifteen bombs by the mid-1990s.

Several Arab countries and Iran carried out nuclear R&D to produce (some said) an "Islamic bomb." Iraq's "Osiraq" nuclear plant was destroyed by an Israeli air attack in 1971. Still, Iraq continued its nuclear programs—discovered by outsiders only after Desert Storm.

Several countries conducted serious research but later claimed to renounce the nuclear weapons option: Argentina, Brazil, Taiwan, South Korea, and North Korea.

South Africa secretly manufactured a half dozen nuclear bombs but then destroyed them in the late 1980s.

Can the Genie Be Put Back in the Bottle?

Seeking to freeze the nuclear weapons club, U.S. and Soviet negotiators in 1968 drafted the **Nuclear Nonproliferation Treaty (NPT)** and asked all states to sign. The pact permitted states with nuclear arms to keep them, but banned other states from acquiring them. Many governments welcomed the idea, but others protested "unfair discrimination" against nuclear weapons have-nots.

Britain backed the NPT but France and China refused to join unless

21. Seymour M. Hersh, *The Samson Option: Israel's Nuclear Arsenal and American Foreign Policy* (New York: Random House, 1991).

UN Security Council Resolution 687, passed April 3, 1991, ordered the elimination of Iraq's nuclear, chemical, and biological weapons programs and missiles with ranges over 150 kilometers. It also authorized inspections to ensure compliance. Here, in August 1991, a group of UN Special Commission inspectors stands at the base of Iraq's 300-mm. long range "supergun."

the U.S. and USSR began to disarm. Beijing called for abolishing all nuclear weapons (leaving the world's largest manpower supply untouched). Meanwhile, it pledged never to initiate use of nuclear weapons.

Why should have-nots forgo nuclear arms? The NPT obligated the nuclear haves to (1) share nuclear technology for peaceful uses with NPT signers; (2) shield signers from nuclear blackmail or nuclear attack; and (3) negotiate "in good faith" to end their own nuclear arms competition.

Some countries found such assurances weak or wanted their own nuclear weapons no matter what. The countries most likely to cross the nuclear threshold—India, Israel, Argentina, Brazil, Pakistan, and South Africa—did not sign the NPT, at least initially. So their nuclear ambitions were unfettered.

But most countries joined the NPT and it entered into force for them in 1970. Signers included many states that could build nuclear weapons but chose not to—Japan, the two Germanys, Italy, Czechoslovakia, and Sweden. Some other states signed the NPT but acted as though they sought to buy or build the bomb anyway. They were free to continue research and could withdraw from the treaty on just three months' notice.

The NPT worked far better than many analysts expected in the 1970s. Argentina and Brazil renounced their local arms race and joined the NPT in the 1980s. South Africa dismantled its secret arsenal and then joined the NPT in 1991. This reduced the number of nuclear haves from seven to six—the Big Five plus Israel. France and China grudgingly joined the NPT in 1992.

The nuclear club expanded from six to nine when the USSR disappeared in late 1991. Newly independent Ukraine, Kazakstan, and Belarus inherited major parts of the Soviet arsenal, but they too joined the NPT as nuclear have-nots and transferred their nuclear arms to Russia. That left six countries with deployed nuclear arms. By the mid-1990s eight or nine countries had renounced nuclear weapons after possessing them or approaching the threshold: South Korea, Taiwan, Argentina, Brazil, South Africa, Ukraine, Kazakstan, Belarus, and perhaps North Korea. Two more stopped just short of deployment: India and Pakistan. All these decisions were influenced by U.S. sticks and carrots.[22] United Nations inspectors destroyed many of Iraq's nuclear weapons facilities in the 1990s.

More than 170 states met in 1995 and debated whether to extend the NPT. Many have-nots complained that the Big Five plus Israel still had nuclear arms; Teheran denounced U.S. efforts to block Russian technology sales to Iran. Despite these and other complaints, the conferees voted on May 11, 1995, to extend the NPT without time limits. They concurred that nonproliferation conduced to a more stable world.

The NPT became the centerpiece of a multifaceted security regime to limit the spread of nuclear and other weapons of mass destruction. Each component of the regime, however, faced serious challenges, as noted in Table 6.2.

If all else failed, the nuclear haves could still try to destroy incipient

22. Mitchell Reiss, *Bridled Ambition: Why Countries Constrain Their Nuclear Capabilities* (Baltimore: Johns Hopkins University Press, 1995).

Table 6.2   Elements of the Nonproliferation Regime

A Growing Infrastructure	Problems
The **International Atomic Energy Agency (IAEA)** was established in 1957 to promote the peaceful uses of nuclear energy. It also monitors NPT compliance.	Too little money, too few staff, and too weak a mandate for its duties. Efforts in 1990s to expand its mandate to inspect beyond declared facilities encountered much resistance.
Nuclear test limitations include the 1963 limited nuclear test ban and the 1996 comprehensive ban on all nuclear tests.	India refused to sign both agreements and prevented the 1996 ban from entering into force.
Nuclear-free zones were agreed on for Antarctica (1959), Latin America (1967), the South Pacific (1985), Southeast Asia (1995), and Africa (1996).	No agreement was reached on the Middle East, South Asia, or most regions where the Big Five operated militarily.
The **NPT** bans further spread of nuclear weapons. Signed in 1968, it entered into force in 1970 and was renewed in 1995 without a time limit.	Not signed by Israel or major threshold states such as India.
The **MTCR** (Missile Technology Control Regime) was established in 1987 to curb the spread of military missiles. By 1997, it had twenty-eight members and three "adherents"—the PRC, Israel, and Ukraine.	The regime had many loopholes. The Big Five exported anti-ship cruise missiles to more than forty countries. China transferred ballistic missiles and their components to Pakistan and Middle Eastern buyers.
After the Gulf War a **UN Special Commission** worked with the IAEA to neuter all Iraqi mass destruction weapons and plants.	Iraq hid whatever it could from the inspectors. France and Russia wished to relax the pressure.
The **BWC** (Bacteriological and Toxin Weapons Convention of 1975) banned possession of biological weapons.	Lacked verification procedures. Iraq cheated, and perhaps Russia. Laboratories in U.S. and elsewhere opposed intrusive inspection.
The **CWC** (Chemical Weapons Convention of 1992) banned production and use of chemical weapons and required their destruction within ten years.	The treaty entered into force in 1997 but without U.S or Russian ratification. Washington feared that the Russians withheld data; Moscow balked at the cost of destroying chemical agents.

Table 6.3 Is Nuclear Spread Inevitable? Is More Better?

Out-comes	How Likely is Nuclear Spread?	
	Inevitable	Avoidable
Good	More is better.	Individual states should go all out to join the club.
Mixed	The worst dangers can be managed.	Be selective: Permit only "stabilizing" proliferation.
Bad	Expect catastrophe and build defenses.	Proliferation can be halted and perhaps reversed.

Table 6.4 The 1994 Ukrainian Debate: Should Kyiv Keep Its Soviet-Era Nuclear Arms?

Yes	No
Nuclear forces will deter Russian bullying or invasion.	Nuclear suicide is not a credible threat.
Nuclear forces are much cheaper to maintain than conventional forces.	Russia might sabotage or destroy our weapons with a first-strike.
We will be able to bargain from strength on disputed issues such as the Black Sea Fleet and Crimea.	We lack effective command and control procedures.

23. Barry R. Schneider, "Nuclear Proliferation and Counter-Proliferation: Policy Issues and Debates," *Mershon International Studies Review* 38, no. 2 (October 1994): 209–234.

24. Scott D. Sagan and Kenneth N. Waltz, *The Spread of Nuclear Weapons: A Debate* (New York: Norton, 1995); John J. Mearsheimer, "The Case for a Ukrainian Nuclear Deterrent," *Foreign Affairs* 72, no. 3 (summer 1993): 50–66; and Steven E. Miller, "The Case Against a Ukrainian Nuclear Deterrent," ibid., 67–80.

25. See John Lewis Gaddis, "The Long Peace: Elements of Stability in the Postwar International System," *International Security* 10, no. 4 (spring 1986): 99–142.

nuclear facilities elsewhere. But this "Osiraq option" (named for Israel's attack on Saddam Hussein's Osiraq plant) would be an act of war and could release radioactive materials into a wide area.

Is More Better?

Why struggle to halt nuclear spread?[23] As we see in Table 6.3, some realists say that "more is better." Nuclear spread, they say, would extend deterrence and prevent bullying. Neorealist Kenneth Waltz favors only a gradual spread of nuclear weapons to give actors time to adjust to a changing structure; other realists favor only selective proliferation to great powers such as Germany and Ukraine.[24]

"More is worse" analysts fear that reason may not prevail. The more nuclear actors, the more chances of a nuclear strike—by mechanical or human error, by madness, or by calculation. Nuclear terror may have contributed to the "long peace" between Moscow and Washington, but that peace benefited also from overall power parity, spy satellites that reduced the fear of surprise attack, some tacit "rules of the road," absence of territorial claims, and lack of historical wounds to avenge.[25] None of these factors eases tensions between Ukraine and Russia; North and South Korea; India and Pakistan; or in the Middle East. Absent these factors, nuclear arms could easily inflame rather than stabilize.

Let us consider how the arguments for and against nuclear weapons may have played out in Ukraine and North Korea in the early 1990s. We begin in Kyiv (see Table 6.4).

If Ukraine kept nuclear arms, Moscow warned, Russia would not implement START 1 or START 2. But Washington offered Kyiv substantial economic and diplomatic incentives to renounce nuclear arms. U.S. intervention succeeded. Ukraine in 1994 ratified START 1, joined the NPT, and promised to send all nuclear warheads on Ukrainian soil to Russia provided that Ukrainian ownership of the fissile fuel in the weapons be recognized. A similar pattern took hold in Kazakstan and Belarus. At Kazakstan's request, U.S. planes removed some 600 kilograms of highly enriched uranium from Kazakstan in late 1994. In 1995 all nuclear warheads were removed from Kazakstan to Russia. In 1997, however, Russia protested Kazak plans to have a U.S. airplane with sensors measure radioactivity near the former Soviet nuclear test site close to the Kazak-Russian border.

How did the situation look in North Korea? Pyongyang signed the NPT in 1985, but the U.S. warned the IAEA (see Table 6.2) that North Korea was cheating—diverting sufficient fissile material from its Soviet-made nuclear reactor to make four to six bombs by 1994. Pyongyang put off any IAEA inspections until 1992 and refused in 1993 any special inspections of facilities that U.S. intelligence suspected of housing fissile material. Moreover, North Korea was building two larger reactors that would permit it to produce thirty nuclear bombs a year by the late 1990s. When the UN Security Council in 1993 demanded that North Korea permit "special inspections" of suspected nuclear material storage sites, Pyongyang said it would withdraw from the NPT. We can guess how North Koreans saw their options (see Table 6.5).

President Clinton seriously considered military action to take out the DPRK nuclear facilities in 1993, but North Korean and U.S. diplomats began to talk. By 1994 they had reached a deal that permitted each side to back away from war. Their deal was not an "agreement," since mutual trust was absent. Rather, it was an "agreed framework"—a schedule of steps that each side would take so long as the other did its part. The DPRK would remain a full party to the NPT. North Korea would freeze its nuclear activities and dismantle its nuclear facilities. It would permit some IAEA inspections immediately and more later on. In exchange, the U.S. would arrange to supply North Korea with two light-water reactors (not suited for producing fissile materials) and heavy oil (good for heating but not for tank fuel) to make up for the energy lost by taking its existing reactor off line. Washington would also reduce barriers to trade and investment and gradually normalize relations with Pyongyang, provided that North Korea reciprocated by curbing its missile exports to Iran.

U.S. negotiators got built-in guarantees. The deal delayed most concessions until North Korea implemented key provisions. No oil arrived until the freeze on nuclear facilities began. No significant nuclear component would arrive until IAEA inspectors had accounted for past plutonium production and placed it under safeguards. Doors opened to peace.

Yes, Pyongyang drove a hard bargain. By violating its NPT and IAEA commitments, North Korea extorted over $4 billion worth of power supplies. South Korea would build the reactors. Seoul and Tokyo would pay for the reactors; the U.S., for the oil. Still, $4 billion was trivial next to the costs of war—a bargain price for arms control.

"Loose Nukes"

The nuclear threats arising from the former Soviet Union were more difficult to control than when the Kremlin ruled its empire with an iron fist. The good news was that tactical nuclear weapons were returned to Russia from the Soviet border republics in 1991–1992 and that Ukraine,

Table 6.5 The 1994 Debate in North Korea: Should the DPRK Continue Its Nuclear Weapons Development?

Yes	No
We must practice self-help because Moscow and Beijing deserted us for the West.	Our economic plight compels us to join the world economy while preserving our system of government.
Even a few bombs can deter enemy attack and give us leverage; the U.S. talks big but does little.	If we go nuclear, South Korea and Japan may follow. Better to strike a deal with the U.S. that isolates South Korea.
Our foes will not dare attack us because they do not want a major war. Besides, we can blow up South Korea's reactors.	Hanging tough is pointless. No one will attack us if we renounce nuclear arms. The U.S. promises us energy assistance.

Kazakstan, and Belarus forswore nuclear arms. The bad news was that the former Second World overflowed with nuclear arms and fissile materials. Underpaid Russian scientists and colonels might sell a ball of plutonium or even a warhead from Russia's stockpiles. Nuclear smugglers were arrested in Russia, Germany, and Eastern Europe. One investigator said the Russian navy guarded its potatoes better than its nuclear fuel.[26]

Russia and the U.S. agreed in 1992 to a Weapons and Nonproliferation Agreement to control fissile materials.[27] Under the **Cooperative Threat Reduction Program** (funded by the 1991 **Nunn-Lugar Act**), the U.S. Congress allocated $100 to $300 million annually to facilitate denuclearization and demilitarization of Russia, Ukraine, Kazakstan, and Belarus, and to reduce the threat of NBC weapons proliferation.[28] But Russians complained that the U.S. kept its purse strings tight while some U.S. officials charged that the Russian Ministry of Atomic Energy and the Russian military shielded their secrets and assets from outsiders.

The hoped-for peace dividend proved difficult to collect. Swords to plowshares—military **conversion**—went slowly in the U.S. and Russia. Both Washington and Moscow wanted to keep weapons labs and production lines open. Who could know what future needs might be? Firms long accustomed to dealing with government officials could not easily produce for civilian markets. Backed with Nunn-Lugar funds, some U.S. firms tried to enlist former Soviet arms builders in civilian enterprises, but the match was often jarring. Should former missile makers now produce soft drinks?

The genie was out of the bottle. It was not clear how many masters the genie would serve.

CONVENTIONAL ARMS PROLIFERATION

Mass destruction weapons are comparatively cheap. Most arms spending is for conventional weapons. The world arms trade declined in the late 1980s but the apparent success of U.S. "smart bombs" against Iraq in 1991 increased demand for U.S. exports.

Double standards prevailed. Washington called for mutual limits on arms sales after the Gulf War, only to step up arms transfers to Israel and other clients. U.S. exports accounted for about 42 percent of the international arms trade in the mid-1990s—total value about $40 billion in 1996. U.S. military aerospace exports alone jumped from about $8 billion to $11 billion in 1996. Runners-up were the UK (22 percent of the total arms trade in 1996), France (14 percent), and Russia (9 percent). Unable to compete with the U.S. in high performance conventional arms,

26. William C. Potter, "Before the Deluge? Assessing the Threat of Nuclear Leakage from the Post-Soviet States," *Arms Control Today* 25, no. 8 (October 1995): 9–16; see also the U.S. National Academy of Sciences report on excess weapons plutonium, summarized in ibid., 17–20.

27. Moscow and Washington built upon precedents. The NSG (Nuclear Suppliers Group) was established in 1974 to regulate nuclear exports, and the INFCE (International Nuclear Fuel Cycle Evaluation) in 1977 by both suppliers and importers to control nuclear energy.

28. See William S. Cohen, *Report of the Secretary of Defense to the President and Congress* (Washington, D.C.: Government Printing Office, April 1997), 61–67.

China and Russia sold missiles and nuclear equipment to the Islamic world. But Saudi Arabia and Egypt were the world's largest importers in 1996, each of which favored U.S. products. And tiny Israel exported weapons worth twice as much as China's exports.[29]

Washington explained that U.S. exports helped "maintain the balance of power"—whereas those of Russia and China destabilized it. U.S. and other arms exporters justified exports by the benefits to domestic industry: Without foreign sales, unit costs would be much higher at home. Furthermore, they said: "If we don't sell abroad, our rivals will. How can we keep our technological edge without foreign sales?"

In 1991–1992 the United Nations established the Registry of Conventional Arms. Perhaps **transparency** would inhibit the arms trade. UN members were supposed to volunteer data on the number of weapons— from tanks to missiles—imported or exported. But voluntary obligations were easily skirted. Officials in Chile reported one thing to the UN, another thing to the IMF, and something else in the national press.[30]

Attempting to increase transparency, more than thirty states adhered to the 1996 "Wassenaar Arrangement"—a voluntary system to coordinate national controls on the export of conventional arms and dual-use technologies by promoting information exchange through a consultative forum. As of 1997, the U.S., UK, France, and Russia belonged, but not Israel or China or any Arab country.

A major threat to life and limb comes from one of the cheapest and most common weapons—land mines. More people have been killed by land mines than by NBC weapons. In the mid-1990s there were at least 85 million mines beneath the soil of sixty-four countries—from Afghanistan to Cambodia to El Salvador. Mines are easy to plant but difficult to remove. To neutralize a $5 mine can easily cost $1,000. But consider also the cost of mines not cleared: lives lost, bodies maimed, farm lands unplowed; the costs of caring for invalids (such a burden that many were executed by their own families in Afghanistan). Humanitarian agencies sought in the 1990s to persuade all UN members to ban the export of antipersonnel mines. But demand and supply (from forty-eight manufacturing countries) remained high.

Canada and NGOs led the fight for a global ban signed in Ottawa by more than one hundred countries in 1997—minus the signatures of the U.S., Russia, and China. Beijing and others liked land mines cheap and dirty. Washington wanted to ban all but high-tech mines that deactivated after a specified time and insisted on the right to retain mines on the North–South Korea dividing line.

Land mines infest the globe. Cheap to produce, they are difficult, dangerous, and expensive to disarm. Here, UN peacekeepers from Bangladesh instruct a Cambodian soldier on how to deactivate mines. A ban on land mines was signed by nearly 100 countries in 1997— but not by the U.S., which insisted it be allowed to maintain mines to defend South Korea from the North.

29. *The Military Balance, 1997/98* (London: International Institute for Strategic Studies, 1997), 264–265.

30. See Edward J. Laurence et al., *Arms Watch: SIPRI Report on the First Year of the UN Register of Conventional Arms* (New York: Oxford University Press, 1993).

WHAT PROPOSITIONS HOLD?
WHAT QUESTIONS REMAIN?

INTERDEPENDENCE, MUTUAL GAIN, AND OPENNESS

If all nations disarm, will there be peace? Not unless human life and institutions are transformed. States arm because they fear and fear because they arm. If all swords become plowshares, some humans will still menace others with slings and clubs. David's "dual-purpose" sling sufficed to kill Goliath.

Mutual vulnerability makes the security dilemma pervasive. As a result, real security must be both mutual and universal.[31] But this insight is difficult to implement. Like the hunter who leaps for the hare, governments often pass up potentially large mutual gains for small, one-sided gains available here and now.

Secrecy often amplifies insecurity. Governments prefer to plan and negotiate armaments behind closed doors. Former Secretary of State Henry Kissinger used "back channels" to Moscow that bypassed Congress and even the official U.S. negotiating team. Not surprisingly, when the White House presented SALT 1 as a done deal, the Senate complained. Secrecy can blind even the secret-holders. Had MIRVs been debated more openly, they might have been curbed—to mutual advantage.

The Arms Control Paradox

Here is the paradox: Arms controls are easiest to negotiate when they are not needed—when relations are so cordial that neither party fears the other. Still, the record shows that arms limitations are possible even when tensions run high. Thus, Washington and Moscow negotiated and implemented SALT 1 while the Vietnam War raged; they concluded the INF Treaty while the Reagan White House backed anti-Communist guerrillas worldwide.

Is Parity Necessary for Arms Control?

Must rivals have the same quantity and quality of arms before they can trim forces? The answer is no. Many arms accords have been concluded despite deep asymmetries. Trade-offs may be paid in multiple currencies. Soviet leaders often focused on economic gains from arms control while U.S. leaders sought strategic stability. Contrary to realist doctrine, arms accords often permit mutual but unequal gain.

The "multiple symmetry" model distorts history and offers bad advice. It exaggerates the action-reaction behavior of competing actors. The USSR never tried to match the U.S. Navy nor did the U.S. emulate the large Soviet army. *Sufficiency* is a better guide to policy than matching.

31. Both conditions were stressed by Soviet President Gorbachev in the late 1980s. See Clemens, *Can Russia Change?*, chaps. 7–8.

Each society should listen to its own drummer—not mechanically mimic others.

Prevention is easier than cure. It is more feasible to ban a weapon before deployment than after. But preventive measures are difficult to adopt during periods of technological ferment.

Does Arms Control Save, Make, or Lose Money?

The economic impacts of defense spending are complicated. Military outlays can pillage wealth. But they can also benefit an economy if they nourish technology, work habits, and infrastructure. The U.S. interstate highway system and the Internet resulted from defense programs. Taiwan, Singapore, and South Korea for decades spent much more of their GDP on defense than Japan did, but also achieved high growth. North Korea outspent South Korea on military preparedness, but stagnated economically.

It is difficult to turn swords into plowshares—even more difficult in former Communist economies than in free market economies. Efforts in the 1990s to convert some of Russia's military industries to civilian mixed with all the other problems of switching to a market economy. Managers of military plants resisted efforts to end their subsidies. Where would they get capital to develop new products? Joint ventures with U.S. companies scored some successes but were hobbled by many problems.[32]

Former Communist states such as Slovakia found that to make autos instead of tanks would require much retooling and retraining. It was easier to turn out Soviet-designed tanks and planes for Third World markets. For similar reasons, Russians in the 1990s armed China, while the U.S. supplied big spenders in Taiwan and Saudi Arabia.

32. Kevin P. O'Prey, *A Farewell to Arms? Russia's Struggles with Defense Conversion* (New York: Twentieth Century Fund, 1995).

The global arms trade declined as the Cold War ended, but partly revived as many governments sought weapons like those used in the Gulf War. During President Bill Clinton's first term, U.S. Secretary of State Warren Christopher often tried to persuade Syrian President Hafez al-Assad to make peace with Israel. But Syria wanted Israel to return the Golan Heights, which many Israelis saw as essential to their security.

Memo to the President:

Are Negotiations Good for Arms Control? Is Arms Control Good for Peace?

START and other arms accords may be steps toward a world where brute force plays a declining role next to soft power, where fitness and well-being are measured not by warheads but by fewer infant deaths and more education. The net impact of arms control on peace and security is unclear. Significant arms limitations have been negotiated and implemented: Some treaties have probably reduced the danger of war and saved money; arms talks have kept channels open and contributed to détente. But disarmament negotiations and propaganda have also spurred distrust and arms competition. Despite many treaties, the USSR and U.S. by 1990 possessed nearly 50,000 nuclear warheads. Each country is obliged by 2003 to cut to no more than 3,500 strategic nuclear warheads. Even then, however, our arsenals will be larger than when the NPT was signed in 1968, and the U.S. will probably retain nearly 7,000 more warheads in storage for deployment if conditions change.

How Much Is Enough?

U.S. defense spending declined from 6 percent of GDP in 1990 to 3.5 percent in the late 1990s.[33] But Americans have yet to collect a substantial peace dividend. In constant dollars the U.S. defense budget in the late 1990s was still fourth-fifths its level in the late 1980s. U.S. defense outlays in the late 1990s exceeded the combined military budgets of all other industrialized countries, perhaps the entire world.

Can the U.S. cut its defense budget and apply the savings to infrastructure improvements, health, education, or tax savings? The answer hinges on the tasks assigned to U.S. forces.

When the USSR disappeared, the Pentagon decided that its mission should be "two plus." It needed forces to fight and win two regional wars like the 1991 Gulf War nearly simultaneously, even while carrying out peacekeeping or humanitarian missions—without allies, if need be.

Some hawks accepted the two plus standard but complained that the Pentagon was asking for too little money and too few personnel to carry out the two plus mission. They urged more spending both for combat readiness and for procurement of new weapons.

Doves said that the two plus mission was not necessary. No rogue state in the late 1990s had even half of Iraq's assets before the Gulf War. Even if they did, the U.S. could and should count on fighting with partners—not alone.

Isolationists said that two plus was too much. They wanted a "Fortress America" guarded by SDI.

Some idealists said two plus might be too little. They wanted the U.S. to be able to serve as world policeman.

Some critics said "one plus" would suffice, because two simultaneous regional challenges are unlikely.

We owls believe that the Pentagon's two plus standard offers a prudent middle ground between the other extremes. It also provides a foundation for dealing with conflicts larger and smaller than two regional wars. It seeks cooperation with partners but could perform its tasks without them. It takes account of near- and

---

33. In 1997 the Pentagon sought budget authority for $251 billion in fiscal year 1998. But this reckoning omitted other defense-related activities that accounted for about 2 percent of GDP. They included interest on the public debt due to previous defense outlays—more than $100 billion; Department of Veterans' Affairs costs—more than $38 billion; civil defense expenditures—more than $32 billion, mostly for military pensions; intelligence—about $28 billion; international security assistance—at least $6 billion per year; assessed payments for UN peacekeeping—$1 billion in 1994; and operational costs—at least $1 billion in a quiet year.

intermediate-term needs while making judicious investments in long-term research and development.[34]

The fact is that already in 1994 the U.S. almost found itself at war with both Iraq and North Korea. Rogue regimes are weaker now than Iraq in 1990 but may have hidden resources. The two plus standard permits a hedge in case China or Russia becomes aggressive.

We need to do more to bring Russia and China into cooperative security programs. We could get by with much smaller forces if we had greater confidence that Russia and China would partner with us for mutual gain.

Americans' willingness to contain rogue governments depends on technologies that keep U.S. casualties low. The U.S. effort against Iraq in 1991 exploited a "system of systems"—coordinated intelligence and precision targeting. But success in the Gulf War also depended on substantial forces quickly transportable over vast distances. We must continue to invest in quantity as well as quality.

Cutting military forces and research can save money today but compel sharp increases later. If demobilization invites aggression, peace dividends can evaporate. Compared to fighting, arms at the ready are cheap. The two plus standard is right.

Twelve Policy Guidelines

Let us be neither hawks nor doves. Better to be wise like owls. Here are twelve guidelines:[35]

1. Maintain a credible but nonprovocative deterrent, but reduce reliance on nuclear deterrence over the long run. It would be imprudent to scrap all nuclear weapons if only because scientists will still know how to make them. But we should encourage Russia to join us in cutting our nuclear weapons to a number well below one thousand.

2. Develop a conventional (and more credible) deterrent.

3. Maintain the ABM regime. Develop theater defenses to protect against regional threats, but avoid measures that could undermine Russian or Chinese confidence in their present deterrents.

4. Lengthen the fuse. Prevent war by miscalculation or accident. Strengthen intelligence and command and control systems.

5. Prevent and control crises.

6. Continue to block horizontal proliferation of mass destruction weapons.

7. Pursue nuclear and conventional arms control.

8. Link arms control analysis and defense planning. Avoid propagandistic and political distractions.

9. Keep the "two regional wars plus" standard. It provides a hedge against many dangers.

10. Restructure and improve our capacity to resist terrorists, home-grown and foreign, some of whom may have mass destruction weapons.

11. Strengthen the UN, IAEA, and other international security regimes for arms control, verification, and enforcement.

12. Reduce the root causes of arms and diffidence: transform relationships.

---

34. Even with a budget oriented toward two plus wars, the Defense Department felt compelled to cut back on its planned spending for new weapons. Infrastructure costs, headed by operation and maintenance, consumed the lion's share of the budget. See U.S. General Accounting Office, *Future Years Defense Program: DOD's 1998 Plan Has Substantial Risk in Execution*, GAO/NSIAD-98-26 (Washington, D.C.: Government Printing Office, October 1997).

35. See also Graham T. Allison, Albert Carnesale, Joseph S. Nye, Jr., eds., *Hawks, Doves, and Owls: An Agenda for Avoiding Nuclear War* (New York: Norton, 1985).

KEY NAMES AND TERMS

antiballistic missile (ABM)
arms control
Baruch Plan
Conventional Forces in Europe (CFE)
    Treaty
conversion
cooperative security
Cooperative Threat Reduction
    Program
disarmament
Intermediate-Range Nuclear Forces
    (INF) Treaty

International Atomic Energy
    Agency (IAEA)
joker
minimum deterrent
multiple individually targetable
    reentry vehicles (MIRVs)
multiple symmetry
national missile defense (NMD)
nuclear, biological, or chemical (NBC)
    weapons
Nuclear Nonproliferation Treaty (NPT)
Nunn-Lugar Act

second-strike
security
security regimes
smart bombs
Strategic Arms Limitation Talks (SALT)
Strategic Arms Reduction Treaty
    (START)
Strategic Defense Initiative (SDI)
theater ballistic missile defense (TBMD)
transparency
triad

QUESTIONS TO DISCUSS

1. "Arms limitation efforts have succeeded only when the weapons at stake are obsolete or otherwise redundant." Is this an accurate assessment?

2. "Arms control negotiations have been counterproductive. At best they created an illusion of progress while the tools of war multiplied." Evaluate.

3. "The strongest power, to retain its hegemony, should strive for supremacy in the quality and quantity of arms." Evaluate.

4. How have the nuclear haves sought to limit the supply of nuclear arms? How have they sought to reduce demand for them?

5. Advise Washington: Should the Pentagon deploy or only research a national missile defense system?

6. Advise Moscow: Should the Kremlin comply with CFE? With START 2?

7. Advise Kyiv: Should Ukraine be faithful to the NPT?

8. Advise Pyongyang: Should North Korea strive to obtain nuclear arms—either openly or clandestinely?

9. Advise Beijing: Should the PRC condemn, ignore, or support U.S. efforts to build theater ballistic missile defenses?

10. Might there be value in alternative approaches to security, for example, nonviolent sanctions?

RECOMMENDED RESOURCES

BOOKS

Blacker, Coit D., and Gloria Duffy, eds. *International Arms Control: Issues and Agreements.* 2d ed. Stanford, Calif.: Stanford University Press, 1984.

Bremer, Stuart A., and Barry B. Hughes. *Disarmament and Development: A Design for the Future?* Englewood Cliffs, N.J.: Prentice Hall, 1990.

Bunn, George. *Extending the Non-Proliferation Treaty: Legal Questions Faced by the Parties in 1995.* Washington, D.C.: American Society of International Law, 1994.

Clemens, Walter C., Jr. *Can Russia Change? The USSR Confronts Global Interdependence.* New York: Routledge, 1990.

Encyclopedia of Arms Control and Disarmament. 3 vols. New York: Scribner's, 1993.

Garthoff, Raymond L. *Detente and Confrontation: American-Soviet Relations from Nixon to Reagan.* Washington, D.C.: Brookings Institution, 1985.

Harvard Project on Cooperative Denuclearization. *Cooperative Denuclearization.* Harvard University Center for Science and International Affairs, Harvard University, Cambridge, Mass., 1993 [part of a series].

Holloway, David. *Stalin and the Bomb: The Soviet Union and Atomic Energy, 1939–1956.* New Haven, Conn.: Yale University Press, 1994.

Institute for National Strategic Studies. *Strategic Assessment.* Washington, D.C.: Government Printing Office, 1995– . Annual.

Rhodes, Richard. *The Making of the Atomic Bomb.* New York: Simon & Schuster, 1986.

SIPRI Yearbook [title varies]. Stockholm: Stockholm International Peace Research Institute, 1970– . Annual.

U.S. Arms Control and Disarmament Agency. *Documents on Disarmament.* Washington, D.C.: Government Printing Office, 1960–1986.

U.S. Department of State. *Documents on Disarmament, 1945–1959.* 2 vols. Washington, D.C.: Government Printing Office, 1960.

U.S. Senate. Committee on Foreign Relations. *Disarmament and Security: A Collection of Documents, 1919–1955.* Washington, D.C.: Government Printing Office, 1956.

JOURNAL

Adelphi Papers

WEB SITES

Arms Control Association
    http://www.armscontrol.org/
Arms Sales Monitor
    http://www.fas.org/asmp/asmind.html
Center for International Security and Arms Control
    http://www-leland.stanford.edu/group/CISAC/
NGO Committee on Disarmament
    http://www.peacenet.org/disarm/
Stockholm International Peace Research Institute
    http://www.sipri.se/index.html
U.S. Arms Control & Disarmament Agency
    http://www.acda.gov/
War, Peace and Security Guide to Arms Control
    http://www.cfcsc.dnd.ca/links/peace/disarm.html

NEGOTIATING CONFLICT: HOW CAN FOES BECOME PARTNERS?

THE BIG QUESTIONS IN CHAPTER 7

- What are the options for dealing with conflict?

- How should you blend carrots and sticks to influence others?

- Is it best to "fight fire with fire"?

- When should you be tough? When should you be conciliatory?

- How can you get more of what you want without fighting?

- How can you escape the vicious cycle of distrust when dealing with a strong and determined adversary?

- How can you minimize criticism from domestic foes when making peaceful overtures to adversaries abroad?

- What risks can you take for peace? Can you be sure that foreign foes will not abuse your efforts to move toward peace?

- Did the Cold War rivals ever reduce tensions for more than a year or two?

- How can you replace conflict and distrust with a strategy of peace and mutual gain?

- What kinds of leaders have been the most effective negotiators?

- What strategies work best between and among actors who are at once partners and rivals?

How to Deal with "Koraq"? . . . *Your government faces a mean adversary—Koraq. Its government has been condemned by the United Nations for repressing its own people and for blowing up an Air France and a JAL airliner. Koraq's top leader is an enigma—sometimes smiling but usually menacing. He holds dozens of your business people and journalists captive—charged with espionage. He threatens to take adjacent lands by force. Intelligence studies estimate a "medium likelihood" that a desperate Koraq may lash out at its neighbors or your country; if so, there is a "high likelihood" it will use some of its 1,000 tons of chemical weapons including nerve gas. Your satellite imagery suggests that Koraq possesses five or more nuclear warheads.*

As National Security Adviser to the White House, it is your job to advise the President: Should your forces attack before Koraq becomes even stronger? You may win, but the costs could be high. You would prefer to resolve differences without war, but you are reluctant to make concessions. You don't want to look soft. Domestic foes may accuse you of cowardice. If you give Koraq an inch, it may try for a mile.

Is it even thinkable to cut a deal with Koraq's leader? If not, should you isolate, weaken, and perhaps overthrow him?

Has niceness ever worked in dealing with hard-line foes? You study the precedents: For decades Washington and Moscow were locked in protracted conflict. So were Washington and Beijing, and Beijing and Moscow. Each bilateral confrontation shaped the other to form a "great power triangle." Each conflict heated up and cooled down, leaving embers that still glow. You note that mainland China and "island China," Taiwan, are torn between conflict and conciliation; this is true of North and South Korea as well.

Do the experiences of Beijing, Moscow, Washington, Taipei, and the two Koreas offer any guidelines for coping with Koraq?

CONTENDING CONCEPTS AND EXPLANATIONS

WHEN TO BE TOUGH? WHEN TO BE CONCILIATORY? HOW?

States and other IR actors have interests that harmonize or conflict with those of other players. If they harmonize, the parties may collaborate to enhance parallel or shared objectives. If they clash, they confront each other as adversaries. Tensions may escalate from harsh words to threats to open hostilities. Détente (the relaxation of tensions) is also possible. Moving away from confrontation, actors engage in trade, form an alliance, reach an entente (understanding), achieve solidarity, and confederate or unite. A warming trend toward accommodation is a **rapprochement**. But détente need not produce entente or solidarity; smiles and sweet talk could be tricks intended to get the other side to lower its guard.

As we see in Table 7.1, the parties to a conflict may fight or withdraw. They may also try to divide the values at stake or transform the relationship and create values together. To divide or create values, however, requires cooperation. If you are a conditional cooperator, how can you induce the other side to cooperate? Should you be tough or conciliatory?

Table 7.1 Four Responses to Conflict

	Passive	Active
Negative	Surrender values (retreat)	Claim values (fight)
Positive	Divide values	Create values for mutual gain

When the Soviet alliance and USSR itself had dissolved, why keep NATO? Should the former foes meet to drink tea and plant flowers? In 1992 there was talk of Russia's joining NATO. By 1997, however, NATO was expanding eastward and Kremlin leaders complained that the West was again dividing Europe.

How should you blend sticks and carrots? Do you begin with a threat or a smile? If the other side frowns, how long do you keep smiling?

Tit-for-Tat

The computer tournament described in Chapter 1 found that the winning strategy in repeated plays of Prisoner's Dilemma is a variant of tit-for-tat (TFT): Cooperate on your first move and thereafter match the other player's previous move. Start off nice and never initiate toughness, but be "provokable"—immediately respond to toughness with toughness. However, you should also be "forgiving"—return to cooperation as soon as the other side cooperates.

TFT pleases realists. This behavior sends a clear message that you will punish force with force but reward cooperation.[1] The TFT approach will elicit good, cooperative outcomes and minimize poor ones. Both sides learn to forgo immediate gains in favor of long-term rewards.[2] The downside is that if both sides follow TFT, just one tough move puts them on an endless treadmill of mutual defection. Once mutual defection begins, it persists. This explains why the Cold War "conflict spiral" was so hard to break. Washington and Moscow usually matched each other's tough deeds and ignored tentative smiles. The security dilemma aggravated their relationship. One side's defensive steps looked threatening to the other. TFT logic pressed for multiple symmetry or better. Furthermore, U.S. and Soviet TFT was self-righteous. Each side reasoned: "They started it, we're just paying them back in kind."

TFT also took hold at the **demilitarized zone (DMZ)**, the no-man's land buffer zone between North and South Korea established by the 1953 armistice.[3] Representatives of the United Nations Command and North Korea met weekly in a Quonset hut at **Panmunjom** in what became a ritual of mutual acrimony. Each blamed the other for violating the armistice. An atmosphere of mutual distrust and disdain reigned. If a North Korean gave an American a piece of paper with his left hand—a sign of contempt—the American usually accepted it with his left.[4]

How to Reverse a Conflict Spiral: True GRIT

How could the parties shift from "fighting fire with fire" to "enlarging the pie" for mutual gain? An alternative approach suggests that one side make unilateral but contingent concessions. Psychologist Charles E. Osgood in 1962 proposed reversing the conflict spiral by **GRIT—graduated reciprocation in tension-reduction**.[5] Either side might take the first step, but the stronger party could better afford the risks.

1. When Queen Elizabeth visited San Francisco to see President Reagan in 1983, she observed that the Union Jack was flown upside down. The gaffe may well have been inadvertent. Still, when Reagan visited the queen on her royal yacht *Britannia*, the U.S. flag dangled upside down. If allies teach one another lessons in this manner, foes are even more inclined to do so.

2. Robert Axelrod, *The Evolution of Cooperation* (New York: Basic Books, 1984); and Axelrod, "An Evolutionary Approach to Norms," *American Political Science Review* 80 (1986): 1095–1111.

3. The July 27, 1953, armistice was signed by U.S. General Mark Clark, Commander-in-Chief, United Nations Command; Kim Il-sung, Supreme Commander, [North] Korean People's Army; and Peng Dehuai, Commander, Chinese People's Volunteers. The agreement provided also for a Neutral Nations Supervisory Commission.

4. The UN command reported more than 1,000 armistice violations just in 1968–1969, leaving 221 killed among UN personnel, 96 South Korean civilians dead, and over 600 North Korean infiltrators killed south of the DMZ. The North replied by accusing the "U.S. imperialist aggressors" of more than 7,000 violations in 1969.

5. At tense moments in the Cold War some Westerners called for unilateral disarmament. Their slogan: "Better Red than dead." But no Western government seriously considered this option. Charles Osgood hoped to break the impasse. See Osgood, *An Alternative to War or Surrender* (Urbana: University of Illinois Press, 1962); see also Amitai Etzioni, *The Hard Way to Peace: A New Strategy* (New York: Crowell-Collier, 1962).

Presidents Bill Clinton (U.S.) and Boris Yeltsin (Russia) tried to convert the détente forged by their predecessors into a long-term partnership. But Yeltsin's Russia felt cut off from the West by the eastward expansion of NATO—a spike in the wheels of cooperation. When the two men met in Helsinki, Finland, in March 1997, Clinton offered Russia a consultative voice in NATO—not the full partnership that Washington would soon offer to three former Soviet allies. Unable to prevent NATO expansion, Yeltsin accepted and both sides declared victory. But tempers continued to simmer in Moscow.

Before embarking on GRIT, the initiator must make clear to the other side its intent to get off the treadmill. Here is the message it must communicate:

We are embarking on a strategy to reduce tensions. We will make several unilateral initiatives to demonstrate our good will. We shall give you time to show your good will. We shall proceed to larger concessions and compromise accords if you reciprocate. But unless tension-reducing moves become mutual, we will revert to TFT.

GRIT may face many pitfalls. First of all, a friendly gesture may be misconstrued. Thus, in 1970 a U.S. Army lieutenant in the United Nations Command at Panmunjom decided to improve the climate by smiling at North Korean soldiers in the Quonset hut instead of glaring sternly. When a North Korean indicated that he wanted to pass, the American smiled and made way for him. Shortly thereafter the American found himself surrounded by several North Koreans who began to jostle him. They interpreted his conciliatory gesture as weakness.[6]

GRIT could not begin with good will gestures by a low-level officer. For GRIT to work in this instance, the U.S. president or head of the UN (U.S.) team should have announced a new strategy—and made sure that North Korean leaders and troops got the message.

A second pitfall is that small steps may lead nowhere. To be safe, the initiator usually begins with symbolic gestures. The other side may interpret these as cheap tricks and not reciprocate. Neither side wishes to be fooled.

6. Walter C. Clemens, Jr., "GRIT at Panmunjom: Conflict and Cooperation in Divided Korea," *Asian Survey* 13, no. 6 (June 1973): 531–559 at 548.

Third, the initiator may renounce GRIT if the other side takes too long to respond. During this interval, the initiator's leaders are exposed to domestic criticism as well as external risk.

Fourth is the **monkey wrench problem**. Domestic foes or jealous clients can throw a monkey wrench that disrupts the process of tension-reduction. Détente is a fragile flower, easily crushed.

Fifth, governments are not monolithic. Bureaucratic inertia and vested interests can throttle GRIT. Purveyors of propaganda and "dirty tricks" may continue their standard operating routines—business as usual.

Finally, momentum may be hard to sustain. The first steps toward conciliation may come cheap, while further moves encounter profound obstacles, as we shall see in each case study.

Triangular Diplomacy

If there are three parties to a conflict, **triangular diplomacy**—the attempt by one party in a dispute to exploit differences between two others—may be useful. When Washington perceived that China and Russia were rivals, several U.S. presidents hoped that a U.S. carrot to China would act like a stick against Russia. Each corner of the triangle was a giant or potential giant. The U.S. had the world's largest economy; Russia/USSR, the largest territory; China, the largest population.

Did good relations between two corners of the triangle depend upon tension between another two? Or could relations have been positive among all three? Realists advised triangulation, believing that "the enemy of my enemy is my partner, at least for now." Idealists prescribed friendship among all three—win-win-win. The interdependence school saw triangular diplomacy as another form of exploitation that might yield short-term gains but then backfire. Given their mutual vulnerability, the three great powers were most likely to enhance their long-term objectives if they could cultivate three-sided cooperation.

Which school, if any, was right? Let us review some cases that illustrate how varying blends of niceness and toughness shaped IR in the late 20th century.[7]

COMPARING THEORY AND REALITY: STICKS AND CARROTS

THE GREAT POWER TRIANGLE

The world's power structure was essentially bipolar from 1945 until the late 1980s. The image of bipolarity was strong in the 1950s when Beijing's

7. One book on tension-reducing strategies concluded that niceness won out over harshness. See Joshua S. Goldstein and John R. Freeman, *Three-Way Street: Strategic Reciprocity in World Politics* (Chicago: University of Chicago Press, 1990). Their analysis, however, depends heavily on "event" data banks based on newspaper accounts that are quite incomplete. Thus, journalists did not know until 1963 that Moscow and Beijing had signed a defense technology pact in 1957 and immediately quarreled about its basic terms.

leaders publicly followed Moscow's line. But they openly split from the Soviet camp in the 1960s and began to play an independent role.

Soviet power declined in the 1980s, as we saw in Chapter 5, while China grew stronger. By the 1990s the balance was unipolar, leaving China with a potential to challenge the U.S. or cooperate for mutual gain.

The Spirit of Geneva, 1955

The first summit meeting between Soviet and Western leaders since World War II took place in 1955. The Big Four (Britain, France, the U.S., and the USSR) met in Geneva to discuss divided Germany, arms control, trade, and cultural exchange. The meeting generated a **Spirit of Geneva**—the first détente in a decade. How did it come about?

After Josef Stalin's death in March 1953, his successors signaled that they wanted better relations with the West. President Dwight D. Eisenhower decided to test Soviet intentions. He instructed his speechwriter: "Let us come out, straight, no double-talk, no slick sophisticated propaganda devices—and say: this is what we'll do—we'll withdraw our armies from there if you'll withdraw yours. . . . The slate is clean—now let's begin." Eisenhower wanted to "make a serious bid for peace."[8]

Eisenhower delivered his "Give Peace a Chance" speech on April 16, 1953. He said he would believe in Moscow's desire for peace when that desire turned into "deeds," for example, an armistice in Korea and a peace treaty for Austria. Washington, he said, would then be ready to negotiate on German unification and disarmament.

The Soviets liked this new tune so much that they published Eisenhower's full text in the Communist Party newspaper, *Pravda,* and the government organ, *Izvestiia.* Within months the Kremlin endorsed the Korean armistice and relaxed its grip on Austria. The new party secretary, Nikita Khrushchev, wanted a GRIT-like approach to East-West differences. President Eisenhower also favored détente. Soviet Foreign Minister Vyacheslav M. Molotov and U.S. Secretary of State John Foster Dulles, however, preferred East-West confrontation. They and other hard-liners helped Soviet-U.S. relations zigzag between hostility and conciliation.[9]

Khrushchev gradually dominated the Kremlin's "collective leadership." He championed "peaceful coexistence" with the West and allowed for "many roads to socialism" within the Communist camp. However, Khrushchev used sticks as well as carrots to deliver this message. He saw peaceful coexistence as a way to defeat the West without war.

8. Quoted in Deborah Welch Larson, "Crisis Prevention and the Austrian State Treaty," *International Organization* 41, no. 1 (winter 1987): 27–60 at 36. See also Matthew A. Evangelista, "Cooperation Theory and Disarmament Negotiations in the 1950s," *World Politics* 42, no. 4 (July 1990): 502–528.

9. The 1955 and 1963 cases described here and in the next section are documented in Lincoln P. Bloomfield, Walter C. Clemens, Jr., and Franklin Griffiths, *Khrushchev and the Arms Race: Soviet Interests in Arms Control and Disarmament, 1954–1964* (Cambridge, Mass.: MIT Press, 1966).

TIMELINE: RISE AND DECLINE OF THE GENEVA SPIRIT IN 1955

3/19
Soviets propose international controls of nuclear disarmament

5/1
Soviet bombers overfly Red Square to impress Western observers

5/10
Soviet diplomats endorse West's disarmament principles

5/14
Soviets create Warsaw Pact alliance

5/15
Big Four recognize Austria's independence

7/18–8/23
Big Four hold summit meeting in Geneva

8/12
Soviets announce 640,000-man troop reduction

August
Soviets conduct H-bomb tests

10/27–11/16
Big Four foreign ministers' meeting in Geneva ends in acrimony and Spirit of Geneva wanes

As we see from the timeline, both sides mixed conciliatory with harsh moves. Neither Moscow nor Washington gave GRIT a chance, because each side sent contradictory messages. Each side behaved as though it was caught up in an approach-avoidance syndrome. It wanted but did not want an accommodation.

When Soviet negotiators accepted British-French arms control proposals as the basis for negotiations, the Western Big Three developed second thoughts. Eisenhower may have wanted arms control, but his secretary of state and top Pentagon officials favored continued arms competition—even deadlock—to arms control. In September 1955 the State Department reneged and placed a "reservation upon all of its pre-Geneva substantive positions" on arms control. When the Big Four foreign ministers met in Geneva in October–November 1955 to follow up on the July summit, Dulles and Molotov made sure that the talks ended in renewed hostility.

No corner of the great power triangle pursued a clear line toward the other two. Stalin had bullied the Chinese Communists for decades. After Stalin's death, Khrushchev wanted to put Sino-Soviet relations on a more friendly footing. In 1954 he traveled to China and met with Mao Zedong. But the two men quickly came to despise one another. One was a miner's son who spoke in peasant proverbs; the other saw himself as a great military strategist and a poet. In 1954–1955 Moscow and Beijing began to compete for the good will of Indonesia and other nonaligned countries.

But some elements of GRIT and triangular diplomacy entered into Chinese-U.S. relations. Premier **Zhou Enlai** began to play China's own peace card. He called in April 1955 for Chinese-U.S. negotiations on Taiwan, then under the protection of the U.S. Navy. In July Beijing released eleven U.S. airmen imprisoned in China and suggested talks with Washington. Chinese and U.S. ambassadors met in Geneva in August, just after the Big Four ended their own Geneva Conference. The ambassadors scored no breakthroughs, but Beijing and Washington developed this format and used it on several occasions before normal relations were established in the 1970s.

For most of 1955 the great power triangle showed a small but uncertain positive sign between Washington and Moscow, a possible shift from minus to plus between Washington and Beijing, and both plus and minus elements between the two Communist giants (see Figure 7.1).

Fig. 7.1 Détente and Tension in 1955

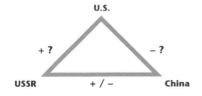

In March 1963 President John F. Kennedy asks: "How can the U.S. step back from the Cuban precipice and—at the same time—curb China's nuclear weapons program?"

Kennedy reviews the record. U.S. relations with the USSR have fluctuated between détente and hostility since Stalin's death. The Spirit of Geneva and several later détentes proved short-lived. It seemed that some demon kept inserting a monkey wrench to sabotage the process. In 1956 relations soured due to troubles in Hungary and Egypt; in 1960, a U.S. spy plane was shot down just before a summit meeting.

The Spirit of Moscow, 1963

Kennedy decided to break the post-Cuba logjam. On June 10, 1963, Kennedy made a speech at American University in Washington—"Toward a Strategy of Peace."[10] There is no record that Kennedy read Dr. Osgood, but JFK's words and deeds looked almost like textbook GRIT. "Peace," Kennedy said, "is a process, a way of solving problems." It did not require an end to all quarrels, but only a mutual tolerance and submission of disputes to a "just and peaceful settlement." Kennedy altered U.S. perceptions merely by talking about Soviets as fellow human beings. "No government or social system is so evil that its people must be considered as lacking in virtue." He hailed the "Russian people for their many accomplishments." He said that "no nation . . . ever suffered more than the Soviet Union" did in World War II. Kennedy urged attention to "common interests and to the means by which . . . differences can be resolved."

Kennedy announced that test ban negotiations would begin soon in Moscow and that the U.S. would not conduct further "nuclear tests in the atmosphere so long as other states do not do so."

The message got through. As in April 1953, when *Pravda* and *Izvestiia* printed the full text of Eisenhower's speech, the two Soviet papers published Kennedy's June 10 speech. Suddenly, Soviet jammers let Voice of America broadcasts get through. Khrushchev responded with a conciliatory speech of his own on July 2. Khrushchev personally welcomed the Western diplomats on July 15, after having ignored the Chinese who had arrived ten days before.

GRIT can be subverted by third parties. Both China and West Germany worried that U.S.-Soviet détente might harm their interests. Trying to ease West German fears, Kennedy visited West Berlin and reaffirmed U.S. support for the beleaguered city. The Soviets, however, scorned Chinese objections to conciliation with Washington.

Where there is a will, ways will be found. Having talked fruitlessly for years, U.S. and Soviet negotiators (joined by British) wrapped up negoti-

10. For the background, see Robert F. Kennedy, foreword to Walter C. Clemens, Jr., ed., *Toward a Strategy of Peace* (Chicago: Rand McNally, 1965), xiii–xv; for the speech text, see ibid., 22–30.

How Better U.S.-Soviet Relations Hurt Sino-Soviet Relations

Even though Khrushchev and Mao did not get along, Moscow and Beijing enjoyed a brief honeymoon in the mid-1950s. It ended for many reasons. Basically, China challenged Soviet leadership and became too aggressive for Moscow's tastes.

Visiting China on his way home from the U.S. in 1959, Khrushchev criticized Beijing for being too belligerent about Taiwan and warned: "We cannot use our fists to test the stability of capitalism." Mao Zedong resented such advice and fumed that "some people have come into our own house to bully us." In 1960 the Kremlin cut off all economic aid to China and withdrew all Soviet technicians.

China feared that Moscow and Washington were negotiating a nuclear test ban to prevent China from developing its own nuclear bomb. Beijing warned Moscow several times in 1962–1963 not to sign an arms agreement with Washington.

The Soviets replied that a test ban was not in the cards. On June 9, 1963, Moscow changed its tune. The Kremlin gave Beijing advance notice of what Kennedy announced the very next day: that "high-level discussion will shortly begin in Moscow looking toward early agreement on a . . . test ban treaty." Even so, the Kremlin kept open its options: The Soviets invited a high-level Chinese delegation to arrive in Moscow ten days before the U.S. and British test ban delegations.

Moscow responded publicly to Chinese charges that the Soviets were "capitulating" to U.S. imperialism. The Soviet Communist Party sent an open letter on July 14, 1963, reminding Beijing that "the nuclear bomb does not adhere to the class principle—it destroys everybody within the range of its devastating force."

ations in days and initialed a limited nuclear test ban on July 25. This spawned a new climate—the "Spirit of Moscow."

But challenges to the new mood came fast and furious: The FBI arrested a Soviet agent in New York and two days later the KGB arrested a U.S. professor in Moscow—tit-for-tat? Kennedy himself demanded and got the professor's release without derailing détente. The Pentagon won Kennedy's permission to resume underground nuclear testing. The Kremlin denounced Washington for going against the Spirit of Moscow. Khrushchev warned Communists not to allow détente to produce "moral and spiritual demobilization."

How could Moscow and Washington sustain momentum toward tension-reduction? Moscow introduced some high-sounding peace proposals even though they were known to be unacceptable to Washington. But British, Soviet, and U.S. negotiators found another quick and easy accord: a "gentlemen's agreement" on October 3, 1963, not to orbit nuclear weapons in space. Relations were also lubricated that same month by Soviet purchase of U.S. wheat. The Soviet buyers agreed that the wheat would be transported on U.S. ships manned by union labor.

On October 10 Khrushchev signed the test ban and gave the U.S. ambassador a letter for Kennedy. It suggested that the two countries turn to other "ripe" issues such as Berlin, nuclear proliferation, bombs in orbit, and fear of surprise attack. A guarded U.S. reply was authorized ten days later. Due to a clerical error, however, it was not sent. The White House did not discover the slip-up until December—after Kennedy was dead.

Soviet-U.S. détente survived Kennedy's murder in November 1963. JFK's successor, President Lyndon B. Johnson, said that he wanted to sustain Kennedy's policies. On December 13 Khrushchev announced a cut in the Soviet military budget. At year's end he praised "disarmament by mutual example"—the same idea as GRIT. In April 1964 each leader—Johnson, Khrushchev, and British Prime Minister Harold Macmillan—made a vague pledge that his country would reduce production of fissionable materials.

The Spirit of Moscow aligned the U.S. and USSR more closely than they had been since 1945, while Sino-Soviet relations hit new lows. Still, Moscow spurned U.S. suggestions of joint pressures against China. The Chinese, despite their hostility to the test ban, told U.S. diplomats in private that Beijing did not oppose all arms controls. These conflicting trends are reflected in Figure 7.2.

Soviet-U.S. cooperation wilted after Khrushchev's ouster in October 1964—the same month that China conducted its first nuclear test. The new Leonid Brezhnev–Aleksei Kosygin regime faced a new monkey wrench—escalation of the war in Vietnam. U.S. bombers began to pound North Vietnam in February 1965, just as Prime Minister Kosygin was visiting Hanoi!

Fig. 7.2 Détente and Tension in 1963

In January 1969 newly inaugurated President Richard Nixon ponders: *"How can the U.S. improve relations with the USSR and normalize relations with China, while making a graceful exit from the Vietnam War? Should Washington now focus on Moscow or Beijing, or both?"*

The "China Card" and/or SALT in 1972

President Nixon and National Security Assistant Henry Kissinger hoped to use triangular diplomacy—play the **"China card"** to win concessions from Moscow and the "Soviet card" to influence China. The Kremlin tried to deflect Washington from exploiting the Sino-Soviet conflict.[11] But history taught Kissinger that "it is usually more advantageous to align . . . with the weaker of two antagonistic partners, because this acted as a restraint on the stronger." His approach dovetailed with Beijing's, for China had long followed the principle *yi yi zhi yi*—"Use one barbarian against the other."

How could the Nixon administration explore with Beijing the prospects of a fresh start? Washington had no representatives in mainland China, because it did not recognize the Communist government. U.S.

An architect of détente in the 1970s, former U.S. Secretary of State Henry Kissinger testified before the U.S. Senate in 1988 regarding the INF Treaty signed in 1987. Kissinger criticized some particulars of the INF accord but supported it as useful for preserving the NATO alliance. In 1997, he opposed giving Moscow a consultative voice in NATO, fearing it would disrupt the alliance.

11. Henry Kissinger, *White House Years* (Boston: Little, Brown, 1979), 173, 191–192.

ambassadors in Warsaw and Geneva had often met with their Chinese counterparts, but that dialogue belonged to a tension-filled past.

Washington began in mid-1969 to use "unilateral steps, intermediaries, and public declarations" to communicate with China. The latter included a public hint that Washington was prepared to accept a Chinese recommendation that the two countries agree to principles of peaceful coexistence; the easing of restrictions so that a U.S. tourist could buy $100 worth of noncommercial goods made in China; and easier permission for scholars, journalists, and members of Congress to travel to China.

Nixon also told leaders of Pakistan and Romania—both close to Beijing—that he wanted better relations with China. Beijing quickly signaled a response. It released two Americans whose boat had drifted into Chinese waters.

Using a Pakistani air marshal as go-between, Kissinger in October 1969 informed Beijing that the U.S. was withdrawing two destroyers from the **Taiwan Strait**—the narrow water wall separating "island China" from mainland China, which U.S. ships had patrolled since the Korean War. Other U.S. warships would continue to transit the Strait, but Washington meant to remove an "irritant."

As tensions grew along the Soviet-Chinese border, Nixon in November 1969 declared that the U.S. "shall provide a shield if a nuclear power threatens . . . a nation allied with us or . . . a nation whose survival we consider vital to our security." In effect, he offered to protect China against Soviet attack! In December China released two other U.S. yachtsmen and invited the U.S. ambassador to visit the Chinese embassy in Warsaw—through the front door.

Nixon and Kissinger followed some but not all of the principles of Osgood's GRIT strategy. They initiated small steps that, if reciprocated, could snowball. Contrary to Osgood's advice, however, they did not begin with an open and clear explanation that the White House was embarking on a new strategy. Instead, they conveyed their orientation to Beijing indirectly and hoped the Chinese would smile back. They enjoyed secret diplomacy and claimed it was necessary to fend off domestic critics in case Beijing spurned U.S. overtures.

Washington entered into what Kissinger called "an intricate minuet" with Beijing "so intricately arranged that both sides could always maintain that they were not in contact." Between November 1969 and June 1970 there were at least ten instances when U.S. officials abroad talked to Chinese at diplomatic functions—four times initiated by Chinese.[12]

12. Kissinger, *White House Years*, 187–188. By contrast, when the author (W.C.) tried to talk with Chinese students at Moscow University in 1958–1959, they walked away, refusing to talk with an American "until Taiwan is liberated."

In December 1970 Pakistan's president sent a message handwritten by Premier Zhou Enlai for Pakistan's ambassador to read to Kissinger. It invited a special U.S. envoy to Beijing to discuss "the vacation of Chinese territories called Taiwan." The White House sent back an unsigned, typed reply on Xerox paper (not official stationery). It welcomed discussions in Beijing on the "broad range of issues which lie between the *People's Republic of China* [emphasis added] and the United States, including the issue of Taiwan."

Here was another change—cheap, but potent: Washington began to speak not of "mainland" or "Communist" China but of the "People's Republic of China." Washington had long called the Communist Chinese capital by its former name, Peiping; now it used the Communists' terminology, Beijing (or Peking)—"northern capital." (This offended Chiang Kai-shek Nationalists who thought of Nanjing—"southern capital"—as China's true capital.) Zhou Enlai told a Japanese visitor in April 1971 that he "took specific note of the fact that for the first time an American President called China by its official name."

On March 15, 1971, Washington removed all restrictions on travel to China, adding: "We hope for, but will not be deterred by, lack of reciprocity." Two days later Beijing denounced what it called the "renegade" Soviet regime in terms that told Kissinger: "The Soviet Union had replaced us as [China's] principal enemy."

Beijing now used sports to continue GRIT. Later, this was called **ping-pong diplomacy**—using sports to shape state-to-state relations. On April 6 Chinese officials invited to Beijing a U.S. ping-pong team then in Japan, having been authorized by Mao himself to do so.[13] When the Americans arrived in Beijing, Zhou Enlai hosted a banquet and announced "a new chapter" in Sino-U.S. relations. As Kissinger observed, Zhou "knew how to make gestures that could not be rebuffed." He was preparing the Chinese public and party leaders for a shift. His tactics implied too that, if official Washington held back, Beijing could appeal directly to the American people.

Kissinger had prepared for this moment a list of "unrejectable steps"—stages of trade relations that could be expanded as Beijing reciprocated. Responding to Beijing's ping, Nixon ponged: He approved the sale of French trucks to China even though they contained U.S.-made engines.[14]

On April 14—as the U.S. table tennis players got a warm reception in Beijing—the White House announced relaxed U.S. restrictions on trade

13. While in Japan, a U.S. player hitched a ride with a Chinese van and received a gift. He reciprocated with a gift the next day and hinted a desire to play in Beijing. Soon the Chinese Foreign Ministry debated the issue. It leaned toward inviting U.S. journalists rather than ping-pong players. Zhou asked Mao what to do. He was silent for days, leading the Foreign Ministry to phone Japan and say no. When Mao replied affirmatively, the Foreign Ministry switched gears.

14. Kissinger, *White House Years*, 712.

with China. The previous day Kissinger informed the Soviet chargé d'affaires of the impending shift and assured him it had no anti-Soviet intent. "This is the conventional pacifier . . . by which the target . . . is given formal reassurance intended to unnerve as much as to calm, and which would defeat its purpose if it were actually believed."[15] Nixon on April 21 declared he would cooperate with an invitation for the Chinese table tennis team to visit the U.S.

Nixon and Kissinger, although devoted to *realpolitik,* were acutely aware of how low-level exchanges might evolve into accords of high political significance. But they paid for their close-to-the-vest diplomacy. Ignorant of the new approach to China, Secretary of State William Rogers and Vice President Spiro Agnew spoke out like a broken record from the past. Rogers even stated in April 1971 that a presidential visit to China could not take place until Beijing complied "with the rules of international law." Fortunately for détente, Zhou Enlai listened to Kissinger instead of Rogers.

Kissinger explained that his secret diplomacy and back channels sought to circumvent normal procedures. But for every agency excluded—usually the State Department—he became dependent upon another's facilities—increasingly, the CIA's. Kissinger blamed the State Department for its tendency to circulate every cable throughout its bureaucracy.

After long and secret preparations, Kissinger on July 9, 1971, flew to Beijing from Pakistan. All went well. On July 15 Nixon told the world about Kissinger's trip and announced that he too would visit China. In February 1972 the famed anti-Communist clinked glasses with the world's leading revolutionary, Chairman Mao Zedong. Meanwhile, Kissinger and Zhou drafted the **Shanghai Communiqué**, which defined the framework for normalization.[16] Ronald Reagan, then governor of California, quipped that the Nixon visit to China had been a great television "pilot" and should be made into a "series." When he became president, he helped to do so.

How did U.S. rapprochement with China in 1972 affect U.S. policies toward the USSR? Washington's new China card probably made the Kremlin—and Hanoi—more anxious to strike their own deals with Washington. Plans were laid for Nixon to visit Moscow in May 1972 and sign major arms accords with Brezhnev. Washington also pressed for a peace treaty with Hanoi. On the eve of his planned summit, Nixon sharply raised the ante by intensifying bomb raids on Hanoi and its port Haiphong, where Soviet ships were anchored. Nixon gambled and won. Despite U.S. escalation in Vietnam, Brezhnev did not rescind his invita-

15. Ibid.

16. Without naming the USSR, the document denounced efforts by any other country to establish "hegemony" or "collude" with other countries to "divide up the world into spheres of interest." In effect, Washington pledged not to cooperate with Moscow against Beijing.

Taiwan was the major sticking point. The communiqué stated Beijing's view that Taiwan is a "province" of China and Washington's that Taiwan is "part" of China. The U.S. favored a "peaceful settlement of the Taiwan question by the Chinese themselves." The U.S. tried in vain to get a commitment from Beijing not to "liberate" Taiwan by force, but Beijing refused, saying that Taiwan "is China's internal affair."

tion to Nixon. The Kremlin did not permit an embarrassment in a remote region to prevent accords on arms, trade, and other concerns vital
to Soviet interests. And Hanoi soon returned to serious negotiations with
U.S. representatives in Paris.

The triangle showed a strong plus between Washington and Moscow,
a growing plus between Washington and Beijing, and a very strong negative—deep conflict—between Moscow and Beijing (see Figure 7.3).

Kissinger achieved normalization with Beijing and détente with
Moscow. But was so much secrecy necessary or desirable? Probably not.
Open diplomacy based on public discussions at home and abroad would
probably have yielded the same gains without the associated costs. Improved relations with China met little opposition in the U.S., but the
rapid reversal of U.S. policy surprised and offended Tokyo and Taipei.
Japan and Taiwan, each a key U.S. ally, wondered how far they could
count on the U.S.

The White House played its China card like a club. But was this toughness needed? The Kremlin had its own reasons to pursue arms control
and trade with the U.S. China needed the U.S. as much as or more than
Washington needed Beijing. Seeing both Moscow and Beijing shift toward Washington, Hanoi feared isolation. But neither Moscow nor Beijing exerted much pressure on Hanoi to come to terms with Washington.

Gorbachev GRIT

Moscow's belligerent foreign policy helped bring the U.S. and China
together in the early 1980s. As Washington and Beijing teamed up, the
USSR acted like a cornered bear. By late 1984/early 1985, however, the
Kremlin sought détente with the West and, by 1986, with China. Mikhail
S. Gorbachev, Communist Party leader after March 1985, talked and acted
as though coached by Western exponents of GRIT and interdependence.
But whereas Dr. Osgood expected the stronger side to take the first steps,
Gorbachev initiated a strategy of tension-reduction even as his country
was tottering. Gorbachev's policy was manifest and persistent, despite re-
buffs abroad and criticism at home.[17]

Gorbachev in 1985–1987 softened previous Communist doctrine on
many points. For example, he argued that the needs of all humanity—not
the working class revolution or a state's national interest—should guide
policy. All countries are interdependent even though contradictions
among them continue. War can no longer be an effective way to pursue
policy. Even local wars can escalate. Conflicts must be resolved by dialogue. Soviet-U.S. military parity and nuclear deterrence do not guaran-

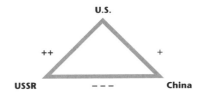

Fig. 7.3 Détente and Tension in 1972

17. On the Gorbachev revolution, see Walter C.
Clemens, Jr., *Can Russia Change? The USSR Confronts Global Interdependence* (New York: Routledge,
1990).

Tit-for-Tat on Spies

Complaining about Soviet espionage, the U.S. government in 1986 ordered Moscow to curtail sharply the number of personnel in its Washington embassy. Gorbachev responded TFT. He told the Soviet politburo that the Americans behaved "like bandits. . . . This hostile anti-Soviet action cannot be left unanswered." He ordered Soviet support staff out of the U.S. embassy in Moscow, leaving the Americans empty-handed. Gorbachev did not fear U.S. reprisals, he said, because Soviet-U.S. ties were limited anyway.

Personal chemistry as well as power relationships shape world politics. Presidents Mikhail Gorbachev (USSR) and Ronald Reagan (U.S.) got along well despite many personality and cultural differences. Here the two men shake hands after signing the INF Treaty in Washington in December 1987.

18. Gorbachev also pledged to withdraw significant Soviet forces from Afghanistan before 1986; hoped for normalized relations between Vietnam and China; and promised a "positive reply" to China's request to build a railroad linking its Xinjiang-Uygur region with Soviet Kazakstan. He also offered to cooperate with Beijing in outer space and to train Chinese cosmonauts.

tee peace. Military deployments should be guided by "reasonable sufficiency"—adequate for defense but inadequate for attack.

Unlike Nixon and Kissinger, Gorbachev and his aides communicated their new line directly to their colleagues. Gorbachev told his diplomats not to act like "Mr. *Nyet*." Gorbachev's meetings with Western and Third World intellectuals became front-page news throughout the USSR.

Gorbachev broke from TFT with a series of dramatic moves. As we saw in Chapter 6, Gorbachev accepted several arms accords that trimmed Soviet forces more than Western. Also, the Kremlin held to a unilateral moratorium on nuclear testing for eighteen months and permitted U.S. scientists and seismic equipment near Soviet test sites. Gorbachev unilaterally cut Soviet military personnel by one-tenth and pledged to restructure remaining units in strictly defensive configurations. He withdrew Soviet forces from Afghanistan and supported arrangements to end regional conflict in Cambodia, southern Africa, the Persian Gulf, and the Middle East. Gorbachev also lowered emigration barriers for Soviet citizens and curtailed repression of political dissidents. He moved to make the USSR a participant in world commerce and science.

Not every Gorbachev move inspired confidence. For example, the nuclear test moratorium pushed the White House where it did not wish to go. Gorbachev officially began the Soviet moratorium in 1985 on the fortieth anniversary of Hiroshima—August 6. This played well in Japan but not in Washington.

Détente did not proceed in a straight line. As noted in the sidebar, Soviet-U.S. relations were often strained even in the Gorbachev years. For a time official Washington played down Gorbachev's concessions. President Reagan believed in negotiating from strength and continued pressures to force back what he called the "evil empire." When Reagan and Gorbachev met face-to-face, however, they got along well. Reagan came to agree with British Prime Minister Margaret Thatcher that Gorbachev was, at last, a Soviet leader with whom the West could do business.

Gorbachev had no China card, because Beijing's leaders were hostile to Moscow. But Gorbachev employed GRIT-like moves to win Chinese confidence. In 1986 he repudiated "selfish attempts to strengthen [Soviet] security at others' expense" and called for "new and fair relations in Asia and the Pacific." He stressed Moscow's readiness to deepen economic and other ties with China.[18] Far from trying to exclude Washington, as his predecessors had done, Gorbachev affirmed that the U.S. was "a great Pacific power."

Three years of conciliating China paid off. Gorbachev visited Beijing in May 1989—the first summit between Soviet and Chinese leaders in thirty years. In 1989–1990 each leg of the triangle was positive for the first time since 1945. It turned out that two positive legs did not require a negative (see Figure 7.4). None of the great powers had to exploit differences between the other two to advance its interests.

How to Blend "Niceness" and "Toughness"

We have seen four cases where niceness helped elicit niceness. In Table 7.2 we consider each case's basic parameters.

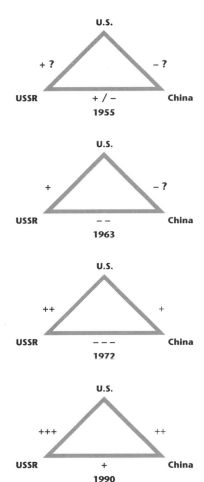

Fig. 7.4 Changing Parameters of the Great Power Triangle

Table 7.2 Four Cases of Tension-Reducing Initiatives

	1955 (USSR→U.S)	1963 (U.S.→USSR)	1970–1972 (U.S.→PRC)	1985–1989 (USSR→U.S.)
Initiator	**Khrushchev**	**Kennedy**	**Kissinger**	**Gorbachev**
Lead from strength?	No	Yes	Mixed	No
First steps symbolic or substantive?	Both	Symbolic	Symbolic	Both
Open or covert?	Open	Both	Covert	Open
Did the other side abuse?	No	No	No	No
Use triangle card?	No	No	Yes	No

In each instance the initiator took risks. Each worried about opposition both at home and among allies. The good news is that GRIT-like moves were seldom abused. There was rarely a long lag between conciliatory initiative and positive response. Usually the first GRIT-like moves elicited a positive response within months. But movement toward reconciliation never developed in a straight line. It moved in zig-zag fashion. Two or three years of testing were usually needed to cultivate a new "spirit." Neither covert nor triangular diplomacy was essential for GRIT to succeed.

CROSS-STRAIT GRIT

GRIT-like policies also helped mainland and island China to moderate their conflict. In 1949 the Communists forced the Nationalists to retreat to Taiwan and a few offshore islands. Still, each side claimed to rule all of China. The Communists called their state the People's Republic of China (PRC); the Nationalists, headquartered in Taipei, called theirs the Republic of China (ROC). The PRC and ROC waged an intense cold war (occasionally hot) across the Taiwan Strait for decades after 1949.

Beijing initiated tension-reducing moves with Taipei in 1979—the same year that Washington shifted U.S. recognition of "China" from the ROC to the PRC. But the ROC leadership did not respond in any positive way to Beijing's overtures until 1986. The smaller, more vulnerable party was suspicious and reluctant to lower its guard. In the 1980s the Communists in Beijing governed nearly a billion people; the Nationalists in Taipei, about 21 million.[19]

As Osgood recommended, it was the larger, stronger party that took the initiative and persisted with many small steps until the other side reciprocated. But Beijing departed from Osgood's prescription by launching initiatives on highly sensitive issues. Thus, the PRC government called for an end to military confrontation with Taiwan and proposed high-level talks on "reunifying the homeland." Beijing also offered cooperation in other, less sensitive realms—shelter for fishermen, visits to relatives, sports, science.

Taiwanese businessmen wanted access to the mainland market. They got there in the 1980s through Hong Kong—still a British colony until 1997. ROC authorities said in 1985 that they would neither "encourage" nor "interfere" with indirect trade between island and mainland China. In 1986, however, ROC President Chiang Ching-kuo hinted that ROC policy to the mainland should also change.

An external event in 1986 spurred the first direct talks between Taipei and Beijing officials. After a defecting Taiwanese pilot flew a cargo plane to the mainland, airline representatives from both sides met in Hong Kong to discuss the plane's return to Taiwan. A few months later—practically on his deathbed—President Chiang lifted Taiwan's martial law and the ban on ROC civilians' visits to the mainland.

In the late 1980s Taipei took many small steps to improve relations with Beijing. The ROC reduced and then eliminated rewards offered to defecting PRC pilots, lifted restrictions on the import of selected raw materials from the mainland, permitted PRC students studying in the U.S. to visit Taiwan, and welcomed ROC-PRC-Singapore police cooperation against criminals.

Following a request by the ROC president in May 1990, the PRC president in September announced that Beijing had pulled back all combat troops from Fujian Province opposite Taiwan. In the early 1990s Taiwanese investment in mainland China soared; so did visits, mail, and telephone calls. In 1993 both sides agreed to regular consultations on is-

19. Jun Zhan, *Ending the Chinese Civil War: Power, Commerce and Conciliation between Beijing and Taipei* (New York: St. Martin's, 1993).

sues of common interest. Washington tried to maintain good relations with Beijing while nourishing informal ties with Taipei. Russia and the ROC also reached out to each other. A positive sign linked each player (see Figure 7.5).

Optimists noted that commerce, kinship, and a shared civilization encouraged closer ties between Taiwan and the mainland. Taiwan had the largest per capita dollar reserves in the world, while the PRC had the fastest rate of economic growth. Taiwanese were expert in business but mainlanders were learning fast. Taiwan had technology and capital; the PRC had cheap but skilled labor.

But a potential monkey wrench became a Damocles Sword in 1995. Beijing had long threatened to fight Taiwan if it declared independence from the rest of China. In the 1990s, however, the ROC began to seek its own seat at the United Nations. When Washington allowed ROC President Lee Teng-hui to make a "private" visit to Cornell University (his alma mater) in 1995, Beijing responded vigorously. It suspended official meetings with ROC officials and began launching ballistic missiles into the sea north of Taiwan. A U.S. warship returned to the Taiwan Strait on December 19, 1995—the first time since 1979. The aircraft carrier *Nimitz* passed through, Washington said, because of bad weather elsewhere. Tension as well as tension-reduction could be fine tuned.

Cross-Strait tensions eased briefly in early 1996. Presidents of forty-three ROC and PRC universities met in Taiwan and called for closer academic cooperation to usher in "the Chinese century." In February–March 1996, however, tensions in the South China Sea worsened. China brought back large military forces to Fujian Province and conducted live-fire training to invade Taiwan. Some PRC officials threatened to nuke Los Angeles if the U.S. stood by Taiwan. But two U.S. aircraft carrier flotillas assembled 200 miles southeast of Taiwan (400 miles from China proper) and the U.S. Secretary of Defense boasted that the U.S. had the "best damn navy in the world." Fine-tuning became a shouting match.

A small, vulnerable client state helped trigger the long war between Athens and Sparta and between the two alliances in 1914. Clients in Cairo and Jerusalem nearly brought Moscow and Washington to blows in 1973. Now the fate of Taiwan renewed enmity between the PRC and the U.S.

"Firm containment" or "flexible engagement"? The Clinton administration sought to show firmness even while continuing its strategy of engaging China in constructive relationships. Washington reasoned: "We don't know if China will evolve into a peaceful member of the interna-

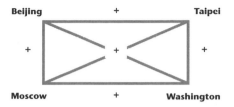

Fig. 7.5 Four-Cornered Cooperation in 1993

True GRIT or no GRIT? Both South and North Korean representatives said they wanted better relations, but neither side went very far to promote reconciliation. Shown here in February 1997, ROK troops check barbed wire entanglements along the demilitarized zone between North and South.

tional community or an imperialist bully. But if we launch a tough containment policy, we are sure to get a foe. If we continue our search for a peaceful engagement, there is hope for a constructive future." Such reasoning was logical, but had failed in the 1970s to constrain Soviet imperialism. Meanwhile, every computer-aided-design software package that the U.S. sold to China increased the PRC capacity to "nuke Los Angeles."

The return of Hong Kong to China in 1997 ushered in a new phase of PRC-ROC relations. If China kept its word and implemented a policy of "one country, two systems," Hong Kong might remain an outpost of economic and civil liberties. This would make affiliation with the PRC more thinkable for Taiwan. If Beijing repressed Hong Kong, however, that would fuel Taiwan's drive for independence. But life is sometimes not so simple. Shortly after Hong Kong's reunion with China, the ROC government abolished its self-proclaimed status as a province of China—a possible move toward breaking formal ties with the mainland. On the other hand, PRC companies based in Hong Kong began to invest in Taiwan—with ROC permission. Commerce might tame politics.

GRIT ACROSS THE DMZ

GRIT can fail—especially sham GRIT, when one side (or both) fakes its desire for reconciliation. South Korea (officially, the Republic of Korea, or ROK) and North Korea (the Democratic People's Republic of Korea, or DPRK) were different from Nationalist and Communist China. Since 1953 the South had become prosperous and confident; the North, an impoverished hermit kingdom under the world's longest-reigning dictator. Still, North Korea in the 1960s and 1970s often proposed steps that could have led to reunification. South Koreans then were reserved. They had not forgotten North Korea's massive attack in 1950 and its many acts of terrorism since.

As in Taiwan, greater prosperity made ROK diplomacy more confident. In the early 1980s Seoul proposed a summit meeting with Pyongyang and twenty pilot projects to help North and South cooperate. Now it was the North Koreans who balked. They demanded withdrawal of U.S. troops from Korea as a precondition for high-level dialogue.

A pattern emerged: North Korea demanded "all-or-nothing" while South Korea advocated "step-by-step" reconciliation. This was not GRIT but a propaganda war. Each side put the onus for stalemate on the other. Neither side made concessions to show its sincerity. Each preferred TFT.

In 1991 things changed. As its Soviet patron expired, North Korea for the first time acknowledged the ROK government as a legitimate entity and signed with it a treaty banning nuclear arms from the Korean peninsula. Seoul affirmed that U.S. nuclear arms had been withdrawn. Both sides agreed to a summit meeting in Seoul.

In the early 1990s the ROK had a negative relationship with the DPRK but positive ties with Beijing, Moscow, and Washington. North Koreans connected positively with no one. Still, Pyongyang had two aces: The DPRK army—much larger than the ROK army—was deployed within easy striking distance of Seoul. Second, the DPRK might "go nuclear."

What to do? North Korea was sealed off—one of the most closed societies in the world. U.S. policy-makers wondered how to draw North Korea from its shell and persuade its leaders to forgo nuclear weapons. Should Washington try to conciliate the North by cancelling the annual maneuvers conducted by U.S. and ROK forces? Or stage them again to intimidate the North and please hard-liners in the South? Could U.S. bombers or missiles mount "surgical strikes" to wipe out DPRK nuclear facilities? Even if they hit their target, radiation might spread. North Korea threatened to ignite a firestorm in South Korea.

Amid rising tensions, Kim Il-sung in 1994 met with two U.S. groups making "private" visits to Korea. Evangelist Billy Graham went to Pyongyang with a Columbia University professor who grew up in a missionary family in Korea. Next, Kim Il-sung met with former president Jimmy Carter. These unofficial meetings with North Korea's dictator set the stage for renewed negotiations between DPRK and U.S. diplomats. Neither Graham nor Carter officially represented the U.S., but each had close ties with the White House. Private (Track II) diplomacy opened the way to official (Track I) diplomacy.

In October 1994 North Korean and U.S. officials approved the "agreed framework"—a schedule of steps to provide nuclear reactors to the DPRK while denying it the capacity for nuclear weaponry—described in Chapter 6. To implement these undertakings, of course, would be complicated.[20] Though isolated and in need, North Korea upped the ante. It tried to exclude South Korea and deal only with the U.S. It wanted not just the reactors but also—gratis—the supporting infrastructure and communications links. When Washington stood firm, however, Pyongyang backed down. It agreed that South Korea would supply the reactors.

Like Kissinger and Zhou Enlai in the early 1970s, Washington and Pyongyang tried to sustain the momentum of tension-reduction. Small steps might have large consequences. Pyongyang and Washington in Jan-

First Steps May Lead Nowhere

Table tennis helped break the ice between Beijing and Washington. Could it do the same for the two Koreas? South and North Korea agreed to field a unified table tennis team for the world championships in 1991. But would it train in North or in South Korea? And what would be its official name? Lengthy negotiations produced two compromises: The team would train in Japan; it would be called "Korea."

Ping-pong reunited some Koreans. In Japan a DPRK ping-pong official met his sister for the first time in four decades. She had gone south during the Korean War while he remained in the North.

Washington in 1991 welcomed moves to ease North Korea out of its isolation. Recalling how ping-pong helped melt the ice between Washington and Beijing in 1971, the U.S. offered to send a soccer team to North Korea and invited the joint Korean table tennis team to visit three U.S. cities. But sports diplomacy faltered. Korean sport unity turned out to be a one-shot deal. In September 1991 both North and South Korea joined the United Nations as separate states.

20. James Goodby and William Drennan, "Koreapolitik," *Strategic Forum* 29 (May 1995): 2

Severe economic problems in North Korea made Pyongyang more receptive to U.S. proposals for four-way talks with Seoul and Beijing to make peace on the Korean peninsula. Here, a fourteen-year-old girl in Anju City, DPRK, forages for food in April 1997.

uary 1995 began to dismantle the trade embargo each had imposed forty-five years before. Each side would now permit direct phone calls and financial transactions. Washington would permit U.S. steelmakers to buy magnesite from North Korea to line their blast furnaces. DPRK and U.S. journalists could now open news bureaus in each others' country. The U.S. State Department said that further relaxation of economic sanctions would depend on progress on the "nuclear issue" and on DPRK restraint in exporting missile technology.

While U.S.-DPRK relations improved somewhat, those between the two Koreas languished. Some U.S. experts suggested arms control measures to build confidence between Seoul and Pyongyang: greater transparency for each side's military forces; constraints on military deployments near the DMZ; a "nonoffensive defense" military posture to replace any capacity for deep penetration across the DMZ, verified by the UN and observers from each side; a direct communications link between the ROK and DPRK defense ministers; reduced military forces (U.S. as well as Korean) on each side of the DMZ; and promises by Washington, Beijing, and Moscow not to circumvent the DPRK-ROK accords.

Even as the October 1994 deal began to be implemented, however, tensions again worsened between the two Koreas. Severe floods and other problems reduced North Korea's harvests and food supplies. The DPRK regime urged its people to get by on two meals a day—one if they could manage. South Korea sent rice, but Pyongyang refused to say thanks. Instead it arrested some ROK fishermen on charges of spying. Millions of North Koreans faced starvation, but South Korea blocked outside food aid until Pyongyang changed its tune. Even as Pyongyang began to receive more food and other assistance from outside, a North Korean submarine crashed onto the South Korean coast, disgorging a dozen commandos, whom the South Koreans hunted down.

Some ROK officials feared that a dying North Korea might still launch a last-ditch attack. Others feared the DPRK might open its borders and deluge the ROK with millions of refugees. Still others hoped the DPRK would collapse and bequeath its nuclear arsenal to the South.

Pyongyang in 1997 continued to bargain hard. The NGO Oxfam (Oxford Committee on Famine Relief, founded in 1942) and UN observers concluded that North Korea was on the brink of mass starvation. Two years of flood had been followed by a prolonged drought. The world mobilized to send food, but Pyongyang still balked at direct talks with South Korea. Even as DPRK diplomats met with U.S., PRC, and ROK negotiators at Columbia University, Pyongyang demanded the withdrawal of

U.S. troops from the peninsula and cancellation of U.S.-ROK maneuvers scheduled for late 1997 in Japan. A "German" solution became more thinkable: collapse of the Communist government, leading to the merger of non-Communist and Communist regions, endorsed by the great powers. In the winter of 1997–1998, however, the South Korean economy shuddered, throwing many people out of work and helping to elect a new, more liberal president, Kim Dae Jung. Would less hubris in Seoul and Pyongyang favor North-South accommodation?

The sustainer of dialogue was not the two Koreas but the U.S., which tried to push both of them to a settlement.

GREAT PERSUADERS

Each movement toward détente and each agreement we have studied depended upon conditional cooperation. Individual negotiators dealt with problems and found ways to reach agreements useful to each side. These individuals embodied many of the "qualities of the effective negotiator" listed in Chapter 1. Each seemed to understand GRIT theory intuitively.

Of the major statesmen in the great power triangle, Kissinger was probably the most skilled negotiator, followed closely by Zhou Enlai. Kissinger and Zhou pursued their own versions of GRIT with signals that could not be rebuffed and which, if criticized, could be denied. Both men knew the issues well and could identify ways to bridge differences.

Despite a weak hand, Gorbachev did what he could to save the Soviet system and join the First World in a joint quest for peace and prosperity. He demonstrated how tension-reduction could be pursued for years to overcome the other side's distrust.

President Reagan did well in fostering détente with Gorbachev. Though Reagan did not study the issues carefully, he could negotiate from great strength. He enjoyed solid domestic support even as Soviet power steadily declined. He charmed many Soviets as well as Americans.

To learn how these negotiators and their advisers thought about their diplomacy and how they graded one another, read the memoirs of Zbigniew Brzezinksi, James Baker, Carter, Anatoly Dobrynin, Gorbachev, Andrei Gromyko, Kissinger, George Shultz, and Cyrus Vance. Readers of Chinese and Russian will relish the memoirs of interpreters for top PRC and Soviet leaders. Works by and about the lead U.S. negotiators with the Balkan states and North Korea, Richard Holbrooke and Robert Galucci, are also quite informative.

In 1997–1998 a new potentially great persuader appeared. Iran's newly

Ranking Great Persuaders

Following is a tentative ranking of some statesmen and diplomats active in the great power triangle. Ratings are based on their strengths in the fifteen traits of a strong negotiator outlined in Chapter 1. Kissinger scored highest, followed by Zhou Enlai; Khrushchev and Brezhnev ranked at the bottom.

Henry Kissinger (strong in 2, 4, 7, 8, 9, 10, 12, 13, 14, 15)

Zhou Enlai (strong in 1, 2, 8, 9, 10, 11, 12, 13, 14)

Jimmy Carter (strong in 2, 5, 6, 9, 11, 12, 13, 14)

Mikhail Gorbachev (strong in 1, 8, 9, 11, 12, 13, 15)

John F. Kennedy (strong in 4, 8, 10, 11, 13)

Ronald Reagan (strong in 3, 8, 13)

Andrei Gromyko (strong in 1, 2, 10)

Nikita Khrushchev (strong in 10, 11, 15)

Leonid Brezhnev (strong in 10, 11)

KEY:

1 = conversion power
2 = knowledge   3 = domestic support
4 = management   5 = empathy
6 = integrity   7 = timing
8 = communication
9 = constructive imagination
10 = toughness
11 = flexibility   12 = stamina
13 = personality   14 = draftsmanship
15 = achievement drive

SOURCE: Evaluations based on formal ratings by former U.S. ambassador Hermann Eilts; professors Roger Kanet and David Mayers; Dr. Jun Zhan; and the author.

elected president, Mohammed Khatami, aimed multiple conciliatory messages at the U.S. Like other practitioners of GRIT, he had good things to say about the "people" of the other camp. Both Teheran and Washington shared mutual interests in oil and gas. An opportunity for sports diplomacy arose when Iranian and U.S. soccer teams were matched to play each other in 1998. But convergent interests faced heated opposition from hard-liners on each side.

WHAT PROPOSITIONS HOLD? WHAT QUESTIONS REMAIN?

HOW TO MAKE GOOD WILL CREDIBLE

Reconciliation begins when parties decide to "give peace a chance." No government initiates or reciprocates tension-reducing moves unless cooperation promises a better return than confrontation. A tough value-claimer will not forgo hard-line exploitation unless it believes that value-creating may produce better results.

A strategy of peace is a wager that dangers can be minimized and assets enhanced by détente. This was the bet made both by Moscow and by Washington in 1955, 1963, 1972, and the late 1980s.

Either strength or weakness can motivate efforts to reduce tensions. Beijing leaders initiated tension-reduction with Taiwan from a position of growing strength; Taipei did not reciprocate until it felt secure. On the other hand, North Korea maintained its aggressive diplomatic style even after its economy had practically collapsed.

Each party must show that its "niceness" is a strategy—not a stratagem. Except for the two Koreas, however, none of the cases we have studied shows much chicanery. Neither the initiator nor the reciprocator exploited the process of tension-reduction to harm the other side. A series of conciliatory moves usually generated a positive response by the other side—often within days or weeks. The long interval between Beijing's initiatives and a positive ROC rejoinder was the exception—not the rule.

Still, niceness without bargaining power might get nowhere. Without some capacity to hurt as well as help, a negotiator's carrots may be devoured and yield nothing in return. Without sticks, conciliation may be fruitless.

The problem in tension-reduction has been how to sustain it—not to begin it. Having backed away from confrontation, it is difficult to proceed toward cooperation.

Memo to the President: In dealing with Koraq, we must negotiate from strength. We must be firm but not provocative. If Koraq steps up its threats to us or our friends, we should respond in kind. If the Koraqis offer a conciliatory gesture, however, we should not abuse it.

Since our overall position is stronger than Koraq's, we can better afford to take risks for peace. But we do not court needless rebuffs. Test the waters quietly to learn whether the time is ripe—whether, despite its tough exterior, Koraq may be ready, for its own reasons, to improve relations with us.

If conditions seem favorable, announce our intention to reduce tensions by a series of steps to move us from confrontation toward cooperation. Make clear, however, that this process will require reciprocal moves by the other side. Carry out a series of unilateral initiatives and give the other side time to respond. Promote open communication—at home and abroad—as circumstances permit. If the other side reciprocates, graduate from symbolic to more substantive initiatives. But respond firmly to rebuffs or defection.

With Koraq the question is how to move from confrontation to détente. With other countries the issue is how to avoid renewed confrontation. This challenge is severe with great powers such as Russia and China whose power position has quickly shifted. Many leaders in such countries are anxious either to regain their past clout or exploit their new power. We should cultivate a positive symbiosis that includes both Russia and China—networks of complex interdependence to promote mutual gain and transcend differences. If peaceful engagement fails, however, we must contain and isolate aggressors, preventing coalitions that threaten peaceful states.

KEY NAMES AND TERMS

"China card"
demilitarized zone (DMZ)
graduated reciprocation in tension-reduction (GRIT)
monkey wrench problem
Panmunjom
ping-pong diplomacy
rapprochement

Shanghai Communiqué
Spirit of Geneva
Taiwan Strait
triangular diplomacy
yi yi zhi yi
Zhou Enlai

QUESTIONS TO DISCUSS

1. How does GRIT differ from TFT? What are the pitfalls of each approach? The potential gains?

2. Why and how can a government use triangular diplomacy?

3. Did détente between two of the three great powers depend upon tension between one of them and the third?

4. How did Track I and Track II diplomacy interact in PRC-ROC and DPRK-ROK relations? How could both tracks be used to foster détente between two other countries?

5. Select a country today that resembles "Koraq." As adviser to the White House, which approaches to conflict and conflict resolution do you recommend?

6. Can GRIT be adapted not just to reduce tensions but to sustain positive ties when tensions develop, for example, between Washington and Moscow?

7. Compare two leading foreign policy-makers today with two analyzed in this chapter. What are their strengths and weaknesses?

8. How do historical memories impede accommodation? What can be done to deal with them?

9. Reflect on your failure or success to "make up" with a friend. Compare similarities and differences between your experience and one of the cases in this chapter. How are personal relations alike or different from those between governments?

RECOMMENDED RESOURCES

BOOKS

Armstrong, Tony. *Breaking the Ice: Rapprochement between East and West Germany, the United States and China, and Israel and Egypt.* Washington, D.C.: U.S. Institute of Peace, 1993.

Baker, James A., III. *The Politics of Diplomacy: Revolution, War & Peace, 1989–1992.* New York: G. P. Putnam's, 1995.

Brzezinski, Zbigniew. *Power and Principle: Memoirs of the National Security Adviser, 1977–1981.* New York: Farrar, Straus, Giroux, 1983.

Chang, Gordon H. *Friends and Enemies: The United States, China, and the Soviet Union, 1948–1972.* Stanford, Calif.: Stanford University Press, 1990.

Christensen, Thomas J. *Useful Adversaries: Grand Strategy, Domestic Mobilization, and Sino-American Conflict, 1947–1958.* Princeton, N.J.: Princeton University Press, 1996.

Clemens, Walter C., Jr. *The Arms Race and Sino-Soviet Relations.* Stanford, Calif.: Hoover Institution, 1968.

———. *Can Russia Change? The USSR Confronts Global Interdependence.* New York: Routledge, 1990.

Dobrynin, Anatoly. *In Confidence: Moscow's Ambassador to America's Six Cold War Presidents (1962–1986).* New York: Times Books, 1985.

Kissinger, Henry. *The White House Years.* Boston: Little, Brown, 1979.

Mayers, David. *The Ambassadors and America's Soviet Policy.* New York: Oxford University Press, 1995.

Osgood, Charles E. *An Alternative to Peace or Surrender.* Urbana: University of Illinois Press, 1962.

Shultz, George P. *Turmoil and Triumph: My Years as Secretary of State.* New York: Scribner's, 1993.

Zelikow, Philip, and Condoleezza Rice. *Germany Unified and Europe Transformed: A Study in Statecraft.* Cambridge, Mass.: Harvard University Press, 1995.

JOURNALS

Asian Survey
Beijing Review
China Daily (Beijing)
Current Digest of the Post-Soviet Press (formerly *Current Digest of the Soviet Press*)

Far Eastern Economic Review
Free China Journal (Taipei)
Issues and Studies (Taipei)
Journal of Conflict Resolution
Negotiation Journal

WEB SITES

NATO
http://www.nato.int

C H A P T E R   E I G H T

NATIONALISM AND WORLD ORDER: PEOPLES AT RISK

THE BIG QUESTIONS IN CHAPTER 8

- Why do many people see others in terms of "us vs. them"?

- Are "nations" born or manufactured?

- Is every nation a state? Every state a nation?

- What do minorities want? How do majorities respond?

- Are there ways to give minorities "voice" so that they are not overwhelmed by majorities?

- How can local ethno-nationalist conflicts affect IR?

- Why could many become "one" in the U.S. but not the USSR?

- Why have Singaporeans prospered while Sri Lankans fought?

- Why have the Swiss stayed together while the South Slavs split asunder?

- Can outsiders help? What options stand before the international community?

- Will nationalism be supplanted by another principle of identification? If so, will it be narrower or broader?

The UN Secretary-General requests that you head a panel to study ethnic and nationalist conflict worldwide. You and your colleagues must draft an action plan to protect peoples at risk. You know that pride in one's own people is basic to most societies. Ethnic ties and nationalism are among the most powerful forces in world affairs. Are they good or bad? They energize cultures and build states, but they also lay waste. Most wars since 1945 have been internal, fueled in large part by ethnic hatreds. Their furies killed millions and turned millions more into refugees.

You ask: "What are the roots of conflict? Do the links of trade and cyberspace mitigate or sharpen friction? What can outsiders do to prevent or moderate contention and replace it with—if not affection—order?"

You wonder: "Can our lives have no meaning, can we not prosper unless we belong to a larger community?" You think back on Aristotle's teaching that humans are "political animals": To be fully human, we must associate with a political community. But with whom or what should we identify? Family? Clan? Tribe? City-state? Race? Class? Profession? Faith? Empire? Gender? All humanity? All living things? Since the late 18th century, more and more people have answered: "Our nation."

Can the narrow passions of tribe, sect, or nation be supplanted by a quest for mutual gain? You and your panelists look for lessons in three very different countries that have coped with and benefited from ethnic and cultural diversity—the U.S., Singapore, and Switzerland. Can these positive examples be replicated in other multiethnic societies?

Your panel considers what each society can do to save itself and what outsiders can do to help. To make recommendations you must first review both theory and facts.

CONTENDING CONCEPTS AND EXPLANATIONS

THE DOCTRINE OF NATIONAL SELF-DETERMINATION

A doctrine of **national self-determination** took shape in 19th-century Europe and won strong endorsement from Woodrow Wilson in 1917–1919.[1] The doctrine has four articles of faith:

1. Every person belongs to a nation. **Nation** here means "people"—not any people but those among whom one is born, a particular people such as the Japanese.[2]

2. It is good and natural for nations to feel **nationalism**—a sentiment that "my nation is great and warrants my loyalty."

3. All nations (or at least the larger ones) deserve political expression in a nation state.

4. Every nation-state has its "legitimate" and "vital" national interests.

BEFORE NATIONALISM: "US VS. THEM"

Most peoples have been—and many still are—**ethnocentric**: They see themselves at the center of all life.[3] Ethnocentrists define themselves as fully human; outsiders are "barbarians" or "foreign devils." Ethocentrists view the world as "us vs. them."[4]

1. Prussian-born scholar Johann Gottfried Herder in the late 18th century taught that being a citizen was not sufficient. To live with meaning, a person must be part of a nation (*Volk*). Herder contended that every people has its own spirit (*Volksgeist*). Georg Hegel added in the 1820s that every *Volk* needs its own state (*Staat*). "All worth that the human being possesses . . . he possesses only through the State." Herder's nationalism was pacifistic; Hegel's lent itself to violence.

2. French *nation*, Spanish *nación*, and Italian *nazione* all derive from Latin *nasci*—to be born. People in general is in French *peuple*; in German, *Leute*; and in Russian, *liudi*. A particular nation is *nation*, *Volk*, or *narod*, respectively. The German *Volk* is akin to "folk" as in folk songs.

3. The Chinese termed their country the Middle Kingdom. Chinese people are "central country people"—*zong guo ren*, while foreigners are "outside country people"—*wai guo ren*. But both terms share the root *ren* for "people" (represented as 人 —resembling a two-legged human).

4. Language differences set people apart. Terms such as the Greek *barbaroi*, Russian *nemtsy*, and Hebrew *goyim* (non-Jews) all imply human incompleteness since these persons could not communicate with the in-group of "real persons." John A. Armstrong, *Nations before Nationalism* (Chapel Hill, N.C.: University of North Carolina Press, 1982), 5.

PEACE AT LAST! WE ARE VICTORIOUS!

WHAT DO YOU MEAN "WE", YOU MODERATE SWINE...

DANZIGER
The Christian Science Monitor

Many "nations" are not "nations." Afghans fought together to drive local and Soviet Communists from power in the 1980s, but then turned on one another.

Ethnic comes from the Greek word *ethnos,* which meant "another people"—outsiders who had their own **ethos** or set of standards and values.[5] From "ethos" (how a people does behave) we get "ethics" (how people should behave). The word history reveals a deep problem: How can there be a common ethical code for all ethnic groups if each plays by its own rules?

Ethnocentrism is old but nationalism is fairly new. Ancients had their tribes, city-states, and empires, but few if any had nation-states, states celebrating the ethos of one major ethnos. Thus, Athenians and Spartans shared a common language and gods but each group gave its political allegiance not to Greece but to its own city-state (*polis*).[6] Athenians saw Spartans as a different ethnos with a different ethos.

Rulers of ancient empires, however, were elitist—not nationalist. The rulers of imperial Egypt, Persia, and China esteemed their own **culture**—their ethos—not their nationhood. The ancient polity that most resembled a modern nation-state was Israel—first under King David and later under the Maccabee dynasty. Israel combined the unifying spirit of "God's Chosen People" with the structure and symbols of a nation-state—a unifying capital, belief-system, and laws.

Until the 19th century, most humans identified with the village or land where they lived, hunted, or farmed—not with some abstract "nation."[7] No modern form of nationalism is much more than five hundred years old. Nationalism arose in England under Henry VIII and later emerged in Holland, the U.S., and France.[8] Napoleon carried the flame of nationalism to Germany, Russia, Spain, and as far as Egypt. Over time, other peoples caught the spark—from Latin America to Africa. Demands for a Jewish homeland arose again at the end of the 19th century. Many of today's nationalisms took shape only after World War II.

IS NATION AN OBJECTIVE OR SUBJECTIVE REALITY?

Can "nation" be defined in objective terms? Josef Stalin tried to do so. He wrote: "A nation is a historically constituted, stable community of people, formed on the basis of a common language, territory, economic life, and psychological make-up manifested in a common culture."[9]

But few nations, if any, fit Stalin's criteria. Ultimately, nationhood is a subjective reality. A nation is any group of people who believes or feels it is a nation. It is an imagined community because most members can never meet one another personally, yet they choose to emphasize what unites them rather than what separates them.[10]

5. Greek *demos* meant city people—those who live in a *polis. Ethnos* meant country people—outsiders. The adjective *ethnikos* meant "foreign" and was used in Greek translations of the Bible to render the Hebrew *goyim.* From *ethnikos* comes "ethnic." To study Native Americans the U.S. government established a Bureau of Ethnology.

6. The presumed Indo-European root *dem* gave Latin *domus* (home), from which English got "domestic" and "domain." Greek *demos* probably meant the households in an area—the inhabitants. From this root English took "democracy" and "demography." Indo-European *pele* probably meant high, fortified place, from which Greek got *polis,* from which English took "politics" and "police."

7. Italian nationalists derided *campanilismo*—the world view of persons whose perspective stopped at what they could see from the local bell tower (*campanile*).

8. Liah Greenfeld, *Nationalism: Five Roads to Modernity* (Cambridge, Mass.: Harvard University Press, 1992). Two centuries before Henry VIII, however, English writers discussed an English "nation," while Chaucer in 1386 wrote about someone who, alas, had to travel to a "Barbre nacioun." For a catalog of national and ethnic stereotypes, see Shakespeare's *Merchant of Venice* (1596). Portia scorns each type but also dislikes a man whose clothes and behavior are from "every where."

9. J. V. Stalin, "Marxism and the National Question" (1913), in Josef Stalin, *Marxism and the National-Colonial Question* (San Francisco: Proletarian Publishers, 1975), 15–99 at 22.

10. Benedict Anderson, *Imagined Communities: Reflections on the Origin and Spread of Nationalism,* rev. ed. (London: Verso, 1991).

Nationalists feel that "we as a nation have had a great past and, working together, will build a great future." Nationalists usually look back as well as forward. If necessary, they invent a new past.

Nationalism is sometimes a secular religion—a belief that each person should feel a deep, perhaps supreme loyalty to the nation. For extreme nationalists, the nation is the tree; the individual, a branch. The tree nourishes the branch but can live without it; the branch can be sacrificed for the tree.

Nationalisms come in all sizes and shapes. Some are comparatively liberal, open and tolerant; others are more **authoritarian,** closed and aggressive. Two kinds of nationalism have sparked conflict in the 20th century: **Expansionist nationalism**, as in Nazi Germany, seeks to conquer outsiders; **intermingled nationalism**, as in Bosnia, may generate ethnic struggles among close neighbors.

Nationalism is not identical to patriotism—devotion to one's fatherland (*patrie* in French). Patriotism may—but need not—be nationalist or ethnocentric. A patriot in country A need not deny the value of country B. Still, both patriotism and ethnocentrism can lead to fear of foreigners, or xenophobia, as well as to racism, chauvinism, and other aggressive forms of nationalism.[11]

11. "Chauvinism" denotes an aggressive, showy patriotism. The term derives from Nicolas Chauvin, a soldier devoted to Napoleon.

Your panel wonders: "What makes individuals feel bonded in one nation? Why do they emphasize what unites them rather than what divides them?" You identify many wellsprings of nationalism:

Spiritual need: Nationalism can give meaning to life after traditional ways and extended families disappear.

Territory: People often believe their land is sacred.

Mission: Many peoples believe they are "chosen" by God or Fate to do great things; some feel entitled to exploit the non-elect.

Conquest and indoctrination: Diverse peoples have been conquered and molded into a single unit such as the "United Kingdom of Great Britain and Northern Ireland." Some groups forget their separate origins; others do not.

External threats: Outside pressures help to forge "national" unity. This tempts politicians to manufacture foreign bogeys if they are not visible.

Why Did Estonians Remain Estonians?

Estonians have lived on the shores of the Baltic Sea for thousands of years. From the 13th century, however, they were ruled by Danes, Germans, Swedes, and then Russians. In the 19th century most Estonians were still peasants, but modernization buttressed nationalism. The introduction of railroads permitted church choirs from scattered parishes to come together for festivals of traditional Estonian music. People met, recalled, celebrated, and strengthened their common heritage. Tsarist Russian and later Soviet officials tried to throttle Estonian nationalism, but Estonians (as well as neighboring Latvians and Lithuanians) persisted with nation-wide music festivals and other ways to affirm their identity. Their drive for independence in the 1980s became a "Singing Revolution." Still, no person has "Estonian" stamped on her or his genes. Today's Estonian way of life derives from an ancient peasant ethos heavily influenced by outside cultures. Even Christianity was an alien import.

Gender: Men do not want to be "emasculated" or their women to be ravished by outsiders. Nationalists of both sexes worship the "mother" or "father" land. Many women praise their heroic men.

Fear of extinction: Many groups fear their genes and cultures will be overwhelmed unless they unite and fend off outsiders, including would-be rapists, spreaders of alien genes.

Mobilization: People must be mobilized to feel a common nationalism. Both democracies and dictatorships mobilized nationalist sentiment in World War II.

Leaders: Some leaders genuinely believe in a national cause; others—entrepreneurs of nationalism, many of them scholars, lawyers, and even physicians—provoke and exploit national sentiments to increase their own influence.[12]

Modernization: Nationalism nourishes and is nourished by modernization—roads, mass communications, industrialization, urbanization, education, and political participation.

But modernization can also undermine national identity. The global spread of products—McDonald's, Microsoft, and MTV—fosters a "McWorld" culture threatening the uniqueness of each "na-

Mobilizing the Disadvantaged for a Sacred Cause

Some analysts say that nationalism has replaced religion, but the two have often worked as partners—as in Catholic Poland, in Buddhist Sri Lanka, and in many Islamic countries. Iran's ayatollahs tapped the alienation of Iran's disadvantaged to support their theocracy. The ayatollahs' regime formed a three-million-strong volunteer force of *Bassiji* ("those who are mobilized") to help fight Iraq in the 1980s, often with suicidal mass wave tactics. When that war ended, the *Bassiji* were directed in 1993 to struggle against the bullets of "cultural corruption" such as lipstick and Western videos that, said Commander Ali Reza Afshar, "make our young impotent to rebuild the nation."[1]

1. One Iranian professor complained that the *Bassiji* "give 15-year-old boys, or unemployed slum dwellers, guns and send them into the streets." They "gain power over the professionals and the elite they believe looks down on them." Chris Hedges, "Mobilzing Against Pop Music and Other Horrors," *New York Times*, July 21, 1993, A4.

12. Two historians at Rwandan National University "manufactured doctrines of Hutu ethnic supremacy depicting all Tutsis as a malignant cancer in the nation's history that deserved to be excised once and for all." Michael Chege, "Africa's Murderous Professors," *The National Interest*, no. 46 (winter 1996–1997): 32–40.

Why Did Colonists Become "Americans"?

In the 17th century England's colonies in North America dealt with the motherland far more than with one another. In the 18th century, however, they were linked ever closer by trade, publications, mail, travel, and the exchange of ideas. As colonists exchanged goods and ideas more with one another and relatively less with the English motherland, they came to feel more "American" and less "English." But external pressures catalyzed their union—the taxes and Red Coats of King George III. Even then, less than half the colonists were devoted to independence. Even they needed to be mobilized and led.[1]

1. See Richard L. Merritt, "Nation-Building in America: The Colonial Years," in *Nation-Building*, ed. Karl W. Deutsch and William J. Foltz (New York: Atherton, 1966), 56–72.

Fig. 8.1 Possible Synergies Among Nationalism, Modernization, and Internationalism

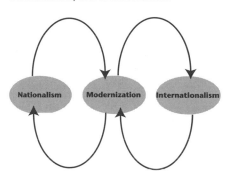

tion."[13] To resist these pressures some peoples become even more ethnocentric. Figure 8.1 depicts the possible synergies among nationalism, modernization, and internationalism.

Economic interdependence: If people depend upon one another as economic partners, they may begin to feel as one. The logic of interdependence may integrate entire countries, then regions and continents, finally the world. Humans, however, are not purely economic animals. Canada and the U.S. are each other's biggest trading partners, but each retains its own national identity.[14] Mutual economic links did not preserve Yugoslavia or the USSR. They may not suffice to forge a truly united Europe.

Organism or artifice? Nationalism arises in different ways at different times and places. But as we see from the Estonian and other cases, nationalism is not "primordial"—not inherent in genes, territory, or even language. History makes and constantly remakes what we call "race," "nation," "culture," and "language."

Will There Be a United States of Europe?

Will the logic of interdependence soon push Italians and Belgians to value "Europe" above their own "fatherlands"? There is no easy way to integrate separate nations into unified regions. In the late 20th century Europe's commercial elites favored an integrated Europe, but many ordinary Danes, Germans, and Spaniards preferred their national institutions. Indeed, majorities in two of the most affluent countries, Switzerland and Norway, repeatedly voted against closer ties with "Europe." In the 1990s Europeans were much further from the preconditions for unity than Americans in the 1770s.

IS THERE A "NATIONAL" INTEREST?

Realists say that each nation has its own interests and that competition between conflicting national interests drives IR. Thus, some Americans argued that it was a vital U.S. national interest to build and dominate the

13. Benjamin R. Barber, *Jihad vs. McWorld* (New York: Ballantine, 1996); Ezra Suleiman, "Is Democratic Supranationalism a Danger?" in *Nationalism and Nationalities in the New Europe*, ed. Charles A. Kupchan (Ithaca, N.Y.: Cornell University Press, 1995), 107–121.

14. Seymour Martin Lipset, *Continental Divide: The Values and Institutions of the United States and Canada* (New York: Routledge, 1990).

Panama Canal. Later, Panamanian nationalists countered that it is their sacred national interest to own and control the canal. Critics deride "national interest" as a propaganda myth. Individuals and groups within each country disagree on what its interests require. Experts disagree whether control of the Panama Canal is important for U.S. interests.

IS EVERY NATION A STATE? EVERY STATE A NATION?

A state is not necessarily a nation. How common is the "nation-state" where nation and state are one? The global pattern is summarized in Table 8.1.

The table shows that nearly one-third of the world's states have populations 90 percent or more homogeneous. Most of the world's great powers have one ethnic group that makes up at least 70 percent of the population. Indeed, this is so for about 60 percent of all states. But even homogeneous states may fracture for other reasons: China is divided by dialect and wealth; Egypt by religion and class; Somalia by clan. Nor does a strong majority guarantee tolerance. The vast majority in Rwanda and Burundi are Hutus, but they have several times tried to wipe out the Tutsi minority—perceived exploiters.

Two of the largest states are extremely heterogeneous—consisting of many nations or ethnic groups. India is 72 percent Indo-Aryan but only 28 percent Hindustani; Indonesia is 46 percent Javanese. Both countries experience much ethnic and religious turbulence.

Table 8.1 How Ethnically Homogeneous Are the World's States in the 1990s?

Proportion of Dominant Ethnic Groups (percent)	Number of States (total = 179)	Proportion of 179 States (percent)	Examples
95–100	37	21	Denmark, Egypt, Japan, North Korea, South Korea, Portugal, Somalia
90–94.99	20	11	Armenia, China, Germany, Italy, Rwanda, Sweden, Vanuatu
70–89.99	51	28	Azerbaijan, Romania, Russia, Singapore, Slovakia, Sri Lanka, Switzerland, Ukraine, United Kingdom, U.S., Vietnam
50–69.99	29	16	Belgium, Benin, Estonia, Kyrgyzstan, Serbia, Trinidad
30–49.99	31	17	Bolivia, Bosnia (1992), Ethiopia, Kazakstan, Zambia
1–29.99	11	6	Chad, Nigeria, Papua New Guinea, South Africa, Zaire

SOURCES: Central Intelligence Agency, *World Fact Book* (Washington, D.C.: Government Printing Office, 1990 and 1993), and *Narody mira: istoriko-etnograficheskii spravochnik* (Moscow: Sovetskaia entsiklopediia, 1988).

Is Canada a "Nation"?

How many nations are in Canada? One, two, or a hundred? A plurality—about 40 percent—of Canada's 28 million population in 1994 had roots in the British Isles. Some 27 percent were descended from French settlers. The French language had equal rights with English, but most people outside Quebec used English in schools and business. Other minorities included persons of Italian, Ukrainian, Chinese, and "First Nation" (indigenous) origin. Even English-speaking whites were split by regional and economic interests. Calls for secession were heard not only in Quebec but also in Anglophone provinces.

In October 1995 the secessionist movement failed by a small margin in a referendum—49.42 percent to 50.58 percent—though 60 percent of French-speaking whites voted for independence. English speakers and immigrants, about 18 percent of Quebec's population, voted against secession. The Cree and Inuit of northern Quebec held their own plebiscites and voted to remain in Canada. Quebec Premier Jacques Parizeau blamed what he called the "ethnic vote" for frustrating the will of "true Quebecers."

Ottawa portrayed Canada as a prosperous mosaic of cultures. But many French-speakers said their language and culture were given second-class status by the Anglophone majority. In 1995, Parizeau received a vigorous welcome by supporters who wanted Quebec to secede.

Ethnic Minorities: Peoples at Risk

The globe also contains thousands of minority ethnic groups—peoples without their own states. They make up about a billion people—a fifth of humanity. Many minorities feel unrepresented or even exploited. The "Minorities at Risk Project," undertaken at the U.S. Institute of Peace in Washington, analyzed 233 "politicized communal groups" (each numbering at least 100,000 persons) during the period 1945–1989. Most were "have-nots" who felt they suffered discrimination, but 25 groups were advantaged "haves," such as whites in South Africa. They too were minorities at risk—from retaliation.[15] In Africa more than two-fifths of all people belonged to minorities in the 1980s, compared with about one-tenth of the inhabitants of Western democracies and Latin America.

How do such peoples show their feelings? Nonviolent political action by such minorities more than doubled in the years 1950–1990 while violent action quadrupled. The Communist world was fairly quiet until the late 1980s when the Soviet and Yugoslav realms began to explode, for example, in Tajikistan and Bosnia.

Contending ethnic groups focus on perceived injustice—"what is" compared with what members believe "should be." Dissatisfied ethnic

Fig. 8.2 Percentage of Language Users in Quebec, 1991

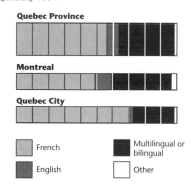

Quebec Province

Montreal

Quebec City

French

English

Multilingual or bilingual

Other

15. Ted Robert Gurr et al., *Minorities at Risk: A Global View of Ethnopolitical Conflicts* (Washington, D.C.: U.S. Institute of Peace, 1993).

How Nationalism Made and Split Eurasia's "Heartland"

Czech nationalists (backed by Woodrow Wilson) created Czechoslovakia in 1919 from the Austro-Hungarian Empire. The Czech majority dominated politics. Minorities—Slovaks, Germans, Hungarians, Poles, Gypsies—felt slighted. Hitler asserted Germany's right to incorporate all German irredenta. The 1938 Munich agreement authorized Germany to annex Czechoslovakia's largely German-speaking Sudetenland, whereupon 400,000 Czechs moved out. Hungary and Poland then grabbed border regions heavily populated by their irredenta, while Slovakia separated and became a German puppet state. The remaining Czech lands became a German protectorate in 1939. After Hitler's defeat, Czechs returned to the Sudetenland and some 3 million Germans were expelled. Slovakia was reincorporated in a unitary Czechoslovakia in 1945, obtained federal autonomy in 1968, and became independent in 1993. Thus, contending nationalisms created, destroyed, and partitioned Eurasia's "heartland" many times in just over eight decades.

groups demand more honor, clout, wealth, land, jobs, or other values; often they feel deprived relative to other groups.[16] Minorities base their claims to entitlement on many factors: alleged racial superiority, history (who got there first), revenge (for previous wrongs), numbers (share in the population), and divine calling. Race, religion, and culture can interact with nationalism to fuel a politics of rage.

Depending on how a people's claims are met—or frustrated—its demands may escalate. The lowest demand is for corporate status—recognition as a distinct minority with equal or special rights, for example, by religious or linguistic groups. Next come demands for **autonomy**—self-government within the state. These are often made by **indigenous** peoples, for example, Navajos.

The most radical demand is for **secession**. A minority may claim the right to form or join a separate state. **Irredentism** is a nationalist movement demanding union of irredenta—a people ruled by an alien government—with kinfolk in their own nation-state.[17] How such demands ripped apart Czechoslovakia is summerized in the sidebar.

Methods of Dealing with Ethnic Minorities

Demands of ethnic minorities have been met by policies drawn from a wide menu of tough and conciliatory measures.[18] Ethnic demands can be met differently in unitary, federal, and confederal systems. A **unitary state** monopolizes power at the center and grants limited powers to local communities. A **federation** balances power between the center and the states. A **confederation** has a weak center and keeps most power in the local units.

Hard-Line Ways to Eliminate Ethnic Differences. Elimination of ethnic differences is most easily accomplished in unitary systems. Methods include top-down pressures and education to encourage **assimilation** (absorbing minorities into the dominant culture, for example, fusing Bretons and Basques into "French"); **genocide**, the systematic annihilation of whole peoples (Jews and Gypsies under Hitler); and forced population transfers such as those listed in the sidebar on page 225. Other hard-line ways to manage ethnic differences include control by one ethnic group (whites in the U.S. South before the 1960s) and partition (apartheid in pre-1990s South Africa).

But repression often generates a backlash. Even when an ethnic group has been "cleansed," its remnants may retaliate for many years afterward. Thus, Armenian assassins stalked Turkish diplomats around the globe in

16. Let us call this perception of relative deprivation "RD." Ted Gurr suggests that RD → Frustration → Action. The model is suggestive but does not specify *who* or *how many* of the group must feel deprived for its action to begin (or end).

17. The term "irredenta" is from the Italian for "unredeemed"—a reference to Italian-speakers under Austrian rule before World War I.

18. See John McGarry and Brendan O'Leary, eds., *The Politics of Ethnic Conflict Regulation: Case Studies of Protracted Ethnic Conflicts* (London: Routledge, 1993), 4.

the 1990s to revenge alleged Ottoman massacres before and during World War I.

Conciliatory Ways to Manage Ethnic Differences. Methods include integration into a common civic culture that does not obliterate but rather accommodates differences; enlisting ("coopting") minority elites (attempted in USSR); affirmative action (U.S. in 1970s); mediation by outsiders (Zimbabwe in 1979); arbitration (Hopi-Navajo dispute in 1980s);[19] one-person, one-vote, but with institutionalized protection for the minority (Zimbabwe, the new South Africa); and **power-sharing**— assuring each segment of society a voice in decisions and a share in public resources (Switzerland since 1943, Belgium since 1970, South Africa in the 1990s).

Power-sharing (also known as "consociational democracy") and special protection of minorities depart from the winner-take-all stance of **majority rule**. If one ethnic group has more than half the votes, it can pass laws that favor its interests while restricting others. Minorities may reject such democracy. Our case studies will detail how power-sharing has worked in Switzerland and failed in Yugoslavia. We shall see that if a minority has "voice" within a system, it is more likely to be loyal and less likely to "exit"—separate from—the system.[20]

Self-Determination vs. World Peace

Demands for **self-determination** by individuals or groups within existing states can convulse the entire international system. Outsiders—the United Nations and individual states—are torn between two principles: respect for state sovereignty and respect for human rights. The first principle dictates non-intervention in the affairs of sovereign states and support for existing borders; the second, a need for intervention when human rights are at risk.

Supporters of non-intervention hold that outsiders should let ethnic groups within a state settle their own disputes. The United Nations and its members should act, if at all, to quash secessionist movements. The United Nations should not allow minorities to alter boundaries or create new states. Any attempt to change borders will produce greater suffering than that it is meant to address.

Interventionists support the interests of human rights and peace over state sovereignty. Where human rights are abused, peace is at risk. And maintenance of international peace and security is the primary reason for the United Nations. Civil strife inevitably leads to refugee flows and other dislocations that burden other states.

Some Targets of Ethnic Cleansing

Ethnic cleansing is a euphemism for forced population transfers or genocidal murders. The term was used by Serbs and others in the former Yugoslavia to justify their genocidal massacres, rape, and forced population transfers of one another in the 1990s. Dispersal and enslavement of conquered peoples have occurred since ancient times.[1] Ethnic cleansers have targeted

Muslims and Jews in 15th-century Spain

Huguenots in 16th- and 17th-century France

Native Americans from the 15th through the 19th centuries

Armenians in 19th- and early 20th-century Ottoman Turkey

Jews and Gypsies in Nazi Germany

Chechens, Crimean Tatars, and others in Stalin's USSR

Germans from the Sudetenland in 1945

East Indians in Uganda in the 1960s

Chinese in Indonesia in the 1960s

Tutsis by Hutus in Burundi and Rwanda in the 1990s

1. See Andrew Bell-Fialkoff, *Ethnic Cleansing* (New York: St. Martin's, 1996). For a review of writings on genocide, see Irving Louis Horowitz in *American Political Science Review* 87, no. 2 (June 1993): 530–531.

19. Mediation and intervention are analyzed in Chapter 9.

20. See Albert O. Hirschman, *Exit, Voice, and Loyalty: Responses to Decline in Firms, Organizations, and States* (Cambridge, Mass.: Harvard University Press, 1970).

Ethnic groups Hutus and Tutsis vied for power within Rwanda. In 1994 Hutu militants tried to wipe out Tutsis but failed (though they murdered 700,000). Caught between the Tutsi-dominated Rwandan Patriotic Front and hard-line Hutus were ordinary people like this Hutu refugee girl, looking for her parents among corpses of hundreds of refugees who attempted to flee to Zaire (Congo).

21. The peacemakers gave some but not all peoples a choice. Communities living along Germany's borders with Denmark and Poland could vote whether to join Germany or its neighbor. But the peacemakers prohibited the German-speaking Austrians from ever joining Germany; they put millions of Germans and Slovaks in one country dominated by Czechs.

The League Covenant consigned some "less advanced" peoples to administration by "advanced nations" under the League of Nations "mandate" system. Thus, South West Africa (a former German colony) became a mandate of South Africa.

22. The United Nations crushed a movement in Katanga Province to secede from the former Belgian Congo in 1960. But Singapore left the Federation of Malaysia without a fight in 1965, while Bangladesh—aided by India's military—broke from Pakistan in 1971.

International law and organization have been erratic in dealing with these issues. The League of Nations Covenant (1919) omitted any mention of national self-determination. Woodrow Wilson and other statesmen at Versailles agreed that it was impossible for each nation to have its own state.[21] Instead the League labored to promote *minority* rights, especially in the new states of Eastern Europe.

The post-1945 legal order focused on *human* rights—not minority rights. The UN Charter endorsed the principle of national self-determination but did not declare it a legal right. The Charter called on states with "trust territories" (such as Belgium, trustee of Rwanda-Burundi) to promote self-government there. The Charter emphasized self-government of particular territories—not of nations or peoples.

Most UN members backed independence for Europe's colonies such as India, but did little for ethnic minorities or nations within existing states (such as Estonia in the USSR). Without UN support, most secessionist movements failed from 1945 to 1990.[22] When the Second World collapsed in 1991–1992, however, UN members quickly recognized most of the new states that emerged from the USSR and Yugoslavia; also Eritrea, which had struggled to separate from Ethiopia since 1962.

The boundary between inter-state and intra-state problems became fuzzier. In 1991–1992 minority rights again became an international concern. The U.S. State Department and the European Union demanded that the breakaway republics of Yugoslavia "guarantee ethnic and minority rights" and respect the "inviolability of borders." But this was to square the circle: How could each ethnic group enjoy self-determination in a multinational state without changing borders or moving populations?

Ethnic ferment encouraged outside intervention. Some top Russian leaders claimed the right to protect 25 million Russians living in former Soviet republics from Estonia to Kazakstan. Moscow also sided in the mid-1990s with Abkhazians wishing to transfer their territory from Georgia to Russia.

Foreign meddling can turn an intra-state problem into one between states. Thus, U.S. and some Russian leaders backed different horses in Yugoslavia and Georgia. U.S.-Russian discord on such matters roiled the entente sought by Presidents Bill Clinton and Boris Yeltsin.

Worldwide in the mid-1990s some 30 million people sought refuge from communal violence. Their numbers burdened host countries already facing heavy unemployment. West Europeans in the 1990s tightened their border controls, rules on asylum, and procedures for naturalization. Neo-Nazi and nativist movements pressed to exclude or evict foreigners.[23] Do victims of ethnic strife have any legal rights in the countries where they seek asylum? Do rights come only with citizenship? There were no easy answers.

Your panel decides to compare three multiethnic societies that have held together with three that have failed. Was there some recipe for success? For disaster? You hope eventually to carry out many case studies, but you begin with three comparisons—the U.S. and USSR, Singapore and Sri Lanka, and Switzerland and Yugoslavia. You look for lessons—both for individual societies and for outsiders, including the United Nations: How can harmony replace hate?

COMPARING THEORY AND REALITY: SELF-DETERMINATION AND WORLD ORDER

CASE I: WHY DID THE U.S. HOLD WHILE TWO RUSSIAN EMPIRES COLLAPSED?

Despite its conflicted race relations, the U.S. expanded and held together in the 19th and 20th centuries while most other states experienced revolutionary change and/or major territorial losses. Indeed, two Russian empires collapsed—the tsarist in 1917 and the Soviet in 1991. Many features that helped make "one from many" in the U.S. were lacking in the

23. The European Court of Justice guaranteed social rights to workers and their families within the European Community regardless of their immigrant status.

France favored immigrants from Poland (part of Western Christendom) over North Africans. But France naturalized more outsiders than Germany, where citizenship depended upon descent ("blood"), while birth on German soil did not count. Roger Brubaker, *Citizenship and Nationhood in France and Germany* (Cambridge, Mass.: Harvard University Press, 1992); compare Harry Goulbourne, *Ethnicity and Nationalism in Post-Imperial Britain* (New York: Cambridge University Press, 1991). See also *Daedalus* 126, no. 3 (special issue: "A New Europe for the Old?") (summer 1997).

Table 8.2 Comparing U.S. and Soviet Integration (1990)

Variable	U.S.	USSR
Population size	Large (250 million)	Large (291 million)
Civilizations	One, plus others in an evolving synthesis	Several distinct
Major ethnic groups	75 percent Anglophone white; 12 percent black; 9 percent Hispanic; 4 percent other	51 percent Russian; 15 percent Ukrainian; 6 percent Uzbek; 4 percent Belarus; many others
Languages	One official plus some bilingual education	One countrywide official language plus official languages of each republic
Government	Federal democracy	Authoritarian "union" under Communist dictatorship
How formed?	Mainly voluntarily	Unity imposed by Moscow
Ethnic segmentation by political unit	None, except for Indian reservations	Each union-republic named for an ethnic group (Kazaks, Chechens, and others)
History of ethnic conflict?	Yes, especially whites against Indians and blacks	Yes, with genocide in 1930s and 1940s
GDP per capita	Very high	Low to medium

SOURCES: World Bank, *World Development Report* (New York: Oxford University Press, annual); U.S. Department of State, *Country Reports on Human Rights* (Washington, D.C.: Government Printing Office, annual); and U.S. Central Intelligence Agency, *World Factbook* (Washington, D.C.: Government Printing Office, annual).

USSR.[24] Some key differences between the two societies are summarized in Table 8.2.

Civilization

The most general form of culture is the mother **civilization** from which each country builds its way of life. The U.S. was rooted in Western civilization but moved in the 20th century toward a new way of life enriched by African, Hispanic, Asian, and other influences.

Nearly three-fourths of the Soviet population were Slavs rooted in Eastern Orthodox civilization. The many ethnic minorities of the USSR kept their distinct identities far more than did minorities in the U.S. Russians remained distinct from Lutheran Estonians and Latvians, Catholic Lithuanians, Sunni Muslims of Uzbekistan, Shiite Muslims of Tajikistan, and Buddhists abutting Mongolia.

In the late 20th century the U.S. no longer resembled a melting pot so much as a mosaic in which each stone kept its luster and reflected the brilliance of others. The USSR remained a patchwork quilt of clashing colors. Why did no unified "Soviet nation" emerge despite long efforts to promote "brotherhood" and "convergence"? In brief: repressed nationalism.

Voluntary vs. Coerced Participation

24. Walter C. Clemens, Jr., "Who or What Killed the Soviet Union? How Three Davids Undermined Goliath," *Nationalism and Ethnic Politics* 3, no. 1 (spring 1997): 136–158.

Most of the individuals and new territories joining the U.S. did so voluntarily. (Exceptions include Native Americans, Africans, Hispanics in annexed Mexican lands, many Hawaiians, and Inuits.) The Russian state was built and sustained by force—from Lithuania to Vladivostok—though some minorities (such as Georgians and Armenians) at times welcomed Russian protection against Ottoman Turks.

Segmentation

Countries can be segmented—partitioned, divided—by natural borders (for example, rivers), by ethnicity, or by other criteria. No U.S. "state" represented a single ethnos, though some cities were dominated by German-Americans and other "hyphenated" minorities. By contrast, the structure of the Soviet Union enshrined territorial ethnicity. Not only were its fifteen union-republics named for ethnic groups clustered there (Ukraine, Armenia, Turkmenia) but so were over twenty autonomous republics and regions (Tataria, Yakutia).

Language

The U.S. had essentially one language, which most immigrants wanted to learn.[25] By contrast, most Soviet republics were allowed to keep using the local language, though Russian was promoted as the language for communicating countrywide. The Kremlin tried to gut minority languages and cultures of local symbols and replace them with "socialist" emblems, but the effect of Moscow's policies was to keep local languages and nationalisms alive in most republics.[26]

Democracy vs. Autocracy

U.S. democracy gave hope to most ethnic minorities that they could improve their lot by working within the system. Majority rule favored the entrenched majority—the largest minority was nearly disenfranchised until the 1960s. A different system such as proportional representation would have assured better representation for minorities, but might have been very divisive. Proportional representation, as in France, would give a party seats in Congress proportional to the number of votes it receives countrywide and thus foster many parties.

Tsarist Russia and the USSR, by contrast, were ruled by autocrats, secret police, and a rigid bureaucracy. Outside the ruling elite, no group—least of all ethnic minorities—had a voice. Stalin established the facade of a federal system but real power remained in the Communist Party and its top leader. When the party lost its ability to intimidate, the system collapsed.[27]

The North's victory in the U.S. Civil War in 1865 made clear than no state could secede from the Union. By contrast, the Soviet Constitution

25. At times, however, foreign languages were the medium of instruction in some U.S. public as well as parochial schools, and bilingual schools became common in the late 20th century. See Lawrence H. Fuchs, *The American Kaleidoscope: Race, Ethnicity, and the Civic Culture* (Hanover, N.H.: University Press of New England, 1990), chap. 24.

26. In the 1920s it appeared that 192 languages would be treated as official. See Yuri Slezkine, "The USSR as a Communal Apartment, or How a Socialist State Promoted Ethnic Particularism," in *Becoming National: A Reader*, ed. Geoff Eley and Ronald Grigor Suny (New York: Oxford University Press, 1996), 203–238 at 214–216.

27. But on Stalin's "big deal" with the privileged sectors of society, see Vera S. Dunham, *In Stalin's Time: Middle Class Values in Soviet Fiction*, rev. ed. (Durham, N.C.: Duke University Press, 1990).

Protesters in Vilnius demand independence from the USSR for Lithuania, Latvia, and Estonia. This April 1990 demonstration formed part of a "Singing Revolution" by which Balts mobilized world opinion for their cause. The three Baltic republics helped catalyze the breakup of the USSR in 1991.

allowed the union-republics to secede. When the Communist dictatorship weakened in the 1980s, Estonians and others quoted the USSR Constitution and said: "We have the right to secede."

Many—probably most—non-Russians felt exploited by the Russian-dominated center. Many Russians, in turn, disdained non-Russians as ingrates and trouble-makers.

Had the USSR been an economic success, national differences might have been subdued, but this is not certain. It was the country's wealthiest republics—Estonia, Latvia, and Lithuania—that led demands for secession, while the poorest regions—those of Central Asia—favored continued union.

Lack of democracy and free expression made the pot boil. Not until 1987 did the Kremlin encourage the Soviet media to address national complaints even somewhat openly. By then it was too late: Grievances erupted like a volcano, opening wounds instead of healing them. A Soviet scholar compared the USSR with India. Both contained multiple civilizations and languages; both were segmented. India was much poorer and its central government weaker. Despite decades of communal violence, India held together. Freedom to speak, write, and organize politically acted as safety valves absent in the Soviet system.[28]

CASE II: WHY DID SINGAPORE PROSPER AND SRI LANKA IMPLODE?

Just to the south of India is another spinoff from the British empire with democratic institutions—the island of Sri Lanka, earlier known as

28. India, he thought, was moving toward the Swiss power-sharing model. See A. A. Prazauskas, "Ethnoregional Political Cultures and the Problem of National-State Integration in India and the USSR," *Vostok* 5 (May 1991): 38–51. For a more complex picture, see Salman Rushdie, *The Moor's Last Sigh* (New York: Pantheon, 1995).

Table 8.3 Comparing Singapore and Sri Lanka (1993)

Variable	Singapore	Sri Lanka
Population size	Small (3.2 million)	Small (18 million)
Civilizations	Four	Two, plus Western
Major ethnic groups	78 percent Chinese; 14 percent Malay; 7 percent Tamil	74 percent Sinhalese; 18 percent Tamil; 7 percent Moor
Languages	English and three other official	One official; two "national"; English
Government	Authoritarian	Majority-rule democracy
How formed?	Mainly voluntarily	Unity imposed on rivals by European imperialists
Ethnic segmentation by political unit	None	De facto in two, mainly Tamil, provinces
History of ethnic conflict?	Little	Much
GDP per capita	Medium high ($15,730)	Low ($540)

SOURCES: World Bank, *World Development Report;* U.S. Department of State, *Country Reports;* and U.S. Central Intelligence Agency, *World Factbook.*

Ceylon. In the 1970s many social scientists regarded Sri Lanka as a model developing country. In 1983, however, Sri Lanka fell apart, torn by one of humanity's oldest ethnic/religious conflicts. Nearby is Singapore, also an island nation of many cultures once tied to the British empire, but one that has enjoyed social peace and ethnic harmony. Why these differences?

Modernizing Nationalism

Like Venice and Hamburg in the Middle Ages, Singapore shows how a commercial city-state can be a major actor in world affairs.[29] Transformed under imperial British rule from a malarial fishing village into a great port, Singapore became independent in 1965. Dominated by ethnic Chinese, the government has labored to protect each ethnic group while unifying all through common symbols.

Singapore's authoritarian, unitary form of government has fostered economic modernization and curbed ethnic contention. It has focused not on the past but on the present and future. It promotes use of English but also accepts Chinese, Tamil, and Malay as official languages.

Singapore has promoted a unifying nationalism based on pride and hope in the island nation's achievements. English, along with skyscrapers and apartment blocks, is an import without local roots. Like the U.S., Singapore tells its various peoples to bond in a new nationalism. (The U.S., however, treasures the language and traditions of its founders, glories in several hundred years of U.S. history, and builds upon thousands of years of Western civilization. It looks back as well as forward.)

Critics say that Singapore's authoritarian government—a blend of Big Brother and McWorld—has stamped out cultural differences and freedom of expression. Others see the regime as an enlightened despotism. Both admirers and critics agree that economic and social progress benefits from ethnic calm, while ethnic harmony benefits from prosperity.

How a Model Developing Country Ran Amok

Much richer than Singapore in natural resources, Sri Lanka remained much poorer. Sri Lanka's per capita income grew at half the pace of Singapore's in the last quarter of the 20th century.

Singapore used unitary state power to enforce mutual tolerance. But democracy failed Sri Lanka, because Sinhalese—three-fourths of the population—abused their power. The majority used government to prop up its language and religion.

Many Sinhalese are ethnocentric. They consider themselves the "Lion People" and protectors of Buddhism. For the Sinhalese popular mind, a

29. On Hamburg and the Hanseatic League, see Klaus Friedland, *Die Hanse* (Stuttgart: Kohlhammer, 1991).

multi-racial or multi-communal state is "incomprehensible."[30] Many Sinhalese see themselves as racially and religiously superior to the Tamil minority. Sinhalese are Aryans who migrated from northern India over two thousand years ago. Tamils are Dravidians, often darker and shorter than Sinhalese, from southern India. Most Tamils practice Hinduism. Some two-thirds of Tamils are "Ceylonese Tamils"—offspring of ancient settlers; only they are politically active. The other third are "Estate Tamils"—poorest of the poor, descended from migrants who arrived in the late 19th/early 20th century to work on tea plantations. Imperial Britain imposed order on Ceylon from the early 19th century until 1948. With independence came majority rule and renewed ethnic conflict. The Sinhalese majority cut back the numbers of Tamils in higher education and civil service, where Tamils held more jobs than their share of the population.[31] Like Singapore, Sri Lanka could have adopted English as its official language to transcend local language differences and step into world trade. Instead, the Sinhalese-dominated government made Sinhala the official language in 1956. When Tamils objected, Sri Lanka's prime minister offered to make Tamil an "official" language for the two Tamil-majority regions. For this effort he was killed by a gang supported by Sinhalese business interests and some Buddhist monks.

Some Tamils tried to work within the system—in parliament and the press. But others became frustrated. Initially they had demanded only cultural rights or autonomy for Tamil regions. Now some demanded an independent Tamil state—"Eelam." Proponents of violence silenced voices of moderation. The most militant fighters were semi-educated rural youths without jobs, spurred on by charismatic leaders. Like Palestinians confronting Israel, young Tamils asked: "What have we got to lose?"

Systematic warfare began in 1983 after Tamil "Liberation Tigers" massacred Sinhalese in remote regions and Sinhalese took revenge against Tamils in the capital.[32] Violence fed violence. Extremists murdered kinsmen who favored ethnic conciliation. As we shall see in the next chapter, India in 1987 stationed 60,000 peacekeepers in Sri Lanka to curb hostilities. But young Tamils fought the Indian troops as well as Sinhalese and Muslim civilians. The Indian Army gave up and returned home in 1990.

In 1994 Sri Lankans elected a new prime minister—Chandrika Bandaranaike Kumaratunga. Her father was the prime minister killed by Sinhalese extremists in 1959; her mother was prime minister in 1971 when Sinhalese Marxists attacked the government; her politician husband, Gamini Dissanyanke, was killed in 1994 by Tamils.[33] Prime Minister

30. K. M. de Silva, *A History of Sri Lanka* (Delhi: Oxford University Press, 1981), 4. See also Dennis Austin, *Democracy and Violence in India and Sri Lanka* (New York: Council on Foreign Relations, 1995), and essays on South Asia in Joseph V. Montville, ed., *Conflict and Peacemaking in Multiethnic Societies* (New York: Lexington Books, Macmillan, 1991), chaps. 15–19.

31. British colonial administrators steered U.S. missionary educators toward Tamil communities. The result was that Tamils were better prepared on average for professional life than Sinhalese.

In early 1983 I walked along the Colombo beach with a Tamil, an ex-civil servant forced into early retirement. From memory he recited Shakespeare sonnets and fragments of Ralph Waldo Emerson's essays. He also knew the great Hindu classics. Although the days were balmy, his heart was heavy, fearing a storm to come. Months later I got a shaky letter from the north; his home in Colombo had been burned and he was on the run.

32. The young Tamils learned guerrilla tactics and fanaticism from a Sinhalese youth group, the People's Liberation Front or JVP, which in 1971 fought Sri Lanka's government for three months with home-made weapons before being brutally repressed. See A. C. Alles, *Insurgency—1971* (Colombo: Colombo Apothecaries' Co., Ltd., 1979); see also de Silva, *A History*, 540–548.

33. Hamish McDonald, "Politics by Murder," *Far Eastern Economic Review* 157, no. 44 (November 3, 1994): 14–15.

Kumaratunga wanted ethnic peace. Tamils replied to her extended hand by sending suicide missions to ram ships of the Sri Lankan navy. The Tigers' leader relished power and did not wish to share it with anyone. Each side used any lull in the fighting to rearm.

More than 40,000 civilians and 30,000 troops from both sides died between 1983 and 1995. But neither side gave up. Colombo offered autonomy to the Tamils in 1995, but the Tigers fought on. Sri Lankan troops captured Jaffna in 1996, but the Tigers kept up guerrilla warfare. They blew up the Central Bank in Colombo and scared off Australian and West Indian cricket players from taking part in championship matches in Colombo. A Tamil in Jaffna told a visitor: "You see us living in darkness. But some day we will get our freedom."

CASE III: WHY DOES SWITZERLAND PROSPER WHILE THE SOUTH SLAVS FIGHT?

Switzerland is the world's oldest democracy and has one of the world's highest incomes. It has experienced no foreign wars and almost no civil strife since the 19th century. Though Swiss use four different languages and practice two major faiths, most consider themselves members of a single Swiss nation.[34] Yugoslavia—land of the South (*Yugo*) Slavs—was the least repressive Communist state and one of the richest. Yugoslavia split from the Soviet bloc in 1948 and asserted its nonalignment with Moscow or the West. Like officially neutral Switzerland, Yugoslavia armed heavily and trained its reserve forces to foster national unity and discourage invaders. Yugoslavia also had a federal structure and power-sharing arrangements similar to Switzerland's. When the 1984 Winter Olympics convened in Sarajevo, Yugoslavia looked more "First" than "Second" or "Third World."[35] Why then did Yugoslavia disintegrate in 1990? There was no single cause. As Table 8.4 on page 234 shows, there were both similarities and differences between Switzerland and Yugoslavia.

Unity From Below and From Above

Switzerland began as a defensive alliance of just three cantons (similar to U.S. "states") in 1291. Gradually, other cantons joined to form a confederation. Switzerland still calls itself a confederation, but—like the U.S. after 1787—it became a more centralized federation in the 19th and 20th centuries.

By contrast, Yugoslavia did not emerge from the free choice of the South Slavs. Unity was imposed from above after World Wars I and II—

34. See also Carol L. Schmid, *Conflict and Consensus in Switzerland* (Berkeley: University of California Press, 1981), chaps. 3 and 4; and Jonathan Steinberg, *Why Switzerland?*, 2d ed. (Cambridge: Cambridge University Press, 1996).

35. Appearances can deceive. Los Angeles looked integrated as it hosted the Summer Olympics in 1984. A few years later it was racked by race riots.

Table 8.4 Comparing Switzerland and Yugoslavia (1990)

Variable	Switzerland	Yugoslavia
Population size	Small (6.7 million)	Medium (23.9 million)
Civilizations	One	Three
Major ethnic groups	74 percent German; 20 percent French; 4 percent Italian; 1 percent Romansch; 49 percent Roman Catholic; 48 percent Protestant	36 percent Serb; 20 percent Croat; 9 percent Muslim; 8 percent Slovene; 8 percent Albanian; 6 percent Macedonian; 5 percent "Yugoslav"
Languages	Three official plus one national	Four official, plus others
Government	Federal democracy with extensive power-sharing	Authoritarian confederation under Communist Party
How formed?	Mainly voluntarily	Unity imposed by Communist dictator
Ethnic segmentation by political unit	De facto in most cantons	Much ethnic intermingling in key republics, but most republics are named for an ethnic group
History of ethnic conflict?	Little	Much
GDP per capita	High ($32,680)	Medium ($3,060)

SOURCES: World Bank, *World Development Report;* U.S. Department of State, *Country Reports;* and U.S. Central Intelligence Agency, *World Factbook.*

by a king in 1919 and by Communist dictator Tito in 1945. Yugoslavia's unity depended on a strong center; Switzerland's, on strong cantons. Yugoslavia was less than the sum of its parts; Switzerland was more.

Civilization

While all Swiss came from a single Western civilization, three civilizations clashed in Yugoslavia: Serbs saw themselves as defenders of Orthodox Christianity against the Islam of Bosnian Muslims and Albanians and the Western Christianity of Croats and Slovenes.

The demarcation lines between Western and Orthodox Christians dated from the third and fourth centuries when the Roman Empire and Christianity split into a branch based in Rome and another in Constantinople. Islam entered the scene in the 14th and 15th centuries when Ottoman Turks penetrated the Balkans, conquered Constantinople, and converted Bogomil Christians to Islam. To be sure, the three civilizations coexisted peacefully for long intervals, but entrepreneurs could evoke nationalist passions by invoking past injustices and bloodletting.

Serbs recalled how their ancestors were defeated by Muslim Turks in 1389. Closer to hand, they recalled that, when Croatia became a Nazi puppet state during World War II, its rulers carried out forced conversions to Catholicism and massacres of Orthodox Serbs in border regions. One in six Serbs under Croat rule died in the war—more than 300,000. Had so many Serbs not died then, Serbs might well have been a majority (not a mere plurality) within Yugoslavia—even in Bosnia—in the 1990s.

Segmentation

Segmentation plus equal rights facilitated solidarity in Switzerland. German, French, and Italian are official languages throughout the country while Romansch is termed a "national" language. Ethnic lines were more clearly defined in Switzerland than in Yugoslavia. A single language dominates most Swiss cantons. Swiss can assume that language boundaries will not be altered—they have changed little in a thousand years.

Yugoslavia was more complicated and changing. Following the Soviet model, Communist leader Marshal Tito in 1945 made the country a federal republic similar to the USSR. It consisted of six republics, most of which were ethnically mixed (see Map 8.1 on page 236).

Serbs were more like Russians than like Swiss Germans. German-speakers made up three-fourths of the Swiss citizenry. Their security and identity were not at risk. They could afford to be solicitous about speakers of French, Italian, and Romansch.

Russians made up slightly more than half the Soviet population, but Serbs (plus their cousins in Montenegro) made up only a two-fifths plurality in Yugoslavia. They ruled not just Serbia but tried to dominate all of Yugoslavia through their overrepresentation in the Communist Party, the military, the secret police, and the entire government bureaucracy. Just as Moscow was capital of Russia and the entire USSR, Belgrade was capital of Serbia and Yugoslavia. Like Russia, Serbia was itself a mini-federation containing several smaller republics.

Serbs felt themselves to be a minority at risk in three regions: The republic of Croatia had a border region, Krajina, abutting Serbia and Bosnia, with many Serbian villages; the republic of Bosnia-Herzegovina ("Bosnia") and its capital Sarajevo were pastiches of Muslims, Serbs, and Croats; and the region of Kosovo had a large Albanian (mainly Muslim) majority (nine to one in 1990) but was administered by Serbs who often used force to intimidate the majority.

Stratification

In Switzerland there is no rigid overlap of ethnicity with religion or wealth. Speakers of German and of French include both Catholics and Protestants (unlike Canada, where most Francophones are Catholic). In Switzerland income differences do not correlate with language. Some

The Yugoslav Federation

The six republics of Yugoslavia in 1945 were as follows:

Slovenia

Croatia

Bosnia and Herzegovina

Montenegro

Macedonia

Serbia (including the autonomous provinces of Vojvodina and Kosovo, raised to autonomous republic status in 1971)

Map 8.1   Ethnic Conflicts in the Former Yugoslavia, 1991

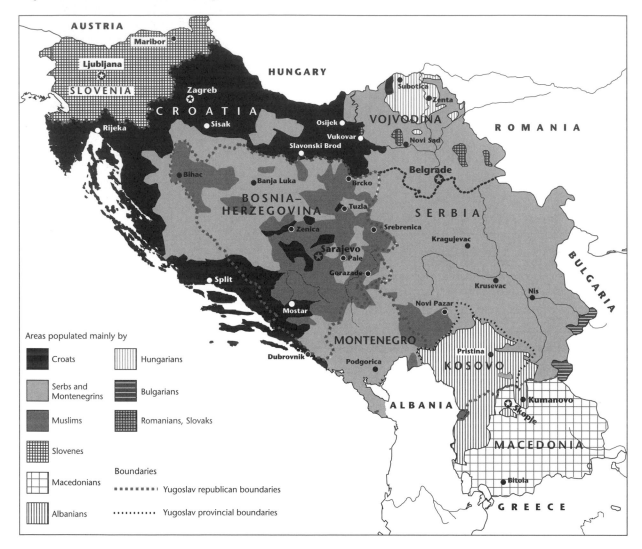

French-speaking cantons, such as Geneva, are wealthy but others are not; the same holds for German-speaking cantons. Switzerland's deepest antagonisms are not ethnic but urban-rural and those between young and old.

Racial and physical differences have divided Americans, Soviets, Sri Lankans, and Singaporeans (among others). But they have played little or no role in Switzerland or in differences among Serbs, Croats, and Bosnian Muslims. Most Swiss and South Slavs cannot be distinguished by their appearance. Unlike the Swiss, most South Slavs speak the same language—Serbo-Croat, though they use different alphabets to write it and have regional dialects. The Yugoslav Constitution declared the languages of all the country's nationalities to be equal. Only in the armed forces was the Serbo-Croat language mandatory.

But Yugoslavia was stratified and each ethnic group felt exploited by another. The two richest republics, Slovenia and Croatia, complained that they were taxed to benefit the center and the poorest republics.[36] Christians feared Bosnian and Albanian Muslims. Ethnic Albanians and Hungarians chafed at Slavic dominance. Serbs felt that Serbia's borders had been shrunk just to make others feel better. All groups feared Serbian imperialism.

Power-Sharing

The Swiss practiced power-sharing at every level of society. In the federal government and in private organizations such as the National Soccer Association each ethnic group was assured a voice. The government's executive body, the Federal Council, consists of seven members—usually four German-speakers, two or three French, and sometimes an Italian—with its chair (the federal president) rotating each year. The Swiss legislature has two houses. The upper house, like the U.S. Senate, assures two seats for each canton.[37]

Power-sharing of a kind existed also in Yugoslavia—at least on paper. In 1974 President Tito rammed through a new constitution that weakened central power and made Yugoslavia a loose confederation. The executive looked much like Switzerland's Federal Council with the presidency rotating each year. The 1974 constitution took Kosovo and Vojvodina from Serbia and made them autonomous republics—a move that angered nationalist Serbs.

The reality was that Yugoslavia, like the USSR, was dominated by the Communist Party and its top leader. Tito's leadership kept Yugoslavia together. After his death in 1980, each ethnic group became more restive. A new strongman emerged in Serbia—Slobodan Milošević. The longtime Communist became an entrepreneur of Serbian nationalism. "Slobo" became president of Serbia in 1989.

The Breakup

Slovenia and Croatia became separatist while Serbia was irredentist. If other republics split from Yugoslavia, Milošević warned, Serbia would act to expand its borders and recover its irredenta.[38] Milošević used what had

36. In Yugoslavia, as in the USSR, the richest republics took the lead in demanding independence. These republics were also those closest to Western Europe: Slovenia and Croatia and the three Baltic republics—Estonia, Latvia, and Lithuania. One of India's richest regions, the Punjab, was most assertive about its rights.

37. The power-sharing approach helps cope with class and religious differences in Austria, Belgium, and the Netherlands, but has had less success in Lebanon, Malaysia, and Cyprus. Power-sharing is like "a delicately but securely balanced scale." A rival approach, that of top-down control (as in Israel with its Arab minority), is like "a puppeteer manipulating his stringed puppet." See Kenneth D. McCrae, "Theories of Power-Sharing and Conflict Management," in *Conflict and Peacemaking in Multiethnic Societies*, ed. Montville, 100.

38. Reflecting the clash of civilizations, the Vatican recognized predominantly Catholic Slovenia and Croatia even before the European Union did in January 1992.

been the Federal Yugoslav Army (with its mainly Serbian officer corps) to take from Croatia the borderlands heavily populated by Serbs.

Bosnia became the next battleground. Of Bosnia's 4,355,000 people, Muslims made up nearly one-half—1,905,000; Serbs came second (1,364,000); then Croats (752,000). With much higher fertility than the others, Muslims could expect one day to make up a clear majority.[39] This worried the Serbs, who feared Islamic fervor. Few Bosnian Muslims practiced Islam with more than routine devotion, but Serb demagogues recalled how Bosnian Muslims cooperated with Croat Fascists in World War II; they warned that Muslims in Sarajevo wanted to establish an Islamic theocracy linked with Iran and Turkey.[40]

If Bosnia remained part of Yugoslavia, Bosnian Serbs would feel protected from Muslim excesses. But most of Bosnia's Muslims, many Croats, and some Serbs wanted to form an independent Bosnia. It would be a secular, multicultural, and multiethnic state of individual citizens. For power-sharing to work in Bosnia, proportional representation was insufficient. But Serb leaders demanded a Bosnian state of equal nations—each with a veto on major decisions. If that were impossible, Serbs would separate, partition the country, and drive out Muslims from ethnically mixed areas.

As in Sri Lanka, majority rule in Bosnia sparked open warfare. Responding to a suggestion by the European Union, Bosnia's government in February 1992 organized a referendum—a popular election on whether to secede from Yugoslavia. Most Muslims and Croats voted for Bosnia's independence, but Serbs stayed away, fearing they would be outvoted. Power-sharing collapsed. In April 1992 Europe and the U.S. recognized Bosnia's independence, but war had already begun. Bosnian Serbs armed and staffed by the ex-Federal Army seized whatever land they could within Bosnia, just as other Serbs had done in Croatia. Ethnic cleansing and genocide commenced.

UN mediators recommended "cantonization" of Bosnia—three cantons: one for Muslims, one for Serbs, and one for Croats, with power-sharing in the capital Sarajevo. But a clean-cut partition was impossible without many population transfers (ethnic cleansing). Furthermore, Serbs controlled 70 percent of Bosnian territory in the mid-1970s and were reluctant to give up what they had won. Muslims refused to recognize Serbian conquests or give the Serbs more than their population numbers might warrant.

The barbarism practiced by the South Slavs against each other in the 1990s mocked all religions. No group was innocent, but a CIA study con-

39. Most Bosnians had been Bogomil Christians for more than a thousand years—an egalitarian sect persecuted both by Orthodox and Western Christian armies. But in the 15th century many Bosnians converted to Islam—the faith of their Ottoman Turk conquerors. Some Bosnian Muslims became landlords and tax collectors for the Ottomans. Class as well as religion divided them from their Christian neighbors.

40. To be sure, Alija Izetbegović, elected president of Bosnia-Herzegovina in 1992, called for pluralism. But in 1970 he had advocated an Islamic government—from Morocco to Indonesia. Muslims, he wrote, should "destroy the existing non-Islamic power" and "build up a new Islamic one."

Possible Mass Graves
Kasaba/Konjevic Polje Area, Bosnia

Unclassified
Jul 95

Recently disturbed earth
Vehicle revetment

Genocide got a new name in the 1990s—
"ethnic cleansing"—as the South Slavs killed
or removed one another from ethnically mixed
villages and regions. Here an aerial photo
shows possible mass graves of Bosnian
Muslims murdered by Serbs.

cluded that Serbs were responsible for 90 percent of ethnic cleansing and genocide. In 1992 alone Serbs systematically raped more than 40,000 Bosnian Muslims and destroyed every major repository of Bosnian Muslim culture.[41]

Multicultural cooperation was lived every day in Sarajevo by the staffs of besieged hospitals, the newspaper *Liberation,* and several radio stations. The Bosnian government's seven-man executive body in the mid-1990s included President Izetbegović and two other Muslims, two Croats, and two Serbs—an ethnic balance as in Switzerland. Worn down as they were by years of siege, however, distrust mounted among the three groups.

Switzerland showed that persons of diverse languages and religions can generate a civic culture based on mutual gain. Among the South Slavs, however, efforts to create power-sharing and tolerance failed. As before World War I, the Balkans in the 1990s remained a powder keg.

WHAT PROPOSITIONS HOLD? WHAT QUESTIONS REMAIN?

Our world is torn between forces that unite and divide humanity. Nationalism operates at all levels of international relations. On Level 1 it inspires individuals to create and to destroy; on Level 2 it energizes and tears apart entire countries; on Level 3 the ideal of the nation-state pro-

41. Some Croat residents of Switzerland traveled to Bosnia for "rape weekends."

vides the organizing principle of the international system, but it blocks movement from anarchy toward a supranational authority; on Level 4 irredentist nationalism is a powerful transnational movement; and on Level 5 nationalist self-seeking and violence threaten the entire biosphere.

Why Do Some Societies Live in Harmony while others self-destruct? Your panel sums up its findings in the form of policy recommendations for individual societies and for the international community:

Guidelines for Dominant Groups in Multiethnic Societies

1. Promote a sense of participation, equal opportunity, and mutual gain among all members of society. Avoid a "tyranny of the majority."

2. Accommodate diversity. The U.S. originated in one civilization but is now fusing others. Singapore is manufacturing its own civilization from many. Switzerland arose from one civilization but had to accommodate diverse tongues and two religions. The USSR, Sri Lanka, and Yugoslavia did not accommodate their diverse civilizations.

3. Remember that prosperity is a result and a tool of ethnic harmony. The three successful societies we have studied were not always rich. Their wealth is more the result than the cause of their successful integration. They did not suffer the ethnic strife that sunders Sri Lanka.

A wealthy society can share the wealth to reward and encourage integration. But this risks a backlash: Slovenes and Croats chafed at taxes to help poorer regions of Yugoslavia; a majority of white Americans balk at affirmative action even though most favor equal opportunity.

4. Bury your hatchets. Do not be haunted by tribal myths of past defeats and glories. Despite the Civil War and racial conflict, Americans elected five Southerners president in the 20th century and blacks won prominent roles in big city and national politics.

5. Discuss openly what are the deep needs and interests of your society and its parts. Open debate filters out bad ideas and increases the likelihood that decisions will be durable.[42] There is no "national interest" etched in stone.

6. Try to understand minorities within your own society and why they fear exploitation. Support their languages and cultures without spawning separatism.

Guidelines for Ethnic Minorities

1. Uphold your interests but avoid needless provocation of other ethnic groups.

2. Protect and enhance your own culture but do not spurn the dominant one.

42. See Robert A. Dahl, *Democracy and Its Critics* (New Haven, Conn.: Yale University Press, 1989).

3. Do not forget your past but live in the present and look to the future. Isolation and local self-sufficiency are becoming less feasible. Many of the world's most affluent and cultured societies speak a language that few others share—Swiss-German, Finnish, Swedish, Danish, Norwegian, Dutch, Flemish. With most of the outside world they use English. Who can say how long these tongues will survive? For now, they flourish.

4. If you face repression, try to mobilize the international community. But recognize that the United Nations and its members have limited will or capacity to intervene. Ultimately most peoples at risk must rely upon their own resources.

Options for the International Community

The United Nations and its member states face a range of options for dealing with peoples at risk.

• *Status Quo Orientations*

1. Hands-off. Let the contenders settle their own problems.

2. Maintain existing borders. Do not allow minorities to alter boundaries or create new states.

• *Strengthen Preventive Diplomacy*

3. Develop early-warning indicators. Interview refugees. Study satellite images to learn whether fields are planted and harvested on schedule.

4. Legislate. Revise and alter international law to give more protection and voice to minorities within international organizations.[43]

5. Try to transform conflict by promoting economic and social change.

6. Monitor. Observe and report on cease-fires, human rights, and elections.

7. Mediate. Promote negotiations between disputants and, if negotiations stall, propose solutions.

• *More Forceful Interventions*

8. Employ deftly the tools of diplomatic recognition, nonrecognition, and derecognition.[44]

9. Utilize conditional economic aid and sanctions.

10. Intervene with force to keep peace or make peace.

Our panel rejects do-nothing options. Why? Ethnic persecution violates international law, spawns refugees, and triggers war—civil and across borders. The panel favors preventive diplomacy (Options 3 to 7). More forceful interventions can be dangerous and costly. If used, they require great skill and commitment. Halfway measures may make thing worse.

---

43. For suggestions, see Gidon Gotlieb, *Nation Against State: A New Approach to Ethnic Conflicts and the Decline of Sovereignty* (New York: Council on Foreign Relations, 1993).

44. The West gave some moral support to Estonia and other republics trying to break from the USSR but did not recognize their independence until Soviet power collapsed. By contrast, the West jumped to recognize the states wishing to secede from Yugoslavia. Nonrecognition—at least for a time—might have cooled tempers there. Later, the West derecognized Serbia in some ways to punish its aggressions.

KEY NAMES AND TERMS

assimilation	ethnocentric	majority rule
authoritarian	ethos	nation
autonomy	expansionist nationalism	national self-determination
civilization	federation	nationalism
confederation	genocide	power-sharing
culture	indigenous	secession
ethnic	intermingled nationalism	self-determination
ethnic cleansing	irredentism	unitary state

QUESTIONS TO DISCUSS

1. What is a nation-state? How common are nation-states in IR?
2. What is the difference between an ethnos, a nation, and a state? Give examples.
3. Name four sources of nationalism. Which were most important in the U.S.? In Russia? In Sri Lanka?
4. Are human rights the same as minority rights?
5. What factors undermined the unity of the USSR, Sri Lanka, and Yugoslavia?
6. What factors helped the unity of the U.S., Singapore, and Switzerland?
7. Can ethnic minorities dominate a country? How?
8. For a realist, which goal would have priority—human rights, minority rights, or national sovereignty?
9. Are multicultural studies good or bad for a country with many ethnic groups?
10. Which options for the international community should be developed? Which avoided?

RECOMMENDED RESOURCES

BOOKS

Anderson, Benedict. *Imagined Communities: Reflections on the Origin and Spread of Nationalism.* Rev. ed. London: Verso, 1991.

Cobban, Alfred. *The Nation State and National Self-Determination.* Rev. ed. New York: Thomas Y. Crowell, 1970.

Deutsch, Karl W. *Nationalism and Its Alternatives.* New York: Knopf, 1969.

Diamond, Larry, and Marc F. Plattner, eds. *Nationalism, Ethnic Conflict, and Democracy.* Baltimore: Johns Hopkins University Press, 1994.

Gellner, Ernest. *Nations and Nationalism.* Ithaca, N.Y.: Cornell University Press, 1983.

Greenfeld, Liah. *Nationalism: Five Roads to Modernity.* Cambridge, Mass.: Harvard University Press, 1992.

Gurr, Ted Robert, et al. *Minorities at Risk: A Global View of Ethnopolitical Conflicts.* Washington, D.C.: U.S. Institute of Peace, 1993.

Halperin, Morton H., et al. *Self-Determination in the New World Order.* Washington, D.C.: Carnegie Endowment for International Peace, 1992.

Horowitz, Donald L. *Ethnic Groups in Conflict.* Berkeley: University of California Press, 1985.

Hutchinson, John, and Anthony D. Smith, eds. *Nationalism.* New York: Oxford University Press, 1994.

Juergensmeyer, Mark. *The New Cold War? Religious Nationalism Confronts the Secular State.* Berkeley: University of California Press, 1993.

Montville, Joseph V., ed. *Conflict and Peacemaking in Multiethnic Societies.* New York: Lexington Books, Macmillan, 1991.

Smith, Anthony D. *National Identity.* New York: Penguin, 1991.

Spiegelman, Art. *Maus: A Survivor's Tale.* 2 vols. New York: Pantheon, 1986, 1991.

Szporluk, Roman, ed. *National Identity and Ethnicity in Russia and the New States of Eurasia.* Armonk, N.Y.: M.E. Sharpe, 1994.

JOURNALS

Nationalism and Ethnic Politics
Nationalities Papers
Nations and Nationalism
Third World Quarterly

WEB SITES

Association for the Study of Ethnicity and Nationalism
http://158.143.104.181/depts/european/asen

Baltics Hotline
http://www.viabalt.ee

Canadian government
on intergovernmental affairs
http://206.248.74.98/ro/doc/rescen.htm
on Quebec
http://206.248.74.98/ro/doc/bibesec1.htm

Red Book of the [Minority] Peoples of the Russian Empire
http://www.eki.ee/books/redbook (*detailed information on the peoples who did not have their own union-republics*)

U.S. Baltic Foundation
http://www.idsonline.com/usbf/

U.S. Institute of Peace (*many projects including aspects of nationalism*)
on religion, nationalism, and human rights
http://www.usip.org/research/rehr/relignat.html
on beliefs, ethnicity, and nationalism
http://www.usip.org/research/rehr/belethnat.html
on former Soviet Union bibliography
http://www.usip.org/grants/Book%20pages/B-CIS.FSU.html
special report on Tajikistan
http://www.usip.org/oc/sr/tajik2.html

INTERVENTION AND MEDIATION: HOW CAN OUTSIDERS HELP?

THE BIG QUESTIONS IN CHAPTER 9

- What can an outside mediator do that disputants cannot do for themselves?

- Why do some interventions succeed and others fail? Is there a science—or at least an art—to mediation?

- For good results, must the mediator bring carrots and/or sticks to the table? Can soft power alone suffice?

- Does personality count or is the mediator just another spoke in the wheels of international machinery?

- What can we learn from mediation efforts in the Middle East and the Balkans? What has been the role of hard and soft power?

- What can be done to reduce buck-passing and spread the burdens of third-party interventions to keep the peace?

- What role is there for the United Nations? What role for its members acting without a UN mandate?

The UN Secretary-General asks you and your panel to probe deeper. You have reviewed why peoples are at risk and suggested how ethnic groups can reduce conflict and create values together. But what if there is an impasse? How can outsiders—"third parties"—help? Your panel has already suggested a wide range of actions. But the Secretary-General wants you now to spell out the principles and techniques by which the United Nations and its members can intervene to curtail conflict—within and between states.

The Secretary-General wants you to consider many forms of intervention—from mediation by diplomats to peace enforcement by soldiers. He wants you to consider not only actions authorized by the UN Security Council but actions by member-states without a formal UN mandate.

Quickly you recall the many efforts by UN representatives and those of other countries to prevent or end conflicts around the globe. The record is mixed. Some interventions have eased bitter conflicts; others have achieved little or backfired. What have been the ingredients of success and failure?

You promise the Secretary-General to review the patterns of third-party interventions and distill lessons that may guide the United Nations and its members.

CONTENDING CONCEPTS
AND EXPLANATIONS

WHAT CAN OUTSIDERS DO THAT DISPUTANTS CAN'T DO FOR THEMSELVES?

Imagine that John and Regina decide to separate. How should they divide their shared property? John walks to work and listens to music at home. Regina drives and goes to concerts. Reasonably, they agree that John may take the compact disk player and CDs; Regina, the family car. But John also demands custody of the dog, because the sound equipment is worth less than the car.

A month after the split, John and Regina solicit help from a "Post-Settlement Embellishment Service." If the mediator knows the true preferences of each side, she or he may suggest improvements on deals struck by two antagonists. The intervenor learns that John now sees the dog as a nuisance and that Regina deeply misses her pet. The intervenor suggests that John transfer Fido to Regina. Each party is better off, including Fido.[1]

If the intervenor could help each side *after* their initial settlement, why not invite an outsider at an earlier stage? A related question: If knowledge of each party's preferences promotes mutual benefit, should governments play their cards close to the chest?

Why mediate? Mediators can win influence, access, glory, material rewards, personal satisfaction, and insight. Sometimes they do good. The century's most dedicated mediator, former President **Jimmy Carter**, explained that his Christian "faith *demands* that I do whatever I can" wherever and whenever.[2]

But mediators often suffer ridicule or worse. Some peacemakers have been assassinated, for example, UN Middle East mediator Folke Bernadotte in 1948. UN Secretary-General Dag Hammarskjöld died in a plane crash as he supervised UN intervention in the former Belgian Congo in 1961. Other cases will be noted.

PEACEFUL SETTLEMENT OF DISPUTES
AND PEACEFUL CHANGE

An ounce of prevention is worth a pound of cure. The UN Charter (Chapter VI) calls for diplomacy to prevent disputes from erupting into war. It obliges parties to a dispute to "seek a solution by negotiation . . . mediation . . . arbitration, judicial settlement, resort to regional agencies

1. Howard Raiffa, "Post-Settlement," *Negotiation Journal* 1, no. 1 (January 1985): 9–12.
2. Jim Wooten, "The Conciliator," *The New York Times Magazine,* January 29, 1995, 28.

How Does Arbitration Differ from Judicial Settlement?

Arbitration is adjudication of a dispute by one or more arbitrators who are selected by the disputants and whose decision the disputants agree in advance to accept as binding. Like a judge, an arbitration tribunal decides cases. But unlike the parties before a court, who cannot choose the judge, the actors who agree to arbitration choose who is to adjudicate their case. Often three arbitrators are chosen to assure a swing vote. A panel of arbitrators was set up by the 1899 Hague Convention for the Pacific Settlement of Disputes, but it is not a permanent court—only a list of arbitrators from whom disputants may choose. By contrast, a *permanent* world court consisting of fifteen judges was established in 1920 under the League of Nations to hear cases brought to it by states and international organizations. This **International Court of Justice** became a basic organ of the United Nations in 1945, and continues to hear cases at The Hague.[1]

What Is Wrong with This Advice? A former U.S. diplomat warns that arbitration allows a third party to determine your country's destiny. "Arbitrate only if you manifestly have principle on your side but are so weak that you must call on others to enforce it."[2]

This is poor advice on two counts: First, the strong as well as the weak may benefit from arbitration, because it offers a way to resolve a dispute short of war. Second, regardless of the decision, you can hardly count on "others to enforce it." Article 94 (2) of the UN Charter provides that if a party refuses to carry out the obligations incumbent in an International Court decision, the other party may appeal to the UN Security Council, which may make recommendations or take action to give effect to the judgment. As of 1998, however, the Security Council had never acted on this authority.

1. The work of these bodies is reviewed regularly in the *American Journal of International Law.*
2. Charles W. Freeman, Jr., *The Diplomat's Dictionary*, rev. ed. (Washington, D.C.: U.S. Institute of Peace, 1997), 28.

Between a Rock and a Hard Place: Negotiation, Judicial Decision, or Mediation?

Greece in 1996 planted its flag on an islet close to the Turkish coast. The islet was inhabited only by goats, but Greece claimed that international law (treaties of 1932 and 1947) gave it the right to these rocks and the mineral wealth around them. Turkey disagreed and mobilized forces to expel the Greeks. Athens proposed to Ankara that they submit the case to the International Court of Justice. Ankara refused. Turkey thought the existing law unfair and, confident of its greater strength, suggested bilateral negotiations. A U.S. mediator persuaded each side (nominal allies in NATO) to pull back its forces, leaving the claims unresolved.

or arrangements, or other peaceful means of their own choice." Chapter VI authorizes the Security Council to recommend "procedures or methods" to resolve disputes. If the Security Council investigates and finds that the dispute may endanger the peace, it may even *recommend* (not decide) the terms of settlement.

The parties to a dispute may prefer to sort out their own problems. But if their direct talks fail, they may accept mediation or arbitration. In 1871, for example, London and Washington submitted to international arbitration a U.S. claim for damages incurred during the U.S. Civil War. The panel awarded damages to the U.S., saving each side from a prolonged contest.

THE SPECTRUM OF INTERVENTION—PASSIVE AND ACTIVE

Third-party intervention is intervention by outsiders—governments, the UN, NGOs, private individuals—not parties to the dispute. The spectrum of intervention runs from smiles and handshakes to jeeps and armored cars. In this chapter we focus on the form of intervention known as mediation.

Mediation is a process of conflict management in which an outside or "third" party helps disputants accommodate their differences. Mediation is usually less threatening than a court. The mediator does not judge the disputants but helps them decide for themselves how to manage their differences. Governments usually shun judicial proceedings if vital interests are concerned, especially if the judge might rule against them. They may believe that the existing legal order is unjust or passé (see the lower sidebar on page 246) and hope that the mediator may help generate new rules.

The mediator may use her/his **good offices**—the unbiased use of one's formal position—to facilitate communications between the contestants. The first steps are called **prenegotiation**. In prenegotiation the facilitator may help to set the agenda, propose meeting sites and procedures, generate a constructive ambience, and sponsor a fact-finding enquiry to collect and analyze relevant information (also buying time during which tempers may cool). A more active mediator may formulate solutions and even encourage, manipulate, or bully the parties to accept a settlement. The mediator may also serve as catalyst, educator, translator, definer of standards, expander of resources, bearer of bad news, agent of reality, or scapegoat.

Conflict resolution is removal of the causes and manifestations of conflict. It includes **peacemaking**—mediation and other tools to settle disputes without war; **peacekeeping**—the interposition of lightly armed forces between consenting disputants to deter fighting or monitor a

How an Objective or Even Random Standard Can "Mediate"

Archeologists from three countries were invited to Egypt in 1902 to study the three pyramids at Giza. George A. Reisner, the head of the U.S. team, recalled: "Everyone wanted a portion of the Great Western Cemetery." Seated on the hotel veranda, the three teams discussed how to allocate the cemetery. They divided it into three strips; put into a hat bits of paper marked 1, 2, and 3; and allowed Reisner's wife to draw out the papers. She then "presented them to each of us. The southern strip fell to the Italians; the middle to the Germans; and the northern strip to me. Then we proceeded to divide the pyramids." (Notes by Reisner at the Boston Museum of Fine Arts.)

A Master Mediator: Teddy Roosevelt

President Theodore Roosevelt convened and mediated the 1905 Portsmouth (New Hampshire) Conference that ended the Russo-Japanese War and the 1906 Algeciras (Spain) Conference that calmed tensions between France and Germany over Morocco. Roosevelt gradually expanded his role from facilitator to formulator and manipulator. He made no threats and promised rewards to no one. "TR" did not even attend the Portsmouth or Algeciras meetings. He kept abreast by telephone, telegram, mail, and visits from U.S. and foreign participants. He nudged the negotiators from afar.

In 1905 TR persuaded Kaiser Wilhelm to urge Tsar Nicholas to make concessions to Japan. A year later, however, it was Wilhelm who spurned compromise with France. But

the Kaiser capitulated when TR threatened in a private message to publicize a letter from the German ambassador (a sports partner of TR) committing Berlin to accept whatever deal Roosevelt thought reasonable.

When news came that Russian and Japanese negotiators had agreed to peace terms, TR exclaimed: "This is magnificent. It's a mighty good thing for Russia, and a mighty good thing for Japan. And," he added, thumping his chest, "a mighty good thing for *me* too!" Roosevelt's efforts helped maintain an Asian balance of power favorable to U.S. interests and commerce. In 1905 he wanted to curb Japanese expansion; in 1906, German. He also won the thanks of millions and a Nobel Peace Prize.

SOURCE: Eugene P. Trani, *The Treaty of Portsmouth: An Adventure in American Diplomacy* (Lexington: University of Kentucky Press, 1969), 141.

Not Every Third-Party Intervention Is Beneficent

Self-appointed British and French mediators gave Czechoslovakia's Sudetenland to Hitler in September 1938. Prague did not request this intervention; Czech representatives were not even allowed into the meeting. Betrayed by their allies, the Czech authorities pulled their troops from the Sudeten forts, giving Hitler easy access to the entire country.

cease-fire; **peace enforcement**—the use of well-armed forces to restore or impose peace; and **peace building**—structural measures to generate a positive peace. Note that peace enforcement can require heavy combat, as in Korea, or only intimidation, as in the Balkans in the late 1990s.

WHAT ARE THE INGREDIENTS OF A SUCCESSFUL MEDIATION?

For mediation to work, the dispute must be **ripe**. The disputants may welcome mediation if their dispute is long and complex, their own negotiations have stalled, and/or the costs of continued conflict are painful. Each side hopes the mediator will help resolve their dispute, but they may also hope for "side-payments" (perhaps an aid package or diplomatic recognition contingent on a peace accord). In addition, if the talks or the accord fail the disputants know that the mediator may be blamed rather than themselves. But there is no way to know in advance just how ripe a dispute is for settlement.

Governments and international organizations attempted to mediate international disputes hundreds of times in the 19th and 20th centuries. Nongovernmental organizations and individuals also mediated on many occasions. Table 9.1 lists many of the 20th century's major efforts at international mediation. It notes the main resources used and whether the mediation achieved success—defined as three years or more of negative peace.

Starting in 1995, the Clinton administration tried to promote a dialogue among Protestant "Unionists" seeking to keep Northern Ireland part of the United Kingdom, "Republican" Catholics trying to fuse it with the Republic of Ireland, and the UK and the Irish governments. Gerry Adams, head of the political wing of the IRA, Sinn Fein, wanted to negotiate with the UK government and Unionists. But Provisional IRA militants often acted as though bombs were more eloquent than words.

Table 9.1 The Track Record of 20th-Century Mediation: No Recipe for Success

Dates	Disputants	Mediator	Good Offices	Formulate Solutions	Manipulate	Help Elections	Economic Sanctions	Economic Carrots	Peacekeepers	Enforce Peace	Military Threats	Military Action	Succeed (S)/ Fail (F)
1905	Japan-Russia	U.S.	X	X	X								S
1906	France-Germany	U.S.	X	X	X								S
1938	Germany-Czechoslovakia	UK, France, Italy		X	X								F
1948	Arabs-Israel	UN	X	X	X								F
1966	Pakistan-India	USSR	X										F
1970–90s	Hopis-Navajos	U.S.	X	X	X			X					F
1977–78	Ethiopia-Somalia	USSR	X	X	X			X			X		F
1978–84	Chile-Argentina	Vatican	X	X	X								S
1978	Egypt-Israel	U.S.	X	X	X			X	X				S
1979	Rhodesian factions	UK	X	X	X	X		X	X				S
1982	UK-Argentina	U.S.	X		X								F
1987–90	Tamils-Sinhalese (Sri Lanka)	India		X	X				X	X	X	X	F
1988	Namibia-South Africa	U.S. and others	X	X	X	X		X	X				S
1988–90s	Nagorno-Karabakh	USSR/Russia		X	X						X	X	?
1990–91	Iraq-UN	USSR, Jordan		X	X								F
1990s	Cambodians	UN	X	X	X	X		X	X				?
1992–	Haitians	UN, U.S., Carter	X	X	X	X	X	X	X	X	X		?
1992–94	Somalis	UN, U.S.	X	X	X			X	X	X	X	X	F
1993	Israel-PLO	Norway	X										S
1993–94	Estonia-Russia	U.S.			X			X					S
1993–94	Ukraine-Russia	U.S.		X	X			X					S
1993–	Israel-Syria	U.S.	X	X	X			X	X				?
1993–	Ireland, UK, Northern Ireland	U.S.	X		X			X					?
1994–	Macedonia-Greece	U.S.	X	X	X			X	X				S
1991–94	South Slavs	UN, EU	X	X	X		X		X		X	X	F
1994–	North Korea, South Korea, U.S., Japan, China	U.S.	X	X	X		X	X	Inspectors		X		?
1995–	South Slavs	U.S.	X	X	X	X	X	X	X	X	X	X	?

Economic and military levers are sometimes useful, but the mediator depends heavily upon personal qualities. They include "the patience of Job . . . the wit of the Irish . . . the broken-field dodging abilities of a half-back . . . the hide of a rhinoceros." To these we may add the insights of a psychiatrist; faith in free choice rather than dictation; trust in human potential, with its strengths and frailties; plus the ability to distinguish the available from the desirable.[3]

Let us convert these concepts into operational guidelines and then examine their validity in major cases.[4]

3. William E. Simkin, *Mediation and the Dynamics of Collective Bargaining* (Washington, D.C.: Bureau of National Affairs, 1971), 53.

4. These principles derive from works by Fisher, Raiffa, Zartman, and others cited in the Recommended Resources at the end of the chapter. The principles also distill the "art of the deal" (see Chapter 1) and the techniques used to reconcile victors and vanquished (Chapter 2), moderate rivalries (Chapters 3, 6, 7), and identify tradeoffs in trade and environmental disputes (Chapters 11 and 14).

THE MEDIATOR'S HANDBOOK: HOW TO BRIDGE DIFFERENCES

Your Qualifications

1. Knowledge: Know the issues, the personalities, their interests, and their domestic setting.

2. Timing: Present your initiatives when conditions are ripe, for example, when key players are tired and no longer trust in self-help. If you enter early, before the conflict escalates, the parties may not listen. If you wait until the disputants beg for outside help, you may gain influence, but only after much destruction.

3. Trust: Cultivate the confidence of each side, but make the most of any bias imputed to you.

4. Endurance: You may need to travel far and work around the clock.

The Disputants

5. Participants: Limit the number of parties represented but include all those essential for success.

6. Negotiators: Encourage the parties to assign negotiators with the authority and skills conducive to productive negotiations. For highly sensitive issues, bring top officials into the negotiation.

7. Empathy: Help each side to "walk in the other's shoes." For example, have each side write down what it thinks are the interests of the other party and then have members of the opposite delegations discuss their papers one-on-one.

9. Cultural sensitivity: Reduce misunderstandings rooted in cultural differences.[5]

Techniques for Crafting an Accord

10. Agenda: Establish an agenda and setting (public or private) conducive to "business" rather than to propaganda.

11. Generate constructive ideas: Get the parties to brainstorm before asking them to commit. Distinguish the contours of a possible deal from a formal commitment.

12. **Positions vs. interests:** Focus on interests—not positions. (For examples, see Table 9.2, page 262.)

13. **Reservation price (RP):** Learn the RP or walk-away price of each disputant—its minimum acceptable terms. Help disputants to set responsible RPs and weigh the costs of no agreement.

14. Openness: Encourage candor about interests, RP, and other considerations shaping each side's negotiating position.

5. Some theorists argue that professional diplomats acquire a language of their own that transcends their origins. But Raymond Cohen, *Negotiating Across Cultures: Communication Obstacles in International Diplomacy* (Washington, D.C.: U.S. Institute of Peace Press, 1991), provides ample evidence of culturally related obstacles to understanding among diplomats. Furthermore, few heads of state or of independence movements are professional diplomats.

15. Packaging: "Fractionate" the issues into smaller, more negotiable parts or "link" them into a comprehensive settlement.

16. Integrative bargaining: Expand the available goods; avoid "distributive" haggling on how to split an existing pie.

17. Creative tradeoffs: Overcome asymmetries in assets by creative tradeoffs, for example, "land for land" or "land for peace." Discourage demands for equality (for example, 100 acres or planes for each side).

18. Problem-solving rules: Generate objective criteria by which to solve problems, for example, scientific information.

19. Best alternative to no-agreement (BATNA): Show each party it can gain more through accommodation than from its BATNA. Deflate unreasonable expectations and loosen commitments.

20. **Single negotiating text (SNT):** Rather than debate rival proposals, develop and refine an SNT to clarify where the parties agree and disagree.

21. "Dance of packages": Lead the disputants toward the efficient frontier for joint gains. (Up to that frontier, sketched in Figure 1.5, page 29, both sides may gain; beyond it, only one party gains.) An initial package might favor A; the second package, B; as preferences are discussed and revealed, a third or fourth package may yield values for both sides.

22. **Leverage:** Utilize sticks and carrots—penalties and rewards. Offer sweeteners to compensate parties for concessions. Pressure them with deadlines. If necessary, threaten to break off the talks, mount an economic blockade, suspend aid, launch a military intervention.

Sustaining the Accord

23. Publicity: Advertise the agreement and its contribution to mutual gain.

24. Protection: Make sure that other concerned parties "get on board" or at least do not sabotage the deal. Insulate the accord from crises elsewhere that could torpedo the deal.

25. Implementation: Help to implement the accord and verify compliance with personnel, forces, or funds from individual states, the United Nations, or a regional organization such as the Organization of American States.

26. Transcend differences: Foster a web of positive ties.

Let us see whether these guidelines are supported by experience. What factors contributed to mediating success or failure?

Why Didn't the UN Do the Job?

Why did Carter and Holst do what might have been done by the United Nations? The United Nations is many things—but certainly not a monolith. "UN" troops are UN in name only. They may wear "blue helmets," but each soldier belongs to a single UN member country—Fiji, France, Sweden, and others. The "United Nations" is the nearly 200 member states that constitute it and operate its six organs and many specialized agencies (see Chapter 15).

Article 99 of the UN Charter gives the Secretary-General authority to bring to the Security Council any matter that may threaten international peace and security. Article 99 opens many possible avenues of preventive diplomacy. Working closely with the Security Council, Secretary-General Javier Pérez de Cuellar in the 1980s created a UN office to collect early-warning data on conflicts, helped mediate an end to the Iran-Iraq war, and dispatched teams to monitor elections in Nicaragua and help draft a constitution for Namibia. But the Secretary-General seldom takes initiatives involving hot spots where the great powers clash head on, as they did in Vietnam and in the Middle East.

The Secretary-General has asked that member states designate stand-by military forces for UN missions, as required by Article 43 of the UN Charter, but this has not happened. Instead, every peacekeeping mission is improvised. As a result, forces usually arrive late where they are urgently needed. They are often weakly coordinated, poorly equipped, and underfinanced.

6. Milton J. Esman, "A Survey of Interventions," in Esman and Shibley Telhami, eds., *International Organizations and Ethnic Conflict* (Ithaca, N.Y.: Cornell University Press, 1995), 21–47 at 26–30.

COMPARING THEORY AND REALITY: LESSONS OF THIRD-PARTY INTERVENTIONS

CAN THE HOLY LAND BE MADE WHOLE?

President Jimmy Carter did the "impossible" when he brokered peace between Israel and Egypt in 1978. But Norwegian Foreign Minister **Johan Jorgen Holst** facilitated in 1993 an even more "impossible" accord between Israel and the Palestinian Liberation Organization (PLO). How could a mediator from tiny Norway achieve as much as the president of a superpower?

The United Nations has been active in the Middle East since 1947, when a Special Committee appointed by the General Assembly recommended that Palestine (since 1920 under UK administration) be divided between Arabs and Jews. After Arabs rejected partition, Israel declared its statehood in 1948. War erupted. UN mediators negotiated two cease-fires. UN mediator Ralph Bunche, successor to the murdered Folke Bernadotte, won the Nobel Peace Prize for his interventions in 1948–1949. A UN Truce Supervision Organization monitored the armistice, and the UN Relief and Works Agency (UNRWA) was established to assist Palestinian refugees. Both organizations continued to exist in the 1990s, along with several other UN contingents that monitored and policed Israel's borders. By the 1990s UNRWA was serving nearly three million Palestinian refugees—one-third of them living in sixty-one camps. The down side: UNRWA programs relieved pressure on Jordan, Israel, and other countries to settle the refugee problem.[6]

Peacekeeping and refugee relief in the Middle East constitute a major burden on UN finances. Here is the dilemma of UN intervention: It can buy time—a breathing space—but it seldom settles anything. Why? The United Nations, in all its diversity, is often too neutral or too partial. When Egypt demanded withdrawal of the UN troops policing Egypt's border with Israel, the UN Secretary-General abruptly withdrew them, whereupon Israel launched a pre-emptive strike against Egypt. Had the Secretary-General found some reason to dig in his heels and delay the withdrawal, the 1967 Six-Day War might well have been avoided. The UN lacks the carrots and sticks to motivate disputants to give up something in exchange for something.

Both the Arab states and Israel have disliked many UN actions and judged the body too partial to the other side. Following the Six-Day War in 1967, however, the UN Security Council unanimously approved a well-balanced Resolution 242. It asked the parties to trade land for peace—

"withdrawal of Israeli armed forces from territories occupied in the recent conflict"[7] in exchange for an end to the "states of belligerency" between the Arab states and Israel. Arabs would have to acknowledge the "independence of every State in the area," but Israelis would have to arrange "a just settlement of the refugee problem."

But Resolution 242 was not implemented and Arab-Israeli relations remained tense. Egypt and Syria attacked Israel in 1973 but were driven back. The parties then accepted a cease-fire negotiated by U.S. Secretary of State Henry Kissinger and later approved by the UN Security Council. Kissinger's subsequent "shuttle diplomacy" between Israel, Egypt, and Syria produced several agreements for partial disengagement of Israeli and Arab forces.

Kissinger was the first of many U.S. diplomats to mediate in the Middle East. Israel did not trust any other country or the United Nations. Egyptian President **Anwar Sadat** and some other Arab leaders thought they could count on Washington to play the honest broker.

Following the 1973 war, Sadat sought peace. To break the diplomatic logjam, he embarked on GRIT-like gestures.[8] In November 1977 Sadat invited himself to Jerusalem and told the Israeli parliament that he wanted to remove the "psychological barrier" between Arab and Jew. Sadat endorsed UN Resolution 242 but also demanded "self-determination" for Palestinians.

Peace negotiations in the Middle East are far more complicated than were those in 1905 between Russia and Japan (see the lower sidebar on page 247). President Roosevelt faced only two main disputants. Mediators in the Middle East have faced dozens. No single actor can make peace among Arabs and Israelis, but any can *brake* and even *break* movement toward peace. Hard-liners in Israel, Syria, Iraq, Saudi Arabia, and the USSR sometimes acted as "spoilers."

Jimmy Carter and Camp David, 1978

Sadat's 1977 visit to Jerusalem sparked several rounds of Egyptian-Israeli talks, but Israeli and Egyptian negotiators soon hit a dead end. At that point President Carter invited President Sadat and Israeli Prime Minister Menachem Begin to join him at Camp David, the presidential retreat in Maryland. Each leader, with advisers in tow, arrived there in September 1978. They expected to stay just a few days but remained for thirteen in cramped quarters pervaded by "cabin fever."

The dispute was ripe for a settlement but many problems remained. Carter saved the day by skillful use of mediating techniques, by the lever-

7. Despite Arab and Soviet protests, Israeli and U.S. negotiators kept the resolution from specifying withdrawal from "all" or even "the" territories—thus leaving a loophole for Israel to retain some territories, for example, East Jerusalem. The equally authoritative French version of the resolution, however, does not specify "the" territories.

8. As we saw in Chapter 7, GRIT stands for graduated reciprocation in tension-reduction.

In 1978, U.S. President Jimmy Carter mediated the Camp David accords between Egyptian President Anwar Sadat and Israeli Prime Minister Menachem Begin. Here the leaders celebrate the Egyptian-Israeli Peace Treaty signed at the White House on March 26, 1979. At Camp David, however, Carter had to meet with each man separately because they did not get along.

age he brought to bear, and by his personality and persistence.[9] Since Sadat and Begin drew sparks, Carter met with each separately. The U.S. team prepared twenty-three versions of a single negotiating text.[10] The SNT pressured each side to say "yes" or, if it said "no," to offer a constructive alternative and to disclose its reservation price.

Carter drew heavily on trust and legitimacy. He began as a facilitator but soon became a formulator and manipulator. He used superpower leverage to clinch the deal.

In the end, Carter, Begin, and Sadat "agreed to agree." They signed one document committing Israel and Egypt to enter a peace treaty within three months. The treaty, concluded in March 1979, offered "land for peace" (the basic quid pro quo when Israel dealt with other neighbors for the rest of the century). Israel got peace with Egypt but had to withdraw from the Sinai Desert, captured in 1967. Egypt had to demilitarize most of the Sinai and permit a Multinational Force and Observers to be deployed there, a force that included both U.S. and Soviet personnel.[11]

Both worn down and elated, Sadat accepted a package far short of his original goals. Camp David left Palestinians in limbo. Sadat also failed to obtain any mention in the treaty of East Jerusalem, which Israel regarded as part of its capital—a unified Jerusalem. Many Arabs treated Sadat as a traitor, and some Arab governments severed ties with Cairo for a decade. Sadat was assassinated in 1981.

9. William B. Quandt, *Camp David: Peacemaking and Politics* (Washington, D.C.: Brookings Institution, 1986); Jimmy Carter, *Keeping Faith: Memoirs of a President* (New York: Bantam, 1983), esp. 322–344; and William B. Quandt, *Peace Process: American Diplomacy and the Arab-Israeli Conflict since 1967* (Washington, D.C.: Brookings Institution, 1993).

10. Carter, *Keeping Faith*, 322, 340–344.

11. This and many other relevant documents are in *The Middle East*, 7th ed. (Washington, D.C.: Congressional Quarterly, 1991), 302 ff.

Johan Jorgen Holst and the 1993 Oslo Accords

Camp David left Palestinians worse off than before. Peace with Egypt gave Israel a freer hand to deal with Palestinians in the Israeli Occupied Territories. They suffered from sweep arrests, deportations, and confiscation of land by Israeli forces. Based now in Tunis, PLO leader **Yasser Arafat** renounced terrorism and called for separate Palestinian and Israeli states in Palestine. But Israel refused to talk with the PLO.

By 1991 there were some 5.5 million Palestinians—nearly half of them under Israeli rule. The Palestinian-Israeli confrontation became riper after the 1991 Gulf War. Many Palestinians cheered when Iraqi missiles descended on Tel Aviv. Many Israelis saw that their security required cooperation with all their neighbors, including the Palestinians. Iraq's defeat led Arafat to grope for improved ties with the West.

Enter the Norwegians. Starting with personal contacts by a Norwegian social scientist and his diplomat wife, the Norwegian Foreign Ministry used its good offices to help PLO representatives and Israelis to meet in Oslo without public knowledge.[12] Roughly twenty meetings were held, from January to August 1993. On occasion the participants gathered at the home of Foreign Minister Holst, who later explained: "We tried to design a format which would bring the conflict down to human scale and create a human atmosphere." Often the Norwegians did not sit in on the PLO-Israeli exchanges but were briefed afterwards. Having heard each side's version, the Norwegians sometimes suggested ways to bridge differences.

The **Oslo Accord** produced results that stunned the world. Israel and the PLO announced in August 1993 a joint Declaration of Principles (DOP) providing for an interim period of limited Palestinian self-rule. A final settlement would be negotiated within five years. Meanwhile, Palestinians would have administrative and financial autonomy in Gaza and the West Bank. Disputes between Israel and the Palestinians would be settled by a joint committee or referred to arbitrators with both sides' consent.

The great gain for Israel and the PLO was mutual recognition and a commitment to live next to each other in peace. Like Camp David, the Oslo Accord was fuzzy. The Israeli-PLO declaration was another "agreement to agree" that did not satisfy hard-liners on either side. The DOP left major questions unanswered, but its defenders saw it as a step toward a larger settlement.

Oslo showed that U.S. pressure was not essential for Israel to reach an

Three Negotiating Styles at Camp David

Of the three Camp David protagonists, Carter ranked first in the fifteen traits of an effective negotiator (see Chapter 1).[1] He was strong in every respect except rapport with the home front. Begin placed second. He ranked very high in knowledge, toughness, stamina, ability to leverage assets, and competitive spirit. He was a stickler for detail. In contrast, Sadat focused on general principles. Sadat ranked high in "nice" qualities such as flexibility, empathy, and tolerance. Begin lacked the winning personality of Sadat; he showed little flexibility or capacity to identify mutually useful solutions. The Israeli leader bargained from material weakness, but got what he wanted.

1. Rankings are by Hermann Fr. Eilts, U.S. Ambassador to Cairo during the Camp David era, and by professors Roger Kanet, David Mayers, and the author (W.C.).

12. Jane Corbin, *Gaza First: The Secret Norway Channel to Peace between Israel and the PLO* (London: Bloomsbury, 1994); and David Makovsky, *Making Peace with the PLO: The Rabin Government's Road to the Oslo Accord* (Boulder, Colo.: Westview, 1996), with documents and references to other key writings.

Map 9.1 The Oslo Accord

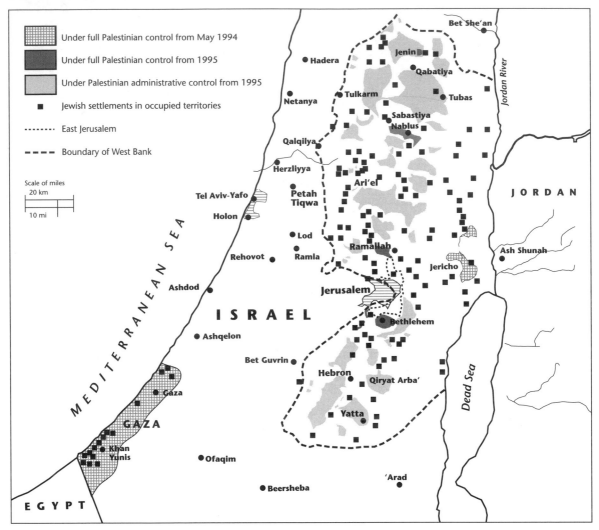

accord with the PLO. But the parties wanted and got Washington's official endorsement. In September 1993 the DOP was signed at the White House by the Israeli Foreign Minister and a PLO negotiator and "witnessed" by the U.S. Secretary of State and the Russian Foreign Minister. U.S. officials approved a commitment by Israel and the PLO to work for a "Marshall Plan"—outside development aid—for the West Bank and Gaza. U.S. and European officials promised to chip in. As we see from Map 9.1, Israel surrendered very little control to the PLO; on the other hand, any diminution of territory could be critical for a country just one or two dozen miles wide at strategic locations.

Israeli Prime Minister Benjamin Netanyahu met Palestinian Authority President Yasser Arafat for the first time on September 4, 1996, in a summit on the Israeli side of the Erez border crossing from Gaza City. Netanyahu pledged to honor the 1993 Oslo Declaration of Principles. But soon after, his government modified the Israeli pullout plan and backed Jewish settlements in areas Palestinians saw as theirs.

Secrecy was probably needed to commence the Oslo talks. But the announcement of the DOP as an accomplished fact shocked many Palestinians and Israelis. Failure to inform the home front about the course of negotiations cost PLO and Israeli officials much domestic support. Palestinian and Israeli hard-liners tried to sabotage the accord (see sidebar). An Israeli assassinated Prime Minister Yitzhak Rabin.

Norway contributed a positive setting. Like Carter in 1978, Holst was persistent and constructive, and profited from expert advisers.[13] While some Israelis and Egyptians blamed Carter for what they viewed as undesirable aspects of Camp David, Israelis and Palestinians could not fault Holst: He helped them analyze options but did not advocate terms.

13. Like Carter in 1978, the Norwegian Foreign Minister gave generously of himself. Worn down by many long meetings and travels, Holst died in January 1994 at age 56. "The moment he entered the peace process, it was in the center of his life until his last breath," said Shimon Peres; Yasser Arafat called Holst "a great peacemaker."

The Peace Destroyer's Handbook: How to School a Suicide Bomber

Martyrs are made, not born. Trainers from the Islamic Resistance Movement know the steps to take to mobilize a young man to detonate the land mine attached to his leg in order to kill Israelis and thwart the peace process between Israel and the PLO:

1. Find a likely candidate. He is single, aged 18 to 24, with a relative wounded, jailed, or killed by Israelis. He is often despondent and angry. He is unemployed and has had trouble finding a bride. He believes that this life is nothing, while a wonderful Paradise awaits Martyrs. He sees Israelis as monsters and remembers his grandparents' tales about life before Israelis took their land in 1948—"how no butter ever tasted so sweet, no grapes were ever so juicy." He believes that a Martyr's family will be honored and subsidized for decades.

2. Cultivate and deepen these convictions.

3. A week before the bombing is planned, show him how to explode the bomb.

4. In the days before the mission, sit him with a mullah and chant relevant scriptures.

5. On the prescribed day, send him off with assurances that his mission is sacred even though the Koran forbids suicide and murder of innocent civilians.

FROM CIVIL WAR TO MAJORITY RULE IN SOUTHERN AFRICA

The obstacles to conflict resolution in southern Africa rivaled those in the Middle East. As we see in Map 9.2, many wars racked Africa in the late 20th century. Still, blacks and whites there managed to avoid all-out war between races. A keystone in the broader peace was peace in Rhodesia—after 1980, Zimbabwe.

Rhodesia in the late 1970s was the last African colony tied to Europe. Though the country's population of six million was 98 percent black, a white minority ruled. In 1965 this minority government declared Rhodesia's independence from Great Britain. London refused to permit Rhodesia's independence without assurances of majority (black) rule. The UN Security Council imposed mandatory economic sanctions on Rhodesia (the first time the United Nations had taken such an action). Meanwhile, black guerrillas fought government forces.

Lord Carrington at Lancaster House

Margaret Thatcher became Britain's prime minister in May 1979 and authorized her Foreign Secretary, Lord Carrington, to work out a settlement granting Rhodesia independence under majority rule. Carrington convened the principal Rhodesian players for talks at Lancaster House in London.

Why did Carrington succeed when earlier mediation efforts by the previous Labour government and by U.S. Secretaries of State Henry Kissinger and Cyrus Vance had failed? A number of reasons may be cited:

1. Prospects of a quick victory on the battlefield had dimmed for each party in Rhodesia's civil war. The hurting stalemate made a mediated settlement more attractive.

2. Carrington simplified negotiations by persuading the anti-government blacks (divided along ethnic lines) to form a single team facing the whites and their new prime minister, a black bishop.

3. Economic squeeze: Rhodesia's economy increasingly suffered from war, United Nations sanctions, and white flight.

4. Minority protection: The new constitution assured political representation for whites and protection for their property. It could not be altered for at least seven years.

5. Like Carter in 1978, Carrington was persistent and creative. The talks started in September 1979 and continued until all parties signed a settlement in late December. It was Carrington and his team—not the imme-

Map 9.2 Africa's Wars and Conflicts, 1980–1996

In the mid-1990s a state of armed conflict existed in Sudan, Liberia, Somalia, Uganda, and the Zaire-Rwanda-Burundi border region, while conflicts in Sierra Leone and Angola diminished. In 1997 Zaire was renamed Democratic Republic of the Congo. Repeated massacres in Algerian villages since 1996 led the European Union to demand admission for EU investigators in 1998.

diate parties to the conflict—"who were constantly looking under the rocks, trying to find a solution, and suggesting alternative routes." It took the weight of Thatcher's government to conceive, negotiate, impose, and implement a settlement. British policy toward Rhodesia-Zimbabwe in 1979–1980 was so even-handed that no one—left or right, white or black—could deny the legitimacy of the new arrangements.[14]

6. Outside approval: The settlement was endorsed by neighboring African "Front Line" states. The Carter administration hinted that Washington would aid Zimbabwe's reconstruction. Moscow did not act the spoiler.

7. International implementation: A Commonwealth Monitoring Force

14. Stephen Low, "The Owen-Vance Period: 1977–1979," *Perspectives on Negotiation: Four Case Studies and Interpretations* (Washington, D.C.: Center for the Study of Foreign Affairs, U.S. Department of State, 1986), 165–170; Jeffrey Davidow, "Lancaster House Negotiations," ibid., 170–179.

of 1,500 troops supervised a cease-fire and disarmament of 20,000 guerrillas; a Commonwealth Observer Group spent seven weeks observing the 1980 elections.

One ethnic group and its leader, Robert Mugabe, dominated Zimbabwe from 1980 into the 1990s. But Carrington gave Zimbabwe's peoples a chance to build their lives in peace.

Peace Throughout Southern Africa

The demise of the Cold War facilitated accommodations across southern Africa. Washington helped broker Namibia's independence from the Republic of South Africa (RSA) in 1988. With cooperation from the USSR, Cuba, the RSA, and Portugal, the U.S. arranged peace between rival factions within Angola and Mozambique.[15] No outside mediator negotiated an end to racial apartness (apartheid) in the RSA. As in Rhodesia, however, UN economic sanctions and ostracism pressured whites to accept majority rule.

UNRESOLVED CONFLICTS: MEDIATIONS THAT FAILED

"Superpower" Failures at Home and Abroad

Not every mediation succeeds. U.S. Secretary of State Alexander Haig failed in 1982 to prevent Argentina and the UK from fighting over the Malvinas/Falkland Islands. U.S. diplomats, sometimes backed by the Marines, tried and failed to pacify Lebanon. Within the U.S., federal mediators in the 1980s and 1990s could not readily accommodate overlapping Hopi and Navajo claims to lands in Arizona sacred to both peoples—even with side payments of cash and land.[16]

Soviet/Russian leaders also tried and failed. In 1966 Premier Aleksei Kosygin arranged a cease-fire between Pakistan and India, but the resultant "spirit of Tashkent" quickly vanished.[17] In 1977–1978 the Kremlin sought to arrange peace between its existing clients, Somalia and Eritrea, and Ethiopia, where leftist officers had seized power. When Eritrea and Somalia balked, the USSR (plus Cuba) sided with Ethiopia.[18] In 1990 the Kremlin tried but failed to prevent war between Iraq and the UN coalition.

In the 1990s the Kremlin sought to influence quarrels among the peoples on Russia's borders, for example, in Armenia and Azerbaijan. Russia's military and economic pressure could readily tilt the local balance of power. But this kind of leverage is not conducive to a lasting settlement.

15. Mark N. Katz, ed., *Soviet-American Conflict Resolution in the Third World* (Washington, D.C.: U.S. Institute of Peace, 1991); and Chester A. Crocker, *High Noon in Southern Africa: Making Peace in a Rough Neighborhood* (New York: Norton, 1992).

16. In the 1980s federal mediators ruled that some 10,000 Navajos had to move elsewhere—either on or off the Navajo reservation—even though such uprooting broke the Navajo way of life and often led to suicide. When Navajos resisted, Hopi and Navajo leaders together with U.S. officials looked for tradeoffs that might assuage both sides—cash, land trades, awards of land managed by the U.S. Forest Service, which Congress would have to approve. See Emily Benedek, *The Wind Won't Know Me: A History of the Navajo-Hopi Land Dispute* (New York: Knopf, 1992); David M. Brugge, *The Navajo-Hopi Land Dispute: An American Tragedy* (Albuquerque: University of New Mexico Press, 1994); and "Alexander Cockburn's America: The Navajo Indians Are Resisting Pressure to Capture Their Lands," *The New Statesman* 126, no. 4333 (May 9, 1997): 32.

17. Tahir Amin, "The Tashkent Declaration: A Case Study—Third Party's Role in Resolution of Conflict," *Islamabad Papers*, No. 8 (Islamabad: Institute of Strategic Studies, 1980).

18. Marina Ottaway, "Soviet-American Conflict Resolution in the Horn of Africa," in *Soviet-American Conflict Resolution*, ed. Katz, 117–138 at 131.

Russia's every word and deed are suspect. The Organization for Security and Cooperation in Europe (OSCE) has tried to mediate in the Caucasus, but it has too little clout; Russia, too much.

Rajiv Gandhi in Sri Lanka

India actively supported Sri Lanka's Tamils in their struggle for independence. But when Sri Lanka's Army advanced on the Tamil city of Jaffna in 1987, Indian Prime Minister **Rajiv Gandhi** pressed for a cease-fire between the Sri Lankan government and Tamil rebels. The "Accord," enforced by an Indian Peacekeeping Force (IPKF), pledged that Sri Lanka would become a multi-ethnic state. The government would be decentralized and each province would have more control over its affairs. The accord required a cease-fire within 48 hours; within 72 hours, Tamils were to surrender all their weapons. The Sri Lankan government in Colombo gave India a virtual veto on its foreign policy in return for Indian support for Sri Lanka's territorial integrity.

Why did Prime Minister Gandhi intervene? He sought to prevent a massacre of Tamil civilians by the Sri Lankan Army, improve the image of his own Congress Party after recent election losses, smother separatist efforts by Tamils and others within India, and prevent the U.S. Navy from getting a base in Sri Lanka.

Instead of saving Tamils from Sinhalese forces, however, the Indians found themselves fighting the Tamil Tigers. The Tigers refused to disarm and then wait for Colombo to share power. After suffering more than 1,000 deaths, Indian "peacekeepers" finally exited in 1989–1990. But the Tamils persisted: In 1991 "human bombs" blew up both Rajiv Gandhi and Sri Lankan President Ramasinghe Premadassa.

What went wrong? First, suspect motives: Many Sri Lankans saw the IPKF as Indian imperialism. Second, sequencing: The accord required Tamils to disarm immediately. Third, distrust: Tamils feared that Sinhalese leaders would renege on promises. Fourth, missing players: The peace process left out both Tamil and Sinhalese militants. Finally, passion: Desires for revenge and glory outweighed fear and exhaustion.

A constructive mediation would focus on interests—not positions (guideline 12 in The Mediator's Handbook). As Table 9.2 suggests, some form of power-sharing might accommodate most Sinhalese and Tamil interests. But no mediator could surmount the demand of many Sinhalese that their religion, culture, and language be dominant.

Table 9.2 Positions vs. Interests in Sri Lanka in the 1990s

Disputants	Positions	Interests
Sinhalese majority	Sri Lanka must remain a unified state dominated by Sinhalese vaues and people	Territorial integrity and sovereignty; noninterference from India; secure access to all ports and territory; prosperity; freedom from terrorists; free practice of Buddhist religion and use of Sinhala language; allegiance of all peoples to the Sri Lankan state
Tamil separatists	Tamils must have a separate state in the north and east of the island	Equal treatment in schools, jobs, resources, language, religion; political representation in Colombo plus local self-government; prosperity; freedom from terrorists; free practice of Hindu religion and use of Tamil language; confidence in democratic processes

Northern Ireland

Similar problems bedeviled Northern Ireland, where a Protestant majority for centuries had repressed the Catholic minority. After nearly three decades of sitting on the fence, the U.S. government intervened in 1995 to promote dialogue among all parties—Catholics and Protestants of Northern Ireland, the UK, and the Republic of Ireland. Like the Tamil Tigers in 1987, the Irish Republican Army (IRA) refused to surrender their arms or give up terrorism until their demands were met. In February 1996, a week after Tamils blew up the Central Bank in Colombo, the IRA broke a seventeen-month cease-fire with a bombing campaign in central London.

The UK government, like the Sri Lankan, waited so long to offer concessions that the other side—the IRA—developed an all-or-nothing mentality. The Labour government that took power in 1997 showed more flexibility. Meanwhile, two island outposts of British colonial rule remained torn by ethnic and religious strife.

Somalia, Haiti, Cambodia

The 1980s and 1990s saw the emergence on every continent of **failed states**—places where the central government broke down, leaving various factions to struggle for power. They included Somalia, Haiti, Cambodia, Liberia, Bosnia, Afghanistan, and Zaire-Congo. Other countries teetering on the brink of failure were Macedonia, Rwanda, Colombia, Tajikistan, and perhaps even Pakistan. The reasons for "failure" were diverse in each case. They ranged from ethnic discord to the withdrawal of superpower influence to mounting population-economic-environmental pressures to the passing of aged dictators.

Somalia in the 1980s became the exemplar of a failed state. One out of eight Somalis died from starvation or clan warfare. At the request of the

UN Security Council, the U.S. in 1992 led a multinational force into Somalia to assure food deliveries. Soon, "mission creep" began as U.S. forces sought to arrest one clan leader and impose order. After more than a dozen U.S. soldiers died, U.S. forces withdrew in 1993. A second UN force tried to keep the peace in 1993–1995, but it had fewer resources and a larger territory to cover. As happened elsewhere, the Security Council issued big orders without the means to carry them out.

Again authorized by the Security Council, a multinational force led by the U.S. intervened in Haiti to oust a military junta and reinstate the country's elected president. As noted later in this chapter, nothing happened until Jimmy Carter met with the junta and U.S. forces were airborne. The junta then departed, but chaos returned. UN observers plus troops and police from various countries tried to put Haiti on the road to democracy and economic development, not easy after two centuries of repressive dictatorship.

By far the biggest and most expensive UN intervention was in Cambodia. In 1991 UN representatives negotiated a truce between factions that had fought one another since 1970. With Security Council approval, the UN Secretary-General arranged an election held in 1993. Just three military advisers remained to assist the Secretary-General's representative.[19] Meanwhile, money continued to flow in. From 1991 to 1997 the United Nations, the World Bank, the U.S., Australia, and other individual countries sank more than $4 billion into Cambodia to promote peace, self-government, and prosperity—but all in vain. In 1997 Hun Sen—the same dictator who ruled Cambodia in the 1980s—evicted or killed his opponents and regained supreme power. In Hun Sen a Communist passion for total control exploited a Cambodian tradition of god-king autocracy.

Can outsiders change countries such as Somalia, Haiti, and Cambodia? Consider this precedent: Following the U.S. Civil War, federal troops—relatively stronger than most UN forces—occupied the former Confederacy for twelve years. When the troops withdrew, much of the old order reemerged. To uphold democracy in Cambodia the United Nations would need an army of peace enforcers and peace builders—not mere peacekeepers. This could not be a one- or two-year assignment. The same holds for the former Yugoslavia.

SOFT AND HARD POWER IN THE BALKANS

Why did UN representative Cyrus Vance and European Union (EU) mediator Lord David Owen fail to halt "ethnic cleansing" among the South Slavs in the early 1990s? Why did U.S. mediators do better in

19. For history and documents, see *The United Nations and Cambodia, 1991–1995* (United Nations, N.Y.: Department of Public Information, 1995).

Fig. 9.1 Too Many Cooks, Too Many Ingredients in the Balkan Broth in 1995

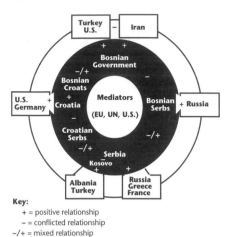

Key:
+ = positive relationship
– = conflicted relationship
–/+ = mixed relationship

20. Former UK Foreign Secretaries Lord Carrington and Lord Owen represented the EU in the former Yugoslavia; Vance, U.S. Secretary of State for President Carter, represented the UN. Other experienced mediators such as Norway's Thorwald Stoltenberg and Sweden's Carl Bildt took a turn, but none got very far with the South Slavs. Private citizen Jimmy Carter also flew in for a few days and arranged a short-lived cease-fire.

21. The Vance-Owen Plan would have divided Bosnia into ten cantons. This plan offended the ideal of multicultural internationalism and the legal principle of territorial integrity. For a defense of the plan, see David Owen, *Balkan Odyssey* (New York: Harcourt, Brace, 1996).

Not all mediation is constructive. The Vance-Owen plan developed by UN representative Cyrus Vance and European Union representative Lord David Owen proposed to divide Bosnia into cantons for each ethnic group. Critics said the plan, never implemented, would have rewarded Serbian aggression and confirmed that three ethnic groups could not live together.

1995–1998? Here is a mystery with many parts: Was not the South Slav dispute "ripe" for settlement years before the U.S. intervened? Were not the UN and EU mediators experienced diplomats who had done well in previous mediating endeavors?[20] Were not the UN and EU peace plans similar in many essentials to the U.S.-designed agreement accepted by the South Slavs in Dayton, Ohio, in November 1995? Did not this agreement "reward aggression" and split Bosnia along ethnic lines?[21]

Why Intervention Faltered in the Early 1990s

The problem was not misunderstanding. Neither language nor cultural misunderstandings obstructed peace in the Balkans. Bosnians, Serbs, and Croats all spoke Serbo-Croat. Most of their leaders—historians, poets, lawyers, and physicians—were also fluent in English.

Many problems undermined mediation efforts in the early 1990s. First, there were too many cooks in the Balkan kitchen—and none with the means to do the job. Each cook was following a different recipe or no recipe at all. Before the U.S. intervention in 1995, no would-be mediator in the Balkans spoke for a strong, unified political entity. Both the United Nations and the European Union were internally divided. The U.S. tilted toward Bosnia; Russia and France favored Serbia; Germany backed Croatia; China preferred non-action. Besides the major actors shown in Figure 9.1, there were many domestic factions and other bit players.

There was no unified "UN" force in the Balkans. The main units came from France and Britain, but other "blue helmets" arrived from countries as small as Estonia and as large as Russia. Coordination was a nightmare.

Some units played favorites. Finances were muddled. Some "UN" forces were paid for by their own countries, others from the UN peacekeeping budget; some got side payments from black marketeering.

The UN chain of command resembled a dog chasing its tail. The local commander (usually British or French) could not use military force without the approval of the UN Secretary-General or his local representative, Yasushi Akashi. But Akashi often vetoed military actions favored by Western governments or approved the moves too late for them to succeed.

UN forces in the Balkans also suffered from "mission creep." At first their job was to protect food convoys; next they were tasked to preserve certain towns as "safe havens"; later, they were told to destroy Serb mortars and artillery menacing Sarajevo. When the United Nations authorized NATO planes to attack Bosnian Serb installations in May 1995, the Serbs grabbed UN peacekeepers and held them as human shields to deter more NATO raids.

What Produced a Breakthrough in 1995?

The U.S. sat on the sidelines in the early 1990s, cheering or sniping as UN and EU mediators pursued peace in the Balkans.[22] In August 1995, however, President Bill Clinton decided that the U.S. should intervene energetically, and sent Assistant Secretary of State **Richard E. Holbrooke** to mediate a Balkan peace. Holbrooke had long sought power, fame, and a place in history.[23] He quickly became the most forceful mediator of the 20th century.

Why did Clinton decide to act? Two reasons were uppermost. First, power politics: The longer the Balkan conflict dragged on, the more it exposed differences within NATO. It also had the effect, repugnant to Washington, of raising Iran's international stature, as Iranian volunteers trained and armed Bosnians. Second, moral outrage: In August 1995 TV viewers from Karachi to the White House saw images of children in Sarajevo mangled by a Serb mortar attack and of the frozen human limbs protruding from a mass grave near Srebrenica, a UN "safe area" where an estimated 5,000 Muslim men were murdered.[24]

Holbrooke's mission began with tragedy. Three of his fellow diplomats died when their armored car slipped off the mountain road to Sarajevo, a route they took because Bosnian Serbs refused to guarantee their safe passage by air. Holbrooke accompanied their coffins back to Washington but soon returned to the Balkans, determined that his colleagues would not have died in vain. (What role is there for luck? If no U.S. diplomats

22. The U.S. ambassador to Denmark told me in 1992: "We are waiting for the Europeans to realize that they can't do the job."

23. Michael Kelly, "The Negotiator," *The New Yorker*, November 6, 1995, 81 ff.

24. Lightly armed Dutch peacekeepers did nothing to stop the murder. They had called for air strikes, but the French general commanding "UN" forces refused. When he finally did act, it was too little too late.

Terms of the Dayton Accord, November 21, 1995

The **Dayton Peace Accord** preserved the fiction of an integral Bosnian state but divided Bosnia into a Croat-Muslim federation and a Bosnian Serb Republic. The central government with a rotating presidency would remain in Sarajevo. Each faction—Muslims, Croats, Serbs—would retain its own army. A side deal authorized the U.S. to train and equip the Croat-Muslim federation so that it could hold its own against Bosnian Serbs.

The Bosnian Serb Republic got 49 percent of the land—roughly where the armies stood in late 1995. All refugees got the legal right to return home. Persons indicted by the International War Crimes Tribunal in The Hague could not hold elected office. Dayton promised Serbia that UN economic sanctions would be lifted but denied Belgrade access to World Bank loans until Serbs showed compliance with the peace accord.

Dayton replaced lightly armed "UN" peacekeepers with more than 60,000 heavily armed NATO forces—one-third of them Americans. Their mandate was much clearer than that given earlier to the UN "blue helmets." NATO troops were to supervise the peace and, if necessary, *impose* peace. The NATO forces were commanded by a U.S. general not subject to the United Nations. A side agreement continued a peacekeeping role for Russian forces, commanded indirectly by the U.S.

25. Roger Cohen, "Taming the Bullies of Bosnia," *The New York Times Magazine,* December 17, 1995, 58 ff; see also Joe Klein, "Setting the Table," *Newsweek,* October 16, 1995, 68 ff.

had died, would Holbrooke have been so tenacious? If Holbrooke's vehicle had overturned, would his successors have been so effective?)

Why were the disputants more ready to accept a mediated settlement in fall 1995? One reason was that those who had sought ethnic purity were already gratified by massacres or conquest. Another was that the Croats and Muslims had gained the upper hand, compelling the Serbs of Bosnia and of Croatia to retreat. The Serbs outside Serbia, meanwhile, had lost the support of Serbian President Slobodan Milošević, now tired of the war he had fomented. In 1995 Milošević was seeking an end to the UN economic sanctions that hamstrung Serbia. Bosnian Serbs agreed to let Milošević represent them in late 1995 negotiations, but later complained that he had betrayed them.

Holbrooke's resources were far superior to those of the EU and UN mediators. Carl Bildt, the EU representative in 1995, had to use a calling card to make phone calls; Holbrooke had mobile phones linked to the full communications machinery of the U.S. government. A comparative unknown, Bildt once depended on Holbrooke to liberate him from interrogation by UN (French) peacekeepers at the Sarajevo airport.

Both lion and fox, Holbrooke met Croat, Bosnian, and Serb leaders in their offices, palaces, and hunting lodges. He mixed walks in the woods and jokes over plum brandy with intense pressure and manipulation. Earlier Holbrooke gave a green light to Croats to retake the Krajina region. Now he ordered them and their Bosnian allies not to take Banja Luka, the main Serb town in Bosnia, even though it had been the site of much ethnic cleansing. Why? An outflow of Bosnian Serb refugees into Serbia proper might lead Milošević to scupper the evolving deal.

When the Bosnian Muslims refused a cease-fire in October 1995, Holbrooke introduced a U.S. general with intelligence reports ("invented," some say) showing that Bosnia's position was precarious. The message: "Get a cease-fire now before the Serbs counterattack."

All parties submitted to a cease-fire in October. Holbrooke then summoned them to a Dayton, Ohio, Air Force base (not too comfortable and a vivid reminder of U.S. hard power) for talks that ended only when an accord was reached—a process that lasted twenty-one days. When the delegates bickered, Holbrooke presented them the three widows and six fatherless children of the U.S. diplomats who died near Sarajevo. The message: "You owe them peace as a memorial." Bosnia's Prime Minister Haris Silajdžić said he was overwhelmed.[25]

As we see from Table 9.3, the Bosnian Serbs had many reasons to reject the Dayton Accord.[26] They were forced rather than persuaded to submit to it. They would be tempted to scuttle it after foreign troops went home. Having allowed Milošević to speak for them at Dayton, they now accused him of betrayal.

As we see in Map 9.3, Republika Srpska, Serbian Republic of Bosnia, encircled the rest of Bosnia and Herzegovina—the Croat-Muslim Federation. Republika Srpska had two political centers, one in Banja Luka to the northeast and another in Pale to the southwest. Soon Bosnian Serb politicians in Banja Luka contested those in Pale. While Bosnian Serbs bickered among themselves, Bosnia's Croat-Muslim Federation became more cohesive and, thanks to U.S. trainers and equipment, stronger.[27]

Holbrooke acted as fireman. He met with Bosnian, Croat, and Serbian leaders in February 1996 and in August 1997 and got them to reaffirm their Dayton commitments. NATO gunships flew overhead in 1996 as NATO ground troops demanded that Bosnian Serbs permit a check of their equipment. NATO's hard power provided serious leverage, but for how long would it work? How long would Western publics be willing to

Table 9.3 Hard Choices for Bosnian Serbs

Losses If We Agree to the Dayton Accord	Gains If We Reject the Dayton Accord
We must forsake the cause of Greater Serbia.	We remain loyal to the Serbian and Orthodox cause.
We cannot win more territory and must give up some we now control.	We may be able to hold on to our present territory and gain more.
Many Muslims and Croats may return to our villages and towns.	We can keep our territory ethnically clean.
We permit foreigners to dictate what we do.	We defy NATO, the Croats, and Muslims. Russia and Serbia may help us.
The War Crimes Tribunal may arrest our leaders.	The War Crimes Tribunal cannot reach us.

Gains If We Accept Dayton	Risks If We Reject Dayton
Peace.	The war goes on.
An opportunity and perhaps funds to rebuild.	Little chance to rebuild.
Promises that we can return to lands lost.	We could be driven from our present territory.
Trade and other exchanges with Serbia and outside the Balkans.	Isolation. Belgrade may further reduce our supplies.
Little threat to our religion.	Possible Muslim-Catholic conquest.

Map 9.3 Bosnia and Herzegovina After the Dayton Accords

The Brcko area was sought by the Croat-Muslim Federation and the Republika Srpska. Located in the forty kilometer Posavina corridor, Brcko links the eastern and western parts of the Republika Srpska. Dayton provided for binding arbitration within a year, but the arbitrators postponed a decision in 1996 and again in 1997.

26. Compare with the Bosnian Serb outlook in 1993 in Roger Fisher et al., *Beyond Machiavelli: Tools for Coping with Conflict* (Cambridge, Mass.: Harvard University Press, 1994), 65.

27. Leonard J. Cohen, "Bosnia and Herzegovina: Fragile Peace in a Segmented State," *Current History* 95, no. 599 (March 1996): 103–112, and related articles in that issue. See also the report by Enis Dzanić and Norman Erik in *Jane's Intelligence Review* (December 1997).

invest money and risk lives to keep the Balkans quiet? Would the South Slavs revert to their old ways when the outsiders left?

But could there be peace without justice? Some observers argued that stability was more important than bringing accused war criminals to trial. But the U.S. insisted that NATO troops in Bosnia could and should arrest any persons indicted by the International War Crimes Tribunal at the Hague. Usually, NATO troops looked the other way when an indicted offender drove by.[28] In 1997, however, some UK troops in the NATO force arrested a few mid-level Serbs suspected of war crimes and sent them to the Hague Tribunal. Croatia, to get U.S. aid, sent a few of its accused war criminals to The Hague.

MEDIATIONS WITH SOFT POWER

Many persons won Nobel Peace Prizes for peace work without economic or military levers. Among Americans so honored were Theodore Roosevelt, for his 1905 and 1906 mediations; Ralph Bunche, for brokering an Arab-Israeli cease-fire; Martin Luther King, Jr., for nonviolent actions to reduce racial discrimination; and Elie Wiesel, for remembering the Holocaust and protesting genocide. Wiesel's words to President Clinton helped trigger U.S. activism in the Balkans in 1995.

The century's leading free-lance mediator was Carter. In May 1994 he affirmed a democratic election in Panama. In June he met with Kim Il-sung and set the stage for official U.S.-DPRK negotiations. In September he persuaded Haiti's generals to step aside. In December 1994 Carter arranged a short-lived cease-fire in Bosnia.

Carter's personality and negotiating techniques were often effective. Still, behind the private envoy loomed enormous hard power. While Carter talked to Kim Il-sung, for example, the Pentagon was actively preparing for another war on the Korean peninsula.[29] And Haiti's junta gave in only after a U.S. invasion force was in the air. Carter's team (which included Senator Sam Nunn and retired General Colin Powell) had persisted beyond the deadline set by the White House. Carter was unorthodox but often effective.

Religious leaders can provoke or restrain violence. Quakers helped promote peace talks between the Nigerian government and secessionist Biafra in 1970. The Vatican in 1978–1984 mediated a dispute between Chile and Argentina over the Beagle Channel.[30] Bishop Samuel Luiz Garcia in the mid-1990s brokered a cease-fire and negotiations between Mayan Indians and the Mexican government. Some South Slav priests and mullahs worked for reconciliation in the Balkans.

28. Theodor Meron, "Answering for War Crimes: Lessons from the Balkans," *Foreign Affairs* 76, no. 1 (January–February 1997): 2–9.

29. Carter phoned the White House as President Clinton discussed possible military action against North Korea. Asked whether the terms that Carter had discussed with Kim Il-sung were satisfactory, Clinton stipulated additional DPRK concessions before he would send U.S. negotiators to meet with North Koreans in Geneva—concessions that Carter secured.

30. This and many other cases are detailed in Thomas E. Princen, *Intermediaries in International Conflict* (Princeton, N.J.: Princeton University Press, 1992).

WHAT PROPOSITIONS HOLD? WHAT QUESTIONS REMAIN?

Outsiders can help to manage, if not resolve, conflicts. Intermediaries can help antagonists shift from mutual pain to mutual gain. If the settlement offers mutual gain, the parties may grow to transcend their conflicts. But clumsy, half-hearted interventions can make things worse.

INGREDIENTS FOR EFFECTIVE MEDIATION

Disputants must see how a negotiated settlement could be their best alternative to no agreement. The concept of ripeness, however, explains very little, for disputants often spurn a possible deal even though conditions seem ripe. Readiness to settle is unpredictable.

History reveals no correlation between the kinds of leverage used and mediation success. Mediation that used only soft power succeeded in 1905 to end the Russo-Japanese War and in 1993 to initiate peace between Israel and the PLO. Blends of tangible and intangible power fostered Egyptian-Israeli peace in 1978 and the next year in Zimbabwe. Washington's mix of economic sweeteners and diplomatic pressures helped persuade Ukraine, Kazakstan, Belarus, and (with qualifications) North Korea to renounce nuclear arms. Holbrooke used every kind of incentive to nail down the Dayton Accord and sustain it.

When dealing with tough customers, hard power—or least pressure—may also be required. In 1997 it looked as though U.S. envoys Holbrooke and Dennis Ross might have to bully the locals to get the Balkan and the Israeli-Palestinian peace processes back on track. Hard power alone, however, has never sufficed to bring about a lasting peace. Hard power backfired for India in Sri Lanka (1987–1990), achieved for Russia very tenuous cease-fires in the Caucasus and Central Asia (mid-1990s), and failed for the U.S. in Lebanon (1982–1983) and in Somalia (1992–1993).

The personal qualities of individual mediators can be decisive. The Mediator's Handbook outlined earlier in this chapter offers useful guidelines, but they must be adapted to time and place. The Norwegians did little except create a setting conducive to fruitful negotiation. A skilled mediator such as Carter can convert a partially ripe situation into a settlement, for example, by using an SNT. A clumsy mediator such as Alexander Haig or Rajiv Gandhi may botch the opportunity. But some mediators may fail even though they use textbook techniques and great levers.

A mediator resembles a salesman. A word or gesture can make or break a sale. Teddy Roosevelt clinched the Moroccan deal by warning the

Can Educators Help?

Informal exchanges, brain-storming, and simulations can clear the way for formal understandings. Psychology professor Herbert Kelman arranged many informal talks between Greek and Turkish Cypriots; law professor Roger Fisher did so between Georgians and South Ossetians; Israeli professors explored possible terms with PLO officials before and after Oslo. Elementary school teachers brought Israeli and Palestinian children together to paint and discuss their images of peace. In Chapter 15 we shall read of plans to organize a University of the Middle East with campuses in many countries.

Kaiser that he would publish an embarrassing letter if Berlin spurned the terms worked out at Algeciras.

Effective mediators come in many shapes and colors: Roosevelt and Holbrooke were as gruff as Vance and Carter were polite. Vance refused "tricks" and bullying, but ultimately failed in the Balkans. Holbrooke had no such scruples. He pushed and pulled the South Slavs to the table. Lords Carrington and Owen were somewhat formal; most Americans, informal. Johan Holst ranged between these poles.

Successful intervention usually requires a major commitment of time, energy, and other resources—the kind invested at Camp David, Lancaster House, and Dayton. Mediators like Carter, Carrington, and Holbrooke sink their teeth into the problem and do not let go until a deal is reached. Mediation diplomacy can risk both the health and political fortunes of its participants; many in search of peace have died for their pains.

SHOULD A MEDIATOR SUP WITH THE DEVIL?

One diplomat pictured Serbian President "Slobo" Milošević as "the sleaziest person you've ever met" and armed with an IQ of 160. Many mediators felt uneasy dealing with suspected genocidists but did so as part of the job. Still, Lord Owen (trained as a physician) could not bring himself to discuss medicine with Bosnian Serb leader Radovan Karadžić, a former psychiatrist but also an accused war criminal. Owen's partner, Cyrus Vance, thought that a mediator should not see anyone as evil incarnate. But he also thought that compromise with persons as evil as Hitler is impossible.[31]

Carter said that judgments about others should be left outside the meeting room. The mediator should focus the disputants on whether an agreement can advance their interests. "People in conflict have to be willing to talk about ending it, or at least changing it, and there has to be someone willing to talk to them, however odious they are—and that's where I come in."[32]

31. Vance thought, however, that with Saddam Hussein "we probably should have given talks more time." Leslie H. Gelb, "Vance: A Nobel Life," *New York Times,* March 2, 1992, A15.
32. Wooten, "The Conciliator."

Memo to the UN Secretary-General:
The United Nations and its members have a vested interest in preventive diplomacy and, when necessary, effective peace enforcement. Mediation and peace enforcement are far cheaper than war.

But the United Nations has no resources unless member states provide them—no funds, no troops. The UN Secretariat can do little to help peoples at risk without the support or acquiescence of the permanent members of the Security Council. This situation has not paralyzed the United Nations. Even during the Cold War the

United Nations dispatched mediators, observers, and peacekeepers to trouble spots around the world. Still, the most effective meditations have taken place outside the UN framework.

Americans conducted much of the 20th century's mediation work. But no single country can be expected to resolve the many conflicts around the globe. A Camp David or Dayton-type mediation places enormous demands on top officials with other duties.

Why have private individuals and governments usually mediated more effectively than international organizations? UN mediators are circumscribed. They cannot operate out of the public eye (like the Norwegians with the PLO and Israelis). They have few carrots or sticks. They depend upon a fragile consensus in the Security Council.

Despite these problems, we should do whatever we can to make mediation by UN representatives more frequent and more effective. One way is to tighten the links between the United Nations and member states. Thus, we have engaged as mediators two former U.S. Secretaries of State and an ex-prime minister of Sweden. We should do more to strengthen our overall capacity for preventive diplomacy. Most mediation has been ad hoc—an improvised response to a specific challenge. When there are signs of trouble, we should have ample means and clear authority to send observers, monitors, and mediators. The United Nations needs an established procedure for providing mediators to global hot spots. Let us establish a panel of mediators, like the list of arbitrators kept at The Hague—a list from which you, the Security Council, and disputants could choose mediators. Let us have stand-by forces in every major country earmarked for UN service.

Are we our brothers' and sisters' keepers? Yes. Let us help humanity to develop stronger means of preventive diplomacy.

Upon seeing this memo, the U.S. Ambassador to the United Nations decides to forward a copy to the Secretary of State, adding his own P.S.

P.S. to the Secretary of State:

These are good ideas. The U.S. cannot pull all other peoples' chestnuts from the fire. To support the Secretary-General, let us pay our own bills to the United Nations on time. Let's share more intelligence for early warning. Let's commit to submit all our disputes to the International Court of Justice or to a mediator. While we try to strengthen the United Nations, however, be ready to intervene with mediators like Holbrooke or the Marines, or both.

KEY NAMES AND TERMS

Yasser Arafat	Johan Jorgen Holst	positions vs. interests
arbitration	International Court of Justice	prenegotiation
Jimmy Carter	leverage	reservation price (RP)
conflict resolution	mediation	ripe
Dayton Peace Accord	Oslo Accord	Anwar Sadat
failed state	peace building	single negotiating text (SNT)
Rajiv Gandhi	peace enforcement	third-party intervention
good offices	peacekeeping	
Richard E. Holbrooke	peacemaking	

QUESTIONS TO DISCUSS

1. Consider a dispute to which you or your group is a participant. Could an outside mediator advance your interests? How?

2. Why should the U.S. (Canada, Mexico, or any other country) invest time, energy, and other resources in mediating others' disputes?

3. Why do some interventions succeed and others fail? What are the ingredients of an effective mediation?

4. When, and to what extent, does effective mediation require the use of carrots and sticks?

5. Are the mediator's personal characteristics important? If so, give examples.

6. What can we learn from mediation efforts in the Middle East and the Balkans? Why did Carter, Holst, and Holbrooke succeed where others failed?

7. Why has it been easier for individuals and governments to mediate effectively than for the international community?

8. What can be done to reduce buck-passing and strengthen the UN capacity for effective mediation?

9. Imagine that you, representing country X, are the mediator between countries Y and Z. Write down their interests and principles. Formulate two ways that they might be reconciled. Outline the techniques and pressures you can use to achieve a peaceful settlement.

10. Imagine that you have this same task but that you represent the UN Secretary-General, who has been authorized by the Security Council to undertake this mediation. Formulate how the two parties might be reconciled and what techniques and pressures you can mobilize.

RECOMMENDED RESOURCES

BOOKS

Armstrong, Tony. *Breaking the Ice: Rapprochement between East and West Germany, the United States and China, and Israel and Egypt.* Washington, D.C.: U.S. Institute of Peace, 1993.

Bercovitch, Jacob, and Jeffrey Z. Rubin, eds. *Mediation in International Relations: Multiple Approaches to Conflict Management.* New York: St. Martin's, 1992.

Brams, Steven J. *Negotiation Games: Applying Game Theory to Bargaining and Arbitration.* New York: Routledge, 1990.

Damrosch, Lori Fisler, ed. *Enforcing Restraint: Collective Intervention in Internal Conflicts.* New York: Council on Foreign Relations, 1993.

Deng, Francis M., and I. William Zartman, eds. *Conflict Resolu-tion in Africa.* Washington, D.C.: Brookings Institution, 1991.

Fisher, Roger, et al. *Beyond Machiavelli: Tools for Coping with Conflict.* Cambridge, Mass.: Harvard University Press, 1994.

Princen, Thomas E. *Intermediaries in International Conflict.* Princeton, N.J.: Princeton University Press, 1992.

Raiffa, Howard. *The Art and Science of Negotiation.* Cambridge, Mass.: Harvard University Press, 1982.

Stein, Janice Gross, ed. *Getting to the Table: The Processes of International Prenegotiation.* Baltimore: Johns Hopkins University Press, 1989.

Zartman, I. William, and J. Lewis Rasmussen, eds. *Peacemaking in International Conflict: Methods & Techniques.* Washington, D.C.: U.S. Institute of Peace, 1997.

JOURNALS AND JOURNAL ARTICLES

Ethics & International Affairs [special issue: "Intervention"] 9 (1995).

"Flexibility in International Negotiation and Mediation." *Annals of the American Academy of Political and Social Science,* no. 542 (November 1995).

International Journal [special issue: "Intervention"] 48, no. 4 (autumn 1993).

Journal of Conflict Resolution

Journal of Peace Research

Negotiation Journal

"Resolving Regional Conflicts: International Perspectives." *Annals of the American Academy of Political and Social Science,* no. 518 (November 1991).

"Rethinking Peacekeeping [three essays]. " *Washington Quarterly* 18, no. 3 (summer 1995): 49–90.

WEB SITES

Arab-Israeli Conflict and The Oslo Accord
  http://www.aipac.org/hot/dop.htm
  http://www.earlham.edu/~pols/ps17971/ashraam/Links.html

History and Tour of the Camp David Accords from the Jimmy Carter Library
  http://www.sunsite.unc.edu/sullivan/CampDavid-Accords-homepage.html

International Crisis Group in Bosnia (includes oversight of Dayton Accord)
  http://www.intl-crisis-group.org/projects/bosnia/bosnia.htm

International Mediation Dataset Collection
  http://www.incore.ulst.ac.uk/cds/metadata/mediatn.html

Power Sharing and International Mediation in Ethnic Conflicts (Copublished by the United States Institute of Peace and the Carnegie Commission on Preventing Deadly Conflict)
  http://www.carnegie.org/deadly/sisk.html

U.S. Department of Defense Link (activities in Bosnia)
  http://www.dtic.dla.mil/bosnia/index.html

PART 3

International Political Economy

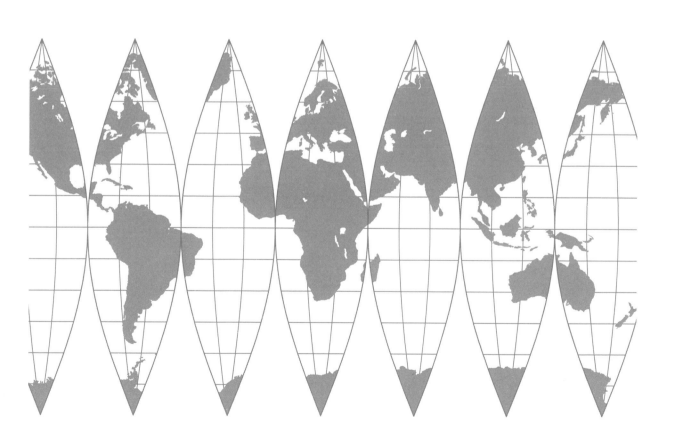

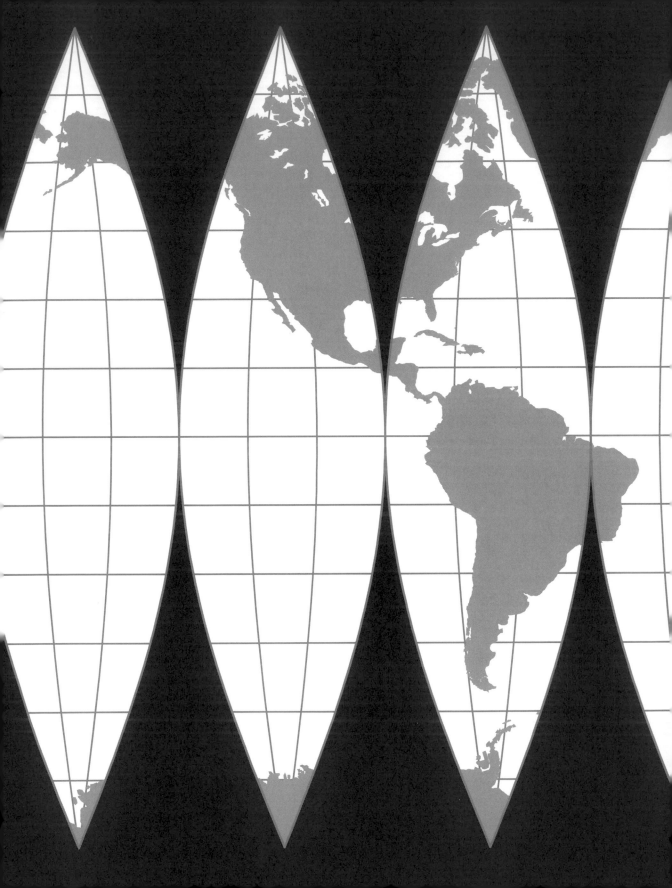

C H A P T E R T E N

DEMOCRACY AND AUTHORITARIANISM: WHAT IMPACT ON INTERNATIONAL PEACE AND PROSPERITY?

THE BIG QUESTIONS IN CHAPTER 10

- What is democracy? How does it differ from authoritarianism?

- Would you expect a democracy or a dictatorship to be more successful in foreign policy?

- How do your expectations fit with 20th-century history?

- Who usually wins when democracies fight authoritarian regimes?

- Do democracies fight democracies?

- Do authoritarian regimes help their societies to become more fit and more affluent?

- Is democracy waxing or waning?

- Would India benefit from a tighter grip at the top?

- Does it matter to India whether Pakistan and China are authoritarian?

- Does it matter to the U.S. whether other countries become democratic?

"Is A Firmer Hand Needed?" ... The President of India is deeply troubled. The world's largest democracy has fallen behind China and other neighbors in economic growth, mass education, and health care. Religious and ethnic strife have risen, leading the President to think about invoking Emergency Powers to govern directly.

The President asks you, a lawyer and university professor in Bombay, to come to New Delhi and review the situation: Is a firmer hand needed to rule India? Is democracy a luxury of the rich? Does India need a more authoritarian government to improve life within the country and wrestle with China and Pakistan? Is it time to change India's constitution?

India's political elite envies Singapore's paternalistic government guiding that country to riches and stability. If just four ethnic groups living in tiny Singapore benefit from a strong hand at the top, might India—one of the world's most populous and heterogeneous countries—also benefit from top-down, centralized governance?

Meanwhile, India's ambassador to Washington discusses these and related questions with her old friend, the U.S. Secretary of State. Is not order better than chaos? Would not Somalia and Haiti also benefit from a strong, authoritarian government? The Ambassador, a student of U.S. history, recalls the question posed by Abraham Lincoln on July 4, 1861: "Must a government ... be too strong for the liberties of its own people, or too weak to maintain its own existence?"

The Secretary of State notes that many Americans are indifferent to the ways that others are governed. A common attitude is: "It's their business—not ours." But other Americans feel a duty to spread good government. Some even believe that U.S. security and prosperity depend upon the spread of political and economic liberty. Assuming they are right, however, the questions looms: What, if anything, can outsiders do to promote democracy where it is weak?

CONTENDING CONCEPTS AND EXPLANATIONS

WHAT IS DEMOCRACY? WHAT IS AUTHORITARIANISM?

What is the impact of democracy and authoritarianism on peace and prosperity? Is the world moving toward democracy or authoritarianism? To look forward, let us go back to the basics—beginning with the ancient Greeks.

Democracy means "people-rule" (*demos* [people] + *kratia* [rule]). There are different kinds of democracy, for example, presidential and parliamentary, as in India. There is majority rule, as in the U.S.; proportional representation, as in France; and power-sharing, as in Switzerland. Despite their differences, these governments meet certain standards: In a democracy policy decisions are made by officials chosen in fair and free elections, with citizens able to organize parties and interest groups independent of government, without coercion and with non-official sources of information available.[1] The underlying **political culture of democracy** balances rights and duties. It bows to the majority but respects the minority. It recognizes the legal equality of each citizen and the need to pool energies for shared goals. It respects **constitutionalism**—government in which power is distributed and limited by law. A checklist by which to evaluate political and civil liberties is outlined in Table 10.1.

Table 10.1 Is There Democracy? A Checklist

Political Rights	Civil Liberties
1. Is the head of state elected?	**1.** Are there free and independent media?
2. Is the legislature elected?	**2.** Does open public discussion occur?
3. Are election procedures free and fair?	**3.** Does freedom of assembly exist?
4. Do elected officials have real power?	**4.** Does the freedom to organize politically exist?
5. Does competition exist between political parties?	**5.** Are citizens equal under law?
6. Can "outs" replace the "ins"?	**6.** Is there protection from political terror?
7. Is society free from domination by the military, foreign powers, or other tyrannies?	**7.** Are there free trade unions with the right to collective bargaining?
8. With respect to minority freedoms, is self-determination or participation in the political process apparent?	**8.** Are there free religious institutions?
9. Are minorities free from assimilationist pressures?	**9.** Do social freedoms related to gender equality, property rights, and travel rights exist?
	10. Is there freedom from economic exploitation?
	11. Is there freedom from government indifference and corruption?

SOURCE: Adapted from Freedom House survey, as reported in *Freedom Review* (January–February 1997).

1. Robert Dahl, *Dilemmas of Pluralist Democracy* (New Haven, Conn.: Yale University Press, 1982), 11; and Philippe C. Schmitter and Terry Lynn Karl, "What Democracy Is . . . And Is Not," in *The Global Resurgence of Democracy*, ed. Larry Diamond and Marc F. Plattner (Baltimore: Johns Hopkins University Press, 1993), 39–52 at 45–46.

A modern democracy rests upon a strong **civil society**—a domain separate from government where self-organizing groups can articulate values and advance their interests, shielding people from unbridled government and from raw market forces. In Poland, for example, the Solidarity trade union movement in the 1970s–1980s united persons wishing to act "as if they were free" despite the Communist dictatorship. Civil society, in turn, is buttressed by a free market economy in an institutionalized legal framework. A productive economy generates the means to permit the government to carry out its collective good functions and provides a material basis for the pluralism and autonomy of civil society, elections, and government.[2]

Democracy, of course, does not equal capitalism. Democracy is a political system. Capitalism and socialism are economic systems based on the technologies spawned by the Industrial Revolution. Under capitalism, the means of production—land and factories—are privately owned. Under socialism, they are publicly owned—usually controlled by the government. As we shall see later in this chapter, democracy can be threatened by excesses of capitalism or socialism—by abuse of private or public power. But the greatest danger to civil society comes when a single party controls politics and, through its monopoly of government power, also controls the economy, the media, and education. In most of Western Europe there is more public ownership of industry than in the U.S.—without damage to democracy.

In a democracy power flows from the bottom up. In an **authoritarian** system power starts at the top. An authoritarian government demands submission—obedience.[3] The **political culture of authoritarianism** emphasizes duties—not rights. Subjects are trained to want guidance from above. Civil society is weak.

Authoritarian rule may be by one (monarchy) or a few (oligarchy). Authoritarians base their right to rule on a variety of claims, for example, by the will of God, their noble genes or virtue, urgent circumstances, the will of the people, or the needs of history. **Josef Stalin**, Soviet leader from the mid-1920s until his death in 1953, called his system a "dictatorship of the working class." A **dictatorship** means that the leader dictates and the subjects obey.[4] No country is a democracy if one party monopolizes power.

Authoritarian rule need not be a cruel tyranny. It may be benevolent or malevolent; enlightened or ignorant; farsighted or capricious. The major authoritarian regimes of the 20th century, however, have been **totali-**

2. Juan J. Linz and Alfred Stepan, *Problems of Democratic Transition and Consolidation: Southern Europe, South America, and Post-Communist Europe* (Baltimore: Johns Hopkins University Press, 1996), 7–15.

3. "Authority," "authoritarian," and "authentic" come from the Latin and Greek roots for "author" or creator.

4. "Dictatorship"—the rule of a dictator—comes from the Latin for dictate, pronounce, decree. *Dictatus* is the past participle of *dictare*, to pronounce. "Despotism" comes from Greek *despotes*—master, lord—and is related to the Latin *domus* and dominion. Byzantine emperors, princes, and bishops called themselves "despots." Some European monarchs of the 18th century claimed to be "enlightened despots." Despotism in the 20th century has usually meant a cruel absolutism. Oligarchy derives from the Greek *olig*—"few."

tarian dictatorships—political systems seeking total dominion over all aspects of life, including the political, economic, social, and cultural. The totalitarian systems of Fascist Italy and Nazi Germany claimed to embody earlier empires, racial purity, and the genius of their leaders—**Benito Mussolini** and **Adolf Hitler**. Communist regimes claimed to be the vanguard of the proletariat, enlightened by the insights of Karl Marx and Vladimir Lenin. Communist dictators such as Stalin and Mao Zedong asserted their competence to decide literary and scientific questions as well as to orchestrate wars and diplomacy.

WEAKNESSES OF DEMOCRACY

Demagoguery

Many political theorists have regarded democracy as inferior to authoritarian rule. Many ancient Greeks understood "people-rule" to mean "mob rule." The people, they said, were easily swayed by **demagogues**— leaders who inflame popular passions with their rhetoric. Looking at India today, an ancient Greek might worry that each *ethnos* (distinct people, such as the Tamils of south India) has its own demagogues, making a unified polity impossible.

Myopic Foreign Policy

The French aristocrat Alexis de Tocqueville admired the equality and freedom he found when visiting the U.S. in 1831–1832. But his book *Democracy in America* (published 1835–1840) pointed to two major dangers: First, democracy may lead to a tyranny of the majority. Second, democratic governments are ill-suited for foreign policy. They have no capacity for a steady, long-term strategy or for tactical flexibility—the ability to move quickly and reverse fields as circumstances warrant. A democracy "cannot combine its measures with secrecy or await their consequences with patience."

Democracies, Tocqueville added, are inept at starting or ending wars. The *demos* refuses to pay for adequate forces in peacetime. So democracies usually have small armies led by mediocrities. Democracies ignore danger signals that the enemy is approaching. The masses are slow to awake but then difficult to restrain.

Unfairness

Communists and other leftists add to the assault on democracy. They say that democracy may be good for the rich but it is bad for the poor.

The leaders of India live in luxury but do little for the masses. Power feeds on itself. One corrupt party has crowded out others in "democratic" India, Italy, and Japan since the late 1940s.

Uncontrolled Individualism

Political scientists Zbigniew Brzezinski and Samuel P. Huntington compared U.S. democracy and Soviet authoritarianism in the early 1960s. The strength of the U.S. system derived from the close unity between society and the government. But the U.S. government was weakened by its subordination to society—in short, by democracy itself.[5]

U.S. devotion to freedom has worn down the institutions needed to restrain the individual—with disastrous results.[6] One-fifth of all Americans live in poverty; racism and crime are rampant. Less than half of U.S. citizens vote. Nearly one in 190 Americans is in jail.[7]

Still other critics say that democracy is not suited for developing countries. Economic growth requires political order and both must begin with central controls.

STRENGTHS OF DEMOCRACY

Least Bad

"No one pretends that democracy is perfect or all-wise," Winston Churchill told the House of Commons in 1947. "Democracy is the worst form of Government except all those other forms that have been tried." The same idea was expressed by Indian Prime Minister Jawaharal Nehru in 1961: "Democracy is good. I say this because other systems are worse."

Human Fulfillment

To be fully human, Aristotle wrote, requires participation in a political community. "Liberty is not a means to a higher political end. It is itself the highest political end."[8] A black South African woman put these ideas more directly on April 28, 1994. "On this day I became a human being. I can vote for the first time." She could not do so under the previous, authoritarian regime.

Peace and Survival

Another reason to favor democracy is that it promotes life. Contrary to Tocqueville, philosopher **Immanuel Kant** (subject to the Prussian king) predicted in 1795 that the foreign policies of representative democracy would foster peace, law, commerce, and community. How his theory stacks up against reality will be examined later in this chapter.

5. Zbigniew Brzezinski and Samuel P. Huntington, *Political Power: USA/USSR* (New York: Viking, 1964).

6. A Singaporean official noted that the U.S. population grew by 41 percent from 1960 to 1990 while violent crime rose by 560 percent and single-mother births by 419 percent. Instead of doing something to halt this "massive social decay," Americans went abroad preaching "the virtues of unfettered individual freedom." Kishore Mahbubani, "The Dangers of Decadence: What the Rest Can Teach the West," *Foreign Affairs* 72, no. 4 (September–October 1993): 10–14.

7. Adam Przeworski, "The Neoliberal Fallacy," in *Capitalism, Socialism, and Democracy Revisited,* ed. Larry Diamond and Marc F. Plattner (Baltimore: Johns Hopkins University Press, 1993), 39–53 at 40.

8. Lord Acton, *The History of Freedom and Other Essays* (London: Macmillan, 1907), chap. 1.

Political scientist Rudolph Rummel agrees with Kant. Rummel portrays democracy as a method of nonviolence. "Democratic systems provide a path to peace, and universalizing them would eliminate war and minimize global political violence." Rummel adds that democracy has another advantage over authoritarian regimes: "The citizens of democracies are the least likely to be murdered by their own governments; the citizens of totalitarian, especially Marxist systems, the most likely."[9] We shall also compare Rummel's theory with reality.

STRENGTHS AND WEAKNESSES OF AUTHORITARIANISM

Decisiveness

Authoritarians claim to mobilize human and other resources better than democracies. For government to function, disputes must be resolved by one alone—"*uno solo*," as Florentine political analyst Niccolò Machiavelli put it.[10] Authoritarians can indoctrinate and command, tax as they please, keep secrets, and intervene abroad with whatever forces are needed—when they are needed. If they wish, they can redistribute the wealth to promote equality.

For English philosopher Thomas Hobbes, only a strong sovereign could assure safety. Otherwise there would be a "war of all against all."

Authoritarian rule keeps the lid on ethnic and nationalist conflict. Whereas India faces constant ethnic and religious turmoil, China's strong central government keeps its minority peoples under firm control. The Soviet empire repressed the bickering of Central Asians, Caucasians, and East Europeans. The breakup of central control has unleashed chaos where there had been a *pax sovietica*.

When the Kremlin cracked down on Hungarian insurgents in 1956, it did so decisively. When the Kennedy administration sought to overthrow Fidel Castro in 1961, it did so halfheartedly. The Soviet regime was manned by professional politicians schooled in *kto kovo* (who, whom); the U.S. government, by political amateurs.

Brzezinski and Huntington also anticipated that the weaknesses of the Soviet system could be more disruptive than those of U.S. democracy. Dictatorship generated tensions with other social forces and institutions. Still, both the Soviet and U.S. systems had great staying power. Brzezinski and Huntington expected the two systems to change but not converge. They predicted "parallel evolution."

9. Rudolph J. Rummel, *Lethal Politics: Soviet Genocide and Mass Murder Since 1917* (New Brunswick, N.J.: Transaction, 1996), xi. Rummel documents these hypotheses in more than a dozen books. His summation is *Power Kills: Democracy as a Method of Nonviolence* (New Brunswick, N.J.: Transaction, 1997).

10. Harvey C. Mansfield, Jr., *Taming the Prince: The Ambivalence of Modern Executive Power* (New York: Free Press, 1989), 83.

Information Blockage

Authoritarian regimes suffer from information blockage. Messengers fear to tell the bad news. If the boss gets bad news, she or he may not share or discuss it with others. We saw in Chapter 3 how *uno solo* (Khrushchev) initiated the Cuban missile gambit—a policy that could have destroyed the world. In Chapter 5 we noted how the Kremlin resisted installing touch-tone telephones.

Abuse of Power

The more unchallenged the government, the more it is likely to abuse power. As English historian Lord Acton put it (in 1887): "Power tends to corrupt and absolute power corrupts absolutely." But even Lord Acton might have been taken aback by the accuracy of his prediction. As Professor Rummel has documented, 20th-century dictators have murdered their own people by the millions.

COMPARING THEORY WITH REALITY: TRACK RECORDS OF AUTHORITARIANISM AND DEMOCRACY

DEMOCRACIES USUALLY DEFEAT AUTHORITARIAN REGIMES IN WAR

While authoritarian regimes started most of the major wars of the 20th century, they also lost them—usually to democracies.[11] Authoritarian Germany, Austria-Hungary, and the Ottoman Empire were defeated by Western democracies in World War I.[12] The dictators of Italy, Germany, and Japan launched World War II, but were defeated by a coalition that included the authoritarian USSR as well as the Western democracies. When authoritarian Arab states and democratic Israel made war, Israel prevailed. Authoritarian Pakistan was defeated or stalemated several times by India.[13] Democratic Britain defeated the Argentine junta in 1982. The First World prevailed over the Soviet empire in cold war.

Why did democracies fight more effectively than Tocqueville predicted? Authoritarian regimes can reach decisions more quickly than democracies—often the wrong decisions. Germany twice waged a two-front war and then, compounding its follies, took on the world's economic colossus.

Authoritarians can indoctrinate and mobilize their people to obey, but they often inhibit creativity and leadership—also important in war.

Since World War II democracies have usually lost when they fought

11. A survey of all wars between democracies and autocracies, 1816 to 1988, finds that democracies won four out of five. See David A. Lake, "Powerful Pacifists: Democratic States and War," *American Political Science Review* 86, no. 1 (March 1992): 24–37 at 31–33.

12. Authoritarian Russia was defeated by authoritarian Japan in 1905 and by authoritarian Germany in 1917.

13. However, China bested India when they faced off in 1962 over disputed territory high in the Himalayas, deepening India's resolve to become a modern military power.

against national liberation movements. Thus, the Dutch were driven from Indonesia (1949), the French from Vietnam (1954) and Algeria (1962), the U.S. from Vietnam (1973), and the Portuguese from Africa (1975). Why? Many in the West doubted that the cause was just or worth fighting for.

DEMOCRACIES BAND TOGETHER AND RARELY, IF EVER, FIGHT EACH OTHER

Liberal peace theory holds that stable, sovereign democracies seldom, if ever, wage war against other stable, sovereign democracies. This theory is as near to an empirical "law" as exists in IR.[14] It appears to be valid across the seventy or more interstate wars that have taken place since 1815 involving at least 270 states.[15] Far from fighting each other, democracies tend to band together in war.

The theory states: "seldom, if ever." There are possible exceptions, for example, the War of 1812, the U.S. Civil War, the Boer War, and the many European and U.S. battles with national liberation movements. But even these possible deviations disappear if we define four terms precisely:

War means an armed conflict that kills at least 1,000 persons in battle.

Democracy requires free elections in which "practically all adults" have the right to vote. Many countries meet this standard in the late 20th century. For earlier times we lower the bar and count as democracies countries in which at least 30 percent of adult males could vote. Not until the 1850s could most white males vote in the U.S., while women gained suffrage only in 1920; most U.S. blacks found it hard to vote until 1965. It was not until 1971 that the voting age was lowered to eighteen in the U.S. Most other countries were much slower to broaden the voting franchise. Female suffrage existed in very few countries until after World War I. If women's vote had any pacifying effect, it would have had little effect until the 1920s or later.[16]

Stable means established and functioning as a democracy for at least three years.

Sovereign means "recognized as independent by the international community."

Applying these standards, we see that none of the candidate conflicts constituted a war between stable, sovereign democracies: The War of 1812 between the U.S. and Great Britain took place when neither side had wide suffrage; the U.S. Civil War (1861–1865) took place between a democracy and a landed aristocracy that was neither stable nor sovereign; both the

14. Jack S. Levy, "The Causes of War: A Review of the Theories and Evidence," in *Behavior, Society, and Nuclear War,* 3 vols., ed. Philip E. Tetlock et al. (New York: Oxford University Press), 1: 209–333.

15. Bruce Russett et al., *Grasping the Democratic Peace: Principles for a Post–Cold War World* (Princeton, N.J.: Princeton University Press, 1993), 9–20. See also Michael W. Doyle, "Liberalism and World Politics," *American Political Science Review* 80, no. 4 (December 1986): 1151–1169, and his two related articles in *Philosophy and Public Affairs* 12, no. 3 (1983): 205–235 and 12, no. 4 (1983): 323–353; for other references, see Cecelia Lynch, "Kant, the Republican Peace, and Moral Guidance in International Law," *Ethics & International Affairs* 8 (1994): 39–58.

16. In Great Britain a majority of adult males could not vote in secret elections until 1872; even then, some 40 percent of adult males remained disenfranchised. Women did not gain suffrage in France, Italy, and Japan until the 1940s; in Switzerland, until 1971.

Boer War (1899) and the Second Philippine War (1899–1902) pitted democracies (Britain and the U.S.) against liberation movements that were neither settled nor sovereign.

Democracies rarely, if ever, fight other democracies. But democracies have often wielded a big stick. Since 1945 the U.S. has threatened force on hundreds of occasions—usually against Communist governments. Of course, a threat is not a war unless many die.

France and Belgium have intervened often in Africa. U.S. military forces openly intervened in the Dominican Republic (1965), in Grenada (1983), and in Panama (1989).[17] The CIA used covert action to unseat leftist governments in Iran (1953), Guatemala (1954), and Chile (1973). None of these amounted to a "war" (with 1,000 or more deaths). Neither were these interventions approved in advance by Congress; in fact, some were later condemned by Congress.

Why has there been so much conflict between the newly independent states emerging from Yugoslavia (for example, Serbia and Bosnia) and the former Soviet Union (for example, Armenia and Azerbaijan)? Since most of these states claim to be democratic and devoted to free markets, does their behavior contradict the assumptions of liberal peace theory?

Edward D. Mansfield and Jack Snyder argue that new states making the transition to democracy are especially war-prone. Some other analysts reply that all transitional states are war-prone, but that the most aggressive are those moving toward authoritarian rule (as Germany did in the 1930s).[18]

Another view is that the new states' liberalism is genuine but that it resembles Europe's 19th-century liberal nationalism more than the universalist nationalism envisioned by theories of democratic peace.[19]

But elaborate explanations are not needed. The new states of the 1990s such as Armenia and Croatia were more authoritarian than democratic; they were not "stable"; even their independence was in doubt, because foreign influences (especially Russia's) were so strong. If and when they and their neighbors become stable, settled democracies, they may well find other ways to resolve their disputes. Democracy and market orientation, of course, are not the only factors that bear on war and peace.[20]

Another challenge to liberal peace theory comes from a series of "near misses"—cases when democracies came close to war. Defenders of the theory reply that most close calls took place in the 19th century between incipient democracies with limited suffrage. In the last decades of the 20th century there were near misses between Greece and Turkey when

17. In Grenada U.S. forces organized new and free elections; in Panama they installed a president already chosen in free elections.

18. Edward D. Mansfield and Jack Snyder, "Democratization and the Danger of War," *International Security* 20, no. 1 (summer 1995): 5–38, reprinted in *Debating the Democratic Peace: An International Security Reader,* ed. Michael E. Brown et al. (Cambridge, Mass.: MIT Press, 1996), with related articles.

19. Bear F. Braumoeller, "Deadly Doves: Liberal Nationalism and the Democratic Peace in the Soviet Successor States," *International Studies Quarterly* 3, no. 41 (September 1997): 375–402.

20. A comparative study of empires and other large political entities shows that "polities that lose momentum rarely recover it." If so, Russia might not threaten its neighbors much regardless of the condition of its democracy. See Rein Taagepera, "Expansion and Contraction Patterns of Large Polities: Context for Russia," *International Studies Quarterly* 41, no. 3 (September 1997): 475–504.

democracy in one or both countries had been replaced or threatened by military rule.[21]

Why Don't Democracies Fight One Another?

Too Few to Fight. Some critics of liberal peace theory say that the sample is too small to form any empirical "law" of IR. The universe of democratic dyads able to fight one another has been small. Thus, most of the 270 states involved in interstate wars since 1815 were not democracies. There were few democracies until the 20th century, and many are too remote to fight one another, for example, Chile and France. With few potential belligerents, it is not surprising that few democracies have fought each other.

But statistics do not explain the existential transformation occurring since 1945: War has become virtually unthinkable between some countries that fought in past wars. Germany and France are still adjacent. So why is war now out of the question?

Common Interests. Democratic or not, the industrial powers of North America, Western Europe, and Japan shared many common interests that motivated them to band together and not fight one another. All were exhausted by World War II. All feared nuclear war. All feared the USSR and Communist expansionism. All profited from trade. The U.S. hegemon maintained order within the First World.

But common interests and trade ties do not assure peace. They did not prevent Europeans from fighting each other in two world wars. Exhaustion and fear of nuclear weapons did not prevent a long cold war between the USSR and the West. Soviet hegemony did not prevent uprisings in Eastern Europe or border wars with China.

Kant's Synergy. It is difficult to prove why something has *not* happened. But there are good reasons to believe that democracy and peace reinforce each other. The inner logic between self-rule and peace was set out in Kant's essay "On Perpetual Peace" (1795–1796). Kant pointed to the combined impact of representative government, the federation of nations, international law, the spirit of trade, and the growth of a common, enlightened culture.[22]

The key to peace, Kant argued, is *representative* government (which Kant called a "republic" to distinguish it from the direct democracy convulsing revolutionized France as he wrote). Kant gave six reasons. First, where "the consent of the citizenry is required . . . to determine whether there will be war, it is natural that they consider all its calamities before

21. For background, see Graham T. Allison and Kalypso Nicolaidis, eds., *The Greek Paradox: Promise vs. Performance* (Cambridge, Mass.: MIT Press, 1997).

22. Text in Immanuel Kant, *Perpetual Peace and Other Essays* (Indianapolis: Hackett, 1983), 107–143.

they enter so risky a game." By contrast, authoritarian rulers can simply declare war and leave it to diplomats to concoct justifications.

Second, Kant predicted that free, self-governing peoples will tend to form federations to preserve peace and their rights. If a powerful and enlightened people forms a representative government, "it will provide a focal point for a federal association among other nations that will join it in order to guarantee a state of peace among nations . . . and through several associations of this sort such a federation can extend further and further."

Third, since these representative governments will not accept any other government over them, they will have to accept an enlarged body of international law that will "finally include all the people of the earth." As community prevails among the earth's peoples, "a transgression in *one* place in the world is felt *everywhere* [emphases in original]. . . ."[23]

Fourth, representative government and law are linked with commerce. The "*spirit of trade* cannot coexist with war, and sooner or later this spirit dominates every people [emphasis in original]." Those with the most to lose economically will exert every effort to head off war by mediation.[24]

Fifth, common institutions should lead to mutual respect. Language and religion divide men, but "the growth of culture and men's gradual progress toward greater agreement regarding their [common] principles lead to mutual understanding and peace."

The "right to visit, to associate [with other peoples], belongs to all men by virtue of their common ownership of the earth's surface. . . ." An alien has a right to hospitality; he should not be treated as an enemy upon his arrival in another's country so long as he behaves peaceably.

Sixth, as the number of representative governments expands, the bases for peace will become global and perpetual. There must be justice and peace *among* states for it to exist *within* a single state. Civil society cannot flourish in fear of external attack.[25] Kant urged governments to remember that if their policies attempt to do what is *morally* right, peace and other good results will follow. If each state behaves morally, the space between them can become an extension of the rational political community or "civil society" achieved within each state. The international arena then could be dominated not by amoral anarchy but by "pure practical reason and its righteousness."[26]

Kant also realized, however, that the system he outlined would be vulnerable to the wild streak in human nature that could tear down the rule of reason. He cautioned that "from the crooked timber of humanity no

23. On the Kantian tradition in international law, see David R. Mapel and Terry Nardin, "Convergence and Divergence in International Ethics," in *Traditions of International Ethics,* ed. Mapel and Nardin (Cambridge: Cambridge University Press, 1992), 297–322. For a skeptical view, see Jens Bartelson, "The Trial of Judgment: A Note on Kant and the Paradoxes of Internationalism," *International Studies Quarterly* 39, no. 2 (June 1995): 255–279.

24. Kant lived in Königsberg, once a thriving participant in the Hanseatic League of city-states on the Baltic Sea and the Atlantic shores of northern Europe. Subject in 1795 to the King of Prussia, Kant wrote when there were very few representative democracies in the world, but he may have been inspired by the spirit of the "Hansas." He was certainly familiar with British and French writings on democracy and many of the peace plans proposed by other authors.

25. See also the essays in *Kant: Political Writings,* 2d ed., ed. Hans Reiss (Cambridge: Cambridge University Press, 1991).

26. See also Lynch, "Kant, the Republican Peace, and Moral Guidance," 57.

straight thing can ever be made." But he hoped that each individual, reaching upward like a tree for air and sun, would grow straight under the canopy of civil society.[27]

Why the Liberal Peace?

Institutional Limits on the Government's Power to Make War. Kant's first point is the least persuasive. "Peoples" sometimes rise to the idea of a good war. Public opinion and the public's representatives have done little to constrain presidents and prime ministers from using military force.

The Perception of Shared Norms. Kant's fifth point is his weightiest. Peoples that perceive one another as democratic have not fought each other. Indeed, they tend to band together against authoritarians.

As Britain became more democratic in the late 19th century, tensions between London and Washington diminished. In the late 19th century the U.S. and Britain committed themselves to third-party arbitration of disputes they could not resolve bilaterally. Instead of struggle between the imperial hegemon and the challenger, a "special relationship" developed between them.

Perceptions are crucial. France invaded Germany in 1923 to collect war reparations, but few Frenchmen thought of Germany then as democratic, though it had been for four years. Lacking mutual respect, Greece and Turkey have experienced many "close calls."

The Spirit of Trade. Kant did not treat commerce as a cure for war. He avoided the simplistic view of the "Manchester School" economists who, in the 19th century, promised that "the free flow of goods across national boundaries" would erase misunderstandings and ensure peace. Unlike them, Kant insisted that peace depended upon a combination of factors—representative democracy, law, commerce, and mutual respect.

A Social Field. Taken together, Kant's six points read like a description of the European Union and, by extension, the "security community" that links Europe, Canada, the U.S., and Japan. Rummel says that all these factors interact to form a "social field"—an exchange society with a habit of problem-solving by negotiation and accommodation.[28]

DEMOCRATIC STATES ARE THE MOST PROSPEROUS IN HISTORY

Democratic societies have created for their members the highest living standards in history. They are geared to mutual gain and value creation rather than toward exploitation, at least within their borders. The top

27. See the fifth of Kant's nine theses in "Idea for a Universal History with a Cosmopolitan Intent" (1784), in *Perpetual Peace and Other Essays*, 15–39 at 33.

28. Rummel, *Power Kills*, chap. 11.

twenty-five countries on the Human Development Index (HDI) for 1997 were all democracies.

Authoritarian regimes tend to be exploitative. They seek power and/or wealth for the rulers and the "state" rather than the common people. The authoritarian USSR achieved the world's second largest economy, but it focused on steel and cement—not consumer goods. The USSR was more fit for war than for peace. Its longtime core, Russia, placed 67th in HDI rankings for 1997. Most Communist dictators lived in luxury while their subjects scraped by and often starved. Exploitation of the many by the few benefits the regime for a while; in the long run it boomerangs.

The highest placed authoritarian country in HDI rankings for 1997 was Singapore—number 26; of former Communist countries, Slovenia and the Czech Republic scored highest at 35 and 39, respectively; the highest-ranking Gulf oil producer was the United Arab Emirates—44; China ranked 108; Egypt, 109.

Each society's fitness affects not just its own citizens but other states as well. Prosperity in today's world correlates with mutual dependence in trade and with close political and cultural ties.

THE COSTS OF AUTHORITARIAN RULE

The ultimate reason to reject authoritarian rule is that it endangers life. Many authoritarian governments have practiced **demicide**—mass murder of people (*demos*)—at home and abroad. Demicide includes genocide (destruction of a particular people) and other forms of mass murder. It also includes **politicide**—the extermination of political foes. As used here, it excludes war dead. Far more civilians have died at the hands of governments than soldiers have died in combat.[29]

From 1900 to the late 1980s, governments probably murdered about 170 million people, of which some 107 million were killed by Communist regimes. The megamurderers were the USSR (62 million), Communist China (35 million—perhaps more), Nazi Germany (21 million), and Nationalist China in 1928–1949 (10 million). By comparison, the battle-killed in all foreign and domestic wars of the 20th century numbered probably under 40 million.

The most lethal regime (defined by the percentage of its own people killed in a short time) was Cambodia under the Khmer Rouge (1975–1979). Croatia under Ustashi (Fascist) rule in World War II and Mexico in 1900–1920 also ranked among the most lethal regimes of the century.

Individual leaders were crucial. The century's bloodiest are listed in Table 10.2.

29. The following analysis and statistics are from Rudolph J. Rummel, *Death by Government* (New Brunswick, N.J.: Transaction, 1996), and Rummel, *Power Kills*. Rummel's estimates of demicide usually take a middle ground between others' high and low estimates. Russian, Kazak, and Chinese scholars have produced higher estimates than Rummel for some events in their countries.

Table 10.2 Leading Demicidists of the 20th Century

Leader	Ideology	Country	Demicidal years	Millions murdered
Stalin	Communist	USSR	1929–1953	43.0
Mao Zedong	Communist	China	1923–1976	38.0
Hitler	Fascist	Germany	1933–1945	21.0
Chiang Kai-shek	Militarist-fascist	China	1921–1948	10.0
Lenin	Communist	USSR	1917–1924	4.0
Tojo Hideki	Militarist-fascist	Japan	1941–1945	4.0
Pol Pot	Militarist	Cambodia	1968–1987	2.4
Yahya Khan	Militarist	Pakistan	1971	1.5

SOURCE: Adapted from Rudolph J. Rummel, *Death by Government* (New Brunswick, N.J.: Transaction, 1996), 8.

How could a regime do such things? Table 10.3 breaks down Soviet demicide beginning in 1917. Nearly 62 million people died, some 55 million of these Soviet citizens—killed on orders of the "dictatorship of the proletariat" seated in the Kremlin. Lenin began these policies; Stalin and his aides continued them. The persons killed were "not combatants in civil war or rebellions and they were not criminals. Indeed, nearly all were guilty of . . . nothing." They were from the wrong class or nation or race or political faction, or relatives of the above. Some were conquered, like Balts; some were believers in God; some were potential oppositionists, for example, teachers or even Communist leaders. Many were killed just to fill a quota. Very high percentages of those killed were Ukrainians and Kazaks—starved in the 1930s and after World War II.[30] One-third of all Chechens perished when Stalin ordered that they be moved during World War II.

The biggest single mass murder took place during China's Great Leap

Table 10.3 Soviet Demicide Compared to Battle Deaths

Period	Years	Demicide	Battle Deaths
Civil War	1917–1921	3,284,000	1,410,000
New Economic Policy (NEP)	1921–1928	2,200,000	n.a.
Collectivization	1929–1935	11,440,000	200
Great Terror	1936–1938	4,345,000	1,200
Pre-World War II	1939–1941	5,104,000	256,000
World War II	1941–1945	13,053,000	19,625,000
Post-World War II	1946–1953	15,613,000	90,000
Post-Stalin	1954–1991	6,872,000	22,000
TOTAL	74 years	61,911,000	21,404,400

SOURCE: Adapted from Rudolph J. Rummel, *Lethal Politics: Soviet Genocide and Mass Murder since 1917* (New Brunswick, N.J.: Transaction, 1996), 6.
    NOTE: n.a.= not available.

30. Rummel, *Lethal Politics*. Similar estimates were made for briefer periods by Robert Conquest, *The Great Terror: A Reassessment* (New York: Oxford University Press, 1990), and Conquest, *Harvest of Sorrow: Soviet Collectivization and the Terror-Famine* (New York: Oxford University Press, 1987). Rummel's data differ somewhat from those given in Chapter 4. For additional estimates on Russian war losses, see articles in the *Journal of Slavic Military Studies*. For a wide-ranging Russian analysis of human losses in Europe's wars through the 20th century, see B. Ts. Urlanis, *Istoria voennykh poter* (St. Petersburg: Polygon, 1994).

Forward, 1958–1962, when 30 to 40 million Chinese starved to death. Mao Zedong refused to admit that his economic experiment could be so disastrous. He kept himself and the army well nourished but did nothing to relieve mass famine.[31]

Many dictatorships have presided over demicide by famine—in the USSR, China, Ethiopia, and elsewhere. But democracy has nearly eliminated famine. Famine in the 20th century was usually a consequence of poor distribution—not an absolute shortage of food. Food was available—usually within the country—but only at a price that the poor could not pay. Democratic governments develop contingency plans to cope with food shortages or simply pay whatever is required to purchase food at market prices. Indians experienced many famines under imperial British rule, but not under self-rule.[32]

Given this kind of brutality, what can be said in support of authoritarian rule? It has produced demicide on every continent—including the Americas, where Mexico had one of the most lethal regimes of the century. The death toll in Latin America was not so high on a world scale, but the dictators and military juntas of numerous Latin American countries also produced demicide—sometimes, as in Guatemala, under the watchful eyes of U.S. agents. The best that can be said for the Latin American and Iberian dictators is that they generally stayed at home, killing their own people but few foreigners.

Democracies have also committed mass murder—of Native Americans, Australian aborigines, New Zealand Maoris, and the Irish. All the imperialist countries committed demicide as they expanded into Siberia, Africa, Asia, and the Americas. Most of these events took place before the 20th century, directed against persons viewed as alien—a situation quite different from Cambodia, where Communist dictators killed one-third of their own citizens. The U.S., Canadian, Australian, and New Zealand governments have taken some steps toward restitution.

John Donne wrote: "Any man's death diminishes me." Who is not diminished by the murder of 170 millions (more than the entire population of today's Russia)? Demicide is a crime against humanity, as defined by the Nuremberg War Crimes Tribunal. Unfortunately, as we shall see in Chapter 16, there is no permanent court to deal with such crimes.

DEMOCRACY IS SPREADING

Democracy has replaced authoritarianism across much of the planet. Democracy is becoming the global rule rather than the exception. A ma-

31. Jasper Becker, *Hungry Ghosts: Mao's Secret Famine* (New York: Free Press, 1996); Dali L. Yang, *Calamity and Reform in China: State, Rural Society, and Institutional Change Since the Great Leap Famine* (Stanford, Calif.: Stanford University Press, 1996); Tu Wei-ming, "Destructive Will and Ideological Holocaust: Maoism as a Source of Social Suffering in China," *Daedalus* 125, no. 1 (winter 1996), 149 ff.; and Arthur Waldron, "'Eat People'—A Chinese Reckoning (History of Cannibalism in Communist Chinese History)," *Commentary* 104, no. 1 (July 1997), 28 ff.

32. Jean Dreze et al., *The Political Economy of Hunger: Selected Essays* (New York: Oxford University Press, 1995); Amartya Sen, "Food and Freedom," *World Development* 17, no. 6 (June 1989): 769 ff.; Frances D'Souza, "Democracy as a Cure for Famine," *Journal of Peace Research* 31, no. 4 (November 1994): 369 ff.; David Hardiman, "Usury, Dearth, and Famine in Western India," *Past & Present*, no. 152 (August 1996): 113 ff.; and Sugata Bose, "Starvation Amidst Plenty: The Making of Famine in Bengal, Honan and Tonkin, 1942–45," *Modern Asian Studies* 24, no. 4 (October 1990): 699 ff.

jority of the world's inhabitants expect to vote for political leaders in free and fair elections.

The number of democratic states has increased in what Samuel P. Huntington portrays as three large waves, interrupted by two reverse waves in which authoritarian regimes displaced democratic. A third rip tide tugged at the democratic shoreline in the 1990s.[33]

Long wave of democratization (1828–1926)—led by the U.S. and Great Britain, this wave culminated in new states after World War I such as Czechoslovakia and Estonia

Short reverse wave (1922–1942)—led by Italy, Japan, and Germany

Short wave of democratization (1943–1962)—led by Italy, Japan, West Germany, Greece, Turkey, India, and Israel

Short reverse wave (1958–1975)—led by Peru, Brazil, Argentina, Pakistan, and India

Third wave of democratization (1974–)—led by Portugal, Spain, Ecuador, Peru, Brazil, India, Cape Verde, Taiwan, Namibia, Ethiopia, Nepal, the Czech Republic, Estonia, and Slovenia

Reverse wave (1990–)—involves Sudan, Suriname, Serbia, and many ex-Soviet republics

These trends are summarized in Table 10.4.

If we analyze the growth of democracy by region, the same trends are evident, as seen in Figure 10.1.

The OECD countries, already far more democratic than any other region, became still more democratic in the mid-1970s when Portugal and

Table 10.4 Number of Democratic States, Selected Years

Year	Democratic States	Nondemocratic States	Total (percentage)
1922	29	35	64 (45.3)
1942	12	49	61 (19.7)
1962	36	75	111 (32.4)
1973	30	92	122 (24.6)
1990	58	71	129 (45.0)
1998[a]	66	81	147 (44.8)

SOURCE: Samuel P. Huntington, *The Third Wave: Democratization in the Late Twentieth Century* (Norman: University of Oklahoma Press, 1991), 26. Updated by the author (W.C.).

NOTE: Omits states with populations under one million.

a. Assumes that Estonia, Latvia, Lithuania, Ukraine, and Russia are democratic states and all other former Soviet republics are non-democratic; also that Slovenia, Bosnia, and Macedonia are democratic, but that all other ex-Yugoslav republics are non-democratic.

33. Samuel P. Huntington, *The Third Wave: Democratization in the Late Twentieth Century* (Norman: University of Oklahoma Press, 1991).

Fig. 10.1 The Growth of Democracy Since 1960

Index of democracy (most democratic = 10)

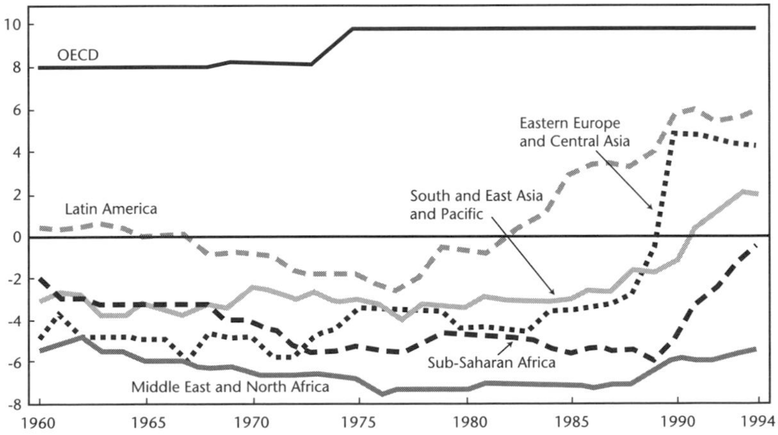

SOURCE: Data from Keith Jaggers and Ted Robert Gurr, 1996, Polity III.

NOTE: Movement toward democracy is shown as movement above and away from the center line. Movement toward autocracy (dictatorship) is shown as movement below the line. Democracy in the OECD countries has been steady except in the mid-1970s when Portugal and Spain became democratic. Eastern Europe and much of the former USSR became more democratic after 1989, but democracy declined in some formerly Communist states in the mid-1990s. Taiwan and several other Asian countries became more democratic in the early 1990s. South Africa led movement toward democracy in Africa in the early 1990s. Most of the Middle East remained autocratic.

Table 10.5 Free Peoples of the World
(in billions and as a percentage of world population)

Survey date	Free	Partly Free	Not Free
1981	1.6 (36%)	0.9 (21%)	1.9 (43%)
1989	1.9 (39%)	1.0 (20%)	2.1 (41%)
1990	2.0 (39%)	1.1 (22%)	2.0 (39%)
1991	2.0 (39%)	1.5 (28%)	1.7 (33%)
1992	1.4 (26%)	2.3 (43%)	1.7 (32%)
1996	1.1 (20%)	2.4 (42%)	2.2 (39%)
1997	1.3 (22%)	2.3 (39%)	2.3 (39%)

SOURCE: Adapted from *Freedom Review* (January–February 1997): 3.

Spain joined the democracies. The number of democracies in Latin America declined in the 1970s but shot up in the 1980s. In 1998 the only dictatorship left in the Americas was Cuba. Most former dictatorships in the Soviet sphere claimed to be democracies in the 1990s, but many remained dictatorships, for example, in Azerbaijan, Tajikistan, and Kazakstan. Democracy gained in Asia and Africa in the 1990s. The Middle East and North Africa remained far more autocratic than democratic.

An even stronger worldwide movement toward democracy emerges from surveys conducted by Freedom House, a nonprofit foundation based in New York.[34] Its representatives study all countries and ask two sets of questions (see Table 10.1). The Freedom House survey ranks each country's political and civil liberties from 1 to 7. Based on these scores, it distinguishes societies as "free," "partly free," or "not free." All "free" and most "partly free" societies are electoral democracies—a total of 118 in 1997. According to Freedom House, in 1997 one-fifth of humanity was "free"—living in 79 of 191 sovereign states; two-fifths, "partly free"—living in 59 states; and two-fifths, "not free"—living in 53 states. The global pattern is depicted in Map 10.1.

Trends from 1981 to 1997 are shown in Table 10.5. Three large shifts stand out: Large numbers of East Europeans moved from "not free" to "partly free" in 1989–1992; Balts, Ukrainians, and Russians made the same move in the early 1990s; and electoral and ethnic violence pushed India from the "free" column to the "partly free" column in 1991–1992.

CAN THE THIRD WAVE HOLD? CAN IT EXTEND FURTHER?

Democracy can be reversed. Most governments over time have been authoritarian. War made the state and the state made war. The government enriched the ruling class. How and why did the few share or surrender power to the many? The process of democratization took place gradually, with many detours and even reversals. It rested on three conditions: a democratic political culture, an institutionalized market economy, and independence from foreign coercion. Can these conditions be fostered worldwide?

Three Prerequisites of Democracy

Political Culture of Mutual Gain and Mutual Respect. In Europe and the U.S. democracy originated in a view that each individual is equal before God and humanity. Democrats distrusted authority and hierarchy. Their ideas drew strength from religious reformers who argued that every

34. Freedom House casts a wider and finer net than Huntington. It surveys 191 sovereign states and 59 related territories—a total of 250 places, whereas Huntington includes only states with one million or more inhabitants. Freedom House has three categories; Huntington just two. That said, their findings are congruent.

Democracies as well as dictatorships have mobilized vast human and material resources for war. In 1990–1991 many U.S. women as well as men risked their lives to protect Middle Eastern dictatorships rich in oil but with very different concepts of women's rights from those in the West.

individual could and should read and interpret scripture for her/himself. Individualism grew in tandem with a print revolution as Bibles and other works were published in tongues commoners could understand.[35]

There are many kinds of democratic political cultures. The U.S. was settled by dissenters—the "Protestants of Protestantism." U.S. democracy originated in individual self-reliance and fear of big government—unlike Canada and some European democracies where people rely more heavily on government. Yet all are democracies. Even more variation exists in non-Western societies.

Most major religions—or sects thereof—have at times buttressed intolerant, authoritarian political systems. In societies where there is only one acceptable religious belief, there is usually but one correct political line. But culture changes. Many Protestant societies were intolerant theocracies but evolved into tolerant democracies. The Catholic countries of Iberia and Latin America seemed for centuries to be bulwarks of authoritarianism, but most democratized in the last quarter of the 20th century.

Before World War II it seemed that Confucian societies defied democratization. In the late 20th century, however, Japan, South Korea, and Taiwan moved toward democracy. China's Communists keep power by totalitarian controls—not by Confucianism, which Mao Zedong tried to obliterate.

Despite some earlier trends, democracy lives in predominantly Hindu

35. The Protestant reformers promoted not just free thinking but literacy, for it was good to read God's word for oneself. The first Bible was published in 1455—in Latin. But soon the scriptures became "user-friendly." Between 1466 and 1526 the Bible (or much of it) was printed in German, Italian, French, and English. More Europeans could then read—and think—for themselves.

Map 10.1 Freedom in the World

SOURCE: *Adapted from Freedom House (1997), updated by the author.*

India and there are ardent democrats in Buddhist Burma, Cambodia, Sri Lanka, and Thailand. Democracy is strong in multi-ethnic, multi-faith South Africa.

The biggest question is Islam. No state with a Muslim majority was ranked as "free" by Freedom House in 1997. About a dozen were "partly free"—Bangladesh, Albania, Jordan, the Kyrgyz Republic, Malaysia, Pakistan, Turkey, Bosnia, and a few more. The others—more than two dozen—were "not free." Many, such as Afghanistan and Iraq, were rated among the least free.

Turkey is the only Islamic country to have experienced long intervals of relatively stable democracy, but even Turkey denies self-expression to its Kurdish minority. Pakistan has been democratic but only for brief intervals between periods of authoritarian rule.[36] Even when signing the UN conventions on human rights, Libya and Iraq added a qualifier: "Islamic law" takes precedence over treaty law.

But Islam is not intrinsically opposed to democracy. The Sufi sect has celebrated individual freedom for many centuries. Chechen intellectuals talked in 1997 about freedom as a value that transcends Eastern and Western civilizations. **Mohammed Khatami**, a senior cleric elected president of Iran in 1997, praised the West for upholding the "idea of 'liberty' or 'freedom,' the most cherished values of all mankind." He noted that the West has cast aside the "regressive thinking that had been imposed on the masses in the name of religion," and "broken down subjugation to autocratic rule." He warned against dogmatic Muslims who would trample religious and intellectual freedom. "If we step on freedom, we will have caused a great catastrophe." Many of Khatami's backers were women and young people, who, at age 15, could vote.

At the time of the Crusades the Islamic world was more enlightened and tolerant than Christian Europe. Outlooks and conditions evolve.

Markets and Middle Class. Democracy thrives on middle-class prosperity that can be achieved only by a market economy. Neither guarantees the other, but each nurtures the other. Some authoritarian regimes have initiated economic growth. None but Singapore has generated high levels of consumer abundance.[37]

"Liberty through the market; no liberty without."[38] Capitalism creates an opportunity for civil society—a social space in which individuals, groups, and institutions can develop free of state control. Without this freedom, innovation is less likely in economics, science, culture, or politics.

Socialist systems, even the most humane, tend toward authoritarian

36. Muslims and non-Muslims have shared power in Lebanon and in Bosnia-Herzegovinia, but non-Muslims have feared that the Muslims would become intolerant when they became a majority. Such fears led to fierce civil war in both places.

37. See Peter L. Berger, "The Uncertain Triumph of Democratic Capitalism," in *Capitalism, Socialism, and Democracy Revisited*, ed. Diamond and Plattner, 1–10, and other essays in this collection.

38. The quote is from Friedrich A. Hayek in 1944. For this and related references, see Raymond M. Duch, "Tolerating Market Reform: Popular Support for Transition to a Free Market in the Former Soviet Union," *American Political Science Review* 87, no. 3 (September 1993): 590–608 at 594.

control. Socialism makes affluence less likely because it inhibits freedom in all spheres. Authoritarian regimes tend to horde resources and production for their own use. They choke private enterprise by making property rights and contracts hinge on the whims of autocrats.[39]

Transitions to democracy are most likely in countries emerging from poverty to middle levels of economic development. In the 1980s this meant per capita incomes of $4,000 to $6,000 per year, distributed so as to have a large middle class. The class must feel that its earnings are safe from inflation or confiscation. Individuals and families must see opportunity for social and economic advancement.

Democracy is both cause and effect of prosperity.[40] As in 19th-century Germany and Japan, the economic takeoff of South Korea, Taiwan, and Singapore in the 1960s took place under authoritarian capitalism.[41] In the 1980s, however, both South Korea and Taiwan moved from authoritarianism toward democracy. The authoritarian state fostered a large middle class and was then transformed by it. The growing middle class demanded a voice. Low-level prosperity and rapid economic growth may be possible without democracy, but not middle- or high-income prosperity. The collapse of many Asian economies in 1997 was blamed on authoritarian cronyism.

Beijing's rulers hoped that China would follow the Singaporean route and not be diverted down the Taiwan–South Korean road.

Independence. Self-rule is impossible while a society labors under foreign oppression. Americans could not be self-ruling when ruled by English laws and Redcoats. Nor could East Europeans while they lived in the shadow of Moscow's Red Army. Bulgarians looked at Moscow and remembered the watchwords acquired during centuries under Ottoman rule: "Bend your neck"—in effect, "Don't raise your head, lest someone cut it off." Many East Europeans wanted self-rule but none threw off Communist hegemony until the meltdown of Soviet power in 1989–1991. Independence achieved, however, most East Europeans found it hard to exorcise the authoritarian strains buried in their political cultures.

Most governments were formally independent at the end of the 20th century. For most, there was no external force compelling them to accept one or another form of government.

The Next Reverse Wave—How Strong?

Disgust with Politics as Usual. The democratic system does not promise successful government, but only a way to change governments

39. Mancur Olson, "Dictatorship, Democracy, and Development," *American Political Science Review* 87, no. 3 (September 1993): 567–576.

40. Kyung-won Kim, "Marx, Schumpeter, and the East Asian Experience," in *Capitalism, Socialism, and Democracy Revisited*, ed. Diamond and Plattner, 11–25.

41. But the economic success of Asia's "Little Dragons" did not hinge on their authoritarian regimes. Rather, each followed an export-oriented trade strategy and benefited from high literacy and the Japanese model. See Jagdish Bhagwati, "Democracy and Development," in *Capitalism, Socialism, and Democracy Revisited*, ed. Diamond and Plattner, 31–38 at 35–37.

peacefully if the public wants a change. If democratically elected governments perform poorly, malcontents may demand an iron fist.

In the 1990s demagogues challenged democratically elected governments on every continent. Their slogans appealed to voters tired of the same old stuff and faces. Like billionaire Ross Perot, who won a fifth of the votes in the 1992 U.S. presidential election, they claimed to be can-do innovators. In 1990 Alberto Fujimori was elected president of Peru on a promise to defeat the Shining Path rebels. Two years later he dissolved Congress and suspended the Constitution. In 1993 Vladimir Zhirinovsky and his misnamed Liberal Democratic Party won nearly a fourth of the votes in Russia's Lower House with promises to restore Russia's glory. Billionaire **Silvio Berlusconi** won just 20 percent of the Italian vote in 1994 but, allied with neofascists and the separatist Northern League, became Italy's prime minister. Berlusconi exploited his personal media empire that included Italy's three TV networks. In the 1990s Europe's authoritarians gathered steam from unemployment and fears that political refugees and "guest workers" drained resources and took jobs from locals. "Skinheads" attacked foreigners.

In 1996–1997, however, many authoritarian demagogues were bypassed or repudiated—including Perot, Fujimori, Zhirinovsky, and Berlusconi. Khatami's election by a large majority showed that many Iranians wanted a more liberal government. If Iran showed a positive example, other Islamic countries might follow. Prospects for democracy in Burma, Cambodia, and many African countries, however, looked grim.

Can Free Markets Destroy Democracy? A more insidious threat to democracy may be posed by the market itself and by the power of mass media technology.[42] What if the forces that control the media in effect brainwash humanity? In that case, the reverse wave would start not in fledgling democracies such as the Kyrgyz Republic but where markets and modern media are already strong, as in Berlusconi's Italy.

Democracies value the individual; markets treat individuals as tools to make money. Democracies value equality; markets foster inequality. Democracies depend on compromise; markets encourage competition. Democracies need a stable, settled electorate; markets and modern technology promote a nomadic life style. Democracies require majority rule with respect for minorities; markets reward self-seeking. Markets and modern technology praise the ephemeral—today's fashion, price differential, sensation.

42. Jacques Attali, "The Crash of Western Civilization: The Limits of the Market and Democracy," *Foreign Policy* 107 (summer 1997): 54–64; see also Claude Moisy, "Myths of the Global Information Village," ibid., 78–87.

Today's market economy requires big money for election campaigns. Television means sound bites and expensive advertising, paid for by lobbies seeking favors. Market elites may win out over democratic elites.

If market masters also commandeer cloning, the vision of **Aldous Huxley**, depicted in *Brave New World*, may be near.[43] Pessimists expect information technology to control people. Optimists forecast the opposite. Perhaps we should suspend judgment and strive for preferred outcomes.

Can Outside Influences Promote Democratization?

Political and economic changes result primarily from developments within each society, but outside influences can help at the margins.

The Power of Example. Good models surpass sermons. Chinese demonstrators in 1989 erected a large Goddess of Democracy resembling the Statue of Liberty.

Teaching. U.S. educators have tried to teach self-government: after 1898 to Cubans, Puerto Ricans, and Filipinos; after 1945 to Italians, Germans, and Japanese; and after 1991 to ex-Soviets and East Europeans. In the 1990s Harvard's John F. Kennedy School of Government offered classes in democratic civil-military relations to Russian and PRC officers. The Soros Foundation provided funds to rewrite Russian history books to foster a civil society.

Advocacy. U.S. ambassadors encouraged democrats in South Korea, Portugal, Uruguay, the Philippines, and many Latin American countries.

Hong Kong before 1997 was strong because it was free. When Beijing crushed demonstrators calling for democracy in June 1989, thousands of Hong Kong Chinese protested. The boy's badge celebrates "Freedom and Democracy." In Hong Kong, as in Beijing, a "Goddess of Democracy" was unveiled. Following Hong Kong's reversion to PRC rule in 1997, could Hong Kong continue to conduct such protests?

43. Published in 1932, before full-fledged Stalinism or Nazism, *Brave New World* depicts a hellish dysutopia in the 25th century.

Eritreans fought a long war for independence from dictatorships—feudal and then leftist—in Ethiopia. Eritrea's national liberation struggle united Christians and Muslims, leftists and moderates. Here, Eritrean women dance and throw popcorn as they celebrate the UN-supervised referendum in April 1993.

Saved by the Web

In late 1996, Serbians in Belgrade staged anti-government demonstrations to protest President Slobodan Milošević's annulment of municipal elections won by his opposition. Milošević attempted to thwart the protests by forcing Radio B-92—the main independent source of Serbian news—off the air, leaving government-controlled media a clear path to influencing the public in his favor.

But the path was not so clear. Students, professors, journalists, and others simply connected to Radio B-92's World Wide Web site, where they could listen to the station's digital broadcasts in Serbo-Croatian and English over audio Internet links. Government officials in Europe, humanitarian agencies, journalists, and supporters continued to receive reports of the protests and, now, of the station closure. With their help, an international Internet campaign pressured Milošević to relent, and Radio B-92 was back on the air just two days after it had been shut down. In addition, the government eased its reactions to the protests and indicated a possible reconsideration of the election annulment.

SOURCE: Chris Hedges, "Serbs' Answer to Tyranny? Get on the Web," *New York Times,* December 8, 1996, 1, 20.

Long ruled by dictators and their thugs, Haitians danced for joy when the military junta was forced out by U.S. and UN pressures in December 1994, allowing Jean-Bertrand Aristide, elected president in 1990, to return from exile in the U.S. But could democracy take root without traditions of mutual respect and amid mass poverty and illiteracy?

But Washington coddled some anti-Communist dictators, spoke softly to Communist regimes when it sought détente, and seldom challenged friendly oil sheiks.

Economic Pressures. UN-sponsored economic boycotts of Rhodesia and South Africa added to pressure on them to become multi-racial democracies. Western aid-givers have sought to condition aid to other African countries on the dismantling of authoritarian rule. Since 1974 the U.S. Congress has conditioned foreign aid, investment, and even trade on the human rights performance of other countries.

West Germany's major political parties subsidized their colleagues trying to democratize Spain and Portugal in the 1970s. Washington subsidized third-wave democratization in Portugal, Poland, and Nicaragua.

Openness. If PCs, Xerox, and the Internet are there, free thought and political competition cannot be far behind. China's great wall cracked. Beijing banned opposition political parties and free trade unions but permitted some Chinese to deal directly with foreign traders and tourists, to travel and study abroad, and to communicate with foreigners on modems.

Addressing a UN-sponsored telecommunications conference in Buenos Aires on March 22, 1994, U.S. Vice President Al Gore called for a planetary information network to promote economic growth, foster democracy, and "link the people of the world." It would "make possible a global information marketplace." He urged that the global information highway be achieved by privatization and competition. Worried about the information monopolies in some Latin American countries, Gore

called for different companies to run "competing but interconnected networks."

Security. Security threats from within or without can destabilize democratic institutions. President George Bush used military force to protect the Aquino government in the Philippines and President Guillermo Endara in Panama from right-wing assaults; President Bill Clinton deployed troops to support democracy in Haiti and Bosnia.

WHAT PROPOSITIONS HOLD? WHAT QUESTIONS REMAIN?

Churchill and Nehru claimed too little. Experience shows that democracy performs far better than authoritarian systems. Democracy has contributed to domestic and external fitness far more than authoritarianism.

Democracy's achievements suggest it may be a superior form of government. Shared democracy is probably the most dependable basis we know for peace. All countries with high domestic fitness (high HDI ratings) are democracies with mixed economies. By contrast, authoritarian governments are lethal to their own subjects and to outsiders.

If peace depends upon democracy and democracy upon a market economy, then peace also benefits from a market economy. Mutual respect and trade permit a positive peace, not just the absence of war.

Memo to the President of India:

More democracy rather than repression will help India cope with its many problems. As in China, India's economy develops not because of central controls but because these controls are being loosened.

Many of our troubles result from illiteracy—not from democracy. Only one-third of our females are literate and just two-thirds of our males are literate. Our democracy should be able to widen literacy and provide health care. Democratic Sri Lanka fulfills these tasks far better than does authoritarian China. One party has held power for too long in India. More competition by other parties would help purge corruption and create more efficiency.

Our federal union has held together because of democracy—not in spite of it. Our ethnic, linguistic, and religious variety is unmatched anywhere—forty-six officially recognized languages plus English. A free press and the right to assembly have permitted each group to express its sentiments openly. The USSR, by contrast, kept a lid on its ethnic grievances. Ultimately the lid blew off and the empire collapsed.

Top-down direction is feasible in Singapore because its three million people are all crowded into a small city-state. By contrast, India is large, equal in area to one-third of the U.S. Managing our lands on the Singapore model is simply not possible. Dependent upon grass-roots development, we need to strengthen our democracy—not weaken it.

Nor can our diversity be compared with China's, where less than 10 percent of the population is non-Han. Even so, China has trouble controlling its Uigur and Tibetan minorities.

Where we have used strong-armed tactics—in Kashmir and in Punjab state—we have created deep, festering wounds. When Prime Minister Indira Gandhi imposed Emergency Rule in 1975–1977, she resolved nothing.

One of India's greatest achievements is that famine has taken few lives since independence. China, by contrast, has lost more than 30 million to famine. The number of deaths resulting from communal strife in India is large, but pales next to the millions executed or imprisoned for political reasons in China.

We need to consolidate democracy and to promote it in Pakistan and China. Were all three countries thriving democracies, tensions would decline and trade increase. We could begin to develop complex interdependence, spend less on arms, and join in nuclear disarmament. We could shape Pakistan's internal politics by taking steps to solve the Kashmir problem, by agreeing to limit or reduce our nuclear weapons capabilities, and by eliminating discrimination against our own Muslims. With Pakistan and China, we could do more to promote educational and cultural exchange. We should emulate the ways that French and Germans have learned to replace enmity with mutual respect and amity.

Having discussed these matters with the Indian ambassador and considered worldwide trends, the U.S. Secretary of State sends a brief memo to the White House.

Memo to the President of the United States:

It is in the U.S. interest to cultivate democracy and market economies everywhere. We cannot be sure that a democracy will not fight another democracy in the future. Still, the spread of democracy may be our best protection against war.

We also know that political and economic freedom boost one another. Market democracies are good for peace, trade, and prosperity.

The U.S. should invest more energy and resources in helping to consolidate and spread democracy. To begin with, we should try to improve our own. The costs of improving our own democratic institutions and fostering them abroad are minuscule next to the costs of war or preparing for war.

KEY NAMES AND TERMS

authoritarian	dictatorship	political culture of authoritarianism
Silvio Berlusconi	Adolf Hitler	political culture of democracy
civil society	Aldous Huxley	politicide
constitutionalism	Immanuel Kant	reverse wave
demagogue	Mohammed Khatami	Josef Stalin
demicide	liberal peace theory	third wave
democracy	Benito Mussolini	totalitarian dictatorship

QUESTIONS TO DISCUSS

1. Does it make any difference for a country's domestic and foreign policy whether its government is authoritarian or democratic?

2. Does domestic policy shape foreign policy or vice versa?

3. Do authoritarian regimes need war? Are they more aggressive than democracies? If so, why?

4. Why do authoritarian regimes have lower living standards than democracies?

5. Why did authoritarian regimes last so long in Eastern Europe?

6. Can a political culture derived from a non-Protestant tradition become democratic? Consider the political impact of other religions such as Roman Catholicism, Orthodoxy, Sunni Islam, Shiite Islam, Buddhism, and so on.

7. Are free markets and democracy compatible?

8. Can democracy be fostered from outside? How?

9. How can market forces threaten democracy?

10. Can democratization be reversed? Where is the third reverse wave most likely? Why?

RECOMMENDED RESOURCES

BOOKS

Brown, Michael E., et al., eds. *Debating the Democratic Peace: An International Security Reader.* Cambridge, Mass.: MIT Press, 1996.

Diamond, Larry, and Marc F. Plattner, eds. *Capitalism, Socialism, and Democracy Revisited.* Baltimore: Johns Hopkins University Press, 1993.

Diamond, Larry, and Marc F. Plattner, eds. *The Global Resurgence of Democracy.* Baltimore: Johns Hopkins University Press, 1993.

Dreze, Jean, and Amartya Sen. *India: Economic Development and Social Opportunity.* New York: Oxford University Press, 1995.

Evans, Peter B., et al., eds. *Double-Edged Diplomacy: International Bargaining and Domestic Politics.* Berkeley: University of California Press, 1993.

Levy, Jack S. "The Causes of War: A Review of the Theories and Evidence," in *Behavior, Society, and Nuclear War,* ed. Philip E. Tetlock et al. (New York: Oxford University Press), 1, 209–333.

Linz, Juan J., and Alfred Stepan. *Problems of Democratic Transition and Consolidation: Southern Europe, South America, and Post-Communist Europe.* Baltimore: Johns Hopkins University Press, 1996.

Putnam, Robert D., et al. *Making Democracy Work: Civic Traditions in Modern Italy.* Princeton, N.J.: Princeton University Press, 1993.

Ray, James Lee. *Democracy and International Conflict: An Evaluation of the Democratic Peace Proposition.* Columbia: University of South Carolina Press, 1995.

Rosenbaum, Alan S., ed. *Is the Holocaust Unique? Perspectives on Comparative Genocide.* Boulder, Colo.: Westview, 1997.

Rummel, Rudolph J. *Power Kills: Democracy as a Method of Nonviolence.* New Brunswick, N.J.: Transaction, 1997.

Russett, Bruce, et al. *Grasping the Democratic Peace: Principles for a Post–Cold War World.* Princeton, N.J.: Princeton University Press, 1993.

Van Wyk, J. J., and Mary C. Custy. *Contemporary Democracy: A Bibliography of Periodical Literature, 1974–1994.* Washington, D.C.: Congressional Quarterly, 1997.

World Bank. *The State in a Changing World: World Development Report 1997.* New York: Oxford University Press, 1997.

JOURNALS AND JOURNAL ARTICLES

American Political Science Review

Demokratizatsiya

Doyle, Michael W. "Liberalism and World Politics." *American Political Science Review* 80, no. 4 (December 1986): 1151–1169.

Ethics & International Affairs

Jaggers, Keith, and Ted Robert Gurr. "Tracking Democracy's Third Wave with the Polity III Data." *Journal of Peace Research* 32 (November 1995): 469–482.

Journal of Democracy

Journal of Peace Research

National Interest

Problems of Post-Communism

Putnam, Robert D. "Bowling Alone: America's Declining Social Capital." *Journal of Democracy* 6, no. 1 (January 1995): 65–79.

WEB SITES

Center for Civil Society International
http://solar.rtd.utk.edu/~ccsi/ccsihome.html *(an information clearinghouse focused on the "third sector" of nonprofit and independent associations)*

National Endowment for Democracy
http://www.ned.org (*the "Democracy Net" of this grantmaking organization, contains listings on all aspects of democracy and offers a newsletter)*

Project Muse of The Johns Hopkins University
http://muse.jhu.edu/muse.html *(networked, subscription access to more than forty journals, including leads to* Journal of Democracy, *and to specific articles, for example Putnam's "Bowling Alone," cited above, which can be found at http://muse.jhu.edu/demo/journal_of_democracy/v006/putnam.html)*

Strengthening Democratic Institutions (SDI) Project
http://ksgweb.harvard.edu/csia/sdi/index.html *(reports on SDI Project in the former Soviet Union)*

C H A P T E R   E L E V E N

THE WEALTH OF NATIONS: WEST MEETS EAST

THE BIG QUESTIONS IN CHAPTER 11

- In what ways did the First World become first—how does the liberal thesis fit?

- If Japan rivals the rest of the First World, does that mean that government guidance and protection work better than the "invisible hand" of free enterprise?

- Does the Clinton administration seek to square the circle when it promotes both free trade and strategic trade?

- Do political or economic conerns play the heavier role as Ottawa, Mexico City, and Washington evaluate their North American Free Trade Agreement?

- Why do some liberals who say they like free trade oppose the World Trade Organization?

- Do the problems of First World economies stem from inability to compete abroad or from inefficiencies at home?

- Should First World governments tilt toward neoliberalism, neomercantilism, a blend, or none of the above?

- Can capitalism survive the end of communism?

"How Can Airbus Win More Market Share?" ... *You are caught*

between the U.S. and Europe. Why? You are the European Union's Commissioner for Competition. Both the Americans and the Europeans claim to favor free trade. But two U.S. aircraft giants, Boeing and McDonnell Douglas Corporation (MDC), plan to merge. Together, they produce 70 percent of the world's civilian aircraft.

Europeans invented the first jet engines and first jet airliners, but Europe's Airbus Industrie in the 1990s won only 30 percent of the world market for medium- and large-size passenger planes. If the two U.S. giants merge, can Airbus remain competitive?

"It's a normal tough brawl between U.S. Inc. and Europe Inc.," said a European industrialist. "As Boeing is America's largest exporter and Airbus is Europe's largest exporter, we're talking about high stakes in an industry where there are no saints." Each company is a symbol of technological prowess for its backers.

European industries are playing catch-up with the U.S. and Japan in many fields. The Americans have a unified market and face just one government. They dominate world sales for military as well as civilian aircraft. Since the Pentagon is ordering fewer planes, U.S. plane makers want to consolidate. That may be good for them, but it's bad for competition. If Boeing and MDC merge, Europe's Airbus has no chance.

How can Airbus win more market share? Should you try to block the Boeing-MDC merger? If so, how? By what law or rules can a European entity block a merger in the U.S.? What penalties can you invoke? If you intervene, will you be upholding or undercutting free trade? If you block the merger, will this really help Europe to compete at the leading edge of modern technology? Or will your success just patch over deep weaknesses?

Whatever you do, there are risks: If you do nothing or if you offend a major European power, this can end your chance to become President of the EU Commission. If you protest the Boeing-MDC merger, the Americans may fight back and humiliate you. They may raise tariffs and start a trade war.

You retreat to your cottage on the North Sea to read up on the wealth of nations. You want to study a basic question of international political economics: Should government guide economic development or merely facilitate it? Did government help or hinder the steps by which Europeans, North Americans, and Japanese became the richest peoples in history? You decide to review the wisdom of Adam Smith, Karl Marx, John Maynard Keynes, and other economic thinkers. But you begin your reading with Charles Dickens' David Copperfield.

CONTENDING CONCEPTS AND EXPLANATIONS

QUALITY OF LIFE

The brutality of England's Industrial Revolution struck Charles Dickens as well as Karl Marx. Dickens recorded how David Copperfield, aged ten, worked in a river-front warehouse overrun by rats. He washed empty wine bottles and pasted labels on new ones for a London wine merchant whose goods were shipped to the East and West Indies. It was the early 1820s and David owed his job to foreign trade, but he would have preferred to stay in school.

The Industrial Revolution began in England about 1780. Before that time, living standards for most Europeans were no better than for most Chinese or subjects of the Ottoman Empire. Famine and plague visited Europe regularly. In the 17th and 18th centuries most Europeans subsisted on bread, often in short supply.[1]

But incomes in England doubled in the sixty years after 1780, and millions moved from the countryside into London and other cities in search of jobs and a better life—a pattern followed in many developing countries in the late 20th century.

London in the early 19th century bore some resemblance to Third World cities of the late 20th century. Not far from the genteel streets where Dickens wrote and where Karl Marx studied at the British Museum, jerry-built rookeries stood back-to-back without drainage.[2] The River Thames was an open sewer whose waters were dumped, untreated, into the cisterns of London householders. Poor people were fortunate if they could use a standing pump turned on briefly once each week. Others bought water from traveling water carts. Typhoid and other epidemics ravaged the poor and did not spare the rich.

Karl Marx predicted a violent revolution in England, but it never came. Instead, incomes rose and England evolved into a welfare state with social security and health care provided by the government. Other Western countries followed in Britain's track, as did Japan, starting in the late 19th century. Most non-Western countries, however, did not or could not soon act on the opportunities presented by the Industrial Revolution. As we see in Map 11.1, many of the world's inhabitants were still poor in the 1990s. How did the West and Japan become rich while much of the world remained poor?

Rich and Poor in the 1990s

Based on their gross national product per capita in 1995, the World Bank classified 210 states and territories by the following categories:

Low-income ($765 or less)—Includes 63 states, such as Albania, Angola, Armenia, Bosnia, Burundi, China, Haiti, India, Nicaragua, and Sri Lanka

Lower-middle-income ($766–$3,035) —Includes 65 states and territories, such as Botswana, Cuba, North Korea, Egypt, Poland, Russia, West Bank and Gaza, and Venezuela

Upper-middle-income ($3,036– $9,385) — Includes 30 states, such as Brazil, Chile, Croatia, Greece, Hungary, South Africa, and Uruguay

High-income ($9,386 or more)—Includes 23 OECD (Organization for Economic Co-operation and Development) countries plus 29 other states and territories such as Aruba, Cayman Islands, Hong Kong, Israel, Kuwait, Singapore, and the United Arab Emirates

1. In 18th-century France bread was the staple food for three-quarters of the population and it consumed half their income. Bread prices doubled in the year before the 1789 revolution. See Simon Schama, *Citizens: A Chronicle of the French Revolution* (New York: Knopf, 1989), 306; and Nathan Rosenberg and L. E. Birdzell, Jr., *How the West Became Rich: The Economic Transformation of the Industrial World* (New York: Basic Books, 1986), 172.

2. A building inspector reported in 1847: Excrement was "lying scattered about the rooms, vaults, cellars, areas and yards, so thick, and so deep, that it was hardly possible to move for it." A public health reformer wrote that these people lived like cattle— "swarms to whom personal cleanliness is utterly unknown." Peter Ackroyd, *Dickens* (New York: HarperCollins, 1990), 381–382.

Map 11.1 GNP per capita, 1995 *(a country's gross national product divided by its midyear population)*

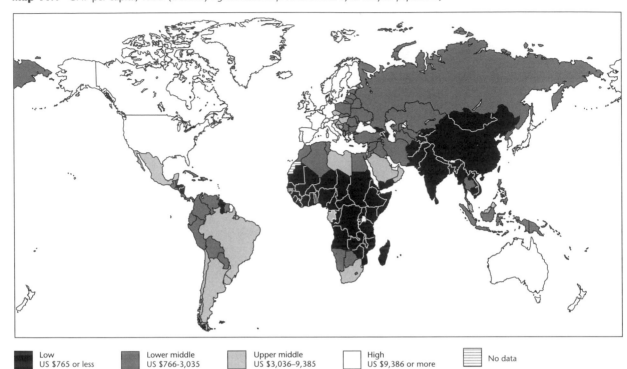

■ Low US $765 or less	Lower middle US $766-3,035	Upper middle US $3,036-9,385	High US $9,386 or more	No data

THE IPE OF VALUE-CLAIMING AND VALUE-CREATION

What can governments do to promote wealth and, if they so choose, human development? Four broad answers have been advocated by contending schools of international political economy (IPE): (1) the imposition of government controls to gain and hold wealth; (2) laissez-faire liberalism that creates wealth by encouraging free enterprise; (3) state intervention to claim and redistribute wealth; and (4) a mixture of private enterprise and public policy to create wealth.

1. Value-Claiming to Get and Keep Wealth: Mercantilism and Neomercantilism

The doctrine of **mercantilism** asserted that wealth is measured by gold and silver in the state treasury.[3] Mercantilist Spain and Portugal hoarded the gold and silver they found in the New World. The mercantilist outlook prevailed in Europe until the Industrial Revolution.

3. Mercantilism comes from the Latin *mercari*—to trade in commodities. This root also gives us "merchant" and "market," but true merchants would be more likely to favor laissez-faire over mercantilism.

Neomercantilism took root in the U.S. in the late 20th century as many Americans called on Washington to buttress U.S. industries against Japanese advances. Neomercantilists want their government to conduct both a vigorous **industrial policy** (to support domestic manufactures) and expansive **strategic trade** (to conquer foreign markets). A neomercantilist spirit pervades Edward N. Luttwak's book *The Endangered American Dream: How to Stop the United States from Becoming a Third-World Country and How to Win the Geo-Economic Struggle for Industrial Supremacy.*[4]

2. The Thesis of Value-Creating Liberalism: Laissez-Faire

Classic **economic liberalism** calls for minimal government intervention—**laissez-faire**. Economic liberalism posits a natural harmony of interest based on enlightened self-seeking. It follows the slogan of the 18th-century French economists who, protesting the heavy hand of government, cried out *laissez-faire*—"let [people] do [what they choose]." (Today's *political* liberals, by contrast, often favor big government.)

The same year that the U.S. declared independence, Scottish economist **Adam Smith** published the classic text of economic liberalism. Smith's book, *The Wealth of Nations* (1776), criticized the mercantilist belief that "to heap up gold and silver" was the readiest way to enrich any country. Smith said mercantilists erred in thinking that "to grow rich is to get money" and that a rich nation, like a rich man, abounds in money. Wealth consists rather in goods for which there is effective demand. Gold, like money, is a means of exchange—not an end in itself. If a country has no gold or vineyards, it may still obtain gold and wine by producing and trading goods wanted in places that have gold and grapes.

Smith stressed the value of complementary exchange. Within each country and across borders there is a natural division of labor based on the **absolute advantage** conferred on each actor by its endowment. Each economic actor is "led by an invisible hand to promote an end which was no part of his intention. . . . By pursuing his own interest he frequently promotes that of the society more effectually than when he really intends to promote it."

Free trade—international commerce without government restrictions or tariffs—should benefit all participants. Government efforts to keep out foreign products are misguided. "If a foreign country can supply us with a commodity cheaper than we ourselves can make it, better buy it of them with some part of the produce of our own industry, employed in a way in which we have some advantage."

4. See Luttwak, *The Endangered American Dream: How to Stop the United States from Becoming a Third-World Country and How to Win the Geo-Economic Struggle for Industrial Supremacy* (New York: Simon & Schuster, 1993).

Is Economic Globalization New?

Karl Marx explained in his *Communist Manifesto* (1848) how capitalism had already created a new system of IPE:

The bourgeoisie [capitalist class] has through its exploitation of the world-market given a cosmopolitan character to production and consumption in every country. . . . It has drawn from under the feet of industry the national ground on which it stood. All old-established national industries have been destroyed. . . . They are dislodged by . . . industries that no longer work up indigenous raw material, but raw material drawn from the remotest zones; industries whose products are consumed, not only at home, but in every quarter of the globe. In place of the old wants, satisfied by the productions of the country, we find new wants, requiring for their satisfaction the products of distant lands and climes. In place of the old local and national seclusion and self-sufficiency, we have intercourse in every direction, universal interdependence of nations.

Still, Smith approved government intervention in three cases:

Defense: Britain should try to give its sailors and shipping a monopoly of British trade, because the country's defense depended on them.

Equal taxation: Imported goods should be taxed at the same rate as domestic goods so as not to give the foreign producer an unnatural advantage.

Tit-for-tat: The state should reciprocate discriminatory policies by other states, but only if there is a prospect of persuading the other side to drop its restrictions.

Students of Capitol Hill politics will not be surprised by Smith's warning that special interest groups will lobby for government favors. He warned that such narrow interests reward legislators who favor laws to keep out competition and punish backers of free trade.

Thomas Jefferson made the case for free trade as well or better than Smith. Jefferson the diplomat also pioneered what we now call **most-favored nations (MFN)** policy. He offered to some twenty European states the lowest tariffs allowed any country by the U.S.—on condition of reciprocity.[5] Then, as now, MFN designations could be a political as well as an economic tool.

As noted earlier, Smith espoused the concept of absolute advantage in which a country exports an item of which it is a low-cost producer. A generation later, David Ricardo in 1817 explained the concept of **comparative advantage**. He showed that market forces direct a nation's resources to those industries in which it is relatively more productive. Like Smith, Ricardo oversimplified by treating labor as the ultimate source of value. He showed that trade benefits both sides when the imported good requires less labor than it would at home and when trade enlarges a country's possibilities for consumption.

3. Value Redistribution to Build a New International Economic Order

Three decades after Ricardo's major work, Karl Marx argued that **capitalism**—private ownership of the means of production—expanded the productive capacities of society. While capitalism was progressive, its fruits were shared unequally. Marx believed that this "contradiction" would cause advanced capitalist societies to explode. He predicted that private enterprise, which impoverished workers, would ultimately be replaced by public ownership of the means of production—**socialism**. Marx ignored market realities: No matter how much a worker produces or earns, no one profits unless the good can be sold.

5. Such agreements, he reasoned, would stop "the right of individual states, acting by fits and starts, to interrupt our commerce or to embroil us with any nation." Letter to James Monroe in 1785, quoted in Willard Sterne Randall, *Thomas Jefferson: A Life* (New York: Henry Holt, 1993), 379. Many treaties between European states included one-sided, unconditional MFN commitments beginning in the 17th century. See T. E. G. Gregory, *Tariffs: A Study in Method* (London: Charles Griffin, 1921), 461.

Like Smith and Ricardo, Marx assumed that the ultimate source of value is labor. Marx believed that capitalists "exploit" labor to get "surplus value" (profits) by paying a mere subsistence wage.

Taking socialism a step further, Communists called for a revolutionary regime to seize all wealth and redistribute it more equitably. But decades went by and the revolution predicted by Marx did not occur. Why not? In his book *Imperialism* (1916) Vladimir Lenin explained that European capitalists had delayed revolution in Europe by investing their surplus capital in what we now call the South. The capitalists bought off European workers with profits gained from exploiting Africans and Asians.

Lenin agreed with Marx that exploitation creates a class struggle within countries. But Lenin added to Marxism the concept of exploitation between units in an international system.

More decades elapsed. Most **less developed countries (LDCs)** of the Third World gained political independence between 1945 and 1975, but many remained both poor and dependent on the capitalist systems of the U.S. and Europe, where workers were less revolutionary than ever.

Why these departures from the predictions of Marx and Lenin? World-system ("dependency") theory answers that underdevelopment is due to structural inequality between rich countries and poor.[6] Imperialists at the core of the system keep its periphery impoverished by unequal exchange: The core exploits LDC labor and raw materials; it levies high prices for its manufactured goods but pays low prices for LDC commodities. At first the North employed mercantilism, then free trade, then its financial power and transnational corporations. The result was the same: dependency for the South.[7]

4. Neoliberalism: Private and Public Cooperation to Create Values

Economists came to perceive choices beyond the simple prescriptions of mercantilists ("hoard"), classic liberals ("keep government out of business"), and Communists ("share the wealth"). British economist John Maynard Keynes wrote in 1936 that government should neither control nor eliminate market activity. Rather, government should manage aggregate demand (by consumers, investors, and government) to compensate for "market failures." Government should "prime the pump" to stimulate business and jobs while cushioning painful adjustments to market dislocations. Instead of hoarding money, government should run deficits if necessary to spur total demand. Growth was the key to prosperity and full employment.

Keynesian principles were accepted by the U.S. and British govern-

How Would Socialism Differ from Communism?

In Marx's vision of Socialism there would still be inequality—but no capitalist exploitation of labor. Socialism would embody the principle: "From each according to his ability, to each according to his work." Only much later, after Socialism had produced great wealth and new work habits, could society adopt the principle of Communism: "From each according to his work; to each according to his need."

6. U.S. scholars have tended to treat dialectical/Marxist theories as empty propaganda. An argument for linking them with traditional and behavioral IR studies can be found in Hayward R. Alker, Jr., and Thomas J. Biersteker, "The Dialectics of World Order: Notes for a Future Archeologist of International Savoir Faire," *International Studies Quarterly[ISQ]* 28, no. 2 (June 1984): 121–142. See also Robert A. Denemark and Kenneth P. Thomas, "The Brenner-Wallerstein Debate," *ISQ* 32, no. 1 (March 1988): 47–65; and Frank F. Klink, "Rationalizing Core-Periphery Relations: The Analytical Foundations of Structural Inequality in World Politics," *ISQ* 34, no. 2 (June 1990): 183–209.

7. Some theorists posited an intermediate "semi-periphery" between the core and periphery. This zone included such cases as Turkey, Portugal, and Argentina, which were difficult to place elsewhere. A major theorist of dependency is André Gunder Frank. See his *Crisis in the Third World* (New York: Holmes and Meier, 1981). On world-system theory, see Immanuel Wallerstein, *Capitalist World-Economy* (Cambridge: Cambridge University Press, 1979), and Wallerstein, *Geopolitics and Geoculture* (Cambridge: Cambridge University Press, 1991).

The international monetary institutions that facilitated post–World War II prosperity were designed at a conference in Bretton Woods, New Hampshire, in 1944. The Western governments turned their back on autarky and committed themselves to international trade, establishing rules for balance-of-payments adjustments and exchange rates. The system changed drastically in 1971 when the U.S. suspended convertibility of dollars into gold.

ments in the late 1930s and 1940s. They were also incorporated into the international monetary system that took shape at a 1944 conference in Bretton Woods, New Hampshire, attended by Keynes. The **Bretton Woods system** extended the idea of aggregate demand management from the national to the international arena. The system sought to establish a climate favorable to expansion of international trade and investment in which individual countries could also pursue "full employment" at home.

The Bretton Woods system and other institutions created in the late 1940s opened the way to a half century of dynamic expansion. The system rested on three pillars: the U.S. dollar, convertible into gold at $35 per ounce; the **International Monetary Fund (IMF)**, established to help countries deal with short-term liquidity problems; and the **World Bank** (formally the International Bank for Reconstruction and Development), tasked to extend long-term loans for reconstruction and development. The first pillar collapsed in 1971, when President Richard Nixon cut loose the dollar from gold and let it float freely against other currencies. The other two pillars evolved to meet the changing needs of global economics.

Working in tandem with the other Bretton Woods institutions was **GATT—the General Agreement on Tariffs and Trade**, established in 1947 to promote reciprocal reduction of tariffs and foster free trade by multilateral concessions. A key GATT principle was that a **rule-based trading regime** is preferred to quantitative targets. The main rule was equal treatment—MFN. Another important rule was a requirement for transparency—publication of all relevant regulations governing imports.

Initially twenty-three states adhered to GATT; by the early 1990s, 125 countries took part in its last negotiating "round." GATT acquired a reputation as the "General Agreement to Talk and Talk," but its efforts paid off. GATT helped industrial countries to reduce tariffs on industrial products averaging 40 percent of product value in 1947 to just 5 percent in the early 1990s. During that time trade in manufactured goods increased at three times the rate of world production.[8]

Starting in 1965, the industrialized countries offered some concessions to developing countries, exempting them from some duties of reciprocity but also weakening their bargaining power. As developing countries became major exporters of textiles and clothing, they faced demands by the U.S. and Europe for **voluntary export restraints (VERs)**—in effect, quotas.

GATT's successes helped in the 1970s and 1980s to foster their antithesis: neomercantilist policies that utilized **non-tariff barriers (NTBs)** to keep out foreign imports. NTBs include government subsidies and procurement policies ("buy national"), health and safety regulations, standards, and even customs procedures (long delays at the dock). Environmental protection policies ("no imports of endangered species or their body parts") can also serve as NTBs.

Desperate to cope with Japan's export power and frustrated by Japan's maze of NTBs, the U.S. departed from the GATT principle of rule-based trade and sought quantitative commitments, for example, a Japanese pledge to import a certain number of auto exhausts, and VERs to constrain Japanese exporters.

GATT's final round of negotiation, the "Uruguay Round," began in 1986 and continued until 1993, when conferees agreed to replace GATT with a World Trade Organization (discussed below), formalized in 1995.[9] By the early 1990s, however, there was no clearcut "North-South" divide in GATT negotiations. Instead, both interests and coalitions cut across traditional lines. The so-called Cairns Group demanding freer trade in agricultural products comprised not just affluent Australia and Canada but ten developing countries—including Argentina, Brazil, Malaysia, and Thailand—along with Hungary.

Neoliberalism adapts classic economic liberalism to an age when industrialized and developing countries are locked in global interdependence. Neoliberals believe in freer trade rather than free trade, because

8. Joseph A. McKinney, "The World Trade Regime: Past Successes and Future Challenges," *International Journal* 49, no. 3 (summer 1994): 445–471 at 447.

9. For an official summary of the Uruguay Round results, see *Focus: GATT Newsletter,* no. 104 (December 1993).

they understand the need for government to shield the domestic economy (including jobs) from radical external stress. Neoliberals trust the invisible hand but believe it must be prodded by late-20th-century international institutions such as the World Trade Organization and an evolving IMF.

How Countries and Firms Acquire Competitive Advantage

The concepts of absolute and comparative advantage explain why the U.S. exports wheat. They do not explain why Japan, with few resources, makes autos so efficiently that they can be sold in Michigan. Technology and management can help firms and entire countries circumvent scarcity. Japan and other countries reduced the U.S.'s comparative advantage in resource endowment by cultivating **competitive advantage**—greater productivity based on better or more factor inputs. Skilled labor and a developed infrastructure were once a U.S. monopoly. No more.

Following are six conditions shaping the international competitiveness of a country's firms. Each attribute can multiply or undermine the power of the others.[10]

1. Resources (human and physical, capital, infrastructure)

2. Demand (domestic and foreign buyer requirements)

3. Proximity of related industries (especially those that are themselves competitive internationally)

4. Firm strategy, structure, and rivalry (how companies are created and managed)

5. Government policies (see four types outlined in the sidebar on page 315)

6. Discontinuities and chance (inventions, for example, in biotechnology; changing input costs such as oil shocks; surges of demand; stock market crashes)

Thus, a combination of human resources, local tastes, and the proximity factor help explain why high-quality leather goods have been produced in Florence for hundreds of years. In the age of globalization, however, proximity of related firms is less important. World-class firms team with distant partners in pursuit of excellence. Cosmopolitan partners offer each other access to the best and latest concepts. Network membership forces learning. Powerful connections open doors.[11]

Thus, IPE theory has progressed from Smith's absolute advantage to Ricardo's comparative advantage to contemporary ideas of competitive advantage.

10. Michael E. Porter, *The Competitive Advantage of Nations* (New York: Free Press, 1990), chap. 3.

11. Rosabeth Moss Kanter, *World Class: Thriving Locally in the Global Economy* (New York: Simon & Schuster, 1995), 88. This idea is embodied in the reorganized format of the journal *Foreign Policy* that appeared in summer 1997 (no. 107).

Four Ways Government Can Shape a Country's Competitive Advantage

Macroeconomic policy to accumulate factors of production, smooth market operations, and protect the environment. Policy instruments include fiscal and monetary regulations to encourage savings and investment; support for education, research, and development; and penalties for pollution and rewards for use of "clean" fuels.

Compensatory policy to assist those injured or left behind by time and social change, for example, retraining workers.

Industrial policy to protect and promote selected industries such as those vital to security or high employment. Industrial policy may subsidize R&D. It may defend local industry by tariffs or by quantitative limits such as voluntary export restraints accepted by others.

Strategic (or "managed") trade policy to promote exports and gain market share abroad in selected industries.

Should You Buy An International Mutual Fund Now?

Are prediction and prescription complicated? Here were just some of the contradictory messages published in the *Financial Times* on April 23, 1997:

Buy! The International Monetary Fund predicts stronger growth for the world's economies in the year ahead, fueled by the engine of U.S. growth.

No! Faster growth will lead U.S. central banks to raise interest rates to curb inflation. British banks should follow suit.

No! Higher interest rates will curb the growth in private investment in emerging markets.

Buy! European economics ministers are trimming their deficits so their countries can qualify for membership in the European Monetary Union.

No! Pressure for lower deficits will curb any movement to create more jobs and reduce Europe's high levels of unemployment.

Buy! The dollar may gain against foreign currencies. When you travel abroad, it will cost you less to stay in Zermatt.

No! When you sell your foreign funds, valued in Swiss francs, you will get fewer dollars back. Also, Europeans will buy less from the U.S.

Caveat emptor.

What is the bottom line for policy-makers at century's end? Is there an ideal mix of bottom-up and top-down economics? Does the U.S. need the same mix as Japan? Does Europe need its own blend?

COMPARING THEORY AND REALITY: BOTTOM-UP AND TOP-DOWN DEVELOPMENT

How did the West become rich? The *thesis* of classical liberalism holds that political and economic freedom, cultivated in England, unleashed human creativity that produced mutual gain in most of the Western world. But the liberal thesis seems to meet its *antithesis* in a "Japan, Inc." advancing and adapting quickly thanks to government direction. Does Japan's rapid rise mean that a top-down, government-backed "industrial policy" works even better than the bottom-up process esteemed by liberals? In this chapter and the next we examine efforts by the U.S. and other governments to find a *synthesis* that supersedes both the bottom-up and top-down models.

THE LIBERAL THESIS OF ECONOMIC AUTONOMY: IS IT ADEQUATE?

The liberal thesis explains the global ascendancy of the West since 1500 by decentralization of authority, experiment, and responsibility. In con-

Fig. 11.1 Technology to Meet Human Needs Can Be Profitable in a Market Economy

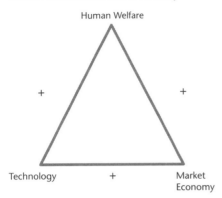

Human Welfare

Technology   +   Market Economy

trast, the centralized regimes of the East—Russia, the Ottoman Empire, China, Japan—enforced an official belief system—even on commerce and weapons development. Lacking any supreme authority, Europe's rival states searched constantly for competitive advantage. Competition sorted out the useful applications of science from the non-useful. Military improvements interacted with technological and commercial advances. A spiral of growth and innovation helped the competitive Western states and their corporations to dominate the globe.[12]

The West grew rich by allowing its economic sector the autonomy to experiment in developing new products, in methods of manufacture, in modes of enterprise organization, in transport and communication, and in capital-labor relations. New market institutions made it possible for innovators to earn high rewards and threatened non-innovators with extinction. Europe's traders jolted consumer tastes with exotic products. Some manufacturers found ways to mass produce and sell goods more cheaply than guilds.[13]

New businesses took many forms. Some were small; some large. Inventors and entrepreneurs needed funding to develop and market their ideas. They were financed in many ways, usually from private sources.

In the West the market served as an experiment linking technology and human welfare. Laissez-faire advanced each of the three variables more effectively than could centralized planning. Figure 11.1 shows how each corner of the triangle boosted the other two. Spurred by the Reformation and the printing press, the spread of literacy was crucial to the growth of democracy, industrialization, and women's liberation. Sweden, the first country to achieve literacy for both sexes, ranked near the top in income and in gender equality at the end of the 20th century.[14]

What does the liberal thesis omit? Many factors other than economic liberalism contributed to the rise of the West—the slow accretion of knowledge and capital over centuries, including science and technology derived from the Islamic and Chinese civilizations; mercantilist and state-sponsored exploration of the New World and its riches; slavery (a source of capital for industry and cheap cotton for textile mills);[15] a strong foundation in agriculture and animal husbandry; protectionist support for infant industries in Britain, the U.S., and Germany; government-sponsored infrastructure development such as the American canals and railroads; government subsidy of agriculture, shipping, and airplane manufacture; and government support for military R&D with spillover benefits for the civilian economy.

12. Rosenberg and Birdzell, *How the West Grew Rich*; and Paul Kennedy, *The Rise and Fall of the Great Powers: Economic Change and Military Conflict from 1500 to 2000* (New York: Random House, 1987).

13. Josiah Wedgwood sold decorated porcelain to the Russian court, but his earthenware pottery transformed the kitchens of the working class in the Industrial Revolution. Wedgwood and a dozen other scientist-inventors belonged to the Lunar Society (so-named because they could ride on wretched roads to meetings held near the full moon). Most were Puritans or Unitarians who believed that the good life is more than material decency; it must be *based* on material decency. J. Bronowski, *The Ascent of Man* (Boston: Little, Brown, 1973), 274–279.

14. Sweden's state church decreed in 1686 that everyone—including children, farm-hands, and maid-servants—should "learn to read and see with their own eyes what God bids and commands in His Holy Word." Most Swedes learned to read within their own families, for there were few schools. By 1740 nearly all Swedes, male and female, could read (but not write)—almost 160 years before general literacy was achieved in England. Egil Johansson, "The History of Literacy in Sweden," in *Literacy and Social Development in the West: A Reader,* ed. Harvey J. Graff (Cambridge: Cambridge University Press, 1981), 151–182 at 157, 180. In 1992 women in Sweden's work force received wages that averaged 90 percent of men's (compared with a 67 percent average in the OECD).

15. Eric Williams, *Capitalism and Slavery* (Chapel Hill: University of North Carolina Press, 1944); also, a book inspired by Williams, Hugh Thomas, *The Slave Trade: The Story of the Atlantic Slave Trade, 1440–1870* (New York: Simon & Schuster, 1997).

Literacy and Economic Growth

Which "came first"—literacy or wealth? Commoners started to read in Europe in the 15th and 16th centuries. Printing presses turned out newspapers and books. Protestant regions such as Sweden and Holland became the most literate and, allowing for resource differentials, more affluent than Catholic regions.

More than half of English men could read by 1760 on the eve of the Industrial Revolution. But New England exceeded Europe in average literacy, because it was settled by literate Europeans. The American rebels in the 1770s could read and think for themselves. Their commerce and cohesion increased with publication of the first newspaper to circulate through the colonies, published by the former printer's apprentice Benjamin Franklin.

The correlation between literacy, wealth, and democracy could be mapped by 1900: The least literate parts of Europe and Russia were among the poorest—and also the least democratic. Authoritarians preferred that their subjects not think for themselves.[1]

For better or worse, literacy also spurred nationalism.

1. Michael Stubbs, *The Social Context of Literacy* (London: Routledge & Kegan Paul, 1986), 82–90, 211–216; and Sidney Pollard, *Peaceful Conquest: The Industrialization of Europe, 1760–1970* (New York: Oxford University Press, 1982), 222, 249, 252.

Many critics challenge the liberal claim that free trade made the West prosperous after World War II. One school holds that free trade was an illusion, because GATT-sponsored tariff reductions did not stop governments from protecting their native industries and farmers with NTBs and subsidies. An opposing school holds that trade liberalization did occur, but that it harmed British and U.S. industry. Free trade, linked to fixed currency exchanges, paralyzed the hegemons while their rivals ascended.

IS JAPAN THE ANTITHESIS OR A VARIANT?

Does East Asia play by rules different from the West? Beginning in the late 19th century, Japan industrialized far more quickly than any Western country. In the 1980s Japan surpassed the USSR as the world's second-largest economy while its per capita income (measured by currency exchanges) exceeded the U.S.'s. Japan accumulated trade surpluses throughout the 1980s while the U.S. trade balance turned negative in 1983 and stayed negative in the 1990s.

Any evaluation of Japanese industrial policy must take into account the fact that Japanese officials saw the economy not just as a means to prosperity but as a platform for national security. Before World War II, Japan's ideology drew upon both mercantilism and militarism. Its slogan was "Rich Nation, Strong Army." After 1945, Japan renounced war but still believed it must master advanced technology, diffuse it, and nurture it. Defense capabilities were embedded in the civilian economy. Japan's post-1945 approach might be called "Rich Nation, Strong Technology."

Four Tests of Industrial Policy Success

A successful "industrial policy" helps an industry grow faster than if left to market forces. Which industries should be encouraged? (1) Industries vital to others—for example, the steel industry, important to automakers; (2) industries with a high value-added per worker; (3) industries with especially good growth potential; and (4) industries targeted for domination by rivals.

The Japanese government promoted the steel industry, even though coal and iron ore had to be imported, helping Japan to become the world's leading steel exporter in the 1970s. But steel met only the first test. It yielded much lower profits than other Japanese manufactures. Japan targeted semiconductors in the mid-1970s and won a large share of the world market. But Japan's semiconductor industry might well have succeeded even without government help. Subsidies were not large, and explicit protection of the Japanese market was removed in the mid-1970s. As with steel, profits were low. But—unlike steel—semiconductors are part of a growing, knowledge-based industry. A delay in shipping semiconductors to the U.S. could keep an American firm from bringing a product to market.[1]

1. Paul R. Krugman and Maurice Obstfeld, *International Economics: Theory and Policy* (New York: HarperCollins, 1991), 274–281.

Japanese firms became world leaders in dual-use (military and civilian) materials and components such as opto-electronics. U.S. science and technology were the stepchildren of the military; in Japan they were its godparents. The U.S. developed two economies—military and civilian; Japan generated a single, integrated economy.[16]

Japan cultivated a strategy of **export-led development**—producing manufactures that win market share abroad and reinvesting the proceeds to cultivate still more economic strength at home. Japan combined industrial policy and strategic trade policy to make its manufactures competitive. This strategy benefited for many years from currency exchange rates that made Japanese products relatively cheaper than U.S. or European.

Critics say that "Japan, Inc." abused free trade—that Japan's Finance Ministry and **Ministry of International Trade and Industry (MITI)** protected Japanese industries and promoted exports to gain control of entire product lines such as semiconductors. Thus, Japan bought two supercomputers from the leading U.S. manufacturer in 1980 and then resisted more purchases while Japanese makers developed their own supercomputers. In 1987 the Nippon Electric Company (NEC) offered a supercomputer to the Massachusetts Institute of Technology for one-third the normal price, which MIT declined after the U.S. Commerce Department threatened to investigate whether Japan was guilty of "dumping"—selling its supercomputers abroad at less than their production price.

Ten years later in August 1997 the U.S. Commerce Department ruled that the NEC had sold its Vector supercomputer at unfair value to the U.S. National Center for Atmospheric Research. The Department imposed anti-dumping duties of 454 percent on the Vector, and duties of 173 percent on Fujitsu supercomputers and more than 300 percent on all other Japanese supercomputers. The duties were expected to shut Japan's leading supercomputer makers out of the U.S. market. NEC spokesmen charged that the U.S. government was closing off its market to outsiders. NEC claimed that its supercomputer needed only eight days to carry out tasks that required one month on a U.S. Cray/C90 machine.

Did Japan's Industrial Policy Succeed?

Other analysts contend that Japan has played by much the same rules as the West but that when the Tokyo government backed some industry (see sidebar) it had very limited success. Had capital been allowed to flow freely to Japan's true strengths, even higher profits might have been real-

16. Richard J. Samuels, *"Rich Nation, Strong Army": National Security and the Technological Transformation of Japan* (Ithaca, N.Y.: Cornell University Press, 1996), 319–321.

Table 11.1 How Important Is Investment in Overall Economic Strength?

Country[a]	Gross Domestic Investment as a Percentage of GDP, 1980	Gross Domestic Investment as a Percentage of GDP, 1995	GDP per Capita, 1995 (in dollars)
India	21	25	340
China	35	40	620
Sri Lanka	34	25	700
South Africa	28	18	3,160
Mexico	27	15	3,320
Brazil	23	22	3,640
Chile	25	27	4,160
Argentina	25	18	8,030
Israel	22	24	15,920
Kuwait	14	12	17,390
Hong Kong	35	35	22,990
U.S.	20	16	26,980
Japan	32	29	39,640
Switzerland	24	23	40,630

SOURCE: Data from World Bank, *World Development Report [WDR] 1997* (New York: Oxford University Press, 1997), Table 13.
   a. Ranked in order of GDP per capita, 1995

Table 11.2 How Important Is Trade in Overall Economic Strength?

Country[a]	Trade as a Percentage of GDP, 1980	Trade as a Percentage of GDP, 1995
India	17	27
China	13	40
Sri Lanka	87	83
South Africa	64	44
Mexico	24	48
Brazil	20	15
Chile	50	54
Argentina	12	16
Israel	91	69
Kuwait	113	104
Hong Kong	181	297
U.S.	21	24
Japan	28	17
Switzerland	77	68

SOURCE: Data from *WDR 1997*, Table 3.
   a. Ranked in order of GDP per capita, 1995.

Table 11.3 How Is Wealth Divided?

Country[a]	Percent Share of Income Of Poorest 20 Percent	Percent Share of Income Of Richest 20 Percent
India	8.5	28.4
China	5.5	30.9
Sri Lanka	8.9	25.2
South Africa	3.3	47.3
Mexico	4.1	39.2
Brazil	2.1	51.3
Chile	3.5	46.1
Argentina	n. a.	n.a.
Israel	6.0	23.5
Kuwait	n. a.	n.a.
Hong Kong	5.4	31.3
U.S.	4.7	25.0
Japan	8.7	22.4
Switzerland	5.2	29.8

SOURCE: Data from *WDR 1997*, Table 5.
   NOTE: Base year not stated, but probably 1995. n. a. = not available.
   a. Ranked in order of GDP per capita, 1995.

ized. One of Japan's great success stories was Honda, run by a maverick who insisted on making autos for export against the advice of MITI.

The main contribution of the Japanese government was macroeconomic—support for education, savings, and investment. For decades the government treated Japan's as a "shortage economy" and rationed both foreign exchange and credit. The government compensated those hurt by social change and retrained displaced workers. As we see in Table 11.1, Japan and several other Asian countries devoted a far higher percentage of GDP to investment than did the U.S. and other representative economies. A high rate of investment, of course, does not assure economic success if other fundamentals are lacking, as in India and Sri Lanka.

Japanese exports in the 1950s and 1960s sold because they were cheap; later they sold because they were superior. Neither price nor quality resulted primarily from government support. Japanese autos and transistor radios acquired their reputation for dependability without any help from MITI. As we see in Table 11.2, however, Japan in the mid 1990s depended less on foreign trade than the U.S. and many other major economies. Hong Kong and Kuwait lived on exports—the former a conduit for Chinese goods, the latter a major oil exporter.

Table 11.3 shows that Japan was also more egalitarian than the U.S. and most other societies whether their incomes were high, as in Switzerland, or low, as in China and Sri Lanka. The absence of data on income distribution in Argentina and Kuwait spoke volumes.

Is Japan Retracing the U.S. Pattern?

Japan's industrialization was mandated from above, but—as in the West—it arose from a decentralized system of land-holding and power sharing. Some leading entrepreneurs in Japan had been samurai warriors. Their behavior in business resembled that of the U.S. "robber barons."

The "catch-up" factor helped Japan. The country that starts from a lower base can shoot up more easily than the leader. A late-comer to industrialization, Japan was like a cross-country skier that follows in another's track. Japan did not take the same risks or invest in untried ideas as Europe and the U.S. had done. Just as U.S. manufacturers improved processes developed in Europe, so Japan improved on those begun in the U.S.

Like the U.S., Japan gained on the front-runner. Both Americans and Japanese did so thanks to their greater efficiency, attention to quality and detail, quick response to new technology, and reinvestment of profits in equipment and plants.[17] Americans visiting Japan in the 1970s and 1980s were struck by the highly motivated work force. Similarly, a British parliamentary study in 1868 noted the clean work places in the U.S., "the care universally bestowed on the comfort of the work people," and workers who "readily produce a new article; understand everything you say to them [and] help the employer by their own acuteness and intelligence."

Lacking comparative advantage in natural endowment, Japan compensated by cultivating its competitive advantage. How much of Japan's excellence came from the top down or the bottom up is in dispute. By 1996, however, all but one of the world's fifteen largest companies were U.S. or Japanese.[18]

THE NEOLIBERAL QUEST FOR SYNTHESIS: THE U.S. IN THE WORLD ECONOMY

Seeking to build U.S. economic strength at home and abroad, President Bill Clinton developed a neoliberal brew of liberalism and neomercantilism. He promoted free trade in tandem with industrial policy and strategic trade. Clinton's "global engagement" also sought to promote development in less developed countries, address environmental degradation, and encourage market reform in the former Soviet empire.

The Clinton Technology Policy

The Clinton administration endorsed an industrial policy that it called "technology policy." It aimed to compensate for "market failure" when private firms do not conduct sufficient research and development.

17. Innovation takes nerve and money. In 1878 the British journal *Engineering* ridiculed Thomas Edison's ideas for an incandescent light for their "most airy ignorance of the fundamental principles both of electricity and dynamics." Edison's ideas, it said, were not for "practical or scientific men."

Andrew Carnegie was then becoming the world's leading steel producer. His secret: high-volume, low-cost manufacturing that exploited the newest technology and sought market share rather than large profits per sale. Smug British steel makers criticized Carnegie's "hard driving" and "scrap and build" policies as wasteful. Carnegie replied: "It is because you keep ... used-up machinery that the United States is making you a back number."

Like some Japanese producers a century later, Carnegie did not have to answer to investors or even to banks. He held more than 50 percent of a limited partnership and was prepared to invest for the long haul. Jean Strouse, "How Economic Empires Are Born," *New York Times*, February 25, 1992, p. A21.

18. Only one was European, Royal Dutch Shell, which placed sixth in size and first in profits. The five largest were General Motors, Ford, Mitsui, Mitsubishi, Itochi; the others were Marubeni, Exxon, Sumitomo, Toyota, Wal-Mart Stores, General Electric, Nissho Iwai, Nippon Telegraph & Telephone, and IBM.

It backed dual-use technologies applicable to commercial as well as military products. Clinton wanted to orient government investment in defense, space, health, and education to strengthen the country's technological base. The Clinton team encouraged private firms to enlarge the information highway within the U.S. and worldwide.

International Trade and Growth: Win-Win

International trade has been an engine of growth. World exports grew at better than 6 percent per year from 1960 through 1995 while world output grew only 3.8 percent yearly. Trade allowed countries to gain from their comparative or competitive advantage.

The Clinton White House embraced "export activism," portraying free trade as a win-win strategy for the U.S. and its partners. The Clinton team claimed that exports led the U.S. economic revival, accounting for nearly four-fifths of the total increase in domestic manufacturing between 1987 and 1993.[19] Clinton in August 1997 said that one-quarter of the country's economic growth in the previous four years came from foreign trade.

Even as the U.S. economy grew, however, the U.S. trade deficit increased, rising to $105 billion in 1995. The imbalance in merchandise trade with Japan rose from $49 billion in 1989 to $60 billion in 1995. The deficit with China also grew. Merchandise trade with the European Union (EU) went from surpluses in 1989–1992 to deficits that reached $13

19. The share of manufactured goods in U.S. exports steadily climbed while that of agriculture, forestry, and mining declined. Aircraft, computers, and office equipment dominated U.S. high technology exports, which totaled $138 billion in 1995. U.S. imports of high technology (mostly electronic products from Asia) amounted to $125 billion in 1995. U.S. Bureau of the Census, *Statistical Abstract of the United States 1996* (Washington, D.C.: Government Printing Office, 1996), Tables 1303 and 1304.

US Government Pushes Asian Nations to Accept Tobacco Exports

DON'T THINK OF IT AS A DEADLY DRUG... ...THINK OF IT AS FREE TRADE.

SENATOR HELMS

DANZIGER
The Christian Science Monitor
Los Angeles Times Syndicate

Free trade can be bad for public health. Even as U.S. authorities sought to limit smoking within the U.S., tobacco interests such as those close to Senator Jesse Helms promoted U.S. tobacco sales abroad. A public health catastrophe awaited many countries as young women joined men in a habit made accessible by rising affluence.

billion by 1995. Why? The Clinton administration explained that Japan and Europe were in the economic doldrums while the U.S. economy expanded. It was natural that Americans would buy from Japan and Europe more than they could sell. Clinton's trade representatives complained, however, that both Japan and China kept out U.S. goods by use of unfair NTBs.

Politics hung heavily over the China trade. From 1989 through 1994 Washington threatened to withdraw MFN status from China unless Beijing improved its human rights practices. Each year Beijing released a few dissidents, and each year its MFN status remained intact. Despite campaign promises that endeared Clinton to the human rights lobby, in 1994 he severed the tie between the MFN designation and China's human rights performance.

Foreign direct investment (FDI) offers a way to take advantage of lower wages abroad and gain access to foreign markets, skirting tariffs, VERs, and NTBs. U.S. businesses invested more overseas in the 1990s but FDI sharply increased in the U.S. By producing in Ohio or Tennessee, Japanese manufacturers could offer their autos directly to U.S. customers. Total FDI in the U.S. in 1994 amounted to more than $3 trillion, while U.S. investments abroad totaled about $2.5 trillion. In 1994 two-thirds of FDI in the U.S. was from Europe; one-fifth, from Japan. FDI concentrated on manufacturing rather than in trade, finance, or petroleum. It produced nearly 5 million U.S. jobs.[20] Japanese investments in the U.S. exceeded U.S. investments in Japan by a ratio of 3 to 1.[21]

What did FDI mean for the U.S. economy? The Clinton team said that it enhanced U.S. competitiveness: Incoming FDI brought new technology and management techniques while outgoing FDI helped U.S. firms to operate abroad. Outgoing FDI cost U.S. workers some low-pay jobs but stimulated other, high-wage jobs at home and abroad.

Mexico, Canada, and the U.S.: Are Free Trade and FDI Win-Win?

How would free trade and greater FDI affect the three North American countries? This question was debated as the **North American Free Trade Agreement (NAFTA)** entered force in 1994. NAFTA established a free-trade area linking the U.S. with its first- and third-largest trading partners, Canada and Mexico.

Arguments for and against NAFTA echoed both north and south of the border, as outlined in Table 11.4. Champions of NAFTA said there would be no "loud sucking sound"—that is, no massive shift of U.S. jobs

20. *Statistical Abstract 1996*, Tables 1288 and 1290.
21. U.S. FDI focused on the UK and Canada. U.S. FDI in tiny Switzerland equaled that in Japan—one measure of how closed Japan was to outsiders. U.S. FDI in Australia was nearly fifteen times more than that in China.

to Mexico. While it was true that U.S. wages in manufacturing exceeded Mexican wages by a ratio of 7 to 1, it was also true that U.S. productivity led Mexico's by a ratio of 8 to 1. This **productivity-compensation balance** differed by industry, as did the cost of relocating whole factories. Manufacturers of heavy trucks and telecommunications equipment would probably choose to stay in the U.S. Makers of clothing and light electronics, on the other hand, might shift to Mexico.[22] Both countries could gain from their comparative advantage.[23] With or without NAFTA, the U.S. would "export" many low-skill jobs.

Before NAFTA, Mexican trade barriers averaged 11 percent on imports compared to the U.S. average of 4 percent. Reducing these barriers could generate more jobs in both countries. Mexicans bought 80 percent of their total imports from the U.S. As more Mexicans received higher wages, they could be expected to buy more U.S. manufactures. Mexico, like Canada, needed the secure access to the U.S. markets that a free trade agreement could provide.[24]

But political considerations rivaled or outweighed economic considerations. Mexican reformers (many with U.S. business degrees) hoped to push-pull Mexico from the Third World into the First. NAFTA could help them succeed with little risk to U.S. interests.[25] Perhaps NAFTA would contribute to democracy as well as to greater prosperity in Mexico. Yet the very day that NAFTA entered force, January 1, 1994, an armed insurrection by Mayan peasants broke out in the state of Chiapas, triggering demands throughout all of Mexico for political and economic reform.[26]

Despite political turmoil in Mexico, trade increased between the three NAFTA economies by 17 percent in 1994. U.S. exports to Canada and Mexico grew much faster than exports to other regions.

President Clinton praised NAFTA as a step toward free trade worldwide. Both U.S. and Latin American officials talked of expanding NAFTA southward, beginning with Chile. But Asians and Europeans feared that NAFTA would reduce their market share in North America. *The Times* (London) accused Clinton of hypocrisy—talking global free trade but working for bilateral and regional deals subject to U.S. domination. Singapore's prime minister in 1994 requested his country's admission to NAFTA. An editorial in the *Far Eastern Economic Review* (June 2, 1994) challenged NAFTA to break from the exclusionary pattern of the EU and admit any country willing to play by its rules. Otherwise, the editorial warned, the world might split into three trading blocs—European, North American, and Asian.

Terms of NAFTA

NAFTA dismantled tariffs on most industrial goods immediately, though trade barriers on some manufactures and agricultural commodities would remain for five to fifteen years. NAFTA included special agreements on services, investment, and intellectual property rights. One effect was that U.S. investors could own and operate firms on the same basis as Mexicans in Mexico and Canadians in Canada. Washington won side agreements to improve environmental protection and labor conditions in Mexico and to deal with possible import surges: If explosive trade growth threatens a domestic industry, a special committee can recommend treaty revisions.

22. In 1993 German automakers BMW and Mercedes-Benz decided to build assembly plants in South Carolina and Alabama—not in Mexico.

23. Gary C. Hufbauer and Jeffrey J. Schott, *NAFTA: An Assessment*, rev. ed. (Washington, D.C.: Institute for International Economics, 1993).

24. Gilbert R. Winham, "NAFTA and the Trade Policy Revolution of the 1980s: A Canadian Perspective," *International Journal* 49, no. 3 (summer 1994): 472–508 at 478 ff.

25. Paul Krugman, "The Uncomfortable Truth About NAFTA: It's Foreign Policy, Stupid," *Foreign Affairs* 72, no. 5 (November–December 1993): 13–19.

26. The rebels, led by several intellectuals, demanded not just land and social benefits for themselves but democracy for all Mexicans. With the local bishop as mediator, the central government promised to meet most rebel demands. Meanwhile the ruling party's candidate in the next presidential elections was assassinated. The peso and Mexican stocks fell sharply—caveat gringo investors hoping for big returns.

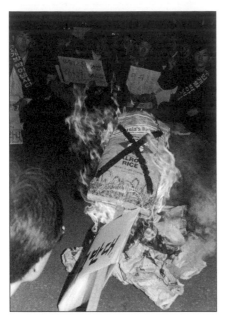

Many countries seek self-sufficiency in basics such as food, but pursuit of this goal can conflict with free trade. Pride as well as economics is at stake. Here, South Korean demonstrators in 1991 burn California rice and other foreign goods.

All calculations as to NAFTA's economic effect were thrown off by a financial crisis in Mexico in January 1995 following a steep devaluation of the peso in December 1994. Mexico's output fell 7 percent in 1995, but the Clinton administration arranged a $50 billion rescue plan with the IMF that quickly stabilized the peso.

Unlike the 1982 peso crisis, when Mexico's import duties rose to 100 percent in an attempt to stabilize the economy, in 1995 NAFTA protected U.S. exporters from increased tariff rates. NAFTA helped shield thousands of U.S. jobs that might have been lost if Mexican tariffs had dramatically increased.

By 1997 the three-way trade of $348 billion represented nearly $1,000 in trade for each of NAFTA's 380 million consumers. Trade between the three partners increased somewhat faster than before the accord. Still, both optimistic and pessimistic forecasts for NAFTA fell short. In 1995–1996 U.S. exports to Canada increased by 26 percent and to Mexico by 11 percent (despite the 1995 financial crisis). Few job losses or gains could be traced to NAFTA. Some other consequences are noted in the following sidebar.

Synergy, Serendipity, and Spillover

Besides trade and jobs, NAFTA had other effects. Mexico tightened environmental protection while NAFTA was being negotiated and kept the controls in place despite the 1995 financial crisis. The U.S.-Mexican border region flourished in 1996 as a kind of "fourth member of NAFTA." With 20 million inhabitants and $100 billion in cross-border trade, the area witnessed 225 million legal frontier crossings each way, mostly Mexican shoppers who spent $22 billion in the U.S. Mexicans re-examined their national identity. More Mexican women joined the labor force, usually at low wages.[1]

Movement toward democracy and clean government in Mexico disappointed liberals on both sides of the border. High-level political assassinations and involvement in drug-trafficking continued or got worse in the mid-1990s. Peaceful Mayan Indians were massacred in Chiapas in 1997 by persons thought to be close to the local government.

1. Bryan W. Husted, "The Impact of NAFTA on Mexico's Environmental Policy," *Growth and Change* 28, no. 1 (winter 1997): 24 ff.; Anthony DePalma, "NAFTA Environmental Lags May Delay Free Trade Expansion," *New York Times,* May 21, 1997, A4; Timothy C. Brown, "The Fourth Member of NAFTA: The U.S.-Mexico Border," *Annals of the American Academy of Political and Social Science* 550 (March 1997): 105 ff.; Isidro Morales Moreno, "Mexico's National Identity After NAFTA," *American Behavioral Scientist* 40, no. 7 (June–July 1997); and Ann K. Nauman, "The Integration of Women into the Mexican Labor Force Since NAFTA," ibid. See also Jon Jeter, "Midwest Cities Turn NAFTA to Their Advantage," *Washington Post,* November 29, 1997, A6. See also David R. D'avila Villers, ed., *NAFTA, The First Year: A View from Mexico* (Lanham, Md.: University Press of America, 1996).

Table 11.4 Possible Gains and Losses Under NAFTA

Arguments For NAFTA	Arguments Against NAFTA
1. Generates economic growth and trade for all three countries	1. Cannot add much to Canadian or U.S. economic growth, because Mexican GDP is small—equivalent to another "Ohio"
2. Creates jobs on both sides of the border; reduces emigration pressures within Mexico	2. U.S. labor unions worry that jobs and investment capital will go south
3. Promotes Mexican expansion led by exports	3. Cheap imports are bad for workers in the U.S. and Canada
4. Encourages U.S. and Canadian investment in Mexico	4. Some Mexicans worry about loss of identity through McDonaldization; some Mexican industrialists want protection from competition
5. Improves bilateral ties and helps promote stable democracy in Mexico	5. It is wrong to treat Mexico as a democracy when it is still authoritarian
6. Improves environmental protection	6. Environmental rules lack enforcement mechanisms

Strategic Trade: Clinton's National Export Strategy

In 1993 President Clinton announced a National Export Strategy to promote exports. The administration acted on four fronts:

1. To reduce controls on high-technology products such as advanced computers and telephone base switching equipment long banned for export to Communist rivals and Third World states seeking nuclear arms;[27]

2. To consolidate all federal export promotion services to facilitate "one-stop shopping";[28]

3. To establish an interagency "Advocacy Network" in the Department of Commerce in behalf of U.S. firms; and

4. To combat the "tied aid" practices of other countries by backing U.S. companies seeking to participate in activities funded by the World Bank (in which the U.S. was the largest player).

Each step had sweeping ramifications for IR. The first move came in March 1994 with the dissolution of "CoCom"—the West's Coordinating Committee on Multilateral Export Controls, which since 1949 had limited technology transfers to Communist countries. Those in favor of lifting controls said that the Cold War was over, that technology spread was inexorable, and that existing restrictions hurt export of U.S. supercomputers. Critics said that dropping export controls was short-sighted, because security interests should override export profits.[29] In 1997 critics pointed to evidence that China had diverted a supercomputer purchased by a Hong Kong firm to a military research institute in Hunan province.

27. AT&T could now bid for $40 billion in phone equipment orders from China.

28. Some information cited here was received by fax within minutes of phoning the U.S. Trade Promotion Coordinating Committee at the Department of Commerce toll-free at 1-800-USA-TRADE and punching document numbers on a menu.

29. Gary Milhollin, director of the Wisconsin Project on Nuclear Arms Control, stated: "The happiest people in the world tonight" are the nuclear bomb and missile makers in "Pakistan, India and North Korea, because they can now obtain, through front companies, computer power that previously was beyond their wildest dreams."

Critics of NAFTA feared a "loud sucking sound" as Canadian and U.S. jobs moved south. Supporters hoped that free trade would boost employment in all three countries. Some U.S. firms established *maquiladora* operations in Mexico—export-processing plants that took advantage of low-wage labor (often female) and proximity to the U.S. border. The costs of complying with environmental and other regulations were also less in Mexico. Despite difficult working conditions, many Mexicans welcomed the regular wages of the *maquiladora* shops.

30. In May 1994 Saudi Arabia gave a $4 billion contract—the biggest telecommunications contract in history—to AT&T after visits to Riyadh by Clinton's Secretary of State and Secretary of Commerce and a Clinton letter to King Fahd. A Canadian and a Swedish firm claimed to have underbid AT&T.

31. Henry R. Nau, *Trade and Security: U.S. Policy at Cross-Purposes* (Washington, D.C.: AEI Press, 1995).

32. Robert B. Reich, *The Work of Nations: Preparing Ourselves for 21st Century Capitalism* (New York: Knopf, 1991).

Why the Competitiveness Obsession?

Did governments worry excessively about the "competitive advantage of nations"?[1] Perhaps the U.S. and Japan were not like Coke and Pepsi—fighting for market share. No major country was like a firm that might "go under." A trade deficit could be interpreted as a sign of strength. If the U.S. trade deficit widened with Japan, it might narrow elsewhere. In any event the U.S. trade deficit was small compared to GDP and virtually invisible next to assets.

Imports from Japan could benefit Western consumers and provide lessons for European and U.S. manufacturers. An industry survey in 1997 revealed that British automakers using Japanese methods had become far more efficient than German or other continental manufacturers.

1. Paul Krugman, "Competitiveness: A Dangerous Obsession," *Foreign Affairs* 73, no. 2 (March–April 1994): 28–44; for criticism and Krugman's reply, see *Foreign Affairs* 73, no. 4 (July–August 1994): 186–203.

The second and third steps made the president into a hawker. He became "CEO, USA" or "Uncle Sam, salesman," taking credit for persuading Saudi Arabia to buy Boeing planes and an AT&T phone system rather than European models. Europeans complained that Washington used political muscle to exclude economic competitors.[30] Some critics argued that Clinton could not have it both ways—free trade *and* strategic trade. Others accused Clinton of ignoring Saudi human rights abuses while harping on Chinese abuse of political prisoners.

A truly strategic trade policy would seek to enhance long-range strategic interests—not business profits. Professor Henry Nau argued that Clinton gave minimal attention to democratic reforms in the former Second World and to halting the spread of dangerous technologies. Instead, the president focused on economic security defined as high-wage jobs and access to foreign markets for U.S. firms. But which was more strategic—access to Japanese car markets or close partnership with Tokyo to deal with North Korea? Geopolitics and military security are, at bottom, more essential to survival than geoeconomics or trade balances.[31]

Technology policy and strategic trade may create more well-paid jobs. But many Americans would need better training to qualify for these positions. The best jobs are taken by "symbolic analysts"—persons who generate and analyze the data and concepts of high technology and global business.[32] IBM's chairman reported in 1994 that U.S. firms were spending $30 billion a year for worker training and losing $25–30 billion as a result of worker illiteracy.[33] In IPE, as in personal life, most problems begin at home.

Most U.S. economic and social problems were "made in the USA"—not the result of foreign wiles. If the U.S. lacked "competitiveness," Americans could blame it on their low rates of savings and investment. Both Democrats and Republicans were loath to raise taxes, cap entitlement spending, or cut defense outlays. The upshot was predictable—crumbling infrastructure; less research; fewer social services; less fitness.

Multilateral Trade: GATT and the World Trade Organization

As noted earlier, the General Agreement on Tariffs and Trade was established after World War II to reduce barriers to international trade. By the early 1990s GATT participants (125 countries) generated 85 percent of world trade. But the U.S. and many other governments wanted a stronger forum. A protracted multilateral negotiation (the "Uruguay Round") produced an agreement in 1993 to replace GATT with a **World Trade Organization (WTO)**. The WTO became a full-fledged international governmental organization, not a mere coordinating secretariat. The WTO's top decision-making forum is a semi-annual ministerial meeting intended to give it more political clout than GATT. The WTO's credibility as an effective fair-trade policeman depends on its dispute settlement system. The WTO had stronger, clearer rules than GATT that applied not just to manufactures but to agricultural commodities and some services such as accountancy.[34] These rules would be enforced by a semi-judicial disputes procedure. Departing from GATT practice, reports by independent panels are automatically adopted by the WTO unless a consensus opposes them. Countries that have had complaints lodged against them may appeal to an appellate body, but its verdict is binding. Thus, WTO members cannot block adverse findings as they could under GATT. If offenders do not comply with panel recommendations, trading partners may claim compensation or, as a last resort, impose tit-for-tat sanctions.

Many members of Congress opposed the WTO because, they said, it challenged U.S. sovereignty, would raise the U.S. deficit by eliminating tariff revenues, would forbid subsidies important to U.S. farmers, and did little to protect intellectual property or promote free trade in services. Environmentalists worried that the U.S. would have to lower its protective standards (for example, barriers to imported tuna caught by methods that trapped dolphins) because the WTO might regard them as ob-

33. The future looked dim. The National Association of Manufacturers reported that 30 percent of companies said they could not reorganize work because employees could not learn new jobs; another 25 percent said that they could not upgrade products because employees could not learn the necessary skills. Louis V. Gerstner, Jr., "Our Schools Are Failing, Do We Care?" *The New York Times,* May 27, 1994, A27.

34. But many services were omitted. U.S. insurance companies and the American Express Company said that they had been let down by U.S. negotiators; Hollywood said that the new regime did nothing to ease access to French theaters and television screens.

How Can the EU Object to the Merger of Two U.S. Firms?

In 1989 the EU declared its approval necessary for any merger of companies with a combined worldwide turnover of 2.5 billion European Currency Units (ecus)—about $2.7 billion—and a combined European turnover of 100 million ecus.[1] It does not matter where the firms are based. If the EU decides that a merger is not "compatible with the common market," the EU can block it. Also, in 1992 the EU and U.S. agreed to limit government R&D subsidies for civilian aircraft.

By its own rules the EU could fine Boeing 10 percent of its worldwide earnings, beginning with any Boeing assets in Europe. President Clinton hinted in July 1997 that the U.S. might reply in kind—perhaps confiscating any Airbus properties in the U.S.

Both the EU and the U.S. claimed to support free trade and to oppose monopolies. In the 1990s the EU usually allowed the U.S. Federal Trade Commission to decide U.S. merger cases and vice versa. So it was unusual but not unprecedented for the EU to protest the Boeing-MDC merger because it had already been approved by the FTC. Earlier, however, the FTC had imposed tough conditions on the merger of two Swiss pharmaceutical companies.

1. The ecu is the international unit of account created for the European Monetary System (EMS), used to denote EMS debts and credits. *The Economist* (March 5, 1988) suggested giving the ecu a different name, the Monnet (for Jean Monnet, a founder of European unity).

stacles to free trade. The Clinton administration replied that the WTO did not threaten U.S. sovereignty. Each country retains the right to make and implement its policy regardless of WTO rulings. Still, U.S. interests benefit from a rule-based regime for international trade.[35]

Advocates hoped that liberalized trade under the WTO would generate more than $270 billion annually in extra world income just from manufactured goods. More trade would mean higher revenues from tax income—not tariffs. The U.S. Department of Commerce hoped that the WTO regime would boost U.S. GDP by 1.5 to 3 percent annually. DRI/McGraw-Hill estimated that trade liberalization would generate 1.4 million jobs (most of them well paid) over ten years.

U.S. Inc. and Europe Inc.

Life isn't fair. Aviation in the U.S. benefited from two world wars and the Cold War. Washington subsidized R&D and mass production of advanced war planes, many sold overseas as well as to the Pentagon. Military R&D and assembly techniques transferred readily to civilian aircraft manufacture. Unlike Europeans, U.S. manufacturers could count on a huge home market. They worked closely with U.S. carriers such as Pan American and TWA that had pioneered world routes. The industry was spiced by flamboyant entrepreneurs and visionaries.[36]

It takes more than subsidies to spawn a world-class industry. Despite government funding, the USSR never produced world-class civilian planes. Soviet engineers built interceptors, satellites, and missiles but lacked any drive to please civilian consumers. Their forte was rugged machinery for hard power.

European aircraft producers found it hard to catch up with the U.S. They had less money than Americans to invest in the 1950s and 1960s, and faced a welter of conflicting demands. Each government favored its own manufacturers and its own flag carrier such as Air France.

Could Europeans skip to the next stage? The British and French governments decided to bolster a strategic industry by co-producing a supersonic transport (SST), the Concorde. Since the U.S. Congress refused to subsidize a similar plane, Britain and France found a niche. Rather than invest in an SST, Boeing built a jumbo jet, the 747. The Concorde was the West's only SST—glamorous but costly. It consumed three times as much fuel per passenger as a Boeing 747. Because any SST generates sonic boom, the Concorde won few overland routes. It earned more glory than profit.

35. Clinton also warned, however, that the U.S. might raise tariffs against violators of intellectual property rights not protected by the WTO.

36. William E. Boeing built his first seaplane next to a lake in Seattle just ten years after the Wright Brothers' first flight.

France and Britain, later joined by Germany and Spain, targeted another niche: They would co-produce a wide-bodied "Airbus" well suited for shorter hauls. The idea was sound but the organization poor. It was a consortium that assigned tasks by quota: Aérospatiale and British Aerospace got the largest jobs because their governments each owned 30 percent of the business; Germany's Daimler-Benz Aerospace and Spain's CASA received fewer jobs—20 percent and 10 percent, respectively.[37]

The Airbus took off only because governments poured some $10 billion into its development and subsidized its early operations. In 1978 the White House called "foul" and threatened to impose anti-dumping duties on Airbus aircraft ordered by Eastern Airlines. To ward off such action, the Europeans agreed in the 1979 GATT treaty to ban uneconomic pricing for airliners. In 1992, as Airbus gained still more market share, an EU-U.S. agreement restricted "launch aid"—the money invested in new models—to one-third of total development costs and required that this sum plus interest be repaid within seventeen years.

The 1992 agreement ended most disputes over existing aircraft but left open the question of who would build a super-jumbo jet capable of flying 550 to 800 passengers over oceans. Boeing proposed joint development with Airbus. By 1995, however, the two sides concluded they could not work together. The European consortium decided to proceed with its own plans for a super-jumbo; Boeing opted merely to enlarge the 747.

All this set the stage for the EU clash with Boeing in 1997 over its proposed merger with MDC. EU Commissioner for Competition **Karel Van Miert** faced all the issues outlined on the first page of this chapter.[38] He opted to fight the merger, taking Europe to the brink of a trade war with the U.S.[39] Van Miert said he was defending "competition," but most observers saw his action as strategic industrial policy writ large. Nonetheless, Boeing backed down and made sufficient concessions to win grudging EU approval for a merger with MDC.

The civil aircraft industry is heavily politicized and closely tied to the defense industry. Airplanes are a major U.S. export. Without them, the trade imbalance would be much larger. Americans buy shirts, cars, and TVs from Asia, but they export airplanes and other high-technology items, along with food and financial services. President Clinton and French President Jacques Chirac became aircraft salesmen. When Saudi Arabia thought of buying planes from Europe, President Clinton got on the phone and reminded King Fahd of who saved his country from Iraq and Iran. The phone call was worth $6 billion in orders for Boeing and

37. For reportage and analysis, see *The Economist, Aviation Week & Space Technology,* and *Europe.* For background, see Lynn Matthew, *Birds of Prey: Boeing vs. Airbus, A Battle for the Skies,* rev. ed. (New York: Four Walls Eight Windows, 1997).

38. The place of the Commission in the overall structure of the European Union is discussed in Chapter 15.

39. The EU's fifteen member-states are consulted on merger regulation but have no formal say in the final Commission decision. The member-states presented a united front though individual states wavered, fearing a knock-down effect on other industries if a trade war erupted. Philip Lawrence and other academic specialists from the UK, Italy, and Germany urged the Commission to block the merger. See "Europe Must Fight US Air Threat," *The Independent,* July 18, 1997.

MDC. In this same spirit, President Chirac persuaded China to buy some Airbus products, if only because France muffled Western complaints about human rights in China.

Van Miert argued that a Boeing-MDC merger would give Boeing the benefit of extensive R&D at MDC paid for by the U.S. Defense Department. He complained also that recently signed exclusivity deals between Boeing and three U.S. airlines would keep Airbus from offering them its super-jumbo for the next twenty years.[40] Boeing made concessions on each point. Boeing would acquire MDC, but agreed to license any patents derived from MDC defense contracts. Second, Boeing would not enforce its exclusivity contracts.

Were these concessions substantial? Chirac and a French commissioner at the EU responded with a resounding *non*. They said the concessions were merely cosmetic and demanded that the EU monitor Boeing's compliance carefully.

Meanwhile, Airbus signed up more than twice as many new orders as Boeing at the 1997 Paris Air Show. And it pressed ahead to introduce a 550-seat plane, the world's largest, by 2003. Boeing, however, made a big splash at the 1997 Moscow Air Show where it exhibited its "Next-Generation" 737-700. Having restrained Boeing, Commissioner Van Miert next took aim at a budding alliance of British Airways and American Airlines.

The bidding never stopped. Lockheed Martin merged with Northrop Grumman and prepared to take on Boeing-MDC in a competition to build the Joint Strike Fighter for the U.S. Air Force and Navy and Britain's Royal Navy. With an estimated worth of at least $210 billion over twenty years, the contract could redefine the industry. British Aerospace was hoping to join Lockheed's bid while Lockheed considered contributing to the proposed Airbus super-jumbo.

WHAT PROPOSITIONS HOLD? WHAT QUESTIONS REMAIN?

ROADS TO WEALTH

Adam Smith was correct. The material wealth of nations lies in their productive capacity rather than their gold hoard. The most productive nations have followed the path laid out by Smith and Ricardo—modified by Keynes. No system has met human needs better than the mixed market–welfare states pioneered in the West. They score higher in measures such as GDP, PPP, and HDI. The average First World citizen lives

40. American Airlines, Delta, and Continental had recently agreed to buy all their planes from Boeing for the next twenty years.

Table 11.5 Why Economies Stagnate, Prosper, or Decline: Three Perspectives

Trend	Top-Down Neomercantilism	Bottom-Up Laissez-Faire and Free Trade	Neoliberal Synthesis
Stagnation	Weak government, poor resources	Excessive government obstructs comparative advantage	Failure to develop competitive advantage
Prosperity	Value-claiming by a strong, "can-do" government that uses industrial policy and strategic trade to limit FDI and achieve a favorable trade balance	Minimalist government that gives a free hand to free enterprise and free trade, in cooperation with WTO, to achieve a high rate of GDP growth	Competitive advantage by wise macroeconomic and technology policies; support for freer trade, combined with NTBs and VERs, conduce to economic growth, competitiveness, and high HDI
Decline	Exhaustion of raw materials or other key inputs; excessive foreign ownership; low barriers to dumping and cheap foreign products, permitting trade deficit and loss of market share	Excessive value-claiming and emphasis on profits, aggravated by excessive defense spending, lead to a low rate of GDP growth	Failure to maintain competitive advantage by effective macro-economic, technology, and trade policies reduces economic growth, market share, and HDI

not "like a king," but better and longer than royalty of past centuries, with central heating, plumbing, a diversified diet, easy access to information and communication, and good health care. Three roads to wealth dominated IPE analysis at the end of the 20th century. The assumptions of each school are summarized in Table 11.5. The fourth alternative, state socialism, had few government backers except in Havana and Pyongyang.

Is there an ideal admixture of government intervention with the market? No formula fits all times and places.

Neomercantilists point to Japan and to the U.S.-European airplane rivalry to argue the need for top-down guidance and industrial policy. Neomercantilists value a favorable trade balance as a way to obtain political as well as economic aims. States with trade surpluses are seen as winners; those with trade deficits, as losers. Taiwan, with the world's largest currency reserves per capita in the 1990s, had more options than Argentina, heavily in debt.

Laissez-faire liberals observe that a favorable trade balance does not necessarily mean that a country "wins." Ordinary Japanese would have a higher living standard if they had access to more foreign products, less costly than home grown, and Tokyo would have less friction with Washington.

Liberals concede that government intervention might be needed in some domains, for example, air traffic control. In most economic spheres, they say, the government is not needed and may do more harm than good. MITI plays at best a supporting role in the Japanese economic miracle. Japan's economic success derives mainly from cultural values—dedi-

cation to education, discipline, a perfectionist work ethic—combined
with high rates of saving and investment. To crack the Japanese market
Americans need to learn the Japanese language and adapt. It took years,
for example, before U.S. auto exporters put steering columns on the right-
hand side. If Americans became more creative, their trade balance would
take care of itself.

The liberal holds that economic success comes not from claiming,
hoarding, or redistributing wealth but from creating values useful to others. In IPE, as in IR generally, the same principle applies: Mutual gain
policies, if followed by each party, enhance the interests of each better
than exploitative value-claiming.

The Clinton White House sought a synthesis by using technology policy and strategic trade to help U.S. industries become more competitive.
But budget-cutting pressures led the White House to do things on the
cheap, for example, cutting back money for welfare, education, and research; promoting U.S. aircraft sales by overseas phone calls; pressuring
new NATO members to buy U.S. weapons; and lifting a ban on U.S. military aircraft sales to Latin America. Here was "government-lite," as one
commentator put it.

IS WIN-WIN POSSIBLE?

It requires an act of faith to trust that an invisible hand will guide all
actors to greater prosperity if each pursues its private good and practices
free trade. If Saudi Arabia buys a 737 or 747 rather than an Airbus, the
near-term and long-term benefits accrue to Boeing, Washington, and
U.S. taxpayers. Saudi Arabia may become locked into its Boeing connec-
tion, depriving Europe of markets and capital for future R&D.

The Boeing-Airbus case highlights the importance of strategic, knowledge-based industries in economic transformation. It suggests that the
ideals of free trade and free competition without government intervention are unattainable in certain industries. It also shows how hard it is for
any country to come from behind in aviation.

Air frames are a strategic industry. Any country that buys its aircraft
from one supplier is hostage to it for spare parts and improved models.
China bought its first Boeing 707s in 1972, immediately after President
Nixon's visit to Mao Zedong. Unwilling then to count on U.S. good will,
Beijing purchased extra planes to cannibalize for parts. By the 1990s mutual trust had deepened so that Boeing operated one of its three largest
overseas centers for spare parts at the Beijing Capital Airport. Boeing sta-

tioned field representatives in eighteen cities throughout China. Leery of dependency, however, China and other countries bought Airbus as well as Boeing products.

The Boeing-Airbus rivalry underscores how global markets can heighten mutual vulnerability. If the two companies had worked together to produce a super-jumbo, there might have been mutual benefit. If only one tries, it alone assumes the risks and possible gains.

The Boeing-Airbus case forces us to look again at mutual gain. Is economic competition zero-sum? Can it be positive-sum? Europe and the U.S., and their aviation industries, wanted to avoid a trade war if only because the two sides needed each other for many reasons. A trade war over aircraft would have inflicted much collateral damage on other businesses and consumers not connected to either Airbus or Boeing.

There were winners abroad as well as in the U.S. when the EU approved the Boeing-MDC merger. Many European firms—Rolls-Royce, GEC-Marconi, Smiths Industries, Snecma, Messier-Dowty—supplied components to Boeing and did not want a trade war. Also, Europeans could benefit when Boeing licensed the results of military research done by MDC.

Both German and Japanese firms had used licenses to co-produce as strategic ladders to advanced aviation technology. Japanese firms succeeded without really flying. They mastered design and integration skills as well as materials to produce major components for U.S. and European aircraft. They often applied the knowledge they had learned from one foreign partner when working with another. Thus, Kawasaki Heavy Industries developed a tool for Airbus from its commercial experiences with Boeing, enabling Airbus to perform tasks it had previously been unable to perform.[41]

For all their relative wealth, European and U.S. manufacturers sought to collaborate with other aerospace firms. In 1997 Airbus planned to create a new 100-seat regional airplane with Chinese and Singaporean aircraft companies. SeaLaunch, a project to launch commercial satellites at sea, combined Norwegian platforms and Ukrainian boosters with Boeing's integrative planning. The first element of the International Space Station was built by a Russian firm under subcontract to Boeing. Boeing was collaborating with other Russian firms to conduct supersonic flights and develop new titanium alloys. By 1997 China had supplied major parts for two thousand Boeing planes and helped design the 737-700 empennage. Know-how, risks, and potential profits were being shared.

41. Samuels, *"Rich Nation, Strong Army,"* 265–266.

Memo to the EU Commission:

Europe is the world's largest market of well-educated, affluent persons. Europeans can compete in nearly any domain. In 1997 several European firms beat out U.S. competitors to build turbines for China's Three Gorges Dam. But to enjoy competitive advantage Europeans must cooperate more with each other. If Boeing and MDC gained strength from merging, why should the components of Airbus Industrie continue to exist independently as costly symbols of national grandeur? We must give up any idea of keeping Airbus Industrie as a consortium of national firms and convert it into a normal, unified business. We must utilize a single currency and master a single language such as English, or become proficient in several European tongues. We must eliminate the festering sore of large-scale unemployment.

IS CAPITALISM DOOMED?

Communism has expired, but will Lenin have the last laugh? He predicted that capitalism will destroy itself. First, by exporting capital to less developed countries, capitalists will give them the means to rival the West. Second, Western capitalists will eventually fight one another over market share. Lenin did not think, as Kant did, that representative democracy would promote trade and stem war.

Lenin's first point gained plausibility with the spread of technology. Many technological breakthroughs occurred in North America, but Japanese, Chinese, and other Asians quickly mastered the know-how and used it to generate competitive advantage.

Lenin's second point has been given a new twist by Benjamin C. Schwarz. He warns that capitalism is doomed because economic imperatives conflict with *realpolitik*. Capitalism thrives on free flows of labor, technology, and money. But each state wants greater wealth and power; each wants to sell, grow, and possess more. Unless the U.S. stands head and shoulders above all rivals combined, movement toward global integration will be reversed. But this kind of hegemony cannot last. Sooner or later, others—perhaps Europe, Japan, or China—will challenge the hegemon.[42]

If Clinton's neoliberal assumptions are correct, international trade can be win-win. Realists and neomercantilists, however, worry that some states will win more than others.

42. Benjamin C. Schwarz, "Is Capitalism Doomed?" *New York Times,* May 23, 1994, A15. For a different tack, see Judith Goldstein, *Ideas, Interests, and American Trade Policy* (Ithaca, N.Y.: Cornell University Press, 1993), chap. 6.

TODAY'S "INVISIBLE HAND"

DANZIGER
The Christian Science Monitor
Los Angeles Times Syndicate

Will an "invisible hand" help the billion or more persons living in poverty today? Some economists argue that handouts retard development. Others contend that aid is necessary for those bypassed by modernization.

Who is right—Lenin, Kant, Schwarz, Clinton? We have no sure answers, but will gather more ingredients for a reply as we examine the dilemmas of development and ecopolitics (Chapters 13 and 14) and prospects for collective security and human rights (Chapters 15 and 16).

KEY NAMES AND TERMS

absolute advantage
Bretton Woods system
comparative advantage
competitive advantage
capitalism
economic liberalism
export-led development
foreign direct investment (FDI)
free trade
General Agreement on Tariffs and Trade (GATT)

industrial policy
International Monetary Fund (IMF)
laissez-faire
less developed countries (LDCs)
mercantilism
most-favored nations (MFN)
Ministry of International Trade and Industry (MITI)
neoliberalism
neomercantilism
non-tariff barriers (NTBs)

North American Free Trade Agreement (NAFTA)
productivity-compensation balance
rule-based trading regime
Adam Smith
socialism
strategic trade
Karel Van Miert
voluntary export restraints (VERs)
World Bank
World Trade Organization (WTO)

QUESTIONS TO DISCUSS

1. How adequately does the liberal thesis account for the rise of the First World? How important were resources extracted from the New World and capital derived from the slave trade?
2. What benefits did Josiah Wedgwood and Benjamin Franklin enjoy that might not have existed for a pragmatic scientist in 18th-century China? Mao Zedong's China? China in the 1990s?
3. If government subsidies helped McDonnell Douglas and Boeing, why didn't they get better results in the USSR?
4. If female literacy and liberation helped Sweden, why do so many women stay at home in equally prosperous Japan and Switzerland?
5. Study Table 11.1. Does domestic investment correlate with overall economic strength? Explain your answer.
6. Study Table 11.2. Do high levels of foreign trade correlate with overall economic strength? Explain your answer.
7. Study Table 11.3. Is wealth more polarized in high-income countries than in low-income countries? Explain your answer.
8. Is NAFTA good for Mexicans? If yes, why? Is it good for Canadians?
9. Are regional trade organizations good or bad for world trade?
10. Does the rivalry of Airbus and Boeing differ from that of Portugal and Holland in the Age of Exploration?
11. Should governments trust in an "invisible hand"? Should they worry about the country's trade balance?
12. Should anyone care where an idea or product originated if we are all part of one global village?

RECOMMENDED RESOURCES

BOOKS

Bhagwati, Jagdish. *The World Trading System at Risk.* Princeton, N.J.: Princeton University Press, 1991.

Brams, Steven J., and Alan D. Taylor, *Fair Division: From Cake-Cutting to Dispute Resolution.* Cambridge: Cambridge University Press, 1996.

Crane, George T., and Abla Amawi, eds. *The Theoretical Evolution of International Political Economy.* New York: Oxford University Press, 1991.

Crosby, Alfred W. *Ecological Imperialism: The Biological Expansion of Europe, 900–1900.* Cambridge: Cambridge University Press, 1986.

Gilpin, Robert. *The Political Economy of International Relations.* Princeton, N.J.: Princeton University Press, 1987.

McClelland, David C. *The Achieving Society.* Princeton, N.J.: D. Van Nostrand, 1961.

Schwartz, Herman M. *States versus Markets: History, Geography, and the Development of the International Political Economy.* New York: St. Martin's, 1994.

Smith, Adam. *The Wealth of Nations* [1776]. New York: Modern Library, 1937.

WEB SITES

Chiapas Rebellion
    http://nt1.ids.ac.uk/cgi-bin/dbtcgi.exe
International Trade Administration
    http://www.ita.doc.gov
NAFTA/Foreign Trade Information System
    http://www.sice.oas.org/
NAFTA text
    http://the-tech.mit.edu/Bulletins/nafta.html
World Bank Group
    http://www.worldbank.org
World Trade Organization
    http://www.wto.org
U.S. Trade Representative
    http://www.ustr.gov/

C H A P T E R T W E L V E

CHALLENGES OF DEVELOPMENT: SOUTH MEETS NORTH

THE BIG QUESTIONS IN CHAPTER 12

- How poor is poor? What share of humanity lives in poverty? Where are they?

- Why are the poor poor? Do the reasons lie abroad or at home?

- To stimulate economic growth, is it more useful to raise the incomes of men or of women?

- Why are 100 million women missing in Asia?

- Is there such a thing as the "happy native," content without industry?

- Isn't it better to be self-sufficient than to depend on trade with others?

- Was there an East Asian miracle? How could Asia's "little Tigers" develop so rapidly despite their poor resource base?

- Does the Tiger model offer lessons for South Asia or Africa?

- Was it wise for Malaysia to press for an end to currency trading?

- What is the most cost-effective spur to economic development?

- How can outsiders help Third World development?

"What Can We Do To Lift South Asia From Poverty?"

The South Asian Association for Regional Cooperation (SAARC) joins seven countries— Bangladesh, Bhutan, India, Nepal, the Maldives, Pakistan, and Sri Lanka. During a two-day SAARC conference in the Maldives, the new prime ministers of India and Pakistan decide to meet one on one. The prime ministers recognize that tensions between their governments spur an arms competition that drains their budgets. But their deepest concern is that South Asia has become the most deprived region on the planet. They ask you, a mutual friend from undergraduate years at Cambridge University, to sit in with them. You are now an adviser to the World Bank and the UN Development Programme. They want to brainstorm with you: "What can we do to lift South Asia from poverty?"

The three of you review the problems: South Asia contains more than one-fifth of humanity, but produces only 1.3 percent of the world's income. More than half a billion people in South Asia live below the absolute poverty line. Nearly half the region's population is illiterate. There are more children out of school in South Asia than in the rest of the world, and two-thirds of them are female. Half the region's children are underweight. UN studies show that gender discrimination is worse in South Asia than in any other region. Defying the worldwide pattern of 106 women to 100 men, in South Asia there are only 94 women for every 100 men.

Despite this deprivation, the governments of South Asia spend heavily on arms. India and Pakistan have two of the world's largest armies. South Asia is the only region where military spending as a share of GDP went up after the late 1980s.

The prime ministers say that they will try to ease political tensions and cut arms spending. But they ask you to draw on World Bank and UN studies to sketch a road map for development. How does South Asia compare with other regions striving for development? What lessons can be drawn from the experiences of East Asia, Southeast Asia, the Middle East, Africa, and Latin America? What, if anything, can outsiders do to assist development? You promise to draft some recommendations before the next monsoon season. For starters, you try to define poverty.

CONTENDING CONCEPTS
AND EXPLANATIONS

HOW POOR IS POOR?

The good news: Human deprivation decreased in the last decades of the 20th century. From 1960 to the late 1990s, child death rates in less developed countries (LDCs) declined by more than half. Malnutrition fell by one-third. The proportion of children not attending primary school fell from more than one-half to less than one-quarter. Life expectancy increased in most countries.[1]

The UN Development Programme (UNDP) defines poverty in two ways: by income and by deprivation. Evaluated by income, anyone with less than $1 purchasing power parity (PPP) per day is poor. In the Caribbean and Latin America, the bar is higher—$2 PPP; in Eastern Europe and the former Soviet Union, $4 PPP; and in the First World OECD countries, $14.40 PPP.[2] The bad news: One-third of humanity suffered **income poverty** in the mid-1990s.

The UNDP also defines poverty as deprivation—lack of choices and opportunity to live a tolerable life. To measure deprivation the UNDP had designed a **Human Poverty Index (HPI)** based on three indicators: a short life, lack of basic education, and lack of access to public and private resources. Further bad news: Human poverty afflicts at least one-fourth of humanity.

Income poverty and human poverty tend to parallel each other, but government services can reduce deprivation despite low incomes, as happened in Cuba. In the oil-rich Arab countries, however, income poverty was cut to 4 percent while one-third of the people still suffered much deprivation.

As we see from Table 12.1, economic growth receded in much of Africa, the former Second World, and the Middle East in 1985–1995. Still, infant mortality dropped sharply in all countries. China and India had lower infant mortality than average for their regions. Average infant mortality in low- and middle-income countries was eight times higher than in high-income countries. Per capita GDP discrepancies were even greater.

In many countries the poverty of women exceeds that of men. This is reflected in the **gender-related development index (GDI)**. In 1997 Canada had the highest GDI and HDI (human development index). The U.S. was fifth in GDI and fourth in HDI. China was 90th in GDI and 93d in

1. United Nations Development Programme, *Human Development Report* [*HDR*] *1997* (New York: Oxford University Press, 1997), 1–13.

2. The OECD—Organization for Economic Cooperation and Development—evolved from the agency that administered the Marshall Plan. This agency subsequently expanded to include Japan, Australia, and New Zealand. In 1994 Mexico joined the OECD and pressures mounted to include East Asian countries such as Singapore and Eastern Europe and Russia.

Table 12.1   Population, Economic, and Health Indicators by Region

Region	Population, 1995 (millions)	Dollar Income Per Capita, 1995	Income Growth Rate,1985–1995 (percent per year)	Life Expectancy at Birth, 1995	Adult Illiteracy, 1995 (percent)	Infant Mortality (per 1,000 live births) 1980	1995
Low- and middle-income countries	4,771	$1,090	0.4	65	30	87	60
Sub-Saharan Africa	583	490	-1.1	52	43	114	92
East Asia and Pacific, including China	1,706	800	7.2	68	17	56	40
South Asia, including India	1,243	350	2.9	61	51	120	75
China	1,200	620	8.3	69	19	42	34
India	929	340	3.2	62	48	116	68
Eastern Europe and former USSR	488	2,220	-3.5	68	low	40	26
Middle East and North Africa	272	1,780	-0.3	66	39	97	54
Latin America and Caribbean	478	3,320	0.3	69	13	60	37
High-income countries	902	24,930	1.9	77	low	13	7
World total (t.) or weighted average (w.)	5,673 t.	4,880 w.	0.8 w.	67 w.	n.a.	80 w.	55 w.

SOURCE: Data from World Bank, *World Development Report [WDR] 1997* (New York: Oxford University Press, 1997), Tables 1 and 6.

How the Poor Define Poverty

"Poverty is hunger, loneliness, nowhere to go when the day is over, deprivation, discrimination, abuse and illiteracy."

—*single mother from Guyana*

"Poverty is the squatter mother whose hut has been torn down by the government for reasons she cannot understand."

—*slum dweller in the Philippines*

Some other answers included "being blind or crippled," "lacking land," "being without a grinding mill," "being unable decently to bury the dead," "having to put children to work."

Source: *HDR 1997,* various pages.

HDI. India ranked 118th in both. The lowest-ranking GDI scores belong to Mali, Burkina Faso, Niger, and Sierra Leone. Of OECD countries, the largest discrepancy was Japan—7th in HDI but only 12th in GDI; similar but smaller disparities were found in Switzerland and Ireland. The largest gap was in Saudi Arabia—62d in HDI and 90th in GDI. Large disparities were also noted in Syria and Algeria while Kuwait and Egypt had much smaller gaps.[3]

Defined by HPI, more than one-fourth of humanity (more than one billion people) was severely deprived. Many were illiterate, lacked access to safe water, lacked food security, and were unlikely to survive to age 40. The largest *number* of poor people was in **South Asia** (the SAARC countries of Bangladesh, Bhutan, India, Nepal, the Maldives, Pakistan, and Sri Lanka). The largest *proportion* of poor people was in Sub-Saharan Africa. Growing rapidly, poverty in Sub-Saharan Africa was expected to encompass half of its people by the year 2000. Income poverty also increased in Latin America. In Eastern Europe and the former USSR income poverty spread in the 1990s from a small proportion of the population to envelope about one-third of the population.

Of developing countries, Trinidad and Tobago had the best HPI rating in the mid-1990s, followed by Cuba, Chile, Singapore, and Costa Rica. Human poverty in these countries was reduced to less than 10 percent of the population.

In the late 20th century incomes fell in more than one hundred countries to levels below those reached one, two, or even three decades earlier. The proportion of poor people rose in Argentina, Honduras, and even the U.S., despite respectable economic growth.

3. *HDR 1997*, Table 2.8.

Inequality rose in many countries during the last decades of the 20th century. The share of global income going to the poorest one-fifth of the world's population in the mid-1990s was just 1.1 percent—down from 1.4 percent in 1991 and 2.3 percent in 1960. The richest one-fifth received 30 times as much income as the poorest one-fifth in 1960; 61 times more in 1991; and 78 times more in 1994.[4]

DEVELOPMENT AND UNDERDEVELOPMENT

The First World's "Great Ascent" from poverty began during Europe's Industrial Revolution and required more than one hundred years to achieve decent living standards and broad opportunities for most people. Another Great Ascent began after World War II and lifted many LDCs from poverty within one or two generations.

For a society, **development** means fulfillment of its potential—economic, political, cultural. A developed society is organized to fulfill potential, however it is defined. Positions of authority depend upon merit—not on heredity, caste, or personal favor. The key to development is knowledge, spearheaded by literacy. A developed society taps individual creativity and cooperation for mutual gain. Such a society will be fit—able to cope with complex challenges.

Morality and economic development coincide: The moral imperative of development is to enlarge the choices available to each member of society. But economic growth also depends upon each person's ability to fulfill her/his potential.

The more development, the easier for a society to be fit; the less development, the harder. Fitness requires high human development and low deprivation. HDI, as we know, reflects health and education as well as income. A less developed society is marked by extreme anarchy or its opposite—rigid order with dependence upon a central authority. Such a society lacks fitness.

Dependency Theory and the World-System

Social scientists disagree about the major sources of underdevelopment. **Dependency theory** (a variant of world-system theory) focuses on external ties. It says that structures of dependency have developed since 1500 that permit the imperialist core (Europe and the U.S.) to exploit and retard the less developed periphery (the South). It calls on developing countries to cultivate self-sufficiency and demand redistribution of global wealth.

Why Did Costa Rica Prosper While Most of Latin America Languished?

Why is Latin America, so rich in natural resources, so poor? Most Spanish and Portuguese explorers and settlers were exploitative and intent on claiming values—not creating them. They used Indians and Africans to do the dirty work on large estates and mines. Owners became rich while workers subsisted. Why did Costa Rica not fit this pattern? One explanation is that it was settled by Basques and others from northern Spain willing to work for themselves and with one another. A nation of "brothers and sisters"—not of rulers and ruled—Costa Rica became a near model of middle-class prosperity, democracy, and peace. A large Basque migration also imparted a liberal dynamism to Chile, but their relative numbers and impact were less than in Costa Rica.[1]

1. Lawrence E. Harrison, *Underdevelopment as a State of Mind: The Latin American Case* (Lanham, Md.: Madison Books, 1985), 55–56. Asked about Harrison's thesis, former Costa Rican president Oscar Arias Sanchez in 1997 said it had some validity but was an oversimplified explanation.

4. *HDR 1997*, 9.

In Rio de Janeiro, Brazil, as in many cities in the developing world, high-rise affluence contrasts sharply with slums crowded by migrants from the countryside searching for jobs and the bright lights of urban living.

Modernization Theory and Internal Problems

Modernization theory asserts that, as societies are organized more rationally and scientifically, economic, cultural, and political changes occur together in predictable ways. The typical trajectory takes the following path: rigid, agrarian society → mass literacy → industrialization → urbanization → mass media → occupational specialization → specialized education → mass political participation → increasingly similar gender roles → high HDI. But stages overlap and stages can be reversed.[5]

Modernization theory grants that external forces have been and still are important. Still, the deepest obstacles to development lie within society—mutual distrust, exploitative patterns of land ownership, corruption, militarism, criminality, and—not least—sexism. Other factors include natural disasters, political instability, communal strife, civil war, and capital flight. These factors reinforce one another and contribute to a **syndrome of underdevelopment**. People feel powerless and exploited—and they are. In PD terms, experience teaches them: "Always defect."

The State. Government can be too strong or too weak. India's rulers attempted after 1947 to control and regulate economic life. The "license raj" (big government) tied India in knots of red tape. When government shrinks, however, social services may disappear, leaving ordinary people vulnerable to exploitation by aggressive entrepreneurs. Russia in the 1990s had a government but one too weak to provide many essential services. "Failed states" such as Somalia had no overall government—just clan rivalry.

Many leaders engage in **rent-seeking**—exploitation of government for personal gain. In 1994, for example, Venezuela's banking system collapsed due to bad debts—loans to powerful friends of bankers. Just before the crash, many "haves" sold their mansions and shipped their money abroad, filling suitcases with cash and taking them on private planes to Caribbean tax havens. They left the country saddled with enormous debts—more than 10 percent of GDP. Worse, in Zaire President Mobutu Sese Seko sold off his country's minerals and stashed his rakeoff (billions) in foreign bank accounts while his subjects lived in misery.

Community. Economics does not predict what kind of politics will exist. But political life strongly conditions economics. Both states and markets operate more efficiently where people feel themselves part of a civic union—a political community in which they have duties as well as rights.[6] Civic virtue—a spirit of mutual aid—shows up in political engagement such as voting, keeping informed on public affairs, and showing concern for other citizens and for public goods.

5. Postmodern countries face different questions: Will computerization enslave or liberate? Will life become more creative or more regimented? How to be trim (not how to subsist)? Ronald Inglehart, *Modernization and Postmodernization: Cultural, Economic, and Political Change in 43 Societies* (Princeton, N.J.: Princeton University Press, 1997).

6. Robert D. Putnam, *Making Democracy Work: Civic Traditions in Modern Italy* (Princeton, N.J.: Princeton University Press, 1993), 156–157.

High socioeconomic development usually requires civic virtue. In a developed society people are linked by a dense network of associations, by active engagement in community affairs, by egalitarian patterns of politics, and by trust and law-abiding behavior. People expect good government and tend to get it.

Inequality. In most LDCs there is a chasm between rich and poor. The rich have access to education and other perquisites of power; the poor do not. The bases of inequality include barriers that keep people "in their place"—social castes, ethnic and religious groups, genders. But the whole cannot advance optimally if major parts lag behind.

Gender Bias. At least 100 million women are missing in India, China, and other LDCs. Why? Many have been aborted or killed after birth. Baby girls have long been unwelcome in China and India because they contribute less than boys to farming and are costly to marry off. China's one-child-per-family policy adds to reasons to do away with girls.[7] In parts of India and China, however, a shortage of potential brides emerged in the 1990s, leading to an upsurge in kidnapping of teenage females.

Gender bias impedes both human development and material advancement.[8] It traps not just women but entire societies in a vicious circle of poverty, illness, and population growth against limited resources. Discrimination against women transmits poverty from one generation to another, because a mother's health and education shape the life chances of her children.

The ill effects of gender bias are most visible in the poorest countries, although bias extends into the richest as well. In poor countries, women are kept illiterate and away from the market economy; they do heavy, monotonous work while also caring for children, spouses, the elderly, and the infirm.

Modernization has helped liberate some women in LDCs, but it has also left many others behind.[9] Women often lack opportunities to acquire the new skills needed for functional specialization—whether in cash-crop farming or in urban factories. Modern farming has created more opportunities for some women; fewer for others.[10] A feminist interpretation of dependency theory asserts that factory owners exploit a docile "reserve army of unemployed women" whose pay and hours can be adjusted to fit the business cycle. Women, these theorists say, are both a sex and a class—the "periphery of the periphery." Imperialism oppresses all Third World people; capitalism, all workers; patriarchy, all women.

The root problem is the expectation—by many women as well as men—that men should dominate society. Only when these attitudes dis-

7. In 1994 the Indian government moved to ban disclosure of an embryo's sex to parents unless it was malformed. Another problem in India is "bride-burning." More than 5,000 brides were killed yearly in the 1990s because their parents failed to deliver an adequate dowry. A quite different custom was banned by British imperialists in 1834: *sutti*—self-immolation of widows, but the practice still occurs in rural areas.

8. *The World's Women 1970–1990: Trends and Statistics* (New York: United Nations, 1991). These realities have been evident for decades. See Irene Tinker and Michèle Bo Bramsen, eds., *Women and World Development* (Washington, D.C.: Overseas Development Council, 1976).

9. When men migrate to cash jobs in towns, the woman's tasks at home and in farming often increase. She may have little time or energy to incorporate ecologically sound practices in farm management. She may be tempted to plant marginal lands to boost short-term income.

10. Mechanized agriculture raised incomes on some farms in the Philippines, permitting some households to hire labor and purchase labor-saving implements. This reduced the number of hours worked by all family members—male and female—and permitted them to engage in more productive work such as trade or raising livestock. Modern seed varieties raised the demand for hired female labor to weed and harvest. But mechanization sometimes lowers female employment. When predominantly female tasks are given over to machines, women are displaced.

Why Women's Work Is Never Done

Repression of women is both cause and consequence of poverty in Africa. Consider the Masai people living near Tanzania's game preserves. Men used to raid cattle and fend off intruders, but—the old ways gone—many now sit drinking a local brew and playing board games. "Men in this community live as supervisors," said a 35-year-old Masai elder, Paritoro Ole Kasiaro. "Men leave the women to do all the everyday activities." Women look after cattle, carry water in jugs from a stream, and ride donkeys to fetch cornmeal from distant shops. They must even maintain the mud and dung hut.

Unlike most Masai men, Kasiaro has attended school and travels eighty miles to meetings of the Regional Council. In 1990 he became an advocate of women's rights and tried to help local women sell jewelry to passing tourists. If they gained income, Kasiaro believed, women would probably buy cornmeal for children. Many men, by contrast, would spend extra cash on liquor. But men controlled the tribe's capital and refused to underwrite their women. To get started, women had to sell their own necklaces.

Kasiaro in 1991 had three underfed wives and three scrawny children; he himself often went hungry; his cattle were dying of disease. He had a fourth wife, age 10, already paid for by his father to her father—before she was born! His life was ruled by custom. He admitted beating a wife when the roof leaks: "Other men will laugh if I don't."

Source: Jane Perlez, "Women's Work Is Never Done (Not by Masai Men)," *New York Times*, December 2, 1991.

---

appear can women take part in modern life on an equal basis.[11] Latin American feminists demand extension of democracy into the private sphere: *"Democracia en el pais y en la casa"* (Democracy in the country and in the home).

Multiple Sources of Exploitation

Multiple forms of exploitation can cause conflict and impede development. Exploitation exists in many settings and contexts—between family members, sexes, ethnic groups, rulers and ruled, bosses and workers, countries, and regions. Exploitation and conflict arise from a common source: viewing others as rivals in a zero-sum struggle for power and wealth. This outlook leads to one-sided value-claiming. If the stronger side exploits the weaker, the exploited may see the relationship as unfair and resist. Exploitation can keep a society backward and provoke civil strife.

Policies that promote mutual gain are more likely to generate prosperity and peace than strategies of exploitation. The fittest societies thrive on complexity, interdependence, and cooperation for mutual gain.

Exploitation by outsiders probably played a larger role in the age of imperialism than in the late 20th century. When a country has been independent for decades, the deepest obstacles to peace derive from the syndrome of underdevelopment noted by modernization theory. Indeed, both prosperity and market democracy can be undermined by rent-seeking politicians and exploitative economic interests.[12] The countries of Southeast Asia confronted all these problems in 1997, as we shall see when we compare theory with reality.

11. In two Indian states where educational levels exceed the national average—Kerala and Tamil Nadu—women farm workers were displaced by men when chemical fertilizer replaced cow dung. Why? Women lacked access to the information provided by extension services. They were less free to travel, less free to communicate with strangers, and less likely to be able to read instructions.

12. Ricardo Hausmann, "Will Volatility Kill Market Democracy?" *Foreign Policy*, no. 108 (fall 1997): 54–67.

The problems of Rwanda, Burundi, and other African countries are difficult for Westerners to comprehend, even though many of these problems arose in the time when European imperialists favored one ethnic group over another and when post-colonial Europeans focused on extracting mineral wealth even if it meant supporting local tyrants.

A country characterized by anarchy or by rigid anarchy will be less able to cope with complex challenges than a society oriented toward mutual gain. But there is surely no one model of development. Every community has its own values, needs, problems, and assets. Still, the path toward modernization pioneered by the West and Japan may suggest lessons for other regions striving to overcome poverty.

Can Outsiders Help?

Is culture destiny? Conservatives say "yes." They believe that since culture is deeply rooted, politics can change little. By this logic, foreign aid is also useless. Worse, it may be siphoned off by the local plutocrats to consolidate their own wealth and power. By contrast, liberals hope that political and economic reforms can change or enhance a culture and save it. They also count on change spurred by communications and interdependence. They hope that, skillfully directed, even limited aid can open up new channels for development.

COMPARING THEORY AND REALITY: WHAT PATH FROM POVERTY?

FOUR ALTERNATIVE ROUTES

What path from poverty? Poor countries assayed four main routes in the last half of the 20th century: (1) welfare without industrial growth, (2) import-substitution, (3) self-reliant Communism, and (4) export-led participation in the world economy. The first three glorified **autarky**—

economic self-sufficiency without foreign trade or aid. By the 1990s nearly all states had embraced variants of the fourth approach.

1. Welfare Without Industrial Growth

Low incomes need not mean poverty. Lacking material abundance, Barbados, Costa Rica, Sri Lanka, and Cuba achieved good HDI scores by investing heavily from limited resources in education and public health. But "doing more with less" does not appeal to LDCs with rapidly growing populations who want higher material standards of living. Even Sri Lanka became disenchanted with socialism in the 1970s and opted for Singaporean-style capitalism. One reason for ethnic conflict in Sri Lanka was that a stagnant economy pushed an expanding population to fight over a shrinking pie. By the time Sri Lanka opted for growth, ethnic strife had become civil war.

Few Cubans reject the welfare state but many would prefer a liberalized political and economic system. In the 1990s, however, they had to endure authoritarian rule or flee.

2. Against Dependency: Import-Substitution and a New Economic Order

Instead of joining the system of world trade, *dependencia* theorists urged LDCs to detach from the system of world trade and unequal exchange. From the 1950s through the 1970s many Latin American, South Asian, and African countries attempted autarky based on **import-substitution**: They tried to become self-sufficient by reducing imports and building up native industries behind high tariff walls. They hoped to earn hard currency by exporting primary commodities and food, but international demand and prices fluctuated wildly. The outcome: Agriculture subsidized inefficient industries that could not compete on world markets. Everyone suffered except government ministers: Quantitative controls on imports permitted them to squeeze the system for private gain.

Trying to beggar their neighbors, South Asian countries traded little with one another. The countries of **East Asia**—Japan, Taiwan, South Korea, Hong Kong, and, eventually, even China—traded with each other, with the rest of Asia, and with the West.[13]

Many Third World governments in the 1970s called for a **New International Economic Order (NIEO)** to restructure the world economy and redistribute its wealth. A majority of UN members endorsed calls for an NIEO in which LDC commodity exports would be protected from price fluctuations and rich countries would transfer more resources to the poor. Western governments resisted the NIEO demands and called for North-South cooperation—not confrontation.

13. Most economists regarded Singapore as part of the East Asian miracle despite its location in Southeast Asia, just south of Malaysia.

Many Third World leaders hoped that the sharp rise in oil prices after 1973 would serve as a tool to redistribute the world's wealth. As it happened, however, oil producers gave away very little of their new wealth. Saudis and Kuwaitis got richer while many LDCs became poorer—some becoming a "Fourth World" of near terminal poverty.

Pressures for an NIEO collapsed in the 1980s. Why? Third World unity was rent by the split into petroleum "haves" and "have-nots"; China and the USSR endeavored to join First World commerce; most regions of the Third World sold more goods to the U.S. than they imported.

Why did the dependency model of LDC solidarity collapse? Dependency theorists blamed manipulation by the world system of finance (even though many Third World economies needed IMF loans to cope with liquidity crises). Liberals and neoliberals blamed the Third World for borrowing too much. Liberalism and neoliberalism offered a rationale for less borrowing, less patronage, less corruption, and more stringent adjustment to reality—lower wages and less welfare.[14]

Dependency thinking lingered in the 1990s. Many LDCs feared that freer trade would benefit the rich and hurt the poor. Some LDC governments worried that the World Trade Organization (WTO) would promote sale of manufactured goods produced in core developed countries while doing little for the periphery.

But free trade can gore some oxen and benefit others. Thus, Ecuador and other Latin American banana exporters cheered in 1997 when the WTO declared illegal European Union quotas and licenses favoring bananas from former British and French colonies in the Caribbean and Africa. Governments in Grenada and Dominica, however, demanded preferential treatment for small LDCs. They warned that the collapse of the banana trade could produce instability across the Caribbean basin and force islanders to switch to more lucrative crops such as cocaine.

3. Self-Reliant Communism

The Communist regimes in Moscow, Eastern Europe, and Asia sought for decades to develop *apart* from the First World. In the late 1940s/early 1950s Soviet leader Josef Stalin urged them all to industrialize to be self-sufficient and generate a working class with a Communist consciousness. Communist China's Mao Zedong, in turn, urged his countrymen to walk on "one leg"—their own, spurning foreign dependence. Perceiving in the 1970s that self-reliance meant backwardness, however, the USSR, Eastern Europe, and China began to cultivate trade ties with the West.

14. Ngaire Woods, "Economic Ideas and International Relations: Beyond Rational Neglect," *International Studies Quarterly* 39, no. 2 (June 1995): 161–180 at 174–176.

4. Export-Led Participation in the World Economic System

Most of East Asia embraced an export-led strategy of economic development based on manufactured goods competitive in foreign markets, adapting the Japanese approach described in Chapter 11. Japan went first, followed by Singapore, Hong Kong, Taiwan, and South Korea—known as the four little **Tigers**. These four began to emulate the Japan model in the 1950s and 1960s; mainland China followed suit in the late 1970s. Each country modified the model to fit its own needs. Together they produced an "East Asian miracle" of rapid growth that contrasted with South Asia's stagnation. Unlike India, the East Asians did not try to buck the system of world trade. Rather, they adapted to the system and used it for their own ends. (Singapore, of course, is really located in Southeast rather than East Asia.)

In the mid-1990s it appeared that other Southeast Asian countries—Thailand, Malaysia, and Indonesia—were repeating the East Asian miracle. Chile, Argentina, and Brazil were also developing rapidly. These latecomers were called **NICs—newly industrializing countries**.[15]

How did the four Tigers do so much with so little? They had some tangible advantages—good harbors, substantial foreign aid from the U.S. or Britain, and investment capital from expatriates. But each had a poor resource base with few minerals or cash crops; each depended on imported energy; each was vulnerable to destructive rains. Each had a dense population relative to the area under cultivation. None had a large domestic market. Except for Hong Kong, each Tiger feared a powerful neighbor and invested heavily in military preparedness.

Nonetheless, each Tiger advanced rapidly from low-income to upper-middle-income ratings. By 1995 all four had high real per capita incomes: Hong Kong, $27,500; Singapore, $22,900; Taiwan, $13,600; and South Korea, $13,100. Despite abundant resources, the other NICs lagged far behind. In 1995 Argentina's real per capita income was $8,100; Brazil's, $6,100.[16]

Let us compare six East Asian countries (Japan, the Tigers, and China) with South Asia (India, Pakistan, Bangladesh, Bhutan, Sri Lanka, Nepal, and the Maldives). Table 12.2 outlines the contrasting policy frameworks of each region.[17]

The East Asians shared five strategies: investment in human capital, outward-looking trade strategies, land reforms and credit reforms to stimulate private initiative, accumulation of physical capital, and comparatively good governance. Let us look at each in turn.

Investment in Human Capital. East Asians invested heavily in high-

15. See World Bank, *The East Asian Miracle: Economic Growth and Public Policy* (New York: Oxford University Press, 1993), and its bibliography.

16. *Handbook of International Economic Statistics 1996* (Washington, D.C.: CIA Directorate of Intelligence, 1996), Table 4. Compare also Argentina and Brazil with other countries in Tables 11.1–11.3 in the previous chapter.

17. See Mahbub ul Haq, *Human Development in South Asia 1997* (New York: Oxford University Press, 1997), 66–78.

quality primary education, accompanied by a largely self-financed university system. By contrast, South Asians heavily subsidized higher education, which benefited the elite coming from better off families. The East Asians started with a higher literacy base, and invested much more heavily to broaden and deepen it. In 1960 Malaysia and Singapore were spending 3 percent of GDP on education—Pakistan only 1 percent. The results were stark: By 1990 only 3 percent of China's adolescent boys and 8 percent of its adolescent girls were illiterate, compared to 24 percent of India's boys and 48 percent of India's girls. In 1997 Singaporean pupils scored highest in the world in mathematics and science.

Universal education quickly became entrenched in the Tiger countries. Females attend primary school at the same rate as males in each Tiger country, though fewer females attend secondary school and college.[18]

Outward-Looking Trade Strategies. East Asians began manufacturing low-tech consumer goods, competing on the basis of low wages, high productivity, and an enlightened export policy. Except for free-wheeling Hong Kong, the East Asian governments protected and favored certain industries.

The four Tigers raised their combined share of world trade from 1.5 percent in 1965 to 8 percent in 1994—almost equal to Japan's 9.1 percent. Each Tiger based its wealth on export of manufactured goods—computers, telecommunications equipment, robotics.[19] In the years from 1970 to 1990 South Korea increased its exports 78 times over; Taiwan, 47 times

Table 12.2 Contrasting Policy Frameworks: East and South Asia

East Asia	South Asia
Investment in human capital	Widespread illiteracy
Macroeconomic stability	Budget deficits/ foreign debt
Relative price stability	High inflation
Liberal approach to trade	Protectionist mentality
Inflow of foreign investments	Foreign aid and loans
Merit-based competition	Feudal patronage
Sound governance	Corruption and inefficiency
Land reforms	Peasants without much land
Efficient tax collection	Tax evasion, loan defaulting
High savings/ investment rates	Lower rates
Invitation to foreign direct investment (FDI)	Hostility to FDI
Public-private sector partnerships	Business as client of government
No open hostility except for PRC-ROC confrontation	Pakistan-India arms race and festering Kashmir dispute

Tiger Women

Did East Asia's "miracle" happen because women were exploited or because they were liberated? Both sexes worked long and hard to make the miracle happen. Exports grew thanks to millions of young women laboring in textiles and other "female industries." Literacy helped both men and women to adjust to urban and factory life. Women moved part way out of their traditional roles, but were still subject to discrimination. Patriarchal traditions worked against females in the Tiger countries. Conditions for women were harshest in South Korea and best in Hong Kong. In South Korea the wage gap between men and women was quite large in the 1960s but had closed somewhat by the 1980s.

Literacy is no panacea. In Thailand more than 90 percent of the population could read in the 1990s. But many girls (and some boys) became prostitutes, largely because their parents or they sought more money. Many prostitutes contracted HIV infections, but some government officials focused on tourist dollars generated by prostitution and on their private bank accounts.

18. As families in Taiwan became smaller and as average incomes increased, Taiwanese invested heavily in the education of daughters as well as sons. William L. Parish and Robert J. Willis, "Daughters, Education, and Family Budgets: Taiwan Experiences," *Journal of Human Resources* 23, no. 4 (fall 1993): 863–898.

19. In 1990 Taiwan rose to tenth place among exporters of machine tools and robotics. In the mid-1990s a Taiwan-based consortium began to produce airplane parts with British Aerospace.

over; Singapore, 34 times over; and Hong Kong, 33 times over. Europe's most prosperous small states, Switzerland and Sweden, increased their exports 13 and 9 times over, respectively.[20] Like Japan, each Tiger exported far more than it imported. In 1997 the World Economic Forum rated Singapore and Hong Kong the most competitive economies in the world, followed by the U.S.

Land Reforms and Credit Reforms to Stimulate Private Initiative. Land reforms took place in Japan, South Korea, and Taiwan under U.S. pressure in the decade after World War II; China gave back land to the peasants in the late 1970s. Land reforms in India made some progress, but not in Pakistan, where rural elites in the 1990s still maintained feudal structures of power.

Farmers need credit but must pay their loans if the economy is to be solvent. Rich landlords often default on their loans in South Asia while many banks there are reluctant to give credit to poor farmers. One success story, however, is the **Grameen Bank**, launched in Bangladesh in 1976. It provides loans (averaging $100) sequentially to poor people, mostly rural women. Peer pressure has kept the default rate to a mere 2 to 3 percent. Having helped 2 million Bangladeshis, the Bank hoped in the late 1990s to serve other LDCs.

Accumulation of Physical Capital. East Asian governments managed to tax incomes and encourage savings; South Asia did less well. Gross saving in East Asia was 34 percent of GDP in 1993 compared to 21 percent in South Asia. East Asians were not born savers. South Koreans saved only 1 percent in 1960; Singaporeans saved minus 3 percent.

Good Governance. In most of East Asia government bureaucracies were efficient; in South Asia, the opposite was true. Corruption in some East Asian countries was rampant, but it was even more widespread in South Asia. The ROK government, however, was both dictatorial and corrupt.

THE ROLE OF WOMEN IN DEVELOPMENT

The greatest untapped source of development energy is women. To release this energy is more difficult than costly, for it requires that both sexes change their attitudes. But the first step in female liberation is neither difficult nor expensive. It is to teach literacy.[21] This requires a strong commitment—from above or from below or by intermediate agencies such as churches and welfare agencies. Development programs have often ignored literacy while funding huge, costly infrastructure projects.

Female illiteracy correlates with low GDP, high population growth,

20. In the same twenty years Japan multiplied the value of its exports by only 15; West Germany, by 12; and the U.S., by 9. Oil exporters such as Iraq and Indonesia increased the value of their exports by about 19; Saudi Arabia, by 11. Calculated from data in *Handbook of Economic Statistics, 1991: A Reference Aid* (Washington, D.C.: Central Intelligence Agency, 1991), 130–131.

From the 1970s through 1990 tiny Hong Kong exported more than any other Tiger. U.S. exports led the world, but were only 4.8 times more than Hong Kong's in 1990; Japan exported 3.5 times more than Hong Kong then and 4.3 times more than Taiwan. Ibid., 134–135.

21. Robert F. Arnove and Harvey J. Graff, eds., *National Literacy Campaigns: Historical and Comparative Perspectives* (New York: Plenum, 1987).

Map 12.1   Eurocentric Visions: How Important Is the South Compared to the North?

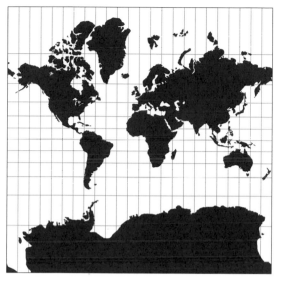

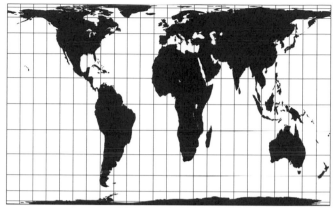

Dr. Arno Peter's projection, dating from 1977, shows areas well, but not shapes. It depicts the relative size of the South more accurately than Mercator's, but shows contours poorly. In reality, Africa is as wide as it is long.

Gerhard Mercator's "Standard" projection above, dating from 1569, places Europe in the center and allots two-thirds of the map's surface to the North. It shows directions and shapes of continents well, but not areas. It makes the South—Latin America, Africa, India, and Australia—look smaller than it is compared to the North. In reality, Africa is larger than the USSR.

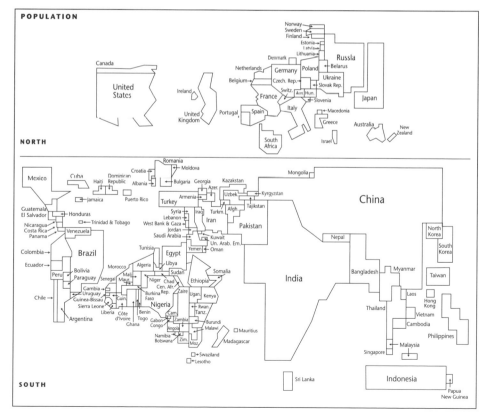

POPULATION

NORTH

SOUTH

A map proportional to population shows China and India as the giants of the world. Russia, though it covers one-seventh of the globe's land surface, looks quite small, not much larger than Japan. Canada, though it covers more land than the U.S., also looks quite small.

WORLD POPULATION NOW GROWING at the RATE of a LOS ANGELES EVERY MONTH

Some social scientists see explosive population growth as a major threat to social stability and environmental protection. But some religious groups and politicians oppose family planning and sex education anywhere. Cornucopians are sure that the earth's resources will suffice. Demographers say that population growth tends to level off with urbanization and affluence. With or without further growth, the combined populations of China and India make up more than a third of the earth's people—a point depicted graphically on page 351. As the maps there show, Westerners have for centuries exaggerated their own place on the planet relative to Asia, Africa, and other regions of the South.

22. Many Nepalese families were still reluctant in the 1990s to educate their daughters—especially if it meant sending them to schools taught by men. But where would Nepal get female teachers unless girls went to school?

23. But 17th-century Swedes learned in family and church settings without schools. Many common people paid to be tutored in 18th-century England. Public schools were important in the U.S.—especially for 19th- and 20th-century immigrants.

24. See Haleh Afshar, ed., *Women, State and Ideology: Studies from Africa and Asia* (London: Macmillan, 1987); Bina Agarwal, ed., *Structures of Patriarchy: The State, the Community, and the Household* (London: Zed Books, 1988).

25. In 1992 the approval of Ireland's highest court was required for a 14-year-old rape victim to travel abroad for an abortion.

26. In Ghana a quarter of all women in the late 1980s wanted no more children, but family planning services reached less than 7 percent of women. Ghana's fertility rate (average number of births for each woman) was then 6.4. In Indonesia, where family planning reached 44 percent of women, fertility declined to 3.3.

27. In Brazil, the health effect was twenty times greater. See Marya Buvinic, "Women in Poverty: A New Global Underclass," *Foreign Policy*, no. 108 (fall 1997): 38–53 at 47.

and high infant mortality—as seen in Figures 12.1, 12.2, and 12.3 on pages 353 and 354. Female education is essential for limiting population growth, cultivating a healthy population, passing on education, and helping women join the work force.[22] Without literacy women are less open to new ideas—unable even to read instructions for medicines. Fertility tends to decrease as women become literate and when they can find jobs in the wage sector. Literacy has steadily increased worldwide, but women still lag behind men in literacy in most LDCs.

In the 1600s and 1700s European countries needed a century or more to achieve widespread literacy.[23] But in the 20th century many countries (Brazil, China, Tanzania, Vietnam) broadened literacy within two decades. Cuba and Nicaragua achieved major reductions in illiteracy within just one year. Centralized political power and modern communications helped all these regimes to telescope the process.

The state does much to shape the place of women in society.[24] It mediates women's lives through its policies on child and health care, education, employment, taxation, and the regulation of wages.[25] In Costa Rica, Korea, and Singapore family planning programs helped reduce birth rates by one-third to one-half between 1965 and 1985. But family planning services do not exist in many countries.[26]

It pays to invest in women. Income in the hands of a mother has an effect on a child's health many times greater than income controlled by the father.[27]

It pays to educate women. If mainly boys are educated, high rates of fertility and infant mortality tend to persist. Various studies show that an

Fig. 12.1   Female Illiteracy (1995) / GNP Per Capita (1994)

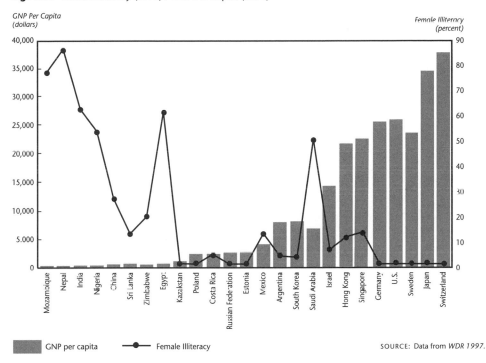

*GNP Per Capita
(dollars)*

*Female Illiteracy
(percent)*

▨ GNP per capita   ●— Female Illiteracy

SOURCE: Data from *WDR 1997.*

Fig. 12.2   Female Illiteracy (1995) / Average Population Growth (1990–1995)

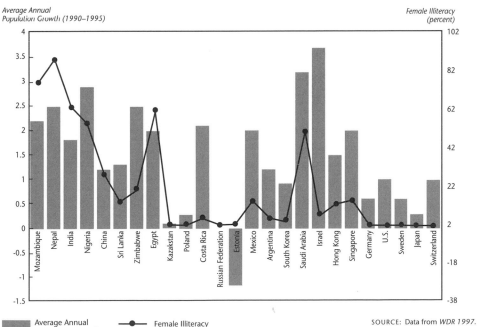

*Average Annual
Population Growth (1990–1995)*

*Female Illiteracy
(percent)*

▨ Average Annual
Population Growth   ●— Female Illiteracy

SOURCE: Data from *WDR 1997.*

Fig. 12.3 Female Illiteracy (1995) / Infant Mortality (1990–1995)

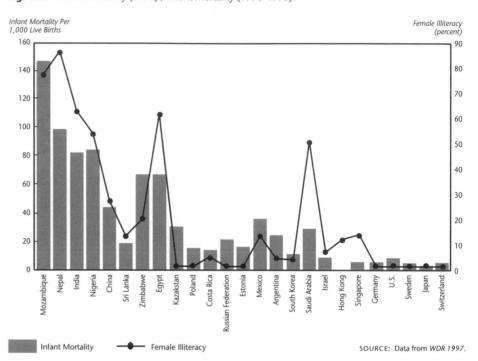

SOURCE: Data from *WDR 1997*.

additional year of schooling for women reduces child and maternal mortality and increases women's earnings by up to 20 percent.[28] From Indonesia to West Africa, girls' education brings them larger earnings. But many governments and many families are reluctant to invest in girls. Some families want their daughters to do housework; others fear they will profit less from their daughters' earnings than from their sons'.

At the end of the 20th century men still command more resources than women in most countries, but the gap is closing. The poorer the society, the larger the gap. The gap is largest in sub-Saharan Africa, next largest in West and South Asia and in North Africa; it is closing more rapidly in Latin America, Southeast Asia, and East Asia.[29]

How successful were Communist revolutionaries at ending sex discrimination? Soviet Communists did much to educate and liberate women—even in Muslim Central Asia. Preventive medicine did much to improve public health. But the net impact of Communism was hard on Soviet women. They joined the labor force but still had to care for the home and queue for groceries. Communism did not end male chauvinism. Russia in the 1980s and 1990s had the highest infant mortality of any developed country. Within the USSR, as elsewhere, female illiteracy was

28. Ibid.; T. Paul Schultz, "Investments in the Schooling and Health of Women and Men: Quantities and Returns," *Journal of Human Resources* 23, no. 4 (fall 1993): 694–734; see also World Bank, *World Development Report [WDR] 1991* (New York: Oxford University Press, 1991), 55. Sri Lanka is a low-income country, but it has low female illiteracy and low infant mortality.

29. T. Paul Schultz, ed., *Investment in Women's Human Capital* (Chicago: University of Chicago Press, 1995). Female access to education is higher in Latin America than in Africa or most of Asia, but machismo still permeates Latin America. Many women attend school, but they experience discrimination and concentrate in only a few academic fields. Nelly P. Stromquist, ed., *Women and Education in Latin America* (Boulder, Colo.: Lynne Rienner, 1991).

Repression of women impedes development in many countries. Here we see delegates to the Non-Governmental Organizations Forum held in Huairou, China, as part of the UN Fourth World Conference on Women, which took place in Beijing in September 1995. Hopes and consciousness were raised; getting governments and entire societies to alter their attitudes was another matter.

highest where infant mortality was highest—in Turkmenistan and Tajikistan.[30]

"Man's work" became women's under Communist rule—from Russia to Vietnam. But Chinese women in the 1980s and 1990s complained of unequal pay and opportunity. Some said that professors altered their exams to deny them better education and jobs. China's one-child policy also increased female infanticide. On the positive side, China's infant mortality declined from 69 per 1,000 live births in 1970 to 38 (compared to India's reduction from 137 to 90).

Many religions have sought to keep women at home and obedient to men. Most Islamic countries in the 1990s are authoritarian and male-dominated. To be sure, women have achieved the pinnacle of power in Bangladesh, Pakistan, and Turkey; a woman has led Palestinians in negotiations with Israel. But women in most Islamic countries have limited access to education and participation in public life.[31] In 1994 Muslim leaders in Bangladesh demanded execution of a feminist writer who called for revision of the Koran's treatment of women. Some Saudi women tried to exploit the Gulf War to establish their right to drive a car, but failed.[32]

HOW CAN OUTSIDERS HELP?

External influences can help or hurt developing economies. Most countries—including the U.S.—have benefited from foreign investment, loans, trade, technology and cultural transfer, brains, and labor.

Foreign aid takes many forms, for example, education. The founder of

30. In the late 1980s infant mortality for the entire USSR was about 25 per 1,000 live births; in Russia, 19 or 20; in Central Asia, between 30 and 75; and in the Baltic, in the low teens. *Naselenie SSSR 1988: Statisticheskii ezhegodnik* (Moscow: Finansy i statistika, 1989), 6, 473 ff.

31. For global trends, see Jane S. Jaquette, "Women in Power: From Tokenism to Critical Mass," *Foreign Policy*, no. 108 (fall 1997): 23–37.

32. Despite relatively high incomes, Saudi Arabia, Kuwait, and the United Arab Emirates had fertility rates higher than 3 in 1989—the Saudi rate was 7.1! In 1989 the infant mortality rate in Saudi Arabia was 67 per 1,000 live births, but that was down from 148 in 1965. Kuwait had reduced its rate to 15 and the United Arab Emirates to 24 by 1989.

More than half of the calves in a Masai village in Tanzania were dying from East Coast Fever. Some village men wanted to spray cattle with chemicals. Women found a cheaper solution: a cattle dip in a blend of chemicals plus local river water. The NGO Oxfam contributed building materials, and villagers pitched in to build the dip. The village charged cattle owners 5 Tanzanian shillings per dip to recover costs of the chemicals and net a small profit. Not trusting their men to do the accounting, the Masai women took lessons in bookkeeping and invented a way to keep the money for other projects.

33. David Halloran Lumsdaine, *Moral Vision in International Politics: The Foreign Aid Regime, 1949–1989* (Princeton, N.J.: Princeton University Press, 1993).

modern China, Sun Yat-sen, studied at Honolulu's Iolani School founded by missionaries to prepare Hawaiians and Asians for Yale. Over time, many Chinese studied in the West and the USSR. Leading figures in PRC nuclear weapon and missile programs had doctorates from the U.S. By the 1990s Taiwan's president and most cabinet members had doctorates from U.S. universities. Many children and grandchildren of Communist China's elite could also be found on U.S. campuses.

Aid was mutual as foreign influences enriched U.S. life. The North transfers much knowledge to the South but the flow of educated humans is mostly South to North. Many scientists and physicians originally educated in LDCs choose to stay in the West.

Some aid is tangible such as food, "turn-key" factories (set up and ready to operate), seeds, irrigation pipes, and armored personnel vehicles (new or second-hand). Some is intangible—a "demonstration effect" (images gathered from foreign troops, tourists, or television) and knowledge (how to farm, speak English, use the Internet, control crowds, win elections, thwart coups). The nonprofit Experiment in International Living organizes home visits in many countries—an educational experience for host and visitor alike.

Many forms of aid do not show up in government ledgers. LDCs that preserve their tropical forests help sustain the earth's climate; they also preserve plants and fauna useful to all peoples. The Rockefeller Foundation sponsored research on hybrid wheat, rice, and other grains that have produced a "green revolution." Oxfam and other NGOs transferred about $5 billion a year to LDCs in the 1990s.

Official development assistance (ODA) comes from governments directly or through multilateral agencies such as the World Bank and the International Monetary Fund (IMF). Narrowly defined, foreign aid means **concessional loans** (loans at less than commercial interest rates) or **grants** (outright gifts) in currency or in kind, such as food. Aid can focus on meeting immediate humanitarian needs, influencing next year's elections, or shaping long-term development.

Never in history did rich countries transfer wealth to poor countries as in the second half of the 20th century. A mix of motives underlay ODA: colonial ties, pride, commercial ambitions, guilt, Cold War rivalry, and a quest for "stability." But moral vision also inspired much aid to LDCs in which donors had few security or trade interests.[33]

Aid may be a mixed blessing that helps some parts of society but harms others. Aid can prop up dictators and enrich corrupt officials; it can prolong fighting. There are dilemmas: Without relief, people die.

With relief, more survive but need food, housing, and jobs tomorrow. Aid may be fruitful and then go sour. Recipients may be grateful or resentful. They may become partners, rivals, or foes.

Outside aid can never substitute for domestic resource mobilization. If a country's internal structure or policies are distorted, outside aid may perpetuate what should be changed.[34]

Donors have altered their strategies like fads. For decades the World Bank lent money for big infrastructure projects such as dams; then it directed funds toward poverty relief; later it conditioned loans on **structural adjustment policies** (freer markets, less debt, reduced welfare, and more democracy). These shifts reflected the policies of influential governments (especially the U.S.) and personal beliefs of World Bank presidents.[35]

In the mid-1990s OECD governments delivered annually less than $60 billion in ODA to LDCs. This amounted to 0.3 percent of First World GDP (about $70 per capita)[36]—not even half of the 0.7 percent goal set by the United Nations and minuscule next to defense spending (2 to 3 percent in the West). Japan (with low defense expenditures per capita) became the largest donor in the 1990s, giving about one-fifth of total ODA. Among OECD states, U.S. aid as a percentage of GDP was the lowest—0.1 percent.

The Clinton administration's fiscal year 1998 budget for International Affairs and its allocations for sustainable development are presented in Tables 12.3 and 12.4. The Clinton team cut the number of countries receiving U.S. aid from about 100 to 55. Czechoslovakia and Estonia, for example, were taken off the recipient list. The **U.S. Agency for International Development (USAID)** administered most U.S. aid programs. It pursued five goals: U.S. prosperity (through trade, investment, and employment); sustainable development; democracy (especially in Eastern Europe and the former USSR); peace; and humanitarian assistance.[37] In the 1990s USAID gave many cash loans—some as low as $10—for small businesses, many run by women. The Clinton team sought more funds for family planning and protection of the global environment. Clinton's "Lessons without Borders" program shared public health techniques developed for Bangladesh with U.S. inner cities, for example, in Baltimore.

More than 150 nonprofit NGOs formed a coalition known as InterAction to support USAID in the 1990s. InterAction claimed that for every dollar its organizations received from the U.S. government, they raised $3 from the U.S. public. The coalition included the American Friends Service Committee, American Red Cross, Church World Service, Islamic Af-

34. Sarah J. Tisch and Michael B. Wallace, *Dilemmas of Development Assistance: The What, Why, and Who of Foreign Aid* (Boulder, Colo.: Westview, 1994), 127; *WDR 1994*, 61.

35. Thus, U.S. ties with Jakarta helped Indonesia's military regime become a favorite World Bank client in the late 1960s and remain so, despite a poor record on human rights and the environment.

Robert S. McNamara became president of the World Bank after serving as U.S. Secretary of Defense. On his compulsions, see Deborah Shapley, *Promise and Power* (Boston: Little, Brown, 1993); on fads, see Paul Mosley et al., *Aid and Power: The World Bank and Policy-based Lending*, 2 vols. (London: Routledge, 1991).

36. *The Reality of Aid 94: An Independent Review of International Aid* (London: Actionaid, 1994), 11 and appendixes.

37. See U.S. Agency for International Development, *Congressional Presentation Fiscal Year 1995*, February 28, 1994.

Table 12.3 International Affairs Budget of the U.S., FY 1996–1998 *(millions of dollars)*

	FY 1996 Actual	FY 1997 Estimate	FY 1998 Proposed
Promoting U.S. Prosperity Through Trade, Investment, and Employment	**974**	**775**	**525**
Export-Import Bank (net)	763	715	630
Food export promotion (P.L. 480 - Title I)	263	151	10
Trade and Development Agency	40	40	43
Overseas Private Investment Corporation (net)	(93)	(131)	(158)
Building Democracy	**1,309**	**1,292**	**1,629**
Newly independent states of former Soviet Union	623	613	900
Central and Eastern Europe	510	475	492
Other countries in transition	143	169	202
National Endowment for Democracy	30	30	30
Multilateral democracy programs	3	5	5
Fostering Sustainable Development	**3,318**	**3,203**	**3,848**
Multilateral development banks, IMF, and debt reduction	1,163	1,013	1,557
State Department and USAID programs	[1,904]	[1,939]	[2,033]
Broad-based economic growth	726	722	755
Health/stabilization of world population growth	743	782	795
Protection of global environment	271	307	342
Democratic participation	164	128	142
Peace Corps and other agencies	249	252	258
Promoting Peace	**6,330**	**6,344**	**6,438**
Regional peace, security, and defense cooperation	5,597	5,528	5,686
Peacekeeping programs	430	417	376
Non-proliferation and disarmament	117	118	127
Counter-narcotics and crime	120	213	230
Anti-terrorism	66	68	19
Providing Humanitarian Assistance	**1,723**	**1,727**	**1,727**
Refugee assistance	721	700	700
Disaster assistance (including transition initiatives)	181	190	190
Food assistance (P.L. 480 - Title II)	821	837	837
Advancing Diplomacy	**5,012**	**5,054**	**5,390**
State Department operations	2,446	2,519	2,576
Machine-readable visa fees	[115]	[137]	140
State Department small programs	38	44	38
USIA information and exchange	1,053	1,029	1,048
United Nations and other affiliates (assessed)	892	882	1,023
USAID operating expenses	524	518	502
Non-state small programs	59	61	63
Special Defense Acquisition Fund	(173)	(166)	(106)
Total, Function 150 (discretionary programs)	**18,491**	**18,227**	**19,451**
Subtotal for Economic and Military Assistance	**11,417**	**11,338**	**11,936**

SOURCE: U.S. Department of State, *International Affairs Function 150: Budget Request and Objectives, Fiscal Year 1998* (Washington, D.C.: Government Printing Office, 1998).
   NOTE: Discrepancies between budget items and subtotals are in the original, perhaps caused by rounding.

rican Relief Agency USA, National Wildlife Foundation, and the US Committee for UNICEF. Nonprofit Sierra Club and profit-oriented solar power groups lobbied for USAID funds to promote sustainable development.

Many forms of foreign aid and influence cost the U.S. and other donors little or nothing. Some examples are goods sent abroad, which are usually purchased in the donor country so that "foreign aid" adds to the

Table 12.4 Fostering Sustainable Development—U.S. FY 1998 Budget *(thousands of dollars)*

	FY 1997 Estimate	FY 1998 Request	Difference
Multilateral Development Banks, ESAF, & Debt	1,012,905	1,557,191	544,286
Multilateral Development Banks	985,905	1,516,191	530,286
International Development Association	700,000	1,034,503	334,503
Global Environment Facility	35,000	100,000	65,000
International Finance Corporation	6,656	0	-6,656
Inter-American Development Bank	25,611	25,611	0
Inter-American Development Bank - Fund for Special Operations	10,000	20,576	10,576
I-ADB[a] Multilateral Investment Fund	27,500	30,000	2,500
Asian Development Bank	13,222	13,222	0
Asian Development Fund	100,000	150,000	50,000
African Development Fund	0	50,000	50,000
European Bank for Reconstruction & Development	11,916	35,779	23,863
North American Development Bank	56,000	56,500	500
Middle East Development Bank	0		
IMF Enhanced Structural Adjustment Facility	0	7,000	7,000
Debt restructuring	27,000	34,000	7,000
State Department and USAID Programs	1,939,050	2,033,100	94,050
Broad-based Economic Growth	722,450	754,600	32,150
Development assistance	495,500	507,500	12,000
International organizations and programs	185,950	206,100	20,150
PL-480 Title III food assistance	29,500	30,000	500
Credit programs	11,500	11,000	-500
Population and Health	782,000	795,000	13,000
Development assistance	757,000	765,000	8,000
International organizations and programs (UNFPA)	25,000	30,000	5,000
Protection of the Global Environment	307,100	341,500	34,400
Development assistance	257,000	290,000	33,000
International organizations and programs	50,100	51,500	1,400
Support for Democratic Participation	127,500	142,000	14,500
Development assistance	121,000	135,500	14,500
International organizations and programs (OAS democracy programs)	6,500	6,500	0
Peace Corps and Other Agencies	251,500	258,000	6,500
Peace Corps	220,000	222,000	2,000
Inter-American Foundation	20,000	22,000	2,000
African Development Foundation	11,500	14,000	2,500
Total Sustainable Development	3,203,455	3,848,291	644,836

SOURCE: U.S. Department of State, *International Affairs Function 150: Budget Request and Objectives, Fiscal Year 1998* (Washington, D.C.: Government Printing Office, 1998).
   a. Inter-American Development Bank.

donor's GDP; salaries for persons from the donor country; surplus food stocks in the donor country used for food aid; and educational programs financed by "counterpart funds" (local currencies owed to the U.S. but expended locally).

For FY 1998 the Clinton administration requested a total of nearly $12 billion for economic and military assistance. The administration also signed orders for military sales amounting to more than $10 billion in FY 1996 and FY 1997. Thus, the U.S. was out of pocket less than $2 billion for all foreign assistance.[38] Since more than one-third of U.S. aid was for mil-

38. U.S. Secretary of State, *Congressional Presentation for Foreign Operations FY 1998*, 654, 707.

U.S. Aid: Who Gets What and Why

From 1961 to the mid-1990s the U.S. provided $180 billion in bilateral economic aid to 153 countries and another $27 billion through multilateral agencies such as the World Bank. After Camp David (1978), Israel and Egypt received the lion's share of U.S. aid—in the mid-1990s 40 percent of U.S. aid, amounting to just over $5 billion. The Palestinians were promised half a million spread over five years. More than half of U.S. aid to Israel and Egypt was for military

assistance and training—that is, for "security" more than "development."

Another pair of star-crossed neighbors, Turkey and Greece, also got large sums intended mainly to balance each other's military prowess. The former Soviet republics got $2.5 billion in 1994, much of it charged to the Pentagon's budget to help them disarm and shift toward people's capitalism. Apart from this strategically motivated aid, little was left for poverty relief and sustainable development.

itary assistance and peacekeeping operations, it properly belonged with expenditures for U.S. security. And since nearly $1 billion was for food aid (Public Law 480—Titles I and II, listed in two places on Table 12.3), this could be counted as a subsidy for U.S. farmers. The bottom line was that foreign *economic* aid cost each U.S. taxpayer on average less than $15 per year in the mid-1990s.

In the mid-1990s foreign aid ($60 billion in ODA plus $5 billion in private donations) made up only one-third of the net flow of resources to LDCs from the OECD countries.[39] The other two-thirds came from trade and investment.

Trade can also transfer resources. Even if oil is omitted, the U.S. ran a substantial trade deficit with Latin America, Asia, and Africa in the 1990s—more than $80 billion per year in 1996–1997.[40] This sum dwarfed U.S. foreign aid (at most, $12 billion).

Some LDCs depend on aid; others do not. For much of sub-Saharan

39. Some OECD countries count the writing off of bad trade debts as aid. Some include funds set aside for foreign refugees.

40. *Economic Report of the President* (Washington, D.C.: Government Printing Office, 1997), Table B-103.

India for decades resisted Western products. In the 1990s New Delhi relaxed the barriers and sought outside investment. Some Indians worried about losing their culture; others about losing their physical well-being.

Africa, ODA exceeded 20 percent of GDP in the mid-1990s. For Mozambique and Rwanda, ODA exceeded 95 percent of GDP. For Cambodia, Laos, and Vietnam aid was over one-third of GDP. At the other extreme, ODA for China and India amounted to less than 1 percent of GDP—a pittance next to foreign investment and trade.[41]

Foreign direct investment (FDI) by the North in the South mushroomed in the 1980s and 1990s—rising to some $200 billion in the mid-1990s. But FDI was concentrated in China and nine NICs such as Malaysia and Argentina. Private investors were chary of higher-risk countries.[42]

The balance sheet must also show remittances from guest workers and emigrants to relatives in the South. These amounted to about $20 billion per year in the early 1990s. For India, Morocco, and Turkey such remittances exceeded ODA.

Debt repayments are a huge burden on many developing economies. From 1983 to 1991 LDCs paid out more in interest than they received in loans. As Table 12.5 shows, such payments amounted to $160 billion in 1992.[43] External debt for the average low- or middle-income country amounted to about one-third of GDP in the 1990s. Debt service consumed about one-fourth of LDC export earnings.[44] In the mid-1990s some lenders offered to reduce or cancel debts of the poorest countries, conditioned on internal reform.

Trade—imports and exports—also shapes net transfers. Trade flows produce huge gains for Japan and the Tigers. China's trade balance was roughly even in the 1990s. But the poorest countries imported goods that cost more than the coffee, cocoa, or sugar that they exported.[45]

The dollar value of U.S. arms sales to the Third World has long matched or exceeded that of U.S. foreign aid.[46] Washington justifies its sales as ways to "strengthen stability" and gain market share. So long as LDC demand is strong, suppliers compete. Even peace-preaching Stockholm bribed Rajiv Gandhi's India to buy Swedish arms rather than French.

WILL VOLATILITY KILL MARKET DEMOCRACY?

The **Association of Southeast Asian Nations (ASEAN)** was formed in 1967 to promote economic and political cooperation among its members and resist great power pressures. One of the world's most successful regional organizations, ASEAN admitted its ninth member in 1997—Myanmar (Burma), which joined Brunei, Indonesia, Laos, Malaysia, the Philippines, Singapore, Thailand, and Vietnam, omitting only one regional state, strife-ridden Cambodia. The ASEAN states contained 450

Table 12.5 Net Transfers to LDCs in 1992
(in billions of dollars)

	Received by LDCs	Paid Out by LDCs
ODA	60[a]	
Private and NGO aid	5[b]	
Migrant remittances	20	
Private investment	120	
Debt service		160
Net receipts	45	

SOURCE: Data from *The Reality of Aid 94: An Independent Review of International Aid* (London: Actionaid, 1994); updated in *The Reality of Aid 1996: An Independent Review of International Aid* (London: Earthscan, 1996).
 a. Includes $12 billion in U.S. assistance.
 b. Includes $2 billion from U.S. sources.

41. *WDR 1997*, 218–219.

42. Ibid.

43. A flood of petrodollars became available in the early 1970s as oil producers placed their swelling revenues in U.S. and European banks. The First World urged Latin Americans and Africans to borrow. Military regimes in Argentina and Brazil led the way: They borrowed huge sums and embarked on bold plans to modernize. Soon they hit a double whammy: Contraction of the U.S. economy eroded demand for Third World exports and U.S. interest rates soared. Latin American and African debtors could hardly service interest payments.

44. For Argentina this was progress, for the country's debt service had consumed a staggering 96 percent of its export earnings in 1989. *WDR 1994*, 206–207.

45. First World protectionist barriers block LDC exports which, if they could be sold, would bring in more than ODA. Meanwhile, subsidies to OECD farmers totaled $180 billion in the early 1990s—three times ODA!

46. U.S. military sales and construction agreements worldwide jumped from $15 billion in 1992 to $32 billion in 1993. The biggest buyers were Saudi Arabia, Kuwait, Taiwan, Greece, and Switzerland. But many poor countries also bought arms. Deliveries, however, were fewer than agreements. See *Foreign Military Sales, Foreign Military Construction Sales and Military Assistance Facts as of September 30, 1993* (Washington, D.C.: U.S. Department of Defense, 1993); see also a study organized by the Stockholm International Peace Research Institute: Herbert Wulf, ed., *Arms Industry Limited* (Oxford: Oxford University Press, 1993), 67–72.

How to Win or Lose Big by Selling Short

Today the baht is worth $10 but you expect its value to drop. You tell your broker to sell baht for you one month from today. Meanwhile, he loans the baht to you at $10. One month from now the price drops to $7. You pay $7 plus interest and pocket the difference. Meanwhile, the Thai government tried to prop up the price. So it bought its own currency—first at $9 and then at $8. Now it has more baht than it needs and can sell them for no more than $7. If the baht had risen, say, to $13, you would have had to pay that price on the appointed day—an enormous loss—plus interest.

"Don't Cry for Me Aseanies"

An evening of skits wound up the ASEAN meeting. Dressed as Evita but not looking quite like Madonna, the U.S. Secretary of State sang out:

Don't cry for me Aseanies,
The truth is I always loved you.
All through the SLORC [Burma's military
    dictatorship] days
And the Hun Sen [Cambodian strong
    man] days. . . .
I came here to talk to your leaders,
But they were all on the golf course
So I went back to Sunway Laguna
And called George Soros,
Talked market forces.
Hatched a conspiracy.
The rest is history.

million people—exporters of shoes, semiconductors, tires, and silks, and the fourth-leading trading partner of the U.S. Old cities such as Bangkok were transformed into stretches of mirrored towers, roads clogged with the sclerosis of new-wealth autos and motorcycles.

Overheating and hubris set in. The currencies of Thailand, the Philippines, Malaysia, Indonesia, and even Singapore fell sharply starting in July 1997. When the Thai baht fell by one-fourth, Thailand's Finance Minister asked the IMF for a special credit line to restore its value.

Malaysia's Prime Minister Mahathir Mohamad took a different tack. He accused international financier George Soros of manipulations to undermine the currencies of ASEAN countries because they admitted Myanmar (Burma) to the organization against U.S. wishes, and because "Jews" did not want to see Muslim countries prosper. (As financial wizard, Soros once gained more than a billion dollars by betting against the British pound, though he claimed in late 1997 to have lost a billion in that year's global markets. As philanthropist, he promoted human rights from Buddhist Myanmar to predominantly Muslim Bosnia.)

Malaysia's foreign minister went further: He said the currency fluctuations were caused by "villainous acts of sabotage"—the "height of international criminality." He promised countermeasures by ASEAN.

As it happened, the July 1997 ASEAN meeting in Kuala Lumpur was attended also by U.S. Secretary of State Madeleine Albright. Her assistant for economic affairs, Stuart E. Eizenstat, denied the Malaysian charge. He argued that "financial markets detected strains in the economy of one of the ASEAN countries [Thailand] and acted accordingly. In an increasingly integrated region this has had a mild spillover effect."

Financial crises of this kind follow a familiar sequence:

Stage 1: Government reforms bring down inflation and open the economy through tariff reductions.

Stage 2: Local and foreign investors plow in capital. Interest rates fall and banks expand credit. Imports rise.

Stage 3: Sated and overextended, households buy fewer durables and spend less. Exports decline. (Thai and Malaysian exports became more expensive because the Thai and Malaysian currencies were linked to the dollar, which appreciated in 1996–1997.) Wages increase more rapidly than productivity.

In Stage 3, developers erect too many office and residential buildings relative to demand. Governments neglect education and infrastructure and do little to regulate banking and finance. The growing trade deficit and strong currency lead government to raise interest rates. Next, government sells dollar and yen reserves to buy its own currency and support its exchange rate. Economic growth slows and tax intakes decline.

Stage 4: Investors withdraw money from the country. The currency depreciates and banks fail. The economy goes into a tailspin. Taxes decline. Bankruptcies spread.

Stage 5: The government asks the IMF to stabilize the currency. Devaluation and structural adjustments ensue.[47]

Such volatility threatens democracy as well as investor confidence. How to minimize volatility? One ingredient is openness. As in diplomacy, so in development: Deception and exploitation backfire. The IMF granted Thailand a loan, but demanded a cutback in government spending, curbs on lending, more transparency, general belt-tightening, and easier entry for foreign banks into Thai operations.

Before 1997 ended the Thai syndrome had spread not just to Malaysia but to Indonesia and South Korea. Despite its appearance as a stellar Tiger, South Korea sought and received the largest bailout in history— more than $57 billion—from the IMF, the U.S., and Japan. Meanwhile, credit agencies such as Moody's Investor Service downgraded Korean government and corporate bonds to junk bond status, making foreign banks reluctant to roll over short-term Korean debts. Newly elected ROK president Kim Dae Jung said he feared the country might go bankrupt.[48]

Were the East and Southeast Asian "miracles" ever real? If so, had they now ended? Did the Thai and ROK economies merely tumble in the familiar business cycles of capitalism or had they entered a tailspin? How far would the repercussions reach? Would Japan, China, and Taiwan catch the same virus?

In late 1997 Taiwan escaped the worst of its neighbors' turmoil. Why? Taiwan still had the world's highest foreign currency reserves on a per capita basis. It did not borrow from abroad to build large projects. It invested more in educating its work force than most Asian countries. Taiwan's banks were not stretched thin in high-risk loans. Taiwan was more closely tied to the Chinese–Hong Kong economy than to Southeast Asia. Taiwan's version of capitalism had been democratic for a decade; capitalism in most of East and Southeast Asia was still strong-man or strong-party capitalism, based on patronage rather than openness. In Taiwan, transparency was high and corruption relatively low thanks to multiparty democracy and a vigilant press.

47. Hausmann, "Will Volatility Kill Market Democracy?" 62.

48. On December 23, 1997, Moody's lowered South Korea's credit rating by four notches—from BBB to B+, the same level as Pakistan and the Dominican Republic, and one notch above Kazakstan, Lebanon, and Paraguay. Three months before, ROK credit was AA–, the same as Italy and Sweden. Critics said Moody's was wrong to downgrade the Korean *government*, which had underborrowed. See *Financial Times*, December 24, 1997, 9.

WHAT PROPOSITIONS HOLD? WHAT QUESTIONS REMAIN?

Wealth-creation and development are complex processes. Each region has its own needs and assets. What worked in East Asia may not work in regions that lack human capital and even markets. Table 12.6 suggests maxims valid for most countries.

Table 12.6 Guidelines for North, South, East, and West

How to Stay Poor	How to Develop Equitably
1. Claim values. Quarrel and fight among yourselves and with outsiders.	1. Create values. Make peace at home and with outsiders.
2. Waste and pollute. Live for today and for yourself.	2. Use resources wisely. Seek sustainable development.
3. Accept fate.	3 "Image" alternative futures.
4. Don't study, invent, plant, save, or invest.	4. Prepare for the future.
5. Multiply so that demand for resources exceeds supply.	5. Adjust population to resources.
6. Ignore public health and preventive medicine.	6. Pursue higher HDI. Promote public health.
7. Keep women down and out.	7. Educate and liberate women.
8. Grow, use, make, market, and sell drugs. Fight over them and markets.	8. Discourage drug cultivation and use, including tobacco and alcohol.
9. Let organized crime flourish.	9. Promote law, order, public safety, private ownership.
10. Shun science and its applications.	10. Cultivate science and its applications.
11. Keep most people in ignorance and illiteracy.	11. Promote mass literacy and numeracy.
12. Exploit and oppress minorities.	12. Give equal opportunity to minorities.
13. Keep land in the hands of a few.	13. Carry out land reforms to promote peace and efficiency.
14. Teach distrust of anyone outside the family.	14. Promote trust and teamwork among all elements of society.
15. Cultivate autarky. Don't specialize or trade. Block imports and pursue import-substitution.	15. Cultivate comparative and competitive advantage. Use an export-led strategy to join international free trade.
16. Avoid risky ideas, inventions, undertakings. Foster an official world view.	16. Promote moderate risk-taking, new enterprises, and new forms of social organization.
17. Reward regime supporters with bribes and kickbacks.	17. Develop a meritocracy. Fight corruption.
18. Depend on central planning; distrust free enterprise.	18. Promote market-friendly government to encourage private enterprise.
19. Shun the outside world or, alternatively, count heavily on outside help.	19. Combine self-reliance with outside aid and investment. Don't count on outsiders for what you can't do yourself.
20. Trust in large and showy projects such as high dams and power stations to win votes and transform nature.	20. Distrust any promised panacea. Make modest adjustments to nature.

Memo to SAARC: Guidelines for South Asian Development

Some of the most weighty factors in development arise from each society's way of life. Try to anticipate what effects your policies will have on values, motives, and attitudes. In the long run these factors will determine whether your policies succeed in speeding economic development. Incentives to achieve can be throttled by too little government or by excessive governmental controls.

Promote Growth with Social Welfare

Neither growth nor social welfare can succeed alone. In Pakistan, for example, growth raised incomes of the poor but social services and schooling lagged. Try to strengthen each link in a virtuous circle: stimulate economic growth ↔ reduce poverty ↔ expand schooling ↔ empower women ↔ improve health ↔ stimulate economic growth.

Here are some specific suggestions:

1. **Tap the poor's most abundant asset—labor.** Utilize market incentives, social and political institutions, improved infrastructure, and technological innovation.

2. **Provide the poor with basic social services.** Growth will languish without schooling, nutrition, health care, and family planning to enable poor people to take advantage of the jobs and other opportunities generated by economic growth.

3. **Promote public health.** Invest more in local clinics than in central hospitals. Train paramedics ("barefoot doctors"). Teach literacy. Make sure that written directions are clear (and certainly not in a foreign language). Promote family planning. Show the benefits of washing and sanitation. Dig wells and latrines and maintain them. Prevent AIDS (5.6 million new HIV infections appeared worldwide in 1996, with 1.7 million deaths from AIDS). Facilitate private sector involvement (as in Tunisia, where eleven large government hospitals were converted into semiautonomous institutions with incentives to improve performance).

4. **Invest more resources in women.** There is an economic case for society to subsidize schooling for women more than for men, because the returns are greater: fewer births, less infant and child mortality, fewer maternal deaths, improved nutrition and schooling for children, plus female participation in the work force.

5. **Establish a social safety net.** Provide cash transfers to the destitute, sick, and elderly and establish a social safety net for others hurt by the shocks of economic development. Provide compensation and retraining for those who lose their jobs.

6. **Promote agriculture.** Encourage and subsidize land reform, free market pricing, local credit unions, producers' cooperatives, roads, access to markets, storage facilities, agricultural research stations, and farm extension services. Study pros and cons of diversified food crops versus single "cash" crops such as tea and jute. Utilize traditional wisdom as well as modern science and technology, safeguard biodiversity including traditional herbs and medicines, integrate low technology with intermediate and high technology, and minimize use of chemical fertilizers and pesticides.[49]

7. **Treat knowledge as an essential** (though insufficient) condition for development. Promote literacy and quality education.[50] Train skilled workers. Induce scientists to work in their native lands. Organize development projects so that they generate skills as well as roads and bridges.[51]

---

49. The pros and cons of the Green Revolution are discussed in Chapter 14.

50. The drive of Thailand and Malaysia toward NIC status stalled in the mid-1990s from a shortage of secondary-school graduates. Many Thais and Malaysians could read well enough to take assembly jobs but were ill prepared for more complicated work.

51. When the U.S. built roads and ports for Trinidad during World War II, the Americans taught locals how to be carpenters and plumbers. When Chinese aid workers built highways for Nepal in the 1980s, they did most of the work themselves.

8. Maximize investment/minimize debt. Invest for growth in infrastructure, agriculture, and industry.[52] Use multiple vehicles—loans, bonds, direct investments—by private investors, national banks and agencies. Encourage local capitalists and landowners to invest at home—not in Swiss or Bahamian bank accounts.[53] Remember that a small loan can transform a life.[54]

9. Join the world economic system. Autarky is a dead end. Use comparative and competitive advantage to find a niche. Diversify. Do not depend on selling the same goods (sugar, coffee, shoes, shirts) that many others produce. Do not count on producers cartels to regulate supply and prices of commodities such as coffee. (Even the oil-producers in OPEC have been unable to control supply and demand.) Seek aid but do not count on charity.

Practice Market-Friendly Government

1. Intervene reluctantly. Let markets work unless they visibly fail. Do not protect domestic manufactures that could be imported more cheaply unless local production offers substantial spillover benefits.

2. Apply checks and balances. Use markets to discipline interventions. Thus, South Korea's government withdrew its support for the heavy chemicals industry when market performance showed that the policy was failing.

3. Intervene openly. Make interventions simple and subject to rules rather than official discretion. For example, use tariffs rather than quotas.[55]

4. Cultivate good governance. Appoint officials on the basis of merit. Eliminate corruption. Develop cabinet stability. Define budgets on time and stick to them. Produce and share meaningful statistics.

Guidelines for the North

1. Think of development, investment, and trade as investment in security. Use your "peace dividend" to invest in development and conflict prevention.

2. Do not promote arms acquisitions by LDCs. Just one arms deal can divert funds that could build one hundred or more schools and clinics.

3. Promote stable democracy. Demand "good governance" and respect for human rights as conditions for any form of aid.[56]

4. Couple relief aid with steps to improve agriculture and self-reliance. Avoid food distributions that re-

---

52. A major demand by Indians in Mexico in 1994 was roads to help them market their produce. Infrastructure needs are the focus of *WDR 1994.*

53. Private investment declined from 70 percent to 53 percent of total investment in Colombia in 1970–1991; in Mexico—gaining in confidence—it rose from 65 to 77 percent. For twenty-one other countries, see *HDR 1993,* 52.

54. Masai women in Tanzania had to sell their necklaces to get started in business. But Nepalese women received United Nations loans to buy looms with which to make woolen goods. Small sums can go a long way where average incomes are less than a dollar per day.

55. *East Asian Miracle,* esp. 347–368.

56. Amnesty International noted in the mid-1990s that U.S. aid went to nineteen countries that tortured prisoners—among them, Israel, Egypt, Turkey, and Colombia.

duce incentives for local growers or perpetuate settle-ment in flood-prone regions. Circumvent dictators who repress their weak and hungry subjects.

5. Implement joint ventures for mutual gain. "Fordism" works better for all parties than exploita-tion. Complementary strengths make it possible to mix and match technology, investment capital, know-how, and labor. But do not permit another Bhopal.[57] Foreign companies in LDCs should observe the same ethical and safety standards as at home.

6. Stabilize currency. Help LDCs to develop a freely convertible, stable currency to control inflation, provide incentives to work and save, and attract investment.

7. Trade. First World countries can make or break an LDC economy by opening or closing their doors to its products.

8. Seek sustainable development—economic growth with environmental protection. Help LDCs to ob-tain non-polluting technologies. Arrange debt swaps, for example, conservation of Amazon jungles for cancel-lation of foreign debt.

Political instability and war are major impediments to develop-ment. Many of Africa's wars arise from the crazy-quilt borders laid down by Western imperialists in the 19th and early 20th centuries regardless of local ethnic patterns and economic needs. Post-colonial wars are fought with weapons made in Rus-sia, Europe, the U.S., and China.

57. Lax standards led to an explosion of a Union Carbide chemical pesticide factory at Bhopal, India, that killed over 3,300 residents and maimed tens of thousands in 1984. Who was responsible? Company offi-cials in Connecticut? Local employees? The U.S. or Indian or local Bhopal government? Should the trial be held in the U.S. or India? Was the U.S. government obliged to extradite Union Carbide officials to India? Finally the Supreme Court of India called on Union Carbide to pay $470 million to settle all claims—a pittance by U.S. standards.

KEY NAMES AND TERMS

Association of Southeast Asian Nations (ASEAN)
autarky
concessional loans
dependency theory
development
East Asia
foreign aid
gender-related development index (GDI)
Grameen Bank
grants
Human Poverty Index (HPI)
import-substitution

income poverty
modernization theory
New International Economic Order (NIEO)
newly industrializing countries (NICs)
official development assistance (ODA)
rent-seeking
South Asia
structural adjustment policies
syndrome of underdevelopment
Tigers
U.S. Agency for International Development (USAID)

QUESTIONS TO DISCUSS

1. What is "development?" Is there a best route to development?
2. Who is poor? By what measure?
3. In what sense is underdevelopment a syndrome? Illustrate principles with examples.
4. Is the U.S. model of development appropriate to the Third World?
5. Is the East Asian model appropriate to South Asia? To Latin America? To Africa?
6. Is it possible to live well on a low income? Look up statistics and compare Sri Lanka and India; Cuba and Haiti; Botswana and Niger.
7. What is the relevance of literacy to development?
8. If Swiss and Japanese women stay at home, why shouldn't Nigerian and Pakistani women?
9. Is the IMF right to demand structural adjustment as a condition for loans?
10. Compare transparency in banking and diplomacy. What are the pros and cons?
11. Why might a government be reluctant to invest in female education?
12. If Germany prospered with less aid than Britain or France after World War II, does that mean that India would be better off with less aid?
13. What sorts of foreign aid are useful? Counterproductive?
14. If you had $100,000 to invest in stocks, how would you allocate it between the First and Third Worlds?

RECOMMENDED RESOURCES

BOOKS

Birdsall, Nancy, and Frederick Jaspersen, eds. *Pathways to Growth: Comparing East Asia and Latin America.* Baltimore: Johns Hopkins University Press, 1997.

Blumberg, Rae Lesser, et al., eds. *EnGENDERing Wealth and Well-Being: Empowerment for Global Change.* Boulder, Colo.: Westview, 1995.

Conrad, Joseph. *Heart of Darkness, with the Congo Diary.* New York: Penguin, 1995.

Dreze, Jean, and Amartya Sen. *The Political Economy of Hunger.* 3 vols. Oxford: Clarendon Press, 1990–1991.

Inter-American Development Bank. *Latin America After a Decade of Reforms.* Baltimore: Johns Hopkins University Press, 1997.

Lerner, Daniel. *The Passing of Traditional Society: Modernizing the Middle East.* Glencoe, Il.: Free Press, 1958.

Naipaul, V. S. *A Bend in the River.* New York: Knopf, 1979.

Summers, Lawrence H. *Investing in All the People: Educating Women in Developing Countries.* Washington, D.C.: World Bank, 1994.

World Bank. *Adjustment in Africa: Reforms, Results, and the Road Ahead.* New York: Oxford University Press, 1994.

World Bank. *World Development Report.* New York: Oxford University Press, annual.

United Nations Development Programme. *Human Development Report.* New York: Oxford University Press, annual.

U.S. Agency for International Development. *Development and the National Interest: U.S. Economic Assistance into the 21st Century.* Washington, D.C.: AID, 1989.

WEB SITES

Asia-Pacific Economic Cooperation (APEC)
http://www.apecsec.org.sg
Association of Southeast Asian Nations (ASEAN)
http://www.asean.sec.org
CARE *(NGO relief organization with branches in many countries)*
http://www.care.org
CARE development resource center
http://www.care.org/devrescenter/index.html
Institute of Development Studies (IDS) *(Sussex, England)*
online information service (Devline)
http://www.ids.ac.uk
references to British Library for Development Studies
http://www.ids.ac.uk/blds/blds.html
addresses of development organizations
http://nt1.ids.ac.uk/eldis/devorg.htm
International Monetary Fund (IMF)
http://www.imf.org
social dimensions of the IMF's policy dialogue
http://www.imf.org/external/pubs/ft/pam/pam47/pam47con.htm
U.S. Agency for International Development (USAID)
http://www.info.usaid.gov
U.S. Peace Corps
http://www.peacecorps.gov
extensive Peace Corps-related sites at CAPCA (Chicago Area Peace Corps Association)
http://www.capca.org/pclist.htm
World Bank
http://www.worldbank.org
World Bank topics on development
http://www.worldbank.org/html/extdr/thematic.htm

C H A P T E R   T H I R T E E N

TRANSITIONS: CAN THE SECOND WORLD JOIN THE FIRST?

THE BIG QUESTIONS IN CHAPTER 13

- Why did the Communist world collapse?

- What kinds of transitions confront the ex-Second World?

- How do you alter an authoritarian political culture?

- Does affluence lead to or follow democratization?

- Does political freedom depend on economic freedom or vice versa?

- Should the transition to a market economy take place gradually or overnight ("cold turkey")?

- Would the onset of democracy bring peace or war?

- Do the same rules for transition apply to all cultures or must they be adapted to local circumstances?

- Can outsiders help in these transitions? If so, how?

- Is aid or investment the more powerful vehicle for change?

- Why has China's economy grown at a rapid pace while Russia's and Kazakstan's have declined?

- Why is it so difficult to get Caspian oil to market?

- How do ethnic problems obstruct commercial oil development?

- Should Kazakstan look east, west, north, south, or inward?

"Which Way Should We Turn?" ... *Your country is five times larger than France but dwarfed by two neighbors—the world's largest state (the Russian Federation) and the world's most populous country (China). Nothing is simple for Kazakstan. More than one-third of your people are Russians. Just across the border in China you have kinsmen. Everyone wants your oil and other mineral resources. The president of Kazakstan turns to you, a trusted comrade from Communist Party times, for help. "Which way should we turn?" he asks. "Should we align with Russia? China? The Islamic world? The West?"*

Kazakstan, like most countries of the former Second World, must make three difficult passages: First, it must replace a Moscow-directed, Communist dictatorship with a more popular government. Second, it must switch from a top-down, command-economy to a market-friendly economy. Third, it must develop an independent foreign policy in a world free of cold war.

Each transition is problematic. And what is good and feasible for Kazakstan depends also on the outcome of similar transitions in other Central Asian countries, in Russia, and in China. Each transition is shaped by many factors: the geopolitics and geonomics of oil; the spread of modern weapons; the strength or weakness of international trade; the engagement or passivity of the U.S. and the European Union. And beyond this, stretched between steppe and mountain, short of water and fearful of earthquakes, you are deeply aware of the fragile biosphere on which all life depends.

CONTENDING CONCEPTS
AND EXPLANATIONS

THE SECOND WORLD: WHY DID IT IMPLODE?

The Second World defied many theorists, both Communist and non-Communist. Karl Marx was wrong. Communism did not arrive first in industrialized England or Germany, but in backward Russia. Communists seized power there in 1917 not because of deterministic "forces" but thanks to forceful individuals such as Vladimir Lenin and Leon Trotsky.

Lenin also erred. Soviet Russia could and did survive without help from a revolution in Europe. Contrary to Lenin's forecasts, capitalist states did not fight each other over markets nor did they launch a serious attack on the "socialist fatherland." U.S. officials in the 1920s erred too when they predicted that the Soviet system would soon fall. Committed to this logic, Washington put off formal relations with the USSR until 1933.

After World War II some Westerners exaggerated Soviet power; some demanded that the West match every arrow in the Soviet quiver (multiple symmetry). Still others erred in predicting that an arms competition would lead inevitably to war.

Few Westerners had any theory to anticipate the rapid and peaceful

The Berlin Wall, built by East Germany in 1961 to prevent more East Germans from moving West, was knocked down in 1989 as the larger Iron Curtain, fortified by barbed wire and machine guns, disintegrated. Here, children play in the rubble of the wall in front of Berlin's old Reichstag building.

collapse of the Soviet empire. "Declinists" forecast a decline of the "super-powers" due to imperial overreach. In 1989–1991, however, the Soviet system collapsed while the U.S. rebounded.

One major IR theory proved completely wrong: There was no last-ditch "hegemonic" war as the Soviet empire crashed. Quite the opposite: U.S. President George Bush tried to prop up the USSR.

As the Soviet empire sank, "endists" pronounced an end to history. To replace the Cold War contest of ideas, they expected the "common marketization" of international relations. But nationalism and holy wars upended endism.

Americans who favored a tough approach to the "evil empire" said that SDI (the Strategic Defense Initiative) and other Pentagon programs of the 1980s had spent the USSR into bankruptcy. They ignored downward trends in Soviet life evident long before SDI began. The militarization of the Soviet society at the expense of economic growth and well-being began decades earlier—under Josef Stalin and then Nikita Khrushchev. Dictatorship and centralized planning neutered creativity. The Soviet system lacked the creative fitness to cope with complex challenges on every front.

The theory best supported by events was George Kennan's forecast that Soviet expansion could be contained until it imploded. But while Kennan in 1946–1947 expected this process to require ten or fifteen years, it demanded more than forty. Kennan later opposed what he called the undue militarization of containment. But scientist and Soviet dissident Andrei Sakharov, as we saw in Chapter 6, thought Stalin would have exploited any U.S. failure to maximize its military potential. Not until Mikhail Gorbachev emerged was there a top Soviet leader not mesmerized by raw power.

As we saw in Chapter 7, Gorbachev proved psychologist Charles Osgood wrong. The Soviet president showed that GRIT (graduated reciprocation in tension-reduction) could be initiated by the weaker party and be maintained for years before the other side (Washington) reciprocated.

Zbigniew Brzezinski was right to underscore the role of "technetronics" in the Cold War. U.S. leadership in the Information Revolution, as we saw in Chapter 5, gained both soft and hard power.[1]

Few observers appreciated the ways that nationalism could and did undercut Soviet power. Despite the East German and Hungarian uprisings in 1953 and 1956, most observers assumed that modernization or Communism had eradicated nationalism. It turned out, however, that

1. Zbigniew Brzezinski, *Between Two Ages: America's Role in the Technetronic Era* (New York: Viking, 1970).

national liberation movements were as weighty as any factor in subverting the Soviet Goliath. A divided Politburo failed to accommodate or repress drives for independence in the Baltic, in the Russia of **Boris Yeltsin**, and in other republics of the Soviet "Union."[2]

TRANSITIONS TO WHAT? HOW?

The major idea underlying Western policy to the former Second World was **liberal internationalism**. It holds that the surest foundation for peace and prosperity is market democracy—a democratic political system and a market economy. These are the essentials of First World development—a path pioneered by the West and adapted by Japan and the Tigers.

Much of the Second World—Eastern Europe, Russia, and most other former Soviet republics—opted in the 1990s to move closer to the First World. Even Outer Mongolia chose multiparty democracy. But China and Vietnam introduced economic freedoms while retaining a Communist dictatorship. Cuba and North Korea kept Communist politics and economics.

Map 13.1 on page 374 shows the Russian Federation and the fourteen other states that emerged from the Soviet Union in 1991. As we saw in Chapter 8, each of these fifteen states had been a "union-republic" in the USSR, each with a constitutional right to secede. The Russian Federation, however, consisted of many units with no constitutional right to secede but insistent on greater autonomy. **Tatarstan**, for example, asserted its "sovereignty" in the early 1990s even though it remained within the Russian Federation. Political activists in the northern Caucasus republic of **Chechnya**, however, demanded complete independence from Russia. Chechens reasoned that they had as much right to independent statehood as neighboring Azeris or, for that matter, Russians.

To join the First World the former Communist states had to make three sweeping **transitions**: to a market economy participating in the World Trade Organization; to a democracy with substantial political and civil freedoms; and to a foreign policy oriented toward peace, law, and conflict resolution.

The stakes were immense. If Russia became a stable democracy, this would provide a sounder basis for peace than deterrence. If Russia developed a vibrant market economy, Russia and its trading partners would become richer. If Russia's foreign policy harmonized with the West's, it would be easier to end conflict in the Balkans and the Middle East. If

2. Walter C. Clemens, Jr., "Who or What Killed the Soviet Union? How Three Davids Undermined Goliath," *Nationalism and Ethnic Politics* 3, no. 1 (spring 1997): 136–158.

Map 13.1 New States Emerged from the Former USSR

China also followed the liberal internationalist route, prospects for peace and prosperity would gain immensely.

How to make these transitions? Analysts disagreed. What is needed to alter an authoritarian political culture? Could the experiences of Spain, Argentina, and Taiwan be relevant to Eastern Europe and Russia? Is affluence a source or a result of democratization? Does political freedom depend on economic freedom, or vice versa?

Should the transition to a market economy take place gradually or instantly ("cold turkey")? Should reforms begin in the countryside or in cities—in agriculture or in industry? Worldwide there were about seventy countries in the 1990s trying to move from autarky toward market economics. Were there rules that applied to any country? Or did the rules have to fit the local culture and circumstances?

Would the onset of democracy bring peace or war? Did peace depend on democracy or democracy on peace?

Could outsiders help in these transitions? If so, how? Should outsiders work with the local governments or try to bypass them? Was it enough for aid workers to know their subject or did they have to be steeped in the local language and culture? Would aid or investment be the more powerful vehicle for change?

For all those unsure how to proceed, Napoleon's advice made sense: *"On s'engage et puis l'on voit."* Begin and then see.

COMPARING THEORY AND REALITY: DISTINCT TRANSITIONS

All Western governments wanted to help the former Communist or Second World to join the First. Was this a pipe dream? Perhaps, but who could have predicted in 1945 that in less than a decade major foes in two world wars would be close allies?

RUSSIA—WHAT PATH?

When the USSR collapsed, no Western elites urged kicking Russia while it was down. Realists wanted to be on good terms with the world's largest country when it bounced back. They wanted Russia to return to the world scene—not like Nazi Germany in the 1930s but like democratic Germany in the 1950s. Idealists hoped for a new world order and trusted that, with encouragement, Russians would embrace democracy. Interdependence thinkers focused on common concerns linking Russia and the West—controlling nuclear spread and pollution, resolving regional conflicts, and trading the goods and services in which each side excelled. Russian rockets and space vehicles could carry U.S. scientific instruments in joint ventures into space.

Why Russia Is Not Germany in the 1950s

Russia in the 1990s, however, was not like Germany after 1945. It more resembled Germany in the 1920s—a country that became ripe for Adolf Hitler.

Unconquered. The USSR had not been defeated in battle. Like many Germans in the 1920s, some Russians blamed their former leaders (Gorbachev and company) for a "stab in the back"—for killing their own empire.

Unoccupied. The USSR was not occupied like Germany after 1945. Western authorities had no power to intervene directly in Russia. They could not remove Communist elites; break up monopolies; rewrite the constitution; issue or control money. Western influence depended mainly on cooptive power—the ability to get Russians to do what the West wanted because *Russians* wanted to.

Unpurged. Unlike occupied Germany and Japan in 1945, the West made no attempt to arrest and charge Soviet leaders with crimes against humanity. While some Russians leveled charges against Gorbachev in his capacity as last president of the USSR, others against those who plotted Gorbachev's overthrow, and still others against those who opposed Russian President Yeltsin in 1993, no one was judged guilty.

Many former Soviet leaders restyled themselves as nationalists—not just in Moscow but also in Minsk, Vilnius, and Tashkent. The old guard had experience and contacts that political novices lacked. Some former Communists, like Southern plantation owners after the U.S. Civil War, did what they could to restore the old ways and block reform.

These former elites continued to play major roles in political, economic, and military affairs. They scratched each others' backs, encouraging corruption as well as inefficiency. Many Russian legislators guarded the old Communist system. The parliament did little to encourage foreign investment. It refused to clarify property rights and make contracts sacred. It favored high taxes that discouraged foreign investors.

Not Fined. The West did not ask Russia for compensation for damages during the Cold War or other wars backed by Moscow. Instead, the West endeavored to help Eastern Europe and the former Soviet republics to rebuild.

Not Forcibly Dismembered. Russia lost many imperial borderlands accumulated by tsars and Soviet commissars. From Estonia to Kazakstan, peoples along Russia's western and southern periphery opted for independence. But no Western state sought territory lost to the Soviet empire. The new Germany did not ask for any of the lands lost in the 1940s to Russia, Lithuania, Poland, and Czechoslovakia. Tokyo, however, refused to aid or invest heavily in Russia until Moscow returned islands taken from Japan in 1945.

Not Forcibly Disarmed. After both world wars Germany was compelled to disarm. In the 1990s, however, Russia was not disarmed. But presidents Bush and Clinton cut U.S. forces unilaterally and sought broader arms accords with Russia. The Kremlin cooperated in some ways but also sold weapons and advanced technologies to Iran and other countries regarded as "rogues" by Washington. Russian forces remained in Germany and in the Baltic states until 1994.

Unstable. Russia was much less stable in the 1990s than West Germany or Japan after 1945. There was constant strife between President Yeltsin and the state **Duma**, the lower house of parliament, where ultra-nationalists and Communists attacked Yeltsin and his moderate course.

Russian Politics: Presidential + Patronage Dictatorship

The transition from totalitarian dictatorship to a more limited government was extremely difficult in Russia and most other Soviet republics. There was no consensus on the proper role of government. Some authoritarians—leaders and followers alike—yearned for the good old days. They preferred Communist "order" over non-Communist anarchy.

In Russia, as in most former Soviet republics, the executive was extremely strong and barely accountable to the legislature. When parliament defied President Yeltsin in 1993, he shut down the parliament and had loyal troops assault the building to drive out recalcitrant parliamentarians. When new elections produced an equally defiant parliament, Yeltsin and his ministers issued decrees without obtaining parliamentary approval. Yeltsin's Russia lacked a responsible system of checks and balances. It had an authoritarian system without authority—what one Russian scholar called "democracy for bureaucracy."[3]

Rent seeking was rampant. Government officials and their cronies found ways to twist the rules for private gain. Opaque and complex regulatory functions could be interpreted by whim. Prime Minister **Viktor Chernomyrdin**, former boss of the oil and gas ministry, quickly became a multimillionaire.

Organized crime skimmed off at least 3 percent of Russia's GDP in the 1990s. Doubts about Russia's future led the newly rich to place much of their wealth in foreign bank accounts or real estate—another 2 or 3 percent of GDP. Enterprises close to the government did not pay their taxes, leading to budgetary shortfalls. In the mid-1990s the Russian government did not pay army officers for six months at a time. Even the military's Strategic Rocket Forces could not pay their electric bills, leading electric suppliers to threaten shut-offs. Still, the armed forces were little diminished since Cold War times. Sullen and resentful, they lost their traditional respect for civilian authority.

Governments in Russia and most former Soviet republics were among the least efficient and most corrupt in the world in the 1990s. They failed to provide law and order; to protect property; to apply rules and policies predictably. Investors did not consider these states to be credible, curtail-

3. Sergei Rogov, "Five Challenges for Russia," *Foreign Policy Research Institute WIRE* 5, no. 7 (April 1997).

ing investment and growth.[4] Ordinary citizens did not trust the government, the police, or the courts.

Privatization created a new Russian elite of robber barons. Government officials awarded controlling shares of former state companies to themselves and their cronies—unelected and largely unregulated coalitions of former Communist apparatchiks and wealthy new bankers. There was little transparency in these transactions. The very banks that arranged "auctions" of state enterprises placed the winning bids. Some individual winners paid with their lives when rivals took revenge through gangland assassinations. In 1995 nine of thirty executives in the Russian Business Roundtable were assassinated. Government was reduced to penury by its inability to collect taxes. In September 1997 Yeltsin announced his determination to control the new capitalists by instituting "clear and equal rules of economic behavior," rooting out corruption, and launching competitive bidding. But some ministers dragged their feet and parliament remained hostile. Yeltsin played off reformist technocrats such as Deputy Prime Minister Boris Nemtsov against old-style Communist Party apparatchiks such as Prime Minister Chernomyrdin. Nemtsov tried to liberate the oil and gas industry from control of the former apparatchiks; Chernomyrdin had reasons to keep it there.

Rebuilding the Economy

For the third time in the century, Russia and Eastern Europe needed to rebuild. After World Wars I and II the Soviet regime had its own vision of what should be done. The Soviets built and rebuilt their state with little help from the West. In the 1990s, however, the Second World lacked any vision except to adapt to First World ways.

Japan stood aloof from Russia, but the Western governments planned and acted together to produce an aid package that would help the former Soviet Union politically and economically. In 1993 the Group of Seven (G-7) major industrialized states agreed to provide $28 billion to stabilize the Russian ruble and to help with balance-of-payments problems. Much of the G-7 aid was distributed through international financial institutions—the World Bank, the International Monetary Fund (IMF), and the European Bank for Reconstruction and Development. Russia became the 165th member of the IMF in June 1992, but Moscow had to borrow $940 million from the G-7 just to pay its dues. And membership did not ensure access to IMF loans. For that, Russia would have to curb inflation, lower its budget deficit, restrict money supply, and meet international debt obligations.

4. World Bank, *World Development Report 1997* (New York: Oxford University Press, 1997), 5. These findings were noted and underscored by some Russian newspapers.

The U.S. sponsored a vast array of aid programs under the 1992 Freedom Support Act "for Russia and the emerging Eurasian democracies." In scope (but not in dollar value) the U.S. programs outdid the Marshall Plan.

Many U.S. programs bolstered private sector activity in the U.S. as well as in Russia. President Bill Clinton pledged in 1993 that half of U.S. aid would go directly to entrepreneurs in the private sector, but it was hard to circumvent the centralized structures and old boy networks left over from Soviet times.

Investment by private corporations and foundations began to dwarf official U.S. aid. Firms such as Coca Cola, McDonald's, and Johnson & Johnson sought footholds in a huge consumer market. Chevron Corporation and other Western firms negotiated joint ventures to extract mineral wealth.

The more centralized and poorly adjusted an economy, the greater the difficulty in making the transition to a market economy. The worse the initial conditions, the greater the need for a package of economic measures that allows prices to be determined by the market without severe inflation. A comparative analysis ranked the former Soviet Union alongside Albania and just behind Bulgaria and Romania in the severity of its problems. Of the former Communist countries of Eastern Europe, the Czech Republic and Hungary had the best circumstances in the early 1990s; Estonia and Latvia were strongest in the former Soviet Union. None of the ex-Soviet states could easily pull itself up by its bootstraps.[5]

The value of foreign aid in reconstructing the former Soviet Union was limited by many factors. First, the amount received was much smaller on a per capita basis than what Western Europe received under the

The Russian flag rose at the Council of Europe in Strasbourg in February 1996 as the Russian Federation became the 39th member of the Council of Europe. But Russians were unhappy that they had no early prospects of joining the European Union, and that NATO was expanding to take in Moscow's former allies in ways that some Russians saw as threatening to Russia.

5. Paul Marer, "Central and Eastern Europe: An Economic Perspective," in *United States Relations with Central and Eastern Europe,* ed. Dick Clark (Queenstown, Md.: Aspen Institute, 1992), 17–26.

Private and Public U.S. Aid to the Former Soviet Union: Examples

• Private aid included the International Executive Service Corps, which provided technical assistance in converting military to civilian industries.

• The Business Information Service served as a clearinghouse to match U.S. investors and businesses in the former Soviet Union.

• The American Bar Association provided legal advisers to the former Soviet Union.

• Partnerships were established with U.S. hospitals to provide training and boost pharmaceutical production in the former Soviet Union.

• The U.S. Department of Energy and the U.S. Nuclear Regulatory Commission provided technical assistance to improve safety of civilian nuclear reactors and improve the efficiency of coal and other heating systems.

• More than five hundred Peace Corps volunteers went to the former Soviet Union to assist in many domains, for example, bookkeeping in rural cooperatives.

Marshall Plan.[6] Net inflow of resources—official aid and private investment—to Eastern Europe was about $20 billion in 1992–1994 and $40 billion to the former Soviet Union. Investors were much more attracted to the Czech Republic, Hungary, Poland, and Estonia than to Ukraine, Russia, or—the extreme case—Tajikistan.

Net aggregate flows to Russia, Ukraine, and Belarus in 1994 amounted to $29 per capita. Half of this amount came from official development assistance—loans and grants, principally from the IMF. There was also direct foreign investment—about one-fifth of the total—and some loans by Western commercial banks.[7] Official U.S. aid to the former Soviet Union amounted to about $4.45 per capita in 1994 (but only $0.71 per Kazak and $1.17 per Russian, while Armenians received $23.24 per capita and Georgians $9.81).[8] No matter how the numbers were interpreted, however, $29 per capita was not a lordly sum to jump start a troubled industrial economy trying to move from central planning to free enterprise.

Second, money arrived in dribbles as donor institutions hedged their bets and conditioned their aid on reforms. Some Russians summarized their predicament: "The West pretends to help us and we pretend to reform."

Third, much of the aid went to the wrong people and places and for inappropriate purposes; some was recycled into Russians' private accounts in Swiss banks or condominiums in Cyprus or Florida.

The Yeltsin government set most prices free early in the 1990s. Russia avoided famine and hyperinflation (defined as 50 percent or more per month) in the early 1990s, but production fell by about 20 percent per year. Savings were wiped out by inflation that reached 20 and 30 percent a month. Pensioners and most people on government salaries saw their buying power evaporate.

Russia's GDP declined sharply between 1991 and 1996, finally stabilizing in 1997. For a country heavily dependent on military industry, the demise of the Cold War was a disaster. Conversion to civilian industry proved very difficult.

In most of the former USSR, Human Development Index (HDI) scores fell steeply. Alcoholism, suicides, and homicides increased sharply. The average life span for Russian men declined in just a few years from 63 to 59 or less. At least one-fifth of Russia's population lived in poverty. Income disparities steadily rose—the richest 10 percent of the population received 23 percent of all income, while the poorest 10 percent took in only 3 percent.[9]

6. Europe—with a population one-third larger than that of the U.S.—received 1 to 2 percent of U.S. GNP for about four years. The $28 billion aid package that the G-7 proposed for the former Soviet Union in 1993 would be less than 0.2 percent of total First World GNP (more than $16 trillion for the OECD). This was a far smaller burden for the donors than U.S. aid to Europe and Japan had been in the late 1940s. On the other hand, the OECD population was nearly three times that of the former Soviet Union. Therefore, even a tiny share of OECD wealth could be a substantial sum—especially when converted into rubles (which traded at more than 1,000 rubles to one dollar in 1993).

7. Data from World Bank, *World Debt Tables* (1996), analyzed by Bartlomiej Kaminski and Zhen Kun Wang in Karen Dawisha and Bruce Parrott, eds., *The International Politics of Eurasia*, Vol. 10 (Armonk, N.Y.: M. E. Sharpe, 1997), Tables 12.1 and 12.2.

8. Calculated from OECD statistics by Peter Dombrowski in *International Politics,* ed. Dawisha and Parrott, Table 10.2.

9. *RFE/RL News Briefs* 3, no. 31 (25–29 July and 1–5 August 1994): 5.

Illness spread because children and others were not vaccinated and often lacked clean water. People ate more starch and less fruit, vegetables, and protein. Cholera broke out in Russia as well as in Daghestan and Azerbaijan. Public health was endangered by Soviet-era ecocide—untreated pollution of all kinds, including nuclear wastes and oil spills—and by still-operating Soviet nuclear reactors.

The Marshall Plan experience suggested that outside aid could help promote economic recovery. But Europeans in the late 1940s already possessed capital, know-how, and entrepreneurial spirit—all lacking in post-Soviet Russia. And while the U.S. provided only a tiny fraction of the funds needed for Europe's reconstruction, U.S. aid catalyzed Europeans to help themselves. Washington pressured them to cooperate with one another as well as with the U.S. The Americans stimulated Europeans to invest in their own future.

Some prerequisites for economic reconstruction are outlined in Table 13.1. Russia in the early 1990s possessed a strong foundation in material resources and basic science, but lacked business knowledge, entrepreneurial spirit, computerization, and—potentially most important—hope. It had little domestic capital and did not readily attract massive foreign investments or loans. Its currency in the early 1990s had little value at home and none abroad. To get what one wanted, Marlboro cigarettes and dollars were the preferred means of exchange.

Germany and Japan had merely to *resume* capitalist ways after 1945, but Russia in the 1990s had to start from scratch. The tasks were immense

Table 13.1 Prerequisites for Economic Reconstruction

	Germany (1919)	West Germany (1949)	East Germany (1949)	Japan (1949)	Russia (1995)	Poland (1995)
Resource base	S	S	M	W	S	M
Technology	S	S	S	M	S	M
Business knowledge	S	S	W	M	W	M
Entrepreneurial spirit	S	S	W	S	W	M
Hope for the future	W	M	W	M	W	M
Capital for investment	S	S	W	M	W	W
Foreign aid	W	M	W	W	W	M
Stable currency	W	M	W	W	W	W
Favorable international environment	W	S	W	S	W-M	M
Domestic stability	W	M	M	M	W	M
Freedom from debts	W	M	W	M	W	M

NOTE: S = strong; M = medium; W = weak.

Poland went "cold turkey" (quickly, with few cushions) toward a market economy in 1989–1990. When price controls disappeared, prices on coal and many other goods skyrocketed while wages rose more slowly. Solidarnösc (Solidarity), the labor and political movement that challenged Communism throughout the 1980s, sought to curb harsh market forces and maintain something of the old welfare state.

and complex. Personal checks and credit cards were almost unknown. Pervasive distrust made deals by handshake unlikely. Contracts were not sacred. Mail was often pilfered. Phones often did not function. Many persons still lived by the unofficial slogan of the 1980s: "They pretend to pay us and we pretend to work."

Strong in human capital but lacking "social capital," Russia's transition from authoritarianism would not be easy.

Russia's traditional culture and its arbitrary government delivered the same message: Hard work and excellence may not be rewarded—they may even be punished. Many Russian fairy tales tell of dull oafs, peasants and princes alike, who get their way by deceit or by magic. This image was not changed in the 1990s as the overnight rich seemed to pull millions from a hat. (Their usual trick, however, involved no magic. Russia's "robber barons" used their privileged positions to sell abroad what had been state-owned resources—oil, timber, gold—and pocket the proceeds.)

Many Russians felt defeated, but Poles felt liberated. Poles had been communized for only forty-five years—not the seventy-four of Russian experience. Even under Communism Poland had known more free enterprise than Russia. Unlike Russia, Poland's population is relatively homogeneous. Poland faced no independent-minded Tatarstan or Chechnya. Polish émigrés were ready and able to invest in their homeland.

Poland went "cold turkey" toward capitalism. Prices were freed overnight. Many people suffered—especially pensioners and others on fixed incomes. Within a year or two, however, the situation improved and Poland moved toward economic takeoff. Production increased and unemployment fell. Inflation was high but manageable—about 30 percent per year. Poland had one of Europe's highest rates of economic growth in the 1990s. If grades were given, Poland in the 1990s would receive at least an A- for transition to democracy, free markets, and a peaceful foreign policy.

Foreign Policy

The CIS and Russia's "Near Abroad." Each of the fifteen Soviet union-republics became a separate state when the USSR dissolved in 1991. Most of the new states on the Soviet periphery had a virtual love-hate relationship with the central core—Moscow, capital of Russia and of the Soviet Union. Most border peoples felt they could not live with or without Russia. At the instigation of Kazakstan, Russia and most of the other ex-Soviet republics formed a **Commonwealth of Independent States (CIS).** The powers of the CIS were ill-defined. It could be a vehicle for close coordination among the former Soviet republics or a mere talk shop. Georgia and Azerbaijan stayed aloof for a time, but by the mid-1990s all former Soviet republics had joined the CIS except for Estonia, Latvia, and Lithuania. The Balts rejected any institution that might again put them under Russia's thumb.

Unlike the Balts, Kazakstan and the other new states of **Central Asia**—Uzbekistan, Tajikistan, Turkmenistan, and Kyrgyzstan—felt extremely dependent on Russia. None had ever been a modern state. Their peoples had been repressed and exploited by the Soviet system. Unsure of their capacities, the Central Asian republics, joined by Belarus (also with no history of modern statehood), were reluctant to break ties with Moscow. In contrast, Ukraine, the Caucasian republics, and Moldova wanted minimal ties with Moscow.

President **Nursultan Nazarbayev** of Kazakstan urged an even closer relationship with Russia than that provided by the CIS. He proposed a "Eurasian Union," but won few backers. By the late 1990s the CIS was more facade than reality. Still, it spawned many working committees. Most important, "CIS" troops—mainly Russians—patrolled many borders of the new Central Asian states.

Some Russians seemed to have an identity problem: They could not be "Russian" without an empire. They voted for rabid nationalists who demanded that Russia retake the Baltic and other borderlands. The Yeltsin government was not openly expansionist, but it coined the term **near abroad** to refer to the littoral of former Soviet republics—from Estonia to Kyrgyzstan. Moscow claimed that it had special security interests in this area and a legitimate right to protect some 25 million ethnic Russians now living under foreign rule.

In the 1980s Russians made up barely 50 percent of the Soviet Union's population; in the 1990s they made up 75 percent of the Russian Federation's people, while a full 20 percent of all ethnic Russians lived outside the Federation. Paradoxes were abundant. The Yeltsin Kremlin asserted that Grozny, capital of Chechnya, belonged to Russia, but that Sevastopol in the Crimea belonged to Ukraine, even though Russians predominated there, because the Soviet government had transferred the Crimea from Russia to Ukraine in 1954.

The Russian Orthodox Church stoked the mood of defiant nationalism. In 1997 Metropolitan Kirill, head of the church's external relations department, opposed ratification of START 2 because it was "one-sided." He condemned the inroads of "Western pseudo-culture" on Russian television. The Orthodox Church pressured the Kremlin to restrict the activities of Western missionaries who, Kirill said, were "arrogant" and sought to exploit Russia's economic difficulties. As a reward for its loyalty to the state, the Kremlin allowed the church a leading role in business arrangements to import cigarettes tax-free for resale and to export oil.[10]

Russian troops took part in many ethnic struggles around Russia's periphery. There was no reason to expect a democratic peace. In the mid-1990s Russia was not a stable democracy; neither were most of its neighbors. Quite the opposite. Most were becoming more authoritarian.

In Moldova Russian troops sought to protect Russians and Ukrainians who wanted autonomy. In the Caucasus they threw their weight for and against the governments of Georgia, Armenia, and Azerbaijan. In Tajikistan they fought Muslim influences percolating from Afghanistan.

In 1994–1996 Russian troops tried to prevent Chechnya's secession from the Russian Federation. Yeltsin sought firm control over the oil pipelines passing through Chechnya from the oil-rich **Caspian Sea** region into Russia.

Do governments learn? In this case, no. The Chechnya campaign repeated the Soviet-Afghan disaster, albeit on a smaller scale. After a series of battles that killed at least 35,000 people—some say 100,000, mostly civilians—Russian troops withdrew from Chechyna in 1996, leaving its political status unclear and the land in ruins.

Relations with the West. Yeltsin and his advisers had a tumultuous affair with the West. In the early 1990s there were passionate promises;

10. Geoffrey York, "Church Bolsters Russian Nationalism," *The Globe and Mail* (Toronto), May 31, 1997.

General Lebed Negotiates with the Chechens in Grozny

ALL RIGHT...
YOU CAN
HAVE THIS
PLACE.

The Christian Science Monitor
Los Angeles Times Syndicate

Chechnya never accepted Russian rule—not in the 19th century and not in the 20th century. When Chechens asserted their independence, Russian troops fought in 1994–1996 to keep Chechnya within the Russian Federation. Facing a stalemate similar to that reached earlier in Afghanistan, Russian President Boris Yeltsin authorized military hero retired Lt. General Aleksandr Lebed in 1996 to negotiate a cease-fire that left the future status of Chechnya undefined. Grozny, the capital of Chechnya, lay in ruins, but neither side had severed the oil pipelines that run from Baku on the Caspian Sea through Chechnya into Russia.

next, mutual disillusionment; by 1997, resignation to a strained but sometimes useful relationship.

In 1997 Clinton gave Yeltsin a sharp rebuff. Washington engineered the expansion of NATO to exclude Russia but include three former Soviet allies (Poland, the Czech Republic, and Hungary).[11] Washington hinted that later waves of NATO expansion might take in former Soviet republics such as Estonia. When Yeltsin denounced NATO expansion, Clinton invited Yeltsin to a Denver meeting of the G-7. But the West had drawn a line across Europe, and Russia was on the far side, judged unfit for membership in the premier security and economic bodies of the First World.

Still, the future was open-ended. Neither side wanted to foreclose options. Russia continued to participate in the Partnership for Peace set up by Washington to facilitate peacekeeping missions by NATO and other armed forces. In September 1997, as noted below, Russian and U.S. forces for the first time engaged in a combined airborne operations exercise in a former Soviet republic, Kazakstan.

CHINA—WHAT PATH?

Why China Is Not Russia

Unlike Yeltsin's Russia, Communist China never aspired to join the First World politically. The most likely scenario for China in the early 21st

11. George F. Kennan, Jack Matlock, Paul Nitze, and many other former policy-makers and scholars condemned NATO expansion. See Alvin Z. Rubinstein, "The Unheard Case Against NATO Enlargement," *Problems of Post-Communism* 44 (May–June 1997): 52–60; and Walter C. Clemens, Jr., "An Alternative to NATO Expansion," *International Journal* 52, no. 2 (spring 1997): 342–365.

century would be more of the 1990s—a Communist dictatorship supervising movement toward a market economy. A less likely scenario would see China keep a market economy but add democratization. A third scenario would be disintegration—Soviet- or traditional Chinese-style. Meanwhile, China's external policies could remain peaceful or turn more aggressive.

To gain perspective, let us compare briefly China in the 1990s with the last decade of Soviet rule. The Soviet system lasted from 1917 to 1991; if China's Communist system also endured seventy-four years, its demise would take place in 2023. But history moves at different speeds and in different directions.

The Economy

The Soviet economy became moribund in the 1980s. Soviet GDP never reached half the U.S. GDP. By contrast, the Chinese economy grew rapidly from the late 1970s into the 1990s and could outstrip the U.S. in the 21st century. Encouraged by elder statesman **Deng Xiaoping**, Chinese saved and invested to become more prosperous. China embraced many of the strategies that boosted economic growth in the four Tigers.

When Communists took power in 1949, China was one of the world's poorest countries. Life expectancy then was 35 years; by the late 1990s it had reached 69. Infant mortality declined from 200 per 1,000 live births in 1949 to 42. Fourth-fifths of Chinese were illiterate in the 1950s; in the 1990s, only one-fifth were illiterate.

Much of this progress took place only after the death of Mao Zedong in 1976. As noted earlier, his self-reliance and ideological campaigns did enormous damage. More than 30 million peasants starved in 1959–1962. Even in the 1970s, hungry peasants swamped cities begging for food.

Deng Xiaoping began his economic reforms in 1978 by liberating agriculture from governmental controls. This was in stark contrast to the USSR, where state and collective farms remained the norm from 1928 on. Deng attacked rural poverty on three fronts: (1) land reform—collective farm land was distributed to households; (2) market orientation—government quotas were reduced and peasants were encouraged to sell a variety of products in open markets; (3) price reform—the government raised prices by 22 to 33 percent for many goods. The government also encouraged village enterprises by lowering taxes and allowing them greater autonomy. These reforms brought rapid results: Rural incomes doubled between 1978 and 1984.

In the mid-1980s Beijing switched its attention to industry and exports. The government gave public funds and offered fiscal incentives to develop export industries in coastal regions near Hong Kong and Shanghai and in Fujian province across the Strait from Taiwan. This strategy improved living standards dramatically. By the mid-1990s only one-fifth of the population along the coast lived in poverty, compared to nearly one-half in the interior.

Deng Xiaoping permitted private enterprise in many spheres but maintained state monopolies in most key industries. Beijing officials called their system "socialism with Chinese characteristics." Others called it Communist or Leninist capitalism.

When Deng died in 1997, there were still 118,000 state-owned enterprises, many unprofitable—a huge drain on state finances. In September 1997, several months after Deng's passing, party chief and PRC President **Jiang Zemin** moved the reform process a giant step forward. He called for a transition to a mixed economy—in effect, privatization of state enterprises. He also warned that large job layoffs could not be avoided. If anyone should say that Jiang was betraying socialism, he replied in advance that "public ownership should take diversified forms."

Where would the process stop? Western observers warned that Communist hacks would have to be replaced by profit-oriented managers. To privatize state enterprises would require Chinese or foreigners to buy shares. The country would need an army of brokers and bankers. The Communist Party might have to loosen controls and permit business-related information to flow freely.

Beijing steadily increased its defense spending in the 1980s and 1990s, but China's burden of defense was much smaller than in the USSR. In 1997, however, President Jiang said that the costs of modernizing the armed forces would require China to reduce from 3 million to 2.5 million troops by 2000 (which would still leave the PRC with the world's largest armed forces).

Foreign investors (Taiwanese as well as Japanese and Western) showed great confidence in Chinese economic prospects. Direct foreign investment in China was many times larger than foreign aid.

China is much more vulnerable to environmental catastrophe than Russia. Starvation has ravaged China for millennia. China's billion-plus people inhabit a comparatively small area buffeted by harsh weather, earthquakes, and a shrinking base of arable land. Who will feed China if it suffers two or three years of bad harvests (as in North Korea in the mid-

1990s)? China's import needs could be many times larger than Soviet or North Korean. China has money, but foreign food supplies might not suffice to sustain China for long.[12]

Government and Foreign Policy

No Chinese Gorbachev appeared in the 1990s—no leader offering glasnost, free elections, greater protection of human rights. Gorbachev wanted to save the Soviet system. But his policies helped kill the system before he could rejuvenate it.

Gorbachev invigorated Soviet politics but failed to stimulate the economy. Deng Xiaoping and Jiang Zemin liberated the Chinese economy but Chinese-style free enterprise left the dictatorship untouched. The Chinese became much richer and slightly freer. President Jiang in 1997 called for major economic reforms but rejected movement toward "western-style democracy." Instead he reaffirmed "Chinese-style socialist democracy." Beijing's leaders admired the authoritarian prosperity of Singapore. China, however, much larger and more diverse, is far more difficult to control from the top down.

Like the USSR, China has been ruled by a one-party, centralized dictatorship selected from a privileged nomenklatura. From the 1970s through the 1990s, China was usually ruled by men in their seventies or older. Still, Beijing's leaders in the 1990s were far more confident and alert than those who ruled the USSR in the decades before its demise. Riding the crest of economic expansion, the PRC leaders had the wherewithal to address many problems.

Like the USSR, the Communist Chinese perceive potential enemies on all sides—India, Vietnam, Taiwan, Japan, the U.S., Russia, and even ASEAN (the Association of South East Asian Nations, which includes Indonesia, Thailand, Singapore, the Philippines, Brunei, Malaysia, and Burma).

Taiwan remained a bone lodged in Beijing's throat. Not only did Taiwan achieve high levels of prosperity and democracy, but it also kept traditional Chinese culture far more vibrant than did the PRC. Soviet leaders had faced no similar rival—no free "island Russia" in the Black Sea. Still, China's size and prosperity made Taiwan a problem that could wait.

China in the 1990s focused on internal development, but threatened war if Taiwan opted for independence. If China became much stronger, would it be more aggressive in world affairs? No one could answer with certainty.

China has seldom pursued an expansionist strategy like that promot-

12. Lester R. Brown, *Who Will Feed China? Wake-up Call for a Small Planet* (New York: Norton, 1995).

Many Chinese welcomed the Information Age. Five years after the 1989 crackdown on Tiananmen Square, this Beijing department store promoted modern computers for home and individual use. Could the government keep buyers from the full range of information available by modem?

ed for centuries by Russian tsars and commissars. Even when Chinese ships sailed to Indonesia, Oman, and East Africa in the 17th century, China did not seek to conquer foreigners but rather sought to impress them with its grandeur. China displayed little zeal for distant expansion. Content to receive foreign kow-tows, the Chinese differed from Americans who saw U.S. expansion as the Manifest Destiny of God's Elect.

The U.S. provided the number-one market for PRC exports in the 1990s. A growing level of trade and technology transfer with the U.S. was a reality for China—not the dream it was for the USSR. As of 1997, however, neither China nor Russia belonged to the World Trade Organization. The U.S. opposed China's admission until its economy became more open and more transparent.

Like the USSR, PRC leaders endeavored to master Western technology while limiting "pollution" by foreign influences. But Chinese were far more determined than Soviets to join in international commerce. Membership in the World Trade Organization was a major PRC goal in the mid-1990s. China's elites gained far more contact with outsiders and alien ideas than did their Soviet counterparts. China's young people studied abroad in far greater numbers; many more foreigners worked and invested in China than in the old USSR; the Internet and satellite broadcasting linked Chinese with the wider world far more than had any ties enjoyed by curious Soviets.

Whereas the Soviet regime claimed to endorse human rights as understood in the West, China never did so. Beijing spurned international covenants on political rights, claiming that the PRC government served the people's economic and social rights.

The democracy movement that briefly challenged Communist rule was sternly and effectively repressed in 1989. That movement gave way in the 1990s to waves of collectivist nationalism and individualistic materialism.

Ethnic Issues and Regionalism

The USSR broke up into fifteen independent states in 1991. Could China break up into disparate regions, as had often happened in its past? China's minority problem in the 1990s was far more limited than the USSR's. Half of the Soviet population was non-Russian. China's minorities, even including Tibet, made up less than one-tenth of the population. To be sure, many non-Han peoples were restive. In the Central Asian region of China (sometimes called Chinese Turkestan), there were more than one million Kazaks, **Uighurs** (who speak a Turkic tongue similar to Kazak), and some Tajiks. Many of these minorities took heart from the creation of Kazakstan, Kyrgyzstan, and Tajikistan. Some Chinese Kazaks, Uighurs, and Tajiks wanted to join these new states across the border; some wanted more autonomy within China; some sought an independent "Uighurstan."

The new states across the Chinese border were weak and floundering. But the peoples there were no longer under alien rule and were relatively free to practice their religion. If Uighurs gained more autonomy, other PRC minorities—Tibetans, Mongols, Manchus, Miao, and others—might demand the same or more. Dominoes might fall.

Beijing attempted to settle ethnic Chinese in border regions in an effort to outnumber the indigenous peoples. PRC authorities repressed Uighur and other dissidents with great ferocity. "Wipe them out like rats," a regional official ordered in 1997. Gorbachev's Kremlin, by contrast, seldom used force against demonstrators.

Communist China in the 1990s appeared to have far more staying power than the Soviet system possessed in the 1970s and 1980s. China had no vast empire to collapse; no falling economy to prop up; no dynamic minority to fear. Unlike the USSR, China suffered very little from "imperial overreach."

But appearances could be misleading. Many Western experts credited the Soviet Union with great strength just before the system crumbled. China too might stand on feet of clay. As Leo Tolstoi noted in *Anna*

Karenina, "every unhappy family is unhappy in its own way." Outsiders cannot easily judge how serious are the problems of another family.

KAZAKSTAN—WHAT PATH?

Kazakstan is vast and rich in resources.[13] But it is profoundly troubled. Kazaks want stability and welfare more than freedom. Why? Long repression can deplete spirit.

Why Kazakstan Is Neither Russia Nor China

The country's national identity is unclear. Kazakstan never existed as a separate state until 1991. Before World War II Stalin drew a map establishing boundaries for Kazakstan and four other Soviet union-republics in Central Asia. The process was no more rational or just than the borders that Europeans imposed on Africa.

In prior centuries Kazaks were nomadic herdsmen, gradually subdued by tsarist Russian generals and traders. One-third of the Kazak population perished resisting Stalin's program of collectivization in the late 1920s and early 1930s. In the 1940s Kazakstan served as a dumping ground for other peoples whom Stalin did not trust, for example, Volga Germans and Chechens. It was home to major Soviet facilities for nuclear testing and biological weapons research. Nuclear scientists went back to Russia in 1993, taking their data books with them and leaving Kazaks unsure of how many and where nuclear hot spots existed. Many Kazaks suffer from diseases likely to be triggered by nuclear radiation.

Having killed a large fraction of the Kazak population, the Soviet regime settled Kazakstan with Russians and other Soviet nationalities. In 1997 some 44 percent of the population was Kazak; 36 percent, Russian—many living in the north near the Russian border. Over 120 other minorities—Koreans, Volga Germans, Kyrgyz—made up the other 20 percent. Russian has long been the common language. Only half of Kazaks were fluent in Kazak in the 1990s. Before 1991 very few schools used Kazak for teaching. In the mid-1990s, however, the Nazarbayev government declared that Kazaks and non-Kazaks alike must be fluent in Kazak by 2006 to hold responsible jobs.

Government

Democracy is only a catchword in Central Asia. Most Kazaks see democracy as at best a distant ideal—not the best system for solving present problems. President Nazarbayev dominated Kazak politics even in Soviet times. The Constitution, adopted in a 1995 referendum marred by many

13. In 1993 Kazakstan encompassed 2,717,300 kilometers and was home to 17 million people; the Russian Federation, 17,075,200 kilometers with 149 million people; Ukraine, 603,700 kilometers with 52 million people; France, 547,030 kilometers with 58 million people; and Germany, 356,910 kilometers with 81 million people. Kazakstan is nearly four times the size of Texas.

irregularities, permits the president to legislate by decree. Nazarbayev's term was extended to 2000 by another referendum, also flawed. Nazarbayev in the 1990s tried to maintain good relations with Moscow but allowed few Russians into the top rungs of government.

As in Russia and other CIS countries, corruption was rife in Kazakstan. Nazarbayev's domination of the courts made it hard to root out corruption. There was a going price for many things—from a traffic ticket to university admission. Corruption gave "reform," "privatization," and even "foreign aid" bad connotations. For many Central Asians, reforms and foreign aid enriched the corrupt.

For better or worse, most Central Asians showed little interest in pan-Turkism spearheaded by Turkey or Islamic solidarity pushed by Iran. For outside assistance Kazaks looked first of all to Europe, Japan, the U.S., and Russia; then to Turkey and China; last of all to Iran.[14]

Trying to generate a sense of shared interests in the region, the U.S. in September 1997 used the Partnership for Peace as a way to organize a week-long training exercise in Kazakstan. It involved some 500 U.S. paratroopers and 1,000 soldiers from Russia, Georgia, Ukraine, Latvia, Turkey, Kazakstan, Kyrgyzstan, and Uzbekistan. The aim was to "enhance regional cooperation and increase the interoperability of the Central Asian Peacekeeping Battalion" (set up by Kazakstan, Kyrgyzstan, and Uzbekistan) and build stability in the region. Some forces were flown nineteen hours from their training facility in North Carolina to jump onto the Kazak steppe; forces from Russia and Turkey were also airdropped at the same location.

The Economy

Some Kazaks welcomed market reforms but wanted price controls. With no experience of capitalism, private enterprise got off to a slow start. Much internal trade was by barter in the 1990s.

Kazakstan possesses not only giant oil and gas reserves but rare metals, phosphates, and chemicals. To the southwest, Uzbekistan has one of the world's largest gold mines and is the world's second largest exporter of cotton. Turkmenistan is rich in gas.

An economy dependent upon the sale of minerals is open to the highest bidders. Many foreign companies competed for oil and gas rights. South Koreans bought privatized copper mines and smelters; a Japanese company planned to double the capacity of a rail link at the Kazak-Chinese border—the export route for half of Kazakstan's steel production.

14. Surveys (1993) analyzed in Nancy Lubin, "Central Asians Take Stock: Reform, Corruption, and Identity," *Peaceworks* 2 (Washington, D.C.: U.S. Institute of Peace, 1995): 21.

Kazakstan helped supply the USSR with wheat. In the 1990s two-fifths of Kazakstan's people worked in agriculture, but farming was not profitable, in part because privatized storage and distribution networks exploited farmers. Capital for improvements was hard to come by. Soil erosion and water shortages were severe. Uzbekistan threatened to sharply reduce water flows essential to Kazak agriculture.

Economic and social malaise produced a shocking decline in public health. As one public health expert put it, many people in Central Asia drink from "little more than a sewage ditch." In western regions of Kazakstan and Uzbekistan, more than 100 of 1,000 babies die before their first birthday. In some villages close to the Aral Sea, life expectancy was just 39 years. Life expectancy in Kazakstan declined from 68.6 in 1990 to 66.1 in 1995; PPP declined from US$5,440 to $2,760; HDI fell from 0.848 to 0.685. Ranked 53d in the world by HDI in 1990, Kazakstan was ranked 100th in 1995.[15]

In 1997, however, the economy began to grow after six years of decline. Inflation tumbled from 1,158 percent in 1994 to a mere 15 percent in 1997. The Kazak government floated its second international bond issue in London while, in Almaty, Prime Minister Akezhan Kazhegeldin served champagne to inaugurate the country's stock market. Not many Kazak firms had sufficient transparency (good accounting) to be listed, but foreign investors were hungry for potential growth in a country with fabulous resources.

Foreign Policy: The Great Game of Oil

Kazakstan tilted west in the 1990s—to the main source of capital and technology and the main hope against Russian expansionism. To please Washington, Kazakstan renounced nuclear weapons, returned all Soviet-era nuclear warheads to Russia, and transferred left-over fissionable materials to the U.S.

But Kazak foreign policy hinges on oil. The "great game" that pitted England against Russia in their 19th-century rivalry over Central Asia was revived and globalized in the 1990s. The new great game takes in all the regional players (including Turkey and Iran) plus the U.S., Europe, China, Japan, and even Oman.

The world runs on oil—at least until it runs out or a replacement is found. Many of the world's largest TNCs produce oil or autos that burn oil—from General Motors and Ford to Royal Dutch Shell and Exxon. As we see in Table 13.2, the U.S. was the world's largest oil producer until

15. United Nations Development Programme, *Kazakstan: Human Development Report 1996* (Almaty: UNDP, 1996), 6.

Who Imports What and From Whom?

The U.S. in 1995 imported 8,832,000 barrels per day (bpd) of crude oil and refined products (compared to 6,530,000 domestic production)— 1,475,000 from Venezuela; 1,344,000 from Saudi Arabia; and 1,069,000 from Mexico. Japan imported 5,544,000 bpd. Its largest suppliers were the United Arab Emirates and Saudi Arabia. Western Europe imported 9,531,000 bpd. Its largest suppliers: Saudi Arabia, Russia, Iran, and Libya.

Western Europe and Japan were highly dependent on oil from Saudi Arabia and other Persian Gulf states, while the U.S. was not. Western Europe depended heavily on oil from two states the U.S. treated as pariahs—Iran and Libya.

Proven oil reserves in 1995 (billion barrels) were as follows: Saudi Arabia, 259; Iraq, 100; United Arab Emirates, 98; Kuwait, 94; Iran, 88; Venezuela, 64; Mexico, 50; Russia, 35; Libya, 30; China, 24; U.S., 22. Initial studies suggested that the Caspian region might hold as much or more oil than that held by the Persian Gulf states combined.

Table 13.2 Crude Oil Production, Imports, and Exports
(1,000 barrels per day)

Country	Production						Imports/Exports (1995)
	1970	1980	1985	1990	1993	1995	
U.S.	9,648	8,597	8,971	7,355	6,847	6,530	8,832 (Imports)
Russia	n.a.	n.a.	10,840	10,320	6,838	6,134	3,030 (Exports)
Kazakstan	n.a.	n.a.	460	510	460	410	n.a.
Iran	3,831	1,662	2,258	3,252	3,671	3,654	2,220 (Exports)
Iraq	1,563	2,514	1,437	2,080	448	600	190 (Exports)
Saudi Arabia	3,789	9,903	3,468	6,414	8,087	8,067	7,715 (Exports)
China	602	2,113	2,496	2,769	2,908	2,989	n.a.
Mexico	420	1,936	2,733	2,648	2,673	2,689	1,110 (Exports)

SOURCE: Central Intelligence Agency, *Handbook of International Economic Statistics, 1996* (Washington, D.C.: Government Printing Office, 1996), Tables 48, 49, 50.

NOTE: n.a. = not available.

about 1970, when the USSR became number one. Soviet production fell in the 1990s, however, and Saudi Arabia became the leader. Even so, oil remained Russia's most valuable export in the 1990s.

Complaisant about energy conservation, the U.S. imported nearly twice as much oil as Japan in the 1990s—an amount three times larger than Russia exported. The major suppliers of U.S. imports were Venezuela, Mexico, and Saudi Arabia. Europe depended heavily on Saudi Arabia but also on Iran and Libya—two countries condemned by the U.S. for supporting terrorism. Japan depended on the United Arab Emirates and Saudi Arabia.

The world's greatest proven reserves of oil and gas in the 1990s were in the countries abutting the Persian Gulf, but geologists believed that huge reserves also existed in or near the Caspian Sea. The countries claiming these reserves included Kazakstan, Russia, Azerbaijan, Iran, and Turkmenistan. Lesser reserves lay nearby in Armenia, Georgia, and Uzbekistan. Outsiders wanted to tap, pipe, transport, refine, sell, and use these reserves.[16]

Marco Polo took note of oil near the Caspian Sea in the 13th century. The area became a major producer in the late 19th century, fueling rivalry between Russians, Turks, Persians, Europeans, and Americans. Tsarist Russia fanned tensions between Azeris and Armenians working in oil-rich Baku in the early 20th century, leaving wounds that festered in the 1990s.

Oil production declined in Kazakstan and Azerbaijan in the early 1990s. Without the familiar networks of the Soviet Oil and Gas Ministry, lacking capital and technical expertise, neither Kazakstan nor Azerbaijan

16. Rosemarie Forsythe, "The Politics of Oil in The Caucasus and Central Asia," *Adelphi Paper* 300 (London: International Institute for Strategic Studies, 1996).

could maintain Soviet-era production levels. They looked to outsiders for help. As the sidebar suggests, however, oil wealth is no panacea.

Getting oil from the ground or seabed is the first problem. The second is getting it to market. Most of Central Asia is landlocked. Kazakstan and Azerbaijan must send its oil across or around the Caspian Sea and across others' territories to reach customers. Russian ships carried oil across the Black Sea and out through the Turkish Straits, but the Turkish government wanted to reduce traffic in hazardous cargoes in the congested waters close to Istanbul.

Russian officials followed two contradictory approaches in the mid-1990s. Hard-line Foreign Minister Evgeny Primakov sought to exclude Western interests and establish Russian dominion over Caspian oil. Prime Minister Chernomyrdin, by contrast, welcomed cooperation with the West, if only to secure Western investment and technology for Russia's oil industry.

Primakov's Foreign Ministry claimed in the 1990s that the Caspian Sea is an inland lake and that each littoral state may claim only resources within ten nautical miles of its shores. The rest of the Caspian should be treated as a condominium—its wealth to be shared equally by all bordering states. Most littoral states, however, said that the Caspian is a sea. They would claim all oil wealth between equidistant lines extending out from their shores.

As we see in Map 13.2, Kazaks had five options: (1) Pipe Kazak oil north to Russia and ship it west from Russia's Black Sea port Novorossisk. (2) Ship the oil west across the Caspian and then by land or across the Black Sea to a Greek or Turkish port on the Mediterranean. (3) Send oil by train or build a pipeline east across China to the Yellow Sea. (4) Build a pipeline south across Afghanistan and Pakistan to the Arabian Sea. (5) Send oil south through Iran to the Persian Gulf. None of the oil producers can export oil without the cooperation of one or more of its neighbors.

The interested parties resembled the hunters in Stag Hunt (see Chapter 6). Each was tempted to snatch the hare no matter what the other hunters felt. But the strategy most likely to enhance individual gain was to implement a plan netting "good" if not "great" outcomes for each party. Kazakstan could not afford to alienate Moscow, for it depended on Russia in countless ways. Indeed, the only existing pipeline ran north. All others, in the 1990s, were pipe dreams.

Is Oil an "Open Sesame"?

Ali Baba found a magic formula—"Open Sesame"—to open doors. If the oil riches of Russia and Kazakstan were better harvested and marketed, could petro dollars lift entire countries? There were no guarantees. Petro dollars did little to raise HDI or bolster democracy in countries that reaped the oil bonanza of the 1970s—Mexico, Venezuela, Nigeria, Iran, Saudi Arabia. To generate long-term benefits, oil income must be spread widely and invested wisely. Otherwise, oil wealth can increase corruption and reduce incentives to save and invest. The U.S. benefited from abundant energy resources but neither Japan nor any Tiger used cheap energy or any mineral resource to get rich.

Corruption Is Not a CIS Monopoly

"Don't we all, as we grow older, have nothing more to give than a buck?" This was the rhetorical question put by Roger E. Tamraz to congressional investigators in September 1997. Tamraz stated that he donated $300,000 to the Democratic Party coffers in 1996 so that he could get access to President Clinton. In one of half a dozen visits to the White House, Tamraz succeeded in winning Clinton's attention for a previously rejected scheme for a $2 billion Caspian Sea oil monopoly.

Oil, Politics, and Ethnicity

What happens when oil mixes with politics? Consider the following scenario:

Map 13.2 Potential Outlets for Kazak Oil

Existing Pipelines --- **Potential Outlets**

Imagine that you serve as policy adviser to the president of Kazakstan as he prepares to sign an important oil deal with China. Already in 1997 the Chinese National Petroleum Company acquired mining rights to an oil field in western Kazakstan. It plans to build an oil pipeline from that field across Kazakstan and China to the Yellow Sea. Some Kazak oil will be used in China; some will be exported to Japan. Kazak leaders welcome diversification to make Kazakstan less dependent on Russian and Western markets.

Since last week, however, PRC troops have been engaged in heavy action against Kazak and Uighur separatists in "China's Chechnya"—the Xinjiang-Uighur Autonomous Region of China. Like Chechnya, the republic's indigenous people are Muslims who want an independent "Uighurstan." They resent Chinese settlers in their midst who service PRC nuclear and missile test facilities and explore the oil deposits of the Tarim River Basin near China's border with Kazakstan.

Realpolitik *predicts that you will ignore your ethnic kinsmen in China for the sake of stable relations with a useful and powerful neighbor. But public opinion in Kazakstan is outraged at PRC military action and demands that the Kazak government protect fellow Kazaks and Uighurs. Moscow tells you it will not get involved in these matters. But there are signs that both Moscow and Beijing are promoting Russian separatism in northern Kazakstan. The PRC government hints it will keep hands off your separatist problem if you re-*

nounce intervention in China's internal affairs. The U.S. ambassador tells you his government takes no stand on Kazak-PRC issues except to uphold existing deals between Kazakstan and Western oil companies. He says that Partnership for Peace cooperation is not available for cross-border operations.

This scenario simulates what *could* happen. If any party exploits another, this kind of collision is quite possible. Politics mixes uneasily with oil across Eurasia.

WHAT PROPOSITIONS HOLD? WHAT QUESTIONS REMAIN?

Transitions are difficult—especially when there is little consensus on the destination. "Transition to *what?*" remained a basic question in the 1990s. Most Czechs, Poles, Hungarians, Estonians, and Latvians in the 1990s saw themselves as part of the West and wanted their countries transformed on a Western model. But Russians were not sure of their identity or goals. As in the 19th century, some Russians were Westernizers, while others saw themselves as different—with a pure Russian or Eurasian soul. Many Russians yearned for a more stable, authoritarian government; more state welfare and regulation of the economy; and a great power status befitting the colossus of Eurasia.

Western models were even more suspect in China and Kazakstan, where few people had knowledge of Western values and where economic insecurity was deep and wide. For most Chinese and Kazaks, stability and higher incomes were top priorities, never mind what system provided them.

From a Western standpoint, no former Communist country east of Poland stood on the threshold of First World development. Russia's foreign policy in the 1990s was reasonably cooperative with the West, but the government remained authoritarian and corrupt; the economy a field of chaos. China cooperated with the West on North Korea but stood poised to attack Taiwan. China's economy boomed but retained many barriers to free trade. Beijing refused to pay even lip service to real democracy, human rights, or minority rights. Kazakstan, too, cooperated with the West in foreign policy. But its government and economy sank in an authoritarian swamp.

Given the uncertainties, engagement rather than containment was probably the best course for the West. The West was probably right to do what it could to encourage the former Second World to become more democratic, more market-oriented, more active in supporting international cooperation.

Memo to the President of Kazakstan:

Despite our present difficulties, our long-term assets are strong—provided we use them efficiently and justly. Our poverty, low HDI, and environmental problems are severe. We must use our mineral wealth wisely and avoid the mistakes made by many oil-rich countries. Instead, we should learn from Asia's Tigers: Invest heavily in human capital, promote land reform, improve public health, and provide good governance. Unlike the Tigers, we are landlocked. But we have natural resources far beyond what the Tigers possessed.

We need to cooperate with other states near and far to extract and sell our mineral wealth. Each potential partner presents risk. We should avoid heavy dependency upon any one. The West and Japan are the most reliable partners but also the most distant. Without becoming heavily dependent on Russia, we should try to engage Russians to mutual advantage.

Our oil riches permit and require diversification. We should export in all directions—through Russia, Azerbaijan, Georgia, Iran, Turkey, Greece, and China. We should welcome a Japanese-Chinese venture to pipe our oil eastward. Japanese participation could reduce chances of conflict with China over ethnic issues in Xinjiang.

We must also take account of regional rivalries in Central Asia. Uzbekistan looks expansionist. The Kyrgyz Republic is fragile. Tajikistan is torn by religion and civil war. Turkmenistan is poor, but its gas reserves could make it our partner or our rival. Given these uncertainties, we must take a long-term perspective: We must invest in education and avoid war.

Hungry and insecure, few Russians or Central Asians placed environmental protection or clean-up high on their list of priorities. In quest of oil and oil profits, few Westerners or Chinese gave serious attention to the biosphere. Still, all wealth and health depend on the fifth level of international life, as we will see in the next chapter.

KEY NAMES AND TERMS

Caspian Sea
Central Asia
Chechnya
Viktor Chernomyrdin
Commonwealth of Independent States (CIS)
Deng Xiaoping
Duma
Jiang Zemin

liberal internationalism
Nursultan Nazarbayev
near abroad
Tatarstan
transitions
Uighurs
Boris Yeltsin

QUESTIONS TO DISCUSS

1. What theories have best explained the rise and fall of Communism?
2. What theories help anticipate possible outcomes of transitions away from Communism?
3. Which parts of the former Second World are most likely to join the First World? Can you rank their assets—high, medium, and low?
4. Is Western-style democracy appropriate for all countries?
5. Is a market economy suitable for all countries?
6. If you were a Uighur nationalist in China, how would you relate to Kazakstan?
7. If you were a Japanese civil servant concerned with energy resources, what policies would you recommend Japan take toward Central Asia?
8. An adviser to President Jiang Zemin, what policies would you recommend for securing oil and coping with ethnicity in Central Asia?

RECOMMENDED RESOURCES

BOOKS

Aitmatov, Chingiz. *The Day Lasts More than a Hundred Years.* Bloomington: University of Indiana Press, 1988.

Brown, Michael E., et al., eds. *East Asian Security: An International Security Reader.* Cambridge, Mass.: MIT Press, 1996.

Bueno de Mesquita, Bruce, et al. *Red Flag Over Hong Kong.* Chatham, N.J.: Chatham House, 1996.

Clemens, Walter C., Jr. *Can Russia Change? The USSR Confronts Global Interdependence.* New York: Routledge, 1990.

Dawisha, Karen, and Bruce Parrot, eds. *Democratization and Authoritarianism in Postcommunist States.* Multivolume. Cambridge: Cambridge University Press, 1997–.

———. *International Politics of Eurasia.* 10 vols. Armonk, N.Y.: M.E. Sharpe, 1994–1997.

Holmes, Leslie. *Post-Communism: An Introduction.* Durham, N.C.: Duke University Press, 1997.

Hunter, Shireen T. *Central Asia Since Independence.* Westport, Conn.: Praeger, 1996.

Kim, Young Jeh, ed. *The New Pacific Community in the 1990s.* Armonk, N.Y.: M. E. Sharpe, 1996.

Lijphart, Arend, and Carlos H. Waisman, eds. *Institutional Design in New Democracies: Eastern Europe and Latin America.* Boulder, Colo.: Westview, 1996.

Linz, Juan J., and Alfred Stepan. *Problems of Democratic Transition and Consolidation: Southern Europe, South America, and Post-Communist Europe.* Baltimore: Johns Hopkins University Press, 1996.

Mandelbaum, Michael, ed. *Central Asia and the World.* New York: Council on Foreign Relations, 1996.

Olcott, Martha Brill. *Central Asia's New States: Independence, Foreign Policy, and Regional Security.* Washington, D.C.: U.S. Institute of Peace, 1996.

Ro'i, Yaacov, ed. *Muslim Eurasia: Conflicting Legacies.* London: Frank Cass, 1995.

U.S. Department of State. *Country Practices on Human Rights Practices.* Washington, D.C.: Government Printing Office, annual.

Yergin, Daniel. *The Prize: The Epic Quest for Oil, Money, and Power.* New York: Simon & Schuster, 1991.

Yergin, Daniel, and Thane Gustafson. *Russia 2010 and What It Means for the World. The CERA Report.* New York: Random House, 1993.

Zhao, Suisheng. *Power Competition in East Asia: From the Old Chinese World Order to the Post–Cold War Regional Multipolarity.* New York: St. Martin's, 1997.

JOURNALS

Asian Survey
Central Asian Monitor
China Quarterly
Current History (special issues on Russia, Eurasia, and China)
Europe-Asia Studies
International Affairs (Moscow)
Oil and Gas Journal
Problems of Post-Communism
Slavic Review

WEB SITES

Arms Control Association
   http://www.armscontrol.org
   Arms Control Today (journal)
      http://www.armscontrol.org/ACT/act.html
Brookings Institution
   general information
      http://www.brook.edu
   foreign policy
      http://www.brook.edu/fp/fp_hp.htm
   China
      http://www.brook.edu/fp/subjects/regions/asia.htm
      #CHINA
   Russia
      http://www.brook.edu/fp/subjects/regions/Eurasia.
      htm#RUSSIA

NATO
   http://www.brook.edu/fp/subjects/regions/
   europe.htm#NATO
Federation of American Scientists
   general information
      http://www.fas.org
   NATO expansion
      http://www.fas.org/man/nato/index.html
Kazakstan
   general information
      http://www.kz/
   Interactive Central Asia Resource Project
      http://www.rockbridge.net/personal/bichel/
      kazdescr.htp *(virtual library containing resources
      and references to culture, health, environment,
      and politics relating to Kazakstan)*
Library of Congress Soviet/Russian Archives
   http://www.lcweb.loc.gov/exhibits/archives/intro.html
Russian American Chamber of Commerce
   http://www.rmi.net/racc
Russian/NIS history
   http://www.friends-partners.org/friends/history/
   russian.htmlopt-tables-pc-english *(contains links to
   Russian and NIS history resources and to an online game
   about Romanov Russia)*

PART 4

Building a Better World

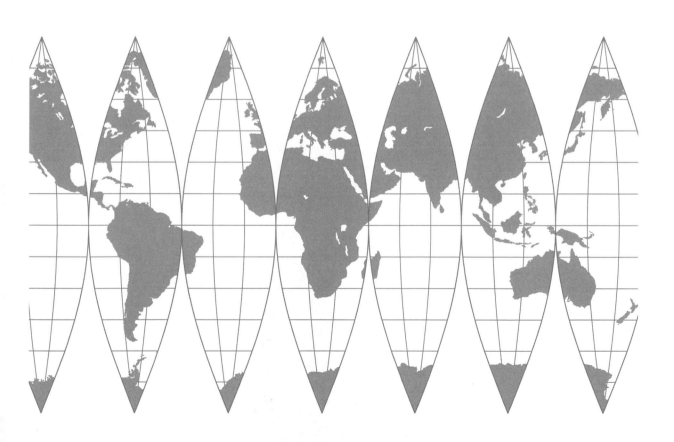

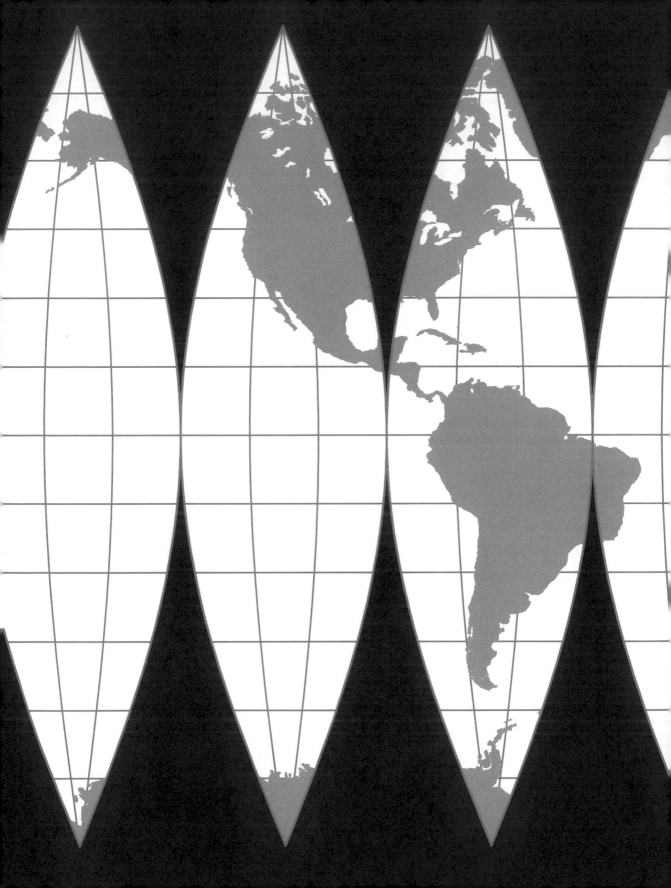

C H A P T E R   F O U R T E E N

ECOPOLITICS: THE HEALTH OF NATIONS

THE BIG QUESTIONS IN CHAPTER 14

- Why should a foreign minister care about the environment?

- Is it possible to have both economic development and environmental protection?

- Are there limits to growth?

- How do international environmental conflicts arise?

- People and resources: Was Malthus right?

- Do population pressures multiplied by resource deficits lead to war?

- How is it that big projects often have complex side effects?

- Is it possible to have "sustainable development"?

- What is the Aswan Syndrome?

- Why care about climate control if "some like it hot"?

- How do mutual gain and conflict/exploitation relate to environmental policy?

What Is a Good Tradeoff? ... *The year is 2012, the place is Rio de Janeiro. As Brazil's Foreign Minister you chair a meeting of negotiators from nearly two hundred countries charged with updating the conventions on climate change adopted at the Earth Summit held in Rio twenty years earlier (1992) and tightened at Kyoto in 1997. The industrialized countries of the North signed a Kyoto Protocol in 1997 pledging them to reduce their emissions of "greenhouse gases" by more than 5 percent below their 1990 levels by the year 2010. The U.S. has fallen short of this target but the European Union and Japan have more than met the goals set in Kyoto.*

Led by Germany, most industrial states are now emitting fewer hydrocarbons into the air than they did in 1990. While the North's emissions decline, however, those of the South rapidly increase. Heavily dependent on coal furnaces, China has now surpassed the U.S. level of emissions. India, Brazil, and Indonesia have all exceeded Germany's level. The North says it is now time for Brazil, China, India, and other newly industrialized countries to pull in their belts too and cut their emissions.

But Brazil's government believes in development—not underdevelopment. It offers tax incentives to transnational corporations such as Volkswagen to help open up Amazonia, the world's largest tropical forest. Most of Brazil's industrialists, miners, big farmers, and timber harvesters resist emissions controls. "It's too early," they say. "First let us catch up with the North." So far, the South has added little to global concentrations of greenhouse gases. In fact, Amazonia has sponged up the carbon released by other countries. "Emissions controls," the industrialists say, "will harm development or profits or both."

Still, Brazilians have reason to want emissions controls. Sao Paulo and other cities are choking on pollution. Scientists say that emissions add to global warming, which leads to rising waters that eat away at Rio and other cities along Brazil's Atlantic coast. The wetter, warmer climate spawns more insect-borne disease.

The Amazon forest, of course, is shrinking as development races ahead. Who can say how much Amazonia is worth to the global environment? What is a good tradeoff? What can you and your colleagues from India and China get from the North in exchange for your taking steps to protect the "global commons"? Brazil's Environment Agency suggests that you promise the United Nations to spend $1 billion per year on emissions controls and conservation if the North compensates Brazil with $1 billion for maintaining its forests. But can Brazil expect compensation for not fouling its own nest? And if the money arrived, how could your government persuade private business interests to redirect their energies?

CONTENDING CONCEPTS
AND EXPLANATIONS

WHY SHOULD A FOREIGN MINISTER CARE ABOUT ECOLOGY?

Why should the Brazilian foreign minister and the U.S. secretary of state concern themselves with air and water quality? These are not the security and sovereignty issues of high politics that occupy top diplomats. Are these not **low politics**—the mundane economic and social concerns that foreign ministers should leave to junior officials or to other departments? The answer is no, for IR, like all of life, depends upon the **biosphere**—the thin sliver of minerals, flora, fauna, and gases that make human existence possible. Humanity—its biological needs, institutions, and behavior—is part of an emergent structure sustaining many interdependent organisms.[1]

Life is easy to destroy but difficult to create. Species disappear at an accelerating rate. One-fifth of all plants and animals could be doomed by 2020 absent more effective steps to save them.[2] Today's willful act may be tomorrow's deficit—trees burned, marginal lands plowed, irrigation canals untended or destroyed. Human-made change helped destroy the biological foundations of ancient Sumerian, Cambodian, and Mayan civilizations. As their way of life teetered, Mayans worried about war, ecological disasters, deforestation, and starvation. "The population rose to the limits the technology could bear. They were so close to the edge, if anything went wrong, it was all over."[3] At the brink of another century, does any of this have a familiar ring?

Stability of habitat is important to humans because it is the system in which they have evolved. Environmental loss endangers their spirits, minds, and bodies. Humans risk closing the door to their future as well as wiping out their past. Endangered species may contain as-yet-undeveloped medicines, foods, drugs, timber, fibers, pulp, soil-restoring vegetation, and petroleum substitutes.[4]

How does all this concern the international political economy (IPE)? Governments and other IPE actors have sometimes led the assault on the habitat. Not only war and power politics but also development, trade, and tourism can degrade the environment. IR and IPE have been part of the problem. Can they be part of a constructive response?

1. Murray Gell-Mann, *The Quark and the Jaguar: Adventures in the Simple and the Complex* (New York: Freeman, 1994), 99–100.

2. See Edward O. Wilson, *The Diversity of Life* (New York: Norton, 1992), 35–36, 346. Wilson's estimate on disappearing species is challenged by some skeptics.

3. Linda Schele, quoted in David Roberts, "The Decipherment of Ancient Maya," *Atlantic Monthly*, September 1991; see also Linda Schele and Mary Ellen Miller, *The Blood of Kings: Dynasty and Ritual in Mayan Art* (New York: George Braziller, 1986), 14–29.

4. Industrial societies now exploit but a tiny percentage of naturally occurring species. Throughout history people have utilized about 7,000 plant species for food, but today we rely heavily on about 20 species, such as wheat and rice. Yet 75,000 species have edible parts; some may be superior to those now used, for example, the winged bean of New Guinea, called a "one-species supermarket."

THE BIOSPHERE AS A LEVEL OF IR ACTION AND ANALYSIS

The biosphere should be seen as the broadest level of IR action and analysis. IR shapes the environment and is shaped by it. This is one point on which many exponents of realism, idealism, and interdependence agree. A realist focused on power and geopolitics must take into account the environment. The realist historian Thucydides analyzed the interface between habitat and power—how the settlement patterns of Greece resulted from stronger tribes pushing out weaker peoples from the most fertile lands.

The health of nations also concerns the realist. Thucydides recorded how war spawns not just battle deaths but starvation and disease. He described how the army of one city-state would besiege another *polis* and then retreat, "laying waste to the fields" as it went. Famine and plague caused more deaths than combat, he wrote.

Disease arising from war has often been far more lethal than enemy action. In the Crimean War (1854–1856), for example, ten times as many British soldiers died of dysentery as from Russian weapons.[5] Influenza in the wake of World War I killed two or three times as many people as the fighting. Better hygiene and preventive medicine reduced the toll from war-induced disease in the 20th century. But more Iraqis suffered from malnutrition and shortages of medicines in the years after the Gulf War than from the fighting in 1991. Humanity remains vulnerable to environ-

5. William H. McNeill, *Plagues and Peoples* (New York: Anchor Books, 1989), 251.

Nuclear testing has ravaged not just human health but the health of the entire biosphere. Here an activist from the NGO Greenpeace in 1995 challenges what France called its last series of nuclear tests, conducted in French-controlled territories in the South Pacific Ocean.

mental dangers triggered by international conflict. Even weather modification is a possible weapon.

Weapons testing and war can damage entire ecosystems. When Saddam Hussein's armies set fire to hundreds of Kuwaiti oil wells in 1991, the blackened air over the Persian Gulf poisoned neutral Iran as well as Kuwait and Iraq; bird and sea life were severely affected. The heavy smoke may also have altered the timing and power of the monsoons that water the Indian subcontinent.

Regardless of power considerations, idealists stress the moral and legal reasons to protect all life. Some idealists make the case for **intergenerational equity**—that each generation should leave to future generations natural and cultural resources equal to those that it has enjoyed.[6]

The interdependence school builds on both realism and idealism to underscore the mutual vulnerabilities of all humans and the biosphere. All peoples and countries have become interdependent—with one another and with their environment. In this context they may seek either to claim values or create them with others. In this sphere, as in others, mutual gain policies work better over time than exploitation.

Ecology (environmental science) and IR can learn from one another.[7] No less than *ecology* and *economics*, IR is concerned with how humans interact with their *ekos* (or *oikos*, Greek for "habitat"). Government leaders and diplomats are responsible first of all for their own country, but many share with environmentalists the goal of making the planet a safer and more salubrious place to live, not just for those alive today but for their descendants; and not just for one or a few peoples, but for all.[8]

WHEN IS ENVIRONMENTAL PROTECTION A SECURITY ISSUE?

Narrowly defined, a security threat presents a direct and immediate danger. But a security threat can also be indirect and long-term—the result of incremental change in several spheres. Two threats probably imperil most humans: Ozone-layer depletion and climate change. The buildup of trace gases due to industrialization has opened holes in the stratospheric **ozone layer**—the zone between 15 and 45 kilometers above the earth's surface that contains ozone, a form of oxygen (O_3)—permitting more ultraviolet rays to strike the earth, raising the incidence of skin cancer and blindness among humans and threatening even plankton in the sea. Climate change, also brought on by industrialization, may produce large-scale economic disruption. But many environmental changes impinge directly on some regions and affect others only indirectly. Deser-

National Interest and the Biosphere

The U.S. Supreme Court backed the interdependence school when it upheld in *Missouri v. Holland* (1920) the right of the federal government to engage in environmental diplomacy. Asserting "states' rights," the state of Missouri sought to prevent a U.S. game warden from enforcing the Migratory Bird Treaty (1918) and regulations made by the Secretary of Agriculture to implement it. But Justice Oliver Wendell Holmes argued "wild birds are not the possession of anyone; and possession is the beginning of ownership." Birds could be in Missouri today but elsewhere tomorrow. "Here is a national interest of very nearly the first magnitude. . . . It can be protected only by national action in concert with that of another power. . . . But for the treaty and the statute there soon might be no birds for any powers to deal with." There is nothing in the U.S. Constitution compelling "the Government to sit by while a food supply is cut off and the protectors of our forests and our crops are destroyed." Therefore, the treaty and statute were sustained.

6. See Edith Brown Weiss, *In Fairness to Future Generations: International Law, Common Patrimony, and Intergenerational Equity* (Tokyo: United Nations University; Dobbs Ferry, NY: Transnational Publishers, 1989).

7. Walter C. Clemens, Jr., "Ecology and International Relations," *International Journal* [special issue: "Earth Politics"] 28, no. 1 (winter 1972–1973): 1–27. See also *International Journal* [special issue "Environment and Development: Rio and After"] 47, no. 4 (autumn 1992).

8. Harold Sprout and Margaret Sprout, *Toward a Politics of the Planet Earth* (New York: Van Nostrand Reinhold, 1971), 28.

tification, for example, may lead to starvation in Africa but not threaten Europe unless Africans attack Europeans or African refugees swarm into Europe.[9]

International environmental conflicts (IECs) may arise from utilization of natural resources that some actors believe cannot be sustained.[10] The depletion may take place directly—within a state (logging in Indonesia) or in a commons (whaling by Norway)—or indirectly (as when sulphur from Russian factories rains down on Norwegian forests). One negative side effect may spawn another, as when deforestation in El Salvador produced "environmental refugees" who crowded into Honduras, sparking a war in 1969. Serious conflicts between states erupt when upstream states close the faucets for tail-enders. Four examples of water-related IECs appear in the sidebar.

Some analysts expect IECs to intensify as states and transnational corporations (TNCs) struggle over increasingly scarce resources.[11] Others believe that a growing abundance removes any need to fight. A third view says that everything hinges on how people think and act. Whether resource shortages provoke conflict depends on **ideational factors**—values, beliefs, institutions, property relationships. These factors shape the behaviors that contribute both to environmental problems and to war, as outlined in Figure 14.1.[12]

Global interdependence, however, means vulnerability. Air and water

9. Marc A. Levy, "Is the Environment a National Security Issue?" *International Security* 20, no. 2 (fall 1995): 35–62.

10. Jon Martin Trolldalen, *International Environmental Conflict Resolution: The Role of the United Nations* (Washington, D.C.: World Foundation for Environment and Development, 1992), 57–60.

11. Lands once deemed worthless, such as the Spratly Islands, have provoked clashes between China and Vietnam. For conflicting interpretations, see Denny Roy and Michael G. Gallagher in *International Security* 19, no. 1 (summer 1994): 149–168 and 169–194.

12. Thomas F. Homer-Dixon, Jeffrey H. Boutwell, and George W. Rathjens, "Environmental Change and Violent Conflict," *Scientific American*, February 1993, 38–45.

Four IECs over Water

1. Anticipating that a dam on the Bafing River built with international financing would raise land values, Mauritania's Arab rulers expelled blacks from the river area, declaring them foreigners—"Senegalese." Blacks in Senegal then destroyed 17,000 shops belonging to Arabs and deported their owners to Mauritania.

2. Turkey controls the flow of the Euphrates River into Iraq and Syria, and diverts it for its multibillion dollar Ataturk Dam irrigation project. Syria backs Kurdish rebels against Turkey, in part to get leverage in the water talks.

3. Israel controls waters valuable to Jordan and to Palestinians on the West Bank and Gaza. Prior to 1993 Israel allotted its settlers on the occupied West Bank four times more water than it did to non-Israeli residents; Israelis were allowed to dig wells that depleted water under non-Israeli farms.

4. Slovakia in the early 1990s rechanneled part of the Danube River and harnessed its power, turning vast wetlands into waste lands—despite Hungarian objections. Budapest had agreed to the project in Communist times, but non-Communist Hungary backed out. Slovakia ignored treaties prohibiting either side from diverting the Danube in ways that altered the common border, impacted negatively on established water conditions, or profited one side only. Slovakia turned down third-parties' proposals to restore the region through a debt-for-nature swap. The International Court of Justice in 1997 treated the river's diversion as an accomplished fact but piously urged both sides to protect the environment.

Fig. 14.1 Ideational Factors Between the Environment and Human Action

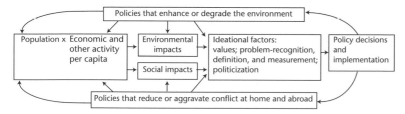

pollution do not recognize the sovereignty of state borders. What begins as a local problem may ripple widely—often unpredictably—through the entire chain of being. As naturalist John Muir put it: "When you try to touch one thing by itself, you find it hitched to everything else in the universe."

If Amazonia is deforested or polluted, this presents an immediate but localized problem for indigenous people. But deforestation also affects the global environment: It shrinks a sponge (or "sink") that absorbs carbon from the entire world, and it releases gases as trees decompose or burn. Even if new trees are planted, decades are usually needed before the new forest acquires a significant ability to store carbons. Biodiversity is even harder to restore. If Sao Paulo and Rio are polluted, a local problem becomes a worldwide problem as gases rising from the polluted cities add to global concentrations. If global weather becomes more volatile, Brazil too is likely to suffer. As Map 14.1 on page 410 illustrates, economic and social developments in Brazil affect the global environment, which in turn affects Brazil.

HOW CAN IR ENHANCE THE ENVIRONMENT?

Environmental diplomacy addresses the interface between habitat and IR. It is practiced not only by governments and international governmental organizations (IGOs) such as the UN, but by private parties—scientists, the media, nongovernmental organizations (NGOs), and TNCs.[13] Environmental diplomacy can utilize many levers: growing knowledge and consensus among experts on environmental problems and options, informed public opinion and environmental awareness, harmonization of policy by various IR actors, carrots and sticks (soft and hard power), declarations of intent (moral force), and bilateral and multilateral agreements (legal force).

Many environmental agreements are bilateral. In 1869 and 1875, for example, Germany and Switzerland signed treaties to regulate fishing in the

13. A major text is Lynton Keith Caldwell, *International Environmental Policy: Emergence and Dimensions,* 2d ed. (Durham, N.C.: Duke University Press, 1990).

Map 14.1 Brazil in the Global Feedback Loop

1. The Amazon Basin, like other forests, traps carbons, but when trees are cut, burned, or left to rot, they release greenhouse gases. The Amazon may hold half of the world's biological riches. It extends into nine countries, but 68 percent of the Amazon Basin lies in Brazil. However, 75 percent of Peru and Bolivia lie in Amazonia, and 45 percent of Colombia.

2. Deforestation takes place rapidly as the area is "developed," with or without government permission or encouragement. Large tracts of Amazonia are owned by foreign companies that receive tax breaks and other financial incentives for building roads and developing Amazonia.

3. Some 400 ethnic groups—estimated at half a million to 2.5 million indigenous people—live in the Amazon Basin. Development of their habitat often leads to cultural genocide and to physical massacres, as among the Yanomani peoples in the northern part of Amazonia. The Basin in the 1990s had 20 million inhabitants. Besides indigenous peoples, there were gold prospectors, coca farmers, rubber tappers, and urban populations.

4. Large dams in the Amazon Basin include Bal Bina, Tucurei, and Samuel. In other parts of Brazil are the large dams Itaparica and Itaipu. They generate power but have dislocated many people, added to deforestation, and degraded natural wonders such as Iguazu Falls.

5. Automobiles and industry create serious air pollution in Sao Paulo, Belo Horizonte, and other Brazilian cities.

6. Most of Brazil's Atlantic coast forest, "Mata Atlantica," has been cut down, opening the way to severe erosion. Rio de Janeiro has been extended into the water on fragile foundations. If ocean waters rise, due in part to global warming, Brazil's Atlantic coast will suffer further erosion.

7. Sources of conflict in the Amazon Basin include drug-trafficking vs. anti-narcotics operations; oil exploration, mining, and other forms of development vs. native peoples and environmentalists; guerrilla insurgents of Colombia and Peru vs. governments and other defenders of the status quo. Outside actors often magnify the conflicts. They include the U.S. armed forces (anti-drug missions), the World Bank, the UN Environmental Programme, the Organization of American States, the Inter-American Development Bank, and Raytheon Corporation.

8. SIVAM (*Sistema de Vigilencia d Amazonia*) is a system of land-based radars and satellites to monitor land clearings approved by the Brazilian Congress in 1996 for development by the Raytheon Corporation and financed by loans from the U.S. Export-Import Bank.

9. Rivalry and some arms competition with Argentina, designated by President Bill Clinton in 1997 as a "non-NATO U.S. ally" and praised by him for officially recognizing that it too should act to reduce carbon emissions, continues.

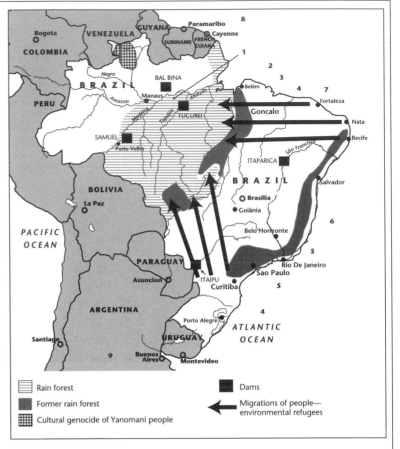

MAP NOTE: Latin America and the Caribbean lost 3 percent of their forest cover in 1991–1995, more hectares than any other region. While 68 percent of Argentina has been "converted," only 28 percent of Brazil had been converted by 1995. But 6 percent of the forests in both countries were converted in the 1980s.

SOURCES: *Oxford Atlas of the World* (New York: Oxford University Press, 1994), 47; "Challenges Facing the Amazon Basin," *Strategic Comments* 3, no. 8 (London: International Institute for Strategic Studies, October 1997); interview with Dr. Maria G. M. Rodrigues, Boston University, 1997; and Lester R. Brown et al., *Vital Signs 1997* (New York: Norton, 1997), 96–99.

Rhine River. More than 130 such agreements had been reached around the world by the 1990s.[14] But many environmental accords are multilateral. A few are outlined in Table 14.1.

Environmental diplomacy often follows a two-stage process: First, diplomats draft and sign a **framework convention** (treaty) stating general objectives but omitting specific methods and commitments. Second, as consensus builds, diplomats adopt supplementary **protocols**—follow-up agreements to specify and tighten commitments. Step by step, this process builds a **regime**—agreed-on rules or understandings. The

14. See Edith Brown Weiss, ed., *Environmental Change and International Law: New Challenges and Dimensions* (Tokyo: United Nations University Press, 1992), 479–490.

Table 14.1 Examples of Environmental Problems, Conflicts, and Negotiated Remedies

Environmental Problem	International Conflict	Negotiated Remedy
Stratospheric ozone layer depletion due to gas emissions	LDCs resist pressures to reduce their emissions	1987 Montreal Protocol, with grace period for LDCs
Greenhouse gases and global climate change	Debate on severity of the problem and who should sacrifice what	1992 Rio Global Climate Change Convention and 1997 Kyoto accords
Acid deposits across borders	Polluters resist pressures from their victims	1979 Geneva Convention for Europe; 1991 Canada-U.S. Air Quality Agreement
Deforestation	Brazil and Indonesia tell the North to change its own practices	Debt-for-nature swaps; 1992 Rio Statement on "All Types of Forests"
Nuclear radiation leakage from reactors	Europeans complain that Moscow told them too late and too little about the 1986 Chernobyl meltdown	1986 IAEA Conventions on Early Notification and on Assistance in Case of a Nuclear Accident
Depletion of fish stocks	Canada vs. U.S.; each country vs. outsiders; Ottawa and Washington claim right to regulate fishing over the continental shelf	Bilateral Canadian-U.S. agreements; 1982 UN Law of the Sea; 1992 Rio Convention on Biological Diversity
Dumping of waste at sea and in LDCs, with or without their agreement	Defenders of global commons and of LDCs oppose dumpers (mainly from the North)	1989 Basel Convention to Control Transboundary Movements of Hazardous Wastes and Their Disposal

process permits countries to "sign on" at the outset even before specific commitments are clear. If supplementary commitments seem too onerous, actors need not sign the additional protocol.

The first UN Conference on the Human Environment held in Stockholm in 1972 led to establishment of the UN Environmental Programme in Nairobi, Kenya. Ten years later, a follow-up meeting was held in Nairobi. In 1992 a third gathering convened in Brazil. The 1992 UN Conference on Environment and Development in Rio de Janeiro—dubbed the **Earth Summit**—became the largest political gathering in history. The conference was attended by some 170 states—over 100 represented by their heads of state or government—and evaluated by 1,500 accredited observers from NGOs and 8,000 journalists. The official meetings were paralleled by meetings attended by 30,000 private citizens from NGOs around the globe.

The 1992 Earth Summit endorsed a series of documents: the Rio Declaration or "Earth Charter," a list of 27 basic principles to govern economic and environmental behavior of states; Agenda 21, action goals in major areas affecting the environment and the economy (nearly 400 pages of small type); a Framework Convention on Climate Change (26 articles and two annexes); a Convention on Biological Diversity (42 articles and two annexes); and an Authoritative Statement of Principles on Sustainable Development of All Types of Forests (15 principles).[15]

15. Michael Grubb et al., *The Earth Summit Agreements: A Guide and Assessment* (London: Earthscan, 1993); for texts, see Stanley P. Johnson, ed., *The Earth Summit* (London: Graham & Trotman/Martinus Nijhoff, 1993).

The Rio accords were long on generalities and short on specific obligations. For critics, the glass was half-empty. For Rio enthusiasts, it was half-full; they argued that such meetings raise consciousness and set the stage for more precise action programs.

MALTHUSIANS, CORNUCOPIANS, AND SUSTAINABLE DEVELOPMENT

The **Malthusian perspective** contends that there are finite limits to growth as expanding human populations deplete resources.[16] This view has its roots in an essay by Thomas Malthus, published in 1798. Malthus predicted that population (growing exponentially) would outstrip food production (growing "arithmetically") unless checked by moral restraints or by war, famine, and disease.[17]

The **Cornucopian outlook**, by contrast, sees life as a horn of plenty that swells with use. Human ingenuity uses the earth to sustain more people than ever—most of them living longer and in greater comfort than their predecessors. Cornucopians are pro-growth: Material well-being is the key that makes everything else possible—including environmental protection. Cornucopians say that Malthus did not anticipate that technology would facilitate vastly larger populations.[18]

"In technology we trust" is the optimists' motto. Technological optimists have wagered that insecticides can wipe out malaria; that nuclear power promises not just weapons but clean energy at a reasonable price; that the Green Revolution can transform agriculture by "miracle seeds" backed by abundant fertilizer and irrigation; that modernization plus affluence will stem population growth; that genetic engineering will produce improved life forms. Each approach, however, spawned negative side effects and much criticism.[19]

Are there no limits to growth? Can demand assure supply? Malthusians fear that there is no technical solution to some problems posed by

16. See the report to the Club of Rome by Donella H. Meadows et al., *The Limits to Growth* (New York: Universe Books, 1972).

17. Malthus warned: "As population doubles and redoubles, it is exactly as if the globe were halving in size, until finally it has shrunk so much that food and subsistence fall below the level necessary for life." Malthus believed that, due to the law of diminishing returns, food production tends *not* to keep up with the geometric progression of growth of population.

18. The Malthusians' viewpoint and Cornucopian economist Julian L. Simon's views may be found in Simon, *Population Matters: People, Resources, Environment, and Immigration* (New Brunswick, N.J.: Transaction, 1990), 374–380.

19. Critics say that the Green Revolution has helped the rich become richer, because only they can afford the necessary fertilizer. If big farms become more efficient, poor farmers are displaced. Over time, however, heavy dependence on fertilizer and water leads to diminishing returns. See also Jane Rissler and Margaret Mellon, *The Ecological Risks of Engineered Crops* (Cambridge, Mass.: MIT Press, 1996).

Betting on Resources: How Would You Wager?

Cornucopian economist Julian L. Simon in 1980 wagered Malthusian environmentalist Paul Ehrlich that the price of five metals would decline in the 1980s. At the end of the decade, Simon won hands down. Ehrlich sent Simon a check for $570.07—the decrease in price by 1990 of metals that had cost $5,000 in 1980. How could the price decline? Simon explained: Appearances can deceive. It may seem that some resource is being exhausted—water, energy, soil. But when the problem becomes visible, human reason finds a solution—more of the resource, a substitute, or ways to conserve and recycle. The story is retold in "Environmental Scares," *The Economist*, December 20, 1997–January 2, 1998, 19–21.

A Boost for Skeptics of Malthus

The world population may increase in the early 21st century but then decline, causing social and economic problems. A UN study in 1997 forecast an increase in world population from 5.85 billion in 1997 to 7.29 billion in 2015. But the proportion of people not reproducing themselves was rapidly increasing. In 1997 some 44 percent of the world's women produced fewer than the 2.1 babies needed to keep a population constant. They lived in roughly fifty countries, from Greece to Thailand. By 2015 demographers expected the fertility rate for 67 percent of the world's people to fall below replacement level.[1]

Meanwhile, the International Grains Council forecast in October 1997 that worldwide harvests of wheat and coarse grains such as maize would surpass all records in 1997. Wheat harvests were expected to reach 598 million tons—a 2.6 percent increase over 1996. Consumption was likely to rise as well, especially due to higher animal feed use.

1. Barbara Crossette, "How to Fix a Crowded World: Add People," *New York Times*, November 2, 1997, E1–3.

population growth. So far Malthus' predictions have materialized only in specific regions. But if humans multiply beyond a certain threshold, their support system may crash, leading to a sharp reduction in population.[20]

The limits-to-growth school argues that clean air, clean water, and biodiversity must be protected—now, not later. They fear that environmental problems can grow so quickly against fixed limits that policymakers may have little time to avert disaster.[21]

Cornucopians say that humans can devise answers to shortages and live in peaceful abundance. They advise no costly steps against uncertain risks. They prefer to wait and see.[22]

SUSTAINABLE DEVELOPMENT VS. EXPLOITATION

Is it possible to bridge the gap between the Malthusian and Cornucopian viewpoints? The concept of **sustainable development** calls for economic growth but stipulates that resources be used in ways that can be sustained over time.[23] Think of natural resources as capital assets and their benefits as income. Sustainable development leaves capital assets (soil, water, forests) intact so that future generations can enjoy undiminished income and quality of life. **Carrying capacity** is the level of resource utilization that can be sustained without degrading the resource. This level depends both on nature and on humans—how they utilize the resource can weaken or buttress its carrying capacity.

Critics say that sustainable development is a nice-sounding slogan but solves nothing. At best it offers a goal but gives no practical advice on how to achieve it. As we see in the sidebar on page 414, sustainable development is easier said than done. It can mean different things to different people.

Sustainable development requires a value-creating approach to

20. Positive and negative feedback loops link growth in human population, resource depletion, pollution, and climate change. Each factor aggravates both environmental problems and the aggressive behaviors that exacerbate other shortfalls. A positive feedback loop generates runaway growth: If population increases, requiring ever higher levels of consumption, resources will be depleted. Negative feedback loops tend to hold a system stable for a time. But change in one element propagates change through the system until it comes back to push that element in an opposite direction, which may produce a crash. See Jay W. Forrester, *World Dynamics* (Cambridge, Mass.: Wright Allen Press, 1971), 94–95; and Meadows et al., *Limits to Growth*, 31–37.

21. Imagine a pond where one water lily grows. This plant doubles in size each day. If it expands unchecked, it will cover the pond in thirty days, choking off other forms of life. For days the plant seems small, so you decide not to cut it back until it covers half the pond. But on the twenty-ninth day, only one day remains to save the pond! Meadows et al., *Limits to Growth*, 29.

22. Many Cassandras have predicted a doomsday that never arrived, for example, an end to oil. Even though oil resources have been depleted in some countries, new finds and alternative fuels more than meet global demand. So far the planet resembles a gigantic cave in which, as we reach the limit of one chamber, the door to another opens—even grander than the one just passed.

23. William C. Clark and R. E. Munn, eds., *Sustainable Development of the Biosphere* (New York: Cambridge University Press, 1986); World Commission on Environment and Development, *Our Common Future* (New York: Oxford University Press, 1987).

Diverse Perspectives on Sustainable Development

Radicals say that sustainable development is impossible—a contradiction in terms. They recommend: "Live simply and redistribute the wealth." Other viewpoints regard sustainable development as possible, but recommend different strategies:

Biologist: "Maintain biodiversity."

Geographer: "Preserve renewable resources."

Democrat: "Help people participate in decisions that affect their lives."

Anthropologist: "Do nothing to threaten indigenous cultures."

Engineer: "Trust in technology, for example, recycling."

Cornucopian economist: "Grow the economy to get the wealth and technology to eliminate poverty and green the human habitat."

Moralist: "Preserve the planet for future generations while providing equal access to those now deprived of resources."

Feminist: "Do not condemn women to gathering firewood and carrying water."

Social scientist: "Differentiate: Sustainable development for an Amazon village means something different than for a megacity such as Sao Paulo."

Peace researcher: "Develop and create values to minimize conflicts over scarce or declining resources."

Mutual gain planner: "Enhance HDI at home and across borders. Husband your resources but interact with other societies for mutual gain."

wealth, politics, and the environment. The concept of mutual gain can be adapted to husbanding the biosphere. A short-term emphasis on claiming values for quick, one-sided profits can make development unsustainable. The values at stake are multiple—the resource itself, the interests of the developers, and those of third parties affected by the development. A zero-sum approach to a resource may kill it: A policy that excludes other actors from a resource may lead those actors to sabotage it. In development, as in other spheres, aggressive exploitation can backfire.[24]

HOW THE LOGIC OF COLLECTIVE ACTION CAN DEGRADE THE ENVIRONMENT

As noted in Chapter 1, a **collective (or public) good** is one that all persons in a given community may share, such as common pasture or breathable air. It is a good that, if available to any group member, cannot feasibly be withheld from other members—even those who do not pay for it. Some public goods are part of the natural environment; some are provided by government or other human agencies. Economic activity and **externalities**—unplanned side effects—can add to or deplete public goods.

Some actors try to exploit public goods and obtain a "free ride" based on others' efforts. This "logic of collective action" leads to the underfunding of public goods such as clean air and to behavior injurious to the commons.[25] The lure of parasitism is even stronger across borders. To cope, governments use incentives—rewards for tree planters and penal-

24. Some UN documents refer to exploitation in a positive and a negative sense on the same page. Exploitation comes from the Latin for "unfold." The term long had a positive connotation—tapping a resource. In the 18th century, however, some economists asserted that the exploitation of German peasants by large landowners was unfair. Later, Karl Marx argued that capitalists exploit workers, deriving "surplus value" from their labor. He predicted that this exploitation could not be sustained, for it would trigger a revolution.

25. Mancur Olson, *The Logic of Collective Action* (Cambridge, Mass.: Harvard University Press, 1965, 1971); and Olson, *The Rise and Decline of Nations: Economic Growth, Stagflation, and Social Rigidities* (New Haven, Conn.: Yale University Press, 1982).

ties for polluters. To curb international free riding—for example, dumping wastes—governments set up special regimes.

To "ecologize" or "green" production can make a country cleaner and more efficient while fostering innovative technology. But neighbors who refuse to ecologize also benefit from the cleaner environment while their own industries produce unburdened by pollution abatement costs.

Our case studies show how power politics, the drive for economic development, and the logic of collective action have abetted exploitation of the biosphere. But we shall also see that farsighted diplomacy—by private citizens and NGOs as well as by governments and IGOs—has done much to conserve the planet.

COMPARING THEORY AND REALITY: IS SUSTAINABLE DEVELOPMENT FEASIBLE?

Life can be a gamble. Faust wagered his very soul for earthly pleasure. International actors—governments, TNCs, the World Bank, even the World Health Organization[26]—have often bet that technology can overcome economic and environmental restraints. Each technology has promise, but each entails huge risks. Let us focus first on water power.

DAMMED WATERS AND DAMNED PEOPLE: THE ASWAN SYNDROME

Mastery of water resources has long been a source of power—political as well as economic and social. It was key to the "hydraulic civilizations" of ancient Egypt, Sumeria, India, Sri Lanka, and China. Water politics shapes both development and environmental well-being at the cusp of the millennium.

Disputes over water will intensify as shortages grow more acute. The sidebar on page 408 illustrates the kinds of conflicts that erupt when upstream states close the faucets to tail-enders.

Many 20th-century governments invested in huge water projects. Backers of large dams promise that Big is Beautiful. They promise a panacea: Cheap power! Cheap water! More crops! Development! Independence! But building a dam is like constructing a nuclear plant. It may bring immediate benefits, but also incur heavy long-term costs and negative externalities. Like nuclear power plants, dams often leave a legacy of destruction difficult to undo.[27] The **Aswan syndrome** trusts in the potential gains of large dams while ignoring their possible negative side effects.

Many governments and the World Bank believed that dams meant de-

26. The World Health Organization and its use of chemical sprays against malaria-carrying mosquitoes are discussed in Chapter 15.

27. On the controversial Glen Canyon Dam in Arizona, see "Dams Aren't Forever," by Daniel P. Beard, commissioner of the Federal Bureau of Reclamation in 1993–1995, in *New York Times*, October 6, 1997, A23; see also Walter C. Clemens, Jr., "Nuclear Power: America's Aswan," *Washington Post*, op-ed, April 20, 1975.

What Happens When a River Crosses Borders?

International rivers—systems that border or bisect one or more countries—can be and sometimes are managed cooperatively. But often the riverine states claim values unilaterally. Claims and counterclaims can generate international environmental conflicts. If the upstream state diverts or pollutes a river, the downstream neighbor suffers. Traditional international law offers support for each side, for it holds that "state sovereignty and territorial integrity may not be violated." If the upstream state is "sovereign," it may use a national resource as it pleases. But the downstream state can complain that its "territorial integrity" is violated if a neighbor depletes its water. International law at the end of the 20th century seeks to reconcile conflicting claims by applying such principles as "reciprocity," "community interest," and "equitable utilization." Lacking any accord, states sometimes defend their interests by force.

28. For worldwide statistics, see World Resources Institute, *World Resources 1992–93: A Guide to the Global Environment* (New York: Oxford University Press, 1992), Table 22.2.

velopment. In 1950 the entire world had about 5,000 dams with walls over 15 meters (50 feet) high. In 1986 there were more than 36,200 such dams. But efforts to "tame" nature produced negative side effects that often outweighed the positives. Chastened, few developed countries built large dams in the last quarter of the 20th century. But many less developed countries (LDCs) continued to build or plan them.[28] Here was a parallel with nuclear power: While the U.S. was phasing out nuclear plants and examining alternatives to dams, China wanted more of both.

An International River System: The Nile

For thousands of years Egyptians lived in positive symbiosis with the Nile. They farmed one crop each winter using the rich alluvial deposits and waters of the annual flood. But Egypt's entry into the world economy challenged ancient ways. Ottoman Viceroy Mohammed Ali wanted to sell cotton abroad to finance Egypt's modernization. He, and after 1882 the British administrators of Egypt, sought to cultivate a summer as well as a winter crop. Mohammed Ali and later the British built irrigation canals and dams that increased productivity for a time. But eventually Egypt faced diminishing returns due to two problems that persisted into the late 20th century: First, irrigated land, unless flushed, becomes salty. Second, silt and water-borne minerals build up behind barriers instead of flowing where needed.

The Nile takes water from eight other countries into Egypt. The Blue Nile originates in Ethiopia's Lake Tana while the White Nile drains two lakes—Lake Victoria (bordered by Uganda, Kenya, and Tanzania) and Lake Mobutu (between Zaire/Congo and Uganda). The Blue and White Nile converge at Khartoum in the Sudan, forming one stream that heads north through Egypt. One of the world's two longest river networks, the Nile follows a 6,671 kilometer course north to the Mediterranean Sea.

British engineers early in the 20th century proposed the "Century Storage Scheme" to manage the entire network with reservoirs on the main Nile, the Blue Nile, and the White Nile. But they failed to implement a system-wide solution due to high projected costs and to European wars.

In 1952 Egyptian officers overthrew King Farouk and asserted Egypt's independence from British influence. They endorsed the proposal of a Greek-Egyptian engineer to erect a high dam on the Nile at Aswan. It would symbolize a modern, self-sufficient Egypt; generate hydroelectric power; regulate the annual flood; and facilitate irrigation to feed an exploding population. Some voices again pleaded for a system-wide approach, but the officers did not wish to depend on whomever controlled the Upper Nile—whether British imperialists or newly independent African states.

Washington and London were nearly ready to finance and build the Aswan High Dam but backed out in 1956—miffed over Cairo's refusal to join their anti-Soviet "Baghdad Pact." The USSR stepped in and agreed to construct the dam and finance one-third of its costs. Already Moscow had sold arms to Cairo. Egyptian leader Gamal Abdal Nasser (president after 1954) was anti-Communist, but open to aid from any quarter. Moscow hoped its investment in Egypt would assure Soviet influence throughout the Middle East.

In 1959 Egypt negotiated with the Sudan an agreement that specified how the Nile's waters would be allocated and established an inspectorate to monitor compliance. Egypt paid Sudan to resettle some 50,000 Nubians displaced by the Aswan reservoir.

The Aswan High Dam was built in the 1960s and all turbines were operating by 1970. What did it achieve? The balance sheet is complicated. Some initial gains became later losses. Some results, good and bad, could not be measured in money.[29]

Food. An immense reservoir called Lake Nasser formed behind the dam. Water from the reservoir irrigated new lands but their area did not exceed the old lands lost. Still, harvests increased because irrigation permitted double cropping. Egyptian officials claimed that the dam paid for itself in just one dry year because it helped feed Egypt in a time of drought. Over time, however, farming became more difficult: There was more evaporation and more seepage from Lake Nasser than expected; the reservoir's water level was more variable and its contents more saline than anticipated; irrigation canals clogged with sediment and salt, requiring expensive drainage systems; and soggy soil required costly fertilizers and pesticides. Snail- and insect-borne diseases increased, affecting some 40 percent of Egyptians.

Fishing in Lake Nasser was good, but fishing downstream and especially in the Nile Delta fell sharply as nutrients piled up in silt behind the dam. Transportation of fish from Lake Nasser to northern markets remained problematic.

Power. Hydroelectric power surged and provided half of Egypt's needs in the 1970s. Later, however, Aswan's electric power diminished as more water was needed for agriculture. Turbines had to be replaced. Cracks appeared in the dam.

29. John Waterbury, *Hydropolitics of the Nile Valley* (Syracuse, N.Y.: Syracuse University Press, 1979); Dale Whittington and Giorgio Guariso, *Water Management Models in Practice: A Case Study of the Aswan High Dam* (Amsterdam: Elsevier, 1983); Gilbert F. White, "The Environmental Effects of the High Dam at Aswan," *Environment* 30, no. 7 (September 1988): 4 ff.; G. Burns et al., "Salinity Threat to Upper Egypt," *Nature*, March 1, 1990, 25; and Daniel Jean Stanley, "Subsidence in the Northeastern Nile Delta: Rapid Rates, Possible Causes, and Consequences," *Science*, April 22, 1988, 497 ff. Interview with former U.S. ambassador to Egypt Hermann Fr. Eilts, May 4, 1994.

Culture. Lake Nasser flooded many ancient Egyptian and Roman ruins, though UNESCO moved Abu Simbel Temple to higher ground. Nearly 100,000 Nubians (half of them in the Sudan) lost their traditional way of life when forced to settle elsewhere.

Political-Strategic. For some years President Nasser and many Egyptians gained pride and confidence, defying the West and ignoring most upstream states. Against this came a new vulnerability, for the dam offered a major target for Israeli bombers. There was also dependence—first on the USSR for money, advice, and technology; later on the U.S. for new turbines and for wheat when Egypt's farms failed to feed the country's growing numbers. Displeased by Soviet behavior, President Anwar Sadat broke most ties with Moscow.[30] In the 1980s Egyptian pride turned to anger. Many Egyptians blamed all the country's problems on Aswan.

The high dam was no panacea. Wishful thinking left Egypt and its neighbors with a host of unresolved problems. Counting on more fish and grain, Cairo did little to promote population control. A serious effort at population planning—inexpensive and environment-neutral—would have done more to keep food stocks in line with population than the costly dam. But no serious population control campaigns were initiated until the 1980s.

In the 21st century Egypt will need more water, but so will Ethiopia, the Sudan, and the countries of equatorial Africa. Upstream states could close the spigot. In 1980 Sadat warned that Egypt would fight if Ethiopia interfered with Egypt's historic rights to Nile water. Sadat's successors, however, talked of digging 3,000 wells to tap the desert if Ethiopia dammed the Blue Nile. In the mid-1990s Egyptian leaders talked of building a second main branch of the Nile by diverting water into a channel leading west and north.

The ideal solution—technically and politically—would be an international storage system to meet overlapping needs of the riverine states, but such an undertaking would require unprecedented cooperation and joint planning.[31]

The Aswan Syndrome in India and China

Governments on every continent have dammed waters and damned people.[32] Like the Nubians, long-established communities have been uprooted—from Paraguay to Senegal to Siberia.[33] Millions more are in danger—from Canada to India and China.[34] Threatened communities try to resist powerful governments but usually lose—especially where democracy is weak.

30. Walter C. Clemens, Jr., "Behind Sadat's Eviction Order," *New Leader,* October 2, 1972, 6–8.

31. Whittington and Guariso, *Water Management,* 221. Three of the upstream states, however, cooperated in water surveys by the World Meteorological Organization.

32. S. Robert Aikken, "Hydro-Electric Power and Wilderness Protection," *Impact of Science on Society* 36, no. 1 (1986): 85–96; Fred Pearce, "Building a Disaster: The Monumental Folly of India's Tehri Dam," *The Ecologist* 21 (May–June 1991): 123–128; and Ricardo Canese, *La problematica de Itaipu: analisis de los cuestiones financiereas, economicas y energeticas* (Asuncion: Casillia de Correo, 1989).

33. Michael M. Horowitz, "Victims Upstream and Down," *Journal of Refugee Studies* 4, no. 2 (1991): 164–181; and Anthony Oliver-Smith, "Involuntary Resettlement, Resistance and Political Empowerment," ibid, 132–149. On Siberia, see Valentin Rasputin's novel, *Farewell to Matëra.*

34. What benefits one region may harm another. Many New Yorkers may welcome a larger supply of electricity from Canada. But Hydro-Quebec's La Grand project at James Bay would inundate a Vermont-sized area—home to Crees, Inuits, and abundant wildlife. As flood vegetation decomposes, it releases methane and carbon dioxide and methyl mercury into the water, contaminating the food chain. See Jonathan S. Price et al., "Impacts on Coastal Marshes," *The Canadian Geographer* 36, no. 1 (spring 1992): 8 ff.

Many dams have been financed by the World Bank—one reason that Greenpeace activists in 1994 demanded "no more dollars for destruction" by "World Bankenstein."[35] Bank president Lewis Preston conceded in 1994 that the bank's greatest mistake had been to undervalue environmental considerations. Better late than never, the World Bank in the 1990s gave more weight to ecology.

In the 1980s the World Bank offered $450 million in loans to India to dam the Narmada River. Later, a more environmentally conscious bank pressed India to explain how it would cope with the dam's consequences—environmental disruption and displacement of at least 250,000 people. This led India in 1993 to reject the final $170 million loan installment.[36]

Communist governments have often trusted in large projects to improve on nature.[37] China's National People's Congress in 1992 approved what could be the world's largest water works—the Three Gorges Dam on the Yangtze River. Chinese officials hoped the project, to be built over twenty or more years, would generate power equal to one-eighth of China's 1991 output and prevent floods. An associated project would sluice water by aqueduct 1,500 miles northeast to Beijing.

But many Chinese and foreign observers saw the Three Gorges project as an enterprise with risks and likely costs far outweighing the potential gains. Public debate on the dam was banned after 1989. Prevented from publishing critical analysis within China, some Chinese scientists published their views abroad. Of 2,600 delegates to the 1992 Congress, 177 voted against the dam and 664 abstained.

Top Chinese leaders presided over the initial diversion of the Yangtze in late 1997. The project was expected to flood 24,000 hectares of arable land and displace more than one million people; inundate 350 miles of a canyon that was a centerpiece of Chinese art, history, and culture for thousands of years; and destroy the habitat of a unique dolphin and other endangered species. The dam's design was untested. Accumulated sediments behind the dam could limit its storage capacity. Like Aswan, this could also be a prime bomb target. Cost estimates for the dam ratcheted up from $12 billion in 1993 to more than $25 billion in 1997. Conservationists urged China instead to fix leaking toilets, raise water prices, and build smaller, safer dams.[38]

Technology can make life better. But governments have often opted for big, showy projects rather than seeking **appropriate technology**—whatever scale and type of technology is appropriate to the task. PRC President Jiang Zemin stated that the Yangtze diversion "vividly proves once

35. Some 150 environmental groups in thirty countries organized a campaign "50 Years Is Enough" directed against the World Bank and IMF. The organizers wanted to hold the two agencies accountable to the people whose lives they affect in the developing world. Greenpeace did not wish to destroy the World Bank; it sought to reduce its resources and power.

36. Hamish McDonald, "Closing the Floodgates: New Delhi Rejects a World Bank Loan to Build a Dam," *Far Eastern Economic Review* 156, no. 15 (April 15, 1993): 15. Another analyst feared that the Sardar Sarovar dam would flood 150 villages and force 1.5 million people off their lands. See Damien Lewis, "Drowning by Numbers," *Geographical Magazine* 63, no. 9 (September 1991): 34 ff.

37. Stalin turned Russia's Volga River into a succession of polluted, heavily sedimented lakes behind vast hydroelectric dams. Cotton irrigation projects in Soviet Uzbekistan virtually destroyed the Aral Sea. A dam completed in the 1980s degraded the water of St. Petersburg. For the broad picture, see D.J. Peterson, *Troubled Lands: The Legacy of Soviet Environmental Destruction* (Boulder, Colo.: Westview, 1993).

38. Seth Faison, "Set to Build Dam, China Diverts Yangtze While Crowing About It," *New York Times*, November 9, 1997, 1, 12; Peter Gwynne, "Yangtze Project Dammed with Faint Praise," *Nature*, April 30, 1992, 736; "The Biggest in Question," *The Economist*, March 28, 1992, 97; and Philip M. Fearnside, "China's Three Gorges Dam: 'Fatal' Project or Step Toward Modernization?" *World Development* 16, no. 5 (May 1988): 615 ff.

again that socialism is superior in organizing people to do big jobs." Prime Minister Li Peng said the event showed the "greatness . . . of China's development." The New China News Agency compared the dam with the Great Wall, built 2,000 years earlier. Undaunted by possible side effects, one of the dam's chief engineers asserted: "Basically no technical problem is insoluble."

Why have so many governments tried to replace a natural irrigation system to which farmers and fishermen have adapted with huge ventures that may prove counterproductive? Anxieties about floods and food shortfalls give rise to wishful thinking and gigantomania. The availability of "free money"—public funds or foreign loans—can mean personal profit and more prestige.

HOW TO NEGOTIATE TO PROTECT THE ENVIRONMENT

Let us examine how diplomats have tried to protect the ozone layer and control the buildup of greenhouse gases. Each case is vital, because the biosphere depends upon layers of gases shielding the planet. To understand and regulate these processes is a challenge for scientists, diplomats, economists, and ethicists. By what principle should rights (for example, to pollute and to breathe) and duties (to protect and to share) be allocated?[39]

A "Simple" Problem: Protecting the Ozone Layer

More than twenty states signed the Vienna Convention on Substances that Deplete the Ozone Layer in 1985. Protocols followed. The Montreal Protocol on Substances that Deplete the Ozone Layer—the **Montreal Protocol**—was signed by some fifty countries in 1987 and entered into force in 1989. The parties agreed to freeze and then reduce production and consumption of chlorofluorocarbons (CFCs) and other chemicals believed to damage the ozone layer. The protocol gave LDCs more time to comply than it did to industrial countries.[40]

The Montreal accord was aided by a scientific consensus on the nature of an environmental problem.[41] DuPont Corporation, the major U.S. producer, initially denied that CFCs presented any danger. DuPont later shifted its stance as evidence pointed to holes in the ozone layer; as Congress threatened to limit CFC production in the U.S.—leaving Dupont's foreign competitors untouched; and as DuPont researchers found a possible substitute for CFCs that promised the firm a competitive advantage worldwide.

39. For background, see Committee on Science, Engineering, and Public Policy, National Academy of Sciences, National Academy of Engineering, Institute of Medicine, *Policy Implications of Greenhouse Warming* (Washington, D.C.: National Academy Press, 1991).

40. Each industrial country signatory pledged to reduce by 1990 its production and consumption of CFCs to less than 1986 levels; by 1994 to cut CFCs by 20 percent under 1986 levels; and by 1999 to no more than half of 1986 levels. The Montreal Protocol recognized the special situation of LDCs (so-called "Article 5 countries") in which per capita consumption of the controlled substances was less than 0.3 kilograms per year. They would have ten more years in which to comply.

41. See Thomas E. Graedel and Paul J. Crutzen, "The Changing Atmosphere," *Scientific American*, September 1989, 58–68 at 63; and Stephen H. Schneider, "The Changing Climate," ibid., 70–79. Some observers suggested that ozone depletion was a greater issue for fair-skinned, affluent Northerners than for the dark-skinned peoples of the LDCs. Most specialists agreed, however, that greater ultra-violet radiation threatens all living things—even sea plankton.

The 1987 protocol's restrictions on CFC production were ratcheted up after scientific evidence accumulated about the seriousness of ozone depletion. In 1990 the parties reconvened in London and agreed to eliminate completely the production of eight ozone-depleting chemicals by the year 2000 in industrialized countries and by 2010 in developing countries. In 1990 more countries jumped on the bandwagon: Ninety-three countries, including China and India, signed the London protocol.

The Montreal-London accords imposed heavier near-term obligations on industrialized states than on developing countries. First, heavy polluters had to reduce emissions earlier than light polluters. Second, production ceilings were pegged to 1986 consumption levels rather than to a per capita basis. Third, in 1990 the industrialized countries agreed to establish a Multilateral Fund of $240 million to help LDCs convert existing chemical plants, install new ones, and import substitutes.

The ozone limitations had mixed success. The U.S. and Western Europe stopped production of CFCs in 1995 but agreed only that year to phase out another ozone-depleting agent, methyl bromide, by 2010. Many Third World countries continued to produce CFCs, some of which were smuggled into developed countries and sold at high prices. As of 1998, ozone holes over Antarctica persisted. Without the ozone accords, however, worldwide incidence of skin cancer would probably be much higher.[42]

Dealing with Climate Change

There have been ice ages and warming trends without human intervention. But human activities may bring on a **greenhouse effect**—global warming due to carbon dioxide (CO_2) buildup in the atmosphere where it absorbs infrared radiation from the sun-warmed surface of the planet and returns the radiation to earth. By the late 1990s carbon dioxide concentrations had risen by 30 percent and methane concentrations had doubled since pre-industrial times. Environmentalists feared that if CO_2 doubled, weather disruptions would be severe.

But coping with global warming is a far more complicated issue than protection of the ozone layer. It may be the "most monumentous environmental problem in human history."[43]

First, the facts are disputed. The **Intergovernmental Panel on Climate Change (IPCC)**, a scientific body set up by the UN to coordinate and assess climate change, estimated that human-caused emissions of CO_2 and other gases were likely to contribute to an increase in the earth's temperatures of between 2 and 6 degrees Fahrenheit by the year 2010.[44] But not all

42. *Scientific American*, September 1995, 18–19; *Chemical and Engineering News* 73, no. 29 (July 17, 1995): 7–8; *The Nation*, July 8, 1996, 11–16; *UN Chronicle* 33, no. 1 (spring 1996): 73–74; *Forum for Applied Research and Public Policy* 11, no. 2 (summer 1996): 55–64; *Amicus Journal* 18, no. 3 (fall 1996): 35–39; and *Nature*, November 21, 1996, 256–259.

43. Robert Repetto and Jonathan Lash, "Planetary Roulette: Gambling with the Climate," *Foreign Policy*, no. 108 (fall 1997): 84–98 at 84; see also James K. Sebenius, "Designing Negotiations Toward a New Regime: The Case of Global Warming," *International Security* 15, no. 4 (spring 1991): 110–148.

44. Andrew Lawler et al., "Panel Leads the Way on the Road to Kyoto Conference," *Science*, October 10, 1997, 216–219; for a skeptical view, see Sonja Boehmer-Christiansen, "A Winning Coalition of Advocacy," *Energy Policy* 25 (March 1997): 439–444.

scientists agree that the globe's climate is warming. Those who believe it is warming disagree on how quickly and why—how much is anthropogenic (human caused). If warming takes place, its effects are also disputed. Will warming melt polar ice caps (raising sea levels) or add to ice caps (thus lowering seas)?

Second, if warming occurs, it could produce gainers as well as losers.[45] "Some like it hot." Warming could make Siberia and Canada more habitable even as lowlands such as the Maldive Islands and Santa Monica are swallowed by the waves. Not surprisingly, vulnerable lands such as the Maldives formed an Alliance of Small States in the 1990s to promote curbs on CO_2 emissions. Some farms could benefit from more rain but then face more mosquitoes and pests.

Third, warming may result from many basic energy uses—transportation, industry, agriculture, forestry. No single action or substitute can remove the problem. Deforestation releases carbons—as much as one-fourth of global carbon emissions.[46]

Fourth, it is not clear how to allocate costs. What actors should pay what price to curb greenhouse gases? The industrialized North has been the main source of warming gases, but the weight of the South is gaining. One estimate is that half the additional emissions expected in the 1990s and early 21st century will come simply from expanding populations; the other half, from increases in living standards dependent upon fuel consumption. Some developed countries have learned to produce more with less, but most LDCs are reluctant to invest in pollution controls. An Indian study asserted that the First World wants to make LDCs a "sink for the West's dirt."[47]

Fifth, the costs of coping with global warming are uncertain, but cutting emissions could mean less catastrophic flooding, fewer droughts, less erosion, less insect-borne disease, and fewer deaths due to heat.

Sixth, few vested interests resisted ozone-layer protection, but opponents to emission controls include some government officials, producers of carbons, heavy industries, and agribusinesses. A potential blocking coalition straddles North and South.

The threat of ozone depletion was analogous to North Korean and Iraqi attacks on their neighbors in 1950 and 1990. The threat emerged quickly and was well-defined. Climate control is a long-term, multifaceted problem more like containing the USSR. It requires a grand strategy to guide actions in the face of distant, uncertain dangers and changing public sentiment.[48]

45. Many environmentalists warned that to count on gains from global warming would be a high-risk enterprise. For example, whole forests could wither. *Policy Implications of Greenhouse Warming*, 34–43; Schneider, "The Changing Climate," 78–79.

46. World Resources Institute, *World Resources 1992–93*, 125.

47. The study asserted that the West wanted to plant trees in the Third World so that the West could "expand its fleet of cars, power stations, and industries while the Third World grows trees." It chided the Netherlands for funding 250,000 hectares of trees in Bolivia, Peru, and Colombia to offset carbons from two new coal-fired electricity plants near Amsterdam. It derided the notion that such projects were "intergenerational compensation." If cows add to warming, the study advised Westerners to consume less meat and milk. Anil Agarwal and Sunita Narain, *Global Warming in an Unequal World: A Case of Environmental Colonialism* (New Delhi: Centre for Science and Environment, 1991), 23.

48. Levy, "Is the Environment a National Security Issue?" 54.

Designing a New Regime

Uncertainty about danger does not mean that concerned parties should take no action. Even if global warming is a mirage, fewer carbon emissions would benefit public health. The question is how to design a regime—a "law of the air"—that creates value for the conflicting interests at stake.

For starters, an actor could initiate a **no-regrets policy**—a policy deemed useful even if other actors do not reciprocate and even if global warming turns out not to be a problem. Some examples follow:

Agriculture: Introduce adaptable crops. Conserve soil. Save trees and reforest.

Building: Move construction away from areas vulnerable to storms and tides.

Design: Introduce energy saving buildings, transport, and industrial processes.

Fuel: Use natural gas instead of coal or oil. Phase out fossil fuels gradually and replace them with non-carbon energy sources—solar, geothermal, nuclear, hydroelectric.

Taxes: Penalize waste and pollution. An energy tax could discourage gas guzzling autos while reducing smog and easing budget deficits.

Recycling: Capture and reuse methane from mines and landfills.

Like the ozone protocols and the U.S. Clean Air Act, a regime to limit carbon emissions could utilize **entitlements**—permits to pollute to a specified limit. An entitlement regime would require heavy polluters to reduce emissions and permit light polluters to increase emissions. Light polluters might choose to sell their allocations to the highest bidder.

But on what basis would entitlements be assigned? What principles would be fair—and acceptable—to North and South?

Squatters' Rights—The Status Quo. Allocate quotas according to a base line such as CO_2 production in a certain year, for example, A.D. 2000. But making the status quo into a sacred rule would penalize industrial states already efficient in energy use, such as Japan, and LDCs in early stages of industrialization, such as India.

Egalitarianism. Entitle every person everywhere to the same level of emissions. One suggestion is to give each citizen of the planet her/his own emissions allocation card. A precedent exists: The Montreal Protocol allocated CFC emissions quotas equally per capita among the industrialized countries.

Political Obstacles to No-Regrets

As we saw in Chapter 13, China wants to tap the natural gas resources of the Caspian, but pipelines require political stability in China's northwest. Should outsiders muffle their concern for the Uighurs and other minorities in hopes that China can obtain natural gas and burn less coal?

To get natural gas from the Caspian Sea to the West may require pipelines through Afghanistan and Iran. Should the West ignore the domestic and foreign policies of those countries to obtain a cleaner fuel?

The Three Gorges hydroelectric project could also reduce China's dependency upon coal. But some dam labor is forced, more than one million people will be displaced, and biodiversity and natural beauty will suffer. What is the right price for fewer CO_2 emissions?

Whatever the moral and political issues, economic pressures and potential profits in the late 1990s pushed for development.

But this could be a formula for catastrophe. If China and India had a right in 2000 to pollute as much per capita as Germany or Russia, carbon emissions could accelerate virtually unbounded.

If entitlements were assigned to each country on a per capita basis in the 1990s, the South's allowance would shrink as human numbers increased. But if entitlements multiply as populations grow, a limit on global emissions would be pushed into the dim future. One solution would treat the entitlement as a national inheritance to be shared with the newborn. If national allowances were established, governments would have to decide how to allocate permits domestically—to what firms, to what individuals?

Historical Responsibility. Grant each country an all-time quota. Countries such as India that have as yet produced few carbons relative to their current populations would be entitled to pollute heavily for years to come. Countries such as Great Britain would face imminent restrictions because they have been heavy polluters for more than a century.

This approach would do little to curb future emissions by LDCs. And it penalizes today's rich countries for having blazed the paths of the Industrial Revolution.

Sourcing Global Warming. Set quotas by country of origin. This would mean sharp limits on major oil producers such as Saudi Arabia, Venezuela, and Mexico as well as the U.S. and Russia; also for Brazil, Colombia, and Thailand, where deforestation adds greatly to global warming. Saudi Arabia, of course, might respond that it is servicing demand elsewhere. Consumers rather than suppliers should be penalized. Brazil might demand rewards for the forest it has conserved—more valuable than the forest that has been consumed.

Willingness to Pay. Let emissions rights be sold to the highest bidders. But this approach might not be fair to the small or the poor. The dikes protecting small Holland may burst if large Germany buys high quotas; a poor upstart might be unable to compete with richer, established competitors.

Each principle has its drawbacks. But a mix of tradeoffs and linkage possibilities may be discovered in the give-and-take of actual negotiations. Governments usually consider fairness issues in two stages. First they weigh the pros and cons of alternative principles in the abstract. Then they see how the issues play out in bargaining. At each stage LDCs ask: "Does this approach give us room to develop? Are we assured sufficient aid to cover the extra costs of developing with low carbon emis-

The UN General Assembly held a special session called Earth Summit + 5 in June 1997 to review environmental action since the 1992 Earth Summit held in Brazil. Here the UN Secretary-General Kofi Annan looks at an exhibit on food by the Consultative Group on International Research, part of the "Sustainable Development in Action" exhibit in the UN Public Lobby.

sions?" Developed countries weigh potential gains against likely costs at home and abroad.

Two international institutions can help resolve these conflicts. The IPCC, founded in 1988, includes scientists from many countries and has forged a consensus on the facts of climate change. The **Global Environmental Facility (GEF)**, created in 1991, is administered by the World Bank in cooperation with the UN Environmental Programme and the UN Development Programme. The GEF makes grants or loans for projects that respond to global environmental threats that might not otherwise be a top development priority for the country in question.

The 1992 Earth Summit in Rio produced a **Framework Convention on Climate Change (FCCC)** ratified by 167 states. At U.S. insistence the FCCC did not set binding targets or timetables, but it did leave the way open for detailed protocols. President George Bush was cool even to a framework agreement, contending that emission curbs could block economic growth. The FCCC acknowledged that rich and poor states share "common but differentiated" responsibilities for addressing climate change. But Rio set no limits on LDC emissions. Rather, it stipulated that developed countries take the first steps to curb their emissions and also subsidize LDC emission curbs.

More than 160 countries sent delegations to the December 1997 conference held in Kyoto, Japan, seeking to convert the Rio principles into an action program.[49] After many long days and nights, conferees endorsed the **Kyoto Protocol** requiring reductions in emissions of CO_2 and five

49. Officially this was known as the Third Session of the Conference of the Parties to the United Nations Framework Convention on Climate Change.

other greenhouse gases (methane, nitrous oxide, hydrofluorocarbons, perfluorocarbons, and sulfur hexafluorides) by thirty-eight industrial countries and the European Union (EU) to be reached between the years 2008 and 2012. No specific targets were set for developing countries, though they were encouraged to make voluntary reductions. No country is bound by the protocol, however, unless its government ratifies the accord along with a sufficient number of other governments to make it a treaty by March 1999.[50]

Given the diversity of interests, what negotiating techniques helped achieve an agreement that so many states could endorse?

First, the protocol defined obligations only for the major industrialized countries. Developing countries could approve the protocol in 1997 and decide later if they wished to accept curbs on their own emissions. This approach made it easier for developing countries to sign the protocol, but could make it harder to win ratification by industrialized countries. On July 25, 1997, the U.S. Senate, by 95–0, in a nonbinding resolution asked President Bill Clinton not to sign a treaty without emission curbs for developing countries. Some environmentalists hoped that the Clinton administration could twist the diplomatic arms of Brazil, China, and India into accepting some limits before the Senate began debating approval of the Kyoto Protocol.

Some 130 developing countries drew a line at Kyoto and refused to accept even voluntary commitments to reduce emissions. The potential importance of these countries to climate change was undeniable. In 1997 they accounted for only one-third of the world's emissions of greenhouse gases, but contained 80 percent of the world's population. As their economies developed, their emissions would soon exceed those of the West and Japan.

The poor South could prove more vulnerable to climate change than the rich North. Governments in many developing countries had already taken steps before Kyoto to raise prices on fuels that discharge carbons. But many LDCs focused on near- and medium-term economic issues. Thus, Malawi's Minister of Forestry, Fisheries, and Environmental Affairs asked: "How can we devote our precious resources toward reducing emissions when we are struggling every day just to feed, clothe, and house our citizens?"[51]

Second, the protocol represented a compromise on emissions targets for industrialized countries. The U.S. delegation had urged a commitment to cut emissions to equal to 1990 levels by the 2008–2012 period; the

50. Pat Murdo, "Kyoto Pact on Greenhouse Gas Reductions," *JEI Report* [Japan Economic Institute of America], no. 47 (December 19, 1997), and coverage in major newspapers and magazines.

51. F. V. Mayinga Mkandawire, quoted in Calvin Sims, "Poor Nations Resist Role on Warming," *New York Times*, December 13, 1997, A7.

EU had wanted a 15 percent cut below 1990 levels by 2010; Japan proposed an overall cut of 5 percent or less. Since the U.S. population and GDP had grown much faster than Europe's or Japan's in the 1990s, it would be much harder for the U.S. to reduce its emissions to 1990 levels or below. But since the U.S. produced 22 percent of the world's CO_2 emissions, environmentalists called for strong U.S. action. Japan, economists and environmentalists noted, produced much lower emissions than the U.S. relative to GDP.

A compromise was facilitated by eight **reduction differentials**. They ranged from an obligation to cut emissions by 8 percent (for the EU) to a zero reduction (for three states) to a license to increase emissions by 10 percent (for Iceland). The U.S. agreed to cut emissions to 7 percent below its 1990s levels; Japan, already far more energy efficient that the U.S. or Europe, had to cut its emissions by only 6 percent (the same target set for Canada, Hungary, and Poland); Australia had wanted the right to increase its emissions by 18 percent, but settled for a rise of only 8 percent.

There was also some personal diplomacy: U.S. Vice President Al Gore pressured Tokyo as well as the White House to make concessions. Gore phoned Japanese Prime Minister Ryutaro Hashimoto at 2 A.M. and asked Japan to accept a burden of one percentage point more—6 percent rather than 5 percent—for the sake of an overall accord. Conference chair Raúl Estrada-Oyuela put some items to a vote when resistant delegations (such as Iraq) were absent. To win approval of the protocol he deleted references to developing nations in the wee hours of December 11, one day after the original ten-day session was to have ended.

Agreement was facilitated by three forms of emissions credits. First, heavy emitters could purchase part of the quota allowed to light emitters. The fifteen members of the EU could trade emission permits with one another to reach their combined 8 percent reduction. The U.S. could buy and sell permits with others in an "umbrella group" that included Japan, Canada, Russia, New Zealand, and Australia.

Second, industrialized countries could offset their emissions by planting forests or taking other steps to bolster carbon sinks. Third, they could also win credits by investing in projects that help developing countries to reduce emissions.

Washington asked for and got an understanding that emissions by armed forces would not be counted when they were engaged in police or humanitarian missions approved by the UN. "We did not want to create a disincentive for future humanitarian operations," said a Pentagon official.

For better or worse, the Kyoto Protocol set the deadline for compliance more than a decade ahead and said nothing about enforcement. However, it stipulated a follow-up session in Buenos Aires, Argentina, in November 1998, where the agenda would include mechanisms for enforcement and for trading permits. Some environmentalists condemned Kyoto for doing too little; others praised it as movement in a constructive direction, setting the stage to ratchet up obligations for all parties.

A former arms negotiator said that U.S. diplomats at Kyoto had given away the store by departing from the practices followed in the strategic arms talks with the USSR. First, they offered major concessions too early and without getting anything in return, for example, exempting major actors such as China and Mexico from obligatory reductions. Second, U.S. diplomats at Kyoto agreed to major reductions with no workable system to verify compliance by all parties. Third, they jeopardized U.S. sovereignty by inviting intrusive action by the World Bank and other international agencies.[52] Defenders of the Kyoto Protocol said that such criticism was unfair and simplistic. Environmental well-being is not a zero-sum contest and involves far more parties and issues than did the Soviet-U.S. arms competition.

No one really knew whether the Kyoto emissions curbs would help or hurt economic growth. To achieve 1990 emissions levels by 2010 could lower or raise U.S. GDP by 2 percent in worst- or best-case scenarios.[53] A 7 percent decrease in CO_2 emissions in ten years could imply a one-third cut from what they would otherwise be. Americans did not like "carbon taxes" (taxes on the carbon content of fossil fuels) but had already used tradeable-permits to phase out leaded gasoline and to cut sulphur emissions.[54]

Senators from coal-rich states and some business leaders said the cost of complying with Kyoto would be onerous, especially since industrializing countries such as South Korea could make steel and other manufactures with no obligation to ecologize production. But other business executives argued that the new regulations would make U.S. firms more energy efficient and hence more competitive at home and abroad.[55] They said it was feasible to produce electricity far more efficiently (wasting only half instead of two-thirds the energy consumed in generation).[56] The White House said it planned to include in its FY 1999 budget a $5 billion five-year program of tax cuts and other R&D incentives for companies seeking to reduce greenhouse gases.

While Detroit's Big Three groused about California's requirements for

52. Richard Burt, *Washington Times,* December 29, 1997, A12.

53. Such estimates are strongly affected by assumptions. See World Resources Institute estimate graphed in "The Cost of Cooling It," *Fortune,* December 8, 1997, 128–129.

54. Robert N. Stavins, "The New Global Warming Treaty Is Not a Sure Bet," *Newsday,* December 14, 1997, B5.

55. See commentary by Michael J. Gage, "Smart Firms Embrace Kyoto Accord," *Los Angeles Times,* December 31, 1997. President of CalStart, a consortium developing advanced transportation technologies, Gage quoted Michael Porter, cited in Chapter 11.

56. Charles E. Bayless and Thomas R. Casten, "Leave CO_2 to the Entrepreneurs," *Washington Post,* December 31, 1997, 21. For the opinion of some 2,000 economists, see Bette Hileman, "Tackling Global Warming Won't Hurt Economy," *Chemical and Engineering News* 75, no. 7 (February 17, 1997): 9–10.

fuel efficiency, Honda and Toyota had already built and sold cars in Japan that produced zero emissions. To help developing countries curb their omissions, Japan proposed a package known as the Kyoto Initiative: low-interest, forty-year loans to developing countries to promote energy-saving technologies, new or renewable energy resources, forest conservation and replanting. Japan proposed to train 3,000 persons from LDCs in energy-saving technologies and waste disposal. Tokyo also planned to send energy conservation experts to advise and train cadres in developing countries.

"Joint implementation" of emission obligations could funnel large investments in new and clean technologies into developing countries. It could offer a powerful incentive for rich Northern firms to invest in countries such as Brazil and India.

How to Strengthen Winning over Blocking Coalitions

Any environmental convention must appeal to a broad group of countries and diminish opposition from blocking coalitions. The deal must satisfy not just governments but also industries, NGOs, and other interest groups. The experience gained in environmental diplomacy suggests the following guidelines for negotiators:[57]

1. Cultivate scientific consensus. Use the UN Environmental Programme, the World Bank, and other institutions to share information and form joint study groups of private (industrial and NGO) experts as well as governmental experts. Provide advice to governments short on environmental expertise.[58]

2. Promote a voluntary action plan of concerned countries without waiting for conclusion of a formal treaty.[59]

3. Remove penalties for constructive unilateral actions that leave states with higher costs than their commercial competitors. By this reasoning, Japan was awarded a lower target than most other industrialized countries at Kyoto.

4. Work toward a consensus on fairness. Set different tasks for different categories of countries (rich and poor, past and future polluters). This was done for industrialized countries at Kyoto but not for developing economies.

5. Utilize techniques found useful in other negotiating arenas such as a single negotiating text.

6. Utilize linkage. Link environmental concerns with other concerns to establish tradeoffs such as financial compensation for environmental protection.

57. Adapted from Sebenius, "Designing Negotiations Toward a New Regime," and the "Salzburg Initiative" of 120 representatives from thirty-two countries, summarized in Lawrence E. Susskind, *Environmental Diplomacy: Negotiating More Effective Global Agreements* (New York: Oxford University Press, 1994), 123–141.

58. Peter M. Haas, "Introduction: Epistemic Communities and International Policy Coordination," *International Organization* [special issue: "Knowledge, Power, and International Policy Coordination"] 46, no. 1 (winter 1992): 1–35, and other articles in this issue.

59. Thus, a "Carbon Club" took shape in the early 1990s. Led by Germany, a number of countries, including Austria, Denmark, Australia, and New Zealand, pledged to cut their CO_2 emissions by 20 to 25 percent by 2005.

7. Start small and ratchet up as risks become more evident. For example, launch an international tax on emissions at a low rate to collect resources for an environmental fund. Pledge more rigorous emission controls if specified gases exceed a certain level.

8. Avoid an all-or-nothing approach. Fractionate.

9. Emphasize potential gains and compensate LDCs for some costs of greening their production. Create new values, for example, by assuring market access for "green products" (such as nuts and rubber) and by inventing better "debt-for-nature" swaps.

10. Build regimes incrementally. Start with agreement to act but leave open specific decisions on "when, what, and how." This permits the parties to "fall forward" toward tougher obligations as evidence mounts of environmental danger.[60] This approach worked in successive accords to protect the ozone layer, but failed between Rio 1992 and Kyoto 1997 to compel LDCs to accept any limitations on greenhouse emissions.

11. Establish clear procedures for mediation and arbitration of environmental disputes and compliance with obligations, perhaps utilizing the International Court of Justice.

WHAT PROPOSITIONS HOLD?
WHAT QUESTIONS REMAIN?

For most of the 20th century Cornucopians proved to be more correct than Malthusians. Human ingenuity managed to sustain an expanding world population that lived longer than ever. Will the limits to growth become more acute? The future is uncertain. What policies are prudent given these uncertainties?

60. The phrase was coined by I. William Zartman. How important is it to advance quickly to specific commitments? It depends on the issue. The dozen or so extra years required to win U.S. acceptance of deep-sea mining provisions in the Law of the Sea did little harm and produced a more viable treaty. Delay in protecting a threatened species, however, could permit its extinction.

You and Your Southern Seven Colleagues Draft This Memo:

Rio de Janeiro, September 1, 2012

Memo from the Southern Seven:

The governments of Argentina, Brazil, China, India, Indonesia, Malaysia, and Thailand hereby reaffirm our commitment to protecting the environment so long as economic growth continues. In the long run, economic well-being depends upon a healthy environment. In the short and medium run, however, environmental protection can be costly.

We propose to stabilize our CO_2 emissions and maintain our forests at levels reached in 2020. Having con-

tributed little to global warming, we ask compensation for our sacrifices. Each OECD country should contribute 0.05 percent of its GDP to the Global Environmental Fund to be distributed to the Southern Seven for application to "clean and green" technology.

But Saudi Arabia and Venezuela have also drafted a memo on behalf of the Organization of Petroleum Exporting Countries. It reads as follows:

Rio de Janeiro, September 1, 2012

Memo from OPEC:

OPEC members, like other enlightened countries, seek both environmental and economic well-being. Since our populations are small and we have just begun to industrialize, it is premature for us to limit our CO_2 emissions. Since we have literally fueled the industrial transformation of North and South, we ask for three forms of compensation: (1) Freedom from any commitment to limit our carbon emissions. (2) A development fund established by OECD countries to equal the revenues we lose due to reduced carbon use elsewhere. (3) Free access for our scientists and engineers to energy-related R&D of any UN member country.

These two memos represent the logic of collective action. If each country seeks to claim values for itself, the globe's life support system will become more vulnerable. Enlightened self-interest requires joint sacrifices and efforts to promote mutual gain. Following are some policy implications derived from our study.[61]

61. See also Frances Cairncross, "Environmental Pragmatism," *Foreign Policy,* no. 95 (summer 1994): 35–52.

GEOGRAPHY LESSON

NOW, THE WORLD IS MADE UP OF SEVEN CONTINENTS AND FOUR SLICKS...

BIG OIL

DANZIGER
The Christian Science Monitor

The world runs on oil and is being ruined by it. This is the view of many Greens. Not just water but also air and soil suffer from oil pollution. Some oil companies and some scientists say that oil slicks dissipate and cause little lasting damage. Oil companies and oil-rich countries such as Kazakstan hope that demand for oil increases. Americans balk at a nickel or dime increase in gasoline taxes. Some oil companies, however, are investigating alternative power resources.

MAXIMS FOR NORTH AND SOUTH: MUTUAL GAIN OVER EXPLOITATION

1. Integrate environmental concerns into security and economic planning. Understand that exploitation tends to backfire—in fisheries as in other spheres.

2. Preserve the diversity of life. Take preventive action to limit the loss of habitat and species.

3. Be prudent; study emerging dangers; take preventive action. But prioritize: Address clear and present needs such as clean water before investing heavily to deal with remote, speculative dangers.

4. Teach green consciousness ("waste not, pollute not, want not").

5. Think and act locally as well as globally. Clean up your own habitat ("no-regrets" policies) even if others lag. Unilateral action can proceed faster than negotiated accords. To insist upon global action may guarantee no action.

6. Promote population control actively but humanely. Don't passively wait for "development" to lower population growth.

7. Utilize all agents of change—government, markets, international organizations, NGOs, education, science, pop culture.[62]

8. Use environmental issues to promote cooperation—not conflict.

9. Turn swords into green plowshares.

10. Make green profitable—for health, income, and knowledge.

MAXIMS FOR THE NORTH

1. You have a duty and the means to lead. Developed countries are still the key players in resource depletion and pollution. Instead of conspicuous consumption, cultivate models of environment-friendly life styles.

2. Balance domestic and international programs—unlike the U.S., which in the early 1990s spent $130 billion per year for environmental protection at home but only $600 million abroad. Money invested in pollution abatement often goes much further in the South than in the North, where conditions are already better and improvements more costly.

3. Balance trade liberalization and environmental interests. Truly free international trade—without subsidies or non-tariff barriers—can contribute to green prosperity. It rewards efficient producers who deal with the real costs of production and cleanup. But formal steps are needed to ensure that the World Trade Organization does not wipe out environmental restraints. The NAFTA experience shows that trade rules by themselves may neglect the green agenda. Environmental rules are also need-

62. Campaigns and concerts by pop music stars in the early 1990s did more to save Walden Pond (memorialized by Henry David Thoreau) from real estate developers than did local government and conservation societies.

ed, along with institutions to monitor and enforce them. There should be a World Environmental Organization to supervise compliance with environmental treaties and to harmonize environmental goals with free trade. This agency should work hand-in-glove with the World Trade Organization, the World Bank, and the United Nations.[63]

4. Develop environment-enhancing technology and share it globally, for example, farming with fewer chemicals.

5. Make energy generation safer, cleaner, and cheaper. Help repair or replace the Chernobyl-type nuclear reactors of the former Second World. Develop and share renewable energy technology. Emulate California laws requiring low-emission autos.

6. Curb arms transfers to LDCs.[64] Instead of subsidizing weapons, underwrite transfers of medical equipment and energy-saving devices. Assist LDCs to invest in technologies that are most productive and least polluting for the long haul. Redirect weapons laboratories toward R&D for the health of nations.[65]

7. Make LDCs partners in sustainable development and learn from one another.

8. Use both aid and pressure to nudge others toward environment-friendly policies.

MAXIMS FOR THE SOUTH: WHAT IS A GOOD TRADEOFF?

1. Understand that human development and long-term prosperity requires environmental protection now.

2. Promote family planning among males and females. Do not treat population control as a racist scheme to weaken the South.

3. Install green technology appropriate to your needs. Skip earlier and dirtier machinery; avoid expensive retrofitting with pollution controls.

4. Develop transportation and other infrastructure needed to harvest, store, market, and distribute food.

5. Do not put off environmental protection until foreign banks write off LDC debts.[66]

6. Walk on two legs. Take useful technology and whatever other aid you can from rich countries, but know that sustainable development is mainly up to you. Avoid scapegoating the North.

7. Don't waste resources on war, arms, or showy projects.

8. Distrust promises of a quick-fix project to redirect nature.

It is a Faustian dilemma: comparatively cheap, clean nuclear power now with the risk some day of catastrophe. The 1986 meltdown of a nuclear power reactor at Chernobyl in Ukraine poisoned many people locally and spread radiation across Europe. Here, specialists try to monitor radiation at the Chernobyl site. Despite their structural flaws, Soviet-built Chernobyl-type reactors continued to operate in many former Soviet bloc countries in the 1990s. Who would pay to replace them? How else could countries such as Ukraine, Bulgaria, and Lithuania obtain electric power at manageable prices?

63. See C. Ford Runge et al., *Freer Trade, Protected Environment: Balancing Trade Liberalization and Environmental Interests* (New York: Council on Foreign Relations, 1994).

64. By all means avoid using foreign aid funds, as Britain did, for a dam in Malaysia in exchange for weapons orders!

65. The Los Alamos National Laboratory, where the first atomic bomb was built, has become a major participant in the Human Genome Project to analyze the human genetic code. It also houses the GenBank, a national database of all genetic sequence information. All three U.S. national laboratories are studying how to harness fusion energy.

66. Debt has not stopped India and other LDCs from spending huge sums on war and weapons. In the early 1990s they bought more than $30 billion in arms just from the U.S.

If Malthusians are correct, population growth must be curbed. Many agencies concerned with sustainable development promote family planning to give women more choices and to reduce pressure on scarce resources. Here, Moroccan women attend a family planning clinic supported by the UN Children's Fund (UNICEF).

9. Purify and conserve water. Raises prices to encourage efficient use. Plug leaks.

10. Promote sustainable farming with land reform, agricultural extension services, and market-driven pricing. Review the merits of cash crops versus food crops.

The struggle for power and wealth generates much waste and destruction, but—as we see in the next two chapters—international organization and law can contribute to the security and health of nations.

KEY NAMES AND TERMS

appropriate technology	greenhouse effect
Aswan syndrome	ideational factors
biosphere	Intergovernmental Panel on Climate Change (IPCC)
carrying capacity	intergenerational equity
collective (or public) good	international environmental conflicts (IECs)
Cornucopian outlook	Kyoto Protocol
Earth Summit	low politics
ecology	Malthusian perspective
ekos	Montreal Protocol
entitlements	no-regrets policy
environmental diplomacy	ozone layer
externalities	protocols
framework convention	reduction differentials
Framework Convention on Climate Change (FCCC)	regime
Global Environmental Facility (GEF)	sustainable development

QUESTIONS TO DISCUSS

1. Compare U.S. behavior in environmental diplomacy with U.S. behavior in arms control policy.

2. Given the logic of collective action, what is the likely approach of Belgium to tightening limits on CO_2 emissions? How did Belgium's behavior in 1997 square with your prediction?

3. What is Brazil's likely position on CO_2 emissions? To what extent is this policy a reflection of enlightened self-interest?

4. Why does the U.S. often seem to drag its feet on environmental diplomacy?

5. Why did governments develop a regime on ozone-depleting gases more quickly and thoroughly than they did on CO_2 emissions?

6. Why do governments sometimes welcome and sometimes spurn NGO contributions to environmental planning?

7. Was there any alternative open to Egypt in the 1950s other than to build the Aswan High Dam?

8. Should China proceed with the Three Gorges Dam?

9. If you were India's prime minister, what rationale for entitlements would you favor? What if that rationale appealed also to your rivals in Islamabad and Beijing?

10. What role is there for openness in environmental diplomacy?

11. Must we choose between development and environment?

RECOMMENDED RESOURCES

BOOKS

Are Human Activities Causing Global Warming? Washington, D.C.: George C. Marshall Institute, 1996.

Choucri, Nazli, ed. *Global Accord: Environmental Challenges and International Responses.* Cambridge, Mass.: MIT Press, 1993.

Fankhauser, Samuel. *Value Climate Change: The Economics of the Greenhouse.* London: Earthscan, 1995.

Haas, Peter M. *Knowledge, Power, and International Policy Coordination.* Columbia: University of South Carolina Press, 1997.

Haas, Peter M., Robert O. Keohane, and Marc A. Levy, eds. *Institutions for the Earth: Sources of Effective International Protection.* Cambridge, Mass.: MIT Press, 1993.

Han, Robert W., ed. *Risks, Costs, and Lives Saved: Getting Better Results from Regulation.* New York: Oxford University Press, 1996.

Houghton, John T., ed. *Climate Change 1995; The Science of Climate Change.* New York: Cambridge University Press, 1996.

Keohane, Robert O., and Marc A. Levy, eds. *Institutions for Environmental Aid: Pitfalls and Promise.* Cambridge, Mass: MIT Press, 1996.

Porter, Gareth, and Janet Walsh Brown. *Global Environmental Politics.* Boulder, Colo.: Westview, 1991.

Repetto, Robert C. *Trade and Environmental Policies: Achieving Complementarities and Avoiding Conflicts.* Washington, D.C.: World Resources Institute, 1993.

Repetto, Robert C., and Duncan Austin. *The Costs of Climate Protection: A Guide for the Perplexed.* Washington, D.C.: World Resources Institute, 1997.

Runge, C. Ford. *Freer Trade, Protected Environment: Balancing Trade Liberalization and Environmental Interests.* New York: Council on Foreign Relations Press, 1994.

Stone, Christopher D. *The Gnat Is Older Than Man: Global Environment and Human Agenda.* Princeton, N.J.: Princeton University Press, 1993.

Susskind, Lawrence E. *Environmental Diplomacy: Negotiating More Effective Global Agreements.* New York: Oxford University Press, 1994.

World Resources Institute. *World Resources: A Guide to the Global Environment.* New York: Oxford University Press, annual.

Worldwatch Institute. *State of the World.* New York: Norton, annual.

Worldwatch Institute. *Vital Signs: The Trends That Are Shaping Our Future.* New York: Norton, annual.

JOURNALS

Ambio
Amicus
Bulletin of the Atomic Scientists
The Ecologist
Energy Policy
Environment
Journal of Environmental Law
International Organization
Issues in Science and Technology
Natural Resources

Nature
Nucleus (Union of Concerned Scientists)
Policy Review
Public Interest
Science
Scientific American

WEB SITES

Bureau of National Affairs *(global climate change treaty information)*
  http://www.bna.com/prodhome/ens/kyoto.htm
Central European Environmental Data Request Facility (CEDAR) *(a project of the Austrian Federal Ministry for the Environment, Youth, and Family Affairs)*
  http://pan.cedar.univie.ac.at/
CEDAR environmental links
  http://www.cedar.univie.ac.at/env_links/
Earth Negotiations Bulletin (ENB) *(web site of the International Institute for Sustainable Development)*
  http://www.iisd.ca/linkages/voltoc.html
  Linkages *(a multimedia resource for environment and development policymakers)*
    http://www.iisd.ca/linkages/
Foreign Policy
  http://www.foreignpolicy.com *(includes access reports of the IPCC)*
Global Warming
  http://www.earlham.edu/~libr/resource/subjects/warming.htm
Greenpeace International
  http://www.greenpeace.org
  atmosphere page
    http://www.greenpeace.org/catm.html
  climate crisis page
    http://www.greenpeace.org/~climate/index.html

Harvard Environmental Resources Online
  http://environment.harvard.edu/
Liberty Tree *(web site on the science and politics of the atmosphere)*
  http://www.libertytree.org/Trenches/climate/climate.html *(includes background, updates, and links)*
Model United Nations of the University of Chicago Environmental Impact of Dams
  http://synergy.uchicago.edu/munuc/SA_Committees/abstracts/UNEP_abstract_b.html
National Association of Manufacturers (NAM)
  http://www.nam.org/ *(includes references to NAM positions on global warming)*
National Center for Policy Analysis
  http://www.ncpa.org/hotlines/global/gwhot.html *(on globale warming)*
Union of Concerned Scientists
  http://www.ucsusa.org *(or phone 1-800-536-3895 for an educational "global warming kit" on the causes and consequences of climate change)*
United Nations Environment Programme
  http://www.unep.org/
The United Nations Framework Convention on Climate Change (UNFCCC), Secretariat
  http://www.unfccc.de/
UNFCCC Kyoto Conference
  http://www.cop3.de/ *(comprehensive conference information, background information, and official documents in several languages)*
U.S. Environmental Protection Agency
  http://www.epa.gov/

C H A P T E R   F I F T E E N

ORGANIZING FOR MUTUAL GAIN: THE UNITED NATIONS, EUROPE, AND NONSTATE ACTORS

THE BIG QUESTIONS IN CHAPTER 15

- Why do peoples cooperate and organize across borders?

- What is international organization (IO)?

- Does might make right in IR? Is there such a thing as law among nations? If governments obey the law, why?

- Does order come to world affairs because it is imposed from above or because it rises from below?

- What is collective security? Has the principle of "all for one, one for all" ever worked?

- Is there a link between IO and industrialization?

- Is "Europe" a customs union or a supranational state, or something else?

- Is Europe uniting? If so, from below or from above?

- Why expand NATO if the Cold War is history?

- Can IO save lives?

- Is IO anything but power?

- Is the world coming together or flinging apart?

*How to Start Your Own Nonstate Actor.... The
new world disorder challenges both state and nonstate actors. Fed up with governments, you decide to organize a new player, the University of the Middle East, to promote coexistence and development in the region. You plan to have UME campuses
across the Middle East and North Africa within thirty years. UME students and facul-
ty will spend time at one another's campuses, bringing Israelis and Arabs, Christians
and Muslims, into scholarly and social contact. Though your board comes from many
countries, in 1998 your planning sessions take place each Sunday night, often at an Italian restaurant in Boston's North End. Your president is Hala Taweel, sister-in-law of
PLO Chairman Yasser Arafat; other participants include Camelia Anwar Sadat,
daughter of the Egyptian president who signed the Camp David Accords, and Walid
Chamoun, whose Maronite Christian family went to war to rid its native Lebanon of
Arafat's forces in the 1970s. The idea for the university came from an Israeli-American
physicist, Ron Rubin, who was galvanized by the assassination of Israeli Prime Minister Yitzhak Rabin. Many of your board met their opposite numbers for the first time at
U.S. colleges. You get backing from Elie Wiesel, the Nobel peace laureate, and Lea Rabin, widow of Yitzhak Rabin, as well as from a leading Iraqi dissident and assorted foreign diplomats. In 1998 you have $50,000 from donors plus donated office space and
equipment. When you raise $500,000, you plan feasibility studies in three countries
and a pilot summer course in Morocco or Egypt.*

*Is your plan desirable? Is it feasible? Let us see how people have organized to meet
their shared needs. How can their efforts be made more effective?*

CONTENDING CONCEPTS AND EXPLANATIONS

WHAT IS A NONSTATE ACTOR?

International organization (IO) consists of intergovernmental organizations (IGOs) and nongovernmental organizations (NGOs). Early in the 20th century there were some 30 IGOs; by 1950, about 125; in the late 1990s, several hundred.

IGOs can be classified by membership and objectives. The United Nations (UN) seeks universal membership and has many goals; the World Trade Organization is open to all states that qualify but has one main focus. The North Atlantic Treaty Organization (NATO) and the Association of Southeast Asian Nations (ASEAN) are regional organizations with narrower objectives. Some IGOs offer parallel or alternative routes to the same goal. Thus, the UN promises universal security; NATO, regional security.

There are tens of thousands of NGOs seeking diverse goals. An NGO for IR scholars is the International Studies Association (ISA). ISA membership is worldwide. While it is headquartered at a U.S. university, some of its officers are residents and citizens of other countries. The ISA meets in many countries. It cooperates with both NGOs and IGOs and sometimes with the U.S. and other governments.

Nonstate actors in IR are players that are not states. They include IGOs, NGOs, TNCs (transnational corporations), and other actors. Their importance to IR was long obscured by the fact that traditional international law recognized only states as its "subjects." In the 20th century, however, international law began to give legal standing—rights and obligations—to individuals, IGOs, and other transnational entities. Thus the OECD (Organization for Economic Cooperation and Development)—the club of rich industrial nations—and the UN have prescribed codes of conduct for TNCs even though such enterprises are not full legal personalities under international law.[1] But international law and courts lag behind reality in their failure to deal directly with transnational actors with the power to build and destroy. Should not a TNC that pillages a rain forest and destroys a native people's way of life be culpable before some authority other than the local government?

International society, like domestic, depends upon consensus and voluntary cooperation as well as on coercive force and law. The parallels are

1. TNCs are not full legal personalities because they have no legal right to take part in formulation of the norms that are to govern them. When home countries endorse codes of conduct for TNCs and international agencies enact follow-up procedures, the process can generate international law. These norms have a semi-legal character: They are neither entirely non-binding internationally nor entirely unenforceable domestically. See Burns H. Weston et al., *International Law and World Order: A Problem-Oriented Coursebook*, 2d ed. (St. Paul, Minn.: West, 1990), chap. 5 at 612; see also Philip C. Jessup, *Transnational Law* (New Haven, Conn.: Yale University Press, 1956); and Wolfgang Friedman et al., *Transnational Law in a Changing Society: Essays in Honor of Philip C. Jessup* (New York: Columbia University Press, 1972).

Fig. 15.1 Determinants of Domestic and International Society

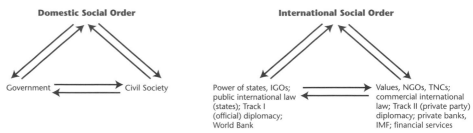

diagrammed in Figure 15.1. Thus we may think of IO as an arena between the realm of government and civil society.

Nonstate actors exist on every level:

Individuals. Persons from many walks of life alter IR. Pablo Picasso expanded our awareness of war with his painting *Guernica.* Mother Teresa organized a global network of hospices. Ted Turner in 1997 pledged a billion dollars to assist UN programs.

Determined individuals—private citizens—did as much or more than governments or IGOs to establish the Red Cross, organize assistance for refugees, and ban land mines. Nobel Peace Prizes were awarded for these and other private efforts.

Individuals and groups can also destroy. An assassination by a Serbian nationalist sparked World War I. The Fatah Revolutionary Council of Abu Nidal, opposing the policies of Palestine Liberation Organization (PLO) leader Yasser Arafat, killed not just Christians and Jews but also fellow Muslims—PLO representatives in Paris, London, and other cities. Disgruntled Egyptians killed peacemaker Anwar Sadat while an Israeli hard-liner derailed the Oslo peace process by shooting Prime Minister Yitzhak Rabin.

State and Society. Ethnic groups and interest groups can shape foreign policy and IR, fueling or moderating conflict. Often they cross borders and join like-minded groups to promote change. For example, many nonstate and state actors in the late 1990s demanded a full accounting by Switzerland and other countries regarding gold deposits before and during World War II.

Interstate (Intergovernmental). The UN and other IGOs owe their existence to states and are part of the state system. Still, they are basically nonstate actors. The UN has few of the coercive powers associated with states. The European Union (EU), by contrast, started as an IGO but began to look and act like a state.

Fig. 15.2 The United Nations System

The Six Principal Organs and Other Units Discussed in the Text

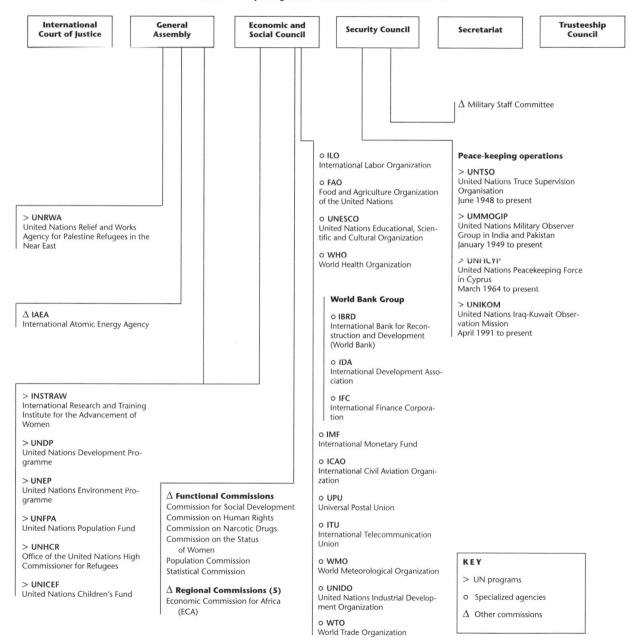

International Court of Justice | General Assembly | Economic and Social Council | Security Council | Secretariat | Trusteeship Council

Δ Military Staff Committee

> UNRWA
United Nations Relief and Works Agency for Palestine Refugees in the Near East

Δ IAEA
International Atomic Energy Agency

> INSTRAW
International Research and Training Institute for the Advancement of Women

> UNDP
United Nations Development Programme

> UNEP
United Nations Environment Programme

> UNFPA
United Nations Population Fund

> UNHCR
Office of the United Nations High Commissioner for Refugees

> UNICEF
United Nations Children's Fund

Δ **Functional Commissions**
Commission for Social Development
Commission on Human Rights
Commission on Narcotic Drugs
Commission on the Status of Women
Population Commission
Statistical Commission

Δ **Regional Commissions (5)**
Economic Commission for Africa (ECA)

o ILO
International Labor Organization

o FAO
Food and Agriculture Organization of the United Nations

o UNESCO
United Nations Educational, Scientific and Cultural Organization

o WHO
World Health Organization

World Bank Group

o IBRD
International Bank for Reconstruction and Development (World Bank)

o IDA
International Development Association

o IFC
International Finance Corporation

o IMF
International Monetary Fund

o ICAO
International Civil Aviation Organization

o UPU
Universal Postal Union

o ITU
International Telecommunication Union

o WMO
World Meteorological Organization

o UNIDO
United Nations Industrial Development Organization

o WTO
World Trade Organization

Peace-keeping operations

> UNTSO
United Nations Truce Supervision Organisation
June 1948 to present

> UMMOGIP
United Nations Military Observer Group in India and Pakistan
January 1949 to present

> UNFICYP
United Nations Peacekeeping Force in Cyprus
March 1964 to present

> UNIKOM
United Nations Iraq-Kuwait Observation Mission
April 1991 to present

KEY

> UN programs

o Specialized agencies

Δ Other commissions

441

How to Make a Better World? Nonstate Actors Speak Out

What if moderators at the Davos World Forum, where top political and economic figures retreat each year to view the IPE from the Swiss mountaintops, asked present and past leaders to give their recipe for a better world? Following might be some of their comments:

Bill Gates: "Universalize the Internet. My company will install the best software in every library."

George Soros: "Open communication."

Ted Turner: "Let CNN bring the world to you."

McDonald's CEO: "Spread the Golden Arches—a sure sign of hygiene and stability. No country with Golden Arches has ever fought another with Golden Arches."

Media mogul: "McDonald's, Coca Cola, and Marlboro are synonymous with the product. World-class brands unite humanity."

Olympic organizer: "Let sports transcend differences."

MTV magnate: "Dance to elevate consciousness."

Gore Vidal: "Beware of military-industrial-media conglomerates striving to control mind and spirit."

Taleban: "Purify. Pray. Jihad. Keep women at home."

Sierra Club president: "Cultivate an environmental ethic."

Montana Militia guerrilla: "Arm to resist black UN helicopters."

Henry Ford: "Go global. I opened a plant in Canada soon after my first U.S. plant. Pay workers a decent wage. Mutual gain."

Lenin: "Let imperialists fight over markets and transfer capital plus technology to Asia and Africa."

Not all of these views have equal weight. Some are incompatible with others. Which do you find most persuasive?

---

2. UN regional offices in the Americas in the 1990s were located in Washington, Havana, Mexico City, Caracas, Bogota, Lima, Asunción, Santiago, and Montevideo. There were another nine offices in Africa; three in Asia; three in the Middle East; and four in Europe. Redundancy and lax financial controls made the global network costly and inefficient.

3. For a more comprehensive picture, see Boutros-Ghali and Pérez de Cuéllar (annual reports of the UN Secretary-General) and the works by Jacobson, Mingst and Karns, and Weiss et al. listed in Recommended Resources at the end of this chapter.

4. As a State Department official in Washington and his Russian counterpart in Moscow talked by phone, they both looked at the same live CNN broadcast of Russian commandos storming the Russian parliament. Strobe Talbott, "Globalization and Diplomacy: A Practitioner's Perspective," *Foreign Policy*, no. 108 (fall 1997): 69–83 at 69–70.

The United Nations has many "Specialized Agencies" such as the World Health Organization (WHO). They too are nonstate actors, though they are funded by governments. The WHO, for example, is staffed mainly by health professionals who focus on their professional tasks and have no coercive power. Once established, IGOs often take on lives of their own, sometimes defying the states that created them. Their bureaucracies are entrenched in Geneva, Vienna, Nairobi, Bangkok, and New York—homes to the UN and other IGOs. Still, the total professional staff at UN headquarters in New York numbered less than 3,000 in the mid-1990s; the WHO staff in Geneva about 700—tiny numbers for bureaucracies that service the entire world.[2] The UN system is outlined in Figure 15.2. Only a few of its activities are discussed in this chapter.[3]

Transnational. NGOs such as the ISA are transnational nonstate actors. So are many religions. Large TNCs such as General Motors command more resources than most states. Many terrorist groups and crime syndicates also cross state borders and shape IR. Communications networks such as Cable News Network (CNN) and the Internet are nonstate actors. CNN presents similar images of reality to viewers in Moscow and Washington.[4] Institutions such as the Rockefeller Foundation, Volkswagen Foundation, and Soros Foundation do much to change IR.

Relations between NGOs and governments are varied and complex. Some NGOs serve governments and get money from them; some partner with governments in a common cause; some are gadflies pushing govern-ments in certain directions; some resist governments; still others are indifferent.

Biosphere. Life's support system is the fifth action level of IR. Its rich-ness and fragility induce new forms of IO to divide resources and to pro-tect the environment.

Which level is most important depends upon the issue at stake, the time, and the place. The interactions among each level, as we have already seen, are conditioned by many factors.

TOP-DOWN VS. BOTTOM-UP ORGANIZATION

Is World Government the Answer?

At the end of the 20th century the European Union was the only IO with some **supranational** authority. Should there be a supranational world government over all other governments and all peoples? If there were a world government, would it stop war? Albert Einstein wrote to Sigmund Freud in 1932, raising these questions.[5] Einstein began: "At pre-sent we are far from possessing any supranational organization compe-tent to render verdicts of incontestable authority and enforce absolute submission to the execution of its verdicts." He inferred an axiom: "The quest of international security involves the unconditional surrender by every nation, in a certain measure, of its liberty of action, its sovereignty." No other road, he thought, could lead to security.

Why did past efforts achieve so little? Einstein thought that "the crav-ing for power which characterises the governing class in every nation is hostile to any limitation of the national sovereignty. This political power hunger" fattens on the greed of arms merchants. The powerful minority indoctrinates the masses, many of whom already possess a "lust for ha-tred and destruction."

Freud replied that he concurred with the gist of Einstein's thinking, but added that early peoples overcame brute force by uniting against it. This was also the origin of law—communal power against individual vio-lence. But if a community joined forces only against one threat, it would quickly dissolve. "Thus the union of the people must be permanent and well organised; it must enact rules to meet the risk of possible revolts; must set up machinery ensuring that its rules—the laws—are observed and that such acts of violence as the laws demand are duly carried out. This recognition of a community of interests engenders among the mem-bers of the group a sentiment of unity and fraternal solidarity which con-stitutes its real strength."

5. The exchange is published in Robert A. Gold-win and Tony Pearce, eds., *Readings in World Politics*, 2d ed. (New York: Oxford University Press, 1970), 86–99.

For today's world, Freud argued, "there is but one sure way of ending war, and that is the establishment, by common consent, of a central control which shall have the last word in every conflict of interest." This required "a supreme court" and "its investment with adequate executive force." Writing in 1932, Freud thought that the League of Nations met the first task but not the second.

Freud hoped that war could be prevented, but he saw positive value even in destructive instincts. He was not sure that they could—or should—be extirpated.

The Einstein-Freud exchange resonates today. Humanity still lacks a supranational authority; human instincts are unchanged; our civilization represses but also applauds violence. Without supranational government, are there other ways to stem anarchy?

Functionalism and Neofunctionalism: From Low to High Politics?

Functionalism offers a route to integration and thence to peace. It assumes that national loyalties can be diffused and redirected into a framework for international cooperation in place of national rivalry. It contends that the best route to peace is to multiply cooperation in low politics, where political obstacles are fewer.

Functionalism thinks of IO as a response to the international political economy. The Industrial Revolution fostered IO. The first modern IGO, the Central Commission for Navigation of the Rhine, was established in 1815 to facilitate traffic by steamship (first built in 1802) as the river passed through seven jurisdictions. Similar IGOs were later established for the Danube, Congo, and Prut rivers and the Suez Canal.

New communication technologies have spawned regulatory IOs, for example, the International Telegraph Union (1865), the Radiotelegraph Union (1906), and the International Telecommunications Satellite Organization (1965). A global public utility outside the UN ambit, Intelsat, provided infrastructure as well as rules for satellite communications.[6]

Between states, there is interdependence—mutual vulnerability. Across state borders, there is globalization. To deal with interdependence and with globalization, states drop their rigid defense of sovereignty: They collaborate to send and receive mail across frontiers; control epidemics; regulate aviation. From such cooperation habits of trust and mutual dependency may develop and spill over into the arenas of high politics. Functionalism counts on "technical self-determination" by experts rather than on the whims of politicians.[7]

Early functionalists urged that nations cooperate in arenas with little political resonance. But **neofunctionlism** favors cooperation in political-

6. Craig N. Murphy, *International Organization and Industrial Change: Global Governance Since 1850* (New York: Oxford University Press, 1994).

7. The theory was articulated by David Mitrany in 1943. See Mitrany, *A Working Peace System* (Chicago: Quadrangle, 1966); see also Ernst Haas, *Beyond the Nation-State: Functionalism and International Organization* (Stanford, Calif.: Stanford University Press, 1963).

Table 15.1 Assumptions of Functionalism and Neofunctionalism

	Functionalism	Neofunctionalism
Image of the World	Interdependence of states	Globalization operating across state borders
Driving Force	Need for technical cooperation by states	Need for supranational authority to coordinate technical cooperation
Attitude to Politics	Apolitical, technical orientation; high politics consensus may arise from low politics cooperation	Ready to confront tough political issues, beginning on a regional scale

ly charged domains where there is also scope for technocrats. Some neo-functionalists focus on regional integration rather than global integration. Jean Monnet, a founder of the European Community, was a neo-functionalist. He sought to build institutions that enshrine cooperation and spill over from one activity to another. For the differing assumptions of functionalism and neofunctionalism, see Table 15.1.

Both proponents and skeptics of functionalism find grist for their mills. Advocates point to the vast increase in the number and scope of international and transnational organizations since the mid-19th century. Nearly every country has become more permeable. Some analysts speak of an "end to geography" because of financial integration and the impact of the information technology revolution.[8] Functionalism and neofunctionalism benefit from and contribute to globalization.

Skeptics doubt the strength of the spill-over effect. They contend that, when push comes to shove, states still defend their sovereign prerogatives. Germany and France fought one another in 1914 and 1940 despite extensive trade and other linkages. Ideology often prevails over interdependence, tribalism over pragmatism, and territoriality over globalism.

COMPARING THEORY AND REALITY: VISIONS OF PEACE, JUSTICE, WELFARE

INTERNATIONAL LAW AND WORLD PEACE

Even without a supranational authority, states for thousands of years have agreed to rules to regulate their behavior—international law. Not until the 20th century, however, was there a strong effort to outlaw war. International law—formal treaties and informal regimes—sought rather to delimit how and when force could be used. Compliance depended mainly on self-interest, for governments valued reciprocity and order over chaos. When vital interests or big gains were at stake, however, they

8. Richard O'Brien, *Global Financial Integration: The End of Geography* (New York: Council on Foreign Relations for the Royal Institute of International Affairs, 1992).

Plebiscites After World War I

The principle of national self-determination was widely implemented in creating the states that emerged from the German and Austro-Hungarian empires after World War I. Plebiscites permitted local populations to choose whether to live in Germany or to join Denmark, Belgium, France, or Poland. There were also plebiscites in the Aaland Islands, in some Austrian borderlands, and in Vilnius. But there were no plebiscites for German-speakers living in the Sudetenland, incorporated into Czechoslovakia, or in South Tyrol, compelled to accept Italian rule. As Woodrow Wilson's advisers warned in 1919, failure to grant self-determination to the Sudetens would later (in 1938) prove "fatal to the new state" of Czechoslovakia. The 1922 vote in Vilnius was skewed by Polish military control and caused conflict with Lithuania until 1939–1940, when the USSR conquered both eastern Poland and Lithuania and transferred Vilnius to the "Lithuanian Soviet Socialist Republic."

9. William J. H. Hough III, "The Annexation of the Baltic States and Its Effect on the Development of Law Prohibiting Seizure of Territory," *New York Law School Journal of International and Comparative Law* 6, no 2 (winter 1985): 303–533.

often departed from established norms. Temptations to defect and go for the hare (rather than cooperate for the stag) have repeatedly injected chaos into the world arena.

Does Might Make Right?

What should—what can—other nations do if one state seizes another's territory by force?[9] Medieval Europe accepted the right of conquest. When a prince seized territory, other parties treated this as an accomplished fact. But recognition by the pope was required to consecrate title and legalize sovereignty. The pope, however, lost influence after the Reformation.

1648. Ignoring the pope, Europe's larger powers in the Treaty of Westphalia claimed the right to withhold and bestow recognition of title. Their approach mirrored balance-of-power thinking: Any change in the number or size of states concerned all states, because such change could upset the equilibrium of power.

1789. The French Revolution injected a new element into the equation: national self-determination. Revolutionary France claimed that it brought liberty to those who wanted it. France annexed Holland, Flanders, and other territories on the ground that these *réunions* represented the free will of the population.

1815. France's annexations were annulled at the Congress of Vienna. Still, plebiscites (popular referenda) became a regular feature of IR, often used to legalize territorial change. In 1860, for example, the Kingdom of Italy annexed the Neapolitan provinces of Sicily, the Marches, and Umbria after plebiscites in each.

Outside of Europe, however, Europeans considered that might made right. When Europeans carved up Africa in the 19th century, they informed one another of their claims—not to obtain recognition, but to prevent friction. Outside of Europe, white race and Christianity offered no protection: In 1900 Britain annexed the Boer Republics in southern Africa by right of conquest.

Might made right for major non-Western powers too. Russia took Siberia and Central Asia by conquest; China conquered Tibet in 1909; Japan forcibly annexed Korea in 1910.

The Stimson Doctrine vs. The Right of Conquest

1919. Woodrow Wilson tried to change the rules. He hoped to prevent aggression by creating a League of Nations that would provide collective security—a system of one for all, all for one against aggression. The

Were Things Different in the Americas—No Right of Conquest?

Westward expansion by the U.S. encountered a maze of conflicting legal principles: Mexican sovereignty; U.S. claims to compensation for alleged attacks by Mexican troops; the people's "will" in California and Texas. When war broke out between the U.S. and Mexico in 1846, the Massachusetts legislature called it a war of conquest, "hateful in its objects." Abraham Lincoln, then a congressman, was skeptical; he wanted to see the spot where U.S. blood had been spilled.

The U.S. Supreme Court in 1849 ruled that war, "declared by Congress, can never be presumed to be waged for the purpose or the acquisition of territory." The Court allowed, however, that the U.S. could expand its territory "to indemnify its citizens for the injuries they have suffered, or to reimburse the government for the expenses of the war. But this can be done only by the treaty-making power of the legislative authority and "is not part of the power conferred upon the President by the declaration of war." Washington claimed some Mexican lands as indemnification and paid for others.

The Treaty of Union of the American States, signed in Chile in 1856, was the first international agreement requiring its signatories not to recognize any territorial change among themselves for any reason. But this attempt to outlaw the right of conquest was undermined when Chile in 1879–1883 annexed Peruvian provinces and Bolivia's entire seacoast. Washington denounced Chile's aggrandizement but did nothing.

League's capacity for collective security, however, was gutted by U.S. nonparticipation and by loopholes in the League of Nations Covenant.

1928. Trying to fill this gap, French Foreign Minister Aristide Briand and U.S. Secretary of State Frank Kellogg drew up the Treaty of Paris, or **Kellogg-Briand Pact**, renouncing war as an "an instrument of national policy." Most countries signed the pact, but it had no teeth—no provisions for enforcement.[10]

1931. Japan flouted both the Covenant and the Kellogg-Briand Pact when its army occupied Manchuria in northern China. Tokyo announced that Manchuria had become "Manchukuo"—a Japanese puppet state.

1932. Kellogg's successor as secretary of state, Henry Stimson, was deeply alarmed by the Japanese moves but his options were constrained by U.S. isolationism and military weakness. Stimson arose at 6 A.M. on January 2 and penned what became known as the **Stimson Doctrine:** The U.S. refused "to recognize any situation, treaty or agreement . . . brought about by means contrary to the Pact of Paris"—in other words, by war.[11]

Stimson's unilateral action helped create international law by consensus. The League of Nations Assembly in March 1932 resolved that it was "incumbent" upon League members "not to recognize any situation, treaty or agreement which may be brought about by means contrary to the Covenant . . . or the Pact of Paris." In 1933 a treaty signed at Rio de Janeiro committed six major Latin American countries to not recognizing territorial aggrandizement by force.

10. The USSR persuaded Poland, Romania, and the three Baltic states to implement the treaty among themselves before it was ratified by the original signatories. Text in *Dokumenty vneshnei politiki SSSR* (Moscow: Politizdat, 1967), 12, 66–70.

11. Godfrey Hodgson, *The Colonel: The Life and Wars of Henry Stimson, 1867–1950* (New York: Knopf, 1990), 158–168.

In February 1933 the League of Nations Assembly condemned Japan and urged members not to recognize Manchukuo. Japan withdrew from the League and, in 1937, resumed its march into China.

The French ambassador to Washington, Paul Claudel, recalled a Chinese saying likening words to "spears of straw and swords of ice." Neither the Stimson Doctrine nor League denunciations sufficed to save China or faith in the League's system of collective security. Washington proclaimed U.S. "neutrality." [12]

When Nonrecognition Counts

But words are not always "spears of straw." When Soviet forces annexed Estonia, Latvia, and Lithuania in July 1940, the U.S. State Department announced that it would apply the Stimson Doctrine to the USSR as it had to armed expansion by Japan, Italy, and Germany. Not only did the U.S. not recognize Soviet annexation of the Baltic republics, but it froze Baltic assets (ships, gold, other properties) in the U.S. to prevent the USSR from taking them. Most countries followed the U.S. lead. Except for Sweden, no European country outside Moscow's sphere officially recognized Soviet rule over the Baltic.

The USSR Congress of People's Deputies acknowledged on December 24, 1989, that the Soviet takeover of the Baltic states had been illegal.[13] This admission ripped all legitimacy from Soviet rule in the Baltic.

The U.S. never closed the Baltic legations in Washington. They were still functioning when the Baltic republics regained full independence in 1991. Washington's refusal to recognize that might makes right helped bring down the Soviet empire.

COLLECTIVE SECURITY: KOREA AND THE GULF WAR

Korea

U.S. diplomacy galvanized the **UN Security Council** to uphold collective security in 1950 and again in 1990. On June 25, 1950—just one day after North Korea invaded the South—the Security Council ordered the DPRK to withdraw. When DPRK troops continued their advance, the Security Council urged UN members to "furnish such assistance to the Republic of [South] Korea as may be necessary to repel the armed attack and to restore international peace and security." On July 7 the Council requested the U.S. to appoint the commander of a unified force under the UN flag to which all members were urged to provide assistance. Sixteen countries sent troops and five others supplied medical units.

12. For the Neutrality Act of November 4, 1939, and modifications urged by the Senate on October 25, 1941, see U.S. Senate, Subcommittee on Disarmament, *Disarmament and Security: A Collection of Documents, 1919–55* (Washington, D.C.: Government Printing Office, 1956), 812–824.

13. *Vestnik Ministerstva inostrannykh del SSSR 2*, no. 60 (January 31, 1990): 7–13.

When and How Can the UN Security Council Enforce the Peace?

The UN Charter gives the Security Council "primary responsibility" for maintaining peace and security and requires UN members to "carry out the decisions of the Security Council." The Charter spells out how the Security Council is to discharge its responsibility. First, it "shall determine the existence of any threat to the peace, breach of the peace, or act of aggression and shall make *recommendations,* or *decide* what measures shall be taken" to restore peace [emphases added]. Next, the Security Council may order "provisional measures" to prevent aggravation of the situation. It may also order nonmilitary actions such as "interruption of economic relations and of rail, sea, air, postal, telegraphic, radio, and other means of communications, and the severance of diplomatic relations."

If the Security Council considers that nonmilitary measures would be or are inadequate, it "may take such action by air, sea, or land forces as may be necessary to maintain or restore international peace and security." "All Members . . . undertake to make available to the Security Council . . . armed forces, assistance, and facilities, including rights of passage" necessary for peace and security. These actions shall be taken by all UN Members "or by some of them, as the Security Council may determine." But Article 51 of the Charter reserves the "inherent right of individual or collective self-defense" *until* the Security Council acts to maintain peace. This article was invoked by NATO to justify a military alliance outside the UN framework.

As we saw in Chapter 4, the fighting soon drew in Chinese "volunteers." An armistice was signed in 1953, but Korea remained divided and UN troops in the South confronted the DPRK into the 1990s—even after both North and South took seats in the UN.

The Gulf War and After

Forty years passed before the Security Council again called for collective action against aggression. For the first time in history, one UN member (Iraq) tried in 1990 to extinguish the sovereignty of another (Kuwait). As in 1950, the U.S. mobilized a collective UN response. But this time the USSR voted with the majority. Presidents Mikhail Gorbachev and George Bush issued a statement: "No peaceful international order is possible if larger states can devour their smaller neighbors." Soviet Foreign Minister Eduard Shevardnadze told the UN on September 25, 1990, that Iraq had "committed an unprovoked aggression, annexed a neighboring sovereign state, seized thousands of hostages and resorted to unprecedented blackmail, threatening to use weapons of mass destruction."

From August 1990 through February 1991, more than a dozen Security Council resolutions showed a wide consensus on the law and how to enforce it. All fifteen Security Council members voted for five of the resolutions. China, however, abstained on the authorization to use force. Only Yemen and Cuba cast negative votes. And while one or both sometimes abstained, even they voted with the majority on five occasions. Outside the Security Council, most Arab states opted to join in military action against Iraq.

How to Get Around the Veto: The Uniting for Peace Resolution

What is the **veto**? UN Security Council decisions require the affirmative votes of nine of its fifteen members (before expansion in 1965, seven of eleven), including the permanent members—Britain, China, France, Russia, and the U.S. Thus each of the "Big Five" can veto or block decisions on substantive issues. This contrasts with the **UN General Assembly**, where a two-thirds majority (or a simple majority on procedural issues) suffices to pass a resolution, even if opposed by any or all of the Big Five. But the UN Charter limits the veto in the Security Council: First, votes on procedural matters may be taken with the approval of any nine members. Second, a state may not vote when it is party to a dispute being investigated by the Security Council. But these exceptions can be readily defeated, for what is "procedural" is itself a substantive issue subject to the veto. Further, one of the Big Five may insist that it is not involved in a "dispute" but only a "situation."

Hence, the Soviet delegate could have vetoed the Security Council decisions on Korea in June–July 1950, but was absent—in protest against the UN failure to seat Beijing's delegate instead of Taiwan's as representative of "China." The U.S. forced through an interpretation that absence did not count as a veto (a position taken already in 1946 when Soviet absence did not stop the Security Council from calling for a report on Soviet occupation of northern Iran).

To circumvent a possible future veto in the Security Council, the U.S. persuaded the General Assembly in November 1950 to adopt the **Uniting for Peace Resolution**. This resolution affirmed the right of the General Assembly to act when the Security Council, "because of lack of unanimity of the permanent members, fails to exercise its primary responsibility" for coping with a threat or breach of the peace. In that event "the General Assembly shall consider the matter immediately with a view to making appropriate *recommendations* to the Members for collective measures [emphasis added]." While the Security Council could make decisions binding on all members, the General Assembly could only make recommendations.

The USSR declared the United for Peace gambit illegal, arguing that the UN Charter gave "primary responsibility" for security to the Security Council. Washington replied that the General Assembly had residual powers if the Security Council were deadlocked. The Uniting for Peace Resolution stood. The General Assembly used it twice in 1956 after vetoes cast by London, Paris, and Moscow to block Security Council action regarding the nearly concurrent UK-French-Israeli invasion of Egypt and Soviet invasion of Hungary. The resolution was also invoked during the 1958 Middle East crisis and the 1960 crisis in the Congo. Even Moscow used it to convene the General Assembly after the 1967 Middle East war. It was revived to deal with Afghanistan (1980), Palestine (1980 and 1982), Namibia (1981), and Occupied Arab Territories (1982).

Some 279 vetoes were cast by permanent members of the Security Council during the Cold War; in the 1990s, however, very few were cast. Enmities declined and informal discussion before votes became more common.

14. For texts of UN Security Council resolutions on the Gulf conflict, see Micah L. Sifry and Christopher Cerf, eds., *The Gulf War Reader: History, Documents, Opinions* (New York: Times Books, Random House, 1991), 137–156.

15. The Security Council called for comprehensive sanctions against Rhodesia in 1966 and for an arms embargo against South Africa in 1977.

On August 2, 1990, just hours after Iraq invaded Kuwait, Security Council Resolution 660 "condemned" Iraq for "a breach of international peace" and "demanded" that it withdraw.[14] Next came a substantive "decision." For the third time in its history, the UN imposed economic sanctions under Article 41 of the Charter.[15] On August 6 Security Council Resolution 661 "affirmed" the "inherent right of individual or collective self-defense" under Article 51. Then, acting under Chapter VII of the Charter, the Council "decided" to "secure compliance" by Iraq with Resolution 660 and to restore the government of Kuwait. The Council "decided" on a total economic boycott: All UN members were to "prevent" any imports from or exports to Iraq and occupied Kuwait, except medical supplies and food. No funds could be transferred to Iraq.

In language similar to the Stimson Doctrine, the Security Council "decided" on August 9 that Kuwait's annexation by Iraq had "no legal validity, and is considered null and void."

Resolution 665 on August 25 tightened the noose. Suspecting that Iraqi ships were off-loading cargoes in Yemen, the Security Council called on UN members with naval forces deployed near Iraq or Kuwait "to halt all inward and outward maritime shipping in order to inspect and verify their cargoes" to ensure compliance with Resolution 661. The vote was 13–0, with Cuba and Yemen abstaining.

On September 24 the Security Council noted that many states were requesting assistance (as authorized by UN Charter Article 50) because enforcement actions were generating "special economic problems." Frontline states Turkey and Jordan were hit hard by interrupted trade with Iraq. Jordan became host to tens of thousands of refugees. Saudi Arabia, Kuwait, the U.S., and other countries began to compensate Turkey and Jordan.

Noting Iraq's continued defiance, the Security Council on September 24 "decided" that all states must deny takeoff, overflight, or landing rights for any plane destined for or flying from Iraq or Kuwait unless it carried medicines or food. All states were ordered to detain any ships of Iraqi registry or deny them entry.

Could outsiders help? On October 29 the Security Council asked the UN Secretary-General, Javier Pérez de Cuéllar, to "undertake diplomatic efforts . . . to reach a peaceful solution of the crisis." He tried, but got nowhere with Baghdad. Nor did the Soviet, French, and various Arab emissaries who also offered to mediate.

Next came an ultimatum: On November 29 the Security Council offered Iraq "one final opportunity": If Iraq did not comply with all UN resolutions by January 15, 1991, the Security Council authorized UN members "to use all necessary means to uphold and implement" the resolutions *and* "to restore international peace and security in the area"—a task that could go beyond fulfilling the resolutions.

Iraq's Foreign Minister Tariq Aziz met U.S. Secretary of State James Baker in Geneva on January 9, 1991, but each side remained intransigent. Meanwhile, the U.S. Congress pondered what to do. President Bush had dispatched a force of half a million to the Persian Gulf (a force equal in numbers to that once deployed against North Vietnam). To order this force to fight, could the president simply use his power as commander-

The Stimson Doctrine and George Bush

Why did Washington respond so forcefully to Iraq's occupation of Kuwait? Was President Bush attempting to uphold the Stimson Doctrine because Stimson, like Bush, had attended Yale University? As it happened, Bush in 1990 was reading Godfrey Hodgson's biography of Stimson, *The Colonel.* (Books count! Kennedy was reading *The Guns of August* before the Cuban crisis.) According to Elizabeth Drew ("Letter from Washington," *The New Yorker,* February 4, 1991), Bush recalled that Stimson addressed his graduation at Andover prep school.

The Bush team jumped from one justification to another—from protecting world oil supplies to saving jobs in the U.S. to eliminating Iraq's weapons of mass destruction. It would have been on a stronger legal footing, however, had it simply reaffirmed the UN Charter and the Stimson Doctrine.

Anger may have also played a role. Perhaps Bush believed that he had been double-crossed after tilting toward Iraq during its war with Iran. He may have been determined to dispel the charge of "wimp." He may have had a visceral dislike of "Sa-dom," as Bush called the Iraqi leader. There may have been revulsion at Iraqi atrocities (some of them detailed by a schoolgirl, who turned out to be the daughter of Kuwait's ambassador in Washington).

in-chief, or did Congress have to declare war? On January 12, 1991, both houses of Congress skirted the constitutional issue. They "authorized" the president "to use U.S. Armed Forces pursuant" to UN Security Council resolutions after "all appropriate diplomatic and other peaceful means" had failed to gain Iraq's compliance.

When the UN coalition opened fire on January 16, the White House proclaimed that the "liberation of Kuwait [had] begun." On February 27, President Bush stated that Kuwait had been liberated and that Operation Desert Storm had ended. The U.S. had led a multilateral force, but supplied most of the men and women and matériel; other states—Kuwait, Saudi Arabia, Japan—subsidized much of the war effort (but left U.S. taxpayers with the tab for medical care and other long-term payments to veterans).

What Did the Gulf War Mean for World Order?

The Gulf War provided history's most successful implementation of collective security—far more effective than the Korean War when the Security Council could act only because the USSR was absent. But the U.S. decision to halt most military operations after Kuwait's liberation left President Saddam Hussein's regime in place. The hegemon stopped moving, and the other partners did too.

The Security Council obliged Baghdad to accept the dismantling of its weapons of mass destruction under international observation. Until compliance was assured, the UN pledged to maintain economic sanctions on Iraq. But Baghdad tried to deceive and intimidate the inspectorate known as the **UN Special Commission (UNSCOM).** The inspectors reported to the Security Council in 1996, 1997, and 1998 that Iraq had probably destroyed many but not all of its ballistic missiles or their warheads, eliminated some but not all of its chemical weapons or production facilities, and hidden biological weapons and documentation.

Is There a Duty and Right to Intervene for Humanitarian Reasons?

Following the Gulf War, France persuaded the UN Security Council to broaden its concept of security. Paris insisted on a right to intervene for humanitarian reasons, backed if necessary by military force.[16] This led to a revolution in UN practice as the Security Council began to justify forceful interventions for humanitarian reasons under Chapter VII as a way to cope with threats to international peace and security.[17] Thus Security Council Resolution 688, adopted on April 5, 1991, condemned Iraq's repression of its own civilian population, claiming that the consequences of

16. The *droit d'ingérence* ("right to intervene") was stressed by Dr. Bernard Kouchner, a founder of Doctors Without Borders. See Kouchner, *Le Malheur des autres* (Paris: Odile Jacob, 1991). Kouchner later became President François Mitterrand's State Secretary for Humanitarian Policy.

17. For a survey of the changing military requirements of UN peacekeeping, see Mats R. Berdal, "Whither UN Peacekeeping?" *Adelphi Paper* 281 (October 1993).

this repression threatened international peace and security. The resolution demanded that Iraq facilitate "immediate access by international humanitarian organizations to all those in need of assistance in all parts of Iraq."

Resolution 688 marked a watershed: Not only did it link domestic repression with threats to international peace, but it compelled Iraq to help NGOs to carry out humanitarian relief for Iraqi citizens. The resolution passed with only ten affirmative votes. China and India abstained, while Cuba, Zimbabwe, and Yemen voted against it. The vote mirrored a growing pattern of assertive support for human rights by the West (usually backed by Russia) and opposition to external probes by developing countries with much dirty (perhaps bloodied) linen to hide.

Resolution 688 was short on specifics, but London, Paris, and Washington claimed its authority to establish "safe havens" for Kurds in northern Iraq. The West also barred Iraqi planes from no-fly zones shielding Kurds in the north and Shiites in southern Iraq. The U.S.-led Operation Provide Comfort air-dropped hospitals for use by Kurdish refugees. UN officials got Iraq to sign a memorandum allowing "humanitarian centers" to be established in both northern and southern Iraq, backed by small contingents of UN guards.[18] After two years, however, Hussein terminated the understandings by which UN guards supported humanitarian activities within Iraq. No Western government wanted to fight Hussein on his home ground on this issue.

The Persian Gulf campaign left many questions hanging: Could the UN ever be sufficiently strong to drive back an aggressor without depending on a leading power? Would—should—the lone superpower ever subordinate its forces to a UN command? How long would rich but militarily inferior countries such as Japan and Germany pay for enforcement actions in which they had little say?

Could the UN prevent disputes such as those between Iraq and Kuwait from becoming hot? There was no assurance that UN members would again fight to protect the small against the strong. In few cases would the legal issues and the oil wealth at stake be so manifest as in the Gulf conflict.

THE UNITED NATIONS AS PEACEKEEPER

Peacekeeping During the Cold War

Peacemaking is defined as actions to resolve conflicts by peaceful means such as mediation and negotiation, as in the Oslo process (see Chapter 9). Peace enforcement is the use of force, as in the Korean and

Who Should Serve on the Security Council?

The UN Big Five—the U.S., the UK, France, China, and Russia—hold permanent seats on the UN Security Council and can veto most substantive decisions. In the 1990s ten other seats rotated for two terms. In 1997 Slovenia became the first ex-Yugoslav state to win a two-year term. The other rotating seats were held by Japan, Brazil, Sweden, Portugal, Kenya, Costa Rica, Gabon, Gambia, and Bahrain. Demands rose for other powerful states to become permanent members—perhaps without a veto. But if Germany got a permanent seat, Italy might object. If India got a seat, what about Pakistan? If Brazil, what about Argentina, Chile, and Venezuela? If Asia and Latin America got a seat, what about the Middle East and Africa? And if the Security Council became much larger, how would it differ from the General Assembly? For thoughtful suggestions on UN reform, see Erskine Childers with Brian Urquhart, "Renewing the United Nations System," *Development Dialogue* (Uppsala: Dag Hammarskjöld Foundation, 1994), 1.

18. Despite the two no-fly zones, Hussein blockaded the Kurdish north and actively attacked the Shiites in the south. The West supported Kurdish autonomy, if only to hurt Hussein, but opposed creation of an independent Kurdistan split off from Iraq. (Turkey worried lest support for Iraq's Kurds strengthen Kurdish separatists within Turkey.) But Hussein cleverly played off one Kurdish group against another.

Persian Gulf operations, to impose or restore peace. Peacekeeping is the interposition of lightly armed forces between potential belligerents to supervise or help maintain peace. Peacekeepers buy time in which peacemakers can resolve conflicts. Their job is conceived as short- or medium-term—not a long-term solution.

Peacekeepers are usually dispatched *with the consent* of the conflicting parties. If the parties are unwilling, however, the Security Council can justify the missions under Chapter VII as a response to threats to international peace and security. The UN Charter has no provisions for peacekeeping, but the UN has sent many observer missions and peacekeepers into the field. The first such mission was improvised in 1948 by the UN mediator in Palestine to supervise the truce between Israel and its neighbors. Between 1948 and the late 1980s the UN dispatched peacekeepers on eighteen occasions.

The timeline shows the scope of UN peacekeeping activities from 1948 through 1990.

Just over 750 UN personnel died in all these operations. They included UN mediator Count Folke Bernadotte, assassinated by Israelis in 1948, and UN Secretary-General Dag Hammarskjöld and seven aides, who per-

TIMELINE: THE TEN COSTLIEST UN PEACEKEEPING MISSIONS, 1948–1990

1948–

UN Truce Supervision Organization (**UNTSO**) ($311 million, 1948–1990)—supervised initial Israli-Arab truces

1956–1967

First UN Emergency Force (**UNEF I**) ($214 million)—stood between Egypt and Israel after the Suez War; withdrawn at Egypt's request just before the Six-Day War

1960–1964

UN Operation in the Congo (**ONUC**) ($400 million)—sought to establish law and order in the Belgian Congo (later, Zaire); included more than 20,000 troops and civilians

1964–

UN Peacekeeping Force in Cyprus (**UNFICYP**) ($636 million to 1990)— supervises the cease-fire between Greek Cypriot and Turkish Cypriot plus Turkish forces

1965–1966

Representative of Secretary-General in the Dominican Republic (**DOMREP**) ($275 million)—observed the cease-fire between the two *de facto* authorities

1973–1979

Second UN Emergency Force (**UNEF II**) ($447 million)—facilitated military disengagement in the Sinai; included more than 6,000 troops from Austria, Canada, Finland, Indonesia, Ireland, Nepal, Peru, Poland, Senegal, and Sweden

1974–

UN Disengagement Observer Force (**UNDOF**) ($452 million)—supervises Golan Heights pullbacks

1978–

UN Interim Force in Lebanon (**UNIFIL**) ($1,762,900,000—by far the most expensive UN peacekeeping mission through 1990)—confirms withdrawal of Israeli forces and helps restore peace and stability in Lebanon

1989–1990

UN Transition Assistance Group in Namibia (**UNTAG**) ($384 million)—promoted early independence for Namibia and supervised free and fair elections

SOURCE: *The Blue Helmets: A Review of United Nations Peace-keeping,* 2d ed. (New York: United Nations, 1990), Appendix 2.

What Can the UN Secretary-General Do for Peace?

The UN Secretary-General has always been caught in a crossfire between conflicting expectations. In 1945 the West wanted him merely to be an "office manager" while smaller countries hoped that he would acquire an independent political role—a counterweight to the great powers. The Charter specified that the winning candidate be recommended by the Security Council—subject to a veto—and then appointed by the General Assembly. The Charter described him as UN "chief administrative officer," but Article 99 gave him the right to "bring to the attention of the Security Council any matter which in his opinion may threaten . . . international peace and security."

The first two men to hold the job, Trygve Lie (1945–1952) and Dag Hammarskjöld (1953–1961), were Scandinavians. Hammarskjöld had modest aspirations when he took the job, but soon saw himself as an explorer: "Working at the edge of the development of human society is to work on the brink of the unknown," he said. Hammarskjöld tried to transform the UN into a dynamic tool of collective security. Believing that Hammarskjöld favored the West, Moscow demanded in 1960–1961 that the Secretariat be headed by a *troika*—a Communist, a neutral, and a Westerner. This idea was rejected, but the next Secretary-General was an inward-focused Burmese, U Thant. In 1971 Washington and Moscow settled on a candidate from neutral Austria—Kurt

Waldheim, whose Nazi background, made public later, left him vulnerable to Soviet blackmail. In 1981 Beijing demanded that the next Secretary-General come from the Third World. The most acceptable candidate was Javier Pérez de Cuéllar from Peru. He was followed in 1991 by the first African to hold the job, Boutros Boutros-Ghali, succeeded in 1997 by Kofi Annan, another African.

Many threats to world peace arose after 1945, but the UN Secretary-General explicitly invoked Article 99 only once to convene the Security Council. Hammarskjöld did so in May 1960 to call the Security Council into session as trouble erupted in the newly independent Belgian Congo. Other Secretaries-General used Article 99 without invoking it directly to convene the Security Council—U Thant during the 1971 Indian-Pakistan war; Waldheim during the 1979 Iranian hostage crisis; and Pérez de Cuéllar during the 1989 Lebanese turmoil.

Critics fault the Secretary-General for not convening the Security Council during the buildups to the Arab-Israeli wars of 1967 and 1973 and the Iraq-Iran war of 1980. Others say the Secretary-General needs up-to-date intelligence from reconnaissance satellites on military flash points. But both BBC and other news media provide ample warnings of mounting crises. What the UN needs is more will power—beginning with the permanent members of the Security Council.

ished in a plane crash in the Congo in 1961. The cumulative cost of all UN peacekeeping missions from 1948 through 1990 was just under $6 billion—a bit less than Israel's defense budget for a single year (1990). These costs and casualties, though tragic, were minimal relative to the losses they helped to prevent.[19]

Peacekeeping in the 1990s

When the Cold War ended the great powers relied more on the UN to maintain the peace. In 1992–1995 the UN conducted operations unprecedented in scope in six states or regions torn by civil strife—Angola, Cambodia, Somalia, the former Yugoslavia, Rwanda, and Haiti.

When civil war and drought brought famine to Somalia, private relief agencies distributed food. As disorder mounted, the UN Security Council

19. Six missions were charged to the regular UN budget; nine of them to special accounts, which some members—led by the USSR, France, and the U.S.—delayed paying for years. Two operations were paid by parties directly concerned (Yemen, by Saudi Arabia and Egypt; West Irian, by Indonesia and the Netherlands); the Cyprus operation was partially financed by the voluntary donations of many countries.

The USSR and France refused to pay for UN operations in the Congo authorized by the General Assembly. When asked for an advisory opinion, the International Court of Justice (see Figure 15.2) held that General Assembly peacekeeping operations should be treated like any other "expenses of the Organization." Nonetheless, the USSR and France held back.

initiated a series of actions under Chapter VII of the Charter.[20] In December 1992 the Security Council recommended steps "to establish a secure environment for humanitarian relief" and welcomed a U.S. offer to lead such an operation. At first the intervention calmed Somalia and made food distribution easier. But when U.S. forces sought to capture a Somali warlord, violence escalated. Somalis were killed; so were UN peacekeepers—Pakistanis and then Americans. After U.S. TV viewers saw charred U.S. corpses dragged through Mogadishu, President Bill Clinton announced an early pullout of U.S. troops, leaving Pakistani and Indian forces to represent the UN.

In 1992–1993 British, Canadian, and French forces in blue helmets operated under a UN flag in the former Yugoslavia. Their job was to ensure delivery of food and medical supplies to besieged communities in Bosnia. But they had neither a UN mandate nor the military strength to overpower Serb and Croat forces obstructing their path. Instead, they had to bargain: Often they paid a road tax—diverting supplies to armed Serbs and Croats—in order to deliver anything to Bosnian Muslims.

The limited UN contingent and NGO aid workers became an obstacle to forceful action to stop Serbian and Croat attacks on Muslim communities. When NATO wanted to bomb Serb artillery pounding Sarajevo, the poorly armed British, Canadians, and French were held hostage, used as human shields to protect Serb and Croat positions.

Both in Somalia and Bosnia some private aid agencies did not want outside military support. They claimed that military escalation made their task more difficult. Still, the NGOs could not stop the fighting. Only when NATO invoked and used hard power did Serbs stop shelling Sarajevo and pull away their cannon and mortars from the surrounding hills.

Could the UN *impose* peace on the South Slavs? Certainly not with a comparatively small, lightly armed force intended only for peacekeeping. Neither the UN nor Europe had the will—or the means—for peace enforcement in the Balkans. As we saw in Chapter 9, attempted mediation by UN and European Union representatives achieved little. They lacked both soft and hard power.

In 1991–1992 the yearly bill for UN peacekeeping missions jumped from $700 million to over $3 billion. UN peacekeeping efforts peaked in 1994 and then—amid disappointments and budgetary shortfalls—declined. UN spending on peacekeeping declined from $3.5 billion in 1994 to $1.2 billion in 1997. The number of UN forces worldwide declined from 76,000 in September 1994 to 19,191 in August 1997.[21] As we see from Table 15.2, few U.S. military personnel were involved in UN missions overall.

20. In January 1992 the Security Council imposed an arms embargo on Somalia; in April it established a UN Operation in Somalia (UNOSOM) to monitor a cease-fire and protect humanitarian relief supplies. Within a few months the UN Secretary-General called for a comprehensive approach to support humanitarian relief and recovery, a cease-fire, a peace process, and national reconciliation.

21. "The Future of UN Peacekeeping," *Strategic Comments* 3, no. 8 (October 1997).

Table 15.2 UN Peacekeeping Missions in the 1990s and U.S. Troop Contributions

United Nations Operation	Date Established	UN Troops	U.S. Contribution
UN Iraq-Kuwait Observer Force	1991	1,085	11
UN Mission for Referendum (Western Sahara)	1991	228	15
UN Observer Mission in Liberia	1993	9	0
UN Observer Mission in Georgia	1993	111	4
UN Observer Mission in Tajikistan	1994	44	0
UN Preventative Deployment Mission in Macedonia	1995	1,158	549
UN Mission in Bosnia and Herzegovina	1995	2,063	226
UN Mission of Observers to Prevlaka	1996	26	0
UNTAES (Eastern Slavonia, Baranja, Western Sirmium)	1996	2,898	35
UN Transition Mission in Haiti	1997	1,405	49
UN Observer Mission in Angola	1997	3,163	0

SOURCE: Adapted from "The Future of UN Peacekeeping," *Strategic Comments* 3, no. 8 (October 1997).

Under the UN flag U.S. troops were most heavily deployed in Macedonia and Bosnia—paid for by U.S. taxpayers. The biggest UN contributor, the U.S., was also its biggest debtor, owing some $1.5 billion by fall 1997. Many states were penny-wise and pound foolish. They left the Secretary-General with empty pockets just as demand for UN services soared around the world.

Washington and London concluded that the UN was ill-equipped for peace enforcement. They wanted the UN to take on only operations that entailed no fighting except in self-defense. France, however, believed that there was a third option: to restore security by force but without designating an aggressor or pre-judging the conflict's political outcome. But most observers believed peacekeeping missions should be rigidly separated from peace enforcement.

Most UN peacekeeping missions lasted only a few years, but some in the late 1990s appeared to be open-ended. Of eight longstanding UN operations (lasting more than five years), U.S. and many UN officials thought that two promoted stability—UNDOF (Israel-Syria) and UNIKOM (Iraq-Kuwait); three achieved partial success—UNTSO (Middle East), UNFICYP (Cyprus), and UNAVEM (Angola); and three contributed only marginally to security—UNMOGIP (Kashmir), UNIFIL (Lebanon), and MINURSO (Western Sahara). Still, U.S. officials saw no reasonable alternative to continuing these operations, because they bought time during which conflicts could be resolved peacefully.[22]

A new pattern took shape after the 1995 Dayton Accords on Bosnia. UN interventions were based on "contracting out" UN jobs, per "consent

22. U.S. General Accounting Office, *U.N. Peacekeeping: Status of Long-standing Operations and U.S. Interests in Supporting Them*, GAO/NSIAD-97-59 (Washington, D.C.: Government Printing Office, April 1997).

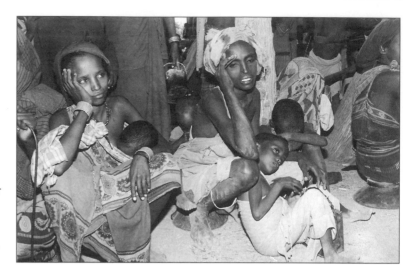

Governments, IGOs, and NGOs seek to cope with complex humanitarian emergencies. In 1992 some 300,000 Somalis fled from civil war and famine to seek food at distribution points supplied by U.S. relief flights. Food was needed, but also order in which to distribute it. When U.S. forces tried to establish order, however, they were repulsed by local warlords.

of the willing." NATO forces replaced those nominally subject to a "UN" commander. Thus, in Bosnia UN Blue Helmets were replaced by a larger and more robust Implementation Force (IFOR) of 60,000 troops from NATO and sixteen other states—later reduced to 35,000 troops in a Stabilization Force (SFOR). These forces, one-third of them from the U.S., kept the local guns silent and permitted economic reconstruction to begin. But even IFOR and SFOR did not compel full compliance with the Dayton Accords. Ethnic differences remained virulent. Few "ethnically cleansed" refugees could return home. The entire operation suffered from Washington's self-imposed deadlines, repeated annually, to pull out after one or two years on the job.

In the mid-1990s the UN also mandated forces from the Commonwealth of Independent States (CIS)—mostly Russians—to guard the borders of Georgia and Tajikistan, and an Italian-led force to restore order in Albania.

Did Intervention Do Any Good?

The Security Council in the 1990s allowed a prominent place for humanitarian intervention backed by force. These operations brought the UN into unknown terrain. They broke new legal ground, but their practical effects were limited. Basically they did too little, too late.

UN failures, as in Somalia, grabbed headlines. But every mission that prevented fighting (for example, in the Former Yugoslav Republic of Macedonia) could be judged at least a partial success. Meanwhile, the learning curve went up as UN officials and governments fathomed the reach of IO in the post–Cold War era.

EUROPE: FROM FUNCTIONALISM
TO SUPRANATIONALISM?

Images of a united Europe inspired visionaries for centuries, but made little progress until after World War II. Three factors contributed to European unity in the late 1940s–early 1950s: revulsion against war, fear of Soviet expansion, and payoffs from the Marshall Plan for European recovery.

As the Marshall Plan wound down, six of its leading participants—France, Germany, Italy, Belgium, the Netherlands, and Luxembourg ("the Six")—established in 1951 the **European Coal and Steel Community (ECSC)** to coordinate production and sales of coal and steel. This organization became overnight the world's closest approximation to a supranational organization. The Six empowered the ECSC High Authority to issue regulations binding on individuals and firms and to collect taxes directly from governments. But the ECSC had no coercive power to implement its decisions.

Jean Monnet, first director of the ECSC, sought to build on its momentum to expand European integration. He wanted to make low politics work for high politics. His neofunctional approach scored a quick victory. The six ECSC states in 1957 signed the **Treaty of Rome** establishing the **European Economic Community (EEC)**. The EEC aimed to create a customs union—a single economic region in which goods, services, people, and capital could move as freely as they do within national borders. The Six also established the European Atomic Energy Community (EURATOM).

The EEC became simply the EC—European Community—as its functions went beyond economics. By 1986 the original Six members had become the Twelve with the addition of the UK, Denmark, and Ireland (1973); Greece (1981); and Portugal and Spain (1986). The Twelve in 1987 agreed to a package of laws known as the **Single European Act (SEA)**, which obliged them to create by 1992 a European market without internal barriers or discrimination and gave new powers to the European Parliament (see sidebar on page 460). Under the act, most decisions could be taken by a simple majority rather than by unanimity, as before. Buoyed by "Europhoria," many members looked forward also to a **European Monetary Union (EMU)**.

In 1993 the EC became the "first pillar" of the European Union. The EU included the EC and two other pillars: one for forging a common foreign policy and another for overseeing justice and home affairs. Unlike NAFTA (North American Free Trade Agreement) and other regional trade organizations, the EU makes trade policies for its twelve members.

How the European Community Functions

European Community governance has been called "bureaucracy tempered by diplomacy." The **European Commission** is the EC executive—the only EC institution that may *initiate* policy. The Commission drafts new policies, implements those already decided upon, and watches over the application of EC rules. As "guardian of the treaties," it takes action against member governments it believes have violated their treaty obligations, for example, on antitrust regulation.

Policies drafted by the Commission must be agreed to by the **European Parliament** and then approved by the **European Council of Ministers** (chaired by rotation, each country having a six-month term).

The European Parliament (518 members in the 1990s) serves for five years and is the only EC body directly elected. It scrutinizes draft EC legislation, questions the Commission and Council of Ministers on their work, and debates topical issues. Since the parliament is an advisory body rather than a true legislature, critics say that the entire EC apparatus lacks democratic accountability. The **European Court of Justice** interprets EC acts and treaties and supports EC law over local laws of member states.

These four institutions take guidance from semi-annual summit meetings of Europe's heads of government—the **European Council**.

Three EC institutions have some supranational competence: the European Commission, the European Parliament, and the European Court of Justice. But both the Council of Ministers and European Council are intergovernmental.

How the European Community Adopts a Law

- **Commission** initiates
- **European Parliament** gives opinion
- **Council of Ministers** adopts common position by qualified majority
- **European Parliament**
  - approves → **Council** adopts act
  - amends by absolute majority → **Commission** may revise → **Council** may adopt
  - rejects by absolute majority → **Council** may act by unanimity

European unity draws on many sources and institutions. Here, the European Council—the summit of the European Union when heads of government and state confer—meets in Turin, Italy, in March 1996. The European Council was created in 1974 and is obliged by the 1987 Single European Act to meet at least twice a year.

Developments within the EC harmonized with three propositions:[23]

1. The EC was more than an "international regime" or "international organization," but was not yet an emerging "superstate." EC member-states retained more sovereignty than they surrendered.

2. The EC embodied a process of supranational decision making—a network of pooled sovereignty. Each unit in the network had strong incentives to interact with other units in the group rather than with outsiders. Common norms were emerging.

3. The process depended on intergovernmental bargains. Each country remained basically sovereign, but there was a "cumulative pattern of accommodation in which the participants refrain from unconditionally vetoing proposals and instead seek to attain agreement by compromises upgrading common interests."[24]

Functionalists looked at these trends and pointed to the influence of transnational interest groups, supranational officials, log-rolling to exchange favors (as in the U.S. Congress), and spill-over effects. They saw EC institutions as independent forces shaping national preferences.

In contrast to functionalists, the school of **intergovernmentalists** stressed the residual power of governments in the EC. It pointed out that individual governments retained sovereignty in most domains and stayed aloof from any all-European endeavors they disliked. Agreements to tighten common institutions resulted from negotiations dominated by the most powerful states—Germany, France, Britain—each constrained by strong internal opposition to European integration.[25]

Meanwhile, Europe in the late 1990s had no shared vision. And one of the best-kept secrets in Brussels was that most "EU" decisions were settled informally in the shadowy Committee of Permanent Representatives before they ever reached ministers.[26]

How Far Can Europe Unite?

Many European business people looked forward to establishment of the **Euro**, the single European currency to be introduced in stages from 1999 to 2002. The Euro could integrate an all-European economy operating on a continental scale like the U.S. If Euro notes and coins replaced national denominations, national prices could be compared more readily. When all banks and insurance companies provide services in a common currency, financial services can also be compared.

A more integrated European economy could encourage mobility of labor and production, thereby weakening existing governments. If compa-

23. See Robert O. Keohane and Stanley Hoffmann, "Institutional Change in Europe in the 1980s," in *The New European Community: Decisionmaking and Institutional Change*, ed. Robert O. Keohane and Stanley Hoffmann (Boulder, Colo.: Westview, 1991), 1–39 at 10, 15–17.

24. Ernst B. Haas, "Technocracy, Pluralism and the New Europe," in *A New Europe?* ed. Stephen R. Graubard (Boston: Houghton-Mifflin, 1964), 64, 66.

25. See Mark A. Pollack, "Delegation, Agency, and Agenda Setting in the European Community," *International Organization* 51, no. 1 (winter 1997): 99–134; and Lee Ann Patterson, "Agricultural Policy Reform in the European Community: A Three-Level Game Analysis," ibid., 135–165.

26. Lionel Barber, "Search for One Voice," *Financial Times*, October 30, 1997, 14, an essay prompted by the book of Belgium's retiring Permanent Representative, Philippe de Schoutheete, *Une Europe pour tous* (Paris: Odile Jacob, 1997).

Nej—no to Danish membership in the European Economic Community. This was the message of some 50,000 demonstrators in Copenhagen in 1972. But most Danes voted for membership in the EEC that year, as did voters in Ireland and the UK. A majority of Norwegian voters, however, preferred their country stay outside the EEC. Greenland, a self-governing region of Denmark, withdrew from the European Community in 1985.

nies do not like the taxes or other conditions in State A, they can more easily move to State B. Companies that adapt to the new environment may benefit while others, slow to change, may not.

But national loyalties still divided Europe in the 1990s. Each country wanted to produce ammunition on its own soil. Firms linked to particular countries (for example, Sweden and France) continued to compete against one another for defense contracts. Three U.S. defense giants had sales of $90 billion in 1996 while eight European firms, competing in the same market, had a combined turnover of less than $60 billion. So long as European governments saw their defense firms as "national," profitability as well as integration would be difficult.[27]

Conflicts could arise from efforts by a European central bank to impose a common fiscal discipline. What if some countries suffer unemployment and want fiscal policies that stimulate production while other countries focus on curbing inflation? Like the U.S. Constitution, the European Monetary Union has no provision allowing disaffected units to secede. If Italy wished to pull out of the EMU, might it have to throw down a gauntlet as South Carolina did before the U.S. federal government in 1861?[28]

Europe led the world in regional integration. But many obstacles blocked unity in the 1990s. They arose from different languages, cultures, levels of economic development, and geography. Cosmopolitan elites speaking English felt at home anywhere; most people spoke only their own tongue and felt at home only at home.

27. Europeans created two new organizations in the late 1990s to integrate their defense market and procurement, but most European countries favored their own industries. If they shopped abroad, the UK and the Netherlands often bought U.S. weapons, but France preferred to find European suppliers. See U.S. General Accounting Office, *Defense Trade: European Initiatives to Integrate the Defense Market,* GAO/NSIAD-98-6 (Washington, D.C.: Government Printing Office, October 1997).

28. See Martin Feldstein, "EMU and International Conflict," *Foreign Affairs* 76, no. 6 (November–December 1997): 60–73.

What Is "Europe"?

How far does "Europe" reach? Does it include Russia? The Americas? Outposts such as New Zealand? Figure 15.3 outlines the many organizations that enmeshed Europe and partners to the east and across the Atlantic.

More than fifty countries—all NATO partners, all of Europe, and all successor states to the USSR—belonged to the **Organization for Security and Cooperation in Europe (OSCE).** Russia in the 1990s wanted the OSCE to supplant NATO, but Western governments deemed the OSCE too large and unwieldy. Its decisions required unanimity—leaving Russia and all other members with a veto.

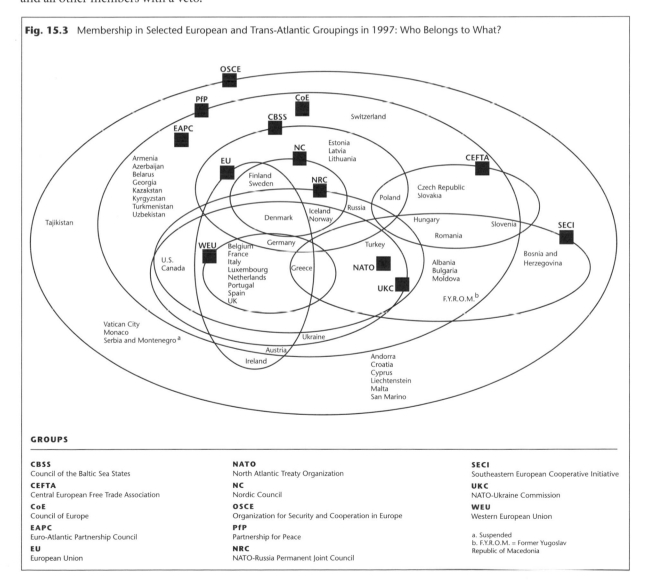

Fig. 15.3 Membership in Selected European and Trans-Atlantic Groupings in 1997: Who Belongs to What?

GROUPS

CBSS Council of the Baltic Sea States	**NATO** North Atlantic Treaty Organization	**SECI** Southeastern European Cooperative Initiative
CEFTA Central European Free Trade Association	**NC** Nordic Council	**UKC** NATO-Ukraine Commission
CoE Council of Europe	**OSCE** Organization for Security and Cooperation in Europe	**WEU** Western European Union
EAPC Euro-Atlantic Partnership Council	**PfP** Partnership for Peace	a. Suspended b. F.Y.R.O.M. = Former Yugoslav Republic of Macedonia
EU European Union	**NRC** NATO-Russia Permanent Joint Council	

The **Partnership for Peace (PfP)** prepared for and conducted peace-keeping missions. Originally conceived as a stepping stone to NATO membership for former Communist states, it included most OSCE members. But it excluded Bosnia, Croatia, and Serbia; Ireland (jealous of its neutrality); Tajikistan (torn by civil war); and mini-states such as the Vatican.

A military alliance founded in 1949, NATO was established to resist attack by the USSR. Washington in the late 1990s pressed NATO to accept into its membership the Czech Republic, Poland, and Hungary, and to consider in the future other states such as Slovenia. Russia and Ukraine acquired consultative status with NATO in 1997 and tried to leverage this into a significant voice. Most U.S. diplomats and scholars familiar with East-West security problems regarded President Clinton's policies on NATO unwise. George F. Kennan warned that NATO's eastward expansion could lead to a major foreign policy disaster. East Europeans concerned for their security (and their pocketbooks) might have better adapted the Austrian model of lightly armed neutrality recognized in 1955 by Moscow, London, Paris, and Washington.[29]

Germany favored opening EU membership to Poland and other East European countries. But many West Europeans did not wish to dilute EU membership and feared competition from the east where wages were lower. Some West Europeans went along with NATO expansion to reduce pressure on the EU to admit the East Europeans.

The **Western European Union (WEU)**, founded in 1955, sought to coordinate the security policies of NATO's European members. Some hoped it could become a European alliance independent of the U.S.

Despite the plethora of organizations outlined in Figure 15.3, none could act forcefully to maintain peace and security except NATO. And even NATO could do little unless the U.S. took the lead. West Europeans had no common policy. Furthermore, Europeans had not modernized their forces in the 1990s and had little capacity to project forces beyond their borders. NATO quality would fall further if East European forces, poorly equipped and funded, were added.

Europe's problems were trivial next to those of the Commonwealth of Independent States. The CIS fell apart in the 1990s as Moscow's heavy hand alienated every member. In 1997 Ukraine began to align with Kazakstan against Russia. U.S. and other Western forces carried out training missions in Ukraine and in Kazakstan, a not-too-subtle reminder to Russia of U.S. power projection assets. Washington backed Kazaks and

29. Walter C. Clemens, Jr., "An Alternative to NATO Expansion," *International Journal* 52, no. 2 (spring 1997): 342–365.

others against bullying by Moscow, in part to assure a U.S. voice on oil allocations.

ORGANIZING FOR HUMAN WELFARE

Apart from security and economic development, international organizations can also foster human welfare. From myriad agencies, let us look briefly at one that promotes public health and another that offers humanitarian relief in wartime.

Serving the Health of Nations

Health issues can be high politics. Bubonic plague, probably carried by ships from Asia, wiped out a third of Europe's population in the 17th century. In an age of global interdependence jet planes carry lethal diseases far more rapidly than the ships that carried the "Black Death."

The **World Health Organization (WHO)** is committed to the "attainment by all peoples of the highest possible level of health." Successor to public health agencies founded in 1907 and 1919, the WHO became a UN Specialized Agency in 1948. It cooperates with scores of other IGOs such as the UN Development Programme and with even more NGOs—from the African Medical and Research Foundation to World Vision International.

In the late 1990s the WHO budget exceeded $1 billion—about ¹⁄₅₀₀th of what governments spent to maintain their ability to kill. Let us examine how the WHO has dealt with several threats to public health.

Smallpox. From its founding the WHO urged its member-states to vaccinate against the ancient scourge of smallpox (see sidebar on page 466). But it was difficult to store and transport the vaccines to less developed countries (LDCs). The cost of a life-saving vaccination was about 10 cents. Still, national governments in India and Africa failed to invest the necessary funds or personnel. Epidemics continued until help came from the outside. Dr. Viktor Zhdanov, a Soviet delegate to the World Health Assembly, began to mobilize broad-scale action in 1958.[30]

In 1966 the World Health Assembly resolved to eliminate the disease entirely. It set up a Smallpox Eradication Unit with a budget of some $2.5 million per year—about 0.6 percent of the WHO annual budget at the time. Assisted by other UN agencies, the WHO brought together the personnel and equipment needed to vaccinate throughout India and Africa. The WHO funded conferences, training courses, fellowships, and consultantships. It also established standards for vaccine quality. It recommended freeze-dried vaccines for remote tropical areas and glycerated vaccines where refrigeration was possible.

UN Specialized Agencies as Nonstate Actors

In the 1990s there were sixteen UN Specialized Agencies, each with its own tasks. They included the WHO, the World Bank, the IMF, the UN Food and Agricultural Organization, the International Civil Aviation Organization, and the International Labor Organization. The Specialized Agencies are coordinated by the UN Economic and Social Council (one of six principal UN organs). A professional orientation usually outweighs the agendas of particular states. Labor and employers as well as governments are represented in the International Labor Organization.

The WHO had 190 member states in 1997. Each member has one vote in the governing World Health Assembly, which meets at least annually. Members pay dues on a scale similar to their UN assessment. The WHO Secretariat is based in Geneva but has branches in each region.

30. Smallpox had nearly been wiped out in the USSR, but epidemics in Iran and Afghanistan spilled over into Soviet Central Asia. Dr. Zhdanov reminded a World Health Assembly gathered in Minneapolis that U.S. President Thomas Jefferson had written to Dr. Edward Jenner, the English physician who introduced the vaccination, commending his discovery as a boon for the future of all peoples. Many epidemiologists trained by Dr. Zhdanov in Moscow took part in the WHO program. The USSR also contributed some 25 million doses of vaccine.

WHO efforts multiplied after 1958, but the eradication program dragged until 1966 for lack of funds and personnel. In 1958 there were five WHO officials working on leprosy and twenty-eight on malaria, but none responsible solely for smallpox.

The Scourge of Smallpox

Smallpox for thousands of years caused 10 percent of all deaths in the towns and cities of Asia and Europe where records were kept. It beset every class and continent. It arrived in North America with settlers and slaves, wiping out much of the Native American population, which had no acquired immunity. But whites were not immune. Epidemics often struck port cities. In 1647 Boston began to quarantine ships with smallpox. An epidemic in Boston in 1677 led to the first medical publication in America. In 1706 a West African slave told Cotton Mather, later president of Harvard College, about inoculation. In 1721 inoculation was introduced into Europe and North America. Fearing the British Army might send persons infected across the lines, George Wash-ington ordered inoculation of his troops in 1775–1776. But not all were protected. The Continental Army might well have taken Quebec City and won all of Canada in 1776 had an epidemic not felled its general and many troops.

The disease was gradually checked in some countries after English country doctor Edward Jenner demonstrated in 1796 how to vaccinate humans against smallpox using cowpox virus. Thomas Jefferson wrote Jenner in 1808 that "mankind can never forget that you have lived. Future nations will know by history only that the loathsome smallpox has existed." For the full story, see Donald R. Hopkins, *Princes and Peasants: Smallpox in History* (Chicago: University of Chicago Press, 1983).

31. In 1980 the WHO recommended that vaccination be stopped since the disease had been eradicated. See F. Fenner et al., *Smallpox and Its Eradication* (Geneva: World Health Organization, 1988). In 1996, two centuries after Jenner invented the vaccine, the World Health Assembly recommended destruction of the world's remaining stocks of the virus and maintenance of the seed virus at a laboratory in The Netherlands. *The World Health Report 1997* (Geneva: World Health Organization, 1997), 89.

In less than a decade—at a tiny cost but with broad East-West-South cooperation—the WHO eradicated smallpox from the planet. The savings made simply by not having to check smallpox vaccination certificates at international airports exceed the cost of the entire eradication program. No value can be placed on the lives saved.[31] Even here, however, there was a risk: If some rogue government kept smallpox in its labs and turned it into a weapon, most people would be defenseless.

Primary Health Care. In 1977 the World Health Assembly decided that the main social goal of governments and the WHO should be world-

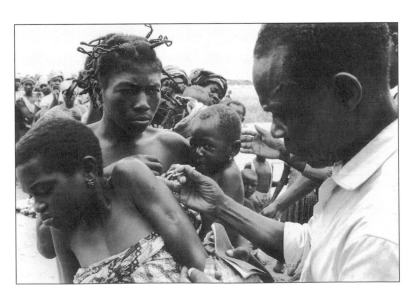

The campaign organized by the World Health Organization to stamp out smallpox required that every human be vaccinated. Here, a WHO worker in 1962 vaccinates villagers in the former Belgian Congo. The disease was eradicated worldwide in the mid-1970s.

wide attainment by the year 2000 of a level of health permitting all people to lead socially and economically productive lives. Affordable "primary health care" should include community education on health problems and prevention; promotion of adequate food, safe water, and sanitation; maternal and child care; prevention and control of endemic diseases; immunization against the main infectious diseases; treatment of common diseases and injuries; and provision of essential drugs.

The WHO estimated that such care could be provided in developing countries for $10 to $15 per person per year (excepting food, water, and sanitation). But in sub-Saharan Africa outlays were only $7 per capita; in South and Southeast Asia they were only $4. By contrast, in developed market economies they reached nearly $600.[32]

In the 1980s only a third of sub-Saharan Africans had access to safe drinking water or adequate sanitation. Roughly half of South and Southeast Asia had safe drinking water but only a fifth to a tenth had adequate sanitation. Lack of safe drinking water and sanitation lead to gastrointestinal diseases—a major child killer. Dehydration can be controlled by oral rehydration therapy (ORT) using a saline water solution that costs pennies—provided mothers possess it and know how to use it. The UN Children's Fund (UNICEF), a UN Specialized Agency that works with the WHO, campaigned to make ORT available worldwide.

For the cost of a few warships all the children in the world could be inoculated against six preventable diseases—diphtheria, whooping cough, tetanus, polio, measles, and tuberculosis. The knowledge and medicines exist. The core administrative structures exist. The missing ingredient is money—or the will to provide it.

Malaria. Another WHO project achieved dramatic results initially, only to boomerang. Malaria once infected 90 percent of the people in Borneo. In 1955 the WHO sprayed the island with DDT to kill the carrier mosquitoes.[33] DDT provided a quick-fix that saved many human lives. DDT was then applied in many countries. But new strains of mosquitoes emerged, bringing with them new forms of malaria. Some experts concluded that screening porches and windows offered a more effective and less destructive approach to malaria control than pesticides.[34] In the 1990s the WHO found in Kenya that insect-treated bednets cut down malaria.

The WHO in the 1990s worked with national health ministries and donors to ensure financial support for seventeen African and three Asian countries where malaria remained endemic. Striving to foster community-based control efforts, the WHO trained entomologists from Asia and Africa in vector control. It provided technical assistance to refugee camps

32. *Global Outlook 2000: An Economic, Social, and Environmental Perspective* (New York: United Nations, 1990), 285–305.

33. Besides killing the mosquitoes that spread malaria, DDT also killed flies and cockroaches—the favorite food of house lizards (geckoes), which then perished. The cockroaches and geckoes killed by DDT were then eaten by house cats. When the cats also died, the rat population soared, bringing with them a sylvatic plague carried by fleas on the rats. Britain's Royal Air Force then conducted Operation Cat Drop, parachuting fresh cats into remote jungle habitats.

34. A. V. Kondrashin and K. M. Rashid, eds., *Epidemiological Considerations for Planning Malaria Control in the WHO South-East Asia Region* (New Delhi: World Health Organization, South-East Asia, 1987).

in Azerbaijan and ten other countries affected by malaria. The WHO malaria experts collaborated with the UN Development Programme in Myanmar; with the World Bank in Bangladesh, Laos, Madagascar, and Vietnam; with the European Union in Indochina; and with European aid agencies in Eritrea, Ethiopia, and Uganda.

Infant Formula. The WHO and UNICEF helped mediate and partially resolve a debate between NGOs and TNCs over infant formula. Two sets of nonstate actors, some allied with governments, faced off. Nestlé and other TNC makers of infant formula touted their product in LDCs using sales personnel dressed as nurses to give free samples to new mothers. Once mothers used the formula, they became physiologically dependent on it when their babies did not suckle.

Public health experts warned that conditions in many developing countries—illiteracy, contaminated water, lack of refrigeration—made infant formula dangerous to public health. Leading pediatricians estimated that ten million cases of infant malnutrition and one to three million deaths occurred yearly in LDCs in the 1970s as a result of mothers ceasing to breast-feed their children.[35]

The World Health Assembly in 1974 warned member countries to review sales promotion of baby foods and to regulate advertisements. But many NGOs took a harder line and demanded a code of conduct. The British group War on Want published a pamphlet called *The Baby Killers* (1974), which was translated in Switzerland under the German title *Nestlé Kills Babies.* Nestlé inadvertently publicized the issue when it sued for defamation. In the U.S. the Infant Formula Action Coalition (INFACT) organized a consumer boycott of Nestlé. After Senate hearings, a meeting between Senator Edward M. Kennedy and infant formula companies produced a request by both sides for a WHO meeting on the issue.

The World Health Assembly and UNICEF in 1981 adopted a Code of Marketing for Breast-milk Substitutes (the vote was 118 for, 3 abstentions, and one—the U.S.—against). The code was non-binding on member governments, but eliminated direct advertising and reduced free sampling and blatant misrepresentation.

The TNCs fought back. Nestlé, Abbot Laboratories, and Upjohn lobbied Washington. The Reagan administration and several LDC governments took no immediate action, but by 1984 over forty countries were moving to convert the code into their domestic legislation. Switzerland and Norway, both major exporters of formula, voted for the marketing code. India passed laws regarding distribution of free samples that were tougher than the code. In the 1990s, however, a major reason to use infant

35. Kathryn Sikkink, "Codes of Conduct for Transnational Corporations: The Case of the WHO/UNICEF Code," *International Organization* 40, no. 4 (autumn 1986): 815–840.

formula emerged: Mothers infected with the human immunodeficiency virus (HIV) often transmit the disease by breast feeding.

HIV/AIDS. Smallpox is gone, but the world faces other epidemics and pandemics. The HIV pandemic spread worldwide in less than twenty years—a reminder that globalization can increase mutual vulnerability. Reported infections worldwide rose from 0.2 million in 1980 to more than 30 million in 1996. Africa had by far the highest rate of per capita infections, but India probably had more HIV-positive people than any other country.[36]

The WHO and other agencies attempted to track the disease and disseminate information on how to prevent and cope with it.

Working in a Joint UN Programme on HIV/AIDS (UNAIDS) begun in 1996, the WHO sought to coordinate a global, regional, and country-level response to HIV. Unlike smallpox, however, the mechanisms by which HIV spreads are many and not well understood. There is no magic shot to prevent it. And drugs to inhibit the disease are expensive. Like smallpox, HIV kills the rich as well as the poor. But poverty, ignorance, and political chaos make preventive action and education difficult.

Complex Humanitarian Emergencies—The Red Cross in Tajikistan

The number of persons fleeing their countries or losing their homes due to conflict more than doubled in the 1980s. The UN High Commissioner for Refugees (UNHCR) reported that 1.4 million such persons received UN assistance in 1961, 5.7 million in 1980, and 27.4 million in 1995. But those needing relief from natural as well as human-made disasters in-

---

Factors Facilitating the Code of Conduct

• The emotional appeal of a campaign for breast milk over infant formula

• A strong consensus on the issues among experts

• A global coalition of NGOs such as the International Baby Food Action Network and INFACT (started in Minneapolis with twenty volunteers and one paid staffer)

• Nestlé's vulnerability to a boycott just as it embarked on a campaign to seek a wider market share for its many products in the U.S.

• The desire of Nestlé and other producers to appear upright and wholesome

• Mediation by UNICEF between Nestlé and its NGO critics

• Rising sales of infant formula to an expanding population regardless of negative publicity.

---

36. *World Health Report 1997*, 124; Lester Brown et al., *Vital Signs 1997: The Environmental Trends That Are Shaping Our Future* (New York: Norton, 1997), 84-85; and *Global Outlook 2000*, 291.

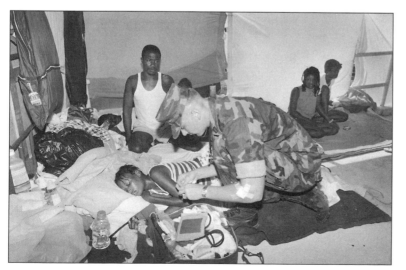

A new and possibly larger threat to public health, HIV supplanted smallpox in the late 1970s and 1980s. Here, a U.S. Navy corpsman in 1993 checks a Haitian refugee believed to be HIV positive. Many Haitian "boat people" fleeing their homeland for U.S. shores were intercepted by U.S. ships and interned at Guantanamo Naval Base, a U.S. facility in Cuba. This woman is on a hunger strike in protest against the refusal of U.S. authorities to give her asylum. Most observers agreed that Washington treated Haitians more harshly than it treated Cuban refugees.

creased from 50 million per year in the early 1970s to some 350 million in the early 1990s.[37] Why? The world had more people, more poverty, more people living in environmentally fragile zones, and more fighting. A vicious circle aggravates the problems: As more official development assistance goes to humanitarian relief, less goes to long-term development. Table 15.3 indicates the extent of human distress.

The end of the Cold War ushered in many **complex humanitarian emergencies**—compounds of dire poverty, hunger, environmental disaster, communal conflict, civil war, displacement of people, and failing economic and political institutions, often complicated by armed interventions from neighboring countries. Challenges for outside nonstate actor aid agencies multiply when local warlords obstruct or abuse humanitarian relief.

For more than a century the Red Cross has tried to lessen the horrors of war. But things were easier when governments were the main combatants. They knew the laws of war and paid some heed to public opinion. They usually permitted the Red Cross to aid prisoners of war, the wounded, and refugees.

In the 1990s relief agencies confronted much fighting by private entrepreneurs. Countries once held together by superpowers were breaking up. Local warlords sought profit or territory for their ethnic group, scorned world opinion, and ignored Red Cross and Red Crescent mark-

Table 15.3   People in Distress in 1996

Country	Population	People in Need (percent of population)	Physicians per 1,000	Infant Mortality (per 1,000 live births)
Afghanistan	22,664,136	3.5 million (15%)	1.00	163
Angola	10,342,899	2.4 million (23%)	0.07	137
Azerbaijan	7,676,953	780,000 (10%)	39.00	25
Bosnia/Herzegovina	2,656,240	many	3.70	n.a.
Burundi	5,943,057	1 million (17%)	0.06	102
Croatia	5,004,112	475,000 (9%)	20.00	10
Eritrea	3,427,883	700,000 (20%)	0.25	105
Ethiopia	57,171,662	2–3 million (3–5%)	0.03	120
Georgia	5,219,810	300,000 (6%)	59.00	18
Haiti	6,731,539	500,000 (7%)	0.22	74
Iraq	21,422,292	2.1 million (10%)	4.00	67
Liberia	2,109,789	2 million (95%)	n.a.	113
North Korea	23,904,124	5 million (21%)	27.20	28
Russia (Chechnya)	1,200,000	350,000 (29%)	47.00	n.a.
Rwanda	6,853,359	1.9 million (28%)	0.04	110
Sierra Leone	4,793,121	1.5 million (31%)	0.07	143
Somalia	9,639,151	1 million (10%)	0.05	122
Sri Lanka	18,553,074	850,000 (5%)	1.40	18
Sudan	31,547,543	4.4 million (14%)	9.00	80
Tajikistan	5,916,373	630,000 (11%)	29.00	47

37. *Vital Signs*, 82–83.

NOTE: n.a. = not available.

Relief agencies were overwhelmed in the mid-1990s by the outpouring of refugees from political turmoil and environmental disaster. Here the UN High Commissioner for Refugees, Sadako Ogata, meets some of the 38,000 Hutu refugees from Rwanda crowding into the Kashuna Camp in eastern Zaire. Among these Hutu refugees, however, were instigators of the recent massacres of Tutsis. How could relief agencies discriminate between innocent refugees and mass murderers intent on resuming genocide?

ings. In 1996 nineteen relief workers were murdered in Chechnya and Africa. Relief agencies often faced multiple clans contesting control of the same city. A local commander's promise of safe passage meant little to an armed teenager at a checkpoint. Warlords in Liberia starved regions to attract food relief; then they stole the food plus the trucks that delivered it. Hutus who led the 1994 genocide in Rwanda used refugee camps in Zaire as bases for military raids back into Rwanda.

Complex humanitarian emergencies renewed old questions for the **International Committee of the Red Cross (ICRC).**[38] Its leaders wondered: If Red Cross workers made war less painful, would this cause more war? Should they ignore politics and act as though each side deserves assistance? Should they welcome or spurn the security that UN or other outside forces could give relief workers?

These questions came to a head in February 1997 when two ICRC aid workers were among sixteen hostages taken by rebels in Tajikistan's civil war. The other hostages included two UN military observers, four workers for the UN High Commissioner for Refugees, five Russian and Tajik journalists, and a translator. The rebel leader abducted the hostages to press the Tajik government for safe passage so a guerrilla force led by his brother could return from Afghanistan.

Responding to the abductions, the ICRC suspended its activities in Tajikistan and evacuated most of its foreign staff to Uzbekistan. The UN told most of its workers to stay indoors. Tajik President Imamali Rakhmanov met with his own security officials, the Russian ambassador, the head of the Red Cross mission, and a UN envoy.

38. The ICRC was founded in 1864 to provide humanitarian aid in wartime. To assure its neutrality, the committee's twenty-five members are all Swiss nationals. It works with national committees of the Red Cross and Red Crescent throughout the world.

ICRC Activities in Tajikistan in 1996

ICRC activities in Tajikistan included the following:

- Visits to 110 detainees held by the Tajik opposition, with arrangements for them to exchange messages with their families
- Nutritional rehabilitation for 5,500 detainees in Tajik prisons (240,000 vitamin tablets, medicines, 165 tons of flour, 10 tons of oil, 113 tons of beans and rice, 2,196 food parcels, 113 tons of high-energy biscuits and milk, 1,347 pairs of shoes, 4,357 blankets)
- Food, plastic sheets, stoves, and fuel to 30,000 people affected by the conflict
- Medical supplies to eight hospitals and six first-aid facilities caring for government and rebel soldiers
- Evacuation of thirty-five amputees to Baku to be fitted with artificial limbs at the ICRC's prosthetic center there
- Seminars and dissemination of printed materials and videotapes on the law of war for officers and soldiers, military academies, the Tajik Institute for Management and Service, the State Medical University, and the Red Crescent Society

WHO teams also worked in Tajikistan trying to control outbreaks of typhoid fever and malaria.

ICRC expenditures for Tajikistan in 1996 amounted to just over $17 million—not much compared to outlays for war or even for peacekeeping. Two-thirds went for relief; the rest for protection, tracing of relatives, health, dissemination of information, operational support, and overhead (5 percent).

39. *ICRC Annual Report 1996* (Geneva: International Committee of the Red Cross, 1997), 219–223.

Rakhmanov's government, dominated by former Communists, had been fighting a coalition of Islamic and nationalist forces for four years. Ethnic, clan, and regional differences also divided the parties. A fragile truce was signed in December 1996. But the war was international as well as civil.

Many cooks stirred the many ingredients. Russia and all of the new Central Asian governments wanted to obstruct the spread of Islamic politics from Afghanistan. They wanted stability and secular government. More than 20,000 CIS troops, mostly Russian, tried to guard the Tajik government. The rebels carried out hit-and-run attacks from Afghanistan and probably got support from Iran and Pakistan. Many thousands died in the fighting, many more were displaced, and more than one million refugees cowered in camps along the Afghan border.

In 1996 the conditions for aid workers in Tajikistan became more precarious. Rebels gained more territory in central Tajikistan and anti-government demonstrations increased in northern Tajikistan. Kidnappings of UN aid workers increased. By late 1996 the ICRC was the only organization working in areas controlled by the opposition. The ICRC tried to give aid to both sides.[39]

The Tajik government accepted humanitarian relief for displaced persons, but denied the ICRC permission to visit government prisons and interview detainees in private. Neither the Tajik government nor the rebels saw the ICRC as a neutral intermediary. Both sides agreed to have the ICRC preside over a prisoner exchange but then dragged their feet.

Nothing was easy. ICRC relief convoys took back roads into rebel-controlled territories. One route wove 2,500 kilometers along the borders of neighboring Uzbekistan and Kyrgyzstan, at up to 4,300 kilometers above sea level, on extremely poor roads, obstructed by military checkpoints manned by the government, the opposition, and CIS border guards.

Was the Red Cross in the forefront of a new world order or did it wage a futile struggle amid growing chaos?

WHAT PROPOSITIONS HOLD? WHAT QUESTIONS REMAIN?

HOPE OR DESPAIR?

IO helps meet human needs that are beyond the reach of local communities and nation-states. A wide variety of international and transnational organizations help people to cope with the dangers and opportunities inherent in interdependence and globalization.

Does the growth of IO give reason for despair or for hope? One image of IR says the glass is half empty; the other, that it is half full. Thus, the realist says that IO is merely another instrument in the struggle for power: Hard-liners will manipulate the Red Cross and other nonstate actors as tools or obstacles to their goals. The realist policy-maker asks: "Should we use or avoid IO to enhance our power?"

The idealist takes hope from the growth of international law and organization. She or he believes the quest to ground IR in law and morality is succeeding. The idealist policy-maker asks: "How can we use or reform IO to achieve our ideals?"

The student of interdependence perceives a shared vulnerability among IR actors that permits both pain and gain. He or she sees global trends that contain a potential for disaster, but also for greater security, prosperity, justice, and environmental well-being. A nurturing structure for mutual gain is emerging, but it can be shattered by numerous forces. The policy-maker oriented toward mutual gain asks: "How can we improve IO to generate values for all parties?"

INTERNATIONAL ORGANIZATION AS AN EMERGENT FORCE

Prosperity in the 19th and 20th centuries depended on IOs that helped to regulate commerce and technology and expand markets. Human life became more complicated, more intertwined, and mutually dependent throughout the 20th century. Survival in the 21st century may depend upon IOs that protect the environment and prevent wars in which weapons of mass destruction might be used.

Governments cannot meet all the needs of modern societies. They delegate, encourage, or permit other actors to pick up and carry on a wide assortment of tasks. Governments have grown accustomed to a range of other actors operating at their side—or even against them—in the world arena.

Everything has increased—world population, the number of states, and the work of IGOs and NGOs. Why? The efflorescence of nonstate actors in the 20th century resulted from and helped cause both interstate interdependence and cross-border globalization. The complex network of IGOs and NGOs can be seen as an **emergent structure** arising from coevolution. This structure is a holistic entity far more than the sum of its parts—the product of coevolution as diverse actors meet their diverse needs. Like a coral reef that sustains and shelters many life forms, IO has evolved and expanded to protect and help people actualize their potential. To be sure, some organizations pursue their own interests at the expense of others, for example, drug traffickers. But many pursue their goals in ways that do no harm or even help many people. A coral reef represents "order for free," because it takes shape spontaneously, without planning. Most components of IO, by contrast, represent human intelligence and volition. The total emergent structure of IO, however, is also "order for free." No one foresaw or planned how its many components would come together.

Like sea anenomes and fish, some IOs do not survive—do not fit with changing conditions. Others, such as the IMF and World Bank, have repeatedly reinvented themselves to promote the goals of their leading members and to meet the needs of developing countries.

Governments have tried to guard their sovereign rights against the expanding competencies of IGOs and NGOs. Also, some NGOs and IGOs have seen each other as rivals. Experience shows, however, that there is room—perhaps a need—for diverse organizations to meet the multiplicity of human needs. Governments, IGOs, and NGOs have learned to work together in many fields—from women's rights to environmental protection to security.

A top-down approach to world government is not feasible. Governments are not about to sign a treaty transferring authority to a supranational institution. Not even the European Union has forged a common foreign or defense policy. How then can still more distant civilizations generate a unified government? And if they did, Juvenal's old question remains: *Quis custodiet ipsos custodes*—"Who shall guard the guardians?"

Collective security has worked twice rather well and could succeed again, but only if a great power spearheads the effort and no other great power objects.

Peacekeeping can be useful if the disputants consent. The costs are trivial relative to dislocations of war. Peacekeeping can help or weaken solidarity among units from different countries.

To impose peace on parties that still wish to fight requires a very strong force and a long-term commitment. In principle a strong UN or NATO coalition should be able to subdue poorly equipped guerrillas. In Africa, Cambodia, and the Balkans, however, results were poor. Outsiders may halt local violence; to remove its deep roots is much harder. And if outsiders succeed in one place, must they extinguish fires everywhere?

Should You Start Your Own Nonstate Actor? ... *Can a handful of pragmatic idealists succeed in founding a University of the Middle East where people from diverse backgrounds study how to coexist and develop for mutual gain? The obstacles are formidable. In the late 1990s tensions mounted between Israel and its neighbors. The sources of conflict intensified—myopia, greed, cultural differences, have and have-not economies, a tenuous balance of power involving weapons of mass destruction—all flayed by entrepreneurs of hate and violence.*

But huge obstacles have been overcome by other individuals and NGOs. Despite the Cold War, Soviet and Western scientists founded the Pugwash Conferences on Science and World Affairs; later, Soviet and U.S. doctors formed International Physicians for Prevention of Nuclear War. Costa Rican President Oscar Arias Sanchez helped mobilize other Latin leaders to press for peace in Central America.[40] Despite U.S.-PRC tensions, the son of Chinese President Jiang Zemin studied at Drexel University and obtained a doctorate. An "American University" has long functioned in Egypt and in Lebanon (though a similar institution was taken over by the Turkish government).

The spirit of the times is on your side. Nonstate actors are getting stronger and filling more niches of human need. Education and peace are prerequisites for development. Politics between governments may not suffice to end the wasteful violence that besets the Middle East. Money will be a problem, but some potential financiers may welcome your effort to replace hate and war with sanity and amity.

Get to yes. Show that you can create values for mutual gain. Join the growing emergent structure of private and public organizations whose pooled efforts help all humanity to live safer and more fulfilling lives. Your success is not assured, perhaps not even likely, but it is worth seeking.

---

40. The Nobel Peace Prize was awarded to the IPPNW in 1985, to Arias in 1987, and to the Pugwash Movement in 1995. Other Nobel laureates mentioned in this chapter were the International Red Cross (1917, 1944, 1963), Frank Kellogg (1929), the UN High Commissioner for Refugees (1954, 1981), Dag Hammarskjöld (1961), Anwar Sadat and Menachem Begin (1978), Elie Wiesel (1986), UN Peacekeeping Forces (1988), Mikhail Gorbachev (1990), and the International Campaign to Ban Land Mines (1997).

KEY NAMES AND TERMS

complex humanitarian emergencies	European Parliament	Single European Act (SEA)
emergent structure	functionalism	Stimson Doctrine
Euro	intergovernmentalists	supranational
European Coal and Steel Community (ECSC)	International Committee of the Red Cross (ICRC)	Treaty of Rome (1957)
European Commission	international organization (IO)	UN General Assembly
European Council	Kellogg-Briand Pact	UN Security Council
European Council of Ministers	neofunctionalism	UN Special Commission (UNSCOM)
European Court of Justice	nonstate actors	Uniting for Peace Resolution
European Economic Community (EEC)	Organization for Security and Cooperation in Europe (OSCE)	veto
European Monetary Union (EMU)	Partnership for Peace (PfP)	Western European Union (WEU)
		World Health Organization (WHO)

QUESTIONS TO DISCUSS

1. What have been the driving forces behind IO? How are they likely to evolve in the 21st century?

2. How did the Stimson Doctrine differ from previous international practice? Did it do any good? How did it relate to collective security?

3. To what extent did UN policy toward North Korean and Iraqi expansion represent collective security?

4. Review the record: What have been the successes and failures of UN peacekeeping efforts? Has the cost been justified?

5. Is Europe uniting as a result of supranationalism or functionalism, or both? What are the obstacles to further union?

6. Has IO done anything for human welfare? Assess the work of the WHO.

7. Consider the role of the ICRC in complex humanitarian emergencies. Should it continue its work? What reforms would you suggest?

8. Do you perceive an emergent structure of IO? If so, is this good or bad?

RECOMMENDED RESOURCES

BOOKS

Beck, Robert J., et al., eds. *International Rules: Approaches from International Law and International Relations.* New York: Oxford University Press, 1996.

Boutros-Ghali, Boutros. *Building Peace and Development 1994.* New York: United Nations, 1994.

Claude, Inis L. *Swords Into Plowshares: The Problems and Progress of International Organization.* 4th ed. New York: Random House, 1984.

Durch, William J., ed. *The Evolution of UN Peacekeeping: Case Studies and Comparative Analysis.* New York: St. Martin's, 1993.

Esman, Milton J., and Shibley Telhami, eds. *International Organization and Ethnic Conflict.* Ithaca, N.Y.: Cornell University Press, 1995.

Evans, Peter, et al. *Double-edged Diplomacy: International Bargaining and Domestic Politics.* Los Angeles: University of California Press, 1993.

Haas, Ernst B. *The Uniting of Europe: Political, Social, and Economic Forces, 1950–1957.* Stanford, Calif.: Stanford University Press, 1958.

Hoffmann, Stanley. *World Disorders.* Lanham, Md.: Rowman & Littlefield, 1998.

Jacobson, Harold K. *Networks of Interdependence: International Organizations and the Global Political System.* 2d ed. New York: Knopf, 1984.

Keohane, Robert O., and Stanley Hoffmann, eds. *The New European Community.* Boulder, Colo.: Westview, 1991.

Lopez, George A., and Nancy J. Myers, eds. *Peace and Security. The Next Generation.* Lanham, Md: Rowman & Littlefield, 1997.

Minear, Larry, and Thomas G. Weiss. *Mercy Under Fire: War and the Global Humanitarian Community.* Boulder, Colo.: Westview, 1995.

Mingst, Karen A., and Margaret P. Karns. *The United Nations in the Post–Cold War Era.* Boulder, Colo.: Westview, 1995.

Pérez de Cuéllar, Javier. *Anarchy or Order: Annual Reports, 1982–1991.* New York: United Nations, 1991.

Ross, George. *Jacques Delors and European Integration.* New York: Oxford University Press, 1995.

Schaeffer, Robert K. *Understanding Globalization: The Social Consequences of Political, Economic, and Environmental Change.* Lanham, Md.: Rowman & Littlefield, 1997.

Simai, Mihaly. *The Future of Global Governance: Managing Risk and Change in the International System.* Washington, D.C.: U.S. Institute of Peace Press, 1994.

Tessitore, John, and Susan Woolfson, eds. *A Global Agenda: Issues Before the 52nd General Assembly of the United Nations.* Lanham, Md.: Rowman & Littlefield, 1997.

United Nations Publications. New York: United Nations, annual.

Weiss, Thomas G., et al., eds. *Political Gain and Civilian Pain: Humanitarian Impacts of Economic Sanctions.* Lanham, Md.: Rowman & Littlefield, 1998.

———. *The United Nations and Changing World Politics.* 2d ed. Boulder, Colo.: Westview, 1997.

Willetts, Peter, ed. *"The Conscience of the World": The Influence of Non-Governmental Organizations in the UN System.* Washington, D.C.: Brookings Institution, 1996.

Young, Oran. *International Cooperation: Building Regimes for Natural Resources and the Environment.* Ithaca, N.Y.: Cornell University Press, 1989.

JOURNALS

American Journal of International Law

American Political Science Review

Daedalus

The Interdependent (United Nations Association of the United States)

International Organization

International Studies Quarterly

Journal of European Public Policy

Reports and Papers (Academic Council on the United Nations System)

UN Chronicle

West European Politics

WEB SITES

Academic Council on the United Nations System
    http://www.brown.edu/Departments/ACUNS/

Action Without Borders: Linking People and Organizations in 120 Countries
    http://www.idealist.org (*NGO hotlinks*)
    http://oneworld.org

European Union
    http://europa.eu.int/ (*official EU homepage*)

International Committee of the Red Cross
    http://www.icrc.org (*official homepage*)

International Institute for Strategic Studies
    http://www.isn.ethz.ch/iiss

United Nations Peacekeeping Operations
    http://www.un.org/depts/dpko (*official UN homepage*)

C H A P T E R S I X T E E N

INTERNATIONAL PROTECTION OF HUMAN RIGHTS: SHAM OR REVOLUTION?

THE BIG QUESTIONS IN CHAPTER 16

- Are we our brothers' and sisters' keepers? Does the answer depend upon religion, color, or culture?

- What is a human right? Where do rights come from?

- Is human rights a Western concept irrelevant to other civilizations?

- How can we reconcile state sovereignty with international responsibility for human rights? Should—must—other governments or the United Nations intervene in societies where human rights are under siege?

- Why do Westerners believe they are entitled to judge what is right or wrong for peoples of Asia, Africa, Russia, and the Middle East?

- How should policy-makers weigh human rights against other policy priorities—survival, trade, environmental protection?

- What kinds of international action have helped human rights? Not helped?

"How Can We Reconcile Ideals with Practical Imperatives?" ...

Human rights are on a collision course with big business, arms control, and environmental protection. Should free speech in China take precedence over multibillion dollar contracts for Airbus or Boeing airliners? Should religious freedom for Buddhists in Tibet and Catholics in Shanghai outweigh huge contracts to French or U.S. firms to build nuclear power stations? Not only would nuclear power plants lock China into long-term cooperation with the West, they would also help reduce emissions of greenhouse gases by replacing coal-fueled power plants.

A majority in the European Parliament demands that the European Commission block exports of high technology to China until it makes substantial progress toward democracy and respect for human rights—not just among Han Chinese but among Tibetans, Uighurs, and other minorities. Key figures in the U.S. Congress make similar demands of the White House. Republican members accuse the Democratic president of waffling on his pre-election commitments to civil liberties in China.

The U.S. president sends the Secretary of Commerce to meet with congressional critics. She warns: "If you condemn Beijing and block exports, the Chinese will buy what they want from Europe or Japan." The European Commission delivers an analogous message to the European Parliament. One commissioner goes further: He urges some parliamentarians to incite the U.S. Congress to take a harsh stand toward China while Europe takes a milder stance. "That way," he explains, "the Americans will alienate China while we scoop up the best deals."

The Secretary of Defense also lectures the U.S. Congress. "We can't afford to drive China into Russia's embrace. And we need Beijing's good will to keep them from selling missiles to Koraq." Next, the Environmental Protection Agency administrator takes her turn on Capitol Hill. Her theme: "Court Beijing to cut global carbon emissions."

A caucus from the European Parliament and the U.S. Congress decides it must take a stand in support of human rights. Unlike many politicians, most caucus members have no ties to the aerospace or nuclear power industries. Indeed, some represent districts with clothing industries threatened by imports from China.

The parliamentarians ask you, a legal consultant to Amnesty International and to Airbus, to review progress on human rights. They want you to answer the question: "How can we reconcile ideals with practical imperatives?"

CONTENDING CONCEPTS AND EXPLANATIONS

DO THE FREE OWE ANYTHING TO THE UNFREE?

Are we our brothers' and sisters' keepers? Traditional *realpolitik* answers "no." But global idealism and interdependence say "yes."

Most readers of this book are among the freest and richest persons who ever lived. But today less than half of humanity lives in free societies. Do the free owe anything to the unfree? Human rights is about liberation from exploitation—the inhumane treatment of some humans by others, as if they were mere tools or objects. Human rights advocates assert the dignity of each person. Some idealists hold that human rights derive from a higher law imbedded in nature or the will of God.[1] Other advocates simply affirm that human rights *should* exist. The interdependence view adds that if the bell tolls for human rights anywhere, it tolls everywhere.

STATE SOVEREIGNTY VS. OUTSIDE INTERVENTION

Like *realpolitik,* traditional international law was state-centric: It dealt mainly with the rights and duties of *states* regarding one another—not with the rights and duties of individual persons or "peoples." If a state injured an alien, the law supposed that the offense was to the alien's state, not to the individual.

Might made right. Traditional international law asserted the king's unlimited power—sovereignty—over his realm. The king could treat his subjects as he wished. This was an issue of "domestic jurisdiction." Outsiders had no legal basis for protesting how a state dealt with its own subjects, except that European princes sometimes claimed the right to protect Christians in the Muslim-occupied Holy Land.

Even while state-centrism prevailed, individual rights received support from different sources—Aquinas, Luther, Hobbes, Locke, Voltaire, Rousseau. But whether they came from God, from Nature, or from contract, individual rights were strongly affirmed in the U.S. Declaration of Independence and in the U.S. Constitution and its amendments.

The state-centric attitude weakened slightly in the 19th century. Throughout the 20th century the pendulum swung away from a rigid defense of sovereignty toward affirmation of universal human rights—

Are Chinese indifferent to human rights? A boy joins student demonstrators on Beijing's Tiananmen Square in May 1989 a few days before they were run down by tanks and troops of the "People's Liberation Army." His banner rejects military rule and bureaucratic tyranny; it proclaims "long live the people" and human rights.

1. For an argument that humans gradually discern the human rights imbedded in the law of nature, see Jacques Maritain, *The Rights of Man and Natural Law* (New York: Scribner's, 1943); and Joseph W. Evans and Leo R. Ward, eds., *The Social and Political Philosophy of Jacques Maritain: Selected Readings* (New York: Scribner's, 1955).

rights to which all persons are entitled. At the end of the 20th century, however, many Third World leaders asserted that each culture has its own values—its own view of human rights and duties.[2] Western demands for universal recognition of specific rights, they said, was another form of Western imperialism. Opposing such relativism, however, former president of Costa Rica, Oscar Arias Sanchez, in the late 1990s called for a universal code of responsibilities as well as rights.[3]

How to Balance "Minding One's Own Business" and Intervention?

Beginning with George Washington, many U.S. leaders have advised their compatriots to avoid foreign entanglements. Thus, John Quincy Adams in 1821 cautioned against joining ostensibly noble foreign causes that "usurp the standard of freedom." As the Cold War began in 1946–1947, diplomat George F. Kennan argued for "containment" of the USSR, but added that U.S. influence abroad could best be achieved by example—never by precept. After leaving government, Kennan often urged Americans to mind their own business. In 1994, celebrating his 90th birthday, Kennan told the Council of Foreign Relations: "There are limits to what any one sovereign country can do to help another."

A more interventionist course was backed by President Theodore Roosevelt. His 1904 State of the Union message declared that, ordinarily, it is more useful "to concern ourselves with . . . our own moral and material betterment . . . than . . . with trying to better the condition of things in other nations. We have plenty of sins of our own to war against [such as] brutal lawlessness and violent race prejudices. . . . Nevertheless there are occasional crimes committed on so vast a scale and of such peculiar horror [that it becomes] our manifest duty to . . . show our disapproval of the deed." Rarely would the U.S. interfere by force of arms, as it did against Spain in Cuba. But it was "inevitable" that a people concerned with "civil and religious liberty" would condemn the "massacre" of the Jews in Kishinev (by Russians) and the cruel "oppression" of Armenians (by Ottoman Turks).

The UN Charter contradicts itself on these matters. Article 1 commits members to respect "equal rights and self-determination of peoples" and to promote "respect for human rights and for fundamental freedoms for all" regardless of "race, sex, language, or religion." But Article 2 asserts that the United Nations may not "intervene in matters which are essentially within the domestic jurisdiction of any state"—adding, however, that this principle "shall not prejudice the application of enforcement measures under Chapter VII" to maintain the peace. This qualification produced a breach in the doctrine of domestic jurisdiction large enough for tanks and war planes to enter.

THE DUTY AND RIGHT TO INTERVENE

At the end of the 20th century some observers insisted that the international community could intervene in any society for three reasons:

2. For the debate on this issue between Singapore's elder statesman, Lee Kwan Yew, and Korean opposition leader Kim Dae Jung, see *The New Shape of World Politics: Contending Paradigms in International Relations* (New York: Norton, 1997), 219–241.

3. Oscar Arias Sanchez, "Global Demilitarization," *Christian Science Monitor*, November 3, 1997, 15.

1. To maintain international security, since civil unrest often spills across borders

2. To uphold human rights, especially the right to life

3. To alleviate suffering caused by famine or other humanitarian crises

Such intervention may be *requested* by a host government seeking assistance, *imposed* upon a government threatening its own people or others, or *provided* to "failed states" where anarchy and banditry have displaced government.[4]

The realities of global interdependence helped to push the dogma of state sovereignty onto the ash heap of history. Broad recognition of transcendent human rights received sustenance from many sources:

The emergence of an international mindset. Nearly unstoppable radio and television waves help people know about famine and massacres in remote places.

Brave individuals. The words and deeds of Ralph Bunche, Martin Luther King, Jr., Mother Teresa, Andrei Sakharov, and Rigoberta Menchu—all winners of the Nobel Peace Prize—echoed around the globe.

The First African American to Win the Nobel Peace Prize

Ralph Bunche was for years the second most powerful official in the United Nations, but at times could not get a room in the best hotels in the U.S. South. The first African American to win the Nobel Peace Prize (1950), he understood that "there could be no national security without civil rights, and there could be no international peace without human rights."[1] Though the only black to graduate from UCLA in 1927, Bunche was class valedictorian. He was in the forefront of building black consciousness in the 1930s and 1940s. As the key UN official dealing with international crises, he practically invented UN peacekeeping.

1. Charles P. Henry, "Civil Rights and National Security: The Case of Ralph Bunche," in *Ralph Bunche: The Man and His Times,* ed. Benjamin Rivlin (New York: Holmes & Meier, 1990), 50–66 at 63. The other essays in the volume examine Bunche as scholar activist, Africanist and decolonizer, and world statesman.

Bold leaders. Presidents Jimmy Carter, Oscar Arias Sanchez, Mikhail Gorbachev, and François Mitterrand raised the priority given to human rights in the world arena.

Nongovernmental organizations (NGOs). Organizations such as the International Red Cross, Oxfam, and Doctors Without Borders (*Médicins Sans Frontières*) intervened where governments did not tread.[5]

A Right to Life: "No Contamination without Representation"

Faced with radioactive pollution of the planet, idealist Eleanor Roosevelt and realist theologian Paul Tillich agreed in the 1950s on the following:

The sovereignty of the human community comes before all others—before the sovereignty of groups, tribes, or nations. In that community, man has natural rights. He has the right to live and to grow, to breathe unpoisoned air, to work on uncontaminated soil. . . . [Emphasis added]

If what nations are doing has the effect of destroying these natural rights, whether by upsetting the delicate balances on which life depends, or fouling the air, or devitalizing the land, or tampering with the genetic integrity of man himself, then it becomes necessary for people to restrain and tame the nations.

This declaration came from an appeal to halt nuclear testing by the National Committee for a Sane Nuclear Policy (SANE), published in the *New York Times,* November 15, 1957. Six months later another SANE petition began: "The World's Peoples Have a Right to Demand No Contamination without Representation."

4. See essays by Robert H. Jackson, Jack Donnelly, Robert Pastor, and Philippe Garigue and others in *International Journal* [special issue: "Humane Intervention"] 48, no. 4 (autumn 1993); Boutros Boutros-Ghali, *An Agenda for Peace,* 2d ed. (New York: United Nations, 1995); Morton H. Halperin and David J. Scheffer, eds, *Self-Determination in the New World Order* (Washington, D.C.: Carnegie Endowment for International Peace, 1992); and Lori Fisler Damrosch, ed., *Enforcing Restraint: Collective Intervention in Internal Conflicts* (New York: Council on Foreign Relations, 1993).

5. See *Life, Death and Aid: The* Médicins Sans Frontières *Report on World Crisis Intervention* (New York: Routledge, 1993).

Is there a human right to be able to walk in one's fields without risk of losing a leg from a land mine? In the 1990s several NGOs focused international attention on the dangers of anti-personnel land mines. More than a thousand NGOs formed a coalition that worked with Canada, Mozambique, Norway, South Africa, and other governments to establish a treaty banning land mines. The International Campaign to Ban Land Mines won the Nobel Peace Prize in 1997. But Washington wanted to keep mines in Korea to thwart a DPRK attack.

WHAT? OUR TECHNOLOGY WORKED PERFECTLY...

LAND MINE MANUFACTURERS IN INDUSTRIAL NATIONS

THIRD WORLD VICTIMS

DANZIGER

The Christian Science Monitor
Los Angeles Times Syndicate

Legal precedent. Individuals, along with corporations and international organizations, have become "subjects" of international law. The European Court of Human Rights (not to be confused with the European Court of Justice) hears complaints by individuals against their own governments.[6]

A growing consensus on human rights norms. Since 1945 most governments formally acknowledge a wide range of human rights. They accept not only the right of each people to live but also to "develop." The tides of human consciousness and law press for liberation.

COMPARING THEORY AND REALITY: REVOLUTIONS IN AWARENESS AND ACTION

BREAKING THE BONDS OF SLAVERY

6. Since 1971 it has become possible for individuals to complain to a UN committee regarding any "consistent pattern of gross violations of human rights and fundamental freedoms." The mechanism by which they may complain ("the 1503 Procedure"), however, does not ensure confidentiality.

7. Martin A. Klein, ed., *Breaking the Chains: Slavery, Bondage, and Emancipation in Modern Africa and Asia* (Madison: University of Wisconsin Press, 1993); and Paul Gorden Lauren, *Power and Prejudice: The Politics and Diplomacy of Racial Discrimination,* 2d ed. (Boulder, Colo.: Westview, 1996).

No problem illustrates better the transformation of international belief and action on human rights than **slavery**—human bondage in which the slave is regarded as the property of the owner.[7] Serfs, by contrast, are in semi-bondage, supposed to have some rights. Slavery is the ultimate exploitation of humans by humans, often imbedded in a structure of coercive repression. Slavery can extinguish mind and soul as well as physical freedom, as we see in the sidebar on page 483.

Slavery was found in Babylon and other ancient cultures. Some Greek,

Enslaving the Mind: The "Mankurt" and the Soviet System

Central Asians recall how the Zhuan'zhuan people advancing across the Sarozek Desert made human robots of young males captured from other tribes. The Zhuan'zhuan placed a wet, sticky camel udder over the victim's shaved head and let it shrink under the desert sun. The pressure on the skull killed most captives but some survived. They lost all memory but became obedient robots well suited for guarding camel herds. Such a being was called a *mankurt*.

Ana, mother of a young man who disappeared in battle, made her way by camel into Zhuan'zhuan territory. There she found her son, now a mankurt. He did not recognize his own mother and shot her with an arrow. Ana's burial place became a revered cemetery for her own people.

The Zhuan'zhuan faded, but much of Central Asia later came under Tsarist Russian and then Soviet rule. The Soviet system also sought to erase memory. It destroyed alleged "enemies of the people" and tried to make them "non-persons."

The mankurt story is passed on by the Kyrgyz writer Chingiz Aitmatov. His novel, *The Day Lasts More than a Hundred Years* (University of Indiana Press, 1988), tells how Soviet authorities also tried to destroy memory: They fenced off the ancient cemetery where Ana lay; refused to use the local language; pressed Kyrgyz and Kazaks to forget their own traditions; took away a school teacher who told his son and his pupils stories not found in the official textbooks.

When Aitmatov was ten years old, his own father disappeared. But Aitmatov could not forget his father. In 1961 Aitmatov dedicated a novella to his father, adding: "Father, I know not where you are buried." Only in 1991, at age 62, did he learn of his father's fate: In 1938 Stalin's secret police had shot his father and 137 other Kyrgyz intellectuals and left them in a mass grave.

Should such things be forgotten? It was not until 1987 that the Gorbachev administration closed Perm 36, the most notorious concentration camp for political prisoners of the former Soviet Union. In 1997 a group of Russian academics decided to preserve the prison complex, isolated in the Urals, as a museum. Its watchtowers once loomed over 2,000 dissidents. One Perm 36 survivor, Sergei Kovalev, in the 1990s still campaigned for human rights, inside and then outside the Yeltsin government. Another surviver, Natan Sharansky, became a major figure in Israeli politics.

Roman, and Arabic writers described other races as subhuman—fit to be enslaved. But Europeans also enslaved and enserfed other Europeans.[8]

When Europeans landed in America in the 16th century, most cultures took slavery for granted. Spanish explorers claimed the New World by a grant from Pope Alexander VI and from King Ferdinand and Queen Isabella.[9] Upon landing the Spaniards read to the natives (in a tongue unknown to them) an order to submit. If the natives obeyed, they would be treated charitably. If they resisted, they would be killed or enslaved. Any deaths and losses would be the natives' fault, for they had been warned. Having justified themselves, the Spaniards enslaved or massacred the natives.

One of the first protests against such practices took place in 1511 in today's Dominican Republic. With the son of Christopher Columbus present in church, Father Anton Montesino chastised the island's Spanish rulers: "You are living in deadly sin for the atrocities you tyrannically impose on these innocent people. . . . What right have you to enslave them?

8. "Slave" comes from Slav—captured and enslaved by West Europeans in the early Middle Ages. German landowners in the Baltic treated Estonians and Latvian serfs as virtual slaves—selling individuals and breaking up families.

9. In 1493 Pope Alexander VI, "by the authority of Almighty God," purported to "give, grant, and assign" to the Spanish king all lands found 100 leagues west and south of the Azores and Cape Verde unless they were already ruled by a Christian prince. But Spain and Portugal in 1494 moved the line westward in a way that put Brazil (discovered later) in Portugal's domain.

What authority did you use to make war against them who lived at peace on their territories, killing them cruelly with methods never before heard of? . . . Aren't they human beings? Have they no rational soul?"[10]

When colonial authorities complained to King Ferdinand, he ordered an end to such preaching. But a former landowner become monk, **Bartolomé de Las Casas**, took up where Montesino left off. His *Brief Relation of the Destruction of the Indies* (published in Seville in 1523) described the massacre and torture (for example, slow grilling over a fire, gagged to muffle screams) of huge numbers of natives in today's Dominican Republic, Mexico, and Guatemala.

Some legal scholars joined Las Casas but others defended Spanish rule. Juan Gines de Sepulveda in 1547 asserted that the Native Americans were "innately servile." The Aztecs, he argued, were "barbarous, uncultivated, and inhumane little men." They cut out hearts and ate the flesh of others. The natives gave up only silver and gold but got in exchange "virtue, humanity, and the true religion."

Spain's Council of the Indies listened to both sides without endorsing either. Still, Las Casas had some impact. In 1573 the Council ordered that the Spanish role in the New World be one of pacification—not conquest. The Spanish crown did not ban force, but it disowned the ruthless methods used by the conquistadores.

As the New World's native peoples perished, Europeans brought in slaves from Africa. Slavery became an integral part of the international political economy: Slaves from Africa cultivated sugar, tobacco, and cotton—producing capital for England's Industrial Revolution. Even Voltaire and other Enlightenment philosophers portrayed blacks as subhuman.

In the late 18th century some English dissenters from established churches—Granville Sharp, Benjamin Rush, James Ramsay, John Wesley—launched the first serious efforts to ban slavery altogether. But while Thomas Jefferson wrote that "all men are created equal," the U.S. Constitution permitted slave imports until 1808. U.S. ships defied European efforts to halt the slave trade. Slavery was not banned in the U.S. until the 1860s. Before and after the Civil War many Americans who demanded the abolition of slavery also worked for women's rights and for universal education—other forms of liberation.

By the mid-19th century the major European powers had abolished slavery in their own realms and had begun to attack slavery everywhere. The 1890 Brussels Conference adopted a treaty abolishing the slave trade and establishing elaborate international machinery to suppress it. Even

10. These words were recorded by Bartolomé de Las Casas. His writings and those of Sepulveda are reprinted in Marvin Lunenfeld, ed., *1492: Discovery, Invasion, Encounter: Sources and Interpretations* (Lexington, Mass.: D. C. Heath, 1991), 199–228.

tighter restrictions were written into the 1926 Slavery Convention and its protocol, as amended in 1953.

A Supplementary Convention on the Abolition of Slavery drafted in 1956 sought to abolish not only slavery but **practices similar to slavery**, such as debt bondage, serfdom, coerced marriage for payment, inheritance of widows, coerced marriage of minors, and branding persons to indicate servile status. But the supplementary convention set up no special body to monitor implementation. It required only that signatories send copies of relevant laws to the UN Secretary-General. Among the countries still not party to this convention in 1997 were Gabon, Guinea-Bissau, and Kenya; also Indonesia and North Korea.

The Universal Declaration of Human Rights approved by most UN members in 1948 provides: "No one shall be held in slavery or servitude; slavery and the slave trade shall be prohibited in all their forms." Virtually the same language is used in the 1966 International Covenant on Civil and Political Rights, the American Convention on Human Rights, the African Charter of Human and Peoples' Rights, and the European Convention on Human Rights.

Apartheid—racial segregation and a racial pecking order—was the law of South Africa until the 1990s. The UN Convention on the Suppression and Punishment of the Crime of Apartheid (1973) imposed individual responsibility on government officials for upholding apartheid. As we see in the sidebar, one such individual sought amnesty by confessing to

Apartheid—racial separation—pervaded South African life before the 1990s. Here we see segregated stands in a sports arena in 1969. Observing racial segregation in U.S. military facilities during World War II, Eleanor Roosevelt persuaded her husband, President Franklin Roosevelt, to begin the work of ending it.

Individuals Responsible for Apartheid: The Banality of Evil

Confronting one of his accusers, police officer Jeffrey Benzien said: "If I say to Mr. Jacobs I put the electrodes on his nose, I may be wrong. If I say I attached them to his genitals, I may be wrong. If I say I put a probe in his rectum, I may be wrong. I could have used any one of those methods." The "probe," one accuser said, was sometimes a broomstick. Accuser Jacobs vividly recalled the "wet bag" at which the policeman was adept: A cloth placed over the head led the victim to the brink of asphyxiation. The now humble officer wondered in 1997 what kind of person could have done such things, but he also believed his work had curbed terrorism. Benzien said he followed orders. One of his superiors admitted that he once held down one of Benzien's victims. See Suzanne Daley, "Apartheid Torturer Testifies, As Evil Shows Its Banal Face," *New York Times*, November 9, 1997, 1, 12.

How Not to Liberate Women

U.S. Surgeon General Dr. Joycelyn Elders declared in 1994 that the U.S. "Medicaid system must have been developed by a white male slave owner. It pays for you to be pregnant and have a baby, but it won't pay for much family planning. White male slave owners wanted a lot of healthy slaves, people to work. We don't need slaves any more. We need healthy, educated, motivated children with hope." The low level of services for poor women contributes to "poverty, ignorance, and enslavement." See *New York Times*, February 26, 1994.

South Africa's Truth and Reconciliation Commission in November 1997.

Despite promises and exhortation, many UN member states permit de facto slavery. A UN study warns: "New forms of servitude and gross exploitation have come to light only in recent years, as violators seek to circumvent laws or to take advantage of changing economic and social conditions."[11] Human rights advocates demand international mechanisms to prevent the sale of children, child prostitution, child pornography, and child labor. Some demand stiffer laws in each country and urge international police cooperation to interrupt and punish the transport of persons in danger of being enslaved. Others (see sidebar) suggest that the long-term solution lies in extending the reach of democracy, improving education and living standards, and supporting social empowerment.

No government espouses slavery. The most blatant forms of slavery have disappeared. But practices akin to slavery continue. They are highlighted in many pages of the U.S. State Department's annual reports to Congress on the conditions of women, children, and labor around the world.[12]

LAWS OF WAR: PRISONERS AND NONCOMBATANTS

Human rights protection crept in through a back door—the rules of war. Europeans long believed they could treat prisoners of war as slaves. As Hugo Grotius, a father of international law, wrote in the early 17th century:

Not only do the prisoners of war themselves become slaves, but also their descendants for ever. . . . By the law of nations those become our slaves who are born of our slave women. . . . The effects of this law are unlimited. . . . There is no suffering which may not be inflicted with impunity upon such slaves.[13]

This view began to change after the 1648 Treaty of Westphalia as prisoners came to be seen as captives of the victorious state rather than of an individual warrior. This led in the 18th and 19th centuries to the practice of exchanging prisoners. In the 19th century the Red Cross and other humanitarian agencies pressed governments to assure humane treatment of prisoners. Conferences held at The Hague in 1899 and 1907 codified the laws of war.[14] These were strengthened in the 1929 Geneva Convention on Treatment of Prisoners. When that convention also proved weak, it was elaborated in three conventions signed in Geneva in 1949. They spelled out duties to prisoners of war, those wounded and shipwrecked, and those wounded on land. A special role was assigned to the International Committee of the Red Cross (ICRC). Hospital ships and medical personnel designated with a red cross (or red crescent or red lion) were to be respected.[15]

11. *Slavery* (UN publication, Sales No. E.84/XIV.1 [1982]).

12. See, for example, reports on Afghanistan, China, India, Kuwait, Sudan, and Thailand in U.S. Department of State, *Country Reports on Human Rights Practices for 1996* (Washington, D.C.: Government Printing Office, 1997).

13. Grotius, quoted in an editorial comment by Theodor Meron, *American Journal of International Law* 85 (1991): 116.

14. The codifying efforts of Dr. Francis Lieber during the U.S. Civil War and the Institute of International Law's 1880 *Oxford Manual* provided a foundation for the Hague conferences.

15. See W. Michael Reisman and Chris T. Antoniou, *The Laws of War: A Comprehensive Collection of Primary Documents on International Laws Governing Armed Conflict* (New York: Vintage, 1994).

The 1907 Hague Conference also established rules for treatment of noncombatants in occupied territory. Private property and family honor, for example, were to be respected. These rules were expanded in a fourth Geneva Convention on the Protection of Civilian Persons in Time of War, also signed in 1949. Not just family honor was to be respected; rape and enforced prostitution were banned. Again the ICRC was given special status.

Most governments acceded to the four **Geneva Conventions of 1949**, though abuses are common. But many guerrillas and warlords do not know of the conventions or choose to ignore them, as we saw in Chapter 15. For its part, Israel denies that the Arab residents of Jerusalem have the rights of noncombatants in occupied territory. Israel treats Jerusalem as regained territory, as Iraq did Kuwait in 1990—putatively the nineteenth province of Iraq.

WAR CRIMES

The actions of Adolf Hitler helped to change human rights law. Following World War II, the victors organized the **International Military Tribunal at Nuremberg** that tried twenty-two German leaders. It found some defendants guilty of

crimes against peace—planning and carrying out wars of aggression contrary to the 1928 Kellogg-Briand Pact on the Renunciation of War;

war crimes—violating rules of war, for example, by waging unrestricted submarine warfare contrary to the London Naval Agreement of 1930; and

crimes against humanity—abusing civilian populations (by murder, deportation, enslavement) in Germany and in occupied territories, contrary to the Hague and Geneva Conventions.[16]

The defense at Nuremberg argued that the accused should not be tried for acts not deemed criminal before 1945. The judges replied that the charter establishing the Nuremberg Tribunal did not invent law. It expressed existing treaty law from 1899, 1907, 1929, 1930—signed and never repudiated by Germany.

Could an individual be held responsible for war crimes? The defense at Nuremberg said "no," because the accused parties merely followed higher orders. The judges disagreed. They held: "Individuals have international duties which transcend the national obligations of obedience imposed by the individual state."[17] "Orders" could mitigate but not excuse the crime.

16. "'Indictment,' 1 International Military Tribunal, Trial of Major War Criminals 29–40 (1947)," in *International Law and World Order: A Problem-Oriented Coursebook,* ed. Burns H. Weston, Richard A. Falk, and Anthony A. D'Amato (St. Paul, Minn.: West, 1990), 150–171. See also Alan S. Rosenbaum, *Prosecuting Nazi War Criminals* (Boulder, Colo.: Westview, 1997).

17. Already in 1919 the Versailles Treaty asserted the right of the Allied Powers to "to bring before military tribunals persons accused of having committed acts in violation of the laws and customs of war." The treaty even called for a court to try the Kaiser "for a supreme offense against international morality and the sanctity of treaties." But Germany in 1919 rejected these articles of Versailles and proposed a tribunal to try leaders of *all* belligerents.

German Chief Air Marshal Hermann Goering (left of center) takes notes on the third day of the Nuremberg trials of accused Nazi war criminals. To his right are Rudolf Hess and Hitler's Foreign Minister Joachim von Ribbentrop. The tribunal upheld the principle of individual culpability for certain kinds of war crimes and crimes against humanity.

Two Positive Replies

Am I responsible for others? Martin Niemöller answered "yes." A German U-boat commander in World War I, Niemöller later became a Protestant minister. He denounced Hitler in the 1930s and was imprisoned at the Dachau concentration camp. A survivor, he later explained:

First they came for the Jews and I did not speak out—because I was not a Jew. Then they came for the Communists and I did not speak out—because I was not a Communist. Then they came for the trade unionists and I did not speak out—because I was not a trade unionist. Then they came for me—and there was no one left to speak out for me.

Factory owner Oskar Schindler also answered "yes." He did not criticize *der Führer.* Instead, he bribed Nazi authorities to spare more than a thousand Polish Jews from the death camps. Viewing the film *Schindler's List* in 1994, many Germans wondered why so few of their compatriots had tried to thwart the Holocaust: "Where was everybody else?"

18. In 1955 five Japanese individuals sued the Japanese government in Tokyo District Court of Tokyo for damages due to injuries sustained by the atomic bombings at Hiroshima and Nagasaki (the Shimoda Case). The Japanese government responded that the U.S. bombings were permitted by international law, because the weapons were new and had never been explicitly banned. The court sided with the plaintiffs saying that states have a duty to refrain from causing unnecessary suffering whether the specific act is regulated or not. The court ruled, however, that the Japanese government was not liable for the damages and that Tokyo had renounced all such individual claims in its peace treaty with Washington.

The court sentenced twelve defendants to death, acquitted three, and gave long prison terms to the others. Similar trials were held for major Japanese leaders. Other persons accused of war crimes were arrested and tried in Yugoslavia, Israel, and elsewhere. More than 10,000 were tried in the USSR; more than 12,000 in West Germany.[18]

GENOCIDE IN PEACE OR WAR

Nuremberg made it explicit: Individuals could be tried for **crimes against humanity**. But Nuremberg also underscored a major gap in the law: Crimes against humanity could be punished by an international court only if they took place in wartime or in preparation for war. The court found that in implementing the Nazi Party's "master race" theory "the conspirators joined in a program of relentless persecution of Jews, designed to exterminate them." But the court claimed jurisdiction only over acts committed as part of Germany's aggressive war—not over persecution of Jews and other civilians in Germany in peacetime. Had there been no war, no international tribunal could have tried Hitler's henchmen for launching the Holocaust.

For millennia governments have massacred their own and other peoples. But in 1948 the United Nations explicitly banned genocide—"people-murder"—and made it a crime under international law whether committed in war or peace.[19] The UN General Assembly adopted unanimously the **Convention on the Prevention and Punishment of the Crime of Genocide** (with abstentions by Saudi Arabia, South Africa, and the Soviet bloc). The convention (treaty) forbids "acts committed with *intent* to destroy, in whole or in part, a national, ethnical, racial or religious group, *as such* [emphases added]." Genocidal acts are defined to include not only killing but "deliberately inflicting on any group conditions of life calculated" to destroy the group including prevention of births and forcible transfer of one group's children to another group. The convention bans not just genocide but conspiracy to commit genocide and incitement to and complicity in genocide.[20] But intent is crucial. Not every mass murder is genocide.

The Genocide Convention makes clear that genocide is not a matter of essentially domestic jurisdiction. Any party to the convention may call upon competent United Nations organs to prevent and suppress genocidal acts. The convention declares that genocidists "shall be punished, whether they are constitutionally responsible rulers, public officials or private individuals." Signatory states are required to pass laws that give effect to the convention.

The Genocide Convention entered force in 1951 and by the 1990s had been ratified by more than 110 countries.[21] But the convention is nearly toothless because no permanent international court has been set up to hear genocide cases.[22] Who will try and punish genocidists? The treaty grants jurisdiction to courts in the very country where the genocidal acts took place—as if an Iraqi court could try Saddam Hussein's actions against Kurds and Shiites![23] The treaty also permits genocidal acts to be tried "by such international penal tribunal as may have jurisdiction with respect to those Contracting Parties which shall have accepted its jurisdiction." Here we have another unrealistic provision. Only if such a court existed and only if Iraq accepted its jurisdiction in advance could Saddam Hussein be tried before it.[24]

Weakening the convention still further, many signatories have entered

19. Raphael Lemkin, a Polish jurist whose family had been wiped out, coined the word "genocide" in 1944 from *genos* (Greek "people" or "race") and *caedere* (Latin "kill").

20. Many terms are ambiguous. What does it mean to kill "a part" of a group? To "conspire" to commit genocide? To be "complicit" in such an act?

21. Even after the UN General Assembly voted for the convention, individual states had to sign and then ratify it. If a state did not sign before the treaty entered force, it could accede. Following are a few patterns:

Country	Sign	Ratify	Accede
China	1949	1983	
Croatia			1992
Estonia			1991
Iraq			1979
Latvia			1992
North Korea			1989
USSR	12/16/49	1954	
U.S.	12/11/48	1988	
Yugoslavia	12/11/48	1950	

SOURCE: *Multilateral Treaties Deposited with the Secretary-General* (New York: Office of Legal Affairs, United Nations, annual).

22. See the report by Benjamin C. G. Whitaker to the Sub-Commission on Prevention of Discrimination and Protection of Minorities of the UN Economic and Social Council (UN Doc.E/CN.4/Sub.2/1985/6).

23. Iraq acceded to the convention in June 1979.

24. *After* the collapse of the Nazi regime, German courts tried and punished many ex-Nazis for war crimes. But Belgrade courts in the 1990s were unlikely to prosecute Serbians for genocidal acts in Bosnia.

A higher percentage of the Cambodian people was killed by Pol Pot's Khmer Rouge regime in the 1970s than by any other demicidist of the 20th century. In 1993 children played next to the "Killing Fields" memorial located on the outskirts of Phnom Penh. Betrayed by his own followers, a frail and broken Pol Pot was subjected to a mock trial in 1997 and put under house arrest.

25. Most jurists agree that the Genocide Convention belongs to the peremptory norms (*ius cogens*) of international law.

26. When Israel apologized, Argentina accepted this as reparation. Israel tried and executed Adolf Eichman under its 1950 law to punish "crimes against the Jewish people" and "crimes against humanity" committed in Europe before and during World War II. See Louis Henkin, *How Nations Behave: Law and Foreign Policy,* 2d ed. (New York: Columbia University Press, 1979), 269–278.

27. The U.S. Assistant Secretary of State in 1959 referred to evidence that in Tibet "the Chinese Communists have committed acts violating the norms established by the Genocide Convention of 1948." But Washington did not then recognize the Chinese Communist regime.

28. The 1949 convention was adopted by more than 150 states, including Yugoslavia in 1950 and the U.S. in 1956 (both with reservations). The convention seeks to protect civilians in the territory of a belligerent state or in occupied territory. It bans "wilful killing, torture . . . wilfully causing great suffering or serious injury . . . unlawful deportation or transfer . . . taking of hostages and extensive destruction and appropriation of property, not justified by military necessity and carried out unlawfully and wantonly." Enforcement provisions are somewhat stronger than the Genocide Convention. Each signatory is obliged to enact laws to provide effective penal sanctions against persons who violate the convention, to search for such persons, and to try them in its own courts or to hand them over to other signatory states for trial.

all manner of "reservations." For its part, the U.S. did not even ratify the convention until 1988—eight years after Communist China. Seeking to protect states' rights, Washington entered five "reservations" so sweeping that Greece, Italy, Ireland, and Mexico called them "invalid" because they violated the "object and purpose" of the convention.

Many jurists say that any state may try a genocidist because genocide is a crime against humanity—like piracy, the slave trade, and skyjacking, all subject to universal jurisdiction.[25] Any state may try pirates, regardless of where the act took place. But when Israeli citizens (perhaps agents) abducted a Nazi genocidist from Argentina and delivered him to Israeli justice in 1960, the UN Security Council asserted that Israel had violated Argentina's territorial integrity and called on Israel to make "reparation."[26]

Governments are reluctant formally to accuse one another of genocide.[27] Pragmatists fear that charges of genocide will only inflame tensions and open a Pandora's Box. Who is to be accused—the prime minister, the field commander, the squad leader, or "all of the above"? And will top leaders be tried even if they are also the ones who negotiate a peace treaty? Whoever is tried, can't their lawyers argue that the accused acted on "orders" or in "self-defense"? If the point is to stop blood-letting, why try to prosecute or punish?

In 1993 Bosnia-Herzegovina went to the International Court of Justice (ICJ) and charged Serbia with violating the UN Charter, the Genocide Convention, and the 1949 Geneva Convention on Protection of Civilians in Time of War.[28] Bypassing many questions about its jurisdiction, the

UN and EU observers and UN Blue Helmets (mostly from Europe) did little to stop or even to protest ethnic cleansing in the former Yugoslavia in the years 1992–1995. No permanent court to hear cases brought under the Genocide Convention existed.

court ruled (13–1) that it could provide provisional relief under the Genocide Convention. The ICJ enjoined Serbia to constrain any military or irregular forces it directed or supported from committing genocidal acts against Bosnian Muslims or "any other national, ethnical, racial or religious group."

Prodded by numerous reports of ethnic cleansing, the United Nations investigated events in the former Yugoslavia. A Commission of Experts noted that the same act could be both a war crime and a crime against humanity. It found that policies aimed at ethnic cleansing had used murder, torture, rape, forcible removal, and wanton destruction of property. "Those practices constitute crimes against humanity and . . . war crimes. Furthermore, such acts could also fall within the meaning of the Genocide Convention." Acting under Chapter VII, the Security Council then established an International Tribunal at The Hague to "prosecute persons [not governments] responsible for serious violations of international humanitarian law" in the former Yugoslavia.[29] A similar tribunal was set up to try genocide cases in Rwanda. In each case the UN member states undercut investigations and the court by withholding adequate funding. There were too few judges, too few courtrooms, and—in Rwanda—too few cells for the accused. By 1997 a few medium-ranking Serbs were convicted at The Hague while some accused Croats and Bosnians awaited trial. NATO troops enforcing the Dayton Accords were reluctant to arrest the big fish, so they roamed free. The Rwanda Tribunal, however, had twenty-three indicted suspects in custody in 1997, including the alleged

29. Snezana Trifunovska, "International Involvement in the Former Yugoslavia's Dissolution and Peace Settlement," *Nationalities Papers* 25, no. 3 (September 1997): 517–536.

mastermind of the killings. One of the indicted was accused of rape and sexual abuse committed during the genocide.[30]

It may be too late to punish genocidal acts that have already taken place. But why not establish a permanent court to hear any future genocide cases? Such a court's very existence might deter future people-murder if ministers, generals, and squad leaders realized they might be punished for genocidal actions. Even Saddam Hussein might pause before gassing a Kurdish village if he could be arrested and tried outside Iraq.[31]

Spurred by NGOs and many small and medium-sized states, a strong movement took shape in the 1990s to establish a permanent International Criminal Court (ICC) to try those accused of genocide, war crimes (including rape), and other crimes against humanity when national judicial systems fail to do so. The court could be a useful supplement to the Security Council, but some permanent members sought to limit the court's powers. Washington, London, and Paris claimed to support the ICC, but worked to subordinate it to their Security Council prerogatives. For example, they proposed that the court's range of prosecutions be approved in advance by the Security Council; they wanted limits on the crimes that could be addressed by the ICC without permission of interested governments. Human Rights Watch and some other NGOs urged that the court be established even if the U.S. and other great powers did not immediately accede.

THE UNIVERSAL DECLARATION AND COVENANTS

In 1948 the UN General Assembly also adopted the **Universal Declaration of Human Rights**. It elaborated civil and political rights such as those enshrined in the U.S. Declaration of Independence and the U.S. Constitution. But it also acknowledged economic and social rights such as "the right to work" and to "just and favorable remuneration."

This distinction between political and economic rights reflected the Western idea of limited government versus Communist demands for government control of the economy. The U.S. was willing to endorse the right to work and to fair remuneration as *goals* but not as government obligations. Communists downplayed "mere" political rights in societies where the rich controlled the media. They said that the right to organize politically is meaningless for people who live in abject poverty.[32]

The Universal Declaration of Human Rights owed much to **Eleanor Roosevelt**, who led the U.S. negotiators and chaired the UN drafting commission. She helped bridge differences between Western and other concepts of human rights.[33]

30. The arrests of more suspects by NATO troops in late 1997–early 1998 and an infusion of money for more judges and cells made the Hague tribunal more credible. See "At Last, a Court that War Criminals Must Take Seriously," *The Economist*, January 31, 1998, 51–52.

31. The UN Security Council *condemned* Iraq in 1990 for violating the 1949 Geneva Convention by its mistreatment of Kuwaiti and third-state nationals, forced population transfers, and destruction of property. But nothing was done to *punish* Iraqi leaders or military officers.

32. Before Gorbachev all Soviet leaders insisted that human rights are subordinate to the needs of the class struggle. They downgraded "bourgeois" political rights (such as a free press) as irrelevant in the Soviet Union's classless society where no contradictions divide leaders from the people. The Soviet system, they said, provides economic rights unknown in the capitalist world. Gorbachev asserted that "all-human" interests take precedence over class and all other interests.

33. Jason Berger, *A New Deal for the World: Eleanor Roosevelt and American Foreign Policy* (New York: Social Science Monographs, Columbia University Press, 1981), 67–74.

A U.S. representative to the United Nations, Eleanor Roosevelt helped forge the consensus that in 1948 endorsed the Universal Declaration of Human Rights.

But the Universal Declaration represented a moral—not a legal—commitment by its signatories. Nearly two decades later, in 1966, the UN General Assembly adopted two follow-up "covenants"[34] that established legal obligations for states that joined them: The **International Covenant on Civil and Political Rights** bound each signatory state to uphold for individuals the rights of expression, of peaceful assembly, of association with others in trade unions, and of taking part in public life and elections. Ethnic and other minorities had "the right, in community with the other members of their group," to enjoy their own culture, religion, and language.

The **International Covenant on Economic, Social, and Cultural Rights** emphasized "the right to work" and to "fair wages and equal remuneration for work of equal value." It spelled out the right of "everyone to the . . . highest attainable standard of physical and mental health," to education, and to participation in cultural life.

Each covenant began by affirming that "all peoples have the right to self-determination" and "may dispose of their natural wealth for their own ends." The political-civil rights covenant obligated each signatory state to ensure to "*all individuals within its territory* [emphases added]" the rights specified without "discrimination of any kind, such as race, sex, language, religion, opinion, national or social origins, property, birth or other status." The economic-social covenant also banned discrimination but gave "developing countries" the option of restricting the economic rights of non-nationals.

34. "Covenant" suggested to Jews and Christians a sacred pact like the one between God and His Chosen People.

Despite signing these covenants, many Asian and African governments continued to assert in the 1990s that their economic conditions and unique cultures exempted them from Western conceptions of human rights. In August 1997 North Korea announced it was withdrawing from the Political Covenant after it was reprimanded for human rights deficiencies and for failing to report on its implementation of the accord. The eighteen-member UN human rights committee responded on October 30, 1997, that no signatory can withdraw from the covenant, which has no provision for termination or denunciation—a deliberate omission, not a mere oversight.

WOMEN'S RIGHTS AS HUMAN RIGHTS

Half of humanity has been subject to discrimination for millennia. Like men, women have been enslaved. But, far more often than men, they have also been raped or compelled to live as concubines or prostitutes, and generally treated as the inferior sex.[35]

Power politics has aggravated the condition of women in many ways. Persecution of witches was endorsed by Jean Bodin (1530–1596), an exponent of mercantilism and state sovereignty, because he saw witchcraft as a form of birth control. Fewer babies would curtail the state's wealth and the armed forces needed for sovereignty.[36] Moving in the other direction, literacy for both genders became the norm in 17th-century Sweden. But though religious reformers wanted all people to read, many religions condone male supremacy into the 21st century.

As we saw in earlier chapters, gynocide—killing female embryos, babies, and even adults—is widely practiced in India and China. Many African girls are still subject to clitorectomy in the name of local "culture." Apart from physical abuse, gender discrimination is still widespread, for example, in wage differentials.

Women's political participation has been curtailed in many societies. The first European country to grant women the right to vote was Finland—in 1906. Women did not win the right to vote in the U.S. until 1920; in Switzerland, 1971. The view that democracies do not fight other democracies (Chapter 10) could not really be tested when half the *demos* had no vote.

The United Nations has treated women's rights as a subset of human rights, to be protected like other rights by law. The United Nations adopted a Convention on the Political Rights of Women in 1952. It asserted that women are entitled to vote in all elections on equal terms with men and

35. The ambiguous status of women is reflected in etymology. Old English *cwene* gives us "queen," but it also meant woman, prostitute, wife.

36. J. Ann Tickner, *Gender in International Relations: Feminist Perspectives on Achieving Global Security* (New York: Columbia University Press, 1992), 81.

to hold public office on terms equal with men. However, the U.S. Senate did not assent to this mild commitment until 1976.

In 1979 the UN General Assembly adopted the **Convention on the Elimination of All Forms of Discrimination Against Women**, which entered force in 1981. The convention banned any gender-based distinction impairing women's "human rights and fundamental freedoms" in any field. It required parties to embody gender equality in their laws and to eliminate prejudices and practices based on alleged superiority of either sex.[37] Iraq and Libya acceded to the convention but entered reservations that put the "laws of personal status derived from the Islamic Shariah" above the convention.[38]

Enforcement of the 1979 convention is lax. Signatories are required to report on laws or other measures adopted to implement the treaty. The reports are reviewed by a committee of twenty-three experts selected by the signatories, and passed on to the General Assembly. Disputes over implementation may be passed to the International Court of Justice, but this has never happened. The only UN body to have been officially censured for gender discrimination is the Commission on the Status of Women—censured for having too many women on it.

The 1949 Geneva Convention on treatment of civilians forbade rape. But ethnic cleansing in ex-Yugoslavia included rape and gynocide. Not only did Serbs drive victims (Muslims and Croats) from their homes, but they often raped them—sometimes locking them into "rape camps." One rapist told his victim: "Now you'll give birth to Serb and get rid of your Croat past." Mothers watched and heard as their young daughters were raped. Many women were killed after the rape orgies. Those who survived physically would not soon get over the trauma. Some gave life to an alien's child or aborted it. Bosnians and Croats also raped, but their actions seemed to lack the strategic purposes of Serbian rapes.

Similar horrors befall women worldwide, for example, in Brazil, Kenya, Pakistan, Peru, and Turkey.[39]

Western governments have led efforts to stamp out trafficking in women and children. International agreements were signed to suppress this traffic in 1904, 1910, 1921, 1933, 1937, and 1948–1951. Despite such accords, this traffic continues.[40]

Efforts to promote women's rights face a huge gap between promises and performance. Some feminist legal scholars doubt that women's lives can be improved by human rights discourse since it has essentially male roots and the "add women and stir" process rarely achieves genuine

37. By 1993 more than 120 countries had ratified or acceded to the convention. The U.S. signed it in 1980 but then did not ratify it. Many non-Western countries endorsed the convention. China signed and ratified it in 1980; Cambodia signed in 1980 and ratified it in 1992; the USSR signed it in 1980 and ratified it in 1981; Afghanistan signed it in August 1980 (nine months after the Soviet invasion), but then did not ratify it; Egypt signed it in 1980 and ratified it in 1981. Three Muslim countries did not sign it, but did accede to it—Bangladesh in 1984, Iraq in 1986, and Libya in 1989.

38. Iraq claimed that the Shariah gave "women rights equivalent to the rights of their spouses so as to ensure a just balance between them." Several governments protested that the Shariah reservation was "incompatible" with the treaty.

39. *Human Rights Watch Global Reports on Women's Human Rights* (New York: Human Rights Watch, 1995), chaps. 1 and 2.

40. In the 1990s girls and women were kidnapped, forced, or lured from Burma into Thai brothels. Occasional crackdowns by Thai police put hundreds of prostitutes in cramped detention for months. Some were released for return to Burma— many HIV-infected. The U.S. Congress was often more outspoken than the State Department in pressing for protection of women in Thailand and other countries. NGOs were even more forthright. For details on Thailand and on Nepal-India and Bangladesh-Pakistan trafficking, see *Human Rights Watch Global Report on Women's Human Rights,* chap. 4.

Why Human Rights Can Affect War and Peace

Aleksandr Solzhenitsyn suffered in and later described the "gulag [prison camp] archipelago" of the USSR. He warned: "Coexistence on this tightly knit earth should be viewed as an existence not only without wars—that is not enough—but without violence, or anyone's telling us how to live, what to say, what to think, what to know and what not to know."

Soviet scientist and human rights campaigner Andrei Sakharov cautioned Washington not to cultivate "a country where anything that happens may be shielded from outside eyes—a masked country that hides its real face." The minimum condition for easing restrictions on East-West trade, Sakharov said, should be unrestricted emigration from the USSR.

equity. Recognition grows that the theory and practice of world politics reflect mainly "male" values. Even the UN Secretariat is notorious for gender abuses.

So long as the treatment of women is regarded as a private rather than a public issue, it will be difficult for international treaties to help women. This attitude adds a layer to the norm of noninterference in domestic affairs.

CAN INTERNATIONAL PRESSURE ENHANCE HUMAN RIGHTS OBSERVANCE?

Should those who enjoy relative freedom be concerned about human rights violations elsewhere? Should not foreign policy-makers focus on their state's security and trade balances and leave human rights to Amnesty International and the International Red Cross? Two Soviet Nobel Prize winners said "no!"[41]

But what can the relatively free do to help the partly free and unfree? Let us examine several major efforts to combine preaching and pressure—carrots and sticks—and their outcomes.

The CSCE-Helsinki Process: Democracies Against Dictatorships

The Conference on Security and Cooperation in Europe (CSCE) opened in Helsinki in 1973. In August 1975 it produced a "Final Act," signed by the leaders of thirty-five states—all NATO and Warsaw Pact governments plus Europe's neutrals.[42] The Final Act offered promises in three distinct realms—security, trade, and human rights. Each country pledged to respect human rights as set out in the UN Charter and Universal Declaration of Human Rights, promote civil and other freedoms and the legitimate interests of national minorities, and uphold "the right of the individual to know and act upon his rights and duties" in the field of human rights.[43]

The Kremlin probably thought that it "won" in the security and trade realms, but humanitarian promises opened the Soviet empire to profound challenge. To be sure, the Helsinki Final Act was not a legally binding treaty. Still, its moral commitments functioned almost like legal obligations. Any alleged violation brought unwelcome publicity and "shaming." The parties committed themselves to what became known as the Helsinki Process—periodic CSCE meetings to monitor implementation of each basket. The signatories stood on trial—permanently. Signatory governments and their citizens could evaluate the human rights performance of any participating state. "Watch" groups of private citizens in

41. Aleksandr Solzhenitsyn won the Nobel Prize for Literature; Andrei Sakharov, for Peace. Sakharov's statement was made to Western reporters on August 20, 1973; Solzhenitsyn's, in his September 1973 statement nominating Sakharov for the Peace Prize.

42. Albania stayed out. Even the Vatican, Cyprus, and San Marino signed.

43. For an analytical history by a U.S. negotiator, and the documents, see John J. Maresca, *To Helsinki: The Conference on Security and Cooperation in Europe, 1973–1975* (Durham, N.C.: Duke University Press, 1987).

THE ACCUSED   SOME ACCOMPLICES

WORLD COURT

SERBIAN LEADERS

BRITAIN   FRANCE   GERMANY   U.S.   RUSSIA

DANZIGER
The Christian Science Monitor

By 1995 the UN had set up a special tribunal at The Hague to hear charges of war crimes in the former Yugoslavia, but many states had reasons not to want vigorous prosecution. The UN kept the tribunal on a very tight budget, though financing improved in 1998.

Communist countries got some protection from Western NGOs and governments who stood by them.

From 1975 until 1990–1991 the CSCE contributed to freer movement of people and ideas within a stable Europe. The CSCE process helped destroy the Communist dictatorships of Eastern Europe and the USSR.

Success, then Failure: The OSCE and Post-Communist Genocide

Five deep problems gutted the ability of the OSCE to serve as more than a talk shop.

1. *No enforcement powers.* The OSCE had no army. At most the OSCE could request NATO or the Western European Union or the Russian-backed Commonwealth of Independent States to act as its agent. But neither Russia nor NATO wished the other to expand its influence. The OSCE and NGOs could bring pressure, but only the coercive power of states could check that of other states.

2. *Voting procedures.* The OSCE could be paralyzed by its consensus requirement. Washington persuaded the OSCE to suspend the unanimity rule and act on a "consensus-minus-one" basis if an OSCE member were the target. This led to the exclusion of Yugoslavia (Serbia), but friends of Serbia could still block actions against it.

3. *Unclear relationship with NGOs.* The increasing bureaucratization of the OSCE could alienate its natural partners such as Amnesty International and Human Rights Watch. Alternatively, the OSCE could be overwhelmed by NGOs. At some OSCE meetings NGOs enjoyed nearly the same speaking rights as government delegations.[1]

4. *Size and heterogeneity.* The original thirty-four members grew to more than fifty with the inclusion of the ex-Yugoslav and Soviet republics, five of them in Central Asia.

5. *Lack of political will.* Europeans gave up "shaming" other OSCE participants. "This is diplomacy—not a boxing ring," said one diplomat. Only the U.S. delegation continued to "name names." It criticized Turkey for torture, Uzbekistan for censorship, Russia for keeping "economic" criminals from Communist times in jail, and others for anti-semitism.

1. Commission on Security and Cooperation in Europe, *The CSCE Implementation Meeting on Human Dimension Issues, Warsaw, Poland, September 27–October 15, 1993,* 103d Cong., 1st sess. (Washington, D.C.: Government Printing Office, 1993).

Washington's role in the Helsinki Process combined Wilsonian idealism and tough *realpolitik* in a "practical, disciplined moralism."[44]

War and genocide in the Balkans and along the old Soviet borders showed that the CSCE and its successor, the Organization for Security and Cooperation in Europe (OSCE), could not keep borders "inviolable" or ensure human rights. The OSCE could *publicize* human rights violations by its members but it could not *stop* them. In the mid-1990s it seemed that nothing short of 30,000 to 60,000 armed forces could maintain order in the Balkans. Even they were slow to arrest indicted war criminals or reverse ethnic evictions.

Pressure and Preaching: The China Case

Should—could—outsiders do anything to back the human rights of Chinese dissidents such as Han Dongfang? A railroad worker in his mid-twenties, Han Dongfang tried to organize other workers during the democracy demonstrations that filled Tiananmen Square in spring 1989. After the "People's Liberation Army" crushed the demonstrators, Han turned himself into the police. At first they offered him tea, but when he denied committing any crime, they locked him up, tortured him, and deliberately infected him with tuberculosis. Fearing he might die, they released him in 1990 but kept him under close surveillance.

In 1992 authorities refused Han's request to hold a one-man demonstration demanding a right for workers to form independent trade unions. But news about Han rippled through China by word of mouth and by radio broadcasts of the BBCand Voice of America.[45] Chinese authorities got rid of Han Dongfang and some other dissidents by giving them exit visas, but other voices emerged.

Washington wanted to nudge China to become a force for world peace, a dependable trading partner, and a supporter of human rights. Each year Congress threatened to cut off most-favored nation (MFN) treatment for Chinese exports unless Beijing conformed to U.S. demands. Congress also barred exports to the U.S. made by prison labor. The Voice of America funneled in criticisms of Beijing's policies to Chinese listeners, undercutting regime efforts at mind control.

The European Parliament (EP) also condemned China's human rights practices. For reasons discussed in the previous chapter, the EP is far more radical than Europe's governments. In 1989 the EP joined with the U.S. Senate to denounce Chinese policies in Tibet. In February 1994 the EP passed a thirty-three-point resolution that called for establishment of a multiparty state in China, demanded release of political prisoners, con-

44. Daniel Patrick Moynihan, in foreword to William Korey, *The Promises We Keep: Human Rights, the Helsinki Process, and American Foreign Policy* (New York: St. Martin's, 1993), xvi.

45. Nicholas D. Kristoff, "Defiant Chinese Dissident Tells of His Ordeal," *New York Times*, April 16, 1992, 1, 6.

demned infanticide, and called for banning goods produced by forced labor. The EP said that economic reforms in China should be accompanied by "the gradual introduction of internationally recognized social standards." It reminded Beijing that China had signed the Universal Declaration of Human Rights. It hoped the Chinese legal system would become independent of political authority. It said any expansion of trade with the European Union should be conditioned on China's ending its system of labor camps. It also urged Beijing to open negotiations with Tibet's Dalai Lama.[46]

Like Soviet authorities in an earlier era, Beijing zealously defended its "domestic jurisdiction" and argued that the Communist government upholds the most basic human rights—to work and eat. Westerners, said Beijing, had no right to preach morality after centuries in which they had treated Chinese as subhuman. Beijing welcomed technology and capital from outside, but condemned Western efforts to spread ideological and moral "pollution."

Candidate Bill Clinton promised to take a tougher look at human rights in China than did President George Bush. As president, Clinton dispatched Secretary of State Warren Christopher to Beijing in March 1994. Shortly before Christopher arrived, PRC authorities released a few prominent political prisoners, but they arrested still more. One of those released, Wei Jingsheng, had already served fourteen years of a fifteen-year sentence. But he was twice taken to police headquarters before Christopher's visit and told to keep quiet.[47] After he talked with the U.S. Assistant Secretary of State for Human Rights, Wei was again jailed.

Neither preaching nor pressure made a discernible impact on PRC authorities. Beijing scorned Western criticisms. China needed the U.S. market but U.S. consumers and exporters also needed China. Beijing counted on U.S. greed to press Congress to renew MFN treatment for China. U.S. business executives chided Christopher for making the U.S. look unstable.

Why did the USSR succumb to human rights pressure while China remained defiant? Moscow accepted the Helsinki human rights commitments in 1975 as part of a larger package that promised the Soviet bloc greater security and trade. But China perceived little threat to its security and counted on MFN no matter what. The Soviet authorities liked to swear their devotion to human rights—partly to claim that the USSR belonged with the West—but PRC leaders did not. The Soviets probably assumed that the Helsinki commitments could be controlled, but Beijing was cautious. China acceded to seven human rights accords in the 1980s,

46. Real power lies elsewhere in the European Union. Still, earlier EP recommendations helped block European trade with Morocco and Syria. David Wallen, "Europe Condemns China," *South China Morning Post*, February 12, 1994, 1–2.

47. In another gesture five U.S. journalists were given a tour of a labor reform camp where Liu Gang, an organizer of the Tiananmen Square protests, was kept and, relatives said, tortured. The cells and cafeteria shown to the journalists were nearly deserted, and they could see Mr. Liu only through a smoked glass window as he walked in the yard with a guard. Patrick E. Tyler, "Chinese Take Journalists on Guided Tour of Prison" and "China Dissident Reports Release," *New York Times*, March 6, 1994.

but usually with enfeebling reservations.[48] Beijing made a sham of human rights.

China in the 1990s. What can outsiders do to help brave individuals like Wei Jingsheng, who risked everything to demand democracy for China? Would human rights in China benefit from a trade cutoff? Many Chinese dissidents thought not. They saw the expansion of Chinese contacts with the outer world as the best basis for liberalization. On the other hand, some Chinese dissidents complained that the West did not protest human rights abuses in China as it did in the old Soviet empire. Westerners, they said, believed that Chinese valued the individual less than Russians.

Few governments in the world have a worse human rights record than China. By the late 1990s things were better than during Mao Zedong's Great Leap Forward (1958–1962) and Cultural Revolution (1966–early 1970s), but China's observance of human rights in the 1990s was bad— just marginally better than Iraq's. There had been no public massacres since Tiananmen Square in 1989, but since that time there had been no large demonstrations to shoot at.

No Political or Civil Rights. Despite some opening up in the 1990s, Chinese had virtually no freedom of speech, press, assembly, or association—and certainly no opposition party (though closely supervised multi-candidate elections took place in villages). Few legal safeguards existed. No due process was observed. Authorities used torture to extract confessions. Prison labor was extensive. Organs of executed persons were sold for transplants.

Social and economic rights were minimal. The new reforms could throw millions out of secure jobs and onto the streets with no safety net. Forced abortions were common. Women received little protection.

Cultural Genocide. An ancient and major civilization, Tibet, was being extirpated. Sinification of Tibetan, Muslim, and other minority regions took place by inundating the local populations with Chinese migrants and by imposing Mandarin as the language of education, government, and economics.

Religious Persecution. Non-approved religious groups were persecuted. The government-sanctioned Catholic Church in China had 70 bishops and about 1,000 priests in 1997. The underground church, loyal to the pope, had 60 bishops and 1,000 priests. During PRC leader Jiang Zemin's trip to the U.S., China released a Roman Catholic bishop after three weeks of detention; he had been caught after seventeen months in hiding.

48. Beijing acceded to the torture convention but said it would not be bound by Article 20 permitting an *outside* commission to investigate possible violations. This meant that China would judge and punish its own torturers. In 1982 Beijing acceded to the protocol protecting refugees, but rejected the treaty's obligation to submit disputes to the ICJ. Beijing also registered broad reservations when it joined the 1949 Geneva convention on protection of victims in war and the 1979 convention banning discrimination against women.

The following analysis is based on many sources, including U.S. Department of State, *Country Reports on Human Rights Practices for 1996* (Washington, D.C.: Government Printing Office, 1997), 616–643.

Indifference to Law. China succeeded in its export-based economic transformation, but Beijing played unfairly. Closing its economy in many ways, China sold five times more to the U.S. than it purchased. Beijing promised many times to crack down on pirating of intellectual property but was slow to act.

Beginning in 1985, the PRC government several times promised to restrain sales of weapons and nuclear weapon technology to countries such as Pakistan, Iraq, Algeria, and Iran but as of 1997 had done little. It blamed sales on "private" parties (often relatives of top rulers). China even diverted a U.S. supercomputer ostensibly intended for meteorology to a weapons design plant. Caught by satellite photos, PRC authorities in 1997 pleaded a misunderstanding.

Despite repression, China in the 1990s opened up. More money, fewer controls, and freer access to information led to more choice in the 1990s.

All these issues came to a head as Jiang Zemin visited the U.S. in fall 1997—swimming at Waikiki, enjoying a state dinner at the White House, lecturing at Harvard, and singing a few bars of Chinese opera to a gathering of Chinese-Americans in Los Angeles.

President Clinton asserted that China's human rights practices were on "the wrong side of history," but he lifted a ban on export of U.S. nuclear power reactors to China after President Jiang pledged not to sell missiles to Iran. Jiang also placed an order for fifty Boeing aircraft worth about $3 billion—some twenty planes more than expected. Business leaders feted the PRC leader at the Waldorf Astoria. Jiang returned home having made no commitments on human rights or Tibet. The long-term impact of his trip, however, could yield surprises. He had met leading members of Congress who also called for a change in China's human rights policies. He had seen and heard human rights demonstrators who followed him to the New York Stock Exchange and to Harvard. Jiang hinted that to see the "specifics" of U.S. democracy was different from reading about them. He allowed at his Harvard talk that Chinese leaders had made some mistakes.

A few weeks after Jiang's visit, dissident Wei Jingsheng was released from prison—on medical grounds—and flown to a U.S. hospital. But Wei quickly moved on to Washington, where he met President Clinton, and New York, where he was honored by the mayor and by Columbia University. *The Economist* (December 13, 1997) pondered whether Wei might follow in the footsteps of Sun Yat-sen, the reformist politician who helped change China in the early 20th century.

THE ZIGS AND ZAGS OF U.S. POLICY
TOWARD HUMAN RIGHTS

Human rights have played an important if secondary role in U.S. foreign policy since 1945. Since the mid-1970s the Department of State has issued a yearly survey on human rights worldwide—***Country Reports on Human Rights Practices***. In the Reagan-Bush years these reports were soft on Latin American dictators, China, and the U.S.'s European allies. In the 1990s, however, the *Country Reports* became more objective, exceeding one thousand pages filled with facts both positive and negative. Thus the 1993 report said of one friendly country: "A wide range of individual freedom is provided for by the Mexican Constitution and honored in practice." But the State Department also reported "the use of torture," "extrajudicial killings," and "electoral flaws" in Mexico.[49]

Starting in 1984 Congress required that the *Country Reports* contain information on workers' rights in countries benefiting from duty-free access to the U.S. market.[50] The yearly surveys have detailed policies by Indonesia, Taiwan, and other friendly countries to block collective bargaining. Beginning in 1992 Congress also demanded that the *Country Reports* provide more information on children, indigenous peoples, and—for recipients of U.S. aid—data on their efforts to curtail military expenditures.

"Doctor, heal thyself." While Washington prodded others, its own performance left much to be desired. Critics wondered how a rich country could permit extreme poverty, racism, and public health problems.[51] They also observed that the U.S. lagged behind most other industrialized democracies in accepting international human rights obligations.

Table 16.1 summarizes the official U.S. position, and those of several other governments, on the major human rights conventions. For comparison, we should note that Finland is a party to every human rights convention except those governing regions outside Europe. Russia, too, is a party to each convention, with the exception of the 1950 European Convention on Human Rights, which by 1997 Moscow had only signed—not ratified. Some of the world's newer states were slow to accede to human rights conventions. Uzbekistan, for example, had by 1997 joined only seven conventions.

Of long-established countries, the U.S. showed the most reserve toward human rights treaties. Some senators refused to approve specific conventions on the grounds that their obligations could violate "states' rights" or lead to anti-U.S. propaganda by governments that did not practice what they preached. To be sure, China and other governments

49. U.S. Department of State, *Country Reports on Human Rights Practices for 1992* (Washington, D.C.: Government Printing Office, 1993), 440–451.

50. This stipulation was part of the Generalized System of Preferences Renewal Act of 1984.

51. These problems are especially acute on Native American reservations.

Table 16.1   Adherence to International Human Rights Conventions as of 1997

Convention	China	India	Iraq	Singapore	U.S.
1953 Slave Trade	O	P	P	O	P
1948 Right to Unionize	O	O	O	O	O
1948 Genocide	P	P	P	P	P
1949 Right to Collective Bargaining	O	O	P	P	O
1949 Prisoners of War	P	P	P	P	P
1949 Civilians in Wartime	P	P	P	P	P
1950 Suppression of Prostitution	O	P	P	P	O
1953 Political Rights of Women	P	P	O	O	P
1956 Slavery	P	P	P	P	P
1957 Forced Labor	O	O	P	P	P
1965 Racial Discrimination	P	P	P	O	P
1966 Civil-Political Rights	O	P	P	O	P
1966 Economic-Social Rights	O	P	P	O	S
1967 Refugees	P	O	O	O	P
1973 Minimum Age for Employment	O	O	P	O	O
1977 Victims of International Armed Conflicts	P	O	O	O	S
1977 Victims of Non-International Armed Conflicts	P	O	O	P	S
1979 Discrimination Against Women	P	P	P	P	S
1984 Torture	P	O	O	O	P
1989 Rights of the Child	P	P	P	P	S

SOURCE: U.S. Department of State, *Country Reports on Human Rights Practices for 1996* (Washington, D.C.: Government Printing Office, 1997), Appendix C.
   NOTE: P = party—either signed and ratified or acceded after treaty entered force; S = signed but not ratified; O = no action taken.

have qualified their acceptance of certain conventions in ways that rob them of meaning. But so, too, has the U.S.

Washington is legally bound by several anti-slavery conventions, by the 1949 Geneva conventions on treatment of prisoners and civilians in wartime, by the refugee protection convention, by the UN Convention on Political Rights for Women, by the Genocide Convention, by the ban on racial discrimination, and by the ban on torture. The U.S. ratified the International Covenant on Civil and Political Rights in 1992, but President Bush (and the U.S. Senate) reserved the right of U.S. states to execute juveniles and to protect hate speech. As of 1997 the U.S. had signed but not ratified the covenant on economic rights, the ban on discrimination against women, the convention on the rights of the child, and the American Convention on Human Rights. Washington refused to sign the 1948 Convention on the Right to Organize, the 1949 Convention on the Right to Bargain Collectively, and the 1950 Convention to Suppress Prostitution.

How could Washington clamor for human rights abroad if the U.S. government did not pledge it at home? Would Americans suffer if all hu-

The Bricker Amendment

The U.S. Constitution makes treaties the law of the land. Treaties can supersede earlier federal and state laws. They can even "federalize" powers reserved to the states. They do not, however, override the Constitution. As the Supreme Court ruled in *Reid v. Covert* (1957), any treaty provision inconsistent with the Constitution would simply be invalid.

Racial segregation and other forms of discrimination long supported or permitted by state laws conflicted with the UN Charter and some human rights treaties. In 1952 a California intermediary court held that the state's Alien Land Law discriminated against aliens and violated the UN Charter. The California Supreme Court struck down the Alien Land Law because it violated the 14th Amendment, but it rejected the view that the UN Charter was self-enforcing. Its provisions could not bind until implemented by state legislation—an interpretation never challenged in the Supreme Court.

Senator John W. Bricker proposed amending the U.S. Constitution to make clear that international agreements are not self-executing and would require implementing legislation before they could be enforced in U.S. courts. The Eisenhower administration defeated Bricker, but paid a price. It agreed not to adhere to any covenant on human rights.

The Kennedy administration in 1963 reversed Eisenhower and asked the Senate to approve three human rights treaties. Four years later the Senate approved a ban on the slave trade; it was not until 1976 that the Senate consented to the treaty giving women equal voting rights with men. The third treaty, on abolishing forced labor, has never been ratified by the U.S.

man rights conventions became the law of their land?[52] If the U.S. were implementing the broadest standards of human rights, would race riots convulse U.S. cities from time to time? If human rights guided U.S. foreign policy, would President Reagan (and his successor) have patronized Saddam Hussein—a butcher of his own people—even winking in 1987 when an Iraqi missile struck a U.S. navy ship?[53]

WHAT PROPOSITIONS HOLD? WHAT QUESTIONS REMAIN?

Human rights have long been championed by global idealists and students of interdependence. But many realists have also come to acknowledge that repression anywhere can threaten international security. Ultimately the defense of human rights is an issue of enlightened self-interest: Because we are interdependent, mutual aid is imperative. Open discussion of these realities at home and internationally is essential to joint value-creation.

Support for human rights has come not only from NGOs such as Amnesty International but from governments. The major Western states have sought to enlarge the scope for outside intervention for human rights.

Sovereignty has been breached, but states are still the main repositories of hard power. Unless states provide coercive power, humanitarian intervention must depend on persuasion. The shortcomings of humanitarian interventions in the 1990s resulted from many factors:

Costs: To pressure other states to alter their human rights practices may jeopardize security and trade and invite counterpressures.

Indifference: No major actor had deep interests in the fates of Kurds, Somalis, or Bosnians.

The logic of collective action: Each potential intervenor hoped the other would do the job. Major actors such as the U.S. cannot actively promote human rights everywhere. Foreigners have often targeted China while ignoring the Sudan.

Opposition and footdragging: Large countries such as China and Indonesia gave neither material nor moral support to human rights interventions. Some Asian countries asserted that each culture has its own approach to human rights; some African governments said that one-party rule was necessary for stability.

Local disunion: Many victims of human rights abuses did little to help

52. See Jimmy Carter, "US Finally Ratifies Human Rights Covenant," *Christian Science Monitor,* June 29, 1992, 19.

53. Walter C. Clemens, Jr., "Goliath and the Exocet," *Christian Science Monitor,* August 18, 1987, op-ed.

themselves. Kurds and Somalis, for example, often placed personal and clan interests first.

Insufficient resources: The UN Secretariat had little money, staff, or authority to coordinate vast operations worldwide.

Inexperience: No one had much experience at the interface between humanitarian relief and peacekeeping.

The necessity for self-help: Ultimately, the advancement of human rights depends more on local than international action.

Universal respect for human rights remains a distant goal. But the scope of state sovereignty has shrunk while international support for human rights has broadened. Many people—individuals and groups—believe that they have a duty and even a right to look after their brothers and sisters worldwide. But China and many other governments assert their sovereignty and reject outsiders' evaluation of their human rights practices.

Memo to the European Parliament and U.S. Congress:

You have practical as well as idealistic reasons to want stronger observance of human rights in China. If one-fourth of humanity is unfree, the rest of humanity is endangered. Human rights means democracy. And democracy means peace. Good things come in a package that includes democracy, stability, peace, and prosperity. In time, scientific advancement and environmental protection will follow.

More East-West trade will not assure democracy or liberate those imprisoned in China and elsewhere for espousing human rights. Expect a constant struggle between practical goals such as profit and power and human rights ideals. Do not buy a simplistic argument that the West must either engage or pressure China. It can do both.

Press for human rights observance everywhere, beginning in Europe and the U.S. Persuade your own governments to enlarge and deepen their commitments to human rights at home and abroad. Support an International Criminal Court with wide powers. Avoid double standards. Apply the same standards to India as to China, to Sri Lanka as to Singapore, to Algeria as to Angola. Do not soften pressures in hopes of getting a contract for your manufacturers of aircraft or power reactors. Let them compete on their own merits.

Do not soften your critique in hopes of persuading China to tighten exports of weapons to other countries. Instead, show Beijing why the spread of such weapons is bad for Chinese as well as Western interests.

Time is probably on your side. The revolution in human rights awareness has gained momentum since the 16th century. It has impacted China only since the early 20th century. But totalitarian controls in China are eroding as they did earlier in the USSR. Make the most of this opening. If Nelson Mandela could become president of South Africa in the late 20th century, who knows what might be possible in China in the 21st? Engage individuals and groups at all levels to discuss and promote human rights. Some Chinese have a vested interest in stability, but others want change. They include many women, ethnic minorities, labor leaders, and intellectuals—artists, humanists, scientists, reporters. Business people chafe at restrictions. Politicians who want unification with Taiwan must demonstrate that human rights are respected in mainland China.

Expect setbacks, but persist.

Individuals make history. After spending twenty-seven years in jail, Nelson Mandela won the presidency of South Africa in 1994. Here Mandela speaks at a Cape Town rally the day before his inauguration. Mandela and former president F. W. de Klerk shared the Nobel Peace Prize in 1993.

KEY NAMES AND TERMS

apartheid

Bricker Amendment

Ralph Bunche

Convention on the Elimination of All Forms of Discrimination Against Women (1979)

Convention on the Prevention and Punishment of the Crime of Genocide (1948)

Country Reports on Human Rights Practices

crimes against humanity

Geneva Conventions of 1949

International Covenant on Civil and Political Rights (1966)

International Covenant on Economic, Social, and Cultural Rights (1966)

International Military Tribunal at Nuremberg

Bartolomé de Las Casas

practices similar to slavery

Eleanor Roosevelt

slavery

Universal Declaration of Human Rights (1948)

QUESTIONS TO DISCUSS

1. To what extent is banning slavery like limiting weapons? How does it differ? Consider the mechanisms and the goals of such limitations. Which levels of action have been most fruitful?

2. How does demicide (Chapter 10) differ from genocide? How does cultural genocide differ from physical genocide? Compare U.S. (Australian, Canadian) government policies toward indigenous peoples with ethnic cleansing in the former Yugoslavia.

3. What right do outsiders have to demand a halt to clitorectomy in cultures where it has long been a tradition?

4. Should outsiders press for an end to child labor (for example, in the carpet factories of Pakistan and India) if families will be plunged deeper into poverty?

5. You are the UN High Commissioner for Human Rights. How do you approach Algeria (or another government) widely believed to be suppressing human rights? The government there blames local terrorists for disturbances and says that outsiders have no right to meddle.

6. As a member of Amnesty International and a stockholder in Boeing Corporation, do you want the U.S. State Department to continue its public reports on human rights in China?

RECOMMENDED RESOURCES

Amnesty International Report. London: Amnesty International, annual.

Donnelly, Jack. *International Human Rights.* Boulder, Colo.: Westview, 1993.

Forsythe, David P. *The Internationalization of Human Rights.* Lexington, Mass.: Lexington Books, 1991.

Human Rights Watch Global Report on Women's Human Rights. New York: Human Rights Watch, 1995.

Humana, Charles, comp. *World Human Rights Guide.* 3d ed. New York: Oxford University Press, 1992.

Laqueur, Walter, and Barry Rubin, eds. *The Human Rights Reader.* New York: New American Library, 1979.

Shue, Henry. *Basic Rights: Subsistence, Affluence, and U.S. Foreign Policy.* 2d ed. Princeton, N.J.: Princeton University Press, 1996.

Tolley, Howard. *The United Nations Commission on Human Rights.* Boulder, Colo.: Westview, 1987.

U.S. Department of State. *Country Reports on Human Rights Practices.* Washington, D.C.: Government Printing Office, annual.

JOURNALS

American Journal of International Law
Ethics & International Affairs
Human Rights Quarterly
UN Chronicle

WEB SITES

AAAS [American Association for the Advancement of Science] Directory of Human Rights Sites on the Internet
   http://shr.aaas.org/dhr.htm
American Civil Liberties Union
   http://www.aclu.org
Amnesty International
   http://www.amnesty.org
B'Tselem: The Israeli Information Center for Human Rights in the Occupied Territories
   http://www.btselem.org
The Carter Center
   http://www.emory.edu/CARTER_CENTER/homepage.htm
The Coalition for International Justice
   http://www.cij.org/cij/
Committee to Protect Journalists
   http://www.cpj.org
DIANA: An International Human Rights Database
   http://elsinore.cis.yale.edu/dianaweb/diana.htm
   http://www.law.uc.edu/Diana/
   http://www.umn.edu/humanrts/
The Global Democracy Network
   http://www.gdn.org/gdn/html
Globalvision's Rights & Wrongs
   http://www.globalvision.org/globalvision/
GILC (Global Internet Library Campaign)
   http://www.gilc.org
GreenNet
   http://www.gn.apc.org
Human Rights in China
   http://www.igc.apc.org/hric/
Human Rights Internet
   http://www.hri.ca
Human Rights Watch
   http://www.hrw.org/

Interaction
    http://www.interaction.org/ia/
The International Committee of the Red Cross
    http://www.icrc.org
International Crisis Group
    http://www.intl-crisis-group.org
Lawyers Committee for Human Rights
    http://www.lchr.org/lchr/
The Multilaterals Project
    http://www.tufts.edu/departments/fletcher/multi
    /humanRights.html
Peace Brigades International
    http://www.igc.apc.org/pbi/
PEN American Center (*writers' organization*)
    http://www.pen.org
Physicians for Global Survival
    http://www.web.net/~pgs/
Physicians for Human Rights
    gopher://gopher.igc.apc.org:5000/11/int/phr/
The Progressive Directory
    http://www.igc.org/igc/issues/hr/or.html

Reliefweb
    http://www.reliefweb.int
United Nations High Commissioner for Refugees
    http://www.unhcr.ch
United Nations Treaty Database
    http://www.un.org/Depts/Treaty/
Universal Declaration of Human Rights (text)
    http://www.hrw.org/universal.html
University of Minnesota Human Rights Library
    http://www.umn.edu/humanrts/
U.S. State Department's Country Reports
    http://www.state.gov
War Crimes Tribunal Watch
    http://www.un.org/icty/basic.htm
Washington Office on Latin America
    http://www.wola.org
WebActive
    http://www.webactive.com

ALTERNATIVE FUTURES: LESSONS FROM THE PAST

THE BIG QUESTIONS IN CHAPTER 17

- Can the world become a better place for life? If so, how? On whom or what does improvement depend?

- What can we learn from IR history? Under what circumstances did it pay for IR actors to pursue a hard line? A win-win orientation? Conditional cooperation?

- Under what circumstances did it pay IR actors to mask their concerns and objectives in negotiations?

- Under what circumstances, if any, was openness a better guide to IR tactics and strategy?

- Looking at the first quarter of the 21st century, what kinds of IR scenarios are most plausible? Can we predict or only sketch if/then alternatives?

- Can unipolarity be beneficent or will it lead to dictatorship?

- Must we assume a collision between today's hegemon and a rising power such as China or the European Union?

- Is the South likely to get poorer or begin closing the gap with the North?

- Is IR likely to be dominated by governments, nonstate actors, or cooperation between a variety of international actors? If by nonstate actors, which kind—NGOs, TNCs, or others?

- Do we have more reason to fear or welcome the global future?

"History Is the Future." *This is a favorite saying of the UN Secretary-General. But she also stands by another belief: "The future is ours to fill." Humanity's future depends on the past but also on what we do in the present.*

She turns to you, a former diplomat turned historian, for advice. You have put aside day-to-day crises and standard operating procedures to write and teach history, utilizing insights gained in arenas where South confronts North and East meets West. The Secretary-General asks you to review IR in the 20th century. Can the world be made safer, more just, more prosperous, more salubrious? What can we learn from the past to guide our policies in the 21st century? Are there lessons for individuals? For governments? For IGOs, NGOs, TNCs, and other international actors?

How do these lessons play out in the alternative futures discernible as we enter the 21st century? Are there any constants in IR? Is change even possible?

IS IT POSSIBLE TO BUILD A BETTER WORLD?

Is it possible to build a better world? Realists reply "no." They maintain that human nature does not change. People in the 21st century will behave much like Athenians and Spartans in the 5th century B.C. They will continue to fear one another and, in preparing to attack or defend, provoke arms races and wars. No one has analyzed IR better than Thucydides when he dissected the Peloponnesian War. We cannot expect to understand IR or prescribe policy better than the ancient Greeks. There are limits to knowledge. Despite scientific advances in many fields, we still cannot fathom leaders such as Saddam Hussein. There are also limits to what humans can regulate. Despite the growth of international law, the 20th century experienced two global wars and many smaller ones. The Damocles Sword of nuclear war hangs by a thread ready and able to end life. Lusting for wealth and power, humans use technology to lay waste to the fishing grounds, the forests, the very water and air on which life depends.

But there are also reasons to believe in the possibility of a better world. The quantity and quality of life has improved dramatically since the 18th century. The planet sustains a steady increase in its human inhabitants. At the brink of the 21st century the average human was healthier and better educated than at any time in history.[1] Infant mortality had fallen sharply even in the poorest countries. Average life spans had dramatically increased. Literacy and basic education were the norm across most of the planet. As resources dwindled, humans learned to conserve them or invent replacements.

What lies behind this capacity for life? Science. Technology. Morality. Organization. Power. Learning.

Scientific Knowledge. Understanding the processes that condition life, humans can extend it. Social science, however, lags behind physical science.

Technology. Applied science provides food and shelter for huge populations; it permits people to travel and communicate globally. Knowledge and technology are great equalizers. In the late 20th century their diffusion permitted India, once ruled by the British raj, to become a center of computer software development, and China to compete with the West and Russia in launching commercial rockets.

Morality. Since the 18th century many people have believed that science, technology, and wealth can and should be used to improve the lives

1. More education did not mean more genius. The 20th century had its Einstein, Picasso, T.S. Eliot, Andrei Sakharov, and Leonard Bernstein. But were they a match for Leonardo, Shakespeare, or Mozart? How did the Left Bank of Paris compare with the agora of ancient Athens? How did 20th-century religious figures compare with those that emerged in ancient India and the Middle East?

2. Ernst B. Haas, *Nationalism, Liberalism, and Progress: The Rise and Decline of Nationalism* (Ithaca, N.Y.: Cornell University Press, 1997). See references in Haas, Chapter 1, to relevant works of other social scientists such as Max Weber, Karl W. Deutsch, James N. Rosenau, Herbert A. Simon, Janice Stein, Raymond Tanter, Larry Laudan, Peter Berger, and Robert L. Rothstein.

of all people, not just privileged elites. Many humans recognize human solidarity across the divides of gender, border, race, religion, language, culture, and class. There is a growing consensus on morality. Most governments endorse the Universal Declaration of Human Rights.

Organization. The modern state helped people organize on a large scale—to establish law and order, tap divisions of labor, produce for broad markets, improve physical security, and establish a welfare safety net. IGOs such as the Universal Postal Union and NGOs such as the Red Cross help states to meet basic needs on a global scale. In the late 20th century, however, the nation-state framework often proved inadequate for dealing with many challenges. The technology of war outpaced organization for peace. Electronic money transfers undermined the ability of governments to control their currency and collect taxes. HIV and drug trafficking mocked national borders.

Experience suggests that humans can and will devise better ways to cope with the dangers and opportunities inherent in mutual vulnerability and globalization.[2]

Power. Human nature may not have changed, but diverse constellations of power may have helped prevent war—a multipolar balance during the 19th century, bipolarity during the Cold War era, and unipolarity in the 1990s. No one has mastered the art or science of peace. Still, it is possible that science, technology, morality, and organization can combine to produce better ways to restrain aggression and promote cooperation.

Learning. Underlying each domain is the ability to adapt and to learn. While physically weak compared to other life forms, humans have brains, nervous systems, and dexterity that enable them to adapt to extreme conditions. Humans have learned from trial and error, including bitter and tragic failures, how to organize to live better.

Today's students of IR can proceed from theoretical insights that the ancient Greeks could only guess at, for example, the mixed nature of conflict. Game theory (launched in the 1940s) deepens our understanding of adversarial relationships—that rivals may have interests in common as well as in conflict, so that, under some conditions, rivals may gain from cooperation. Modern psychology helps explain why actors often misread one another and even their own interests. The better we understand such problems, the greater our chances of finding ways to manage if not solve them.

Diplomatic skills, communication, conflict resolution, and mediation techniques can be taught. The slim book *Getting to Yes* puts forth not just an outlook on adversarial relations but a compendium of negotiating techniques found useful by negotiators in a variety of cultural settings.[3]

What can we learn from the past? Let us analyze the cases studied throughout this book. Under what conditions has it paid off for policymakers to pursue hard-line policies, a win-win approach, or conditional cooperation? For now we focus on the pay-offs for the policy initiator. Later we can consider the outcomes for other actors affected by those policies.

WHICH APPROACH WORKS BEST: WIN-LOSE, WIN-WIN, CONDITIONAL COOPERATION?

The IR experiences recorded in this book confirm the utility of approaching foreign policy in a spirit of conditional cooperation and openness to elicit informed participation by all concerned parties. These conclusions emerge from the cases summarized in Tables 17.1–17.4. In many instances the parties took more than one approach or changed midstream. Thus the tables represent a highly simplified interpretation of complicated, sometimes contradictory events. But while historians may disagree about individual cases, the overall patterns are striking.

Hard-line policies spawned many failures: the Versailles system, defeat for the perpetrators of six major wars, Khrushchev's Cuban gambit, and Communist repression of human potential.

Win-win policies failed to unite Americans after the U.S. Civil War, but a win-win orientation helped cultivate fitness in the U.S. in the 20th century and in post-1945 Japan.

3. Roger Fisher and William Ury, *Getting to Yes: Negotiating Agreement Without Giving In* (New York: Penguin, 1983), available in many languages.

Table 17.1 Approaches and Outcomes in Part 1: Hard Realities, High Ideals, and Global Interdependence

Cases Analyzed	Approach			Outcomes	Interpretation/Other Key Variables that Made a Difference
	Hard-line	Win-win	Conditional cooperation		
How to Win at Peace					
Appomattox and after		◆		–	Soft peace terms abused → repressive occupation of South → lose-lose
Versailles and after	◆			–	Tough terms weakly enforced → German resentment and revisionism → WWII
ERP (Marshall Plan)		◆	◇	+	Need to rebuild + fear of USSR = mutual gain policy → security community
Confrontation					
Cuban confrontation	◆			–	U.S. missile buildup + Khrushchevian risk-taking → confrontation
Cuban stand-down (1962)			◆	+	Sobering dangers → top leaders make concessions → war averted
Why Fight?					
World War I	◆			–	Irresponsible leaders + cult of offensive + nationalism → war
World War II	◆			–	Nationalist militarists in Tokyo, Rome, and Berlin vs. irresolute West
Korean War	◆			–	Egomaniacs + rising confidence in Communism vs. irresolute West
U.S.-Vietnam War	◆			–	U.S. determination to prevent falling dominoes + LBJ insecurity
Soviet-Afghan War	◆			–	Instability in Afghanistan + Soviet determination not to lose a Communist regime
The Gulf War	◆			–	Egomaniac in Baghdad + Iraqi grievances vs.irresolute West
How To be Fit					
The U.S. in the 20th Century		◆		+	Rich resources + freedom + Fordism = mutual gain; deep problems remain
The USSR	◆	◇		–	Rich resources + dictatorship = industrialization + poverty
Japan		◆		+	Industrial policy + consensus = affluence, but modest creativity

NOTE: ◆ = dominant approach; ◇ = partial approach; empty cell = little attention; + = positive outcome for initiator; – = negative results for initiator.

Two major IR achievements hinged on conditional cooperation. The Marshall Plan helped produce a secure and prosperous trans-Atlantic community; U.S. and Soviet management of the Cuban confrontation was a victory for sobriety and peace.

Conditional cooperation helped the U.S. and USSR limit both offensive and defensive arms. However, the Nuclear Nonproliferation Treaty suffered from lack of a deep commitment. It helped limit the nuclear club, but India, Israel, and others refused a have-not status despite U.S. and Soviet blandishments. Conventional arms control foundered on hard-line demand and a win-lose mentality among suppliers.

Conditional cooperation generated several short-lived détentes between Moscow and Washington, setting the stage for an end to the Cold War in the late 1980s. Hope for mutual gain encouraged closer economic ties between Beijing and Taipei, but win-lose hostility kept political differences alive. Hard-liners in Seoul and Pyongyang thwarted ROK-DPRK cooperation.

Table 17.2 Approaches and Outcomes in Part 2: From Anarchy, Order?

Cases Analyzed	Approach			Outcomes	Interpretation/Other Key Variables that Made a Difference
	Hard-line	Win-win	Conditional cooperation		
Arms Control					
SALT 1 and ABM (1972)			◆	+	Offense can beat defense → make the best of mutual vulnerability
INF (1987)			◆	+	Overkill + desire for détente → destruction of new weapons systems
START 2 (1990s)			◇	+/−	Overkill + end of Cold War → U.S. and Russia move toward a smaller deterrent
NPT (1968 into 1990s)			◇	+/−	Nuclear club tries to close the door but three or more states persist
Conventional arms trade		◇		−	Desire for stability vs. profit motive + new weapons technologies + new world disorder → reduced but continued arms transfers
Conflict Management					
Geneva Spirit (1955)	◇	◆		+	GRIT → brief détente cut short by Eisenhower's heart attack + other conflicts
Moscow Spirit (1963)	◇	◆		+	GRIT → détente cut short by JFK's death, Khrushchev's ouster, and Vietnam
Moscow Spirit (1972)	◇	◆		+	GRIT + triangular diplomacy → détente, damaged by 1973 Arab-Israeli War
East-West Détente (1989)		◆		+	GRIT + weakening of Soviet regime + Gorbachev style → end of Cold War
Soviet-PRC Détente (1989)		◆		+	Soviet pullback of forces + Gorbachev style = new Sino-Russian relationship
PRC-ROC (1980s–1990s)	◇	◆		+/−	PRC GRIT + eventual ROC reciprocation = much commerce and less conflict
ROK-DPRK (1970s–1990s)	◆			−	Rival regimes (and once homogeneous people) enmeshed in hostile distrust
Nationalism and World Order					
Unity of U.S.		◆	◇	+	Voluntary union of many cultural and ethnic groups + residue of slavery
Disunity of USSR	◆				Coerced union of many disparate groups fails when coercion weakens
Unity of Singapore	◇	◆	◇	+	Authoritarian government imposes unity from above on small city-state
Disunity of Sri Lanka	◆			−	Affirmative action for Sinhalese majority vs. Tamil demands − civil war
Unity of Switzerland		◆	◇	+	Oldest democracy + local autonomy + power sharing (+ wealth) = harmony
Disunity of South Slavs	◆			−	Enforced union + death of unifying leader + nationalist agitation + war
Mediation					
Camp David (1978)	◇	◆		+	Sadat's confidence + Begin's intransigence + Carter's mediation + U.S. soft and hard power = Egyptian-Israeli peace that omits Palestinians
Lancaster House (1979)		◆		+	Carrington's mediation + isolated minority regime = peace in Zimbabwe
Oslo (1993)		◆		+	Holst's good offices facilitate Israeli-Palestinian accord to coexist
South Slavs (1991–1995)	◇	◇		−	UN and EU mediators and UN forces too weak to stop bloodshed
South Slavs (1995–1998)	◆		◇	+/−	Holbrooke mediation + NATO troops = negative peace and no ethnic harmony

NOTE: ◆ = dominant approach; ◇ = partial approach; empty cell = little attention; + = positive outcome for initiator; − = negative results for initiator.

Positive-sum expectations underlay the relative ethnic harmony of the U.S., Singapore, and Switzerland. In sharp contrast, top Soviet, Sri Lankan, and South Slav leaders followed a hard-line approach to ethnic problems, making conflict likely. Ethnic harmony probably requires confidence that all groups can win.

Conditional cooperation permeated the successful mediation at Camp David, Lancaster House, and Oslo. It also played some role at Dayton, but U.S. intervention among the South Slavs rested heavily on dictation and hard power. U.S. dictation left many parties resentful, like Germany after Versailles. Earlier EU and UN interventions among the South Slavs, on the other hand, lacked force of any kind.

Many steps toward peace—from the Spirit of Geneva in 1955 through the 1990s—suffered from hard-line sentiments that impeded cooperation. Playing it safe or keeping some guns in reserve stoked the security dilemma and mutual distrust.

Peace among democracies benefited from conditional cooperation but depended upon the unconditional belief that democracies would team up for mutual gain. The dictators' exploitation of their own peoples and others assured their ultimate collapse. China's dictatorship softened after Mao but still menaced any who dared dissent.

A win-win confidence in the "invisible hand" helped the West and Japan to achieve mass affluence. Dealing with foreigners, however, Japan sometimes played hardball. Mimicking Japan, President Clinton's synthesis offered vigorous support of U.S. exports. Trying to protect Airbus, the EU Commission took a hard-line approach to the Boeing–McDonnell Douglas merger. Behind NAFTA and the WTO, however, there were win-win assumptions plus expectations of reciprocity.

Win-lose assumptions underlay most efforts at autarky. Asia's Tigers, however, embraced the win-win rationale of free trade even when they protected their domestic markets. China followed the Tigers' path, but shielded an even larger proportion of its economy from competition. Autarky and protectionism sometimes did more harm than good for their practitioners. "Infant industry protection often becomes senile industry protection."[4] For decades governments and their cronies in South Asia also played a version of hardball: They dominated economic life and throttled free competition. Lack of transparency fostered reckless business decisions and economic waste as well as corruption. In the mid-1990s, better late than never, they began to open up.

Transitions were painful in the former Second World. In most former Soviet republics, influential individuals and groups seized what were for-

4. Steven Radiolead and Jeffrey Sachs, "Asia's Reemergence," *Foreign Affairs* 76, no. 6 (November 1997): 44–59 at 51.

Table 17.3 Approaches and Outcomes in Part 3: International Political Economy

Cases Analyzed	Approach			Outcomes	Interpretation/Other Key Variables that Made a Difference
	Hard-line	Win-win	Conditional cooperation		
Democracy vs. Dictatorship					
Democratic peace		◆	◆	+	Established democracies + mutual respect (+ trade) → positive peace
Dictatorial tyranny	◆			−	Dictatorships start and lose most major wars of the 20th century
Indian democracy		◆	◇	+/−	Corrupt system is inept but avoids tyranny, disintegration, and famine
Chinese dictatorship	◆	◇		+/−	Corrupt system mobilizes and educates but also commits demicide
Economic Prosperity					
Economic growth (Western)		◆		+	Free enterprise + literacy + "invisible hand" + technology = Industrial Revolution
Economic growth in Japan	◇	◆		+	Drive to learn/adapt + discipline + industrial policy → rapid ascent
Clinton synthesis	◇	◆		+	Free enterprise + industrial policy + free trade → growth, low inflation
NAFTA		◆		?	Complementary economies at different stages + proximity → hope
WTO		◆	◆	?	GATT experiences → trust in free trade vs. residual protectionism → hope
Airbus Boeing merger	◆		◇	?	Free trade/anti-monopoly policies vs. desire for market share → compromise
Models of Development					
Import-substitution	◆			−	Inability to compete in world markets → attempted autarky → isolation
NIEO	◆			−	Dependency on fluctuating commodity prices → request to share the wealth
Communist autarky	◆			−	Reluctance to depend on capitalist or other foreign systems→ isolation
Tigers		◆		+	Work, education, savings, investment + some foreign aid = Asian miracle
Leninist capitalism	◇	◆		+	Tiger formula minus foreign aid + strong central controls = PRC miracle
South Asia	◆	◇			Central controls + poor education and public health = slow growth
Transitions					
Russia	◆	◆		+/−	Russia in 1990s is not Germany in 1950s; robber baron capitalism + lack of entrepreneurial traditions + poor safety net + mafias = low productivity + income inequality + poor health
Kazakstan	◇	◇	◇	−	Conditions as in Russia + dictatorship + hope for salvation by oil
Poland		◆			Free enterprise not forgotten + some foreign capital + belief in work
Estonia		◆			Conditions as in Poland + Protestant ethic + ties with Nordic countries

NOTE: ◆ = dominant approach; ◇ = partial approach; empty cell = little attention; + = positive outcome for initiator; − = negative results for initiator.

merly state monopolies. These parasite-robber commissars became millionaires overnight, leaving most people worse off than under Communism. Russia, Azerbaijan, and Kazakstan counted on oil wealth. None produced many goods for export, with the exception of arms—still a Russian specialty. By contrast, Poland and Estonia acted like Tigers and embraced a win-win approach to world trade.

A hard-line approach in ecopolitics views even the biosphere in zero-

Table 17.4 Approaches and Outcomes in Part 4: Building a Better World

Cases Analyzed	Approach			Outcomes	Interpretation/Other Key Variables that Made a Difference
	Hard-line	Win-win	Conditional cooperation		
Ecopolitics					
Aswan syndrome	◆	◆		+/–	Trust in the technological quick-fix→ some economic gain + serious environmental and other problems
Amazonian syndrome	◆	◇		–	Trust in natural abundance and development
Ozone diplomacy			◆	+	Expert consensus on dangers/remedies + willingness to apportion costs
Global warming diplomacy	◇		◇	?	Potential disasters vs. limited consensus on dangers/remedies/costs
Does Might Make Right?					
Stimson Doctrine	◆			+/–	Moral-legal pressure → legitimacy denied to Japan, Germany, Soviet conquests
Collective security in Korea	◆			+	UN approval + U.S.-led forces = denial of DPRK annexation of South Korea
Collective security in the Gulf	◆			+	UN approval + U.S.-led coalition = denial of Iraqi annexation of Kuwait
Keeping/Making Peace					
Peacekeeping (1948–1990)	◇	◆		+/–	UN missions→ prevent renewed war in many but not all conflict zones
Mixed missions (1991–1997)	◇	◇	◇	+/–	Many UN missions fail in rebuilding failed states and enforcing peace
Functionalism					
EU as a common market		◆	◆	+	Functional cooperation + common market + peace = world's richest trading bloc
EU as a political union	◆	◇	◇	–	Diversity of interests and cultures = political divergence/impotence
Humanitarian Relief					
Tajikistan		◆		+/–	Neutral relief efforts difficult in civil/international strife
Law and Human Rights					
Slavery	◆			+	Slavery stopped but practices akin to slavery continue in the 1990s
Nuremberg Tribunal	◆			+	Personal culpability for war crimes + no sure enforcement = no deterrence
Genocide	◇			–	No sure enforcement → genocide in Indochina, Bosnia, Burundi, Rwanda
Laws of war		◆		+	Geneva Conventions usually observed by governments but often not by warlords
Universal declaration		◆		+/–	Moral pressure → raised consciousness, but no legal force
Covenants		◆		+/–	Legal obligations undermined by reservations and weak or no enforcement
Women's rights		◇		?	Legal obligations undermined by reservations and weak or no enforcement
Helsinki Final Act (1975)	◆	◆	◆	+	Moral pressures + Soviet desire for trade and legitimacy = growing voice for human rights in USSR and less repression
Human rights in China	◇			–	Outside pressures + FDI + trade = little effect on awakening giant

NOTE: ◆ = dominant approach; ◇ = partial approach; empty cell = little attention; + = positive outcome for initiator; – = negative results for initiator.

sum terms. Builders of large dams and those who clearcut tropical forests do not respect the intricate balances of nature cultivated over time. Some groups profit from pillage, but at a high cost to long-term sustainability.

Environmental diplomacy usually plays catch-up after the damage is manifest. Ozone diplomacy required sacrifices first by industrial economies and later by LDCs. The obstacles to an accord on global warming were more complicated. Restraint by small actors could do little to shape the overall situation. Hard-line profit motives reinforced the logic of collective action.

Hard power plus resolve are needed to restore or enforce peace. The 1932 Stimson Doctrine was tough but, lacking hard power, did not discomfit aggressors except for the USSR, denied legitimacy in the Baltic. Indeed, Washington's principled stand against Soviet annexation of the Baltic republics contributed to their eventual liberation. By contrast, tangible and intangible power merged in the U.S.-UN responses to the Korean War and to Iraqi expansion.

The win win approach proved weak or inadequate in dealing with hard-liners: Southern leaders after the U.S. Civil War; merchants and buyers of conventional arms; protection of human rights by toothless conventions; mediation or peacekeeping when some parties insist on zero-sum policies.

Win-win can be a useful approach to peacekeeping when all parties want peace. But peacekeeping failed between adversaries not content with the status quo, such as the South Slavs. To maintain peace in the Balkans required much hard power.

A win-win strategy helped to build European economic cooperation but failed to generate a common foreign/defense policy. The win-win orientation of the ICRC and other relief agencies did not dissuade warlords in Tajikistan and other battle zones from their *kto kovo* mindset.

A hard line gave a coup de grace to slavery in most parts of the world. It also inflicted punishment on some top Nazi and Japanese leaders for war crimes. Conditional cooperation—an expectation of reciprocity— often moves governments to respect the laws of war regarding prisoners and civilians. Without enforcement, however, most human rights conventions are flouted by dictatorships and sometimes by democracies. Moscow's hope for trade and other benefits induced the Kremlin in the 1970s and 1980s to pledge respect for human rights. But China received massive FDI and trade privileges in spite of its poor human rights performance.

To sum up, win-win policies helped to foster domestic fitness in the

U.S. and Japan; advance ethnic harmony in several multiethnic countries; sustain the democratic peace and unite democracies against dictatorships; spur economic growth within and among free market countries. Faith in free trade arose from trust that an "invisible hand" would promote mutual gain. A win-win approach usefully supplemented conditional cooperation in the ERP, the EU, the GATT, and the WTO.

Conditional cooperation succeeded in cases where rivals had a mix of conflicting and shared interests: reconstructing Europe and Japan after World War II; stepping back from the Cuban brink; limiting the strategic arms race; inaugurating and maintaining six major détentes; mediating between Israel and Egypt, Israel and the PLO, and factions in Zimbabwe; protecting the ozone layer; assuring reciprocal compliance with the laws of war; and obtaining Soviet participation in the Helsinki Process.

As expected, an orientation toward mutual gain served the interests of each party better than exploitation. Value-creating policies assisted actors with roughly comparable assets, such as the U.S. and USSR. But unequal partners also generated mutual gain, for example, the small and large countries that participated in the ERP. Belgium gave and perhaps gained more from NATO than did France. Industrialized and industrializing countries apportioned the restraints needed to protect the ozone layer.

Hard-line policies that aimed to exploit failed in every case studied—often within a few years.

Our second conclusion drawn from our case studies is that, in peacetime, openness and multiparty dialogue are more likely to produce successful policies than decisions hatched in secrecy. The best support for this hypothesis is again the Marshall Plan—conceived behind closed doors but initiated, planned, and implemented openly. But most agreements on security issues were negotiated in secret—even those that generated mutual gain such as the Cuban stand-down, SALT, INF, START, and the Camp David and other mediated accords. While the details were negotiated in secret, the logic of most arms control accords was discussed openly in the West. Most of the numbers and types of weapons at stake were public information. As a result, Western publics and NGOs could be and were active participants in the arms control process. Except for a few privileged scientists and journalists, Communist publics remained in the dark about arms control issues and numbers, informed only after treaties were signed—and even then, only in generalities. Absence of public participation permitted militarization of the USSR beyond any reasonable security need, ultimately weakening the Soviet regime.

If open diplomacy plays to the crowds, of course, it can become a propaganda contest harmful to mutual trust. Both secrecy and propaganda soured most Soviet-U.S. détentes. Thus, President Eisenhower's major proposal at the 1955 Geneva summit was a call for "open skies"—permission for spy planes to cross Soviet and Western territory. The idea had intrinsic merit but it was conceived at a U.S. Marine base by experts in psychological warfare and aimed to put Khrushchev on the defensive.

The only Soviet-Western détente that endured more than one or two years was that pursued by Gorbachev and the Reagan-Bush administrations. It was also the most open and constructive, with little propaganda meant to embarrass the other side.

Openness also proved useful in welding national unity in free societies, cultivating a strong economy, and unleashing science. By contrast, Communist governments have tended to deny the realities of ethnic discontent, falsify production and health statistics, and keep scientific advances secret. Secrecy also shields corruption. In the 1990s business people the world over came to decry corruption, as practiced in Nigeria, Indonesia, and China.

Secrecy is useful if you wish to evade arms limitations or prepare a surprise attack. Openness is good if you wish to rally collective security against aggressors. Saddam Hussein's deceptions kept UN arms inspectors running in circles in the 1990s but also alienated potential patrons in Paris and Moscow.

Secrecy is good if you wish to keep a government bureaucracy or banking system dominated by nepotism and other favoritisms. Openness is better if you wish to clean house, attract long-term credits and investments, and inspire support for bodies such as the UN.

Secrecy is useful if you want to violate human rights without public embarrassments. Openness is good if you campaign against such violations.

An open society—where all citizens may think and express themselves freely and enjoy access to all forms of information—is a prerequisite for other social goals at home and internationally—scientific and technological progress, improved living standards, mutual gain enterprises at home and abroad, détente, arms control, peace, environmental preservation, and justice.[5]

INTO THE 21ST CENTURY: ALTERNATIVE FUTURES

Let us stretch our minds across the first quarter of the 21st century. Our view starts from the pyramid of power outlined in Chapter 5—a unipolar world combining a sole superpower with successive levels of

5. As Andrei Sakharov put it in his Nobel Peace Prize acceptance speech in 1975: "Détente can only be assured if from the very outset it goes hand in hand with continuous openness on the part of all countries, an aroused sense of public opinion, free exchange of information, and absolute respect in all countries for civic and political rights. In short: in addition to détente in the material sphere, with disarmament and trade, détente should take place in the intellectual and ideological sphere."

great, medium, regional, and rising powers. Six scenarios follow, though many variations are possible. Each scenario assumes that technology continues to reduce distance and time, that many means of locomotion and of destruction become cheaper and more widely acceptable, and that mutual vulnerabilities increase. Our first five scenarios assume that governments dominate the world scene; the sixth scenario posits that the processes of globalization elicit world governance by combinations of national, international, and transnational agents. Each scenario blends elements of conflict and mutual gain.

To maximize credibility, each scenario is portrayed as a fact—not what "could," "would," or "should" be. The most familiar scenarios—those closest to the pyramid of power in the 1990s—are listed first.

I. Unipolar Stability

U.S. hegemony is rooted in tangible and intangible assets that show no sign of weakening—a splendid geographical setting occupied by a diverse and well-educated population with freedom to create.[6] The unipolar world continues for decades. It proves to be the most peaceful, stable, and prosperous era in human history. It is a world in which most states deal with global interdependence in a manner that generates mutual gain. It begins to embody the principle: "From each according to her or his ability, to each according to her or his need." There is more value-creation than aggressive exploitation or parasitism.

Unipolarity is more conducive to peace among the great powers than the multilateral balancing of the 19th century, the rival alliances of 1914, or Cold War bipolarity. Great power stability, of course, does not prevent disorder between and within lesser states drifting toward chaos. Outside powers, usually with UN blessing, intervene in some but not all trouble spots.

The U.S. is a new kind of hegemon on the world stage. This *pax americana* is more stable than the ancient *pax romana*, because it rests more on persuasion and cooption than on commands or coercion. The sole superpower seldom acts alone. Washington needs, seeks, and usually gets the support of other actors for its key goals, as it did in forging a policy to contain Iraq and North Korea in the 1990s.

A deal takes shape: Washington does not abuse its power and other countries do not gang up against the lone superpower. This deal is feasible because in the 1990s the U.S. was closer to the UK, Germany, Japan, China, Russia, Brazil, India, Ukraine, and Kazakstan than any one of

6. See Zbigniew Brzezinski, *The Grand Chessboard: American Primacy and Its Geostrategic Imperatives* (New York: Basic Books, 1997).

them was to another. The other major powers have no deep reason, as in 1914, to chain-gang or, as in 1938–1939, to pass the buck.

Economic prospects for most of the world are positive. The world is sufficiently rich and well informed to find paths to sustainable development. The World Bank formulates dependable guidelines by which countries can develop and improve their HDI scores and their GDPs. Russia begins to realize its economic potential. New giants arise—China, Brazil, Argentina, Indonesia, Kazakstan. But none has the wish or the means to challenge the global hegemon.

Europe and Japan remain powerful trading states. Europe, however, is at most a confederation. Real union is infeasible due to language and cultural differences. Most Europeans are more likely to converge against one of their own, Germany, than against the U.S. To avert this, Germany abjures advanced weapons and remains dependent upon the nuclear forces of its NATO partners.

Alliance with the U.S. is still the linchpin of Japan's security. The country's place in the pyramid of power declines as China's strengthens. Japan faces severe limits. Its archipelago remains crowded. The population becomes grayer with fewer workers to support retirees. Japan's foreign markets shrink as Korea and other neighbors fill the same demands at lower prices.

Most Pacific rim economies slow their torrid pace as fresh inputs of labor, capital, and energy become more costly. HIV infections impose a heavy economic burden in several countries. Many workers die young or require expensive drugs to live. Authoritarian rule curtails the once vibrant growth of Singapore and Hong Kong.

II. Fragmented Chaos

Extrapolations often go wrong. How could chaos replace stability? Humans stand at the brink: Mutual vulnerability means that a serious change in any part of the system can ripple and multiply throughout the whole.

First, the biosphere fails to support human life in some places where it flourished in the 1990s. The affluent Pacific rim sits on a ring of fire—volcanoes and fault lines—that devour life and property. Storms and droughts increase due to climate change abetted by pollution and deforestation. Both environmental and economic barriers impede growth. It is easier to call for "sustainable development" than practice it. Global epidemics spread and undermine both physical and financial health.

Second, the rational calm inspired by expanding prosperity is not shared by actors whose deep demands go unmet. Unemployed youth in many LDCs are furious in the knowledge that others live far better than they. Religious and ethnic zealots incite violence. In failing states the road to economic development is derailed by civil strife. As in Tajikistan in the 1990s, many groups continue to fight despite local exhaustion and foreign mediation. In rogue states like Iraq in the 1990s, some leaders throw down the gauntlet to challenge the have-nations.

Third, weapons of mass destruction become more accessible. A single nuclear explosion near a city—set off by mechanical accident, human error, or design—makes Chernobyl and Oklahoma City look like child's play. Besides local deaths, large areas suffer from radiation and disruption. Reports that Iraq is ready to launch anthrax-filled warheads creates panic in Iran and Israel.

When the awakening giant China trembles, there are global repercussions. Millions are unemployed as the country's economy slows. Malthus strikes: China cannot feed itself because too much scarce farm land has been sacrificed to industrialization. Serious environmental problems undermine public health. China's border peoples become more restive. Beijing's dictators are challenged by democratic reformers and regional potentates. As we know from Chapter 10, transitions from or toward dictatorship are dangerous to world peace.

Compounding these problems, the U.S. fails to lead or throws its weight too aggressively. It antagonizes followers or loses them. Washington oscillates between do-nothing complacency and hubristic power. The U.S. home front deteriorates as racial and class cleavages multiply; as Hispanic and other groups reject the long dominant culture; as guns rule some streets and many schools; and as Congress and the public refuse to invest in science, public health, or even in basic infrastructure. Couch potato–fast food obesity and drug dependency impede intellectual, emotional, and physical health.

The logic of collective action takes its toll. Many actors parasite and pass the buck. While more and more individuals "bowl alone"—some of them lost in cyberspace—a global time of troubles engulfs humanity.

III. Challenge to the Hegemon

Nothing lasts. When the U.S. appears weak or overbearing, rising powers challenge the hegemon. Most Chinese remain poor, but the country's enormous GDP permits Beijing to build economic clout and formidable armed forces. China's scientists and engineers move the country to the leading edge of technology. China's oil requirements deepen its motives to hold onto Central Asia and to dominate the South China Sea.

Problems multiply when China cracks down harder on its Uighurs and insists that Japan stop building antimissile defenses. But a more serious threat to stability arises when China demands that Taiwan join in a Beijing-dominated federation. Washington again sends aircraft carriers to the Taiwan Strait. The danger to peace is far greater than when an Austrian archduke died in Sarajevo.

Here the road forks: One path sees China back down before the U.S. show of force. Like Russia's rulers in 1911 and 1962, however, Beijing swears "never again"—never again to retreat before rival power. Since the 1990s PRC strategists have studied how to defeat "a powerful opponent with a weak force in a high tech war."[7] China steps up investment in the sinews of war and prepares for a confrontation one or two decades hence.

The other path also leads to trouble: Washington pulls back while Beijing incorporates Taiwan into China. The PRC proceeds to bully other neighbors—Vietnam, Korea, Japan, Russia, India. Washington wants to contain China, but blows hot and cold—as it did toward Khrushchev in 1958–1962. Emboldened, China marches toward a collision with the enfeebled hegemon, believing it will win the next game of Chicken.

IV. Bipolar Cooperation

China and the U.S. have equivalent GDPs by 2020, but average Chinese incomes are much lower than average U.S. incomes. The two economies are more complementary than competitive. The two countries have no territorial claims on each other. Projects such as the Guangdong Modern Dance Company and the U.S.-sponsored School for Advanced International Studies at Nanjing have convinced people in both countries that mutual gain is possible in culture and science as well as in commerce.

The Taiwan issue no longer troubles PRC-U.S. relations. China adapts the Taiwanese model. Dictatorship gives way to pluralism. Technocrats supplant ideologists in Beijing. Mainland China and Taiwan are interdependent economically but distinct politically. They agree to disagree on politics.

The erstwhile Middle Kingdom keeps to its existing borders and focuses on internal problems. China suffers many of the severe economic and environmental challenges noted in the previous scenario. But the U.S. and other countries give or sell much of what China needs to make

7. See Michael Pillsbury, ed., *Chinese Views of Future Warfare* (Washington, D.C.: National Defense University Press, 1997).

Undetermined Domain . . . Distant Sound . . . Comrade . . . Light

The Guangdong Modern Dance Company blended Martha Graham-style techniques with kung-fu in 1997. Though not literal, their creation "Undetermined Domain" could recall the Tiananmen Square massacre as dancers hurled themselves against a wall onstage—a wall that turned into cages formed from its metal supports. But the specific images of this piece could be universal: Does not every civilization have its Tiananmen Square?

And must not every civilization consider the role of the individual within the group? The piece "Distant Sound" depicted a parade of upright and bent-over women, some of whom attempted to escape from the conformist pattern. The duet "Comrade" challenged Chinese (and others') values by showing how two men could love each other. A soloist (from Tibet) starred in "Light," choreographed to the adagio of Mahler's Fifth Symphony.

"Art is long, life short; judgment difficult; opportunity transient." Goethe's words are inspiration for cooperative ventures between the West and Asia—in dance as in other spheres. The Guangdong Modern Dance Company's tour of the U.S. contributed to a world in which cooperation for mutual gain overshadows rivalry.

The very existence of the Guangdong company underscored the ways in which China had opened up, for it flowed from collaboration initiated in 1990 with the American Dance Festival in Durham, North Carolina, and danced to U.S. as well as Chinese music. In 1997 the group performed at the Kennedy Center for the Performing Arts in Washington, D.C., Connecticut College, Rutgers University, and the University of Washington.[1]

1. See Anna Kisselgoff, "The Person, the Group: Reflections from China," *New York Times,* November 1, 1997, A20.

up its food and other deficits. China is not active at the United Nations but rarely objects to peacemaking, peacekeeping, or peace enforcement activities sponsored by the U.S. and other powers.

V. Multipolar Cooperation

The poles of power are diverse but, on the whole, complementary. Global interdependence links not just the major powers but also North and South. Peace is sustained by the trends anticipated by Kant. Most governments are representative democracies; most belong to a grid of complex interdependence and trade. Cyberspace joins scientists, cultural figures, business people, relatives, and pen pals across the world.

By 2020 Russia and the U.S. have cut their nuclear arsenals to one thousand strategic warheads. China, France, and the UK are authorized, if they wish, to equal that number, but they opt for much smaller arsenals. The military requirements set out in Articles 43–47 of the UN Charter have been fulfilled. The UN Security Council has a Military Staff Committee; most UN members have earmarked forces for use by the Security Council. Collective security is becoming a reality. The tough action taken by the UN against Saddam Hussein in the 1990s encourages confidence in collective security and discourages rogue attacks on the evolving world order. Israel and most of its neighbors are learning how to coexist and trade. The Palestinian Republic is becoming the Singapore of the Middle East.

North-South differences narrow. More Asian, African, Middle Eastern, and Latin American countries enter the path of rapid and sustainable development. New strains of hybrid wheat, rice, maize, and other crops permit nearly every region to become self-sufficient in basic foods—without heavy irrigation or chemicals. Few countries still depend on jute, cocoa, or any other single commodity. Investment in health and education rises dramatically as developing and industrialized countries shift resources from defense to development needs. Biodiversity in the Amazon and other tropical regions is protected and becomes profitable.

VI. Global Governance Without World Government

A transnational civil society is evolving. Like civil society within countries, it shields individual humans and groups from the raw powers of government and market. The transnational civil society develops in tandem with complex interdependence across many countries and regions. Common values—political choice, trust in free markets, respect for human rights—are shared by more than half of humanity. Territoriality weakens as a principle of organization. There is no world government by a supranational authority. National governments remain. But they share power with a medley of nongovernmental agencies—business and labor groups as well as NGOs. Together they form expanding networks of institutions designed to meet a wide range of human needs.[8]

National governments confer among themselves and with responsible specialists from national, international, and transnational agencies. This is functionalism writ large—decision making informed and managed by experts, mediated and supervised by representatives of elected governments. As we see in the sidebar on page 528, the 21st century can build

8. See Wolfgang H. Reinicke, "Global Public Policy," *Foreign Affairs* 76, no. 6 (November–December 1997): 127–138; *Our Global Neighborhood: The Report on the Commission on Global Governance* (New York: Oxford University Press, 1995); and Mihaly Simai, *The Future of Global Governance: Managing Risk and Change in the International System* (Washington, D.C.: U.S. Institute of Peace Press, 1994).

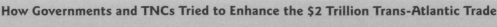

How Governments and TNCs Tried to Enhance the $2 Trillion Trans-Atlantic Trade

The Trans-Atlantic Business Dialogue took place between industrial leaders and officials from the European Union and the U.S. In 1995 they met in Spain; in 1996 in Chicago; in 1997 in Rome. They wanted to increase trans-Atlantic trade—worth more than $2 trillion. Corporate CEOs noted that trans-Atlantic tariffs on most goods averaged a mere 3 percent. A far weightier factor driving up prices was a non-tariff barrier: duplicate sets of regulations on each side of the Atlantic on everything from health and automotive safety to environmental protection. Duplicate testing increased prices for consumers and delayed marketing of new products. Governments and CEOs found a simple remedy—mutual recognition agreements: If a product passes inspection on one side of the Atlantic, it is ordinarily approved on the other. In 1997 the U.S. and EU ratified mutual recognition agreements in five domains including pharmaceuticals, medical devices, and electromagnetic equipment. If either the U.S. Food and Drug Administration or its EU counterpart approved a drug, it would usually be accepted as safe by both. If authorities wished to retest the drug, however, they could.

Corporate leaders and governments also discussed uniform standards for taxation, investment, and prosecution of business corruption. But common standards were difficult to achieve for many reasons. Europe's regulatory system was more decentralized than the U.S. system. Safety and environmental norms were not identical in the U.S. and Europe. The U.S. Congress insisted on higher standards for some foreign products, for example, industrial fasteners, than those it imposed on U.S. manufacturers. The U.S. government resisted pressures from U.S. and EU businesses to drop trade sanctions aimed against Iran, Iraq, and Cuba. Drug companies wanted laws to ban dissemination of their trade secrets on the Internet; other groups lobbied against any form of censorship.

Did all this amount to collusion between bureaucrats and technocrats? Consumer advocates and environmentalists demanded transparency and full reporting. Perhaps they too would be given seats in the trans-Atlantic dialogue.

upon the efforts of governments and industrial leaders in the late 20th century to forge a consensus on shared concerns.

To cope with epidemics, for example, government experts form a committee drawn from national medical boards, the WHO, the ICRC, and the recently formed International Academy of Health Sciences.

To deal with economic issues—currency fluctuations, debt, volatile commodity prices—government experts form a committee drawn from the World Bank, the IMF, leading commercial banks, and the recently formed International Academy of Economic and Social Scientists.

To deal with threats to peace and security, governments depend heavily on the UN Security Council and the UN Secretary-General. Some governments retain nuclear arsenals, but the Security Council has its own rapid reaction force, backed by designated units from most UN members. The UN Secretary-General has a panel of mediators whom she/he can propose to disputants. A committee of elders drawn from Nobel Peace Prize laureates advises the Security Council and the Secretary-General. The International Peace Academy has graduated many diplomats skilled at conflict resolution.

By 2005 the University of the Middle East has received help from some governments and foundations. By 2020 it has trained a generation of men and women more concerned with peaceful development than with sectarian passions. By 2025 they have launched several projects that knit Israel and its neighbors in mutual gain.

World governance is more than the "common marketization" of IR. It is global public policy responding to the dangers and opportunities inherent in globalization.

Which Scenario Is Best? Which Is Most Feasible?

It is easy to say which scenarios are the worst. Scenarios II and III—fragmented chaos and a collision between hegemon and challenger—could destroy many lives and waste valuable assets. The more violence, the greater the suffering and the more difficult the tasks of reconstruction. Wise planners will act to block the roads that lead in these directions.

Any scenario that promotes peace and prosperity is acceptable. But Scenario VI—world governance—has two advantages. First, it postulates development of a truly transnational society. Without such a society, the state system may eventually break down. World governance both requires and contributes to a well integrated global society.[9]

Second, global governance is more likely to cultivate a rich emergent structure able to cope with complex challenges than any scenario that leaves basic tasks mainly to governments. Fitness requires an ability to cope with complexity. Cooperation between governments and non-governmental bodies is more likely to embody the flexibility and reach needed to deal with emerging needs.

ONE WORLD OR MANY?

Realists assert that world politics is still a struggle for power. States are the key actors as they joust to maximize their national interests. Regimes, law, and other forms of international cooperation are ephemeral. They endure only so long as states' interests overlap. Nongovernmental actors shape the periphery—not the vital center—of world politics. Functional cooperation makes life more convenient, but will never supplant the contest of all against all.

Global idealists hold that sovereignty is a deeply eroded myth. Every state is permeable—even hermit dictatorships such as Myanmar. Nearly every state depends upon others near and far. Mutual dependency drives states and other global actors into networks of cooperation—regimes

9. See the alternative paths to world order in Hedley Bull, *The Anarchical Society: A Study of Order in World Politics* (New York: Columbia University Press, 1977), chaps. 10–14.

and organizations. Technocratic cooperation overshadows politics, as in the European Community. What was once the tail begins to wag the dog.

A vision of global interdependence provides a broader framework for understanding the past and planning the future. It underlines the dangers and opportunities inherent in mutual vulnerability—the need to think about means and ends, practicality and morality.

Large parts of humanity are moving toward "one world," but others are left in a time warp. Most of the First World is moving toward complex interdependence and globalization. But more than half of humanity lives in societies so poor and undeveloped that their ties with the rest of the globe are slim and tenuous. They experience the pains but not the gains of interdependence. Bangladesh and Somalia depend heavily upon world markets and international assistance, but they tend to be victims or beneficiaries—not active agents in world affairs. Some are prone to jihads—against outsiders or against one another.

To reduce anarchy we need heightened global consciousness, deeper and more rewarding global relationships, and stronger global institutions.

GLOBAL CONSCIOUSNESS: EDUCATION FOR ONE WORLD

If we are to live in peace and create values together, each person needs education in basic principles:

Empathy—to see the world as others do

Historical perspective—to understand that "everything is the result of everything else"

Respect for other cultures—to admire and enjoy the myriad ways of life across the globe

Reverence for life—to deal with a fecund but fragile biosphere

Responsibility—to consider our place in the great chain of being: our debts to those who lived before, to those less privileged than ourselves, and to those who will follow

POLICIES FOR ONE WORLD

The case studies reviewed here—taken from different times and different places of 20th-century politics—tend to confirm the book's two underlying hypotheses. Informed by this knowledge, you draft your report.

Memo to the UN Secretary-General: *The dynamics of international relations in the 20th century are replete with cases validating the efficacy of the following two guidelines:*

1. The optimal way to enhance each actor's interests is by carrying out strategies aimed at creating values for each party. Value-claiming generates short-term gains that tend to backfire.

2. Policies arrived at openly tend to work better than those conceived and implemented covertly.

These guidelines have an inner logic: The more that policies are discussed at home and with concerned actors abroad, the greater the likelihood of achieving mutual gains valued by each party. The quality of discussion, in turn, depends upon the information and orientation of decision makers and the public. A variable-sum outlook is more constructive than a zero-sum perspective and safer than win-win expectations.

The combined power of these guidelines is best seen in the postwar evolution of the First World—a security and trade community built upon a quest for mutual gain, its contours and defining moments debated openly within and among North America, Europe, and Japan.

Value-creating strategies can be difficult to conceive, plan, and implement due to many factors—bad memories, divergent cultures, asymmetries of power and wealth. We can buy time by negotiating arms control, establishing international regimes, developing trade and educational exchange, utilizing third-party mediation, and fostering dialogue among all segments of global society. If we avoid catastrophe, there is the possibility that a negative-sum or zero-sum struggle may become a variable- or even positive-sum search for overlapping goals. If the relationship between France and Germany can be transformed, why not that between Israel and Syria? If the U.S. and Russia can become real partners, why not India and Pakistan?

Every dogmatism can be a blindfold shutting out light and opportunity from our vision. For Russia to shed Communism was not death but a chance for rebirth. Other societies may also find that by shedding their zero-sum dogmas they are liberated at home and abroad.

Wisdom dictates a quest to nurture value-creating policies with other societies, coupled with awareness that strong currents of anarchy remain.

GLOSSARY

LEARNING ABOUT
INTERNATIONAL RELATIONS

PHOTO AND CARTOON CREDITS

INDEX

GLOSSARY

ABM antiballistic missile defense; constrained by U.S.-Soviet agreements since 1972

absolute advantage concept of market strength based on natural endowment; a premise of Adam Smith's trust in an invisible hand

actor in IR a state, TNC, NGO, or other IR player

Adam Smith a father of economic liberalism, authored *The Wealth of Nations* (1776)

alliance a military partnership stipulating joint action under specified conditions; more loosely, any partnership

Alsace and Lorraine disputed borderlands taken by Germany in 1871 and retaken by France in 1918–1919

anarchy absence of government (though order is still possible)

apartheid system of racial segregation practiced in South Africa until the 1990s

Appomatox Virginia Court House where Confederate General R. E. Lee surrendered to Union General U. S. Grant in 1865; symbol of a conciliatory peace policy

appropriate technology whatever scale technology is appropriate to the task

arbitration binding adjudication by one or more arbiters selected by the disputants

arms control regulation of arms to enhance political, military, economic or other aims; could entail disarmament

Arafat, Yasser chairman of the Palestinian Liberation Organization (PLO) since 1969 and, after 1994, of the Palestinian Authority in the West Bank and Gaza

assimilation absorbing minorities into the dominant culture

Association of Southeast Asian Nations (ASEAN) international organization formed in 1967 to promote cooperation among its members, which in 1997 included Brunei, Indonesia, Laos, Malaysia, Myanmar (Burma), the Philippines, Singapore, Thailand, and Vietnam

Aswan syndrome devotion to high dams and reluctance to face negative externalities—uprooted people, silting, salty soil, diminished nutrients downstream, increased vulnerability

attention space the amount of attention a decision maker can devote to any problem; constrained by fatigue and by multiple demands

autarky economic self-sufficiency and non-reliance on imports or aid

authoritarian top-down governance based on strong leadership rather than democracy

autonomy self-rule

balance of payments accounting of all transactions between one country and the rest of the world

balance of power an ambiguous concept that can mean equality of power, inequality, or any distribution of power, with focus on military and economic assets

Bay of Pigs Cuban coast where anti-Castro exiles, sponsored by the CIA, were defeated by Cuban forces in April 1961

Baruch Plan U.S. proposal in 1946 to create an international authority to control all nuclear weapons and plants throughout the world; inspection and other provisions rejected by Moscow

bean count the most basic assessment of power, counting who has what, for example, how many soldiers, tanks, modems; undervalues intangibles

best alternative to no-agreement (BATNA) a crucial issue in deciding whether to seek a negotiated accord

biosphere the zone of life on earth and the atmosphere that shapes and is shaped by IR; the fifth level of IR action and analysis

Blitzkrieg German for lightning war; combined tank and air assaults followed by rapid infantry advance used by Germany in 1939–1941

bounded rationality the concept that limits on time, energy, and available information constrain the ability of decision makers to process information and act rationally

Bretton Woods system system of international finance established in 1944 based on convertibility of the U.S. dollar into gold and supported by the IMF and World Bank; replaced by floating currencies after 1971

Bricker Amendment U.S. constitutional amendment proposal of the 1950s that called for implementing legislation for treaties (for example, on human rights) before they could become law

buck-passing deferring to another actor to take the first step, for example, to cope with expansionist Germany in the 1930s

Bunche, Ralph Afro-American who served for years as second most powerful official in the UN Secretariat; awarded Nobel Peace Prize (1950) for mediating Arab-Israeli dispute in 1948–1949; helped created UN peacekeeping

Burlusconi, Silvio billionaire media mogul who served briefly as Italy's prime minister in the mid-1990s; exploited his three TV channels for political influence

C³I "C cubed": command, control, communications and intelligence to coordinate warfare from a distance

capital material wealth being used or usable for the production of more wealth

capitalism private ownership of the means of production; for Marxists: private ownership of the means of production, destined to be replaced by socialism

Carter, Jimmy U.S. president who mediated the 1978 Camp David accords and, as a private citizen, the 1994 U.S.-DPRK understandings on nuclear issues

Carthaginian peace total destruction of Carthage by Rome in 146 B.C.; symbol of a vindictive, repressive policy to the defeated

carrying capacity the level of resource utilization that can be sustained without degrading the original resource

Caspian Sea land-locked sea bordered by Russia, Kazakhstan, Iran, and Azerbaijan with vast oil reserves

Central Asia Kazakhstan, Kyrgyzstan, Turkmenistan, Tajikistan, Uzbekistan, and some adjacent parts of Russia and China such as Xinjiang, where more than half the population is Uighur or Kazak

chain-ganging movement in unison, as in 1914 when most members of the two alliances quickly joined one another in war

Chechnya   political entity in the north Caucasus; declared its independence from Russia after the Soviet break-up; attacked by Russian forces in 1994–1996

Chernobyl   site of 1986 nuclear reactor accident in Ukraine; also, the nontechnical name for a type of Soviet-built reactor widely used in Eastern Europe

Chernomyrdin, Viktor   prime minister of Russia for much of the 1990s; former official in the oil industry

Chicken   collision course in which double defection leads to shared catastrophe

China Card   leverage that Washington hoped to use against the USSR based on prospect that that the U.S. might draw closer to a major Soviet foe

Christianity, Orthodox and Western   civilizations sharing much in common, but Orthodox Christianity based in Constantinople, Moscow, and other eastern capitals developed differently and sometimes in conflict with Western Christianity

civilization   the broadest level of cultural identity

civilizationism   Samuel P. Huntington's view that the fault lines of post–Cold War IR are at the meeting places of the world's seven or eight major civilizations

civil society   intermediate institutions shielding individuals from government and from raw market forces

Clausewitz, Carl von   early-19th-century Prussian military strategist who argued that war is the continuation of policy by other (violent) means

Clemenceau, Georges   French premier who pressed for reparations from and repression of Germany after World War I

coevolution   the development of an actor in tandem with other actors and their shared environment

cold war   multifaceted struggle to defeat the other side using many kinds of hard and soft power but avoiding hot war, unless by proxies

collective (or public) good   a good freely available to all, whether produced by human action or nature, thus tempting free-riders

collective security   a system of "one for all and all for one" requiring each party to respond to an attack on another member as an attack on itself

commodity agreement   accord by producers of a primary product to limit production and/or set prices

Commonwealth of Independent States (CIS)   an IGO in which all former Soviet republics participate except for the three Baltic states; the CIS generated many agreements on economic and military cooperation in the 1990s but implementation was weak

comparative advantage   relative advantage of one producer or country; a major reason for international trade

competitive advantage   economic strength based not just on endowment but on many factors including standards set by local consumers and governments

complex humanitarian emergency   problem facing relief agencies in 1990s, often includes consequences of a failed state, poverty, civil war and foreign intervention, environmental disaster, and famine

complex interdependence   a relationship between IR actors characterized by a complex agenda with no hierarchy, interaction on many levels, and bargaining without force

Concert of Europe   periodic meetings of the major powers during the 19th century to deal with threats to stability; a precursor to the UN Security Council

concessional loans   loans granted at less than commercial interest rates

condominium   international order in which two or more actors share power

confederation   a system of governance in which most power resides in the local units

conflict   disharmony, struggle, combat, war—deeper than a dispute; often results from exploitation real or perceived

conflict resolution   removing the causes and manifestations of conflict, for example, by peacemaking or peace building

Congress of Vienna   1815 conference that established a new order in Europe after Napoleon's final defeat; symbol of a firm but conciliatory policy to the vanquished

convention   in IR a synonym for "treaty," often used in environmental diplomacy

Conventional Forces in Europe (CFE) Treaty   1990 treaty limiting tanks, planes, and other weapons from the Atlantic to the Ural Mountains; tilted against Russia after Moscow's former allies aligned with the West

conventional war   war fought by regular forces with tanks, planes, and missiles but without biological, chemical, or nuclear weapons; definition may change over time

Convention on the Elimination of All Forms of Discrimination Against Women   1979 treaty banning gender-based distinctions impairing women's human rights in any field; requires governments to report on laws designed to implement the treaty

Convention on the Prevention and Punishment of the Crime of Genocide   1948 treaty adopted by most governments that bans acts committed with the intent to destroy a "national, ethnical, racial, or religious group, as such"

conversion   the difficult problem of converting military to civilian industry

conversion power   ability to translate hard and soft power into fitness and influence

cooperative security   programs to promote shared security interests between U.S. and partner-rivals such as Russia

coordination game   a game in which the point is to increase the gains for each player

Cornucopian outlook   the belief that human ingenuity ensures that there will be no finite limits on growth, as technology will be used to sustain populations

cost-tolerance   an intangible asset of power, the ability of a society to endure hardship and persevere in war or otherwise

Council on Mutual Economic Assistance (COMECON)   Moscow's anwer to the ERP, an EGO formed in 1949 to coordinate trade and economic policies in the Soviet sphere—from East Germany to Outer Mongolia; Cuba joined in 1972, Vietnam in 1978

Country Reports on Human Rights Practices   annual survey of all countries (except the U.S.) undertaken by the U.S. State Department to assess human rights practices worldwide

crimes against humanity   activities undertaken during wartime or in preparation for war identified by the International Military Tribunal at Nuremberg as actionable before an international court; includes murder, extermination, enslavement, and deportation of any civilian population and persecution on political, racial, or religious grounds

cruise missile   pilotless aircraft, radar and computer guided, armed with nuclear or other warheads

cult of the defensive   military doctrine trusting in the superiority of the defense over the offense

cult of the offensive military doctrine trusting that wars can be won quickly by the side that mobilizes and strikes first

culture way of life, material and spiritual; a matrix of behavior

current account a measure linking a country's international transactions with its national income; includes all sales and purchases of currently produced goods and services, interest income, military transactions, travel and transportation receipts, and unilateral transfers

Dayton Peace Accord November 1995 agreements to end fighting in Bosnia and establish a Bosnian state that included a Croat-Muslim Federation and Republika Srpska; peace to be upheld initially by NATO forces

DDT an insecticide banned for most uses in the U.S. since 1972 but used in many LDCs

deadlock an impasse; in game theory, a condition in which both parties defect, round after round, causing mutual hurt

debt rescheduling renegotiated terms for loan repayment; usually, attenuation

debt service total principal and interest due on a loan each period

declinism view that great powers decline if they overreach, that is, expand too far and spend too much on empire

demagogue leader who arouses popular passions with rhetoric

demicide mass murder of people (*demos*), especially one's own

demilitarized zone (DMZ) an area without fortifications; between North and South Korea, a zone of intense confrontation

democracy governance by the people, usually indirect, by means of freely contested elections

Deng Xiaoping paramount PRC leader from 1977 to 1997

dependency theory variant of world-system theory that sees the world as having an imperialist core with a dependent periphery

détente relaxation of tensions

determinism belief that impersonal forces, not individuals with free will, determine historical outcomes

deterrence restraint of other actors achieved by fear of retribution

development in IR refers to fulfillment of potential by individuals (measured in HDI) or states (economic and political development)

dictatorship governance by an individual or small group with complete authority and unlimited power; may use persuasion as well as force

diplomacy foreign policy, especially by negotiation; includes Track I diplomacy— diplomacy by government officials—and Track II diplomacy—diplomacy by private citizens and organizations

disarmament the reduction or elimination of armaments

Dobrynin, Anatoly Soviet ambassador to six U.S. presidents; an important go-between during the Cuban missile crisis

Duma (also State Duma) the lower house of parliament in the Russian Federation

Earth Summit 1992 UN Conference on Environment and Development

East Asia home of an "economic miracle" led by Japan, followed by the four "Tigers" and by China; the miracle appeared less certain in the late 1990s

ecology study of habitat, environmental science

economic liberalism theory that individuals seeking their self-interest will raise the common good; against government intervention in economic affairs

economic statecraft use of economic rewards and penalties to shape the behavior of other actors in IR

economic warfare boycotts and sanctions meant to punish other actors or slow their development

ekos (oikos) "habitat," Greek root of economics and ecology

emergent structure a holistic entity more than the sum of its parts; a product of coevolution as diverse actors meet their diverse needs, as in a coral reef or, by analogy, the networks of global governance

endism the view of Francis Fukuyama that history—defined as the clash of ideas—ended with the Cold War

entente an understanding, as in the Triple Entente before World War I

entitlement right or permit, for example, to release carbons

environmental diplomacy negotiation and actions at the interface between IR and the habitat, for example, the ozone layer

escalation dominance ability to prevail at any step of the escalation ladder, thus discouraging the other side from escalating

escalation ladder hypothetical steps by which actors move toward greater violence, pausing at intervals that permit the parties to deliberate before intensifying their struggle

ethnic pertaining to ethos

ethnic cleansing forced removal or attempted extermination of an ethnic group

ethnocentrism centering on one's own ethnic group, its merits and problems

ethnos a different people with its own ethos (like Spartans to Athenians); sometimes rendered as *ethnie*, a unit smaller than a nation

ethos a character and moral values of a people

Euro common European currency planned for gradual introduction from 1999 to 2002

European Atomic Energy Community (EURATOM) established in 1957, promotes nuclear energy use in Europe and develops common standards

European Coal and Steel Community (ECSC) the world's premier supranational organization, founded in 1951 by France, Germany, Italy, Belgium, the Netherlands, and Luxembourg to coordinate their production and sales of coal and steel

European Commission executive body of the European Community; initiates policies and "guards" previous EC accords

European Community (EC) collective term for the EEC, the ECSC, and EURATOM; the EC shares five institutions and became the first "pillar" of the EU in 1993

European Council the EU summit: the heads of government meeting twice each year to provide guidance for other EU organs

European Council of Ministers a forum for policy planning by top ministers who meet at least twice a year; chaired by rotation

European Court of Justice judicial body of the EC; rules on legality of acts by the European Commission and on compatibility of national and EC laws

European Economic Community (EEC) established in 1957 by the ECSC states, an agreement to form a common market for the free movement of goods, labor, and capital across national borders

European Monetary Union (EMU) EC goal of a common currency managed by a central bank, mandated by 1991 Maastricht Treaty

European Parliament the only EC body directly elected by voters of the member states; primarily a deliberative body

European Union (EU) formed in 1993, the EU includes the EC as one pillar plus a pillar for forging a common foreign policy and another for overseeing justice and home affairs

ExComm (Executive Committee) fourteen to twenty officials from various branches of government who advised the U.S. president during the Cuban missile crisis

expansionist nationalism a nationalism seeking to displace or rule other nations, for example, Nazi Germany

exploitation utilization of a resource; value-claiming, hard-line treatment of others as foes in a zero-sum relationship

export-led strategy economic development focused on producing goods competitive in foreign markets

externality in economics, any cost or benefit of a good not encompassed in its price; a side effect, positive or negative, for initiator or for third parties

extraction capability ability to mobilize assets, for example, to tax and conscript for public purposes

factor endowment production inputs: land and resources, labor, capital, and skills

failed state country such as Somalia in the 1990s where central government does not function

falling dominoes theory expectation that if a critically positioned actor falls to the other side, its neighbors will also fall; helped to motivate U.S. support for Greece, Turkey, and South Vietnam

Faustian wager risking the future for the present, as with nuclear power, an energy source that can also damage the biosphere

federation political system in which power is divided between the center and the regions

feminism in IR belief that women and their interests have been neglected in the practice and the study of IR

First World the West and Japan, comparatively rich and free

fitness ability to cope with complex challenges

Fordism mass production plant with wages adequate to allow consumerism

foreign affairs any matters that concern a foreign minister

foreign aid any form of assistance across borders—from emergency relief to grants and low-interest loans to education and technology transfer

foreign direct investment (FDI) capital investments including plants in a foreign country; can lower production and transportation costs and surmount local tariffs and NTBs

Fourth World poorest of the poor; includes some Native Americans

framework convention a treaty stating general goals, a commitment the parties expect to spell out in subsequent accords

Framework Convention on Climate Change (FCCC) agreement reached at 1992 Earth Summit, the FCCC provided a foundation for later protocols; stipulated that developed countries take the first steps to curb greenhouse gas emissions and subsidize LDC emission curbs; set no targets or deadlines

free-riding taking advantage of public goods but not contributing one's own share

free trade exchange of goods and services across borders shaped by market forces without tariffs or other government constraint

freer trade neoliberal view that the principle of free trade must be modified to meet the internal needs of each country

frontier of possibilities (Pareto Optimum) area of agreement beyond which one side must lose

functionalism international technical cooperation on common interests, as in the WHO, that can bypass political differences but build habits of trust

fungibility convertability; the extent that an asset (for example, gold, dollars, knowledge) may be traded for another

General Agreement on Tariffs and Trade (GATT) a forum established in 1947 to promote free trade; more than 125 states took part in early 1990s; superseded by the WTO in 1995

Gender-Empowerment Measure (GEM) indicator of participation in economic and political activity relative to gender

Gender-Related Development Index (GDI) HDI corrected for gender differences

Geneva Conventions of 1949 rules for the humane treatment during wartime of the sick, the wounded, prisoners of war, civilians, and others; accepted by most governments but unknown to or not respected by many guerrilla groups and warlords

genocide effort to destroy another people or its culture, banned by 1948 Genocide Convention

geonomics belief that economic strength has eclipsed military strength as a source of influence in IR; rationalizes neomercantilist policies

geopolitics belief that geography plus military assets is key to survival and influence in IR; underlies belief in importance of controlling "heartlands" and choke points at sea

Ghandi, Rajiv prime minister of India in 1987 who used Indian hard power attempting to make peace between the Sri Lankan government and Tamil insurgents

Global Environmental Facility (GEF) created in 1991 and administered by the World Bank in cooperation with UNEP and UNDP, the GEF makes grants or loans for projects that respond to global environmental threats

globalization cross-border ties based on forces that bypass governments, from the Internet to epidemics

good offices using one's position to promote talks between disputants

graduated reciprocation in tension-reduction (GRIT) a publicly announced strategy of initiatives to reduce tensions, steps that, if reciprocated, will be enlarged

Grameen Bank a development bank established in Bangladesh in 1976; provides loans averaging $100 sequentially to poor people, mostly to rural women; spreading in the 1990s to other LDCs

grants outright gifts, either in currency or in kind, such as food

Greenhouse effect global warming presumed to be caused by trapping of solar radiation in the earth's atmosphere due to buildup of carbon dioxide, methane, and other gases

Green Revolution improved agricultural yields due to hybrid seeds, fertilizer, and irrigation

gross domestic product (GDP) total value of goods and services produced within a country; does not include depreciation of resources or machines

gross national product (GNP) GDP plus net receipts from nonresident sources

Group of Seven (G-7) First World economic giants: Canada, France, Germany, Italy, Japan, the UK, and the U.S.—sometimes joined by Russia

groupthink collective opinion shaped by pressures to conform with little room for dissent

Gulf of Tonkin Resolution August 1964 resolution by which the U.S. Congress sanctioned escalation of U.S. military activity in Vietnam; authorized the president to take "all necessary measures" to repel attack on U.S. forces and "prevent further aggression"

hawks and doves hard-liners and conciliators

hard power ability to command others by threat or coerce them by force

hegemonic war fought by challenger to displace hegemon or by hegemon to maintain its position

hegemony leadership, dominion

Helsinki Process follow-on structures and evaluation of progress in implementing the Conference on Security and Cooperation in Europe; Final Act signed in Helsinki in 1975

high politics issues of state security and sovereignty

Hitler, Adolf leader of Germany, 1933–1945

Holbrooke, Richard E. U.S. Assistant Secretary of State who negotiated the 1995 Dayton Accord

Holst, Johan Jorgen Norwegian foreign minister who mediated the Oslo Accord between Israel and the PLO

Hot Line Washington-Moscow crisis communication link established in 1963 using undersea cables; revised in 1971 to use satellite links

hubris arrogant, overweening pride

Human Development Index (HDI) an aggregate measure of development based on health, education, and real GDP; designed and applied by the UNDP

human poverty the lack of choices and opportunity for living a tolerable life; affected at least one-fourth of humanity in the 1990s

Human Poverty Index (HPI) an aggregate measure of poverty based on life expectancy, literacy, and access to public and private resources; designed and applied by the UNDP

Hussein, Saddam president of Iraq, 1979– ; ordered war against Iran in the 1980s and invasion of Kuwait in 1990

Huxley, Aldous author of the dystopia *Brave New World* (1932)

ICBM land-based fixed or mobile intercontinental ballistic missile (range of 3,000 or more nautical miles)

idealism (in IR) theory that IR is or should be a quest for law and morality in international life

ideational factors values, beliefs, institutions, property relationships that shape behavior, for example, toward potential IEC

import-substitution strategy to develop an economy shielded from foreign imports

income poverty a measure of poverty: an income below $1 or $2 in LDCs but with a higher threshold in industrialized countries

indigenous native, for example, "First Nations" of Canada

industrial (or technology) policy government actions to nurture and protect a selected industry or industry in general; an expression of neomercantilism

infant mortality death rate in the first year per 1,000 live births; an indicator of social and economic conditions

influence a measure of change in others' behavior achieved by hard or soft power; a result of power but not identical to it

intelligence information, sometimes secret, gathered about other actors and forces in IR

interdependence mutual vulnerability or sensitivity, with capacity for pain or gain; possible paradigm for IR theory

intergenerational equity obligation of each generation to pass on natural and cultural assets equal to those it enjoyed

intergovernmentalist view that EU is an IGO, more an organization among governments than a supranational body over them

intergovernmental organization (IGO) an IO whose membership consists of governments, for example, the UN and the IAEA

Intergovernmental Panel of Climate Change (IPCC) an international scientific body to assess climate change

Intermediate Nuclear Forces (INF) Treaty 1987 Soviet-U.S. treaty to eliminate all land-based missiles with ranges between 500 and 5,500 kilometers (about 300 to 3,400 miles); verified by on-site inspectors; required destruction of missiles but warheads could be recycled

intermingled nationalism cohabitating nationalisms, often in conflict—unlike intermingled nations, which may coexist peacefully

International Atomic Energy Agency (IAEA) UN agency established in 1957 to promote peaceful uses of atomic energy; since 1970, monitors compliance with the NPT

International Committee of the Red Cross (ICRC) NGO founded in 1864 to provide relief to wounded soldiers and other victims of violence worldwide; an agent of humanitarian diplomacy, the ICRC works with national Red Cross and Red Crescent organizations; the Committee is composed of Swiss nationals who, being citizens of a neutral country, can act as intermediaries

International Court of Justice a principal UN organ; a permanent court of fifteen judges based at The Hague

International Covenant on Civil and Political Rights 1966 treaty that binds each signatory to uphold the individual's right of expression and participation in public life; not ratified by the U.S. until 1992

international environmental conflict (IPC) conflict caused or aggravated by dispute over the environment, for example, a dispute over water

international law treaties and customary behavior; public international law applies mainly to states but is expanding to cover other IR actors including individuals; private international law governs business across borders and helps decide which state's courts have jurisdiction

International Military Tribunal at Nuremberg court that tried German leaders in 1945–1946 and confirmed that individuals could be held responsible for crimes against peace, war crimes, and crimes against humanity

International Monetary Fund (IMF) a UN Specialized Agency founded in 1944 charged with easing the short-term liquidity problems of its members

international organization (IO) IGOs and NGOs

international political economy (IPE) interaction of international economics and politics, for example, on trade and investment

international relations (IR) cross-border interactions, especially political; includes any development, governmental or private, material or spiritual, shaping these interactions

IRBM intermediate-range (1,500 to 3,000 nautical miles) ballistic missile

Iron Curtain Winston Churchill's term for the political, economic, and barbed wire barriers separating Western and Communist Europe during the Cold War

irredentism   nationalist movement demanding union of a people (irredenta) ruled by another government with their kinsfolk in their own nation-state

Jiang Zemin   president of China in the late 1990s who continued Deng Xiaoping's policies aimed at cultivating a freer economy while retaining Communist political rule

joint implementation   a way for industrialized and developing countries to cooperate to reduce gas emissions

joker   an item in a negotiating package sure to cause its rejection by the other side

Kant, Immanuel   18th-century Prussian scholar; helped inspire liberal peace theory of late 20th century

Kellogg-Briand Pact   1928 Pact of Paris renouncing war

Keynesianism   use of government monetary and fiscal policies to stimulate, regulate, and cushion a market economy

Khatami, Mohammed   elected president of Iran in 1997, articulated a GRIT-like policy toward the U.S. people

Kim Il-Sung   leader of North Korea from 1945 until his death in 1994; initiated Korean War

kinetic power   power in action, for example, troops marching

Kissinger, Henry   realist scholar and diplomat; Secretary of State under Presidents Richard Nixon and Gerald Ford

Kyoto Protocol   1997 addition to the FCCC spelling out specific gas emissions targets and deadlines for developed countries but not for LDCs

laissez-faire   strong form of economic liberalism

Las Casas, Bartolomé de   16th-century Spanish priest who sought humane treatment for indigenous peoples of the Americas

less developed countries (LDCs)   poor countries with low incomes; may or may not be developing economically

levels of analysis   distinct but overlapping arenas for IR action and analysis; in this book, individuals, states, international systems, transnational systems, and the biosphere

leverage   the total political, economic, and military power a party or mediator can mobilize to influence others

liberal internationalism   theory that market democracy offers the surest foundation for peace and prosperity

liberal peace theory   democracies do fight but rarely, if ever, make war on other democracies

logic of collective action   to contribute as little as possible to public goods while benefiting from what others contribute

low politics   foreign affairs apart from high politics, for example, trade, humanitarian action, and environmental protection

MacArthur, Douglas A.   Supreme Allied Commander in occupied Japan, 1945–1950, and commander of UN forces in Korea, 1950–1951

Maginot Line   defensive fortifications shielding some but not all of France's border with Germany in the 1930s; skirted by Germany in 1940

majority rule   the method of governance in which the laws are made and enforced according to the desires of the numerical majority

Malthusian outlook   derived from Thomas Malthus, the belief that there are finite limits to growth as expanding human populations deplete natural resources

Mao Zedong   leader of Chinese Communist Party from 1921 and the PRC from 1949 until his death in 1976

maquiladora   export processing plant that takes advantage of low-priced Mexican labor and proximity of U.S. import markets

market   arena where supply meets demand mediated by price

Marshall, George C.   U.S. army general, Secretary of State, and Secretary of Defense; exponent of the Marshall Plan

Marshall Plan   the European Recovery Program (ERP) proposed and funded by the U.S. to promote Europe's reconstruction, 1947–1951; a model of mutual gain

McNamara, Robert S.   U.S. Secretary of Defense during the Cuban missile crisis and initial U.S. escalation of the Vietnam conflict

mediation   a process of conflict management in which an outside or third party helps disputants accommodate their differences

mercantilism   doctrine that wealth consists in accumulating gold bullion or similar forms of wealth

Mikoyan, Anastas   First Deputy Prime Minister of the USSR under Nikita Khrushchev and occasional emissary to Fidel Castro

minimum deterrent   the smallest arsenal sufficient for deterrence, perhaps dozens or hundreds of nuclear weapons

Ministry of International Trade and Industry (MITI)   Japanese agency responsible for protecting Japanese industries and promoting targeted exports

MIRV (multiple independently targetable reentry vehicle)   warhead and guidance system for missiles able to carry multiple warheads each able to target a different object

modernization theory   a developmental strategy stressing that economic, cultural, and political change occur together in predictable ways

Molotov, Viacheslav   Soviet Foreign Minister under Josef Stalin and later under Nikita Khrushchev; a supporter of Stalinism and a hard line to the West

monkey wrench problem   tendency of extraneous events to disrupt the process of détente

Monroe Doctrine   President James Monroe's 1823 admonition to Europeans not to colonize the Americas, coupled with an assurance that the U.S. would not intervene in Europe or Europe's existing colonies; a noninterventionist policy that later set the stage for U.S. interventions "south of the border"; a doctrine that died in the 1960s, if not earlier

Montreal Protocol   1987 agreement to phase out the use of chlorofluorocarbons and halons that deplete the ozone layer

MOOTW   Military Operations Other Than War, Pentagon-speak for everything from peacekeeping to disaster relief to intimidation

Morgenthau, Hans J.   leading U.S. exponent of realism after World War II; author of *Politics Among Nations*

most-favored nation (MFN)   a designation that grants a state the maximum trade privileges afforded to any other; a potential lever in bargaining

MRBM   medium-range (600 to 1,500 nautical miles) ballistic missile

multiple symmetry   a model that says each rival must match or surpass every asset of its adversary or lose the competition

Mussolini, Benito   Italian dictator, 1922–1943

mutual gain shared benefit for parties to a transaction; can be equal or asymmetrical; the result of value-claiming policies or other circumstances

nation a people that perceives itself a nation

national interest hypothetical stake of a nation (i.e., a state) in security or some other value; the realist's basic criterion for action; some interests, however, are ephemeral or pertain only to particular groups

nationalism dedication to one's nation—its past, present, and future; can energize a people and/or foster conflict

National Missile Defense (NMD) goal of U.S. Department of Defense R&D in 1990s to protect the U.S. from "limited strikes, whatever their source"; could violate ABM treaty

national self-determination self-rule by a nation or the right to choose self-rule, for example, by a plebiscite

nation-state a state consisting largely of one nation

natural resources renewable supplies (such as water) and non-renewable (such as oil)

Nazarbayev, Nursultan president of Kazakstan in the 1990s; authoritarian at home, pragmatist abroad; sought to preserve ties with Russia while opening Kazakstan to Western and Chinese oil interests

NBC weapons nuclear, biological, and chemical agents of mass destruction

near abroad Russian term for area formerly occupied by the Soviet border republics such as Ukraine; a concept used to justify Russian interventions in this area

negative peace absence of war, sometimes fragile

negative-sum (lose-lose) an interaction in which both sides lose

negotiation a process by which parties communicate about ways to deal with issues on which they disagree

neofunctionalism orientation to IO that seeks international cooperation on issues that are politically sensitive

neoidealism diverse efforts to update classic IR idealism; ranges from civilizationism and endism to feminism, faith in NGOs, and postmodernism

neoliberalism liberalism modified by Keynseanism and neomercantlism; part of the Western response to Japan

neomercantilism doctrine that wealth depends on a favorable trade balance; encourages industrial policy and strategic trade

neorealism theory that structures of material power determine IR; updates classic realism by greater attention to IPE and to scientific method

New International Economic Order (NIEO) call by LDCs in 1970s for redistribution of wealth and for stabilization of commodity prices

newly industrializing countries (NICs) states such as Thailand, Malaysia, Indonesia, Argentina, and Brazil that adopted an export-led development strategy in the 1980s and 1990s

nongovernmental organization (NGO) a nonstate actor in IR such as Greenpeace or Amnesty International; sometimes referred to as International NGO (INGO)

nonstate actor IR players that are not states; includes IGOs, NGOs, TNCs

non-tariff barriers (NTBs) rules, subsidies, and other bureaucratic measures to limit foreign imports

nonviolent sanctions and resistance moral, political, and economic measures to persuade or pressure others to change their behavior; includes embargoes, strikes, and demonstrations

No-regrets policy actions useful even if other actors do not reciprocate and the possible danger (for example, global warming) turns out not to be a problem

North American Free Trade Agreement (NAFTA) 1994 agreement establishing a free trade area between Canada, Mexico, and the U.S.

North Atlantic Treaty Organization (NATO) military alliance formed in 1949 to protect the West from attack by the USSR; expanded membership after the collapse of Soviet power

Nuclear Nonproliferation Treaty (NPT) 1968 treaty to limit the spread of nuclear weapons beyond the Big Five; signed by most states except those most able and determined to join the nuclear weapons club

Nunn-Lugar Act 1992 U.S. congressional act allocating funds to facilitate dismantling and control of former Soviet weapons

Official Development Assistance (IDA) government aid to developing countries, directly or through the World Bank and IMF

Organization for Economic Cooperation and Development (OECD) the only IO to include all industrial democracies (the "club of rich nations"); conducts research and fosters discussion of common problems

Organization for Security and Cooperation in Europe (OSCE) outgrowth of the Helsinki process launched in 1975, an IGO with more than fifty member states—all of Europe, all members of NATO and the former Warsaw Pact, all successor states to the USSR; meets and acts to promote security and cooperation

Oslo Accord joint Declaration of Principles in August 1993 by Israel and the PLO providing for an interim period of limited Palestinian self-rule; left many problems for future negotiations

ozone layer stratospheric gases shielding earth from ultraviolet rays

Palestinian Liberation Organization (PLO) umbrella organization for Palestinian nationalists, founded in 1964; led after 1967 by Yasser Arafat

Panmunjom meeting place for DPRK and UN negotiators adjacent to Korea's DMZ

Partnership for Peace (PFP) conducts multilateral exercises and peacekeeping missions by most states belonging to the OSCE; a substitute or stepping stone toward NATO membership

peace building structural measures to generate a positive peace

peace enforcement the use of force to uphold or impose peace, for example, the Dayton Accord

peacekeeping the interposition of lightly armed forces to separate combatants with their consent

peacemaking mediation or other diplomatic intervention to promote peace

Penkovsky, Oleg V. a colonel in Soviet military intelligence who transmitted valuable information to British and U.S. agents in 1960–1962

perestroika "restructuring," Gorbachev's economic reforms in late 1980s

ping-pong diplomacy use of sport to signal interest in normalizing relations between estranged countries

plan in Communist economics, physical output goals for one, five, or even fifteen years, often including set wages and prices

polarity (uni-, bi-, multi-) centers of global power—one, two, many

police action military intervention with proclaimed purpose of upholding international law, as in the UN action in Korea, 1950–1953

political culture of authoritarianism trains subjects to want guidance from above; emphasizes duties—not rights; excludes civil society

political culture of democracy balances rights and duties; follows the majority but respects the minority

politicide extermination of political foes

population transfer the systematic movement of a group of people, often against their will

positions vs. interests distinction between sometimes rigid bargaining posture and the deep interests that negotiations could enhance

positive peace not just the absence of war but a stable harmony; may arise from a value-creating order oriented to mutual gain

positive-sum (win-win) an interaction in which both sides win

postmodernism movement that deconstructs IR language and institutions to see what lies beneath the surface

power latent, mobilized, or kinetic means to influence others; includes hard coercive and soft persuasive power

power-sharing governance that ensures each minority or faction a voice, regardless of its electoral or numerical strength

power transition theory belief that a shifting balance of power induces hegemonic war, a war either to uphold or overthrow the existing hegemon

practices similar to slavery activities banned by the Supplementary Convention on the Abolition of Slavery (1956); includes debt bondage, serfdom, coerced marriage, and branding

pre-emptive war first-strike delivered a short time (minutes, hours, days) before the enemy attacks; ordered when foe seems to be embarking on an attack

preferential trade agreement reduces barriers between signatories but does not provide for MFN to others; NAFTA and the EEC are examples of such accords

prenegotiation the process of setting the agenda, developing meeting sites and procedures, and generating a constructive ambiance before formal negotiations begin

preventive war a first-strike delivered months or even years before the shifting balance of power permits the other side to attack and win

Prisoner's Dilemma (PD) game theory exercise showing how distrust and self-seeking can lead to losses for each player

productivity-compensation balance an outcome whereby a highly paid worker who produces more products per hour than a lower paid worker costs less per unit of output; relevant to NAFTA

protocol a code of conduct; an addendum to a treaty/convention spelling out and often tightening obligations

proxy war hot war by clients

psychological warfare efforts to weaken the resolve and confuse the minds of the foe by propaganda, disinformation, and other techniques and to rally support

purchasing power parity (PPP) real GDP per capita

Pyongyang capital of the Democratic People's Republic of Korea

quota quantitative limit on imports or exports

rapprochement improved relations between two previously estranged parties

rational actor model assumption that states are united and rational in pursuit of their "national" interests

R&D research and development

realism (in IR) theory that IR is struggle for power by states

reduction differentials different obligations for different countries, for example, in targets for gas emissions

regime government; in IR, tacit or explicit norms of behavior among states, with or without a formal treaty

rent-seeking exploitation of official position for personal gain

reparations compensation for damages caused by the other side, paid in cash or in kind— labor, coal, ships; indemnities may be paid from gold and currency reserves or from future earnings

reservation price (RP) the walk away price of each disputant; minimum acceptable terms

reverse wave movement to displace democratic with authoritarian regimes, as in Serbia and several other countries in the 1990s

revisionist state one that seeks to revise or overthrow an unfavorable international order

ripeness hypothetical condition making a dispute amenable to mediation

rogue state a state that deviates from generally accepted standards; vicious, unreliable actor, perhaps willing to use poison gas or biological weapons or other mass destruction weapons

Rome, Treaty of 1957 treaty creating the EEC; a second treaty signed the same day in Rome established EURATOM

Roosevelt, Eleanor U.S. humanitarian who campaigned against racial and gender discrimination in the U.S. and later chaired the UN commission that drafted the Universal Declaration of Human Rights

rule-based trade regime a system characterized by qualitative rather than quantitative targets in trade

Sadat, Anwar president of Egypt who agreed to peace with Israel at Camp David in 1978

SAM surface-to-air missile for use against enemy aircraft

secession withdrawal by one unit from an organization or a state, as when Slovakia seceded from Czechoslovakia in 1992

second-strike massive retaliatory blow after suffering a first-strike

Second World the Communist states, especially those obedient to the USSR; did not always include China

security being safe; includes military security (safe from external attack, achieved by military means or by diplomacy), internal security (safe from subversion), food security (safe from hunger), and environmental security (safe from environmental disaster)

security dilemma phenomenon where State A's defensive actions may elicit countermeasures from State B and thus increase State A's insecurity

security regime rules, informal norms, and decision-making procedures designed to overcome the security dilemma

segmentation partitioning a country by natural borders, by ethnicity, and by other criteria

self-determination choosing one's own political identity; the alleged right of a nation to have its own state

self-help realist belief that IR actors must depend upon their own strengths for survival and other goals

separatism nationalist or other political movement seeking self-determination, for example, some Tamils in Sri Lanka

Shanghai Communiqué framework for normalizing PRC-U.S. relations drafted in 1972 by Zhou Enlai and Henry Kissinger

Shiite Islam dissident Muslim sect; politically dominant only in Iran; persecuted in many Sunni-dominated countries

silting silt buildup behind a dam lowering its life span and energy potential

Single European Act (SEA) 1987 agreement by which all EC members pledged to create a European market without internal barriers ordiscrimination by 1992

single negotiating text (SNT) one text accepted or amended by each party in negotiations; used at Camp David in 1978 to define areas of agreement and difference

slavery form of human bondage whereby one individual is considered the property of another; common throughout history but generally banned since the 19th century

smart bombs highly accurate weapons, able to outwit defenses

social learning capacity of an entire society to draw relevant lessons from experience and change its behavior accordingly

socialism public ownership of the means of production; for Marxists, individual income is decided by the quality and quantity of work performed; the views of non-Marxist socialists differ on many points from those of Marxist socialists

soft power the ability to inspire consensus (agreement) and to coopt (persuade others to share the same goals)

South Asian Association for Regional Cooperation (SAARC) regional IGO charged with fostering cooperation among its members: Bangladesh, Butan, India, Nepal, the Maldives, Pakistan, and Sri Lanka

sovereign a supreme power, for example, a king

sovereignty independent, unfettered power of a state in its jurisdiction

Spirit of Geneva first détente of the Cold War, generated by 1955 summit conference in Geneva of French, Soviet, UK, and U.S. leaders

standard operating procedures (SOPs) bureaucratic routines meant to promote efficiency but that sometimes yield rigid and/or inconsistent policies

state key actor in IR; a political entity with a sovereign government controlling a demarcated territory and a permanent population and possessing the legal right to deal with other states

stereotyping casting others in a rigid and simplified mode based on preconceptions and resisting evidence to the contrary

Stimson Doctrine U.S. refusal (1932) to recognize any political or territorial change accomplished by force; the doctrine resurfaced when Iraq seized Kuwait

strategy long-range plan; a military plan

Strategic Arms Limitation Treaty (SALT 1 and 2) froze Soviet and U.S. strategic arms and sharply limited ABM deployment (SALT 1, 1972) and endeavored to limit not just missiles and bombers but the number of warheads they could carry (SALT 2, 1979); SALT 2 was never ratified but each side generally observed it

Strategic Arms Reduction Treaty (START 1, 2) accords mandating not just arms control but disarmament as well; required Moscow and Washington to reduce arsenals to no more than 6,000 strategic nuclear warheads (START 1, 1990) and cut down to no more than 3,500 strategic nuclear warheads by the year 2003 (START 2, 1991); as of 1997, only the U.S. stood ready to ratify START 2

Strategic Defense Initiative (SDI) "Star Wars" plan developed in the 1980s to build an astrodome-like defensive shield to protect the U.S.

strategic doctrine the theory guiding a country's military planning, for example, faith in the offensive or in deterrence

strategic (or managed) trade government intervention to help a country's firms win market share abroad

strategic weapon Russian view: mass destruction weapon that can hit the homeland of a rival power; U.S. view: weapon with a range capable of hitting the U.S. from the USSR

structural adjustment economic reforms required of borrowers by IMF and other lending or donor agencies

submarine-launched ballistic missile (SLBM) mainstay of the U.S. deterrent; SLBMS are accurate and can carry many warheads, and their placement on submarines makes them difficult to destroy

Sunni Islam orthodox faith of most Muslims

supranational authority a government over other governments; a world government

sustainable development economic growth that maintains the carrying capacity of system resources

syndrome of underdevelopment reinforcing patterns of mutual distrust, skewed land ownership, corruption, militarism, criminality, and sexism that instill a feeling of powerlessness among the population

tactics means to a strategic goal; may include one step back to get two steps ahead

Taiwan Strait body of water separating the PRC and ROC, with several ROC-controlled islands

Tarim River Basin PRC area bordering Kazakstan believed to hold major oil reserves

tariff tax on imported goods to shield domestic producers and/or generate revenues

Tatarstan semi-autonomous province of the Russian Federation on the middle Volga; rich in mineral resources

Theater Ballistic Missile Defense (TBMD) U.S. R&D program in 1990s seeking defenses (low- or high-altitude) to protect U.S. forces abroad and allies from short- and intermediate-rangemissiles

third-party intervention mediation or other action by an outside actor not party to a dispute

third wave global movement to replace authoritarian with democratic regimes, initiated by Portugal and Spain in 1974

Third World LDCs or developing countries, mostly nonaligned; includes Group of 77, a UN caucus on economic affairs

Tigers Singapore, Hong Kong, Taiwan, and South Korea who successful adopted Japan's model of export-based development

Tilsit, Treaty of harsh peace imposed on Prussia by Napoleon in 1807, requiring Prussia to cede territory to France and pay indemnities

tit-for-tat (TFT) responding in kind to conciliatory or tough moves by the other side; an alternative to GRIT

totalitarian dictatorship authoritarian government seeking total dominion over all aspects of life including political, economic, social, and cultural

trade imbalance current accounts deficit when value of exports exceeds imports

trading state a country strong in international commerce rather than military power; may utilize strategic trade policy

transitions challenges to the Second World countries that want to join the First; include the transition to democracy, the transition to a market economy, and the transition to a foreign policy oriented toward peace

transnational   that which transcends national borders; contrasted to what is between them (international) or over them (supranational)

transnational corporation (TNC)   a corporation such as IBM that is headquartered in one country but that operates transnationally; also known as multinational corporation (MNC)

transnational relations   the interactions of TNCs and NGOs who engage in activities and possess memberships that transcend official state borders

transparent   open and visible to observers; refers to weapons, bank accounts, corporate accounts, elections, arms trade and is relevant to the utility of openness

triad   deterrence based on three legs: long-range bombers, land-based missiles, and SLBMs; any leg must be able to retaliate if the others are destroyed

triangular diplomacy   juggling or manipulating the conflicting and shared interests of two or three major rivals such as Russia, China, and the U.S.—as when Kissinger tried his China card

Triple Alliance   Germany, Austria-Hungary, and Italy before 1914

Triple Entente   France, Russia, and Great Britain before 1914

Uighur   Turkic-lanugage, Muslim ethnic group in northeast China, some of whom press for greater autonomy and resist Chinese influences

unconventional war   guerrilla or other war that differs from the current convention

UN Development Programme (UNDP)   coordinates development planning in LDCs; produces the annual *Human Development Report*

UN Environmental Programme   established in 1972, monitors the environment and promotes sustainable development; a catalyst for the Earth Summit and efforts at climate control

UN General Assembly   parliament of the world; functions on the basis of one country, one vote, but its resolutions are not legally binding

union-republic   one of fifteen major units in the USSR

unipolarity   world domination by one pole of power

unitary state   centralized state such as China; contrasted with a federal or confederal system

Uniting for Peace Resolution   1950 UNGA resolution affirming the UN General Assembly's competence to act on security issues if the UN Security Council fails to do so

unit veto   ability of each actor to block action by others, for example, by nuclear threat

Universal Declaration of Human Rights   proclamation by the UN General Assembly in 1948 setting forth political, economic, and social standards for all peoples; challenged by concept that human rights mean something different to each culture

UN peacekeeping forces   lightly armed military forces from UN member states deployed as a buffer between hostile parties; sometimes facilitate humanitarian relief

UN Security Council   UN organ with primary responsibility for maintaining peace and security; fifteen members, including five permanent and ten rotating

UN Special Commission (UNSCOM)   inspectorate seeking to discoverand destroy Iraq's NBC weapons after the Gulf War

U.S. Agency for International Development (USAID)   the main foreign aid agency within the U.S. government

value-claiming   strategy to seize goods at other's expense

value-creating   strategy to enlarge the pie for mutual gain

Van Miert, Karel   European Commissioner for Competitiveness who set conditions in 1997 for the merger of industry giants Boeing and McDonnell-Douglas

variable-sum   a non-zero-sum interaction in which each party may win or lose

Versailles system   international order established in 1919; combined a repressive policy toward the losers in World War I with hope in the newly formed League of Nations

voluntarism   belief that free will and individual choice are decisive in human history

voluntary export restriction (VER)   an export quota usually accepted under pressure from an importing country with a large trade imbalance

Waltz, Kenneth N.   exponent of neorealism and pioneer in distinguishing levels of analysis

war   organized violence; a way to continue diplomacy and to claim values

War Powers Resolution   1973 law setting limits to the U.S. president's authority as commander-in-chief and identifying the role to be played by Congress in authorizing force

Western European Union (WEU)   founded in the 1950s, an IGO with a council and an assembly composed of the European members of NATO

Westphalia, Treaty of   1648 peace ending the Thirty Years War and establishing the nation-state as the key unit in IR

World Bank   International Bank for Reconstruction and Development (1944), a UN Specialized Agency charged with promoting economic development using both government and private bank funds; a subsidiary, the International Finance Corporation (1956), makes loans to private companies in LDCs; another subsidiary, the International Development Association (1960), makes "soft loans" to poor LDCs

World Health Organization (WHO)   UN Specialized Agency promoting public health; its vaccination campaign eliminated smallpox, but the WHO in the 1990s faced a resurgence of malaria and a pandemic of HIV-AIDS with no easy answers

World Island   for geopoliticians, Eurasia

world order   a hierarchy of international power with rules favored by the dominant actors, often established after a major war

world-system theory   portrait of a world divided by systems of hierarchy and dependency; the imperialist core exploits and retards the LDCs on the periphery

World Trade Organization (WTO)   an IGO formed in 1995 to promote freer trade; successor to the GATT

Yeltsin, Boris   first elected president of Russia (May 1990); an autocrat who claimed to be a democrat

yi yi zhi yi   Chinese maxim: "Use one barbarian against another."

zero-sum (win-lose)   an interaction in which one side's winnings equal the other's losses

Zhou Enlai   PRC premier, 1949–1976, and foreign minister, 1949–1958; negotiated normalization of U.S.-PRC relations in early 1970s

LEARNING ABOUT INTERNATIONAL RELATIONS:
A Study and Resource Guide

FOCUS AND FOLLOW-THROUGH

To investigate IR on your own, first identify a problem that interests you and that is important. Narrow the topic so you can investigate it in the time available and with the resources at your disposal.

Though you focus on a narrow issue, you must review its history and context. What are the contending schools of thought? Study a variety of secondary sources—not dozens, for there are limits to your time and energy. But read a sufficient kind and number of sources so you become aware of some alternative interpretations. Don't depend on the first book or Internet references you find. Begin with readings and web sites cited in this book's footnotes and Recommended Resources.

Be proactive: Ask what kinds of evidence   historical facts, documents, statistics—you could find to support or challenge the experts.

Allow time for your ideas to germinate. Discuss them with instructors, other students, and with wise persons who do not know the subject matter before deciding on the framework of your investigation. Do so again as you begin to collect evidence and as you draft conclusions. Don't be afraid to ask questions. Talking can help thinking and writing.

Write an outline and use it. Diagram relationships between possible causes and effects. Paste up your outline and look at it as you study and write.

Let us consider two kinds of papers.

REVIEWING WHAT OTHERS HAVE WRITTEN

You may choose to analyze what others have written in a book review (one or two books) or a bibliographic essay (many articles or books). If the latter, narrow the topic to a common theme such as "Outside Aid and Development in Southern Africa since 1975."

In a review your first job is to summarize each work briefly but accurately—its methods, assumptions, findings, and policy recommendations, if any. Second, compare each article or book with others in the field. Third, discuss what you see as the strong and weak points of each. For models, see reviews in the *Mershon International Studies Review* and in the back pages of *World Politics* and *Foreign Affairs;* see also *The Wilson Quarterly, The New York Times Book Review,* and *The New York Review of Books.*

Rather than books, you may review articles on the same topic in different journals. Ask whether the journal seems to favor some world view or methodology. Compare, for example, *The National Interest* with *World Politics.* For a cross-national comparison, compare articles in *Foreign Affairs* (New York), *International Affairs* (London), and *International Affairs* (Moscow). Be aware how outlook and methods can tilt findings.

Or you may compare the opinion essays (called "op-eds"—opposite the editorial page) of newspapers, for example, the *Washington Times* and *Washington Post.* Or juxtapose an op-ed with the analysis in a scholarly journal such as *World Politics.* What is gained or lost in the more pithy presentation?

Hone your language skills by comparing coverage of the same event in *Le Monde* or *Frankfurter Allgemeine* or *Asahi Shimbun* with *The New York Times.* (You may discover that many IR words are similar in most West European and Slavic languages.)

Bibliographic essays may also describe new evidence such as declassified documents. For models, refer to the journals *Diplomatic History* and *American Historical Review.* For starters, analyze the documents in a recent volume of *Foreign Relations of the United States* (listed below).

DEVELOPING YOUR OWN ANSWERS: HOW TO WRITE A TERM PAPER

Building on what others have discovered or argued, develop your own answers to important issues in IR. You may focus on description, on forecasting alternative futures, or on policy prescription.

Narrow the Topic

Pose a sharp question to energize your quest. If interested in war, you should read a few books or encyclopedic surveys to learn how specialists address the big questions. But to write a term paper, focus. Do not tackle "what causes war" in general. Instead, examine factors (long-term, proximate, or catalytic) that may have contributed to a particular war, for example, intensification of the Vietnam conflict in 1965.

Decide on Your Approach

IR rests upon history but is not satisfied with chronological description. It wants to know how, why, and what if. So you need to think how your paper relates to theory. Consider not just one explanation but several competing hypotheses. If you evaluate only one possible explanation, your framework may not be rich enough to deal with the conflicting evidence you discover.

Here are four approaches to theory-building:

1. Test a theory others have advanced, replicating their methods and case studies.

2. Expand a theory by applying it to different times and places from those its authors studied.

3. Apply a theory from another field (psychology, economics, cybernetics) to see how it fits IR.

4. Articulate your own hypotheses about how things hang together.

Each approach has merit. The first is easiest; the fourth, most difficult. Whichever you choose, you must find and analyze data—events, developments, statistics—that falsify or corroborate your expectations.

Before you decide on your approach, however, get some perspective: Read Joseph Conrad's *Nostromo,* Aldous Huxley's *Brave New World,* or Salman Rushdie's *The Moor's Last Sigh* or an epic such as *The Iliad, Mahabharata,* or *Song of Prince Igor.* Balance today's news from the BBC or National Public Radio with some thoughts from Henry David Thoreau's *Walden.* Go for a walk; get some sleep; turn on your mind and your PC and proceed.

Compare Theory and Reality

There are four main routes to compare theory with reality: logic, broad observations, in-depth case studies, and experimentation.[1]

Logic. First, you may depend basically on logic. You may analyze texts or events for their internal logic. For example, if event x took place after event y, x could hardly have caused y. Here you must supplement logic with history. Perhaps you can find out more about the sequence of events than other authors. But it is difficult to write a persuasive IR paper using logic alone. Better to use logic in conjunction with hard evidence.

Broad Observations. A second approach is the broad survey in which you observe a large number of cases—a large *N*. You review many cases—dozens, hundreds, perhaps thousands—to see if a small number of variables co-vary as the theory predicts (the more of x, the more of y).

Several large-*N* studies are reported in this book: war frequency and intensity in Chapter 4; minorities at risk in Chapter 8; the growth of democracy in Chapter 10; economic growth in Chapters 11 and 12. But large-*N* studies can be ex-

pensive and time-consuming. They can also be inconclusive if complicated variables are reduced to a simple sum. Furthermore, cases from different times and places may not be truly comparable.

Still, you can conduct your own broad surveys at little cost. The world has become more porous. Data sources unknown to previous generations are at our fingertips.

Hypothesize, for example, that high defense expenditures correlate with low economic growth or with poor public health. Check out the correlations, if any, using the military "bean counts" offered by the International Institute for Strategic Studies and Stockholm International Peace Research Institute; economic data published by the World Bank in *World Development Report;* and social indicators collected by the UN Development Programme (UNDP) in *Human Development Report.* To manipulate the statistics, access the raw data collected by the World Bank and UNDP available on CD-ROM.

Be aware that attempted precision has many pitfalls. Correlation need not mean causation. The rise or fall of economic growth, for example, might be due more to the weather than to defense spending. Before generalizing from your large-*N* study, read some in-depth cases to get a sense of the many factors that bear on your theme.

In-Depth Case Studies. In-depth case studies offer a third approach to comparing theory with reality. They permit you to analyze the interaction of many variables in a small number of cases—a large-*V* study. You track decisions and outcomes. Which hypothesis best explains the unfolding of words and deeds?

Large-*V* research can be highly rewarding, especially if you can access relevant documents. If interested in war, you might ask: "Why did President Johnson opt to escalate the fighting in Vietnam in 1965 when he doubted that the U.S. could prevail?" Abundant documentation exists—declassified Pentagon, State Department, and White House papers and the private papers and memoirs of other key individuals such as Secretary of State Dean Rusk and Secretary of Defense Robert S. McNamara. Because the documentation is so rich, you will need several competing hypotheses to guide your search.

Here, too, correlation does not mean causation. You might look for the correlation between public opinion surveys and Johnson's policies. But his policies may have been shaped more by some virtually unquantifiable factor such as a desire to adhere to the same path initiated by his predecessor, John F. Kennedy.

Even if you integrate quantitative and qualitative evidence, you may be grasping only a part of the elephant. The level on which you focus may not even be the most decisive. Instead of analyzing top leaders, you might target the Departments of State and Defense to see how they dealt with Vietnam. Did

---

1. For elaboration, see Stephen Van Evera, *Guide to Methods for Students of Political Science* (Ithaca, N.Y.: Cornell University Press, 1997).

mid-level officials support or try to restrain their bosses? Why? What were the roles of standard operating procedures and vested interests?

You might prefer to study how individuals and groups outside of Washington felt about escalation in 1965. Go back to the speeches, diaries, and other writings of student leaders, mothers, draftees, volunteers.

A team approach can generate insights. Partner with others to cover different facets of the same case. Your partner might ask: "Why did Hanoi persist in its campaign to bring all of Vietnam under its control in the face of U.S. escalation?" Still others might investigate the policies of China and the USSR toward Vietnam in 1965. Or why the UN did so little to intervene. Note, however, that evidence on these other actors will be much tougher to obtain than similar information on the U.S. To get reliable documentation on all parties to a conflict you may have to go further back in time, for example, to the wars that began in 1914, 1939, or 1950.

If you do one or more in-depth case studies you should search out large-N studies of similar cases. To learn about such studies has become much easier thanks to computerized searches, for example, PAIS international database (Public Affairs Information Service, New York).

Experimentation. A fourth approach is experimentation. History sometimes provides a laboratory. Thus, the policies imposed by the victors in 1919 and after 1945 can be seen as experiments in the design of world orders. Lessons from these cases, however, did not apply directly to the 1990s, because conditions were so different.

You can conduct your own experiments, for example, using role-playing simulation exercises. Or you can survey the opinions of experts or other sectors of public opinion. With a grant you can commission the Gallup or Roper teams to conduct a survey that tests a hypothesis. Or do your own small-scale survey among students, neighbors, or relatives such as the missile-defense surveys reported in Chapter 6. (Students went into low-income, middle-class, and high-income neighborhoods and then pooled their findings.) You can do such surveys using a written questionnaire or face-to-face discussions or both.

Having done the research, you must write it up. Organization and style are crucial.

How to Organize a Term Paper

Introduction. Tell the reader what you are going to say. What question or questions do you address? How do these questions arise? Why are they important? What answers, if any, have others proposed? How will you answer these questions—with what evidence or by what methods? Summarize your own answer. If you find it difficult to write this introduc-

tion, your own organization or evidence may need more work. If questions persist, try to identify them and thus show that you understand the limits of your work.

The Body. The body of the term paper is where you present evidence and analysis. For example, if you have conducted one or more case studies, the body of the paper will summarize each case. Do not present the history of each case at great length. You must know the background of each case, but do not lay out the chronology in your paper except as necessary to your argument. Instead, cite in a footnote the main background materials you have read and move on to your own analysis.

Conclusions. What propositions hold? What questions remain? If there are policy implications, what are they and to whom do they apply? If more research is needed, what directions might it take?

Style and Content

Style affects content. A sloppy presentation can obscure your meaning, masking the effort you have invested. Make several drafts of your paper. Cut and paste to develop flow. Keep a dust bin (perhaps a separate computer file) for sections you hate to discard but may not be essential to your argument. Read what you write out loud—to a friend or just to yourself.

Write short, snappy sentences and paragraphs. Avoid long sentences and long paragraphs. Avoid passive constructions that sneak in important points as if they were self-evident.

Be clear about pronouns: Whom or what does "it" refer to?

In IR we must be clear about actors: If we say "China" did something, do we mean the country as a whole? The Communist Party leadership? The top leader? His cousins? Or something else?

Review your spelling. If using a computer, use but do not depend on its spell-checker. The machine may not be sure if you want to say discreet or discrete, ethnic or ethic. If you present statistics, look once more at the decimal points.

Check footnotes and bibliography. Double check spellings and numbers—volumes, pages, dates, and so forth. Use whatever format the instructor requests; otherwise, follow the format of journals such as *World Politics* or *International Studies Quarterly* or the guidelines in Kate Turabian, *A Manual for Writers of Term Papers, Theses, and Dissertations,* 5th ed. (Chicago: University of Chicago Press, 1987).

FEEDBACK AND CUMULATIVE LEARNING

Whatever you study and write about, consider it as a brick in an edifice of knowledge and insight that you are building for a lifetime of use. Value the feedback you get from readers. See how your opinions and facts stack up against the tides of change and new information. If you have written about Albania, run a cross-check the next time you meet an Albanian or read about Albania. Current events will take on new meaning when you relate them to the theories and cases you have analyzed. No matter what field of study or work you pursue, IR will be there—an essential element of your context.

REFERENCE WORKS

Encyclopedias, Dictionaries, and Yearbooks

Dictionary of 20th Century World Politics. Ed. Jay M. Sharif et al. New York: Holt, 1993.

Dictionary of Alternative Defense. Ed. Bjorn Moller. London, Adamantine Press, 1995.

Dictionary of American Diplomatic History. 2d. ed. Ed. John E. Findling. New York: Greenwood Press, 1989.

Dictionary of American Foreign Affairs. Ed. Stephen A. Flanders and Carl N. Flanders. New York: Macmillan International, 1993.

Dictionary of International and Comparative Law. 2d. ed. Ed. James R. Fox. Dobbs Ferry, N.Y.: Oceana Publications, 1997.

Dictionary of International Finance. 2d. ed. Ed. Graham Banock and W.A. P. Manser. London: Hamish-Hamilton, 1995.

Dictionary of International Trade. Ed. Edward G. Hinkleman. San Rafael, Calif.: World Trade Press, 1994.

Encyclopedia of American Foreign Policy: Studies of the Principal Movements and Ideas. 3 vols. Ed. Alexander DeConde. New York: Scribner's, 1978.

Encyclopedia of Arms Control and Disarmament. 3 vols. Ed. Richard D. Burns. New York: Scribner's, 1993.

Encyclopedia of Conflict Resolution. Ed. Heidi Burgess and Guy M. Burgess. Santa Barbara, Calif.: ABC-CLIO, 1997.

Encyclopedia of Russian History. Ed. John Paxton. Santa Barbara, Calif.: ABC-CLIO, 1993.

Ethnic Relations: A Cross-Cultural Encyclopedia. Ed. David Levinson. Santa Barbara, Calif.: ABC-CLIO, 1995.

A Global Agenda: Issues Before the General Assembly of the United Nations. Lanham, Md.: University Press of America, annual.

Guide to American Foreign Relations Since 1700. Ed. Richard Dean Burns. Santa Barbara, Calif.: ABC-CLIO, 1983.

Historical Dictionary of Aid and Development Organizations. Ed. Guy Arnold. Lanham, Md.: Scarecrow Press, 1996.

Historical Dictionary of European Organizations. Ed. Derek W. Urwin. Metuchen, N.J.: Scarecrow Press, 1994.

Historical Dictionary of Human Rights and Humanitarian Or-

ganizations. Ed. Robert F. Gorman and Edward S. Mihalkanin. Lanham, Md.: Scarecrow Press, 1997.

Historical Dictionary of International Tribunals. Ed. Boleslaw Adam Boczek. Metuchen, N.J.: Scarecrow Press, 1994.

Historical Dictionary of Multinational Peacekeeping. Ed. Terry M. Mays. Lanham, Md.: Scarecrow Press, 1996.

Historical Dictionary of Refugee and Disaster Relief Organizations. Ed. Robert F. Gorman. Metuchen, N.J.: Scarecrow Press, 1994.

Historical Dictionary of the United Nations. Ed. A. LeRoy Bennett. Lanham, Md.: Scarecrow Press, 1995.

Historical Dictionary of the Word Bank. Ed. Anne C. M. Salda. Lanham, Md.: Scarecrow Press, 1997.

Historical Dictionary of United Nations Educational, Scientific and Cultural Organization (UNESCO). Ed. Seth Spaulding and Lin Lin. Lanham, Md.: Scarecrow Press, 1997.

International Development Dictionary. Ed. Gerald W. Fry and Galen R. Martin. Santa Barbara, Calif.: ABC-CLIO, 1991.

International Organizations: A Dictionary. 4th ed. Ed. Guiseppe Schiavone. London: Macmillan, 1997.

International Relations: A Political Dictionary. 5th ed. Ed. Lawrence Ziring et al. Santa Barbara, Calif.: ABC-CLIO, 1995.

Oxford Companion to Politics of the World. Ed. Joel Kreiger et al. New York: Oxford University Press, 1993.

Protest, Power, and Change: An Encyclopedia of Nonviolent Action from ACT-UP to Woman's Suffrage. Ed. Roger S. Powers and William B. Vogele. New York: Garland, 1997.

The Statesman's Yearbook. New York: St. Martin's, annual. First edition, 1864.

World Factbook. Washington, D.C.: Central Intelligence Agency, annual.

BIBLIOGRAPHIES

Arms Control and Security

The Access Source Guide: An International Directory of Information on War, Peace and Security. Ed. William Kincade and Priscilla B. Hayner. Cambridge, Mass.: Ballinger, 1988.

Arms Control and Disarmament: A Bibliography. Comp. Richard Dean Burns. Santa Barbara, Calif.: ABC-CLIO, 1977.

Bibliography on Peace Research in History. Ed. Blanche Wiesen Cook. Santa Barbara, Calif.: ABC-CLIO, 1969.

Bibliography on Peace, Security, and International Conflict Management. Washington, D.C.: U.S. Institute of Peace, 1993.

The Civil War: A Newspaper Perspective: The New York Herald, The Charlotte Mercury, Richmond Enquirer. (Computer Files). Malvern, Pa.: Accessible Archives, 1994.

Peace and War: A Guide to Bibliographies. Ed. B. A. Carroll et al. Santa Barbara, Calif.: ABC-CLIO, 1983.

The Peace Corps: An Annotated Bibliography. Comp. Robert B. Marks Ridinger. Boston, Mass.: G.K. Hall, 1989.

Search for Security: The Access Guide to Foundations in Peace, Security and International Relations. Ed. Anne Allen. Washington, D.C.: Access, 1989.

Soviet Disarmament Policy, 1917–1963: An Annotated Bibliography of Soviet and Western Sources. Comp. Walter C. Clemens, Jr. Stanford, Calif.: Hoover Institution, 1965.

The Vietnam Conflict; Its Geographical Dimensions, Political Traumas, & Military Developments. Comp. Milton Leitenberg. Santa Barbara, Calif.: ABC-CLIO, 1973.

Countries and Regions

The Access Guide to Ethnic Conflicts in Europe and the Former Soviet Union. Ed. Bruce Seymore II. Washington, D.C.: Access, 1994.

African International Relations. An Annotated Bibliography. Comp. Mark DeLancey. Boulder, Colo.: Westview, 1997.

The Baltic States: Estonia, Latvia, Lithuania. Comp. Inese A. Smith. Oxford, England; Santa Barbara, Calif.: CLIO Press, 1993.

The Chinese Communist Movement; An Annotated Bibliography of Selected Materials in the Chinese Collection of the Hoover Institution on War, Revolution and Peace. Comp. Chun-tu Hsueh. Palo Alto, Calif.: Hoover Institution, 1960.

Guide to the Collections in the Hoover Institution Archives Relating to Imperial Russia, the Russian Revolutions and Civil War, and the First Emigration. Comp. Carol A. Leadenham. Stanford, Calif.: Hoover Institution, 1986.

Guide to the Study of the Soviet Nationalities: Non-Russian Peoples of the USSR. Ed. Stephan M. Horak. Littleton, Colo.: Libraries Unlimited, 1982.

Latin American Political Movements. Ed. Ciaran O. Maolain. New York: Facts on File, 1985.

Leaders of Twentieth-Century China: An Annotated Bibliography of Selected Chinese Biographical Works in the Hoover Library. Comp. Eugene Wen-chin Wu. Stanford, Calif.: Stanford University Press, 1956.

One Nation Becomes Many: The Access Guide to the Former Soviet Union. Ed. Stephen W. Young et al. Washington, D.C.: Access, 1992.

Poland: An Annotated Bibliography of Books in English. Comp. August Gerald Kanka. New York: Garland, 1988.

Poland, Past and Present: A Select Bibliography of Works in English. Comp. Norman Davies. Newtonville, Mass.: Oriental Research Partners, 1977.

Pressure on Pretoria: Sanctions, Boycotts and the Divestment/Disinvestment Issue, 1964–1988: A Select and Annotated Bibliography. Comp. Jacqueline A. Kalley. Johannesburg: South African Institute of International Affairs, 1988.

Revolution and Structural Change in Latin America; A Bibliography on Ideology, Development, and the Radical Left (1930–1965). Comp. Ronald H. Chilcote. Stanford, Calif.: Hoover Institution, 1970.

Russia, the USSR, and Eastern Europe: A Bibliographic Guide to English Language Publications, 1975–1980. Comp. Stephan M. Horak. Littleton, Colo.: Libraries Unlimited, 1982.

Scholars' Guide to Washington, D.C., for African Studies. Comp. Purnima Mehta Bhatt. Washington, D.C.: Smithsonian Institution Press, 1980.

Scholars' Guide to Washington, D.C., for Central and East European Studies: Albania, Austria, Bulgaria, Czechoslovakia, Germany (FRG & GDR), Greece (Ancient & Modern), Hungary, Poland, Romania, Switzerland, Yugoslavia. Comp. Kenneth J. Dillon. Washington, D.C.: Woodrow Wilson International Center for Scholars, 1980.

Scholars' Guide to Washington, D.C., for East Asian Studies: China, Japan, Korea, And Mongolia. Comp. Hong N. Kim. Washington, D.C.: Smithsonian Institution Press, 1979.

Scholars' Guide to Washington, D.C., for Latin American and Caribbean Studies. Comp. Michael Grow. Washington, D.C.: Smithsonian Institution Press, 1979.

Scholars' Guide to Washington, D.C., for Middle Eastern Studies: Egypt, Sudan, Jordan, Lebanon, Syria, Iraq, The Arabian Peninsula, Israel, Turkey, Iran. Comp. Steven R. Dorr Washington, D.C.: Smithsonian Institution Press, 1981.

Scholars' Guide to Washington, D.C., for Northwest European Studies. Comp. Louis A. Pitschmann. Washington, D.C.: Woodrow Wilson International Center for Scholars; Smithsonian Institution Press, 1984.

Scholar's Guide to Washington, D.C., for Russian/Soviet Studies: The Baltic States, Byelorussia, Central Asia, Moldavia, Russia, Transcaucasia, the Ukraine. Comp. Steven A. Grant. 2d rev. ed. Ed. Bradford P. Johnson and Mark H. Teeter. Washington, D.C.: Smithsonian Institution Press, 1983.

Scholars' Guide to Washington, D.C., for South Asian Studies: Pakistan, Sri Lanka. Comp. Enayetur Rahim. Washington, D.C.: Smithsonian Institution Press, 1981.

Scholars' Guide to Washington, D.C., for Southeast Asian Studies: Brunei, Burma, Cambodia, Indonesia, Laos, Malaysia, Philippines, Singapore, Thailand, Vietnam. Comp. Patrick M. Mayerchak. Washington, D.C.: Smithsonian Institution Press, 1983.

Scholars' Guide to Washington, D.C., for Southwest European Studies: France, Italy (Including Ancient Rome), Malta, Portugal, Spain. Ed. Joan Florence Higbee. Washington, D.C.: Wilson Center Press; Lanham, Md.: University Press of America, 1989.

The Small and The New in Southern Africa: The Foreign Relations of Botswana, Lesotho, Namibia and Swaziland Since

Their Independence: A Select and Annotated Bibliography. Comp. L. E. Andor. Johannesburg: South African Institute of International Affairs, 1993.

The Soviet Armed Forces Books In English, 1950–1967. Comp. Michael Parrish. Stanford, Calif.: Hoover Institution, 1970.

Soviet Foreign Relations and World Communism. Comp. Thomas Hammond. Princeton, N.J.: Princeton University Press, 1965.

Economic Development

The European Reconstruction, 1948–1961: Bibliography on the Marshall Plan and the Organization for European Economic Co-Operation (OEEC). Paris: Organization for Economic Co-operation and Development, 1996.

A Select Bibliography on Economic Development, with Annotations. Comp. John P. Powelson. Boulder, Colo.: Westview, 1979.

General

The Access Guide to International Affairs Internships in the Washington, D.C. Area. Ed. Bruce Seymore II and Susan D. Krutt. Washington, D.C.: Access, 1994.

Alternative Approaches to the Problem of Development: A Selected and Annotated Bibliography. Ed. Charles W. Bergquist. Durham, N.C.: Carolina Academic Press, 1979.

Foreign Affairs Bibliography: A Selected and Annotated List of Books on International Relations. Ed. William Langer and Hamilton Armstrong. New York: Harper for Council on Foreign Relations, 1933.

The Foreign Affairs 50-Year Bibliography: New Evaluations of Significant Books on International Relations, 1920–1970. Ed. Byron Dexter. New York: R. R. Bowker, 1972.

International Organization; An Interdisciplinary Bibliography. Comp. Michael Haas. Stanford, Calif.: Hoover Institution, 1971.

International Relations Theory: A Critical Bibliography. Ed. A. J. R. Groom and Christopher Mitchell. New York: Nichols, 1978.

"Significant Books of the Last 75 Years," *Foreign Affairs* 76, no. 5 (September/October 1997): 214–238.

International Law and Commerce

An Annotated and Cross-Referenced Bibliography of East-West Commerce. 2d ed. Comp. Paul Marer. Bloomington, Ind.: International Development Institute, 1980.

Bibliography of International Law. Comp. Ingrid Delupis. New York: R.R. Bowker, 1975.

Canadian Bibliography of International Law. Comp. Christian L. Wiktor. Toronto: University of Toronto Press, 1984.

A Collection of Bibliographic and Research Resources: International Law Bibliography, 1984–1990. 2 vols. New York: Oceana Publications.

The Gulf War 1990–91 in International and English Law. Ed. Peter Rowe. London: Sweet & Maxwell, 1993.

Human Rights: An International and Comparative Law Bibliography. Ed. Julian R. Friedman and Marc I. Sherman. Westport, Conn.: Greenwood Press, 1985.

International Bibliography of Air Law 1900–1971. Comp. Wybo P. Heere. Dobbs Ferry, N.Y.: Oceana Publications, 1972. Five supplements to 1995.

International Law of the Sea: A Bibliography. Comp. N. Papadakis. Alphen aan den Rijn, Netherlands; Germantown, Md.: Sijthoff & Noordhoff, 1980.

International Law, Organization, and the Environment: A Bibliography and Research Guide. Comp. Forest L. Grieves. Tucson: University of Arizona Press, 1974.

Law & International Law; A Bibliography of Bibliographies. Comp. Theodore Besterman. Totowa, N.J.: Rowman and Littlefield, 1971.

Ocean Affairs Bibliography, 1971; A Selected List Emphasizing International Law, Politics, and Economics of Ocean Uses. Washington, D.C., Woodrow Wilson International Center for Scholars, 1971.

Public International Law: A Current Bibliography of Books and Articles. 23 vols. Secaucus, N.J.: Springer-Verlag, 1975–. Semiannual.

Transfer of Technology: A Bibliography of Materials in the English Language: International Law Bibliography. Comp. Betty W. Taylor. Dobbs Ferry, N.Y.: Oceana Publications, 1985.

Methods

Growing Artificial Societies: Social Science from the Bottom Up. Joshua M. Epstein and Robert Axtell. Cambridge, Mass.: The MIT Press, 1997.

Guide to Methods for Students of Political Science. Stephen Van Evera. Ithaca, N.Y.: Cornell University Press, 1997 and its bibliography.

Managing International Conflict: From Theory to Policy: A Teaching Tool using CASCON. Lincoln P. Bloomfield and Allen Moulton. New York: St. Martin's, 1997.

A Primer for Policy Analysis. Edith Stokey and Richard Zeckhauser. New York: Norton, 1978.

Simulated International Processess: Theories and Research in Global Modeling. Ed. Harold M. Guetzkow and Joseph J. Valadez. Beverly Hills, Calif.: Sage, 1981.

CHRONOLOGIES

At War in the Gulf : A Chronology. Comp. Arthur H. Blair. College Station: Texas A&M University Press, 1992.

Chronology, Bibliography and Index for the Group of 77 and the Non-Aligned Movement. Ed. Joachim W. Muller and Karl P. Sauvant. New York: Oceana Publications. 1993–

A Chronology and Fact Book of the United Nations, 1941–1979: Annual Review of United Nations Affairs. Comp. Thomas Hovet, Jr., and Erica Hovet. Dobbs Ferry, N.Y.: Oceana Publications, 1979.

A Chronology of Conflict and Resolution, 1945–1985. Comp. John E. Jessup. New York: Greenwood Press, 1989.

Facts on File (periodical since 1940 and collections on special topics).

The Foreign Affairs Chronology of World Events: Second Edition. 1978–1991. New York: Council on Foreign Relations, 1992.

International Terrorism in the 1980s: A Chronology of Events. Comp. Edward F. Mickolus et al. Ames: Iowa State University Press, 1989–.

Modern China: A Chronology from 1842 to the Present. Comp. Colin Mackerras. San Francisco: W.H. Freeman, 1982.

Presidential Diplomacy: A Chronology of Summit Visits, Trips, and Meetings. Comp. Elmer Plischke. Dobbs Ferry, N.Y.: Oceana Publications, 1986.

Press and Speech Freedoms in America, 1619–1995: A Chronology. Comp. Louis Edward Ingelhart. Westport, Conn.: Greenwood Press, 1997.

South Africa's Foreign Relations in Transition, 1985–1992: A Chronology. Comp. Elna Schoeman. Johannesburg: South African Institute of International Affairs, 1993.

U.S. and Soviet Policy in the Middle East, 1945–56. Ed. John Donovan. New York: Facts on File, 1972.

DOCUMENTS

Documents in International Affairs, 1928–. New York: Oxford University Press, 1929–.

Human Rights in International Law: Basic Texts. Strasbourg: Council of Europe Press, 1992.

U.S. Department of State, *Foreign Relations of the United States.* Washington, D.C.: Government Printing Office, 1861–. Title varies. Publications are by year, region, and specific topic, for example, Paris Peace Conference, 1919 (13 volumes). Contains valuable information on other countries, not just the U.S.

For a list of documents published by various countries, see above, *The Foreign Affairs 50-Year Bibliography.*

STATISTICS

Military Balance. London: International Institute for Strategic Studies, annual.

Statistical Abstract CD-ROM.

United Nations. *Human Development Report.* New York: Oxford University Press, annual.

United Nations, Department of International Economic and Social Affairs, Statistical Office. *Directory of International Statistics.* New York: United Nations, 1982–.

World Bank. *World Development Report.* New York: Oxford University Press, annual.

World Development Indicators 1997 CD-ROM.

JOURNALS

(For more specialized journals, see the Recommended Resources at the end of each chapter.)

Adelphi Papers (London)
American Political Science Review
Asian Security (Tokyo)
Asian Survey
Beijing Review (PRC)
Boundary and Security Bulletin (Durham, UK)
Brown Journal of World Affairs
Daedalus
European Journal of International Relations (London)
Foreign Affairs
Foreign Policy
Global Society (Abingdon, UK)
Greenpeace Business (London)
International Affairs (London)
International Affairs [Mezhdunarodnaia zhizn'] (Moscow)
International Journal (Toronto)
International Political Science Review
International Organization
International Politics
International Security
International Security Review (London)
International Studies Quarterly
Journal of Area Studies (Loughborough, UK)
Journal of Conflict Resolution
Journal of International Affairs
Millennium (London)
Mershon International Studies Review
New Times International (Moscow)
Orbis
Political Science Quarterly
SAIS Review: A Journal of International Affairs
Socialist Affairs and Women and Politics (London)
Survival (London)
Swords to Plowshares: A Chronicle of International Affairs
Wilson Quarterly
World Affairs
World Business and Economic Journal (London)
World Policy Journal
World Politics

ABSTRACTS

International Political Science Abstracts. Oxfordshire: International Political Science Association

PERIODICALS AND NEWS SERVICES

The Baltic Times (Latvia)
Beijing Review (China)
Christian Science Monitor
Corriere della Sera (Italy)
Current Digest of the Post-Soviet Press
Dong A-Ilbo (Republic of Korea)
The Economist (UK)
Financial Times (UK)
Foreign Broadcast Information Service (compiled by region) (Note: FBIS is currently available on-line. Microfiche is available for 1994 and before.)
Frankfurter Allgemeine Zeitung (Germany)
International Herald-Tribune
Japan Times (Japan)
La Nacion (Argentina)
Le Monde (France)
Los Angeles Times
Manchester Guardian (UK)
Neue Zürcher Zeitung (Switzerland)
New York Review of Books
New York Times
Nezavisimaia gazeta (Russia)
El Pais (Spain)
Publico (Portugal)
South China Morning Post (Hong Kong)
Straits Times (Singapore)
Times (UK)
Wall Street Journal
Washington Post
Yomiuri Shimbun (Japan)

WEB SITES

Bibliographies on Peace and Conflict from the University of Colorado at Boulder Peace and Conflict Studies Web site
    gopher://csf.colorado.edu:70/11/peace/biblios
Boston Chapter of the World Future Society
    http://www.lucifer.com/~sasha/refs/wfsgbc.html
ConflictNet
    http://www.igc.org/igc/conflictnet/
Foreign Affairs
    http://www.foreignaffairs.org *(has links to numerous other IR web sites)*

Foreign Policy
    http://www.foreignpolicy.com
The Harvard Program on Nonviolent Sanctions and Cultural Survival
    http://data.fas.harvard.edu/cfia/pnscs/
INCORE: The Initiative on Conflict Resolution and Ethnicity, University of Ulster and the United Nations University
    http://www.incore.ulst.ac.uk/
New Civilization Network
    http://www.worldtrans.org/newcivnet.html
    New Civilization Network Resource Library
        http://www.worldtrans.org/newcivilization.html
Peace and Conflict Resolution Centers
    http://www.pitt.edu/~ian/resource/conflict.htm
Peace and Conflict Studies at the University of Muenster, Germany
    http://www.uni-muenster.de/PeaCon/
Peace and War Section of the American Sociological Association
    http://www.la.utexas.edu/research/pwasa/index.htm
Project Muse of The Johns Hopkins University
    http://muse.jhu.edu/muse.html *(networked, subscription access to more than forty journals)*
Santa Fe Institute
    http://www.santafe.edu/
The Soros Foundation/Open Society Institutes
    http://www.soros.org/
Stockholm International Peace Research Institute
    http://www.sipri.se/
U.S. Institute of Peace
    http://www.usip.org/
War, Peace and Security Guide to Arms Control
    http://www.cfcsc.dnd.ca/links/peace/disarm.html
The Winston Foundation for World Peace: Conflict Prevention Resource Site
    http://www.crosslink.net/~wfwp/
World Citizen Web
    http://www.worldcitizen.org/
World Future Society
    http://www.wfs.org/
The World Game Institute
    http://www.worldgame.org/
    Net World Game
        http://www.worldgame.org/networldgame/index.html
World Government Links
    http://www.worldcitizen.org/links.html

PHOTO AND CARTOON CREDITS

To The Reader: xxxi Jeff Danziger, © 1990 The Christian Science Publishing Society.

Chapter 1: 5 Tim Clary, Agence France Presse/Corbis-Bettmann. 6 Jeff Danziger, © 1995 The Christian Science Publishing Society. 9 UN Photo 158657 by J. Sailas/UNDCP. 11 © Digital Vision. 17 Courtesy of the United Nations, *The State of the World's Women 1985*, illustration by Wendy Hoile. 18 Courtesy of Soros Fund Management. 19 Courtesy of the International Physicians for the Prevention of Nuclear War. 21 (Soviet grain ship) Brenda Hadenfeldt, (silicon chip) © Digital Vision.

Chapter 2: 37 (Berlin Wall) Jeff Danziger, © 1989 The Christian Science Publishing Society, (Bosnian graveyard) Nesad Tinjic. 41 UPI/Corbis-Bettmann. 49 UPI/Corbis-Bettmann. 58 NASA.

Chapter 3: 72 UN/DPI Photo. 76 UPI/Corbis-Bettmann. 80 UPI/Corbis-Bettmann.

Chapter 4: 106 UPI/Corbis-Bettmann. 115 Martin Stuart Fox, UPI/Corbis-Bettmann. 116 Jeff Danziger, © The Christian Science Publishing Society. 122 Richard Ellis, Reuters/Corbis-Bettmann. 125 Jeff Danziger, © The Christian Science Publishing Society.

Chapter 5: 135 (Costa Rican marketplace) Courtesy Eric Wright and Kim Sproule, (Oscar Arias Sanchez), Walter Clemens, Jr. 144 Jeff Danziger, © The Christian Science Publishing Society. 147 Jeff Danziger, © 1995 The Christian Science Publishing Society. 150 © Digital Vision. 155 Jeff Danziger, © 1996 The Christian Science Publishing Society.

Chapter 6: 167 Stanley Troutman, UPI/Corbis-Bettmann. 168 Amen Abzhanovich Khaidarov. 172 Jeanne Nemcek, *The Bulletin*

of the Atomic Scientists. 178 UN/DPI Photo 158470/H. Arvidsson. 183 UN Photo 159491/J. Bleibtreu. 185 Jeff Danziger, © 1996 The Christian Science Publishing Society.

Chapter 7: 191 Jeff Danziger, © The Christian Science Publishing Society. 193 Agence France Presse/Corbis-Bettmann. 199 UPI/Corbis-Bettmann. 204 Tim Clary, UPI/Corbis-Bettmann. 208 Choo Youn-Kong, Agence France Presse/Corbis-Bettmann. 210 Rick Carne, Office of U.S. Representative Tony Hall.

Chapter 8: 217 Jeff Danziger, © 1992 The Christian Science Publishing Society. 223 Andre Pichette, Agence France Presse/Corbis-Bettmann. 226 Pascal Guyot, Agence France Presse/Corbis-Bettmann. 230 Reuters/Corbis-Bettmann.

Chapter 9: 248 Jeff Danziger, © 1996 The Christian Science Publishing Society. 254 UPI/Corbis-Bettmann. 257 Fayez Nureldine, Agence France Presse/Corbis-Bettmann. 264 Jeff Danziger, © 1993 The Christian Science Publishing Society.

Chapter 10: 293 Jeff Danziger, © The Christian Science Publishing Society. 299 (boy at demonstration in Hong Kong) Carl Ho, Reuters/Corbis-Bettmann, (Eritrean women celebrate UN-supervised referendum) UN Photo 159900/M. Grant. 300 Robert Harbison, © 1994 *The Christian Science Monitor*.

Chapter 11: 312 UN Photo 24476. 321 Jeff Danziger, © 1996 The Christian Science Publishing Society. 324 Reuters/Corbis-Bettmann. 326 Gary Massoni, American Friends Service Committee. 335 Jeff Danziger, © The Christian Science Publishing Society.

Chapter 12: 342 UN/DPI Photo by S. Rotner. 345 Jeff Danziger, © 1996 The Christian Science Publishing Society. 352 Jeff

Danziger, © The Christian Science Publishing Society. 355 UN/DPI Photo by Milton Grant, © United Nations. 356 Courtesy of Geoff Sayer, Oxfam. 360 Reuters/Corbis-Bettmann. 367 Jeff Danziger, © 1996 The Christian Science Publishing Society.

Chapter 13: 371 Michael Probst, Reuters/Corbis-Bettmann. 379 J.P. Ksiazek, Agence France Presse/Corbis-Bettmann. 382 Jeff Danziger, © The Christian Science Publishing Society. 385 Jeff Danziger, © 1996 The Christian Science Publishing Society. 389 Will Burgess, Reuters/Corbis-Bettmann.

Chapter 14: 406 Eric Feferberg, Agence France Presse/Corbis-Bettmann. 425 UN/DPI Photo by Milton Grant. 431 Jeff Danziger, © 1990 The Christian Science Publishing Society. 433 I. Kostin, Novosti Press Agency/*The Bulletin of the Atomic Scientists*. 434 UN Photo 156359/J. Isaac.

Chapter 15: 458 Pat Hamilton, Reuters/Corbis-Bettmann. 460 Gerard Fouet, Agence France Presse/Corbis-Bettmann. 462 UPI/Corbis-Bettmann. 466 UN/DPI Photo by B. Zarov. 469 Reuters/Corbis-Bettmann. 471 Agence France Presse/Corbis-Bettmann.

Chapter 16: 479 Arthur Tsang, Reuters/Corbis-Bettmann. 482 Jeff Danziger, © The Christian Science Publishing Society. 485 UN/DPI Photo by H. Vassal. 488 UPI/Corbis-Bettmann. 490 UN/DPI Photo by J. Isaac. 491 Jeff Danziger, © 1992 The Christian Science Publishing Society. 493 UN Photo 23783. 497 Jeff Danziger, © 1995 The Christian Science Publishing Society. 506 UN Photo 186835/C. Sattleberger.

Chapter 17: 526 Jay Anderson, courtesy of American Dance Festival.

INDEX